How to Make It as a Woman

Women in Culture and Society

A Series Edited by Catharine R. Stimpson

How to Make It as a Woman

Collective Biographical History

from Victoria to the Present

Alison Booth

The University of Chicago Press • Chicago & London

Alison Booth is professor of English at the University of Virginia. She is the author of *Greatness Engendered: George Eliot and Virginia Woolf* and editor of *Famous Last Words: Changes in Gender and Narrative Closure.*

The University of Chicago Press, Chicago 60637
The University of Chicago Press, Ltd., London
© 2004 by The University of Chicago
All rights reserved. Published 2004
Printed in the United States of America
13 12 11 10 09 08 07 06 05 04   1 2 3 4 5

ISBN: 0-226-06545-6 (cloth)
ISBN: 0-226-06546-4 (paper)

Library of Congress Cataloging-in-Publication Data

Booth, Alison.
　How to make it as a woman : collective biographical history from Victoria to the present / Alison Booth.
　　p.　cm. — (Women in culture and society)
　Includes bibliographical references (p.　) and index.
　ISBN 0-226-06545-6 (cloth : alk. paper) — ISBN 0-226-06546-4 (pbk. : alk. paper)
　　1. Women—Biography—History and criticism.　2. Biography as a literary form.　I. Title.　II. Series.

CT21 .B515　2004
809′.93592072—dc22

2004003607

To the women in our families
in several countries and of all ages
this book is dedicated in honor of
our great men

Contents

Illustrations

Acknowledgments

Prefaces in collective biographies usually apologize for omissions and often perform what I call scenes of autobiographical dispossession—"where were the eminent models when I needed them?" An "acknowledgments" page serves a different but complementary purpose. It expresses gratitude for an abundance of helpful models, while it confesses to the limitations of any list and the incapacity of words to pay all one's debts. The conventionality of such expressions does not make them the less significant—much as in the formal conventions of the books I examine in this study.

I would like to extend warm thanks to all those who have helped me to complete this project. My work on Anna Jameson and on self-help literature was supported by a fellowship at the Virginia Foundation for the Humanities. The University of Virginia has aided my research in crucial ways, through Sesquicentennial Research Fellowships and Summer Research Grants as well as through the tireless aid of inter-library loan and the excellent resources of Alderman Library online, in special collections, and in the stacks. The dean of the College of Arts and Sciences, Edward Ayers, and the vice president for research and graduate studies, Dr. R. Ariel Gomez, contributed funds toward the cost of publication, and I am grateful to them and to Associate Dean Karen Ryan for this aid in ushering the book into the world. Michael Levenson and the English Department made it possible for me to travel to Australia to present my findings on women's collective biographies and to locate some Australian prosopographies in the State Library of New South Wales. I am grateful for the opportunities to develop portions of this book in keynotes or plenary sessions at the third annual British Women Writers Conference in 1994, the City University of New York Graduate Center Victorian Conference in 1998, George Mason University's Women's Studies Program and English Department in 1999, and the annual Virginia Woolf Conferences in 1997 and 1999. Audiences there and at Narrative and Dickens Project Conferences over the years have supplied me with examples and helped me to develop my concepts of role-model narrative and prosopography.

I remember speculating, circa 1995, that there might be hundreds of these volumes of brief lives of women. At the time it seemed sensible to substantiate that assertion, and Sybil Oldfield was wonderfully encouraging and generous with her own bibliography in progress. Nothing in my first years would have predicted the recent ones spent in archival hunting and tallying of publication rates and tables of contents or the inspiration I have found in such inquiry. I gladly thank David Vandermeulen, who with gentle incisions cut through several knotty questions about the aims and designs of my bibliography. Karen Kates Marshall, director of the Humanities and Social Sciences Services at the University of Virginia Library, earned my gratitude for adopting so warmly the annotated bibliography as part of the library's online resources. I am likewise grateful to the University of Chicago Press for easing the arrangements to publish the basic bibliography in the book while making the annotated version available online. Michael Furlough and Matthew Gibson and their helpful staff in the University of Virginia's Electronic Text Center have dedicated time and resources to developing this site. I look forward to working with them in enhancing its design and capacities.

I wish to thank the research assistants who helped in building and furnishing the bibliography and in obtaining copies of the books: Margaret Cooke, Karen Dietz, Christopher Jackson, Erin O'Connor, and Sarah Whitney. Christine Bayles-Korstch, Regan Boxwell, and Aimee Geoghan helped to complete and correct the "Pop Chart" of famous subjects. The chronological index and the resulting chart of publication rates similarly owe much to both Regan Boxwell and Aimee Geoghan. I thank Regan Boxwell and the generous and expert Rey Antonio of Copying Services for their help in producing the illustrations for the book. The final stages of copyediting were eased by Richard Gibson's alert assistance.

Colleagues at Virginia and elsewhere have read portions of the book and have helped me to refine and shape it. Deborah McDowell, Rita Felski, Chip Tucker, and Patricia Spacks read chapters with the insight and high standards that are so evident in their own work. David Amigoni, Sarah Blair, Janice Carlisle, Jay Clayton, Eileen Gillooly, Leigh Gilmore, Susan Gubar, Margaret Homans, Gordon Hutner, Christine Krueger, Laurie Langbauer, John Maynard, Andrew Miller, Adrienne Munich, Lillian Nayder, Linda Peterson, Jim Phelan, Brian Richardson, Peter Rabinowitz, Kristen Samuelian, Mark Schoenfield, and Hilary Schor have fostered exciting intellectual engagement over the past decade in the often overlapping roles of editor, session organizer, referee, and friend. Susan Lurie and Helena Michie gave astute anonymous readings and then stepped forward as the real people behind my ideal audience. Catharine Stimpson was warm from the start, and I would like to thank her and Susan Bielstein and Anthony Burton at the University of Chicago Press for ushering the book through its stages. Yvonne Zipter has been a pleasure to work with as copyeditor; my readers have her to thank as well.

For permission to reprint portions of "Illustrious Company: Victoria among Other Women in Anglo-American Role Model Anthologies," in *Remaking Queen Victoria,* ed. Margaret Homans and Adrienne Munich (Cambridge University Press, 1997), 59–78, and portions of "Millennial Victoria," *Victorian Literature and Culture* 29 (2001), 159–70, both in chapter 7, I thank Cambridge University Press. I thank Indiana University Press for permission to reprint "The Lessons of the Medusa: Anna Jameson and Collective Biographies of Women," *Victorian Studies* 42 (Winter 1999–2000): 257–88, as part of chapter 4. The Library of the Religious Society of Friends in London kindly provided the image of Jerry Barrett's *Elizabeth Fry in Newgate Prison,* and I acknowledge their permission to reprint it here. Finally, I would like to present *How to Make It as a Woman* to David Izakowitz, Emily Izakowitz, and Aaron Izakowitz as both a journal of those hours apparently alone in my crowded study and a reward book, full of entertainment as well as instruction. But I thank them in person for the good they have done me.

How to Navigate This Book

The magnitude of the sources to which this book refers, from ancient times up to the present, and the uses to which I have put them have required several systems of organization. Critical works are generally cited, via footnote numbers in the text, in notes collected at the end of the book. Early works of collective biography, which are listed chronologically in the bibliography, are referred to by author and date in the text. The collective biographies at the core of this study, which are arranged alphabetically in the second part of the bibliography in a numbered list, are indicated in the text by number, set in brackets and superscript. For example, Lydia Maria Child's book of women who supported eminent men would appear as *Good Wives*.[170] Information on various editions and titles would appear at number 170 in the bibliography printed here, and more complete information, such as the names of the subjects in Child's table of contents, could be examined in the online annotated bibliography, http://etext.lib.virginia.edu/WomensBios/. A reader wishing to identify other works first published in 1833 could turn to the "Chronological Index" (table A1 in this book), where item number 170 is listed with nine other numbers. Figure A1, "Number of Collective Biographies per Year," represents the annual totals in the chronological index; it shows that the rate of ten publications in 1833 was a high point not reached again until a decade later. A reader curious about the popularity of different kinds of subject could note that item 170 is marked "PC," that is, it is an unspecialized collection published between 1830 and 1850 and its list of female subjects contributed to the data represented in table A2, "Pop Chart." (The collections chosen for the Pop Chart samples had to claim to be inclusive, not specializing in one region, occupation, religion, or other category.) Comparing the names in the Pop Chart to the contents in the online entry for Child's *Good Wives* reveals that few of Child's subjects became standard favorites, though

Lady Fanshawe appears for her "Role in Revolution" in four other collections besides Child's during 1850–70; in four collections 1880–1900, and in no collections 1910–30. Such a decline in renown is fairly common. A reader who becomes interested in Lady Fanshawe could trace her story among the adventuresome narratives in chapter 2 (using the general index as guide), and by searching the online bibliography could locate all the other collections, specialized or general, 1830–1940, in which Fanshawe is known to be featured.

I would not want such suggestions to determine how readers use this book. Nor would I maintain that it is necessary to absorb the history of women's biographies or the rhetoric and form of collective biographical history (discussed especially in the first two chapters) to find interest in the female prosopographies that I put on display. Enjoy the pictures, or turn right away to chapter 2 for transgressive performances, or to chapter 3 for pioneering activism.

Of Prosopography and
Collective Biographies of Women

In or about December 1404, the learned Christine de Pizan—born in Venice, educated in the French court, and considered by some to have been the "first professional writer"—began to write *Le Livre de la cité des dames* or *The Book of the City of Ladies.* It was "the first work by a woman in praise of women," according to Earl Jeffrey Richards, whose English translation in 1982 (xxi, xlv) recuperated the work in a feminist context (prior to that, it had been translated into English only once, in 1521 [xix]).[1] The book begins by introducing an autobiographical persona who feels at home in tradition yet excluded by it: "One day as I was sitting alone in my study surrounded by books on all kinds of subjects, devoting myself to literary studies, my usual habit, my mind dwelt at length on the weighty opinions of various authors whom I had studied for a very long time" (3). Interrupting herself, she decides to browse at random and lights on a book of misogynist satire by Mathéolus. This sets her to reviewing the male authorities she has read, which "all concur ... that the behavior of women is inclined to ... every vice" (4). In spite of the authority of her own experience, the narrator concludes "that God formed a vile creature when he made woman," and she utters a lament to God in her despair (5). Naturally, this is just the first beat in a well-orchestrated pageant: Reason, Rectitude, and Justice then appear as three celestial ladies to console and instruct the scholar.

Their method is to assemble a vast, all-female Habitat for Humanity construction crew of about 140 legendary and historical women of many ranks (plus more in groups such as the Sabine women) to build a classified utopia. Rather than receiving sustained biographical treatment, the subjects appear as names and anecdotes in an ancient form of argument by example, governed by typology. Christine learns of the Roman virgin Claudine, for example, who seeing her father attacked during a military parade, forgot "serene conduct" and "boldly planted herself between the swords and lances which she saw drawn on her father and forcefully grabbed the nearest assailant by the throat," defeating the attackers and winning the "praise" of the city (114–15). Claudine serves unconsciously as a pagan precursor of many heroines who appear in volumes published centuries after de Pizan's: on the one hand, Margaret Roper, daughter of Sir Thomas More, or Pocahontas and other rescuers of men and, on the other hand, the Maid of Saragossa and other warrior women (in the mythic, action-hero mode of *Crouching Tiger, Hidden Dragon*). The paragraph on Claudine is followed by "A Woman Who Breast-Fed Her Mother in Prison"—but read on in *The City of Ladies* for yourself or turn to my second chapter, "Heads Turn, Heads Roll," for more of such warm-blooded adventure. That anything might be overheated in these noble deeds of women neither the Christine pupil nor her Virgilian guides seem to suspect. Says Christine to Lady Rectitude, "I have learned a great deal from you: how all things which are feasible and knowable, whether in the area of physical strength or in the wisdom of the mind and every virtue, are possible and easy for women to accomplish" (117–18). All the models are sanctioned, though some derive from such pagan sources as Plutarch (by way of Boccaccio, Ovid, and Beauvais's *Speculum historiale* [Richards, xxxviii–xl]), and some deviate widely from pious feminine scripts of de Pizan's (or Pisan's) day. It is the sort of cracked rhetorical foundation on which collective biographies of women are built.

Although I will devote little attention in this book to medieval or early modern texts, Christine de Pizan is a worthy precursor in the tradition of exemplary biographical collections of women. Volumes of groups of female biographies took hold in England with the development of the printed book and proliferated after the mid-eighteenth century. In every way, the quantity of such books shapes this study. My bibliography includes more than 900 all-female collections published in English between 1830 (when middle-class women's movements and publishing practices became more efficient) and 1940 (before the postwar publication boom produced too many volumes to tally). Many of the subjects and conventions current during the nineteenth century survive only through the first decades of the twentieth. Sybil Oldfield's important annotated bibliography *Collective Biography of Women in Britain, 1550–1900* lists nearly 400 British works, including male-female collections as well as works published before 1830.[2] My scope is American as well as British because publication was so often transatlantic and based on an international exchange of subjects and social movements.[3] Obviously in demand, this crowded field of recognition has largely gone unnoticed. The form might seem to have exhausted itself but for the fact that it is still constantly renewed. There has been a surprising consensus in favor of praise of famous women, as groups of famous men had long been praised.[4] Over the centuries, it seemed that a nation or community was hardly worth its salt without its lists of eminent women. The presenters of these group panegyrics assumed that assortments of female biographies served not only as sound evidence concerning women's nature and as reliable guides to feminine excellence but also as contributions to national history. The collective biographies that I study in this book helped to codify how to make it as a woman. Serving as more than self-help or eulogy, canons of women's lives appear to have been indispensable aids in the formation of nationhood as well as of social difference: a necessary form of prosopography or collective biographical history.

How to Make It as a Woman is the first full-length interpretation of the form in which writings about women continue to appear. My consideration of the prefatory construction of readers and other narrative techniques, of the types and assortments of subjects or thematic principles of collections, of the illustrations, and of various biographers only begins to map what this territory holds. I focus on collections, by men as well as women, that narrate (rather than outline or summarize) lives of three or more subjects exclusively female. Dictionaries and encyclopedias, flourishing from the 1890s, may contribute to nation-building projects more obviously than the volumes of fewer subjects treated at greater length, but the reference works also downplay the self-modeling and literary pleasures offered by more elaborated lives. There were many mixed collections such as *Brave Men and Women,* many more all-male, and many "ungendered" collections that include women in their pages but not their titles—perhaps five times as many altogether as the women-only volumes.[5] Yet I study the difference the category of sex makes in collective ex-emplarity. While I locate a strain of anthologies of African American women in the 1890s, I also question the inscriptions of race and ethnicity in "global" sampling or in celebrations of Anglo-Saxon womanhood. Although individual biographies of women would also reward more study, I favor collections because of the comparative bias that they bring to the fabric of female social roles: the way that a compilation of lives snags or gathers what might appear to be femininity by the bolt.[6]

In form and function, the hundreds of collections of female biographies might be the lost ancestors of late-twentieth-century women's studies. Although these early popular collections require ideological decoding today, their effort to recuperate women of the past seems, oddly enough, never to go out of style. The collection of representative life narratives has contributed to each phase of debate about women's roles and rights since early modern times.[7] Catalogs of notable women have flourished in plain view for centuries, while generation after generation laments the absence of women of the past. A latter-day de Pizan might view commendation of elite women as a part of the problem rather than the solution.[8] Yet the catalogs of exemplary women seem to have been vindicated for placing confidence in the power of biography to shape subjectivities and, by extension, communities. Celebration of historic womanhood necessarily reinforces the idea of gender difference: the norms must be restated when exceptions to them are registered. *How essential to the progress of civilization is notable womanhood—that is, those women who depart from the ways of their sex!*—so the presenters rather illogically affirm, often lauding "manly" deeds or virtues. The Victorian horizon of gender ideology evidently was broad enough to encompass the beautiful assassin Charlotte Corday alongside Joan of Arc, Hannah More, Pocahontas, Queen Elizabeth, and others in a collection titled *Lessons from Women's Lives.*[36] What lessons are these, and what do such disparate models teach in common? Incrementally, across decades of shifting social conditions, these self-contradictory catalogs helped to expand the available praiseworthy roles beyond European upper classes and traditional occupations.

To recognize this intriguing subgenre of biography is to alter some preconceptions of auto/biography studies, literary history, and feminist studies. Studies of biography and autobiography center on individual monographs and rarely reflect on the classic form of parallel lives or notice the formal, rhetorical, and ethical effects of series of subjects. Life writing is a complex social interaction—the narrator, the protagonist, and the audience always collaborate in the narrative—even when there is a single subject. Judy Long emphasizes that all biography entails an "intersection" of "two subjectivities. . . . the subject and narrator."[9] Paula Backscheider rightly extends the sociable intimacies of biography to include the audience as well: "If biographers and their subjects are collaborators, biographers and readers are soul mates."[10] With always at least three parties on the line, biographies become all the more interpersonal in their common multiple formats. Rendering individuals representative of the group, biographies lend themselves to group representation. Most life narratives bear closer comparison to a collection of short pieces than to a novel. In literary collections, the ensemble adds webs of internal cross-reference to each essay, story, or poem; so in biographical collections each life gains comparative dimensions through the others.

A collective biography, like canons and other lists of recognition, poses problems of selection and omission, anxiously conceded in most of the publications in my bibliography. The representative woman is a synecdoche of her type. Yet she must to a degree foil the mimetic claim: she is more noteworthy than the mass of women honored by proxy. Within a finite list, further, no two identical subjects would be warranted and so the category breaks down. What is a woman, if she differs enough from the ahistorical feminine ideal to be narratable and if she differs from other renowned or obscure women enough to retain a name? Along with the hints of missing persons and tenuous distinctions, works in this mode tend to get lost in the shuffle of each season's or generation's efforts to form an adequate list of women's roles. While histories

of literature have demoted didactic biography, histories of biography have neglected collections, especially female multibiographies, in part because these
works seem especially incomplete and transient.

Even feminist studies, whether historical or literary, have for various reasons contributed to the comparative neglect of "records of woman" (to borrow
Felicia Hemans's 1828 title).[11] Accounts of the development of modern subjectivity and middle-class gender ideology, such as Nancy Armstrong's *Desire and
Domestic Fiction,* rely heavily on the novel and conduct literature as discursive
instruments of such development.[12] Yet female collective biographies commonly served as such instruments; indeed, the anthologies of famous women
seem even better designed to model alternative characters and life narratives
than do the conventions of fictional plots or pious advice. Adding to the neglect
of female collective biography, feminist critics have favored autobiography or
have paid disproportionate attention to women novelists and poets. A medium
that honors public figures of various callings and that seems not to qualify as
literature thus may be overlooked, though many women of letters contributed
to it as subjects or presenters. More insidiously, feminist projects of recovery
depend on enhancing the sense of women's suppression in the past.[13] It is as
though searchers compete to be the first to rediscover obscure women, when
in fact so many of the recurrently "obscure" have been recognized time and
again. Indeed, it is impossible to encompass the potential and achievements of
womanhood, to judge by the hundreds of prodigies who impelled themselves
into dozens of books across the decades.

Bursting with the good news that much of women's biographical history is
not lost, yet realizing that many were predisposed not to hear this news, I might
have shared some of Christine de Pizan's despair. Rereading the opening scene
of de Pizan immediately put me in mind, anachronistically enough, of Virginia
Woolf in the British Museum. I plucked from a pile on the floor a fresh copy of
the 1981 edition of *A Room of One's Own* (the flesh-toned one with the faceless,
depressive, Edwardian woman gazing out of the window; my old blue copy
from the 1970s, with the Magritte design and the dated blurbs—"Mrs. Woolf
speaks for her sex with as much fancy as logic"—is full of helpful post-its
and annotations, but its pagination varies from the edition now furnished
to my students). I quickly found the moment when Woolf's narrator, Mary
Beton, opens the library catalog and exclaims to her audience word for word
as I might address my own readers: "Have you any notion how many books
are written about women . . . ? Have you any notion how many are written by
men? . . . But I should need to be a herd of elephants, I thought, and a wilderness
of spiders . . . to cope with all this. . . . In despair [I] began running my eye up
and down the long list of titles."[14] In other words, Woolf offers another, more
recent performance of the woman scholar browsing in search of predecessors
through an overwhelming tradition.

In a reversal of Christine's discovery that a misogynist literature was belied
by a history of great women, however, Woolf's narrator discovers a literature

that presents great heroines—"Clytemnestra, Antigone, Cleopatra..."—contradicted by a history of women's debasement (43). And does Woolf ever mention Christine? They might inhabit different universes, to judge by Woolf's version of women's literary history. I returned to Margaret Ezell's *Writing Women's Literary History,* so important to my project.[15] Ezell highlights the early anthologies of literary women, such as George Ballard's *Memoirs of Several Ladies of Great Britain,* first published in 1752 (78–89); I study these and many other collections that represent all kinds of female vocation. As Ezell observes, Woolf's search for Judith Shakespeare in *A Room of One's Own* helped to persuade subsequent feminist literary scholars that there were indeed no worthy women poets in the sixteenth and seventeenth centuries. Ezell attributes the myth of the silence of the early woman writer to the "limitations of the historiography of [Woolf's] day" (49–50).[16] For generations before Woolf, those who paid tribute to groups of women simultaneously deplored the dearth of female biography. Thus in 1851 Arabella Stuart Willson[886] laments, "How few of the memoirs and biographical sketches which load the shelves of our libraries, record the lives of women!"—as she adds to the hundreds of female biographies *The Lives of the Three Mrs. Judsons.*[17] Even today the lament recurs. Judy Long poignantly recalls her re-discovery of Lini de Vries, "unique, heroic, a model for women of any age.... How had my elite education encompassed such an omission?"[18]

As I sat in my study surrounded by notes, computer disks, photocopies, and books, working on the final stages of a literary history that had become the habit of years, I pondered how to lift the fog that has obscured the (written) lives of women, and how to introduce this wealth of historical material in a compelling way. One approach might simply be to enumerate and display as many of these volumes in as many lights as possible. But such a labor would not leave room for me to mount my arguments concerning narrative construction of women's roles and histories. And it would not do to give the impression that I am collecting antiques in an obsolete form. I turned to my left, to my assortment of anthologies of feminist scholarship, recent variations on the form of women's collective life writing. For instance, *Remaking Women: Feminism and Modernity in the Middle East,* edited by Lila Abu-Lughod: this volume displays a composite image of past and present Eastern womanhood on the cover: a blue-eyed flapper faces forward, partially obscured by a dark-eyed, veiled woman in profile. The short "bios" of the contributors at the back of the book reveal this to be a collaborative project that assists in individual career building at distinguished academic institutions. (It establishes a certain community: only one contributor is a man, and only one has a Western-sounding name, coincidentally with the same surname as mine.) The table of contents offers studies of a range of models of female development in different historical contexts within marginal geographical and cultural zones (readers might find volumes that fit that description on their own shelves). Among the chapters, Marilyn Booth's "The Egyptian Lives of Jeanne d'Arc" seems particularly instructive for my purpose. Booth writes that, beginning circa 1892, "in Egypt, biographies of 'Famous Women' in the early women's press, in the dominant press, and in biographical compendia of notable women . . . constructed a complex narrative of modernity that put female heroines at the center"; the heroines often overlapped with those popularized in Europe and North America in the previous century.[19] But there is little time in this study to more than glance at a few contemporary parallels to my subgenre, such as this auto/biographical collection of women's studies. Nor do we yet have the equivalent of an international Genome Project that would synthesize the prosopographies of women in all languages and eras. Evidently the largest body of such works has been generated in English from 1830 onward.

What characteristics and customs prevailed in such publications? I turned to my right, to the bookcase that holds a chronological sampling of all-female collective biographies (many other volumes lurk in stacks of photocopies behind my back). Any of these *Extraordinary Women*[692] or *Celebrated Women*[175] might serve to give a taste for the kind of reading that was so constantly produced (most often by men) and consumed (presumably most often by women)—from 1845, at least a dozen per year; by 1850, between twenty and thirty annually; in some years (1854, 1900) forty or more. After some hesitation I chose one that is on the latter end of the period of my bibliography but representative of a Victorian "city of ladies." Characteristically, the presenter/biographer, subjects, and implied reader(s) seem to constitute themselves a cohort, as they measure certain differences and exclusions.

In 1915, the American Sunday-School Union published, in Philadelphia, an illustrated volume of nine biographies, *Women Who Have Ennobled Life* by Lilian Whiting.[862] Bound in faded lavender moiré cloth, with gilt lettering and purple and gilt decoration on the cover, it includes black-and-white photographic reproductions of portraits, homes or sites, statuary, and facsimiles of letters, as well as an abundance of verse (most of the lives begin and end with poetic quotations, and all are interlaced with them). These and other features seem designed to induce a certain highly reputable pleasure.[20] Presumably the book offered edifying entertainment to "Mrs. A. M. [F]rase[r] / 1228 2nd St., Loraine. O.," who signed and dated (1929) the flyleaf of the copy now owned by the University of Virginia. Inside, she would have encountered detailed, active, laudable lives of eight Americans and one Englishwoman, all of whom were celebrated internationally during the nineteenth century (the last having died in 1910): Elizabeth Barrett Browning, Mary Ashton Livermore, Louisa May Alcott, Margaret Fuller d'Ossoli, Mary Lyon, Harriet Beecher Stowe, Frances Elizabeth Willard, Harriet Goodhue Hosmer, and Julia Ward Howe. To the well-known outline of their careers Whiting added considerable biographical documentation of these women's overlapping circles, in a sort of cross-referencing, mutual multibiography (thus, e.g., the Brownings' "ideal social life in the beautiful 'Flower City'" included Stowe, Fuller, and Hosmer, amid a list of their mutual friends [31]).

Whether the first owner of this book felt invited to join this distinguished register is impossible to know. Probably it was a more recent student and not Mrs. Fraser who underlined in pencil large portions of Alcott's instructive biography, as for instance: "No aspirant in all the literary guild ever more innocently and unselfishly longed for fame and gain than did Louisa Alcott" (87). The book was checked out as recently as 1991, perhaps as a ready digest of information on these reforming writers and artists. Beyond these clues and the rhetorical designs in the volume itself, there are few indications of the responses of generations of readers of this or the hundreds of other such collections that had been published for well over a century before 1915.[21]

The biographer Lilian Whiting has left more evidence as to her intentions. Writing from "The Brunswick, Boston," she prefaces the collection with "Just a Word" on her "selection" among those "whose lives and work have contributed to the . . . higher life of humanity." The "sympathetic" reader will not, she hopes, question the omission of "many . . . equally worthy of attention." She chose her subjects according to "temperamental attractions"—and perhaps it was easy to identify with women of her acquaintance or one degree of separation (5–6). (On a typical occasion, she heard Harriet Hosmer read aloud from Hosmer's correspondence with the Brownings [232].) Though she does not say so, the selection favors the Boston intelligentsia and their associates at home and in England and Italy, a "brilliant coterie . . . in those mid-nineteenth-century years" (244). Indeed, she cannot remark on the narrowness of the list because like most compilers of short biographies she claims comprehensiveness even as she apologizes for absences. According to the custom of prefaces, Whiting acknowledges other possible stand-ins for her types: Vittoria Colonna was educator Mary Lyon's "predecessor by more than three centuries"; the names of Lucy Stone, Rosa Bonheur, Frances Power Cobbe, and so on might well be added (5–6). Some of the possible others "visit" the collection: "Lady Henry Somerset, the close friend and constant coworker of Frances Willard for the causes of temperance" (6) appears in a portrait that accompanies Willard's biography. Similarly, a photograph of the "Statue of Florence Nightingale, in Santa Croce, Florence," interrupts Julia Ward Howe's biography.[22] Dr. and Mrs. Howe had visited the Nightingales in England, and Dr. Howe "encouraged" Florence to take up "the great work."[23] If too many figures of ennobling women and their patrons begin to intermix here, the reader should recall Whiting's advice: "we" should "study" the subjects for similarities within variety, "finding in each one common chord; one golden thread running through all these lives; one aim investing each with its crowning grace,—that of *Christian womanhood*" (6). It matters little which parts of the whole performance we understudy; it is a collaboration.

Presumably, the readers and the writer learned to join that host of model womanhood. Though some of the short biographies seem more realistic than others, the pressure of the whole—according to the presenter, at least—is to reduce differences among women to a single message. The life of the leader of the temperance movement Frances Willard is more abstract than any, a repetitive effusion on "the angelic type of womanhood" (187).[24] Seven pages of encomium pass before Willard's parentage and birth (a common beginning of a "life"). A few small flaws are allowed: "she was no expert at household tasks" (195). But her triumphant public life is followed by tributes (she died in 1898): "In the national Capitol at Washington has been placed a statue of Frances Willard;— the only woman in the United States, as yet, to be so honored. It was unveiled on February 17, 1905" (206). The woman who "would have been as capable of addressing Queen Victoria as 'My dear sister,' as she would of thus speaking to her seamstress" (187), was in the end "named our 'Uncrowned Queen'" (207).[25]

Some work of national and international class consolidation was performed here, raising a standard for Evangelical social ministry. Yet Whiting's word notwithstanding, most of these women took a defiant step away from convention at some point; all of them exercised agency in ways that would still be commended today. (Significantly, only the writers in Whiting's list—Barrett Browning, Alcott, Fuller, Stowe—are much celebrated in the lists of the past quarter century.) Preparation for the sweet hereafter was not exactly their daily contemplation as they became famous for their achievements. Clearly a conventional married domesticity was no prerequisite for inclusion in the volume. And the women differ from each other in their remarkable careers. The sculptor Harriet Hosmer, for one: opposite the famous photograph of Hosmer in beret and short skirt atop a sturdy ladder while at work on a cloaked male statue three times her size, Whiting describes the "Arcadian freedom and simplicity" of the artist's life in Rome (210).[26] It is indeed difficult to see Hosmer, protégée of the lesbian actress Charlotte Cushman, harmonizing with one chord of holy ministry to humanity, just as it takes some effort to place Margaret Fuller, transcendentalist lecturer, feminist, and political journalist, as devout Christian *tout court.* And that friendship between Lady Henry Somerset and the divine Frances Willard piques a twenty-first-century person's desire to know more.

Each life in this collection would reward close reading. Like Whiting, I have to offer an apology for selection, have to place an extra burden on each example to represent a type. In fact, I must be selective in my examinations of individual texts. Like de Pizan, I will have to perform a scholar's kind of reading, "browsing here and there" (3). The difficulty of choosing among multiplicity is also an opportunity: a benefit of collective biographies. Multiple lives, however eulogistic, help to resist the preeminence of a heroic individual. The differences among the narratives also challenge the claim to represent universal womanhood. Further, group biographies suggest the interdependence and social construction of identities. I find a perverse sort of hope in the failure of the prosopographical selection to close ranks and declare adequacy. A theme, with repeated variations, segues into something different than the single pattern of notes that first met the ear.[27]

Collective biographies offer many such rhetorical advantages. The argument implied in selection and arrangement prevents the illusion of a transparent, objective account of a person's life. Collections of lives can rarely disguise their didactic purpose. A collective biography requires an additional rhetorical frame besides that of any biography: the definition of the category or principle of selection, even at the apparently empirical level of inclusive reference works. The anthology of the great teaches greatness, of women womanhood, of writers what it takes to make a writer. Few presenters in the collections I examine hesitate to advertise the profit to be gained from the discursive exchange. A collection also promises practical assistance similar to that of *Reader's Digest*. One buys the value added by the compiler and publisher, who spare one the cost or effort of acquiring various written lives for oneself or of reading as many lives at greater length. The well-designed collection, in addition, may teach a crucial social skill: comparative judgment of personality. A collection may add to this, above all, the encouraging view that noteworthy lives differ enough from each other to leave space for others to join them.

The form of collective biography has persisted because of such rhetorical benefits and because of its potential as historiography. Biography in general has had an ambiguous status as either history or literature or as both.[28] At least since Plutarch (first century A.D.), "particular" or biographical history has been offered as a more illuminating means of reviving the past than "universal" political history. Arguably a collection has even more claim to being historiography than does an individual biography, as several lives begin to plot common historical ground. As history, the collective female biographies raise familiar problems. Many collections refer to history in their titles and claim to improve the reader's knowledge as well as character. Yet the biographical history of women seems even more partial and unreliable than the history of men. The treachery of existing records of women was one of the daunting obstacles when feminists took up (once again) the challenge of writing women's history in the 1970s. In 1975 Gerda Lerner objected to "compensatory history" of "women worthies": "The history of notable women is the history of exceptional, even deviant women, and does not describe the experience and history of the mass of women."[29]

The fallacy of most histories of women has been to survey the individuals whose records remain. Thus, Stephen Watson Fullom's well-meaning *History of Woman* (1855) might almost have been assembled from headlines of women in male-centered political events: "Several illustrious women figure in the dark annals of the English civil war, and the heroic Countess of Derby, who resisted to the last the haughty power of Cromwell, and the gentle Countess of Sunderland, may be numbered among the foremost. Lady Fanshawe and kindly Lucy Hutchinson have themselves written the stirring tale of their lives."[30] Quite so: women of rank who wrote their own lives, or who shared beds, drawing rooms, or battlefields with ruling men, endured to find their place in histories and biographies. Collective biographies like most histories rely heavily on what are called secondary sources: previous auto/biographies or historical accounts. The situation is not always radically improved by the new social history. In 1992, Elise Boulding's *The Underside of History* reflects a far broader and better-documented perspective than Fullom's but relies as well on selective biographical archives, as in the section "Women Adventurers," where one encounters some stars of popular Victorian collections, for example: "Flora MacDonald is perhaps the most famous of the eighteenth-century adventuresses."[31]

In short, until quite recently the history of women even more than of men has exhibited a bias toward well-documented elites. Only a small portion of the brief lives of women claim to be drawn from life or from original research. By and large, we are given *re-nown*. Yet the volumes endorse a surprising range of women of different social origins and circumstances, and many a collection expresses the desire to honor neglected heroines of hearth or mission field, or the victims of racial, class, or other prejudice. As a group, the collective biographies tend to subvert the conventions of rank or wealth, giving the genteel-poor social worker more status than the society hostess. The objects of the heroines' charitable or courageous deeds receive a liberal humanitarian respect, and with a few partisan exceptions, the subjects receive praise in spite of particular political or religious affiliations. For all the harm done in its name, there was great opportunity in the international maternalist mission along the lines of Frances Willard, which placed progress for educated women in Anglo-Saxon Protestant nations at the vanguard of civilization.[32] Although generations of assorted exemplars fail to integrate many women into a "universal" history, that does not imply that this subgenre also fails in its other cultural assignments. The effects of role model anthologies, as they might be called, are multifarious, while they reward examination as precedents for the kinds of collective biographical construction that today dominate discourses of difference and identity.

How Do We Do Prosopography?

Although this book seeks to reveal the contours of a specialized subgenre within the span of a long century, it also invites readers to see decidedly old-fashioned texts through postmodern spectacles, in light of today's consumption of personalities and construction of communities. I highlight representations of "nameable" history, or what I call prosopography, from the ancients to the present. "Prosopography"—literally, the writing of masks—is sometimes used as another term for collective biography or "multibiography." Lawrence Stone defined prosopography in 1971 as "the investigation of the common background characteristics of a group of actors in history by means of a collective study of their lives."[33] The term does have associations quite different from my own project, but even these connotations confirm the suggestiveness of multiple representations of social types. Certain nineteenth- and early-twentieth-century positivist or eugenicist studies, by Jean Louis Giraud, Francis Galton, Charles Beard, Sir Lewis Namier, and their followers, engaged in prosopography of the biographical background of political or cultural elites.[34] Linda Colley, in her study of Namier, notes that early- and mid-twentieth-century prosopography, in spite of its conservative allegiances and an unexamined faith in empiricism, could present an instructive social challenge to "heroic history."[35] In quite a different mode today, medievalists and classicists engage in prosopography as they examine the scant data of military, religious, civic, or numismatic records for signs of life in lost epochs.[36] Certain branches of sociology depend on comparative analysis of vital statistics; Pierre Bourdieu's *Distinction* is prosopographical, for example.[37] In general, prosopography suggests methods of interpreting patterns in partial collections or of memorializing the clustered remains of lives.

My claim is that group biohistoriography or prosopography has been instrumental in constructing modern subjectivities and social differences. Prosopography thus personifies what Raymond Williams calls "selective traditions."[38] For emerging nations, peoples, or subjectivities, the selected lineage of life narratives helps to constitute "imagined communities," according to Benedict Anderson's conception. To shape the story of a nation is to conspire in forgetting much of its past, as Renan famously observed, but it also is to invent an antique origin and lineage. Thus in Anderson's vision, modern nationhood aligns with "the inner premises and conventions of modern biography and autobiography."[39] The narratives that replace lost memory of birth or of a beginning develop "*genealogically*" for the person or the group; "the nation's biography" forms itself on memorialized "deaths."[40]

Since the earliest writing, life stories have associated with funereal occasions and memorials. Sacred texts such as the Bible have striven to preserve the biographical genealogy of a people always beginning in dispossession and bereavement. The elegiac matter of auto/biography finds its partner in the absences of history. Both narrative forms, auto/biography and history, in a sense anthropomorphize lost time. Thus, in Mary Evans's phrase, the subjects of life narrative are themselves "missing persons." Their represented presence signals what has been left untold—both "the silent millions of people" and the minutiae of experience.[41] I like the daunting polysyllable "prosopography" for the very reason that it seems to mourn the loss of the missing. Etymologically, "prosopography" is affiliated with "prosopopoeia"—according to the *Oxford English Dictionary* (2d ed.), "a rhetorical figure by which an imaginary or absent person is represented as speaking or acting" or "by which an inanimate or abstract thing is represented as a person." It suggests the rhetoric that would animate and replenish the past through an ironically distancing address to an audience over the dead body of an interlocutor. In poststructuralist poetics, prosopopoeia, which might simply be a fancy term for "personification," acquires the problematics of figuration itself. As Paul de Man influentially notes, prosopopoeia—"to *give* a face," mask or voice to an absence—is the trope not only of lyric but of autobiography.[42] I would stress the point that biography exploits the energy of this trope—life writing is *prosopoetic*.[43] The mirrored solitude of a lyric moment becomes a public, broadcast funeral oration, expanding into a sort of parade or pageant of the figures who acted throughout history. As the root association of person with "mask" suggests, the image of a face or body plays an important part in these collective representations.

As if motivated by the memorial impulse, many branches of academic study today build on group biohistoriography. Not only verbal and visual portraiture but naming is crucial to this practice, as in the ancient device of assembling symbolic genealogies through the epithets of heroes. The semiotician Anna Makolkin finds a *"biographical onomopoesis"* in the biography that recognizes national heroes: "the distance between the hero's birth and his death is basically a map of this onomastic progression from a common proper name to the name-allegory."[44] This is true not only of such legendary heroes as Moses or Alexander or of the rulers for whom a period or cities may be named: Elizabethan; Washington, DC. Prosopography also encourages the conversion of many names into types, into Carlylean indefinite articles or collective nouns: "a Boswell," "a Jane Austen" or "the Beats," "the Encyclopédistes." Naming similarly gives form to narratives of disciplines. Ideas or terms become identified with the adjectival surname of the eminent originator ("Marxist," "Foucauldian," "Kristevan") or an entire oeuvre takes on the proper name (as when one "reads Irigaray" or "reads Sedgwick"); theories or "approaches" find representation through published equivalents of the team photo of such famous figures.[45] Everyone—not just within Western conference-going circuits but everyone in literate, historicized cultures—knows the distortions in such selective name giving, just as everyone has been disturbed by the brevity of renown, a reverberation of one's own mortality. The effort to give face or voice to a perishing heritage or ideals perhaps shows most in representative lists of eminent people that leave so much to be desired by being so unrepresentative.[46] Prosopography, in other words, figures "Who Is Not Who," just as a narrative must fail to fix either the ineffable complexity of life or the infinite regression of beginning.

The inadequate naming of parts for the whole lies at the core of the canon controversies. Collective biography, like canon building in general, attempts to consolidate imagined communities and subjects according to the institutionalization of collecting that developed with the rise of consumer culture.[47] With the increasing value placed on secular self-development and individual rights came a broadening range of biographical recognition, which circulated in collections targeted at disenfranchised groups. The practice "saves face" for the group by displaying a collection of model subjects. As Erving Goffman long ago observed, "once a person with a particular stigma attains high occupational, political, or financial position . . . a new career is likely to be thrust upon him, that of representing his category."[48] The alternative prosopography accumulates tales of triumph over systematic adversity or stigma (overcoming obstacles is the basic unit of all life narrative, the biographeme, perhaps). Triumphant models for women and minorities construct a target audience that shares that specially vindictive adversity, as though exceptions prove, and improve, the rule. In this context, the assemblage of notable women of history offers closer parallels to the antiquarian pursuits or compilations of folklore that proliferated from the eighteenth century onward (George Ballard, an early biographer of women, was an antiquarian) or to the postbellum and early-twentieth-century efforts to preserve oral narratives of former slaves than to the metropolitan museums or Euro-American universities established during the same periods. The latter supported the canons or traditions of the center, whereas the prosopographies of women belong with projects of recovery at the margins of modern national formations (as when revivals of Scottish ballads accompany a nineteenth-century reinvention of Scotland). The supplements acknowledge the ephemeral quality of what they would preserve; they come with built-in multiple ports for add-ons, to be upgraded or replaced.

Prosopographies engage the conventions not only of naming and collecting but also of canons and lists in general. At the new millennium many have perceived the flaws in list making.[49] Lists may have a dull syntax, may seem superfluous, yet they rouse a competitive desire. Much of the recognition of women, as of other marked social groups, has consisted of lists of names. You may already have begun to keep score for the famous women listed in this study. Nevertheless, I am not offering a corrected list of the greatest women of history. I would underline here the necessary incoherence and lacunae of catalogs, as finite selections require differences among their items. Any collection may be constituted by "the fact that it *lacks* something."[50] As Marjorie Garber observes of canons of great books, they betoken "an anxious fantasy of wholeness" always already lost.[51] Even the most authorized signs, like icons in a temple, confirm the absence of the signified for which they solicit recognition or worship. A community's pantheonic series, as they might be called, engender pandemonium within the unity they stand for. Conflict among the subjects, unruly implications, and arbitrary substitutions to cover glaring absences—such are the unpresentable habits of prosopography.

Although I focus on book-length compilations, prosopography takes many forms and may be embodied in quite different media. Indeed, because debates over canons have tended to focus on literature or the arts, it is easy to overlook the wide range of media and contexts in which communities seek to register and memorialize their coherent existence in space and time. I shall try to draw comparisons across discourses and eras without losing distinctions. Etymologically, a "canon" was a model sculpture, and a lingering religious connotation associates a representative list with the images of saints on a holy edifice.[52] Commonly, personified histories take concrete spatial form, as in Mount Rushmore or halls of fame.[53] Whether for the dominant group or for its minorities, the figurative series tend to be associated not only with quasi-sacred locations but also with spectacles, rituals, and holidays. National role-model lists often mark themselves on a calendar, as in saints' days or the months devoted to women's history or African American history.[54] Early catalogs of women were often dramatized as visions incorporating a public spectacle (as in Chaucer [1372–86] or de Pizan [1405]), and there has been a leaning toward pageantry since then (as in Cicely Hamilton's 1910 suffrage play, *A Pageant of Great Women*[373] or Caryl Churchill's 1982 *Top Girls*).[55] Much like other representations of the great and good, catalogs of women may be monumental or spatial, in a range of forms: noblemen's galleries of beauties (e.g., Steinman[753]); the Hall of Woman at the 1893 World's Columbian Exposition; Judy Chicago's installation *The Dinner Party*, with its symbolic place settings for the famous women of history; the National Museum of Women in the Arts; and many others.[56] Visual representation seems inherent in prosopography, as the mask or *prosopon* suggests; theories of identity and ethics from Lacan to Levinas stress the sight of an other's embodiment or face. Accordingly in the collections I study, the portrait collaborates—in sometimes lively contention—with the name and the narrative in the effort to summon a woman as she once was.

Partial series of names, images, and life narratives, then, may prosopoetically articulate a collective past or a community ideal. They may memorialize a heritage or mourn the dead as much as they forecast a future through the audience response. After September 11, 2001, the landscapes of some cities in the United States featured prosopographical collaborations such as the street shrines seeking to capture name, face, written voice, material traces of the dead.[57] The *New York Times* in their daily section B and on their Web site featured a series of prosopographies reconstructing the community that has been violated: "A Nation Challenged: Portraits of Grief." These elegant, abbreviated lives, far too many, remain freshly difficult to read in spite of the repeating formulas. Each name is followed by a title summarizing the person's life and a few short, well-crafted paragraphs emphasizing character more than event, and whenever possible quoting family or friends; the text accompanies a smiling photograph—all in the effort to resist the mass reduction of living persons to untraceable materiality and fading memory.[58]

Prosopography may require only a name, as in the generations of collective memorials to the war dead in villages and cities in the United States and Europe. Maya Lin's *Vietnam Veterans Memorial* in Washington, DC, a chevron cut in the earth, spreads an inclusive rather than selective list suitable for an age not of heroes but of social history and horizontal representation. The more than fifty-eight thousand names inscribed on the wall, a collective epitaph, invite prosopopoeia, while the monument participates in the spatial prosopography of the United States on the mall as a whole.[59] On a landscape of personified nationhood, prosopographies of marginal social groups may stake out different claims to recognition, shifting the emphasis from memorials of the missing to tributes to the neglected (the affect is of vindicated pride rather than grief).

The Rotunda and the adjoining Hall of Statuary in the U.S. Capitol, for example, attempt to realize federal prosopography, imagining origins and development of an empire that subordinated first peoples as though without the aid of genocide or slavery.[60] In this concrete, neoclassical group narrative, women participated as the war-bonneted statue of Liberty above the dome, as the allegorical figures in the dome's fresco, *The Apotheosis of Washington,* and as wives at the margins of a few of the paintings. Until recently, Pocahontas (a star of many nineteenth-century collections of women's biographies) was the only female to have both name and animation within the arena of the Rotunda: either rescuing John Smith or undergoing her conversion to Christianity. Evidently, a statue of Frances Willard in 1905 and of other women thereafter, placed on the periphery of the Rotunda, had not infiltrated the Capitol sufficiently. By 1996, the omission of women from the ever-more-crowded inner circle of paintings and statuary in the Rotunda itself had become glaring enough for Adelaide Johnson's composite statue of Lucretia Mott, Elizabeth Cady Stanton, and Susan B. Anthony to be raised by Congressional order from the crypt a floor below, where it had loitered since its unveiling with feminist fanfare in 1921.[61] This awkward triumvirate provokes some of the usual objections to a set of representative figures: Why these middle-class, Anglo American women of 1848 and no others? Why a set of women rather than an individual? If the Rotunda is improved with at least an afterthought of historic womanhood, the whole nevertheless may be an irredeemable project of national forgetting—erasing unwanted versions of America—through memorials to elites.

The Capitol itself begs an allegorical reading as a model of prosopography in the modern European and North American contexts that I feature in this study. Adelaide Johnson's statue may represent the collective female biographies repeatedly rearranged, hidden in the crypt, resurrected, and reinserted in the colloquium of elite men without much destabilizing effect. For centuries, the causes of the marginal—of women, workers, people of color, the colonized or disenfranchised or disabled—have been promoted by sets of exceptional lives. A bouquet of role models is somehow just the thing to inspire individual emulation and group advancement. The ironies of this perpetual practice do not, I think, render it pointless or especially harmful—unless temporary recognition, which has its influence on ideology and self-fashioning, is mistaken for other forms of restitution or progress. The selective tradition of the marginal group may be flawed: just these three New Englanders—a statue more instructive than aesthetic. Such limitations are equally true, however, of the surrounding discourse (the Rotunda and Capitol as a whole), which really ought to include— in an era that monitors the fair share of recognition I can't help feeling what's missing—some triumphant figures of feminism and civil rights.

Prosopographies in Proportion

What share of biographical history have women been able to claim? How widespread is collective biography and the subset of all-female volumes? These questions relate to the long-standing debates about women's disproportionate exclusion from the canon. The history of collective biographies of women presents a contest for recognition similar to that in disciplines in the humanities in the later twentieth century: comparatively evanescent, marginal lists and somewhat more durable prosopographies for the whole.[62] Under the separate rubric of women's cultures, scholars may have reestablished enough female models to achieve nearer parity—or more historically accurate proportions—of women and men in a potential tally of all participants. A gender-integrated overview is rarely attempted, however. Joanna Russ charged in 1983 that textbooks and syllabi seemed incapable of accommodating women writers at more than 5–8%, though "the personnel change rather strikingly" to maintain the same proportion.[63] The percentages of the underrepresented have risen since 1983, as a glance at recent anthologies and curricula suggests. Yet the change largely consists of additions: a course in Asian American women writers or the *Norton Anthology of African American Literature* alongside the *Norton Anthology of English Literature.* Still the recuperative and the "comprehensive" activities run parallel to each other.

It would be extremely difficult to measure the proportions of men and women in life writing over time. Most critics of biography have not just avoided that difficulty but have striven for the opposite of an accurate measure: a purified, partial record. A very small homosocial canon of biography suppresses the obvious "feminine" associations of the genre itself with the mortal, embodied person and private life.[64] While criticism of biography has been preoccupied with a few full-length classics that seem to transcend the matter of the age, much of the material that we know as biography is collective and contingent.[65] The majority of biographies in English are not full-length, separate lives of eminent men but more miscellaneous records, some of which include or concentrate on women.[66] While only a few women's lives—Joan of Arc, Florence Nightingale, Queen Elizabeth I, and a handful of others—ever attract as much lasting notice as famous men, most men or women must cohabit in the annals, and most have only a small allotment of page space. Classic individualist biography resembles an imperiled work of art in an age of mechanical reproduction.

A bibliography of all-male or mixed collections would be vast indeed. Although collective biographies are an especially transient population, a few names or works endure as their prosopographical purpose retains respect: Suetonius, Plutarch, or Vasari; Aubrey, Walton, or Johnson; *The Dictionary of National Biography* and *Who's Who;* Emerson's *Representative Men* or Carlyle's *On Heroes, Hero-Worship, and the Heroic in History.* Single biographies fare somewhat better, from Boswell's Johnson to Gaskell's Brontë to Edel's James. But usually it is the eponymous protagonist that endures more than the biographer or the work. Thus certain autobiographers, who in turn become subjects of biographies, stamp their surnames on the monument: Augustine, Goethe, Rousseau, Franklin, John Stuart Mill, Cardinal Newman, and Henry Adams. It is as though the written record were merely the frame or display case around the authentic original.[67] No single collection of women has become a landmark since Chaucer (1372–86).

The recognition that multiplicity may be built into the foundation of biography surfaces only rarely.[68] Paul Sturges affirms that "the oldest established version" of biography is "collective," from "lives of saints" to "lives of 'worthies.'"[69] Thomas F. Mayer and D. R. Woolf retrace the varieties of collective exemplary lives, based on ancient models, that were fostered as "a subgenre of history" in early-modern Europe.[70] Reed Whittemore is one of the few critics to consider the effects of this rhetorical form: "Writing dozens of related biographies and giving them a common ideological and cultural context is a very different act from taking on an individual in isolation."[71] Margot Peters indeed draws a distinction between Plutarchan sets and the "modern" comparative "group biography" that sheds new light on a "well documented . . . individual" or that "allows a writer to recover the lives of persons who may not warrant separate volumes."[72] Ancient as well as recent prosopographies render subjects as representative interrelated types in the service of civic modeling and national pride. Few have remarked that collective biographies serve to consolidate genders or other social categories. This oversight has been encouraged because many a collection appears oblivious to its own criteria of selection (as when several women crop up in a volume of England's "worthies"). Yet prosopographies scarcely mask the desire to regulate differences, even when their express intentions are to set the record straight.

William Hazlitt provides an instructive example of the effort to separate canons by sex and nation in the early nineteenth century.[73] Hazlitt's prosopography *The Spirit of the Age* appeared first serially in the *New Monthly Magazine* in 1824, two years before Anna Jameson's series *The Beauties of the Court of King Charles the Second* was published there. Hazlitt's perceptive and influential work exclusively samples the British male; woman must be the matter of the age. Yet seventeenth-century predecessors in this genre (John Aubrey, Thomas Fuller, or Samuel Clark) had included a few women, and twenty years later, Richard Henry Horne's *A New Spirit of the Age* would name eight women in his more populous table of contents.[74] Hazlitt's spirit is exceptionally masculine. His critical canon *Lectures on the English Poets* is likewise masculine, in contrast with such precedents as Theophilus Cibber's *Lives of the Poets of Great Britain and Ireland* (1753). Yet it is false to say that there are no women in Hazlitt's *Lectures;* a few are crowded into the "Living Poets" section in a brief women's auxiliary outside his canon. "I am a great admirer of the female writers of the present day; they appear to me like so many modern Muses. I could be in love with Mrs. Inchbald, romantic with Mrs. Radcliffe, and sarcastic with Mme D'Arblay: but they are novel-writers. . . . The first poetess I can recollect is Mrs. Barbauld." After reminiscent praise for Barbauld, he slips in a mention of Mrs. Hannah More: perhaps still living, she is certainly prolific, but he can give no personal account of her works. Thence he moves to a diatribe against the puppetry of "Miss Baillie," whose "baby-house theatricals" have "such a *do-me-good* air," and then, as he says, "the transition . . . is not far" to insulting a male "lady-like poet," Samuel Rogers.[75]

Hazlitt covers the range of approaches to female traditions within this small window of opportunity for women writers in his volume: gallantry, nostalgic admiration, neglect (Why should anyone read Hannah More today?), and hostility. A nod to the distaff side does contribute to an air of completeness, as well as to a manly definition of the English tradition. A new de Pizan would have found in *Lectures on the English Poets* some cause for discouragement. Yet Mary Hays and others had already offered consolation in the form of female prosopographies, and from the 1830s onward the equivalents of the Ladies Reason, Rectitude, and Justice were always ready to present female models in favorable light. As the century advanced it became commonplace that the spirit of the age needed *Eminent Women of the Age.*[630]

Through the past two centuries the form of collective biography—with a bias toward the male educated elite of a nation—flourished almost unremarked. William Howitt's *Homes and Haunts of the Most Eminent British Poets* (1847) helped to establish a lucrative line of biographical piecework that continues to support literary tourism to this day.[76] Rather than allying with travel narrative or literary criticism as in Howitt or Hazlitt, collective biography might serve intellectual history, as in Bulwer Lytton's *England and the English* or, much later, Vernon Louis Parrington's *The Colonial Mind.*[77] In 1940, Leonard Russell edited a collaborative set of portraits, *English Wits,* with contributions by Wyndham Lewis, Desmond MacCarthy, A. J. A. Symons (and one woman, Olga Venn); Mary Russell Mitford, the sole female subject, brings up the rear of a parade that begins with Alexander Pope.[78] Portraits of "movements" or diachronic samplings of a cultural type often have been written as crossover trade books by professors of English, as in Richard D. Altick's *The Scholar Adventurers;* tales of forgeries and rivalries, lost manuscripts, and intrepid hunting all might be the stuff of "Noble Deeds of Anglo American English Professors," circa 1950.[79] Meanwhile, women writers continued to present groups of women in mainstream biographies for adult, nonspecialist readers.[80] Men, however, also remained active in the promulgation of female multibiography, with the occasional negative modeling.[81] The tidal wave of representation of female biography under feminist auspices still surges; I would not even begin to catalog the many albums of foremothers published by university presses in the past three decades.[82] Some recent critical prosopographies have narrated collective lives as they reflected on the practice. Among impressive examples are Phyllis Rose's *Parallel Lives: Five Victorian Marriages* and Henry Louis Gates Jr.'s *Thirteen Ways of Looking at a Black Man;* Rose acknowledges the model of Plutarch's *Parallel Lives of the Greeks and Romans,* and Gates recognizes the burdensome tradition of "Representative Negroes."[83] Few presenters or critics of this biographical mode, however, seem aware of its long history and significance.

The prevalent forms of women's intellectual and cultural history and the multitude of women preserved in them have been more than passively overlooked; the existence of such records has been actively denied. Carolyn Heilbrun accordingly affirmed, in *Writing a Woman's Life* and elsewhere, that it became possible to write a woman's life only around 1970. Heilbrun in fact would have agreed that there had been biographies of women, but she claimed that the master narratives—public history, classic biography—omit women's lives and that the few published female biographies were ironed into a single pattern for domestic use.[84] Heilbrun's own recent triple memoir of Clifton Fadiman, Lionel Trilling, and Jacques Barzun expresses a shared memory of lack: *When Men Were the Only Models We Had*.[85] Although memoir is entitled to its mythic proportions, only rarified senses of "models" and of "we" could make the statement true: there were models of successful women in many cultural fields—if not high-powered female professors at Columbia with a general audience of intellectuals—available in publications of the early and mid-twentieth century.

There are some reasons for telling the story that a period of deprivation has been followed by restitution. Men did claim the lion's share of all forms of auto/biography and almost the whole "kill" of criticism on these forms before the later twentieth century. And it is true that daylight now shines on a greater variety of women from the past than ever before. Neglected forms of writing such as diaries and letters receive increasing attention. Interest in all modes of autobiography has grown with the rise of studies of gender and race and the recovery of narratives of trauma, survival, or resistance. Many recent articles in *Biography, Auto/biography Studies: a/b* and *Prose Studies* consider lives of women and people of color. The scope of recognition has extended to working-class auto/biography, slave narratives and minority or "multicultural" autobiographies within the United States, and lives of those in underdeveloped nations.[86] Individual biographies of women have proliferated, and some feminist studies of biography have followed.[87] With the usual focus on the solitary full-length life, critics such as Linda Peterson, James Eli Adams, and Trev Broughton examine the memorial writings of Victorian men as well as women to ask questions concerning class, gender, and sexuality.[88] Poststructuralist conceptions of subjectivity have inflected a few studies of biography, such as those by William Epstein and the contributors to Rhiel and Suchoff's collection *The Seductions of Biography*.[89] Yet much of the renaissance of recognition for women seems oblivious to the history of life narrative or, rather, depends on a foreshortened perspective on that history that confirms the absence of records of women and of various marginalized groups until some variable starting point in the mid-twentieth century.[90]

As Sybil Oldfield has shown, "a great many women have not been 'hidden from history' as orthodox feminist historiography has so often maintained." Oldfield paraphrases Gerda Lerner's observation that women "have had to reinvent the wheel of women's history generation after generation. . . . whereas men could live within history." While Lerner correctly identifies an element of recurrence in the records of women, Oldfield rightly objects to the notion that women have gone missing in history. Oldfield's bibliography *Collective Biography of Women in Britain* helps to relocate "women's persistent presence in that often naive but always influential mode of history—the collective biographies of Western Europe, most of them written by men."[91] The naïveté that

Oldfield perceives in collective biographies of women cannot be ascribed simply to women as writers, subjects, or even readers. It was widely assumed in the nineteenth century, as Kate Flint has shown, that any reading (by males as well as females) entailed "identification" and, hence, the imprinting of "desirable moral and social qualities," as the prefaces of contemporary "brief biographical compilations" claim.[92] I am tempted to attribute a kind of permanent inexperience not to a female audience but to the genre itself, as though women's biographical history were always to be compiled as if for the first time. Both the amplitude and the neglect of these influential records strike me as remarkable. The exhilaration of rediscovery, however, takes on a certain pathos when I see that the act of unburial must be so often repeated.

The Designs of This Book

How to Make It as a Woman models different approaches to this large and unfamiliar body of texts. The alternate elevations or cross-sections place these works in literary history, contemporary context, and the histories of feminist and biographical criticism; feature some of the subjects and their typical narratives; and introduce some of the presenters and their address to readers. Chapter 1, "Self-Help History: Presenting Models of Womanhood," characterizes the role of the presenter in a historical context of self-help and role modeling, suggesting the auto/biographical theme of dispossession underlying prosopographical representation. Although the presenters' rhetoric, selection, and portrayal of subjects are perhaps most central to the instructive mission of these works, I shift emphasis in chapters 2 and 3 to the more entertaining roles of the subjects themselves. Chapter 2, "Heads Turn, Heads Roll: Heroic Types from Judith to Clara Barton," develops from the patterns of exceptionally enduring types that may be remembered or replaced in later generations—a limited role call that I term "compulsory typology." Although new roles may emerge, such as the nurse, in a given collection, the niche is considered sufficiently occupied if either Florence Nightingale or Clara Barton is present. (Some collections are sorted by role, as in groups of queens, nurses, writers, missionaries, or by other categories such as region or religion.) Many of the celebrated heroines played sensational parts in biblical or classical zones, revolutions or wars, and European courts or theaters. Frequently, a beauty who turns heads appears on the scene when heads roll; the tales exhibit a great deal more action—bondage, decapitation, spying, escape—than gained entree to the parson's parlor through the three-decker novels or domestic manuals. I feature a common story in which the wife or lover rescues the condemned man from prison, employing cross-gender or cross-class disguise, perhaps herself becoming imprisoned or suffering martyrdom (from Eponina to Lady Russell and Flora MacDonald), as well as that of the innocent woman who commits murder—or enters battle— to save her people from tyranny (from Judith to the Maid of Saragossa). These and other complementary narratives, including the old conventions of captivity narratives and the new story of the angel in the bureaucracy (those "nightingales" of the 1860s, Sister Dora and Clara Barton), emerge from interracial conflict or war. Illustrations represent the fallen or dismembered male body below the battlefield nurse, warrior woman, or other upright heroine—as though in revenge for the history of the nude.

In the third chapter, "How to Minister as a Woman: The Likes of Elizabeth Fry, Mary Carpenter, Dorothea Dix, and the Three Mrs. Judsons," I begin with the premise that the social work performed by most of the subjects in these collections mimics that of the volumes themselves. In the course of the nineteenth century, queens, saints, performers, and women of letters were joined by women who reformed the panoply of Foucauldian institutions, from prison, to school, to church, to hospital, to the very halls of government, while women missionaries induced parallel reforms in foreign lands. The ideal of the lady—uniting aristocratic leisure, Christian sacrifice, and the code of feminine influential altruism—melds with the paradigm of exertion, leadership, fame, and material gain, until "the mission" has become "the career" by the early decades of the twentieth century. Thus, the title page of Whiting's *Women Who Have Ennobled Life* displays the epigraph, "'For this cause came I into the world'—'not to be ministered unto, but to minister.'"

The fourth chapter continues the focus on nineteenth-century middle-class subjects but also includes some female presenters as the service that the subjects perform shifts from philanthropy to literature. "The Lessons of the Medusa: Anna Jameson and Mutual Multibiography" studies Jameson's work and reception within a network of women of letters. Jameson's collective biographies of women illustrate a range of models from the progressive Portias to the transgressive Lady Macbeths to the self-immolating Ophelias. Jameson herself has been obscured by misconstructions of her persona, yet she proves a worthy ancestor of different modes of feminist criticism today. The fifth chapter, "The World's Fair Women; or, Racial Progress in the Nineteenth Century," turns from the modeling of certain benevolent missions to the arguments concerning woman's role in interracial, national, and global histories. Prosopographies before and after the abolition of slavery in the United States, and during the expansion of imperialism in the early twentieth century, attempted universal biographical histories calibrated by gender and race. It was a longstanding precept that the status of woman was the measure of civilization. Sarah Hale issues Anglo-Saxon, Christian, imperialist propaganda along with her praise of all notable women of all eras. Other presenters promote their own versions of timeless universal gender or national narratives of individual women. At the time of the World's Columbian Exposition in 1893, numerous "global" prosopographies of women provoked an urgent need for African American female prosopographies.

In the final two chapters, I return to matters of literary history and feminist critique that have governed the status of female prosopography. In chapter 6, "Writing Women's Lives, Revisited: Virginia Woolf and the Missing Canons of Biography," I feature Woolf's split role as doyenne of modernist biography and as sponsor of gynocriticism. I retrieve some of the female collective biographies generated in the vicinity of Bloomsbury before I correct some of the astigmatisms in visions of life writing. The concluding chapter, "Our Queen Victoria: Feminist Prosopography," reviews a history—up to the present—of Anglo American female prosopography through representation of Victoria. While many anthologies from the 1840s till well past her death feature the eponymous heroine of the age, second-wave feminist literary studies, in turn, seem peculiarly drawn back to biographical interest in the queen herself, who stands for the sovereign subject in spite of her immersion in collective constructions. Unresolved contemporary issues concerning aesthetic value, canonicity, gender coding of work and sexuality, and the class status and legitimate ancestry of the feminist academic herself seem displaced into the Gilbert-and-Gubar canon and onto the Homans-and-Munich queen.

Before I turn to a brief history of female collective biography in English, I should note a few more important aims of the book—with a few roads not taken—and offer a quick guide to the common conventions in lives of famous women. Engaged as I am with myriad bids for the attention of aspiring readers, what I offer cannot be a publishing history, an analytical bibliography of the printed books as physical objects, or a contribution to *l'histoire du livre*.[93] Rather, I participate in the historical studies of women's relations to writing, publishing, reading, education, and vocation during the nineteenth century by Nina Baym, Martha Vicinus, Sally Mitchell, and others.[94] By training and inclination, I concentrate on feminist interpretation of narrative form in historical contexts. At the same time, I diverge from the study of a female literary tradition as I and others have practiced it. Although I discuss some of the prominent compilers of women's biographies, particularly in a network of Victorian women of letters—and although many authors enjoy popularity in these volumes—this study downplays the concept of an author, as these publications value collaboration and imitation rather than originality. The professionalization of authorship and struggle for copyright are scarcely visible in a subgenre that almost everyone regarded as useful or ornamental packaging for reproductions of priceless originals.[95]

I have chosen to examine as thoroughly as possible the great variety of female prosopography in book form, setting aside the numerous individual biographies published in book series and the many brief lives in magazines. It would be rewarding to study the concurrent developments of serialized print and popular prosopographies. As Annette Wheeler Cafarelli claims, "print culture" itself, particularly in serial forms, encouraged an "aesthetic of fragmentation" and the habits of reading "discontinuous narratives."[96] Multibiographical books have a longer history than do journalistic series, and indeed they predate printing. In modern book form, collective biographies, along with monographic biographies, make greater claim to permanence and to the edifying power of histories than do the short lives of women or men appearing in periodicals.

Magazines invariably include many other solicitations of reader attention besides the women's biographies they may reproduce. Volumes that consisted exclusively of biographies of women must have been marketed on the presumed value of such reading, as well as, probably, on the prestige associated with such subject matter or with ownership of elegant editions (the only advertising to appear in such collections consists of publishers' catalogs).

Concerned as I am with the way these works interpellate readers (loosely translated, "to call into identity"), I nevertheless have not undertaken a study of reader response or a reception history. Such collections were rarely reviewed and seldom distinguished by author or title and were thus unlikely to be recalled as formative childhood reading or discussed in memoirs, letters, or essays. Undoubtedly, demand for such books was partly driven by Sunday school and missionary societies, schools and libraries, and parents (as in late-Victorian juvenile series), but it would also have been spurred by individual readers who spent discretionary money on the increasingly inexpensive varieties of volumes available after midcentury. Once the texts were acquired or borrowed and read, the effects are likewise unknown. Did readers change their actions in order more closely to resemble eminent women, or were these role models rather fantasy illustrations of female fate removed from ordinary conditions, or exceptions that forestall any need to change the rules? Answers to such questions are as elusive as the response of Victorian schoolchildren to the prize books of fiction, history, or biography produced and awarded for their moral benefit.[97]

There was plenty in these life narratives to appeal to readers. A set of conventional elements recurs in the tales in different combinations, ordering, or emphasis, usually with a significant shift away from novelistic marriage plots toward ambition or vocation. Very often, a chapter will begin with *birth,* closely allied with native soil and nationhood as well as ancestry and class status, and it will end, very often, with *death,* sometimes lingering and always hopeful of reward. Considerable interest attaches to graves as well as birthplaces of famous women. In between, the elements vary in prevalence, the one essential element being *vocation or work*—including precocious learning, acts of charity, spiritual vision, works of genius, even feats of entrepreneurship—and its common associate, *deeds,* which subsumes travel, combat or rescue, and revolution or reform that requires confrontation with male rulers. Most tales include some certification of *prestige,* a cluster of traits associated with birth, class, and privileged zones (e.g., nature, Paris), but often confirmed later in life when the heroine is recognized by a poet or receives an audience with royalty or a reward from the state. Equally important to the exemplary power of the tale is *influence*—featuring scenes of instruction or conversion (with testimonial weeping) of everyone from children to pupils to politicians to natives—and some form of *religion,* with variations that I shall note in later chapters.

Other expected topoi turn out to be optional. On the one hand, short lives may dwell on the *body,* specified as vigorous, frail, beautiful, or pitiably ill;

love, including suitors rejected or happily won, with some few instances of martyrdom for love or grieving widowhood or, occasionally, a positive portrayal of lifelong female companionship; or *family,* requiring exemplary conduct as daughter, wife, or mother or resourcefulness when husband or father fails to provide or is captured or incarcerated. On the other hand, the body, love, and family may be ignored almost entirely in the telling of a woman's public career. While each of the above story elements may occur in male biography and in novels, men's lives mute the matters of the body, influence, and family. Most nineteenth-century novels, in contrast, suppress female vocation and force a heroine to pay for any deeds or for the wrong kind of love.

Female prosopography thus controverts the conventions of the novel, men's biography, much of history, and advice literature in portraying female agency. Readers most likely engaged with such narratives not to observe variations on conventional options but to recreate impressions of women who had really lived, in both senses of that phrase. The presentation is not always realist, but much of the power of these publications must lie in the invitation to revisit actual lives. I want to emphasize the typological patterns of such prosopographical works without abstracting the appeal of the historical women. Given the thousands of subjects and hundreds of collections that exist, I can characterize only a few of the heroines, such as Judith or Charlotte Corday, Elizabeth Fry or Mary Carpenter. Similarly, I leave unexplored most of the labyrinthine by-ways of historical authentication of the biographies (what, e.g., is the currently plausible history of Zenobia of Palmyra, and what sources guided the redactors who put her tale in currency in collective biographies?). It is with the reiterated narratives, the ostensibly true legends, that I have to do. I prefer to err on the side of the amateur woman reader of the day, or what Anna Makolkin calls the "zero-degree biographee": the capable but uncritical reader who accepted as plausible a cornucopia of heroines—often in the style and scale of Scott's historical fiction—and who perhaps derived pleasure, instruction, and designs for living as much from the folkloric actions and images as from the didactic framework.[98] While parents and teachers smiled on biography as "good for you," girls like Austen's Catherine Morland might find female multibiography much more palatable than "real solemn history" and discover in its pages a supply of incident worthy of romance or gothic fiction.

Types and Chronotopes of a Subgenre

To attempt a full history of collective biography would be to break the contract of selective arrangement to which readers expect biographers or historians to adhere. Even to limit my attention to collections of women's biographies published in English in the past two centuries would nonetheless swell this book beyond the weight that any coffee table could bear. A panorama of female prosopography should range far beyond Anglo American contexts in the nineteenth and early twentieth centuries. For instance, it should feature ancient Chinese collections of women, medieval lives based on classical models, humanist catalogs in the modern vernaculars of Europe, the series of exemplary women that were modeled on classic Arabic collections and published in early twentieth-century Egypt, and the feminist-inflected "area studies" of women around the world today.[99] While nations frequently shared each other's famous women (as the Egyptians lauded Joan of Arc or the New England astronomer Maria Mitchell), some form of female prosopography seems to be a necessary component of nationhood. As Geraldine DeLuca put it in a 1986 omnibus review of young adult biographies of women, "I cannot imagine a civilized culture without this uneasy amalgam of history and the novel."[100]

Undoubtedly there were many contributing factors in the "rise" of collective biographies of women. Antecedents of the texts in my bibliography predate modern publishing, the enfranchised middle class, Enlightenment individualism, the novel, and the other "heroes" credited with the invention of the modern subject. A conspicuous starting place would be the lists of legendary women circulating internationally among European, classically educated writers in the vernacular; the templates were Christian hagiography, while the sources might be pagan, as in Boccaccio's (1361–75), Chaucer's (1372–86), or de Pizan's (1405) catalogs.[101] The international *querelle des femmes* continued through the sixteenth and seventeenth centuries in many representations of "lives of illustrious women."[102] As Mary Garrard has illustrated, Renaissance and baroque paintings and engravings of "*femmes fortes*" often cast contemporary eminent women as reincarnations of "predecessors," such as Marie de' Medici or Anne of Austria as Minerva; early modern biographies drew analogies between Catherine de' Medici and Artemisia or between Blanche of Castile and Judith and Esther.[103] This pattern of compulsory typology—justifying as well as constraining the avatar in terms of a great woman of the past—prevails in collective biographies of women to this day.[104]

The English fashion for collections of celebrated women, like fashion in other respects, often took its models from the French. Various French and English compilers in the seventeenth century began to popularize—beyond a court audience—a canon of female eminence, as in Madeleine de Scudéry's *Les Femmes illustres ou les harangues héroïques* (1642), published as *The Female Orators* in London in 1714.[105] Plundering each other, many later collections relied on the Abbé de Brantôme's *Le Livre des dames*, a gallery of contemporary or recent European queens and noblewomen first published posthumously in Holland in 1665 as *Vie des dames illustres* (*Lives of Illustrious Dames*) and soon appearing in recurrent English editions.

A neoclassical passion for universal typology prevails in several seventeenth-century British catalogs of woman. Thomas Heywood was an ambitious synthesizer of woman before the Interregnum in Britain; he might be seen as compiling a Yeatsian *Vision* or symbolic universe. *Gynaikeion; or, Nine Books of Various History concerning Women, Inscribed by the Names of the Nine Muses* (1624; later published with a title that begins, *The Generall History of Women* [1657]), and another venture by Heywood, *The Exemplary Lives and Memorable Acts of Nine of the Most Worthy Women of the World: Three Iewes, Three Gentiles, Three Christians* (1640), include the sort of personnel that staffed *The City of Ladies*: Deborah, Judith, Esther, Boadicea, and the Amazon Penthisilea.[106] In *Gynaikeion,* Heywood humbly submits "a Collection of Histories, which touch the generalitie of Women, such as have either beene illustrated for their Vertues, and Noble Actions, or contrarily branded for the Vices, and baser Conditions.... Here thou mayest reade of all degrees, from the Scepter in the Court, to the Sheepe-hooke in the Cottage: of all Times, from the first Rainebow, to the last blazing Starre: of all knowne Nations, ... of all Faiths; Jews, Pagans, or Christians: of all Callings" ("To the Reader," n.p.). A universal handbook, whether of or for women or both, has a lot to cover.[107]

An examination of Heywood's elaborate "index or table" reveals little that is historical or even humanly female: Nemesis, Fortune, Ceres, Morning and Night, the Sybils of Delphi, and many others parade by before Semiramis or other women of historical standing appear (122). Belatedly he addresses Queen Elizabeth: "That as you are the last of these in this my Catalogue by order, posterity may reckon you the first amongst the Illustrious by merit" (125). Anticipating modern self-help reliance on identification, he explains: "The purpose of my tractate, is to exemplifie, not to instruct; to shew you presidents of vertue ... ; and that setting so many statues of honour before your eyes, ... each heroick and well disposed Ladie, or woman lower degreed ... may out of all ... apprehend some one thing or other worthie imitation ... and everie of you fashion her selfe as complete a woman for vertue, as *Apelles* made up the purtraiture of his godesse, for beautie" (118–19). Patchwork girl, indeed; the power of stories to model subjectivity would seem to be remarkably old news.

Heywood's enthusiasm for comprehensive sampling was shared somewhat later in this period by prosopographers of men and women such as Thomas Fuller, whose *History of the Worthies of England* (1662) includes "all the women ... preserved as part of local tradition" in England.[108] John Shirley's *The Illustrious History of Women* (1686) centers on women in Heywood's manner, and in 1688, Nathaniel Crouch matched Heywood's endeavor with a similar pattern of nine types (and four of the same names) under the pseudonym Robert Burton: *Female Excellency; or The Ladies Glory* (reissued in 1728, and in 1765 retitled *The Female Worthies: Or, the Ladies Glory*). Burton's address "To the Reader" seems to anticipate the constructivist argument (and reliance on precedents) that developed through the nineteenth century (John Stuart Mill says pretty much the same in *The Subjection of Women*): "Though Women from the injurious estimates of the World, have been commonly reckoned uncapable of noble Undertakings ... consider how many outward Advantages Men are allowed above them ... and if Women had the same Helps, I dare not say but they would make as good Returns, of which there have been many famous Instances in former Ages."[109]

Though in some respects these early collections of women in modern English anticipate the form that would flourish in the nineteenth century, in other ways they help to measure a dramatic change in register, from mythology and sacred history to the emergent national history. The most dramatic development in the tradition of female multibiography comes with the advent of brand-new model women, particularly those of middle rank, distributed among the subjects handed down from antiquity. Although this partly entailed the process of secularization that affected all genres of writing, the subjects continued to serve some religious themes. "History" itself might quickly supply the sacred or legendary, as when the Reformation generated its own books of martyrs, with numerous women among the men.[110] In the eighteenth century, middle-class models of learning and the arts began to join the mighty or the holy; in the nineteenth century, these types were joined by women of social service and reform and by missionaries of religion or of causes metaphorically associated with religion (as in Josephine Butler's "crusade" or the temperance "mission").

Another line of development for modern female prosopography might be traced less in the shifting types of subjects and more through the earliest women presenters. Female historians and literary scholars resurface if one looks past the standard genres, as Natalie Zemon Davis, Nina Baym, and others have done.[111] In early modern Europe, upper-class widows and nuns often recorded dynastic or monastic memoirs.[112] As a few female historians later flourished, such as Catherine Macaulay in England (1731–91) and later Emma Willard in the United States (1787–1870), women in both countries began to produce biographical collections that reward consideration as historiography. In the antebellum United States, a number of women historians emerged who nevertheless wrote national histories largely devoid of female agents.[113] Yet American women did begin, in the 1830s and 1840s, to produce "particular" histories of women: biographical collections that portrayed female participation in the public sphere. On both sides of the Atlantic, when Victorian women wrote history, it largely took the form of biographical collections of women.[114] As Rohan Maitzen has pointed out, for Victorian women writers, female biography was actually the main avenue into historiography, an opportunity to assume the authority of nonfiction prose.[115] A woman who presented the biographies of women writers, actresses or courtesans, missionaries, reformers, queens, or saints found she could simultaneously write on serious subjects—art, history, religion—and share in the celebrity and cultural capital of her prototypes, while affirming women's historical roles and contributions to learning.

A history of female collective biographies in English would need to trace not only the rise of women's historiography and the emergence of middle-class women's vocations but also the changing conditions in publishing within interdependent social and economic developments. The production of multi-biographical books expanded with modern publishing practices (as small-scale booksellers gave way to increasingly specialized editorial, printing, and retailing enterprises), influenced by the decreasing cost of paper, mechanized printing, and improved transportation for greater ease of distribution (especially in North America, where obtaining books remained difficult well into the nineteenth century).[116] The economic transformations of the later eighteenth and early nineteenth centuries had increased the proportion of families with the literacy and disposable income for reading and the conditions for conspicuous leisure among women, with an attendant elaboration of an Evangelical domestic ideology formulated as "woman's mission" or "the cult of true womanhood."[117] The contributing social changes—including initiatives in both Britain and the United States, at different times, for education of both sexes and several classes and for emancipation or enfranchisement of Catholics, slaves, workers, provincial interests (beyond London and New England), and women—are too many and perhaps too familiar to analyze here. It is nevertheless certain that collective biographies of women flourished from the 1830s and accompanied the various pulses on behalf of broadening recognition for the above social elements.

The rates of publication (see app. fig. A1) suggest that collective biographies of women tripled and quadrupled in popularity across the decades. In the 1830s, most years yielded seven to nine collections; by the 1840s, annual rates of ten to fifteen were common, with twenty in 1848 and twenty-two in 1850. The year 1854 brought forty-two collective biographies. From 1850, most years exceed twenty volumes, and through the 1880s and 1890 a rate above thirty per annum became common enough, with high points (thirty-nine to forty-three) in 1893–95 and 1900. Variations within such counts offer few clues as to their causes, especially given the different motivations and production schedules of book projects and the inconsistency of reprinting (the counts include later as well as first editions).[118] Yet in broad outline, it seems that peaks coincide with periods of economic prosperity, public agitation for rights, and newly minted celebrity careers. Crises such as the U.S. Civil War and World War I might be expected to have an impact (at least on the price of paper) and may have, in fact, contributed to dips in their wake, but new female subjects became prominent through these events. The relative declines in some years of the twentieth century may reflect not only the economy but also social changes that made commendation appear more old-fashioned and less effective than other available modes of women's advancement.

The books themselves display changing designs and expectations. The more sporadic publications of the early nineteenth century were usually unillustrated and tailored for the broadest market. The mid-nineteenth century's increasing variety included expensive steel-engraved formats suitable for the annual gift book or for school-prize presentation, as well as more practical formats and increasingly specialized themes.[119] Beginning in the 1870s, but especially during the period 1890–1920, highly colored, gilded, curlicued covers and numerous children's-tale illustrations adorn many female collective biographies, issued in lap size (octavo) for private reading rather than table size (quarto) for shared display. From the 1870s onward, official commemorative projects led to collaborative volumes by women of a region or group, as in the cataloging efforts of states in preparation for the 1893 World's Columbian Exposition or the tributes to pioneer Australian women in the 1930s, a period of centennial celebrations. New lives came into the mix with increasing speed and quantity, as more women participated in newsworthy events or became celebrated for their own successful careers. Such careers in turn sponsored collections of that category. Articles in magazines and newspapers, memoirs, volumes of letters, or more rarely the full-length authorized biography supplied the material that rapidly disseminated through the selections of famous lives. By no means are these volumes addressed solely to girls.[120] Across the later Victorian decades, prefaces often took up the question of emancipation and progress for women rather than the task of modeling youth. At the same time, some collections signaled discriminating taste, literary refinements, or scholarly pretensions.

Instead of a genealogy of authors—the standard organization of literary history—the subgenre of prosopography requires attention to changes in the principles of selection and commendation of model subjects. In general, two strains competed for prominence in the prosopographies of women: learning, which I shall associate with George Ballard, and piety, codified early on by Thomas Gibbons. The most influential English prototype of the turn to women of learning was also one of Europe's first explicitly national tributes to female achievement, Ballard's *Memoirs of Several Ladies of Great Britain Who Have Been Celebrated for Their Writings or Skill in the Learned Languages, Arts and Sciences* (1752), a collection of lives that "best deserve our imitation" (53). Ballard's work much deserved imitation; *Memoirs* was perpetually reissued or repackaged through the nineteenth and twentieth centuries. By 1827, Anna Maria Lee's *Memoirs of Eminent Female Writers, of All Ages and Countries* added to a swelling stream of biographical literary anthologies.[e.g., 349; 372; 385] Simultaneously, the pious tradition developed, as in Thomas Gibbons's 1777 *Memoirs of Eminently Pious Women, Who Were Ornaments of Their Sex, Blessings to Their Countries and Edifying Examples to the Church and World,* again frequently amplified or repackaged by later editors and again raising the honor of British womanhood (the forty-eight subjects in the 1804 edition, edited by George Jerment, overlap with only seven subjects in Ballard's list, also of forty-eight). Yet Gibbons soon reappeared in an American guise (edited by Daniel Dana in 1803, and in 1815 by Samuel Burder), and pious themes prevail in most collections of that time period. In the long run, however, Ballard's standard outlasted Gibbons's. Whereas models of piety live presumably quieter lives and vanish in a generation, some women writers lay claim to recognition across the centuries.

In the nineteenth century it was a commonplace that relative degrees of civilization could be measured by the standing of women in each country and that much of the good found in history could be attributed to woman's influence. Laura C. Holloway, in the preface to her 1883 *The Mothers of Great Men and Women, and Some Wives of Great Men,*[411] declares, "The deeds of heroism in every age have been the indirect, if not the direct, work of women, and most frequently of mothers" (n.p.). Thirty years earlier, Sarah Hale, editor of *Godey's Lady's Book* and ambitious prosopographer of "all distinguished women" in her 1853 *Woman's Record*,[362] had declared that "the true progress of every race is marked in the condition of the women." The Anglo-Saxon Christian nations, by that measure, were indisputably the most advanced (564).[121] Yet the moral progress initiated by women articulates itself in a distinctly literary, rather than religious, tradition among women. Hale readily reconciles the Ballard and Gibbons strains, as *Woman's Record* overwhelmingly favors pious writers. In both her journal and her encyclopedia, Hale recruited women to authorship and arguably was "a pioneer in the professionalization of authors, male and female."[122] Hale and her successors even claimed that the woman of genius might be both a good woman and a survivor—as though to counteract the myths of Corinne or LEL (Letitia Elizabeth Landon) or even Charlotte Brontë.

Many collections are sponsored by religious societies (as was Whiting's), and many narratives conventionally attest to the heroine's youthful piety or early conversion. Although some collections are sectarian (and most of the new recruits are Quaker, Methodist, or Unitarian), the prosopographies have more to gain from affirming an ecumenical Christian cause indistinguishable from the cause of global womanhood. Highlighting the aim of religious instruction, many collections feature heroines of the Bible; there were at least two dozen publications similar to Charles Adams's 1854 *Women of the Bible*.[2] Various religious groups honored their own canons of women, as does the aptly named Charles Wesley Bouy's 1893 *Representative Women of Methodism*.[130] And the lives of missionaries seem to have whetted an appetite, throughout the last three quarters of the nineteenth century, in at least fifteen publications along the lines of Augustus Robert Buckland's 1895 *Women in the Mission Field, Pioneers and Martyrs*.[128]; 123

Not all the subjects are European or Christian. At times, Jewish women form a commendable set.[72; 473; 493; 508; 742; 851; 930] Grace Aguilar assembled two volumes of *The Women of Israel*,[19] with an exceptionally long publication run (1845 to at least 1917). The Jewish Aguilar protests that presenters of biblical women attribute progress for women "to Christianity alone," as though "the law of Moses sank the Hebrew female to the lowest state of degradation." "We feel neither anger nor uncharitableness towards those who would thus deny to Israel those very privileges which were ours, ages before they became theirs," but Aguilar must correct the false claim "lest . . . the young and thoughtless daughter of Israel may believe it" (1:8–9).[19]; 124 Mrs. John A. Logan's comprehensive collaboration from 1912, *The Part Taken by Women in American History*,[516] includes a chapter titled "Jewish Women of America" (counterpart to chapters on Catholics and "Christian Science").[125] Rarely, collections admit a modern Jewish woman such as Rachel, the early-nineteenth-century French actress who in spite of early poverty retained "the hands of a princess," according to Alfred de Musset.[624, pp. 362–71] Nevertheless, the Christian, European middle class appears to set the standard for all humanity. An Asian woman may join the list either as a famous ruler (thus Tze-hi, the Empress Dowager of China[712]), as an exotic beauty of rank, or as a model of the benefits of Christianity and European education.[137; 271; 367; 611; 928] Toru Dutt of Calcutta (1856–77) was posthumously well received as "an educated Hindu" who had acquired "the natural speech of a Parisian lady" and whose poetry and other writings caught the attention of Edmund Gosse. Her story combined the conventions of the learned dying "poetess" and the innocent singer of native lore.[624, pp. 530–45; see also 156; 624; 626; 628]

The religious nationalism at stake in these female prosopographies may coincide with Ballardesque promotion of women's cultural achievement, as I have suggested. Influenced by the feminism of the 1790s, women themselves began to contribute different forms of biographical history of women. Mary Hays, proponent of Wollstonecraftian feminism, published *Female Biography,* appearing in 1803 in London and 1807 in Philadelphia, and *Memoirs of Queens* in London in 1821, the latter designed to promote "the moral rights and intellectual advancement of *woman*" through "records of female eminence and worth" (v–vi).[126] Anna Jameson, initially more conservative than Hays, became an outspoken model and advocate of "difference" feminism; by the later 1820s, she launched a series of popular collections in the common categories—beauties, mistresses, queens—that acknowledge women as historical counterparts to men. Such works as *Memoirs of Celebrated Female Sovereigns*[453] of 1831 successfully bridged the transatlantic markets and the transition from a phase of postrevolutionary reaction to a Victorian code of domesticity.[127]

In the 1840s, some multivolume collections—remarkable for being based on archival research—staked a definitive claim for women in national history: Agnes Strickland and Elizabeth Strickland with the sixteen-volume *The Lives of the Queens of England, From the Norman Conquest,*[763] published over the period 1840–48; Louisa Stuart Costello's four-volume *Memoirs of Eminent Englishwomen,*[200] which appeared in 1844; Mary Anne Everett Green [Wood] with the three-volume *Letters of Royal and Illustrious Ladies of Great Britain*[341] in 1846; and, from 1849 to 1855, the four volumes of *Lives of the Princesses of England;*[342] and Elizabeth Ellet's *Women of the American Revolution,*[259] which enjoyed many reprintings in two or three volumes, beginning in 1848.[128] While the scholarly standards for such biography became more demanding over the decades, the professionalization of history gradually edged out the amateur biographical historian, while at the same time the demand that biography measure up to belles lettres demoted most collective biographies.

Across the decades, the titles of these collections echo and rearrange themselves in the manner of Gertrude Stein. A single collection may appear in strangely mutable forms. For instance, Lydia Maria Child's collection of 1846–50, *Biographies of Good Wives,*[170] was first published as *Good Wives* in 1833.[129] Portions of the latter also appeared, in 1848, in "Miss M. Kendrick's" *Gift Book of Biography for Young Ladies.*[484] As an entire collection, *Good*

Wives had reincarnations as *Celebrated Women* (1858) and *Married Women: Biographies of Good Wives* (1871): nearly forty years of a much imitated type, the wives of great men, under shifting titles.[130] Throughout the central decades of the century, "good" women paraded before the public eye, modifying the definition of goodness constructed in the Gibbons tradition. Charlotte M. Yonge, best known for her novels ("The Author of *The Heir of Redclyffe*") and her *Book of Golden Deeds*,[925] also produced a collaborative collection in 1862, *Biographies of Good Women*,[924] which had the same thirty-year longevity, from the 1860s to 1890s, as her *Deeds*. Other titles sounded the note of the "good" while also capitalizing on the market for juvenile literature: Lydia Huntley Sigourney's *Great and Good Women: Biographies for Girls*[720] (1866, and continuing in print in the 1880s); or Catherine Mary Macsorley's *A Few Good Women, and What They Teach Us: A Book for Girls* of 1886.[536] By World War I, the definition of good might appear quite distinct from its early meanings, as in Cecil Ker's 1916 *Women Who Have Made Good*.[485] During the same period, many piecemeal offerings to children presented the childhoods of eminent personages,[148; 289; 692; 734; 818] with increasing emphasis on militaristic valor and national service.[131] Characteristically these offered "his" and "hers" versions of such generic titles as *Historic Girls*[114; see also 409] (an 1887 sequel to *Historic Boys*). The fusion of titles and long reprint lives of many collections support one harmonious story of model womanhood—or more immediately, they signify the opportunism of publishers and the sense that presenters claimed little credit. Given the carelessness with titles and contents, one suspects that few works ever earned the sort of audience loyalty that induces parents to supply the book in their own children's formative years, yet some collections remained in print long enough to be enjoyed across generations.

Like the titles, the illustrations served as important guides to reader response that were nevertheless beyond the biographer's control. Almost all volumes published after midcentury included at least a frontispiece, with often as many as ten or twelve portraits of the subjects, and the larger format, more expensive Victorian volumes were lavishly illustrated. Illustrations may be the first cause of a publication, as in "books of beauty" such as the Findens' *Portraits of the Female Aristocracy of the Court of Queen Victoria,* first published around 1839 and then again a decade later.[297] However realist the text, the portraits in most collections romanticized freely, until cheaper photographic reproduction led to a new regard for the individual's genuine appearance. Sometimes the engravings copied oil paintings taken "from life," yet very often the artist resembled an illustrator of fiction or even served the function of an advertising agency, furnishing daydream types. As in a Revlon ad campaign in the 1990s in which a row of models with slightly shifting contours and hair shades was presented as "the most beautiful women in the world," images in many Victorian volumes formed idealized comparative series. Even in support of a history of women, collections may, like Hollywood historical dramas, depict fashions of female features and coiffure as if they were ahistorical and universal.

Certain illustrations led an itinerant life from publication to publication (tracing sources would be another detective project). Queen Elizabeth, painted by Edward Corbould and engraved by William Holl, appeared in Appleton's luxuriant New York edition of Agnes Strickland's *The Queens of England*[764]; this same adult, equestrian, imperious Elizabeth, engraved by Buttre, adorns James Parton's "Girlhood of Queen Elizabeth," contrasting with all the other illustrations in the 1888 collection *Daughters of Genius*[624] (fig. 1). While the same image may circulate, the illustrations of different subjects often look

Fig. 1 *Queen Elizabeth* by Edward Corbould, engraved by William Holl. From Agnes Strickland and Elisabeth Strickland, *Queens of England* (1851),[764] and Mary Howitt, ed., *Biographical Sketches* (1868),[424] and engraved by J. C. Buttre in James Parton, *Daughters of Genius* (1888).[624]

Fig. 2 Cleopatra by Charles Staal, engraved by Edwards, from Mary Cowden Clarke, *World-Noted Women* (1857),[174] and Frank Boott Goodrich, *World-Famous Women* (1891).[331]

alike, not only within a volume but across different collections. Appleton's also published Mary Cowden Clarke's *World-Noted Women*,[174] in which designs by Charles Staal, engraved by Francis Holl, make Sappho and Aspasia, Petrarch's Laura and Lady Jane Grey look like pairs of twin sisters from the same family.[132] Charles Staal became something of an implied historian of woman, as what might have been his favorite model or his feminine ideal donned various period costumes and accessories. Cleopatra (fig. 2) is hardly the effulgent seductress in the barge like a burnished throne or the martyred lover with the asp but, rather, the royal matron and thinker bravely facing her regrets. Certainly she has no African features here or in other images in the Victorian collections, and her draperies would be suitable for a performance of *Lady Macbeth* on a nineteenth-century stage.[133] This same Cleopatra reappeared as the frontispiece in Frank B. Goodrich's *World-Famous Women*[331] when it was reissued in 1891.[134] In Clarke's 1857 album,[174] Cleopatra's avatar, Joan (fig. 3), is more of a girl, without jewelry or dark charms, grasping a cruciform sword (and a tentative riding crop?) before her fanciful feminine armor and midcentury crinolined skirt; the tents of war behind her might be the curtains

Fig. 3 *Joan of Arc* by Charles Staal, engraved by G. H. Mote, from Mary Cowden Clarke, *World-Noted Women* (1857).[331]

of a Victorian drawing room. Joan of Arc adorns the covers or frontispieces of many collections; as possibly the most frequently illustrated heroine, she prompts curious solutions to the puzzle of a warlike yet feminine saint, similar to Lucy Snowe's compromise when acting a male role in Brontë's *Villette*.

Transcultural anachronism prevails. Pocahontas (fig. 4) is permitted to be brave, with her peace pipe and a shawl held over the breast that is bared in other illustrations of this ancestress of Virginians, this Christian convert who died in England.[173; 331] Pocahontas's hair and expression nearly match those of Florence Nightingale (fig. 5), though the crossing of their arms is reversed. Nightingale, whose Crimean war campaign began in 1854, was thirty-eight years old when Clarke's *World-Noted Women* was published three years later. Her image evidently was still flexible in the public imagination, as the different style of figure 8 suggests. Staal's version in Clarke (perhaps drawing on an early portrait) affirms Nightingale's familiarity to her near kin, the readers,

Fig. 4 Pocahontas by Charles Staal, engraved by B. Eyles, from Mary Cowden Clarke, *World-Noted Women* (1857).[331]

with her unambiguous corset, crucifix, and nearly direct gaze.[135] With some frequency, the same subject bears no resemblance to herself in different portraits: an elaborate historical painting of "Mrs. Fry Reading to the Prisoners in Newgate, 1816" (fig. 20), relying on the famous portrait of the Regency Quaker in her tall cap, completely contradicts the midcentury lady represented in a simple frontispiece, "Mrs. Fry in Newgate," the sole illustration in Russell's *Extraordinary Women*.[692]; 136

Eminent Women of the Age,[630] by James Parton and others, exhibits a different style of illustrations from Clarke's *World-Noted Women,* with a similar tendency to meld a collective likeness. The frontispiece reproduces the famous portrait by Edouard Dubufe or Dubuffe of the celebrated painter of animals, Rosa Bonheur. In it, Bonheur looks like a boy in spite of her skirts, one hand, holding a drawing pen, resting on the shoulder of a friendly bull (or is it a cow?), portfolio cradled under her other arm (fig. 6). At the end of the volume,

Fig. 5 *Florence Nightingale* by Charles Staal, engraved by G. H. Mote, from Mary Cowden Clarke, *World-Noted Women* (1857).[331]

a head-and-shoulders image of the sculptor Harriet G. Hosmer in boyish haircut, white collar, and loose bowtie might be a close-up of Rosa Bonheur (this also is "Engd. By Augustus Robin, N.Y."; fig. 7). (Dubufe's half-length portrait of Bonheur [after 1853; engraved by Oliver Pelton] also resembles Hosmer's image.) As it happens, the Bonheur and Hosmer portraits were originally taken from life, and these women seem not only to have worn similar masculine attire from the waist up and to have adopted similar hairstyles but also to have had a similar kind of energetic, dark good looks. Opposite the frontispiece of Bonheur, Florence Nightingale appears in a title page vignette as a slightly Spanish or at least Catholic maiden (remember the controversy over her having hired nuns as nurses), with a flower in her hair and a crucifix at her throat, eyes veiled in reading a small book like a breviary. This image had earlier graced Clark's *Portraits of Celebrated Women*,[173] in a different engraving (fig. 8). Though this Nightingale bears a slight resemblance to Margaret Fuller (in Parton's *Eminent Women*), she resembles no one so much as the version of young Queen Victoria in Parton (also by Perine). That Parton's homier sisterhood share names and

Fig. 6 *Rosa Bonheur* by Edouard Dubuffe (or Dubufe), engraved by Augustus Robin, from James Parton et al., *Eminent Women of the Age* (1869).[630]

attributes with the elegantly elongated images in Clarke's *World-Noted Women* says much about the collective, optimal representation in such volumes. The images ignore historical and cultural differences and rely on a prop box full of iconography; presumably readers did not ask what the original person "really" looked like, but sought their own mannequin likenesses.

In general, illustrations increased in number from the middle of the century; volumes after 1860 rarely omitted portraits unless they were willing to forfeit the juvenile or popular market. The high-action plotting of children's fiction at the turn of the twentieth century was anticipated in 1862 by Joseph Johnson's *Clever Girls of Our Time*,[466] with its eight engravings of similar scenes that invite the (youthful) fantasy of performing passion or genius before an audience: for example, "Miss Browning [*sic*] witnesses the drowning of her Brother"; "Catherine Hayes singing in the summerhouse" (in both compositions, observers in the left background support the heroine who looks away to the right); "Malibran declaiming on the stairs" (a spectacled man listens

Fig. 7 *Harriet Hosmer,*
engraved by Augustus Robin,
from James Parton et al.,
Eminent Women of the Age
(1869).[630]

Eng.ᵈ by Augustus Robin.N.Y.

through a door under the stairs to the unselfconscious operatic rehearsal).[137] In works not designated for young readers, the most common convention was the head-and-shoulders portrait, in later decades a photograph with enlarged signature. Recent or living famous women began to appear as a series of idiosyncratic individuals with credentials, seniority, and respectable fashion, like members of a board rather than a host of seraphim.[138] Sometimes homes and haunts or period scenes were added, as in the illustrations of biographies today. The forty-one illustrations in Creighton's 1909 *Some Famous Women*[207] alternate, in the twentieth-century manner, the standard engraved bust of the eminent woman with images of historical context and setting ("Whitby Abbey," "Knights Jousting") and portraits of kings and ministers. More sober or critical works might omit illustrations even at a time when inexpensive books displayed them. C. A. Sainte-Beuve's *Portraits of Celebrated Women*[697] in 1868 included a frontispiece of Mme de Sévigné, but in its third edition (1895) it omitted that sole image.

While the illustrations may be the first appeal to a reader's attention, the volumes make strong arguments by the less direct means of structure, generally according to time, space, or both. History and geography form the axes that in a sense graph the acceleration of the narratives. Some inclusive volumes are organized alphabetically, but often a smaller sampling will choose among various ways to represent historical time: a chronological sequence of individuals; the grouping of subjects in sets of different "ages" (as in classical, early modern, and recent); or the synchronic selection from one period. Women may personify epochs and religious movements, as in *Heroines of the Crusades*[91] or *Ladies of the Reformation*.[30] Some tables of contents appear arbitrary, but others provide chapter titles that designate types (see chap. 2). Separate chapters may further collect subgroups of women, sometimes blood relations or career companions, sometimes anonymous groups. The plan of a calendar is rather rare in book form; the fact that lives might be arranged in the order of the subjects' birthdates would seem to have little effect on the interpretation (to any but astrologers).[139] Although it would be rare today to suggest that women of achievement function as saints did hundreds of years ago, there is still a penchant for all-female calendars (and not just of the pinup variety). Carrie Chapman Catt edited the *Woman's Century Calendar,* published in the same year as the first *Who's Who,* 1899, and today the Library of Congress annually publishes *Women Who Dare,* serial tributes to the woman of the month.[140] Underlying such temporal patterns are the prevailing historical arguments,

Fig. 8 *Florence Nightingale* by J. B. Wandesforde, engraved by J. C. Buttre, from D. W. Clark, *Portraits of Celebrated Women* (1863);[173] and minus background and ornate frame, as frontispiece, engraved by G. E. Perine, in James Parton et al., *Eminent Women of the Age* (1869).[630]

either of degeneration or more often of progress through generations of women. In addition to historical time, the collections ring changes on narrative time: "duration" or the balance between narration and scene; the entire lifespan or the pivotal action. Collections of peak episodes may be historical (often concerning war), yet historical context may be minimized in order to abstract the action or the virtue that the deed exemplifies, to be repeated in different times.

Just as temporal order associates these works with historiography, so does spatial or geographical demarcation.[141] Many volumes designate or imply British, American, European, or regional boundaries. Commonly, all the subjects in a collection represent a single native land. Elizabeth Ellet's several collections did much to establish American womanhood, as in the many editions of *The Women of the American Revolution*[259] or her *Pioneer Women of the West*.[256]; [142] Phebe A. Hanaford (biographer of George Peabody, Dickens, and Lincoln) compiled a biographical history with a temporal title, *Women of the Century*,[376] and with chapters according to vocational category (e.g., "Women Physicians") but with a profoundly national aim, as the capitalized dedication attests: "TO / THE WOMEN OF THE SECOND CENTURY / OF THE UNITED STATES OF AMERICA, / THIS RECORD OF THE WOMEN OF THE FIRST, / WHOSE LIVES WERE FULL OF USEFULNESS, AND THEREFORE / WORTHY OF RENOWN AND IMITATION, / IS NOW INSCRIBED." Narrower still than such patriotic lists are state prosopographies such as *The Women of New York*[261] or the six exclusive registers of the women of Georgia between 1902 and 1941.[87; 139; 284; 599; 665; 801] The scope may be transatlantic or transchannel, as in Bethune's *The British Female Poets*[76] (Philadelphia) or Kavanagh's *French Women of Letters*[477] (London and Leipzig), and there is a small tradition of tributes to "fair Hibernians," as in Hamilton's *Notable Irishwomen*.[371; see also 83; 193; 318; 319; 534; 608]

Collections may, in contrast, present farflung geographical or national origins, usually with an attempt at historical reach as well. In the seventeenth and eighteenth centuries, presenters often projected a universal history of woman, much as Heywood or Burton had done. Thus in 1766 came an anonymous offshoot of Ballard with a satisfying title that begins, *Biographium Faemineum: The Female Worthies; or, Memoirs of the Most Illustrious Ladies, of All Ages and Nations, Who Have Been Eminently Distinguished for Their Magnanimity, Learning, Genius, Virtue, Piety, and Other Excellent Endowments.* . . . The "all ages and nations" ambition appeared on occasion through the 1830s and in several instances during the 1850s and 1860s and flourished once more in the early decades of the twentieth century, as in the ten-volume collaboration *Women: In All Ages and in All Countries*.[899]; [143] The synoptic scope persisted even among the increasingly specialized designs at the turn of the twentieth century. Thus, the encyclopedic *Famous Women: An Outline of Feminine Achievement through the Ages*[17] appeared in New York in the same year, 1928, that *Women of the West: A Series of Biographical Sketches of Living Eminent Women in the Eleven Western States of the United States of America* came out in Los Angeles.[79]; [144]

The prevailing Anglo American axis was only occasionally made explicit, as in *Memoirs of Eminently Pious Women of Britain and America*[41] (a probable adaptation of Burder, Gibbons, and Jerment [1815]). Title pages may indicate simultaneous publishers in London and New York or suppress foreign origin altogether. H. E. Marshall's *Boy-Kings and Girl-Queens* (1914), obviously not exclusively female, acknowledges publication only in the United States. Marshall's preface, however, explains that "the stories are taken from the history of our own land and from that of our near neighbours France and Germany." "Our own land" clearly refers to Britain, not England; "Scotland alone furnishes enough to fill a large book," Marshall observes, conceding the necessary omissions to sample the entire kingdom.[145] Narratives of monarchy, of course, would have Old World settings and often were imports, but citizens of the republic increasingly wrote and read the lives of sovereigns without compunction.[146] Anglo American collections, moreover, frequently include representatives from several European countries, often with a disproportionate French sample. I suggest that this French infiltration—the ubiquitous Joan of Arc aside—results from the continued impact of the salons and the written recognition of Frenchwomen since the seventeenth century, as well as the conspicuous roles women played in the events of the French Revolution and Napoleonic era. Protestant Anglo-Saxon women might have been superior in morals and discipline, but Frenchwomen undoubtedly enjoyed more leading roles among men in their nation's upheavals. The English-speaking prosopographies served, it seems, as a middle-class Victorian substitute for the riskier and more rarefied salons.

With their various settings of the chronotope, nineteenth-century collective biographies of women increasingly specialized in their principles of selection. Relations to famous men often introduced female subjects to the annals, as in Child's original collection *Good Wives* or in collections of wives of prime ministers and presidents.[147] Sisterhood, most often used in the quasi- or truly Catholic sense,[506; 234; 457; 549; 727] is sometimes featured as a family relationship, whether to men (*Little-Known Sisters of Well-Known Men*[648; see also 690; 875]), women (Hannah More or Charlotte Brontë and her sisters[794; 685]), or both.[199; 870] Much credit is awarded to mothers, again either in the families of the great—as in Sarah Ellis's *The Mothers of Great Men*[262] and many others[e.g., 22; 70; 93; 135; 411; 700; 840]—or in religious roles.[e.g., 38; 391; 640] Mothers also stand as counterparts to "forefathers" (e.g., *Pioneer Mothers of the West*[305]). *Christian Mothers: Saviours of Society*,[347] an Irish Catholic publication, concludes with a tribute to "the world-wide influence" that "the Irish Mother" exerts through emigrant "daughters," who import into the United States or "the English-speaking colonies" the devout religion of their "home" (52). The topic of family relations neatly intersects with national or cultural genealogies.[148] Records of the loves of missionaries, rulers, or writers may warrant somewhat constrained biographies of the women themselves (as in *Love Affairs of Literary Men*[663] or *The Women Napoleon Loved*[415]). Yet such recognition may have shifted the credit to the women (as happened for Zelda

Fitzgerald or Eleanor Roosevelt when biography gave them their due). Often, when "relative" models came to wield power, it was as single women (regents, widows, spinsters, or royal mistresses).

Frequently, the *feme sole,* or legally autonomous woman, became associated with negative models, the "bad" women. Presenters might place the heroine of sexual ventures in a frame of disapprobation, while middle-class readers could always savor the aristocratic codes of conduct in Whitehall or Versailles.[149] A few early nineteenth-century collections figured women as outsiders, such as the anonymous *The Female Revolutionary Plutarch* (3 vols., 1803) and *Eccentric Biography . . . Actresses, Adventurers, Authoresses, Fortunetellers* (1803), yet collections built around the idea of transgression became scarce during the nineteenth century. Titular boldness returned only in the era of the New Woman, as explicit moral advice became less palatable and new theories of gender and sexuality filtered through to a general audience. If many presenters circa 1850 subscribed to the view of women's moral superiority, many circa 1920 adhered to the notion of archetypes of gender or to popular Freudianism. Myths of eternal feminine types seemed to serve the purpose of placing the presenter and reader on the more solid ground of rational civilization, watching in fond amusement the passions of womanhood. There was increasing demand for models of latitude, not only the slight titillation of such works as *Lives of Twelve Bad Women,*[830] but also role modeling for girls in *Adventurous Women.*[703] With the renewed international women's movement came prosopographies of female political resistance once more, as in *Seven Women against the World.*[328]

Just as subjects may be collected according to a common theme of good or bad character, they may be sorted according to their work or achievements. Before 1870, few volumes grouped examples by a single vocation, apart from collections of writers, missionaries, or queens. Gradually, artists and performers, who had peppered Victorian collections, claimed their own separate volumes as well. Ellen Clayton assembled not only *Queens of Song*[179] in 1863 but also *English Female Artists* in 1876.[176] The American Elizabeth Ellet made no earlier claim to a large company of American women artists, compiling instead her 1859 *Women Artists in All Ages and Countries,*[258] but in 1919, Lorado Taft produced *Women Sculptors of America.*[781] Collections exclusively of actresses, as opposed to male and female thespians, appeared after the turn of the twentieth century, as in *Twelve Great Actresses.*[680]; 150 Other vocational categories became standard, as collections resembling Samuel Smiles's biographies of engineers developed for women as well, in the manner of *Woman in Science* (1913),[590] or *Makers of Nursing History* (1928),[636] or in increasing varieties, *Heroines of the Sky* (1942), or *Women Doctors of the World* (1954).[151]

The multibiographies not only organize subjects by occupation, but they also strike the notes of rank and class. Whereas the middle and upper ranks enjoy a near monopoly, a few dramatic exceptions from working classes merited inclusion. Jenny Lind provides a favorite example: "We marvel how one who sprang from the ranks of the poor should have risen to give the keenest delight to all who were privileged to listen to her, from the monarch to the peasant, and yet have preserved the same child-like and beautiful simplicity of character with which she set forth" (121).[731] Lind might be the predecessor of the twentieth-century starlet discovered working in the drugstore. The celebrated Sarah Martin was an orphaned Yarmouth seamstress who dedicated herself to instructing prisoners till she herself took on the stature of middle-class philanthropists. She rivaled male ministers, according to Sarah Hale: "Such a life . . . should be included in collections of biography, and chronicled in the high places of history . . . , and children [should] associate the name of Sarah Martin with those of Howard, Buxton, Fry—the most benevolent of mankind" (414–15).[362] Lind's celebrity was built on journalistic records of her tours, whereas Martin herself wrote effective accounts of her instructive program. Inevitably collections are biased toward literate women of means who left records. Yet women of impoverished origin who shone in the arts did gain an entree without having written their own memoirs.

If somewhat permeable in terms of class or national origin, the collections seemed "naturally" to have been rather homogeneous with regard to race. Mainstream American collections of women after the Civil War might have included a handful of African American heroines; some white women editors featured as many women of color (two to four per collection) as did mixed-sex African American collections, and often the same few.[152] Phebe Hanaford, in *Women of the Century*,[376] whose dedication I noted above, includes among many biographies Frances E. W. Harper, Sojourner Truth, and Phillis Wheatley, as well as the ever-popular Pocahontas.[153] By the 1890s, African American anthologies of women emerged in explicit parallel to the Anglo American collections, particularly on the occasion of the World's Columbian Exposition. Meanwhile, under Jim Crow conditions, collections purporting to represent all women continued to appear without any racial variety. Other than Pocahontas, Native Americans—or any ethnic varieties within the United States—remained invisible through the 1940s at least.

Heterosexuality—again "naturally"—has been the default mode, though many "chaste" women of the past would be read quite differently today. Through 1940 I have not found a single biography that thematizes lesbianism, though women known to love women do gain recognition—for their achievements. Certain kinds of "manliness" have long been favored in collections. Mythical stature has protected some cross-dressing women from censure; some who enlisted to follow their sweethearts, or to serve as spies or messengers, or to contribute to a naval campaign are honored for that feat.[154] Ménie Muriel Dowie gives a somewhat mocking cheer for *Women Adventurers*:[243] "two soldiers, one sailor-soldier, and one modern officer" remarkable for their disregard of social codes of all kinds. The many women pirates' lives were "smeared with so much coarseness and triviality" that they did not make the cut for this volume (xvi–xviii). Dowie's ideal of an adventurer is the "lady" who makes a kind of vocation of "mischance" (xviii–xix). The subjects in this volume struck her instead as a "classic jest": "common" women of a bygone time (x, xviii). *Women Adventurers* unites reprints of the original first-person narratives with contemporary affidavits and images of Mme Velazquez (1876), Hannah Snell (1750), Mary Anne Talbot (1809), and Mrs. Christian Davies (1740), famous for their performances as men. In chapter 2, I will illustrate a companion theme, the many women who rescue a male prisoner by dressing him as a woman.

With the modernist shift in biography, some collections of women adopted not only Stracheyan satiric polish but also aestheticism and concise psychological insight. A provincial example shows the widespread influence of the fashion for brief impressions: Lois Oldham Henrici's *Representative Women: Being a Little Gallery of Pen Portraits,*[397] which includes elegant photographs and accounts of the achievements of contemporary arbiters of taste such as Edith Wharton and the designer Elsie de Wolfe, as well as pioneers such as Marie Curie and Jane Addams. The agenda of Henrici's collection is the uplift of the race through the labor of progressive womanhood (Olive Schreiner and Charlotte Perkins Gilman echo throughout). Such a cosmopolitan and reforming blend, with a strong flavoring of the presenter's personality, has a successful American model in Elbert Hubbard's many volumes in the series *Little Journeys to the Homes of the Great,* including *Little Journeys to the Homes of Famous Women,*[425] which unites literary tourism, the personal impressionistic essay, and biographies of women writers. Both Henrici's and Hubbard's publications, like many in the decades around the turn of the century, are finely decorated in art nouveau style and seem to instruct the reader in the Arts and Crafts lifestyle (Henrici's title and her publisher, the Crafters, signal direct imitation of Hubbard's own bookmaking enterprise, the Roycrofters).

Other contemporary collections similarly served as guidebooks to literary high culture. Esther Singleton undertook a series of popularizations of cultural expertise resembling Hubbard's (including numerous travel books with the formula of *As Seen and Described by Great Writers*). Her 1907 catalog *Famous Women as Described by Famous Writers*[724] suggests that women are rather like Paris or Japan: prestigious historic locations that inspire great writing. The collection includes such pieces as Swinburne's Mary, Queen of Scots; Alexandre Dumas's Marie de Mancini; Mrs. Jameson's Duchess of Cleveland; Sainte-Beuve's Duchesse de Maine; and entries by the historians James Anthony Froude (Lady Jane Grey) and John Richard Green (Elizabeth I). Not incidentally, literary prestige collaborated with portraits of high rank. In the broadest Bloomsbury orbit, Philip Guedalla designed his *Bonnet and Shawl: An Album,*[352] dedicated to Edmund Gosse, with aspirations to both urbanity and aesthetics: a set of "real" wives—Carlyle, Gladstone, Arnold, Disraeli, Tennyson, and Palmerston are their surnames—complemented by comic sketches of the "ideal" wives of Henry James, Swinburne, and Edmond de Goncourt.[155]

Whereas the mass of collections resists even the general categorization that I have offered here, trends in the interrelation of subject, presenter, and audience do emerge. The aura of unique heroism evaporates in the crowded atmosphere: catalogs of greatness cheapen it, in the etymological sense of marketing it. The coveted agency seems to redistribute from pedagogical presenters to subjects and, thence, to the audience. In the middle decades of the nineteenth century, rather anonymous authorities vigilantly structured the proper education of women and the proper feminine virtues. By the outset of the twentieth century, collections more commonly praised the extremes of individual women across the ages and provided for a more active reader, one who would choose her own career. At the same time the presenter played a more individualized role. Of course, Boswell was neither the first nor the last homodiegetic narrator of biography—or presenter within the telling. Increasingly, popular prosopographies modeled the presenter as social companion of the subjects or as investigative reporter or interviewer.

Simultaneously, the subjects became less august and remote; the audience approximated more closely the life patterns being represented. Though the modern reader might have been more explicitly hailed as a young girl, she was invited to form her own judgments and life story. The replication of the hundreds of collections may have rendered the unique, heroic, beautiful, or great not only nearer but also reproducible. The self-help power of female collective biographies seems indeed to be generated by the friction among the three parties to the narrative exchange, who readily change places. A reader of a successful woman's life identifies with her, emulates her; she may possibly become, in turn, an eminent woman, perhaps a writer of tributes to famous women, and eventually find her own story circulating in the lists of recognition, part of a cohort that reforms the character of the nation.[156] If most readers remain uncelebrated, many collaborate in the work originated by the subjects or take part as presenters. Whereas some Victorian collections cautioned a humble admiration from afar, by the 1920s, the question had become, "What have these women that you have not?"[157] With a little effort, you too could become one of the finest models of womanhood.

World-Noted Women, Celebrated Women, Eminent Women, Notable Women—there can scarcely be enough of such women to go around all the albums of great figures. A preface often alluded to many similar works in an attempt to justify an addition to these ranks. The sense that no list was adequate and that categories as well as individual exemplars competed for attention, however troubling to the responsible compiler, nevertheless provided his or her rationale for presenting new piecemeal goods. While mass-produced models seemed to superimpose restrictive gender codes on the audience, at the same time they strove to diversify in order to increase demand for yet another collection. The differences among models and collections betray the instability of every foundational term in this arena, from exceptionality and fame to women and history. The standards of exemplary conduct for European and American middle-class women, far from being determined and timeless, require perpetual remodeling.

Self-Help History

Presenting Models of Womanhood

Worthy lives make self-improving reading. As Thomas Salter advised in *A Mirrhor mete for all Mothers, Matrones, and Maidens* (1579): "You shall never repeate the vertuous lives of any such Ladies as, *Claudia, Portia, Lucretia* and such like were, but you shall kindle a desire in [maidens] to treade their steppes, and become in tyme like unto them."[1] For centuries, no one seems to have doubted the personal lessons of biography, lessons at the same time of great importance in forming future citizens. Collective biographies of women, with subtitles such as *A Book for Young Ladies,* obviously had designs on the audience.[175; 178] Perhaps their contribution to collective development is less conspicuous, though works billed as *Biographical Studies of Women Who Have Made History*[11] aimed at nothing less than a revision of social history.[2] Victorian biographies confess to much the same designs as the sixteenth-century handbook (or mirror) of character, though with considerably greater proximity between subjects and audience and with gradually increasing value placed on the idiosyncratic or aesthetic. Lydia Huntley Sigourney expresses a standard conviction in her preface to *Examples from the Eighteenth and Nineteenth Centuries*: "The study of the lives of the great and good, like that of grand and beautiful pictures, gives present pleasure and lasting remembrance. What we thus contemplate and admire, may become . . . a pattern of life" (5).[718]

How indeed does this work? What is the constructive power of life narrative? By what means is the personal mode of life narrative transposed into the collective, political register of history? I suggest that answers to these large questions lie in the three-way rhetoric of life narrative. The encounter of presenter, subject, and audience provides the competitive triangulation that propels desire and narrative, according to a standard model.[3] Part of the attraction of life writing must derive from the fact that it moves among three positions in the manner of actual social interchange—as when two people discuss a third person's character or deeds—with the advantage of more controlled, textual conditions.[4] The fantasy of complementary mirroring, of self-recognition in the likeness of another, is shattered by the asymmetry of a third term that generates change and development. Thus, the presenter might be regarded as a persona for "history," for a dialectic that propels identification toward the collective.

To understand the anomaly of "self-help history," I sample a range of discourses from different contexts and, accordingly, will incur a degree of anachronism. Salter's sixteenth-century "Mirrhor" does share traits with self-help prosopographies in the twenty-first century. Yet the differences between them—or more pertinently, between Victorian and recent rhetorical constructions of women's lives—show that conventions of modeling have indeed changed over the centuries. "How to Make It as a Woman," hardly a Victorian locution, became conceivable in part through the reiterations of various representations of successful development for women. I will sketch some early formulations of the power of biographical narrative and offer a group portrait of nineteenth-century presenters and their positive and negative modeling of subjects before I examine the ethical standing of biography and the discourses of self-help and role modeling today.

During the youth of the novel, when it generally had the sort of reputation now enjoyed by violent video games, printed lives of the great and good were the prescribed inoculation—immediately to cure the reader but ultimately to restore the health of the community.[5] The novel's excessive influence in remapping racial and cultural geography, as well as its restless plots of individual development beyond the control of elites, made it appear to be an instrument of untrammeled social change.[6] Yet while the novel was regarded with suspicion, there was a consensus that biography had a beneficent effect. This benefit was attributed to what in recent terms would be called identification, a process that remains as mysterious as other dynamics of desire.[7] Perhaps because biography seems to spark identification that is guided by the presenter and limited by the conventions of social reality, it was trusted more than the novel. Now, however, the relative standing of the genres has reversed. Biography was downgraded at the end of the nineteenth century with the increasing literary stature of the novel. As professional critics jettisoned nonliterary ballast from the airship of literature, biography could be discarded as useful rather than literary. At the same time, professional historiography dismissed such collections of female biography as Elizabeth Ellet's or Agnes Strickland's as sentimental "pen portraits."[8] Self-help, exemplary biography, and identification with heroes or role models all became associated with uneducated or feminine audiences. It was not always so.

Henry Fielding's fictional history of Joseph Andrews ironically begins by insisting that examples take effect in person, without any intervention:

> It is a trite but true observation that examples work more forcibly on the mind than precepts. . . . It is more strongly so in what is amiable and praise-worthy. Here emulation . . . inspires our imitation in an irresistible manner. A good man therefore is a standing lesson to all his acquaintance, and of far greater use in that narrow circle than a good book.
>
> But as it often happens that the best men are but little known, . . . the writer may be called in aid to spread their history farther. . . . He may perhaps do a more extensive service to mankind than the person whose life originally afforded the pattern.[9]

Human beings may embody lessons to each other, but the greatest benefit requires circulation by a third party. In this description of biographical modeling, the subject does little more than *be* a "standing lesson," while the audience rather passively yields to "irresistible" desire to follow examples. It is the writer/presenter who capitalizes on these propitious intersubjective conditions; the medium of transmission exercises a determining power.[10] Fielding nowhere maligns the didactic program or suggests that "we" are feminine, weak, ignorant, or unoriginal to imitate the example of goodness.

Samuel Johnson, who so often personifies the beginning of modern biography as well as the new type of the man of letters, focuses on the reader's response more than the presenter's patterning agency, yet he too affirms a kind of social warranty in the reader's involuntary identification with models of character in like circumstances. In *Rambler,* no. 60 (October 13, 1750), Johnson finds in biography "an act of the imagination, that realises the event [of others' happiness or calamities] however fictitious, or *approximates* it however remote. . . . We feel, while the deception lasts, whatever motions would be excited by the same good or evil happening to ourselves" (my emphasis). Johnson spatializes identification as an increase in proximity, while his contemporary usage—"motions would be excited"—reveals the physical metaphor in our own term, "emotions." No form of writing "can be more delightful or more useful" than biography, as "none can more certainly enchain the heart by irresistible interest, or more widely diffuse instruction to every diversity of condition."[11] Johnson is our contemporary in favoring realist detail of everyday, private life to convey the genuine individual, yet he retains a classic approval of instruction and veneration. Represented lives are irresistible. The conviction, shared by Fielding and Johnson, that life narratives are "useful" in modeling character generated the demand for prosopographies as both self-help and collective historiography. Sets of exemplary lives accumulated a social archive and projected, through audience emulation, into the future. From Benjamin Franklin's *Auto-biography* to George Craik's *Pursuit of Knowledge under Difficulties,* and well into the twentieth century in spite of critical dissent, life narrative continued to be encouraged as a means of self-improvement for men and women of all "conditions."[12] Thus when John Edward Bruce compiled *Short Biographical Sketches of Eminent Negro Men and Women* in 1910, he invoked Dr. Johnson to support his "hopes" that these "moral portraits" will "beget a desire of imitation" in the next generation.[13] When Mary-Ellen Kulkin appealed to school librarians in 1976 to improve the quality of role-model biographies, she urged the new ethical imperatives of that era: the biographies should be accurate, without "sexism, racism, and classism," and not "so burdened with moral lessons" as to "have a discouraging effect."[14]

The intended use of collective biographies declares itself boldly in many a preface. Two characteristic modeling exercises illustrate the aims well: collections from the beginning and middle of the nineteenth century that had some staying power among publishers in Britain and the United States. In 1804, the Reverend George Jerment took up Thomas Gibbons's 1777 *Memoirs of Eminently Pious Women* (see my introduction, 30) and extended it to two volumes with the addition of nine Scotswomen and a broader sampling of classes.[15] Jerment circularly affirms the self-replication entailed in such a collection: "The lives of persons eminent for piety and distinguished for Christian experience, if related with fidelity and judgment, are among the most valuable presents that can be offered to the Christian reader" (Gibbons and Jerment 1804, 2:1). (Unlike many collections after the beginning of Victoria's reign some thirty years later, Jerment's addresses readers of both sexes.) The reproduction of the Bible's "miniature-portraits of distinguished women" is particularly reliable (1:vii–ix); Jerment would be rewarded if "others, and particularly young ladies, be excited to imitate mothers in Israel" (1:xi–xii). Jerment issues an apology for omitting "many names of equal worth." Finally, he announces a justification for the study of women in terms that bridge the eighteenth and nineteenth centuries: "The Female sex, at all times, and especially in a frivolous and giddy age, are objects deeply interesting to every man of sense, sensibility, morality, and piety.... Women possess vast influence" (1:v). The Christian man of feeling is counseled in 1804 to study the best examples of feminine influence, a concept even more emphasized in the ensuing decades.

Consider a second, contrasting example of typical modeling moves. Miss M. Kendrick in 1848 rather impersonally presents the plain, unillustrated *Gift Book of Biography for Young Ladies*:[484] "The following little Work has been written under the impression that Biography might be made the source of information and amusement, and at the same time arouse those finer faculties of our nature.... The following choice selection has been made, from the conviction that the noble examples it exhibits are peculiarly calculated, under the blessing of God, to induce the reader to strive to imitate such excellencies" (v–vi). The passive voice ("has been written under the impression"; "has been made, from the conviction") suggests an obedient guiding principle and a firm consensus ("our nature"); reader response follows of course. This is a British production, but the title page gives credit to Mrs. L. M. Child as coauthor. The preface acknowledges that four of the twelve biographies are reprinted from Lydia Maria Child's *Good Wives,* which was published in the United States in 1833. Kendrick's collection ends with "Concluding Remarks"—a rare feature—commending Bible study and the Christian life. But unlike Jerment, a man speaking to men and women, Kendrick addresses girls: "My dear young friends" (265–70). Unlike Child, she employs an intrusive narrator; the short lives by Kendrick frequently break out into sermons on conduct.[16] The young ladies summoned in the title are schooled in the contours of their class and warned against ambition. Thus, the early deaths of Charlotte, Princess of Wales, and Lady Jane Grey seem logically to follow from their "exalted station" (265). In contrast, the "bright example" of Hannah More is safely admired at a distance: "You may neither possess her capabilities nor sphere of action; but you may humbly imitate her line of conduct" (267). This limited franchise of emulation carries with it a promise that one may in turn be gazed on as a subject: our "conduct" matters "because our example is often influential when we are unconscious of it" (268). Such a claim for the mutually formative effects of social subjects anticipates more recent sociological formulations, as when Pierre Bourdieu declares, "the history of the individual is never anything other than a certain specification of the collective history of his group or class."[17]

These two quasi-collaborations—of Gibbons and his later editor Jerment and of Kendrick with her earlier source, Child—begin to illustrate the presenters' dedication to social construction. From the more entertaining to the more instructive ends of the spectrum, the designs practice on the reader; the teaching is supposed to *take.* Such discursive power may come as no surprise to early twenty-first-century readers, though it was under a cloud in literary studies for most of the previous century. The formative and restorative power of narrative is now broadcast news—across disciplines and in and out of the academy— as though it were the philosopher's stone, genetic raw material, or panacea.[18] Not only postmodernists but also humanist social scientists, lawyers, and clinicians presuppose that identity is constructed of stories.[19] The shifts toward narrative "have been variously dubbed 'interpretive turn,' 'discursive turn,' 'cultural turn,' and . . . 'post-structuralist turn.'"[20] In part, this theoretically informed shift responds to feminist and other political criticism that challenged the universality and objectivity of traditional disciplines. In other respects, it may be symptomatic of the dispersed authority and diffusion of information in consumer culture. Whatever the contributing causes, many fields have come to favor collecting life stories as evidence or as therapeutic process.[21] To tell one's story, to attend to a collective telling of the past, is to take trauma in hand and begin the healing or reparation. Nineteenth-century presenters, without anticipating recent discourses of victimization or rights, share a belief in the restorative and documentary effect of personal narrative.

How to Be a Presenter

What do presenters hope to achieve in their prosopographies? What do presenters do, and who or what are they? In the following chapters, I shall introduce many individuals who commend models of female excellence. Here I need to establish that "the presenter" is a position occupied by several people: original composers of individual lives, an editor or a compiler who assembles abridgments or paraphrases of the originals, or a publisher (commercial house, religious society, or school committee), as well as illustrators, printers, and others who design the book's form. For this reason, I prefer the term "presenter" to "biographer." For most purposes, it is sensible to unite the ideological and material conditioning of the book, the person named on the title page, and the speaker of the preface or interjected commentary as a sort of implied presenter. In advice literature, it is difficult to imagine an implied author who is not in close unison with the voice of the text, who does not sincerely adhere to the precepts put forth. Just so, presenters of celebrated women generally appear to be advocates of women, according to their lights. But of course those lights may slant in contrasting directions, according to the choice of subjects and the particular gender ideology or social agenda of the volume but not according to the sex of the biographer. Only late in the nineteenth century do a few female biographers dedicated to feminist activism stand out from the reformist consensus, while after 1900 a few male compilers mock the sex in a way almost unknown since the eighteenth century.

The preface or foreword to a biographical collection holds important clues to the presenter's purposes and the reader's expected response. An introductory address, an opportunity few presenters miss, generally relies on the following conventions. The most important moves might be termed *apology,* in the sense both of asking to be excused and mounting a defensive argument. In this tactic, the presenter may express humility, avow borrowing from other sources, justify making this addition to a crowded field of publications, regret inevitable omissions, and yet uphold this selection on its merits. The convention of humility seems quite justified when the compiler's task mainly has been that of sampling, rephrasing, and arranging. The apology affirms that the present models exemplify traits of missing women. It thus entails two interrelated conventions, *exemplification* and *construction of the reader.* In exemplification, the preface asserts that biographies shape character and that female biographies model girls or women. To construct the reader, the speaker mentions or addresses the audience and solicits its response. As a form of self-help, collective biographies hail the reader: advising her to be content with her narrow sphere, urging her to step out of it, warning her to avoid the errors of some historical women, adjuring her to acquire the qualities of others. Generally these expressions adjust the levels of intimacy or distance.

These levels in turn relate to the effort to integrate self-help modeling with communal instruction, hence the fourth common theme: *women's historiography.* Many presenters claim women's importance in history, trace progress in terms of the condition of women, celebrate women's unsung heroism, and directly revise the stories of history to include women. The collection may also support women's rights or women's claim to moral superiority. While all biographical collections implicitly shape race, class, nation, and religion, these differences may remain muted in a preface. Some, however, will state what also may be registered in a title or table of contents, the *claims of race and nationhood.* Just as the criterion for advanced civilization was the status of women, so praise of eminent women became a patriotic and forward-thinking utterance; less often, this utterance sought support from examples of inferior races that abused their women. A final set of common references concerns *religion,* a major theme in the biographies, as I have noted. Spiritual goodness seems essential to the concepts of exemplification—the subjects have it—and construction of the reader—the reader should have it. Some collections attest to the faith of the presenter, serve as instruments of particular sects, or offer the lives as devotional exercises; other volumes advocate nonsectarian, unified missions.

The presenter is a rather anonymous collaboration. Prefaces are usually brief and formulaic, in the tone of the public speaking of the day. Often they eschew the use of the first person, and other than the occasional anecdote or the name, date, and location at the end, little identifies the individual(s) who composed or edited the work. A few introductions develop lengthy arguments, according to the opinions of the presenter or the lenience of the publisher. They may summarize a history of women, offer capsule lives of famous women not featured in the volume, or, in an enhanced version of women's historiography, comment on current women's movements or trends in women's behavior, often critically.

Individual participants in this collaboration nevertheless merit some attention. It is not an exaggeration to say that thousands of editorial and compositional man-hours were devoted in the nineteenth century to laying the groundwork for women's studies. A few women began to generate catalogs of women when it became clear, after 1775 (and Ballard's second edition [1775]) that such books would indeed sell, and by the 1830s female-authored collections regularly appeared. Even into the twentieth century, however, the majority of presenters of all-female collections of lives were men.[22] Like other work on Grub Street, it was a man's job; for all we know, though, it may have been a daughter's or a wife's job in some instances where the man's name or no name appears to sign for the volume. Often a professional writer or a clergyman with a family to support offered his own answer to the question of what women had contributed to civilization. In the United States, enterprising male writers initiated popular anthologies of female subjects, among them Samuel Lorenzo Knapp (whose *Female Biography*[492] was in currency from 1833 to 1868), Samuel Griswold Goodrich ("author of Peter Parley's Tales," whose *Lives of Celebrated Women*[332] was in print 1843–76), Jesse Clement (whose *Noble Deeds of American Women*[182] was in print 1851–75), and Frank Boott Goodrich (whose *World-Famous Women*[331] was in print 1859–91 [see my introduction, 35, n134, regarding its illustrations and shifting title]). Among the most prolific collective biographers of women in any period were two American men, James Parton, whose anthologies burgeoned between 1868 and 1890 (at least seven large collections of lives, of which five are exclusively female[624–26; 628; 630]), and Gamaliel Bradford, whose female multibiographies span 1916–30.[101–4] But no compiler of women's lives produced more volumes than the Englishman William Henry Davenport Adams, who became a veritable workshop of collective biography; of twenty-nine collections, he assembled exclusively female groups under ten different titles[6–15] (with some reproduction of material), primarily in the 1880s.

Meanwhile, women seeking to earn a living as writers could meet a demand while gaining some access to public realms of discourse, including historiography. When women did engage in biographical production, they were likely to present a selection of their own sex.[23] I consider more fully the female presenters because women's multibiography takes on an additional role-modeling dimension when presented by a woman, who herself belongs in the target audience of a woman's model life narrative and who might in turn join the series of exemplary subjects. A famous woman writer such as Anna Jameson or Agnes Strickland serves as a shadowy attendant in the glowing chambers of the queens or saints she represents and as a goal in the middle distance for her female readers, who are likelier to attain to learned authorship than to sovereignty or beatitude.

Like other kinds of published prose in the nineteenth-century, biography could be considered a "sage discourse" or a form of hackwork, depending on the circumstances. Miriam Elizabeth Burstein detects in some collective biographies "the writer's need to answer the simultaneous call of morals and mammon, in double-quick time."[24] Yet in the hands of many presenters, effective portraiture went well beyond hasty imprints of the standard woodblocks for children. Throughout the mid-nineteenth century, a number of professional British and American writers, even those who enjoyed the higher prestige of the sage or the higher income of the novelist, turned to collective female biography. Clearly, the nineteenth-century women who contributed to this genre regarded it as continuous with other forms of social service in which they might engage, perhaps as an incremental advancement of civilization through influence on the reader.[25] Among the women writers who contributed to the form, in addition to Jameson, Strickland, and Mary Cowden Clarke there were authors of advice such as Sarah Ellis and Lydia Maria Child, eminent authorities such as Harriet Martineau or Sarah Hale, the novelists Charlotte M. Yonge and Harriet Beecher Stowe, and the feminist activists Bessie Rayner Parkes and Millicent Garrett Fawcett. Most contributed to the genre of multibiography only once or twice in their careers. Beginning in 1850, Julia Kavanagh produced four massive female prosopographies, including antecedents of academic feminist criticism, *English Women of Letters* and *French Women of Letters*,[476–79] while Margaret Oliphant helped to standardize an English biographical literary history (predominantly male) in the 1880s and 1890s, adding her contribution to an all-female collection, the multiauthored *Women Novelists of Queen Victoria's Reign*.[607] Jennie Chappell's three volumes (and one reissue of two together[160–63]) of assorted "noble workers" such as the Baroness Burdett-Coutts, Frances Willard, Mrs. Fawcett, and Frances Ridley Havergal were published (mostly by Partridge) between 1898 and 1933; the Evangelical missionary framework belies the well-narrated, realistically detailed portraits of powerful and successful women.

Like some literary working men, some women besides Chappell pursued this profitable line in series of collections—for example, Ellen Creathorn Clayton, who is named as author of six collections, including the unusually specialized *English Female Artists, Female Warriors,* and *Queens of Song,* published by Dean or Tinsley between 1859 and 1879.[175–80] Sara Knowles Bolton produced sixteen collective biographies, four exclusively of women;[96–99] the 1892 edition of *Famous Types of Womanhood* credits her as the even-handed distributor of recognition to *Poor Boys Who Became Famous, Girls Who Became Famous, Famous American Authors, Famous English Authors, Famous American Statesmen, Famous English Statesmen, Famous European Artists,* and *Famous Men of Science,* each selling for $1.50. Crowell's "Mrs. Bolton's Famous Books" stretched beyond Bolton's death in 1916. There is a 1949 edition of a collection first published in 1886, *Lives of Girls Who Became Famous*[98] (the publisher's copyright is renewed from 1923 onward). Women unknown in Bolton's day blend into the alphabetical series, without byline: the African American singer Marian Anderson; an Australian nurse, Elizabeth Kenny; and major figures of our contemporary repertoire, Helen Keller, Eleanor Roosevelt, Amelia Earhart. The industry of Mrs. Bolton's Famous Books is self-perpetuating in every sense, yet it always verges on anonymity. Bolton, like Clayton and many others, failed to gain a foothold herself in the biographical registry. The current obscurity of once-celebrated women and their circles of commendation suggests that exclusive communities will be excluded in turn.

Whether signed by a single male or female biographer or by several people, whether assembled by posthumous teamwork or rivalrous lifting, Victorian female prosopography was a collaboration.[26] This was not the altruism of the beehive; the exchange of personae could be as ruthless as market competition, as when certain Victorian women of letters limited or submerged each other's effects through mutual recognition (see chap. 4). Yet to compile women's lives in the Victorian period was to support a diffuse argument about women's contributions to the progress of the world. In Bolton's words, "The power of true womanhood, in all civilized lands, is increasing year by year" (preface, n.p.).[97] Collections at times impaled famous women with domestic morals, as Sophia Goodrich Ashton labels "Charlotte Brontë [*sic*], the Worthy Daughter."[37] Yet the prevailing claim supported world-shaping careers open to female talent.

Especially in multiauthored texts, the collaboration of a specific imagined community is a featured effect. In the interaction that I call mutual multibiography, contributors in turn become each other's subjects. A complex anthology by men and women by James Parton and others, *Eminent Women of the Age*[630] (illustrated as I described in the introduction), sorts forty-seven entries by calling: queens, mistresses, feminists, actresses, and writers, from Margaret Fuller to Elizabeth Barrett Browning, with subprosopographies such as "woman as physician," contributed by Horace Greeley, T. W. Higginson, James Parton, several ministers, and a professor, in addition to such notable women as Fanny Fern (Mrs. James Parton—by no means the only wife to appear in a husband's volume), Grace Greenwood (contributor to *World-Noted Women*[174]), Elizabeth Cady Stanton, and Mrs. Lucia Gilbert Calhoun (contributors to *Our Famous Women*,[758] below).[27] Fern, Greenwood, and Stanton appear as subjects as well as contributors in Parton's omnibus, along with Lydia Maria Child and Lydia Huntley Sigourney, both themselves collective biographers elsewhere. This accommodating volume of 1868 glances at the small as well as the great and manifestly advocates increasing opportunity for women in the era of Reconstruction.

In Parton's collection, Elizabeth Cady Stanton, a national heroine to this day, receives a lengthy and glowing biography by Theodore Tilton, followed by her own contribution in the form of compiled memoirs of fourteen participants in the "Woman's Rights Movement," including their correspondence. Stanton tells, for instance, of first meeting Lucretia Mott in London on the momentous occasion of the World's Anti-Slavery Convention: "I shall never forget the look of recognition she gave me when she saw that I already comprehended the problem of woman's rights and wrongs. She was the first liberal-minded woman I had ever met, and nothing in all Europe interested me as she did" (371).[630] Stanton's chapter as a whole, then, is an intricate prosopographical sketch that mixes biographies and autobiographies to establish the mutual recognition of leaders in the women's movement across the United States, a microcosm of Parton's entire collection.[28]

Fifteen years later, another massive collection again appeared in Hartford, *Our Famous Women*.[758] The thick leather-bound, "Superbly Illustrated," collection ("Sold Only by Subscription") contains thirty short biographies by "Twenty Eminent Authors," all women. Twelve of the contributors also appear as subjects. As the table of contents shows (fig. 9), there is a chain stitching of mutual representation among the names, in one instance (Rose Terry Cooke and Harriet Prescott Spofford) a direct exchange of lives of each other. Harriet Beecher Stowe, author, becomes Harriet Beecher Stowe, subject; one of Stowes's subjects, Mrs. A. D. T. Whitney, presents Lucy Larcom, who presents in turn Clara Barton; a contributor, Julia Ward Howe, earns her own tribute by her daughter Maud Howe, and so on (Elizabeth Cady Stanton contributes a biographical piece on Susan B. Anthony, as she did in *Eminent Women*[630]).[29] On the whole, the subjects are better known today than are the presenters.

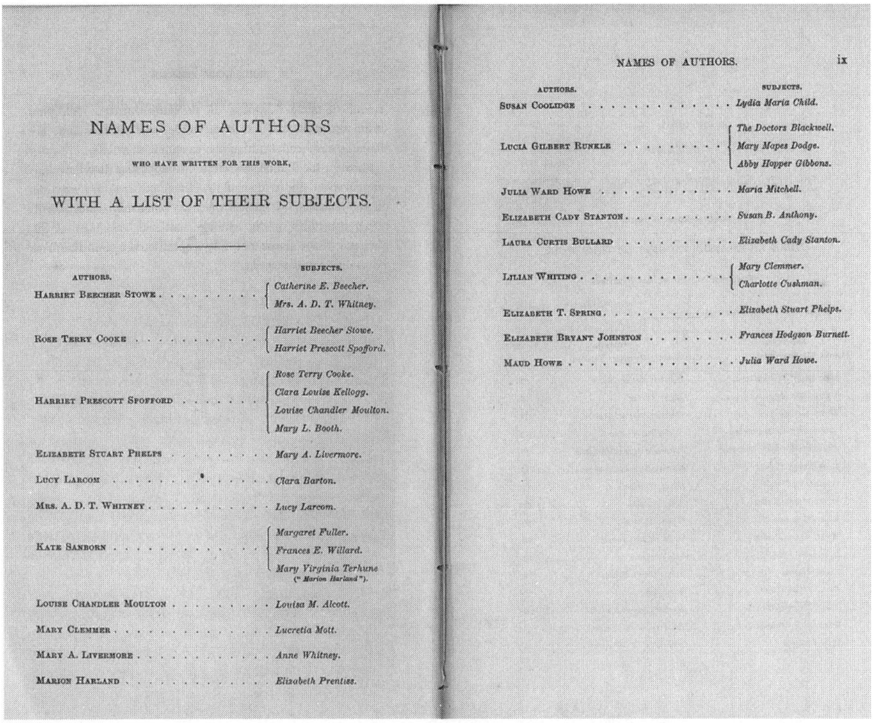

NAMES OF AUTHORS

WHO HAVE WRITTEN FOR THIS WORK,

WITH A LIST OF THEIR SUBJECTS.

AUTHORS.	SUBJECTS.
Harriet Beecher Stowe	*Catherine E. Beecher.* *Mrs. A. D. T. Whitney.*
Rose Terry Cooke	*Harriet Beecher Stowe.* *Harriet Prescott Spofford.*
Harriet Prescott Spofford	*Rose Terry Cooke.* *Clara Louise Kellogg.* *Louise Chandler Moulton.* *Mary L. Booth.*
Elizabeth Stuart Phelps	*Mary A. Livermore.*
Lucy Larcom	*Clara Barton.*
Mrs. A. D. T. Whitney	*Lucy Larcom.*
Kate Sanborn	*Margaret Fuller.* *Frances E. Willard.* *Mary Virginia Terhune* ("*Marion Harland*").
Louise Chandler Moulton	*Louisa M. Alcott.*
Mary Clemmer	*Lucretia Mott.*
Mary A. Livermore	*Anne Whitney.*
Marion Harland	*Elizabeth Prentiss.*

NAMES OF AUTHORS. ix

AUTHORS.	SUBJECTS.
Susan Coolidge	*Lydia Maria Child.*
Lucia Gilbert Runkle	*The Doctors Blackwell.* *Mary Mapes Dodge.* *Abby Hopper Gibbons.*
Julia Ward Howe	*Maria Mitchell.*
Elizabeth Cady Stanton	*Susan B. Anthony.*
Laura Curtis Bullard	*Elizabeth Cady Stanton.*
Lilian Whiting	*Mary Clemmer.* *Charlotte Cushman.*
Elizabeth T. Spring	*Elizabeth Stuart Phelps.*
Elizabeth Bryant Johnston	*Frances Hodgson Burnett.*
Maud Howe	*Julia Ward Howe.*

Fig. 9 Table of contents, Harriet Beecher Stowe et al., *Our Famous Women* (1884).[758]

It is hard to imagine Clara Barton, Frances E. Willard, the Blackwells or the elderly astronomer Mitchell taking time out of their prominent international careers to write biographies (deceased subjects—Beecher, Fuller, Mott, Child, Cushman—obviously no longer participated in the textual meetings of this community). Yet in their day Stowe, Mary Livermore, Howe, and Stanton, stretched to the limit of public demand as celebrities, chose to contribute to this memorial.

The roster of subjects contrasts with the illustrated title page (fig. 10): the seated woman with telescope and globe denotes Maria Mitchell, who discovered a comet; the woman standing between an easel and a classical female bust suggests the sculptor Anne Whitney; the nurse kneeling to refresh the wounded soldier in a war-ravaged landscape alludes to the several medical women and Civil War nurses within. Properly, the illustration should give pride of place to a woman at a desk employed in that least picturesque of activities, writing; *Our Famous Women* are almost all women of letters in some phase of their careers. The woman at the podium addressing a large crowd might also be a suitable emblem for many of these women. The publishers of *Our Famous Women* valiantly advertise "an entirely new work, full of romantic story, lively humor, thrilling experiences, tender pathos, and brilliant wit, with numerous anecdotes, incidents, and personal reminiscences." The standard "publisher's

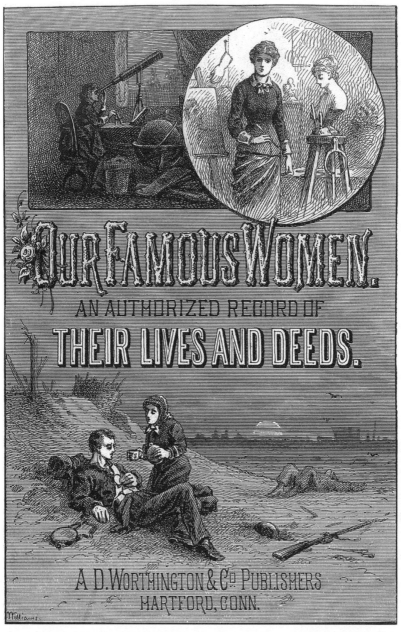

Fig. 10 Title page, illustrated by T. W. Williams, Harriet Beecher Stowe et al., *Our Famous Women* (1884).[758]

preface" condones yet another collection because "the simple story of what a few women have done would prove an inspiration and incentive to the many women who long to do." The volume is "authorized," we learn, by the subjects, who permitted friends or relatives to present their lives for the common good. The selection is *"representative"* of "a range of endeavor and achievement," within the "national" scope (1884 ed., v–vi)—in fact, a New England, cosmopolitan, liberal selection. The ministering women whom I portray in chapter 3 either find a place in this American collection or are represented by typological proxies.

Readers today are likely to read such prosopography as an exclusive club. It is true that collective biographies, like clubs, may be heightened by vigilant gate keeping but also by the possibility of admission. Many in the immediate audience of these prosopographies must have felt invited into alternative life patterns because of the limits placed on the circuit of communication: our famous women. While the series of eminent women slides into a superimposed portrait of female heroism, the table of contents—a menu of models chosen to appeal to a range of tastes—confirms that womanhood may range beyond the obscure wife, mother, or mistress, the fabled pair of angel or whore. Unlike most novels, these narratives give considerable narrative space to different norms; not only do these works claim that their heroines actually lived and achieved recognition, they also defy the privileging of one heroine, with her small cluster of foils and rivals. Why always Dorothea?—let us consider the lives of many Saint Theresas. Why always the romance plot?—take note of female *Bildung* or even epic. This is a form that shapes subjects and communities: self-help history.

Biography Is Good for Us

While presenters succeeded in fusing narratives of individual and collective development, the effort showed: the aims of forming (feminine) subjects and the aims of historiography often conflicted. Historical women differ in broad outline and in detail from "good" women. As George Eliot's narrator in *The Mill on the Floss* (1860) sums up the traditional outlook: "The happiest women, like the happiest nations, have no history." According to ancient authority the better the woman, the less that is known or said about her.[30] Most midcentury collections affiliated with conventional standards of feminine domestic virtue and counseled the reader to content herself with local influence in obscurity. This would suggest that such works served as brakes rather than pistons in historical progress for the middle-class Anglo American women they invited on board. Yet any such collection implies commendation of the women whose excesses made a mark on the broadest historical canvas. John S. Jenkins, launching *Heroines of History*[461] with a dedicatory epistle to his friend S. Sheldon Norton, Esq., explains that his ten renowned subjects "were not *perfect* women" (only the "simple-minded . . . Bard of Rydal Mount" could imagine such), but *"famous* women, and so lifted 'above mortality.'"[31] The actions or traits of more recent or more eminent women may be too widely known to conform to a moral. Conversely, earlier or more remote milieus seemed to permit lax behaviors that "civilized" standards had outgrown, while goodness supposedly enjoyed more favorable conditions in recent Christian Anglo-Saxon zones. The reader was expected to filter out the sensationalism of royal intrigues, the temptations of the stage, the appeal of well-known suitors, the heat of free-thinking salons to construe these figures as "good" models for middle-class English or American women of the day.

According to their own express aims, in short, the biographies of women available in this period were hardly good for you. Such models as Cleopatra or Catherine the Great may be held up as warnings, side by side with Felicia Hemans or Sister Dora, the poetess and the nurse who were well within middle-class British bounds. To blend a salutary theme, presenters intermix the rhetorical strategies outlined above. For example, Charles Bruce, in *The Book of Noble Englishwomen*,[125] might seem to be all *apology* as he acknowledges his borrowings from Charlotte M. Yonge, Mr. and Mrs. S. C. Hall, Bessie Rayner Parkes, and Julia Kavanagh, his edition's debts to several publishing houses, and his inability "to include the names of all those Englishwomen who have become memorable." But apology instantly leads Bruce to the motifs of *nationhood* and *constructing the reader*: "England has been richly blessed with noble women. . . . Their names will never be erased from our national story"; "the reader will find many familiar names omitted, and many others included . . . [who are] less known; humble heroines" (5). The roster of national excellence somehow begs for substitutions; one could join those humble heroines.

Presenters discovered ingenious strategies for modeling a single feminine gold standard out of unruly individual examples to serve a national purpose. Lydia Maria Child's much reprinted and plundered *Good Wives*[170] evades (as in Kendrick above) the problem of reconciling domestic virtue with historical agency by choosing examples who were dutiful to eminent men. Child's forty-two examples include queens and countesses as well as the wives of poor artists, missionaries, and businessmen, some familiar, others rare, ranging from classical to revolutionary times; English, French, and German or Swiss models dominate (in that order). The 1833 edition appeared as volume 3 of the series Ladies' Family Library, edited by Child; the first two volumes, joint biographies of Mme de Staël and Mme Roland[168] and of Lady Russell and Mme Guyon,[169] contain less "original writing" than quotation of the subjects' own words. In *Good Wives*, in contrast, Child has "quoted sparingly," though relying heavily on others' writings. Having "compressed large books into a few pages," she then wrote "freely whatever was suggested to my mind" (vii–viii).[170] Indeed, Child's preface (reprinted through 1871, with the omission of the above remarks on the previous biographies and her method of compression and paraphrase), suggests the biographer's independent convictions reined in by a wish to please.

Child sounds the usual tropes with interesting variations. Her initial aim appears to be *constructing the reader,* but by the end of the preface the ambition is nothing less than the salvation of the republic. The preface begins, "It was my original intention to have entitled this volume, The Wives of Distinguished Men. But great men have sometimes had bad wives; and I was unwilling to do anything to save such individuals from the oblivion they deserved. . . . It shall ever be my earnest endeavor to write nothing, that can . . . check the progress of good feelings and correct principles" (vi). This *apology* appears necessary since her narrative manner has been criticized: "I have been told that I did not moralize enough"; yet "the beauty of biography" consists in its *exemplification,* that is, "faithful portraits of individuals" for the reader to judge freely (viii). Child willingly provides a moral in the preface: the sacredness of "domestic affection" for the sake of "national prosperity, as well as individual happiness" (x–xi). Her own credentials as a believer in this hearth-side faith may have left her "open to the charge of sentiment and romance," but this is true to her character as a good wife (the volume is dedicated to her husband [x]).

Child's apology simultaneously reforms character and *nationhood:* some readers have objected "that there is not a large proportion of American wives in this volume." Child explains that American wives "furnish no details for the biographer, or any . . . striking anecdote" (ix). America seems to resemble happy women or happy families, all alike and ahistorical.

> I know that good wives and excellent husbands abound in every part of the
> Union; but it must be remembered that I could only give a sketch of those
> whose virtues were in print; . . . our national career has hitherto been too
> peaceful and prosperous to call [female character] into action in a manner likely
> to secure a place in history. . . . We inherit a large share of English reserve,
> added to that strong fear of ridicule, which is the inevitable result of republican
> institutions; we are, therefore, rather shy of publicly expressing our
> attachments in glowing terms; in our distrust of French exaggeration, we
> approach the opposite extreme. (ix)

Multiple signals radiate here. Child's models must already be "in print"; thus the presenter herself must already be a reader of prior texts, a copyist, though she recasts all in her own spirit. ("In print" in the United States in 1833 also tends to mean, "from European sources.") The good wives must have somehow exceeded the bounds of domesticity to have registered in the stock of narratives heightened by (French) romance, imported from the Old World. (Many compilers would soon prove Child wrong: the first two centuries of European settlement had generated rich occasion for female heroism.) As I shall illustrate in chapter 2, Child's subjects often are heroines in rescue adventures; portrayed according to romance conventions, they are hardly patterns of hearthside respectability.

Child ensures a breakdown of separation of spheres: good wives mold "national character" and become oblique leaders of the world.[32] The peaceful and prosperous republic gradually reveals a nastier side: mutual surveillance, "dishonorable competition, and fraudulent cunning"; even "household virtues become neglected and obsolete" in recent generations (xi–xii). (Where are those superabundant happy marriages?) Character is the only safeguard of the nation's destiny; "the actions and motives of each individual . . . affect the character and destinies of his country" (xi–xii). The two meanings of "domestic"— family and national life—emerge as interdependent.

Decades later, other presenters reconcile varied models to a universal standard of "goodness" as a source of historical progress, with England rather than America in the vanguard. Charlotte M. Yonge, in *Biographies of Good Women*,[924] aspires to present a complete historical series that unites as one "bright example." The multiple authors (*Chiefly . . . Contributors to "The Monthly Packet"*) produce a "second series" because they "had omitted many" from the first; yet additional demonstration is hardly needed that all good women strive "towards the same goal" (vii). "The diamond of perfect womanhood has many facets, and through all the light of Heaven is reflected" (vii–xii), as witnessed by the records of diverse women across three hundred years. As in Lilian Whiting's vision of the "one common chord," "golden thread" or "aim . . . of Christian womanhood" (*Women Who Have Ennobled Life* [6];[862] see my introduction, 7–9), Yonge unites a universal feminine ideal. Yet the narratives in Yonge's collection skirt the questionable morals of Italian and French courts, beg pardon for the staunch Catholicism of some, so jarring to "English thought and feeling" (557), and insist on the unrelenting goodness of the famous as well as the more humble models. "Let it not be thought that we are going to write in behalf of the stage," the contributor "E. T." assures us regarding Mrs. Siddons, who had no "choice" concerning her family's profession (429).

More than thirty years later, Rosa Nouchette Carey's *Twelve Notable Good Women of the XIXth Century*[143] presents an entirely different list than Yonge's but in a similar spirit of conglomeration. The tone and ethos of this fin-de-siècle retrospective seem to have modulated in response to competing representations of New Women and suffragettes, allied with aestheticism rather than evangelicalism. To Carey, history presents a pageant of women: "On our little world-stage there enters, one by one, some representative living personality to play her part. . . . How various are the gifts, how diversified and unequal the *rôle,* the *répertoire!*" Less confident than Yonge of the single light of heaven, Carey nevertheless insists that the pageant is well-directed and sequential: first Victoria, then Florence Nightingale, "and following them a noble little band of workers," the "many" who wait on "the few." Faith in the efficacy of models remains firm; constructing the reader and the nation remain crucial. In an age of tawdry publicity, "there is one saving clause . . . the strength and power of example. . . . One might as well throw stones into a pond and expect no eddies or circles, as believe that good works may be done without influencing. . . . May these sketches . . . be read and studied by the women of this generation, and 'go and do thou likewise' be written upon some true heart" (9–11). Comparing the construction of character to a law of physics, Carey betrays the concern that unregulated influences might interfere in the exchange of precept and voluntary emulation. Carey shares a form of Child's conviction that all happy American families are alike: British women of the nineteenth century *are* notably good. The ethics of the age depend on lessons from the national pageant of good women. With the perils of degeneration in mind, few presenters emphasized the contrasts and disparities among the subjects in a collection.

Yet some presenters of good women did spurn the idea of a unified womanhood. Julia Kavanagh, exercising her critical skills on the theme of *Women of Christianity, Exemplary for Acts of Piety and Charity,*[479] envisions her own pageant of women in history. In *apology,* she describes her difficulties in choosing among the "many great and heroic women [who] suddenly seemed to rise from the barbaric gloom of feudal ages, or appeared mingling with strange daring in the strife . . . of recent generations!" She excludes women "whose virtues went not beyond the circle of home," favoring models of "sacrifice." Kavanagh then departs from convention by turning on her predecessors and raising the stakes of the prosopographical project. When she began the lengthy labor:

> I thought of the difficulty of procuring materials, not that the materials would often be imperfect. I did not know then . . . that the good are quickly forgotten. . . . that their history is too often written by the least gifted amongst those who write, and read by the most humble amongst those who read; that the limited sympathies of the biographer, and the fastidiousness of the reader, have united to keep in obscurity the most noble of their race. . . . Biography after biography have I read, and—with some interesting exceptions—I have been struck with their painful and wearisome similarity. Now, this need not be. The good are not alike: they differ from one another as much as other people. The fault must lie with the biographers who praised when they should have painted. . . . I wish I could have changed this; but as I found things told, even so was I compelled to relate them. (3–4)[33]

Not unlike Lydia Maria Child thirty years before, Kavanagh finds herself serving as a medium of previous narratives. Yet she insists, as later feminists must continually remind themselves to do, that women differ among themselves.

The activist Bessie Rayner Parkes in her *Vignettes,*[621] not overtly dedicated to a golden theme of goodness, neither relies wholly on previous publications nor molds her subjects to gendered likenesses: "The twelve women thus depicted, without any attempt at a connecting link between them, are as various in nationality, creed, habits of mind, and daily pursuits as can well be imagined. There is a moral in their utter dissimilarity which I leave to the intelligent reader; but of every one of them it may truly be said that they did worthy work in the world" (vi).[34] That last clause is the kicker. Even when the subjects individually and together challenge a narrow definition for a woman's life, the narratives make them conform to a standard of justification, the secularized mission of "worthy work in the world."

When Louise Creighton published *Some Famous Women*[207] (in London, New York, Bombay, and Calcutta in 1909), the range of vocations and the imperial scope had both expanded. Creighton models career options for the Edwardian girl, even as she writes a prosopographical history of England. The "you" addressed in the preface and in the narratives is distinctly constructed as a schoolgirl, and the "we" belong presumably to a classless female sex across the empire. Creighton presents her twelve subjects in flat, limpid, instructive tone: "In this little book I am going to tell you about some of the women who have been famous in the past." She offers the common apology for omissions but follows up with a common sort of warning: "It was not always the best women who were the most talked about" (xi). The loosely chronological set of twelve subjects culminates in the queen herself (whose domestic-looking image and signature form the frontispiece): "I should like to have told you something about the women doctors, . . . teachers, . . . writers and novelists. From all their lives you would learn one lesson which is set forth clearly in the life of Queen Victoria. . . . The ruler of a great empire has to work as hard as any girl in a factory, and Queen Victoria is known as a great queen, not because she had talents above other women, but simply because she set herself to do her duty in the position in which God had placed her. In that we can all imitate her" (xii–iii; see my chap. 7).

Within this imperial unity, Creighton nevertheless presents distinctive individuals who served an Anglo-Saxon Christian history of the progress of Britain (the sole foreign subject is Joan of Arc [xiii]). The student learns of the material conditions of early women, who were "busy in keeping their houses" and producing goods and were deprived of "book learning" (only recently did people concede that "girls had minds as well as boys" and should be educated [xi]). Readers should avoid the "aimless life led by a great lady in the Middle Ages," Joan of Kent (xii), but recall instead some "women who had no great position in the world" but who "made themselves famous" through "care for the poor and the suffering" (xii). "Amongst our forefathers, the wild German tribes who conquered Britain and made it England, women had always held an honourable place," which led to the ready spread of Christianity (15); queens and consorts helped to convert the early kings.[35] High-born women such as Saint Hilda became foundresses of utopian, almost matriarchal communities (19); Hilda appears to hasten the dawn of English literature through her protégé Caedmon (21–22). Margaret Beaufort in turn led the country out of the unruly days of the War of the Roses and ushered in the etiquette, benevolent household management, charity, and learning that carried forward through the Tudor line (65).[36] Lady Rachel Russell succeeded Margaret Beaufort as the female type whose extraordinary personal influence sustained and improved the character of the people.[37]

Most indicative, perhaps, of Creighton's construction of English history as a series of vignettes of good women is her chapter on Julia Selina Inglis, who wrote a diary of the siege of Lucknow. In Creighton's retelling, the Indian Mutiny remains an inexplicable rebellion "caused by the discontent of the native troops" (112), while the British women and children perform a strange sort of sentimental comedy in a "beautiful . . . calm and peaceful" setting, in spite of heat, starvation, frequent injuries, and deaths (115). The "native butler and nurse" of the Inglis family remain "devoted," and the "busy" but adoring husband, Colonel Inglis, finds moments for intimacy and for group prayers "which were a great comfort" (115). In spite of historical documentation of the mutiny (117–18), "comfort" (119) is the recurring term. Unquestionably, the happy family will be reunited in "England," the last word of the chapter (125). In a domesticated history of the British Empire, Mrs. Inglis becomes a named synecdoche for brave and virtuous womanhood, a member of that body politic represented by Victoria, as well as the descendent of progressive races. An English or English-identified reader gains such a lofty genetic heritage.

Reader, Take Care

Not all collections *exemplify* or *construct the reader* in positive terms. Presenters tag some famous women with warning labels; instead of "do thou likewise," "do thou the contrary." If the theme of goodness encouraged many presenters in a fantasy of universal womanhood or a ballad of national unity, the spectacle of an errant woman required the concept of diversity. No modern presenter would maintain that all women are alike bad. In the course of the nineteenth century, the construction of the audience generally became more positive and trusting and, hence, the frame of judgment more flexible to accommodate deviant subjects. The early implied reader tended to be seen as more susceptible, whereas the later reader enjoyed greater self-determination. Accordingly, negative modeling was more common at the beginning of the nineteenth century than in the middle, whereas in the twentieth century, "tough" subjects sometimes appeared without much censure. Particularly children's texts of the later eighteenth or early nineteenth century retailed punitive or monitory life history. In 1799, Mrs. [Mary] Pilkington's *Biography for Girls* begins with "Louisa Harrington, or, the Victim of Pride," a girl whose vainglorious parents made her "one of the most unamiable girls," capable of spurning a dying urchin whom her own carriage had run over; the spectacle of her heartlessness costs her an eligible match and leads with abrupt logic to early and "unregretted" death (3–32).[38] In 1803, Mary Hays generally reproaches "the follies and vices by which [women] suffer themselves to be degraded" (iv), much in the tone of *A Vindication of the Rights of Woman*.[39] Nevertheless, Hays adopts the more positive strategy of the new century in her collection, *Female Biography:* "To excite a worthier emulation, the following memorial of those women [who] . . . have reflected lustre upon the sex, is presented more especially to the rising generation," who are less corrupted by the artifices of gender—or by novels (1803, v–vi).

Negative modeling did persist into the age of Victoria. Women in high places seemed poised to fall; all eyes may have been on them, but they made perilous models. Queens and female courtiers, favorites in such representative lists because they had front-row seats at the performance of history, naturally became test cases of the standards of femininity. The 1832 edition of Anna Jameson's *Memoirs of Celebrated Female Sovereigns*[453] bears an admonitory epigraph from that model of principled wifely sacrifice in the French Revolution (never mind her lovers), Mme Roland: "Nous sommes faites pour embellir le monde, plutôt que pour le commander." Jameson heaps censure, with zest, both on those who would command rather than adorn or embellish and on those who relinquish command, such as Christina of Sweden, "who gave away a throne from an excess of selfishness." If not for her position, Christina would have "been merely regarded as a vain, clever, and very eccentric woman . . . ; but being placed upon a throne, she appeared extraordinary, and even sometimes great." Nevertheless, "destitute of virtue or common sense, her sex, her learning, and her splendid position only served to render her more conspicuously wretched, ridiculous, and pitiable" (2:5–6). A woman discovers that sovereignty only makes a worse spectacle of any deviation from femininity.

In other early collections, Jameson discovers the proximity of fame and vice, rather as Child finds that distinguished men often had bad wives. In 1831 Jameson (née Murphy) supplied the text for engravings of her father's copies of portraits of women by Lely and others in royal and private collections (commissioned by Princess Charlotte, whose early death left Murphy unpaid for his years of work). The material in *Memoirs of the Beauties of the Court of Charles the Second*[452] presents a challenge to a conscientious age: "But, says Morality, . . . how is the world or posterity benefited by celebrating the charms and the errors of these fair pieces of sin and mischief, who ought rather to do penance with their faces to the wall . . . ? . . . If the severe historian must needs stain his page with that disgraceful era . . . let the poet forget it—let the lover forget it; above all, let women forget the period which saw them degraded from objects of adoration to servants of pleasure" (20). Nevertheless, recent revival of public interest in the Restoration requires that caricatures be corrected; "the innocent should not be confounded with the guilty" (21), and some of the court celebrities were "as blameless as they were lovely" (14). Jameson sees an advantage in heightening distinctions among women.

Conservative presenters throughout the nineteenth century maintained the earlier suspicion of female fame, though fame is what underwrote their selection of subjects. John Maw Darton's *Famous Girls Who Have Become Illustrious Women: Forming Models of Imitation to the Young Ladies of England*[220] primarily exhibits contemporary positive models, including fellow presenter Lydia Maria Child. Darton equivocates on the dubious standards for really famous women of history: "It is possible to deserve fame and yet not be famous"; a life may be "heroic," though known only in one's town or village (v). Biographies might lead dutiful daughters astray. Readers should "emulate" "noble lives" "in the discharge of daily duty," rather than being "mere copyists of the great ones who have emblazoned their names on the roll of fame." The "heroism of the past . . . has shone out the most brightly in the dark and hideous days of the world's history," which have encouraged bad deeds. In this "glorious age" of "Christian civilization," one is unlikely to face persecution (v–viii). Darton thus forms a rather suburban class of "young ladies of England," locating wayward historicity in remote times.

William Russell, Esquire's elegantly written set of twenty-five *Extraordinary Women*[692] takes pains to represent numerous errant examples and to specify why they should not be emulated—a curious expenditure of didactic labor that seems to chime with Darton's warnings. Russell portrays such eccentric wanderers as Queen Christina of Sweden and Lady Hester Stanhope, both learned women of "masculine . . . propensities" (58) who renounced power in their homelands. Catherine II of Russia sold her soul to the "Tempter" for "dominion, glory, riches" and died with a "prolonged scream" in the devil's "choking grasp" (257). Russell spotlights Charlotte Corday, assassin of Marat, venerated by many as "the Jeanne Darc [*sic*] of Liberty," or "the beautiful Nemesis," but in Russell's eyes merely a bloody murderess whose "self-glorifying pagan fanaticism [was] kindled at the pictured pages of Plutarch" (193, 200). (As a girl Mme Roland was similarly disturbed: "Her brain was . . . throbbing with . . . enthusiasm kindled by the magic pages of Plutarch" [42–43].)

Russell's is no relentless catalog of censure, even of foreigners or atheists, however; he begins with a laudatory chapter, "The Maid of Orleans," which unlike the other tales actually suits the subtitle, *Their Girlhood and Early Life.* Mrs. Hutchinson (one of Child's *Good Wives*), shone during the "heroic phase of our national life" (74); although as "feminine" as a "romance" heroine, Hutchinson "stood unflinchingly by her gallant husband" (75) during "the memorable defence of Nottingham Castle" and later when he was condemned to death at the Restoration (81). (An illustration of "Mrs. Hutchinson attending the sick at Nottingham" closely resembles contemporary images of Florence Nightingale, while Mrs. Fry in the frontispiece, Josephine seated in conversation with Napoleon, and other images closely resemble Mrs. Hutchinson.) The typical broad assortment is marketed as models of "girlhood," though the narratives are propelled through years of eminence to violent or sacrificial death. In spite of the presenter's outspoken praise or blame, it is difficult to delimit the volume as role modeling for British or American middle-class girls of the day, not only because of Russell's elaborate syntax but also because of the scenes of murder, battle, and martyrdom, as well as the international mix of high-ranking fame from different periods.

Some presenters, however, begin to question the received legends of villainesses of history, as Jameson began to sort the innocent from the guilty. *Lives of Celebrated Female Sovereigns and Illustrious Women,*[454; 403] ostensibly by

Mrs. Anna Jameson yet edited by Mary E. Hewitt, strays considerably from Jameson's original biographies of queens, adding a frontispiece of Charlotte Corday (no monarch, she). Hewitt's short preface apologizes for including Semiramis, "who is described by one of her historians, as 'a monster, possessed of every vice;' but she lived so far back in the ages of the world, that this account appears, to us, to be merely suppositious [*sic*], and I have chosen to introduce her here, as an example of the indomitable courage and . . . action" sometimes called forth in women. Hewitt attributes Semiramis's ultimate "cowardly submission" to the "fatalism" of "an idolatrous age" (n.p.). Even as she derivatively repeats the warrior-queen legend, Hewitt also offers a glimpse of critical historiography (perhaps monstrous legends mask the reality of "heroines of history").[40]

Models of the distant past require translation into Victorian terms. Mary Cowden Clarke's *World-Noted Women; or, Types of Womanly Attributes of All Lands and Ages,*[174] like other up-market collections for display, establishes its high-art credentials with elegant steel engravings (some noted in my introduction) and with literary allusions.[41] Clarke begins with an epigraph from Shakespeare, "The world's large tongue proclaims you," and a frontispiece of Sappho with a lyre beside a mountain lake, as though to illustrate Mme de Staël's *Corinne*.[42] Clarke cautions that some of her "types," "far from . . . models," should "be beheld as beacons of warning" (3). Like Mary Hewitt and others, however, Clarke dissents from the customary censure of famous women; we must "judge exceptional characters by exceptional rules" and view them by the standards of their day (3). Women's "fervour of character is almost always mistaken. . . . for absurdity or vice" (14). The world proclaims quite a mixed company, including a high proportion of suicides, martyrs, or heroines of ill-fated romance, a high degree of renown, intimacy with poets, or participation in international politics, as well as a high rate of learned women.

Clarke applies traditional judgments of feminine chastity and humility: Lucretia's suicide after a political rape shows a commendable inability "to survive outraged self-respect" (23); Cleopatra is known as "the grandest coquette that ever lived" (61); and Aspasia was "perhaps even more valuable . . . acting *through* [Pericles], than had she been more palpably great in herself" (57). Yet there is an undercurrent of proto-feminist polemic in the book. Clarke blames Margaret of Anjou or Catherine the Great for the ruthlessness that might seem noble in a king but in other ways exonerates them. Catherine was a terrific manager of her time and her many lovers, and Margaret's laughter when presented with the Duke of York's head was probably a sign of "hysterical agitation," natural enough in the circumstances (228). In many instances Clarke designs her heroines to exemplify a fusion of masculine and feminine excellence. Sappho, for example, rather like George Eliot's Alcharisi, was "attractive, as well as gifted—a perilous combination for a woman," driven to fame by her "ardour" and her "consciousness of grace and genius" (15). Aspasia, interestingly, "was a man herself, in every particular but those attractions of her sex which gave her additional influence" (41). "The female mind has frequently a keenness . . . and

an almost instinctive quickness of foresight, which, consociated with masculine calmness and staidness of wisdom, forms an all-potent combination
of intellectual might" (45). Florence Nightingale combines man-womanly "invincible spirit, and softest charity" (404). Praised by the Parisian newspapers
for her elegant "toilet," Nightingale's vocation is condoned as "house-keeping"
(382, 385); in short, she is in every way "a woman for every living woman to
be proud of calling sister" (393). This last statement could be a caption for the
whole book: Clarke implies a solidarity not only among her fellow presenters,
readers, and subjects but also among the varied heroines themselves, across
history (4).

Other presenters of ancient or grand types seem far less troubled than Clarke,
as they never fully face the implications of the narratives they commend. Emily
Owen (publishing as Mrs. Octavius Freire Owen) in *The Heroines of History*[616]
assumes the difficult "duty" of supporting "feminine influence," "the fearful
power our sex can exercise" over "character" and history (5). She appears to
read her own collection as though it were a paean to domesticity as well as to
the advanced stages of Anglo-Saxon civilization. Misogyny is the vice of un-
believers such as Voltaire or of "the darkness of barbarism"; "we leave to the
Hottentots the singular custom of first proving their arrival at manhood, by
beating their mothers" (5). Such slurs support Owen's project of exemplification and nation building. "Biography, like a vast picture made up of a myriad
varied faces," offers guidance to inspire "the young mothers of the future generation" (6–7). Yet Owen's subjects exhibit a remarkable range of action, from the
biblical manslayers Jael and Judith, to the classical warrior queens Semiramis,
Cleopatra, and Zenobia, to Joan of Arc and a "Modern Era" made of stern stuff:
Mary Queen of Scots is said to have married her husband's murderer; Margaret
of Anjou and Catherine de Medici "loved, for their own horror's sake, scenes of
persecution and bloodshed" (270).[43] No excess of good republican wives and
mothers in this lot. Momentarily wary of the general pattern of violence, Mrs.
Owen, like Darton, offers thanks that our times no longer require "performance
of a duty at variance with . . . our woman's nature" (11). One wonders what future mothers would result from taking the impress of Cleopatra—unless they
instinctively take her as a "reproof."

Even sacred history seemed unreliable as a source of models. The common
biblical prosopographies appeared to rely on the notion that women in the
good book must be good. At least the reader of tales of biblical heroines could
be said to be engaged in a good activity. Eliza R. Steele, or "Mrs. Steele," in her
preface to *Heroines of Sacred History*,[752] suggests that her work is preferable
to competing kinds of reading: "In this age of paper, when the world seems
busy 'making many books,'" she regrets that readers seek "some rare novelty"
among "empty husks." "The lover of . . . soul-stirring narration, need not seek
the shelves of romance . . . ; let him open these glowing pages." To encourage
reading of the Bible, Mrs. Steele embellishes the tales of its "most conspicuous
female characters" (v–vi), rather as the heroines of Shakespeare acquire their

own lives. Like Mrs. Owen, Mrs. Steele presents Judith and other biblical women of dubious deeds, confident that their stories will entertain.

Not only high rank, remote times, and sexual transgression required some explanation to Victorian readers. Even British predecessors in moral writing, education, and reform could be controversial as models. In the mid-nineteenth century, Clara Lucas Balfour uncovers "the strange mixture" of qualities in and responses to Hannah More (1745–1833). More's remarkable success inevitably elicited extreme judgments; a later generation's more moderate view puts her in historical perspective: "Her celebrity arose quite as much from the unintellectual character of most women of her time, as from any peculiar excellence in her writings." Yet "a woman who was so praised and so abused, must have been a remarkable character." Thus, we should study "the lesson of her life": "from a comparatively humble station" she rose "to be the favourite companion of the learned and the noble, and the monitor of both peasants and princes," through hard work rather than "brilliant genius." More was, in short, a self-made philanthropist "of whom England may be justly proud" (40–42).[52]

Other presenters carried forward Jameson's line of dubious "court beauties" with lessening concern for what morality said. *The Queens of Society*,[797] by Katherine Byerley Thomson (under the pseudonym Grace and Philip Wharton), offers one response to unreliable models: yielding to the pleasures of gossip. The collection revels in the misdemeanors of the ruling classes. The queens of society deserve their fame not only for wit and beauty but also for learning, literary talent, political leadership, and, yes, amiability or the "appearance of it." Although most of Thomson's examples represent "irreproachable moral character, one or two have been chosen by way of contrast and . . . warning" (iii–v). Lady Hervey, for example, is "not held up as a model nor exhibited as a warning. As a woman of the world she can not be esteemed an object for imitation. As one who, in the midst of great temptations, escaped great perils, she ought not to be pointed out as a delinquent" (287). The equivocal negatives leave the audience to beware. That taken care of, the relaxed (at times muddled) and faintly salacious stories can get under way.

By the first decade of the twentieth century, Thomson's descendents considered a woman of the world a fit object for imitation, though even then remnants of a gendered code of virtue shaped the presentation. Thus W. R. H. Trowbridge in *Daughters of Eve* celebrates Peg Woffington "as the merry magdalen with the heart of gold"; or the Countess Potocka as "the woman of impulse *par excellence*—passionate, ardent, reckless, and warm-hearted" (v).[812] Horace Bleackley writes of Fanny Murray, in *Ladies Fair and Frail*, "For the sins of her youth, which were thrust upon her by wicked men, she offered the atonement of twenty righteous years" of uncomplaining service to her wayward husband. "Long before her death the tears of the recording angel must have blotted her name from his book" (49).[89] Bleackley's pious rhetoric is a bit facetious, but it places his subject in a frame of conventional conduct.

Across the above range of cautionary approaches to negative models, the reader might possibly receive the warnings as a promise that the undertaking was a great deal more entertaining than instructive. To get at the juice, perhaps, one needed to peel off the judgmental rind. Yet both the outward and inward effects were indispensable to the whole. Women were historic because they served the good of humanity and admirable because their transgressions caught them in the web of history. Equivocation in *exemplification* (are the subjects good or merely great?) goes hand in hand with ambiguity in *construction of the reader*. Through it all, everyone presumes that biographies are useful in modeling character and shaping history.

The Ethical Standing of Biography

In the past one hundred years, the uses of biography have gone largely underground. It is no longer so good for you, the subjects are no better than they should be, and the curious voyeur has come out in all of us. The suasive appeal of biographies since 1900 has changed its manner more than its aim, however. Most observers dismiss collective biographies as they ignore the widespread consumption of life narratives of all kinds, preferring to debate the designs of certain full-length, individual biographies of distinguished cultural leaders. In this rarified zone, two sets of questions, those of ethics and of epistemology, swirl around the presenter's treatment of the subject and engagement with the reader. The ethical orientation generally shifted, at the beginning of the twentieth century, from praise to debunking. Whereas many Victorians attacked Froude and others for exposing the flaws in a great man, such qualms succumbed to the public's right to know.[44] The epistemological or representational mode simultaneously moved from public to private, from historical fact to aesthetic perception. Full-length biographies masked their teaching as they authenticated psychological traits and arbitrary gifts rather than modeling the precepts of success.[45] Edmund Gosse, in the eleventh edition of the *Encyclopedia Britannica,* banned any "broad views" from biography, which should simply display "the faithful portrait of a soul in its adventures through life."[46] The inward turn suggested new zones of aesthetic privilege, as though as an end in itself. Yet the swerve away from civic purpose was itself a purposeful, if not fully articulated, avoidance of the ever-widening recognition of hitherto obscured lives. Both epistemological and ethical principles in these debates responded to the crowding at the scene of life writing. To understand the critical neglect of the prevalent influence of prosopography, it helps to review the historical contexts that prescribed different modes of biography.

In the nineteenth century, many groups cast wider nets of recognition through educational projects such as the Mechanics' Institutes and the Society for the Diffusion of Useful Knowledge, the tracts of the missionary societies, journals addressed to working men and women or to ladies and gentlemen, inexpensive encyclopedias, and self-help texts, accompanying the increasing prominence of women as writers (on all subjects) and as educators.[47] As though in defense against such an onslaught, critics began to narrow the definition of literature and to draw a distinction between elite and popular audiences. Richard Altick's historical perspective on Victorian prosopographies is telling: in the "age of biography" appeared many "series . . . of book-length biographies: Eminent Women, English Men of Action, . . . English Worthies, Men Worth Remembering, Lives Worth Living"; "capsule lives" in popular journalism; "biographical encyclopedias" for scholars or for "the self-teaching workman"; "specialized compilations" of "painters, architects . . . Irishmen, saintly women, . . . 'earnest men,' good wives, booksellers"; "a sort of low-brow Protestant *Acta Sanctorum*" of dissenting missionaries, preachers, and philanthropists.[48] The very listing implies a lack of interest, with the distancing effect of population statistics. Like the later Victorians themselves, Altick may wish to stand above the surge of lives, though he writes like a collector rediscovering huge stores.[49]

Most twentieth-century commentators maintain that biography only gained tolerable dignity when realism defeated piety. Albert Britt in 1936 followed Harold Nicolson (who followed Gosse) in promoting objectivity rather than "moral judgments"; "it is only within our own century that the spell of hagiography has been entirely dissipated."[50] Such a redefinition of the genre addresses the relative positions of the three parties: whereas the Victorian reader was guided by a better-informed presenter to observe the subject's example, the twentieth-century reader was often hailed as an equal or even superior to the subject and disliked hearing from the presenter directly. Criticism of biography has often tried to set subject and presenter apart from the audience, in a studio of their own. Yet recently, the empowered audience has seemed to shut out the presenter or mediating frame to gain more immediate access to the subject. Confession is a more favored modern idiom than deposition; biography that teaches, or that enforces a makeover of the audience in the subject's image, threatens the sense of voluntary response or intimacy with an undoctored voice.

Few have praise for life narratives with obvious commercial purpose: celebrity lives from the *People* profile to the ghosted memoir, A&E's Biography network, and Web sites. Entertainment value shades into role modeling and historical instruction, however, in the above venues, on the sports page, or in the materials on multicultural heroes for elementary education. Yet no one seems to object to the traces of veneration in the bestselling portrait of martyred genius or great leader, Virginia Woolf or Winston Churchill, provided the treatment is suitably "magisterial."[51] Readers of the biographies of Dickens by Fred Kaplan, of the Brontës by Juliet Barker, or even of feminist prosopographies for a general audience such as Germaine Greer's *The Obstacle Race: The Fortunes of Women Painters and Their Works* or Elizabeth Longford's *Eminent Victorian Women,* do not suppose themselves to have much in common with purchasers of self-help, viewers of talk shows, or fans of the royals.[52]

As John Guillory observes, a secular literary canon retains its claim to impart a "truth" that rivals philosophy, science, and "scripture."[53] Efforts to purify a secular art of biography fail, as hero worship persists in diversified forms. Models today may be openly revered provided the context justifies a drive for achievement or recognition: in the studies of women, gender and sexuality, racial or ethnic literatures, or multicultural movements; in efforts to redress disability, disease, or trauma; or in most careers that could lead to fame, including government, business, the military, entertainment, athletics, and the arts. According to Linda Wagner-Martin, a feminist biographer may choose a female subject on the basis of "admiration"; it is no breach of contract that the "biographer has somehow identified with the community that surrounds the subject's life" and seeks to provide some form of affirmation to her readers.[54] In contrast, Wagner-Martin rejects scandalous or negative celebrity biographies.[55] Yet from the "unauthorized" to the "high" literary, biography retains its aims to instruct as well as entertain: to shape readers' subjectivity much as in hagiographical conduct books.

Steadily on bestseller lists and prominently reviewed, full-length biographies come in for vicious attack today, generally for a combination of ethical and epistemological errors. In a 1999 *New York Times* editorial, "Just Published: Minutiae without Meaning," Stanley Fish inveighs against biography (he spares autobiography) largely for the disproportion of instruction over entertainment. Readers should pass up biography for "more edifying spectacles like politics and professional wrestling." Fish says he feels nauseated, reading a biography, by the "gap" that opens up between fact and narrative structure, "cause and effect." Once upon a time, biographies had "master narrative models," but now the only honest formulas prevail in celebrity biographies. "Biographers . . . can only be inauthentic, can only get it wrong, can only lie."[56] Why some conventions are admissible, others inauthentic—why some lies entertain and instruct while others make one sick—Fish leaves the reader to judge according to taste. Interestingly, Fish as pragmatist, assessing a convention's failure to work, shades into Fish as judge of character: biographers are poseurs, bunglers, liars.[57] Many defenders of biography as a genre vouch for it as literary art, not historical fact, but if the narrative takes too much novelistic liberty, critics raise an outcry.[58]

Janet Malcolm has offered more astute and developed criticism of monographic biography than has Fish but with similar asperity. Unlike Fish, she is preoccupied with the deed of writing a life, the ethical axis, rather than with the problem of representation. Probing the viper's nest of Sylvia Plath biography, Malcolm asserts,

> Biography is the medium through which the remaining secrets of the famous
> dead are taken from them and dumped out in full view of the world. The
> biographer at work, indeed, is like the professional burglar. . . . The voyeurism
> and busybodyism that impel writers and readers of biography alike are
> obscured by an apparatus of scholarship designed to give the enterprise an

> appearance of banklike blandness and solidity. The biographer is portrayed
> almost as a kind of benefactor. . . . The reader's amazing tolerance (which he
> would extend to no novel written half as badly as most biographies) makes
> sense only when seen as a kind of collusion.

Readers blind themselves to the low standards of this disreputable line of work because they too want to "peep through the keyhole."[59]

With Malcolm's famous criticism in mind, John Paul Eakin traces other episodes in the controversy, suggesting that headlines linking biography to hunting or murder merely exaggerate the actual ethical perils of biography, in which one's privacy—a property—becomes a stolen commodity; one's personhood—identified with a living body—is violated: "The person, embodied in text, made thing, is accessible to harm." Eakin rightly perceives "ethical problems" not only in "unauthorized" biographies but in "collaborative autobiography," particularly ethnography; as Daphne Patai puts it, "The fact remains that it is we who are using *them* for *our* books."[60]

In life writing as elsewhere, the representational and ethical issues fuse; questions of technique meld with matters of property and rights. Both Fish and Malcolm regard biographical narration as a usurpation of the power of the novelist.[61] Breach of genre, however, seems a rather minor offense, and one that hints that the laws of genre have been drawn up in error or were at least meant to be broken. Group life narratives undoubtedly compound the presenter's power, as Patai and Eakin acknowledge. The collection and re-presentation of life stories of dispossessed living subjects resembles the practice of collective biography of historical models, but it raises ethical alarms neither for its excesses of commendation nor for the sorts of crimes detected by Malcolm. If the interests of presenters, subjects, and readers who share social conditions are somewhat at odds (though shared), and if a professional biographer violates one famous subject's privacy, an ethnographer exploits an entire group of unwitting indigenous subjects. The metaphors would be those of imperialism rather than of burglary and banking.

Often the controversies concerning representation and the politics of identity have implicitly engaged in criticism of model biography's ethical dimensions. Many deplore the mass production of personalities and the easy access that lowers the standards and exposes the flaws in the famous or that reduces the political to the personal. Since the 1960s, successive waves of lamentation for a culture of narcissism, a loss of "civil society," have come ashore.[62] The objections to current cultural customs vary, with various degrees of justification, but it seems clear that all are provoked by the actual redistribution of cultural capital that has resulted in part from generations of prosopographies or collective retribution through life narratives. In 1977, Richard Sennett attributed a cultural decline to something like what I call prosopography: "What has emerged in the last hundred years, as communities of collective personality have begun to form, is that the shared imagery becomes a deterrent to shared action."[63] Many more recent observers have questioned contemporary identity politics.[64] From opposing perspectives, all appear to agree that personality has replaced character and artifice has supplanted authenticity or, in James Monaco's words, "celebrity has entirely superseded heroism."[65] Rather than hoping for adaptation through acquired characteristics, audiences eat their champions alive on the magical theory that they become them.

At the same time that critics such as Malcolm defend biographical subjects against the aggressions of biographers and readers, some defenders of moral commendation have spoken up. In a representative moment, Maxine F. Singer's 1991 commencement address at Barnard College waxed nostalgic. In a printed version, she wrote that "young women in the 1930s and '40s . . . had real heroines" like Isadora Duncan, Martha Graham, and Marie Curie. "Heroines, yes, but role models? Most American women of my generation could not have imagined an unconventional personal life, and most lacked the talents" of these heroines. Today people want "a role model's proximal reality" in order to reduce the grandeur that demands difficult aspiration.[66] Yet over a decade later, with anniversary tributes to the heroes of World War II and more recent catastrophes, veneration is back. Gertrude Himmelfarb lauds a Carlylean tradition of biography (perhaps what Fish intends by "master narratives"), and she objects to the modern "valet" spirit that reduces heroes to the sum of their flaws and appetites.[67] Traditional biographers, far from burglars in Himmelfarb's view, are reverent personal servants to the memory of the great man. In effect, Himmelfarb offers a counterpart to Malcolm's rebuke of biographical aggression: praise of the biographer who upholds respectful hierarchy. Both views run counter to the mainstream twentieth-century supposition that biography for well-informed adults objectively represents the private life of the subject, without calling for emulation or blame. Rather than join in the outrage or nostalgia of Fish, Malcolm, Singer, or Himmelfarb, I would ask what produced a notion of pure, uninvested biography in the first place.

Self-Help and Role Modeling

The various objections to contemporary biographical representation have in common a sense that, as Woolf once put it, "human character changed." In general, self-help discourse disavows the possibility of such change: surely the norms are stable, however the individual may develop toward them. Self-help guidance should discourage the relativism of historical perspective, just as conduct literature often defies new models of subjectivity. Yet collective biographies have long functioned both as self-help and as historiography, as though to reconcile subjective and communal developments. If narrative constructs subjectivity, and if reiterated patterns of narrative form imagined communities or collective histories, self-help modeling must have world-shaping consequences.[68] Certainly, self-help biographies once held a strong reputation as effective guidance, especially appropriate for men.[69] Confidence in identification confirmed a general faith in the power of written models to shape mores. Today advice or "human potential" has sunk in status with its broad popularity, as a form of self-deception peculiarly appealing to women.[70] This historical change in self-help's aims from the model public man to the model private woman might in part be accounted for by recognizing the continuing self-help form and function of prosopographies.

Interpreters of self-help have been puzzled to assess the tendencies to exclusivity in what announces itself as an instrument of democratization and to trace the masculinist origins of what has become a feminized genre.[71] In fact, self-help for women flourished alongside that for men, in the form of collections of women's biographies. The most recognized Victorian vocational self-help was addressed as an exchange among men, featuring working men benefiting from industrial expansion, whereas the models of success for women conformed to a more middle-class range of occupations, above all writing, teaching, and social service (most forms of paid work for the female population remained hidden). In the later nineteenth and early twentieth centuries, success literature shifted to promote competitive personality in capitalist enterprise. According to Judith Hilkey, the hefty, expensive success manuals published between 1870 and 1910 in the United States (more than a hundred were in print circa 1900) served as a symbolic "equation of success and manhood."[72] Hilkey notes that some manuals included models of successful women as well as many representative men's lives, but she overlooks collective biography as a contemporary ally of the manuals for men. Success literature continues, with an influx of New Age and therapeutic discourses, to offer multiple exemplary narratives to largely female audiences.

A review of the history of exemplary life narrative, self-help, and role models should correct some misperceptions of these modes as signs of feminine weakness. Not that I wish to defend exemplary biography as a simple tool for uplift. The discourse of role models seems to heighten stratification, exposing the lack in the target audience. As Tim Dean, for example, protests, "Do gay men need heroes more than other people do?"[73] Identification further seems associated with femininity conceived as an inability to maintain proper separation from objects of desire or to attain objectivity.[74] Recent feminists understandably disidentify with the promotion of role models associated with the consciousness-raising period, but as Carla Kaplan insists, the moves of recovery and identification are indispensable in feminist studies, an "archeological imperative."[75] In a parallel realization, Victoria Glendenning admonishes biographers, "We are all . . . in the business of ancestor-worship, even when we demystify and demythologize."[76] Rather than seek universal complements of one's essential self, a searcher for precedents may carry historical and critical maps.

Self-help is unmistakably newfangled, adapted to globalized consumer culture, but its roots run as deep as those of modern biography and the models of individual development generated by the Protestant Reformation and the rise of capitalism.[77] Some of the earliest successes of printers and booksellers were hagiographies, or collections of heroic personifications of a developing community, such as Foxe's *Book of Martyrs* (in print in various forms from 1563). The pilgrim's progress evolved into secular self-making as the traditional external controls of relatively static communities were replaced by the portable self-discipline of mobile subjects in cities and colonies. Following on the eighteenth-century rise of Evangelicalism, self-help began to be articulated as a moral prescription for social reform. Its argument was embodied in the examples of self-disciplined entrepreneurs, learned men, missionaries, explorers, and reformers. G. L. Craik's *The Pursuit of Knowledge under Difficulties*, first published by the Society for the Diffusion of Useful Knowledge in 1830–31, established the plan of working-class male collective biography to model self-improvement.[78] The term "self-help," a rationale for personal progress as an engine of mutual progress, crystallized with Samuel Smiles's international bestseller first published in 1859, though it had appeared earlier in Carlyle's *Sartor Resartus* (1833–34) and in Emerson's "Compensation" (1841).[79]

In its early forms, self-help generally had socially transformative ambitions; it strove for cooperative reorganization for mutual benefit. Smiles has been vilified as a middle-class apologist for individualism and the status quo, a "laissez-faire" traitor to the Chartist movement he first advocated as a journalist.[80] More accurately, Smiles, as "Everyman's Carlyle," had a mid-Victorian confidence in shared progress based on self-denial rather than self-interest; his works effectively served to consolidate the interests of the broadest middle class.[81] *Self-Help* consists largely of a series of short biographies of self-made industrialists, and thus it has been read as a paean to solitary initiative. Yet such readings fail to account either for the sheer quantity of similar life stories or for the omission of personal details: this is mass, common success. Smiles attributes "our power as a nation" to "the spirit of self-help . . . in the English character," which in turn is distributed fairly among "the lives of men unwritten"; like Fielding or Johnson, Smiles trusts that good examples "pass unconsciously into the lives of others, and propagate . . . for all time" (38–39). Nevertheless, Smiles concurs with Fielding that written records afford a more efficient means of distributing the process of identification. Written lives "of great, but especially of good men" serve "as helps, guides, and incentives to others. Some of the best are almost equivalent to gospels" (39).[82] However oblivious to the operations of class Smiles wished to be, his response to economic inequality is frank and practical compared to his utter unconsciousness of gender inequality. Smiles's humble apprentices who rise to become masters of many men have little time for wives or children; few women are mentioned among the narratives of persevering enterprise.[83]

If Smiles secularizes and materializes hagiography, his moral program remains similar to religious discipline. Religious themes pervade self-help modeling in all periods, from Gibbons and Jerment to Lilian Whiting's *Women Who Have Ennobled Life*.[862] In contemporary self-help, therapists usually replace ministers or priests, and introspection replaces the confessional or the protestant self-interrogation.[84] Beyond Christian contexts, New Age self-help guides claim to reconstruct an eternal, divine collective womanhood through the goddess revival, offering a range of narrative models for the reader: "Which Goddesses Are You Ruled By?"[85] If much self-help strives to adjust the reader to broad but inscrutable social codes, the prevailing religious discourse serves an additional need according to Max Weber's sociological model: "'the sense of dignity'" of "pariah" "status groups," who find compensation in "a providential 'mission'" or "a specific honor before God."[86] While advice books may consist of boldface rules and spiritual or religious sermons rather than biographies or typological narratives, they often to this day compile series of model experiences and lives corrected by right living. Much contemporary self-help tells auto/biographical stories as though self-understanding and self-improvement were the only means of change; unhappiness in family, career, or leisure is due to internal causes, and the good reader exercises a choice of models or rules to live by. Maureen Ebben observes that the solutions offered by self-help "are largely personal, private"; the books borrow "the entrenched apolitical discourses of medicine and religion," with the political effect of "pathologiz[ing] behaviors of everyday life" (112, 120).

Role models, like self-help, turn out to be complex interactions with specific historical significance. Role models may be distrusted as simulacra of agency, yet consumer culture places great faith in their efficacy.[87] A "role model" is a narrative construction rather than a person; it is always a three-way discursive exchange, just as autobiography tends to be mediated by presenters (the troublesome slash between genres in "auto/biography" tilts toward the right-hand term).[88] David Amigoni, with the help of Bakhtin, insists on the triangulation in all biographical narrative and adds that the subject itself is not "unitary": "The hero" is "the topic of the utterance, which passes between the sender and the listener."[89] The complexity of this understanding of life narrative or of role models helps to resist the allure of the hero as autonomous individual and to recall the shaping influence of the presenter, the effects of the audience, and the rhetorical occasion or context. In everyday usage, the term "role model" refers to the admired, successful person that an admirer chooses because of some affinity. The (mediated) story of the model protagonist promises to reproduce a tale of obstacles overcome, thus reducing the distance between the original and the copy. Collective representations of models are sorted by categories commonly attributed to birth (sex, race, nationality) as well as those determining weighty social differences (religious or political affiliation, class or vocation), thus reinscribing the principles of difference and inequality as they invite observers to challenge such principles.

In the role market, diversity has functioned like product diversification.[90] Many hope that role models will leap ahead of slow-footed legislation and crippled affirmative action when children and members of marginalized groups choose the right story to reenact. The media constantly solicit us to consume other lives. What Sidonie Smith and Julia Watson write of autobiography, in italics, I would cite emphatically on behalf of biography as well: "*This telling and consuming of autobiographical stories, this announcing, performing, composing of identity becomes a defining condition of postmodernity in America.*"[91] Magazines such as *Women's Sports and Fitness, Career World,* and *Parents',* as well as numerous Web sites, commend affirmative assortments of models ("Every Girl Should Have One") to aid and shape the young or the disadvantaged, particularly in racial and ethnic or gender categories.[92] Thus, for example, a cover of *USA Weekend* displays: "Goal Model: Mia Hamm Leads the USA in This Week's Women's World Cup. She's the new face of a role model. 'I take it very seriously.'"[93] Beyond sports and entertainment, role modeling may be taken in all educational and political seriousness, though it so easily participates in advertising.[94] Whereas the photograph of an unknown model repeats a fashion of beauty without enacting a specific story (thereby licensing the consumer's daydream), the role of the successful, named person implies a repeatable plot, like the conventional parts in drama. The noun "model" evolves into a verb as a subject exhibits or models behavior, the presenter molds or models the subject like clay into an image, and aspirants remodel themselves to match that replicated image.

Role models seldom are presented singly. Trade books of multicultural self-help offer convenient prosopographies, for example, *¡Latinas! Women of Achievement,* edited by Diane Telgen and Jim Kamp (1996).[95] In a textbook format, it features seventy contemporary Hispanic women, each with a full-page photograph and several pages of informative praise. The foreword by Nicholasa Mohr recalls: "When I was growing up female and Puerto Rican in New York City . . . there were no positive role models for me."[96] For the presumed Latina reader, the prospects now are much more open, as the assortment of subjects attests: businesswomen and lawyers, poets and artists, Isabel Allende, Joan Baez, and Linda Ronstadt, the congresswomen Ileana Ros-Lehtinen and Lucille Roybal-Allard—a series of public personalities that solicits a same-sex, same-ethnicity gaze. For the most part, TV celebrity sets the standard for inclusion, and apparent variety shades into interchangeability. Of course, popular commendation is no more credulous among one targeted group than another. One could substitute in the following brackets the appropriate nouns or names from basketball or ballet, Asian Americans or Appalachians: "From their [Hispanic] roots to their current position in [the pop music mainstream], the award-winning [Gloria Estefan] and the [Miami Sound Machine] are the embodiment of the American dream come true." None of the subjects in *¡Latinas!* is simply a mother or aunt from the barrio, one of the obscure survivors who became Mohr's personal heroes.[97] In prosopography, what matters is the collective name recognition, the establishment of a repeatable story; in P. David Marshall's words, "the system of veneration, the process of succession of valued human identities, is more important than what any one of the individual celebrities may represent."[98]

The triangular narrative interaction may be illustrated in a rhetorical performance, the public response to the death of Commerce Secretary Ron Brown in 1996. This event, which has undoubtedly faded in most memories after waves of subsequent catastrophe, serves well as an instance of panegyric, the formula for "commendatory lives" developed in fifth-century-B.C.E. Greece.[99] It particularly illustrates the distribution of agency in role models as in biographies. Common references to role models usually promise optimal self-determination even as they coerce subjects into their mimetic categories. The life held up as a public example resounds within a particular staged space, though it may be on a satellite scale; the rhetorical spotlight on a solitary exception depends on a well-chosen and receptive audience governed by the rule(s) that the life serves to prove or even to break.

A *Los Angeles Times* article reporting on the funeral of Ron Brown in April 1996 described the procession from "the bustling black neighborhoods" to the "marbled monuments of Washington, symbolically retracing the path of his remarkable career." In President Clinton's words, "He proved you could do well and do good—he also proved you could do good and have a good time." Such a moral seems to claim the life as an instructive example for apparently complementary social extremes: baby-boomers and at-risk black youth. The article concludes with a sign that some have chosen to mimic the hero's quest: "Charles W. Saunders, 48, the mayor of tiny Waynesville, Ohio, . . . drove all night . . . to make the funeral. 'If I could use him as a role model to rise higher than a mayor's job, well, I would be very happy.'"[100] Ron Brown's life and death become narratable in terms of their resemblance to other such stories within his own categories—African Americans, males—and according to other narrative types (crossing Dick Whittington with President Kennedy, perhaps). At the same time, it becomes highly iterative because it differs from the common outcome of stories of that origin (the end of Ron Brown's story is not predicted by its beginning, or even its middle). Often the hero or heroine abandons ties, leaves home, resists the claims of affiliation that the audience wishes to reaffirm. Again, the model is not an individual but an interaction of presenter(s), audience, and subject. The subject's deeds (Brown's triumphant progress) and audience's replication of that action (not necessarily as well-publicized as Saunders's journey) both solicit and are solicited by the presenters' act of telling. The aspirant's private hopes for recognition ideally become mutual and performative. It is supposed that Brown would mentor Saunders (noun becomes verb here) if he knew the mayor had elected him as role model.[101]

Agency itself becomes a—perhaps the most—coveted and elusive object of desire in such discursive interaction. Though all participants appear free to choose their roles, these can be as coercive as the market forces that are masked as consumer choice. In some ways Brown had even less choice than Saunders did as to the prescription of his story as a role model, and both seem compelled into a spurious intimacy. Often the figure of greatest agency in the triangulation of the role model is the one who appears asked to do least: the biographer, ostensibly transparent medium for the facts of a life, who shapes the story and the audience. This narrative source need not be clearly personified—it may be a magazine ad, news show, or Web page, for example—nor need the actual authors have decided designs on the character or behavior of the public. The subject-forming function of biography does not depend, of course, on a biographer's conspicuous intentions or on a reader's conscious assent or identification. Indeed, models may be comparatively "unchosen"—parents or teachers—or they may be negative—notorious criminals or failures. And of course they may be consciously resisted or used as guides to opposite behavior. Today we make (negative) examples of those whom we catapult to fame, as in reality TV shows, or of those insiders who once could trade on their success, as in that celebrated model of domesticity, Martha Stewart. But the cautionary or retributive tale has long been a part of collective biographies, as I have shown.

The connection between contemporary role models and the historical roots of women's self-help history—the collections of biographies in this study—may not be short, but that distance describes the changes that have occurred in conceptions of biography as well as in ideology and social conditions. To recognize collective biographies of women as a form of prosopography is to begin to explain the history of self-help. It also suggests that presenters and the audience benefit personally as well as collectively from the compilation of exemplary life narratives. It is a group history that helps the teller reimagine an origin of belonging.

Naming What's Missing

As presenters serve the cause of self-help history for communities of women, they rely on the conventions that I have considered above. In some respects, presenters become autobiographical personae not unlike the audience, prosopoetically giving voice to the absent ideals or buried heritage. In prefaces to collective biographies as well as in other writings, many witnesses appear to sense the possible futility of praising famous women. I close this chapter on the functions of presenters by turning briefly to the conventions of naming what's missing. I will call these conventions *citations of famous women* and *autobiographical dispossession*. The first is the habit of listing by name a series of women, a shorthand version of a collective biography. The second may combine with the first, but requires a searcher, in the manner of Christine de Pizan (1405), who recalls finding no predecessors, no mentors or models, in spite of the possible citations. Both moments in the larger prosopographical project tend to produce a sudden reversal: those absent now appear, those present disappear. In miniature, citations of famous women and autobiographical dispossession illustrate the paradoxes of supplementary prosopographies, as well as the bonding of presenter and audience through an exchange of notable subjects. Often these exchanges center on women writers as the best evidence for women's potential. They make explicit the role-modeling function of subjects and the "self-help" need for such precedents in a collective narrative.

As tributes to historical women gathered during the later eighteenth century, a skeptical observer might question the pertinence of examples of women's achievements. Mary Wollstonecraft, in *A Vindication of the Rights of Woman* (1792), wishes to reason through a political and social theory of gender rather than to admire exceptional women; she names remarkably few women and refuses to "trace the history of woman."[102] She writes, "I shall not lay any great stress on the example of a few women who, from having received a masculine education, have acquired courage and resolution." Her note, inserted after "a few women," specifies "Sappho, Eloisa, Mrs. Macaulay, the Empress of Russia, Mme d'Eon, &c. These, and many more, may be reckoned exceptions; and, are not all heroes, as well as heroines, exceptions to general rules? I wish to see women neither heroines nor brutes, but reasonable creatures" (197).[103] Most of the women she does name elsewhere in *A Vindication* are contemporary or recent women of letters (as Wollstonecraft gives their titles): Mrs. [Hester Thrale] Piozzi, Baroness de Staël, Madame Genlis, Mrs. Chapone, Mrs. Macaulay, and Mrs. Barbauld (227–31, 243n. 2). "I shall not lay any great stress on" lists of exceptional heroines, and yet I list them.

During the ensuing century, countless voices attested to the worthiness of women by citing precedents of achievement. By 1880, Margaret Oliphant might well charge that it was high time to move on to another tactic. In her appeal for economic equality for women of all classes, "The Grievances of Women," for *Fraser's Magazine,* Oliphant sets herself apart from a public-speaking or equal-rights sort of feminist, and adds:

> I may also say that I decline to build any plea upon those citations of famous women, with which even Mr. Mill was so weak as to back up his argument. It does not seem to me of the slightest importance that there existed various feminine professors in Italy, in the Middle Ages, or even that Mrs. Somerville was a person of the highest scientific attainments. I allow, frankly, that there has been no woman Shakespeare (and very few men of that calibre: not another one in England, so that it is scarcely worth taking him into account in the averages of the human race). If such fanciful arguments were permitted . . . Shakespeare embodied all that was noblest in his genius, not in men but in women. . . . All this is however entirely beyond and beside the question.[104]

Oliphant, like Wollstonecraft, seems to indulge in a bit of *occupatio*: "I will not offer one of those pointless lists of names, such as . . ." those she proceeds to name or others like them. By the 1880s, few any longer would say that women were incapable of contributing to civilization, but many liked to point out that men had created the greatest works. (Shakespeare continued to be a favorite refutation—and confirmation—of female greatness, as *A Room of One's Own* suggests.) Both Wollstonecraft and Oliphant would dismiss collective biographies of women as "beyond and beside the question."[105]

Oliphant and Wollstonecraft would have been wrong to suppose that female prosopographies simply idealized a few privileged exceptions. Oliphant, it happens, also misrepresents John Stuart Mill's *The Subjection of Women* (1869), which relies almost as little as Wollstonecraft's *Vindication* on citations of famous women.[106] Mill does refer to notable exceptions: "The Greeks always accounted Sappho among their great poets. . . . There is not in all modern literature a more eloquent vehicle of thought than the style of Madame de Staël" (127–28). But he names these and other writers as anomalies in the midst of explaining the "deficiency of originality" in the works of women (128). Women have been poorly educated "amateurs" (134). "When we consider how sedulously they are all trained away from . . . any of the occupations or objects reserved for men, it is evident that I am taking a very humble ground for them, when I rest their case on what they have actually achieved. . . . Negative evidence is worth little. . . . It cannot be inferred to be impossible that a woman should be a Homer. . . . But it is quite certain that a woman can be a Queen Elizabeth, or a Deborah, or a Joan of Arc" (98–99). Actual examples, impressive as they are, scarcely touch the question of the nature, potential, or rights of women, as Mill demonstrates.

Citations of women's achievements are very "weak" or "humble ground" on which to found a feminist claim, yet Mill, Wollstonecraft, and Oliphant cite the names of famous women even in conceding this. Often the citations concern women of letters or the arts, in nineteenth-century arguments as much as today. Frances Power Cobbe's now-classic essay with the facetious title "What Shall We Do with Our Old Maids?" frequently resorts to catalogs of names, especially those of women writers. The article, provoked by "redundancy" (the statistical surplus of unmarried women in Britain), speaks simultaneously to a dearth. Cobbe acknowledges, as Mill would do a few years later, the limits of women's artistic achievements: "Sappho was a mere name, and between her and even such a feeble poetess as Mrs. Hemans, there was hardly another to fill up the gap of the whole cycle of history. No woman has written the epics, nor the dramas, nay, nor even the national songs of her country, if we may not except Miriam's and Deborah's chants of victory. In music, nothing. In architecture, nothing. In sculpture, nothing. In painting, an Elisabetta Sirani, a Rosalba, an Angelica Kauffman—hardly exceptions enough to prove the rule." Cobbe—obliterating many women you could name where she names "nothing"—characterizes the "feebleness and prettiness" of women's works until a few recent exceptions, Elizabeth Barrett Browning and Rosa Bonheur.[107] Later in the same article, Cobbe waxes more positive, inspired by the prospects for the scientific women, for example, who

> will follow in the steps of Mrs. Somerville.[108] . . . Authoresses are already a
> guild. . . . Let any one read the list of books in a modern library, and judge how

large a share of them were written by women. Mrs. Jameson, Mrs. Stowe, Miss
Brontë, George Eliot, Mrs. Gaskell, Susan and Katherine Winkworth, Miss
Martineau, Miss Bremer, George Sand, Mrs. Browning, Miss Procter, Miss
Austen, Miss Strickland, Miss Pardoe, Miss Mulock, Mrs. Grey, Mrs. Gore, Mrs.
Trollope, Miss Jewsbury, Mrs. Speir, Mrs. Gatty, Miss Blagden, Lady Georgiana
Fullarton, Miss Marsh, and a dozen others. (105)

It is a list that must puzzle most twenty-first-century readers in some of its
entries. And who might be the "dozen others"? The naming suggests a fluid,
incomplete, assailable guild or canon. That a British female literary tradition
has bearing on the circumstances of unmarried women appears to go without
saying.

Faced with the failures of the Mrs. Speirs to rival the Mr. Miltons, commentators have substituted literary heroines for historical women, as de Pizan
and Woolf do. Ruskin, in his lectures on the "separate characters" of men
and women (published as *Sesame and Lilies* in 1865), had based his ideal of
woman's queenly influence on a catalog of Western literary examples, relying
on Shakespeare à la Anna Jameson.[109] "Now I could multiply witness upon
witness of this kind," writes Ruskin. "I would take Chaucer, and show you why
he wrote a Legend of Good Women, but no Legend of Good Men. I would take
Spenser ... " (55). Ruskin seems dazed by the oversupply of feminine excellence in "Shakespeare and Aeschylus, Dante and Homer," tacitly all the more
so because historical conditions have hardly promoted "obedient devotion" to
this ideal (56–57). Ruskin's elegant contribution to self-help literature stumbles
over the gap between (literary) models of womanhood and the actual historical record, again as in de Pizan or Woolf. Although some of my prosopographies feature the heroines of Byron or Browning or Shakespeare,[e.g., 295; 558]
most concentrate on historical rather than literary heroines. In a few cases, a
woman becomes famous as the original of a fictional heroine, as when Elizabeth Starling in *Noble Deeds of Woman* honors Helen Walker, the original
of Scott's Jeanie Deans.[750 (pp. 52–54, 190); also 925 (pp. 337–57)] More important than the
degree of history or fiction is the subject's relation to male-dominated tradition:
Does she help to refute the notion that women will never achieve the highest
greatness?

Ruskin's chivalrous specialization of women might warn us against citations
of famous women, with their water-drop effect on monuments of history. Yet
many others also offer examples of what women had done as though to sidestep
the impossible question of what women might do.[110] The naming of the list of
predecessors often is truly prosopoetic, in the form of first-person elegy that I
call autobiographical dispossession. I sample only a few versions of a common
refrain of bereaved thinking back through our mothers or other ancestors. The
presenter of models places her- or himself in the role of the reader encountering
a dearth of models that only now is fully accounted. Everyone seems convinced
that recognition is being doled out, elsewhere. In the words of a Black History

Month Web site, "other cultures are made aware of their history . . . and we are not."[111] My ancestral pantheon is in ruins, yours clocks a million visitors a day.

In 1976, Mary-Ellen Kulkin collected "models and inspirations for young people" in *Her Way*, an annotated bibliography noted above. She recalls, "I grew up in the 1940s thinking that the only woman athlete was Babe Didrikson, the only woman scientist Marie Curie, and that other than Clara Barton, Florence Nightingale, and some queens and first ladies, the only other women of note were movie actresses . . . [or] the wives, mothers, and daughters of famous men learned about in school."[112] A kind of compulsory typology restricts us to the latest incarnation of the woman athlete, woman politician, wartime nurse. But even these names are remembered now as screen memories then; some other ancestry is withheld. Kulkin deplores the loss of a history of eminent black women; in the 1950s, the young could name "neither Harriet Tubman, Phillis Wheatley, Mary McLeod Bethune, nor Marian Anderson, but Aunt Jemima!" Kulkin has found that honorary catalogs and individual biographies were available to African Americans early in the twentieth century. But she laments, "The relative scarcity of biographies of women in my childhood . . . meant that girls, unlike their brothers, could not find true-life models who would inspire them" (xvi). An excursion into the losses of African American heritage gives way to Kulkin's primary theme, the deprivation of girls, who unlike their brothers lacked adequate role models for achievement. By default, the only children in the 1950s who faced their own mirror images were white boys, and the subject of her pity is white girls like herself.

A comparable citation of a withheld plenitude occurs in Paule Marshall's account of what she missed in Harlem in the 1930s: "No . . . teacher of mine had ever mentioned [Paul Laurence] Dunbar or James Weldon Johnson or Langston Hughes. I didn't know that Zora Neale Hurston existed. . . . Nor . . . Frederick Douglass and Harriet Tubman . . . or . . . Sojourner Truth. There wasn't even Negro History Week when I attended P.S. 35 on Decatur Street! What I needed . . . was an equivalent of the Jewish shul . . . where we could . . . learn about our history."[113] Marshall can now identify by name the heritage she was missing and presumes that Jewish children knew theirs all along (did they seem fully assimilated in the 1930s?).

Carolyn Heilbrun, one of those Jewish children, had her own memory of rereading an absent list through the list that was there. "In the late 1930s and early 1940s I read biographies at the St. Agnes branch of the New York Public Library." She read in alphabetical order and puzzled over the opening of *The Education of Henry Adams*: "'Had he been born in Jerusalem . . . and circumcised in the Synagogue by his uncle the high priest, under the name of Israel Cohen, he would scarcely have been . . . more heavily handicapped in the races of the coming century.'" Heilbrun recalls, "I had to make myself a boy to enter that world [of daring and achievement]; I could find . . . almost no biographies of women at all."[114] The New York child might have recognized herself in the stigmatized Jew; Heilbrun might later have emphasized the pun lurking in

Adams's term, "races." Instead, Heilbrun's theme is the absence of likeness in biographical history for the female subject, whereas Marshall desires models of color, male or female. Both seek a prosopography of their own. Although thousands of women and hundreds of African Americans were preserved in libraries when Marshall or Heilbrun were impressionable young readers, they retroactively give face to a comparative absence.

Such a series of retrospective readings of missing models could go on. I could mention Alice Walker's famous search for Zora Neale Hurston, which Walker superimposes on Virginia Woolf's search for Judith Shakespeare.[115] I could follow Cornel West's prosopographical flourish in *Race Matters*: "How do we account for the absence of the Frederick Douglasses, Sojourner Truths, Martin Luther King, Jrs., Malcolm Xs, and Fannie Lou Hamers in our time?"[116] But I will not. There were, at least, more than enough recuperative catalogs of exemplary women to have given any (middle-class, Anglo American) nineteenth-century woman the ancestry she needed. Perhaps the wish to have missing forebears restored to us, as by the three Ladies in de Pizan's city, impels us toward our goal of restitution. If only, Louise Bernikow hopes, "someday we'll have the story right."[117] Rather, the restorative work is to do over again. What the series of personae ironically collects are empty places for the presenters and audience themselves to fill. The most immediate benefit may be the very insufficiency for which prefaces apologize: the open-ended momentum of "and many others"— the ellipsis of generations. Concurrently, "how to triumph over the adversity of being a woman" becomes "how to join the progress of civilization."

Chapter Two

Heads Turn, Heads Roll

Heroic Types from Judith to Clara Barton

In a classic lament for missing role models, Elizabeth Barrett Browning wrote, "I look everywhere for grandmothers and see none."[1] Barrett Browning has no need to cite the cumbersome list of the maternal generation, models of hampered feminine genius such as Felicia Hemans, "bound fast in satin riband," as the younger poet put it.[2] Symbolically what Barrett Browning would erase were the chronicles of tragic heroism or suffering captivity, the sorts of narratives rendered into verse in Hemans's prosopographical *Records of Woman* (1828). Hemans recalls, for example, that Arabella Stuart was secretly married to William Seymour and both were imprisoned by James I as threats to the crown. Arabella escaped "in male attire" and took sail to meet her husband; their vessels missed the rendezvous, she was recaptured by the king's men, and ended her life as a mad prisoner (3–4). It was not the sort of tale that Barrett Browning intended to reenact, though her own captivity and escape were to become legend. Granted the self-help effect of choosing the right model, the aspiring woman might convincingly claim that the right models did not exist. The most-cited women set dangerous precedents, bright flares shining in dark days. Often what remained was little more than a name, an image from traditions of art, a tragic scene, such as Sappho, Penthesilea, Dido; biblical heroines such as Deborah or Ruth; queens such as Zenobia of Palmyra or Cleopatra.

Yet a contemporary of Barrett Browning, holding in her hands one of the lavish assortments of notable women, might feel in possession of a city's worth of heroic examples closer to home than the lists that were already venerable for Heywood and others in the seventeenth century. Plentiful recent tales of heroism, variants perhaps of the story of Arabella Stuart, would seem very unwise to repeat, though repeated and varied they were. I revive spectacular deeds that seem to scramble gender and class and to wrench history into the realm of romance. Remarkable enough considered as history, these narratives are all the more startling in the context of a discourse of self-help, in which presenters commend the examples as models for feminine character. Although as I have suggested the effort to catalog a history of women remains erratic and endless, it may impart a sense of strength in numbers as well as in the individual acts or careers united in particular volumes. Evidently, European women for some time had been creating an epic heritage without waiting for Barrett Browning's poet, Aurora Leigh, to dare to write in a modern epic form.

"Heads Turn, Heads Roll" is my shorthand for a mélange of gender and race, captivity and rescue in disguise, decapitation, and prostrate or dead men. "Manly" deeds are justified by emergencies, often those of international or civil war or colonial conflict. I present five interrelated varieties under this large theme: first, "Petty Treason, or Prisoners in Drag"; second, "The Judith School of Patriotic Murder"; third, "Captivity and Interracial Crimes"; fourth, "Over His Prone Body, or Martial Arts"; and fifth, "Adventures in Nursing Administration." The limitations of most of these heroic exceptions are obvious; many are not the "grandmothers" a sensible or humanitarian person starting her career would want to follow. Extreme almost in the current popular sense of that word, these action-figure heroines will offer a revealing context for the more mannerly activists in chapter 3. I found it difficult to decide whether Sister Dora and Clara Barton, my final subjects in "Heads Turn, Heads Roll," ought not to belong in the category of institutional reformers in "How to Minister as a Woman." After all, these sorts often share space on prosopographical lists. Such slippage of types or categories faces all presenters, and for this reason I begin with an examination of the efforts at typecasting in some collections—often a matter of apparatus such as titles and ordering—before I revive the more venturesome sorts of tales.

Even in the nineteenth century no one still seriously suggested that Boudicca, Lucretia, the warrior Maid of Saragossa, the scholar Vittoria Colonna, and other notables represented all types of womanhood for all time. This did not prevent collections from attempting a universal catalog of types, however. In female prosopographies, compulsory typology limits the likenesses to reincarnations of earlier types. Obviously, heroes through the ages have been subject to similar mimetic patterning; epithets always seek to make sense of exceptional individuals through analogies to predecessors.[3] In the conditions of scarcity of recognition for women, however, the patterning seems more restrictive. Any new notable woman becomes comprehensible as an imprint of a type: to name a few, the mother of the great man (Susannah Wesley conceived as the English, Protestant Monica [mother of Augustine]); the learned woman (Eliza Carter as the English Aspasia); the woman of genius (Margaret Fuller as the Yankee Corinne). The typological likeness provides an interpretive frame, ostensibly one of honor, but it tends to narrow the potential agency as it praises. Thus when Voltaire (admiringly) labels Catherine the Great as the Semiramis of the North, the epithet may recall its popular narrative: Semiramis, reputed lover of her own son, is said to have seduced one of her soldiers each night and slaughtered him next morning. Antonia Fraser in *The Warrior Queens* writes of "an encouraging (and admonitory) litany" of the names whenever a new female military ruler emerges: "Boadicea . . . Penthesilea, Judith, Semiramis and Zenobia. . . . Elizabeth I and Catherine the Great," all the way to Margaret Thatcher.[4] The analogies erase most individual features of the lives thus linked. I would emphasize that the rhetoric of typology follows patterns of cultural re-membering and forgetting rather than essential archetypes or eternal truths. In specific contexts, typology helps to license some careers, but it prescribes interpretation of them and tends to obliterate the outlying or redundant exam-ples. In the lives of women en masse in my bibliography, the broader effect is a default delete or replace mode.

Compulsory Typology and Amazing Agency

Some collections provide keys within the table of contents to their own typo-logical coding. The realization that impressive women differ widely from each other seems to have exerted a centrifugal force that many collections try to counterbalance with the moral "caption" of a category. The chapter titles and the sequence of subjects may resemble taxonomies, cosmologies, or simply variations on themes. By examining a few examples of this practice, I also will call attention to some of the most popular subjects in Victorian collections. I have devised a measure of the relative eminence of female subjects from this particular historical angle: a tabulation of the more than sixty subjects included four or more times in general collections from the periods 1850–70, 1880–1900, and 1910–30 (see app. table A2). Yet any statistics, no matter how accurate, could never confirm the triumph of certain subjects over others. The very premise of such collections is variable differentiation among a select set, each component of which nevertheless stands as part for whole (representative type) that itself is part of a whole (womanhood). Across centuries and zones, women stand in for each other; absent figures make their presence felt, as any instances of a type do multiple duty.

Some collections display a random order of eponymous chapters. More intriguing is another common practice whereby the headings and chapter titles form a sort of spasmodic argument concerning types of womanhood. Two forms of such proto-discursive titles deserve more remark than tables of contents customarily receive: first, the typological (an epithet or attribute is linked to the subject's name), and second, the anonymous collective (the title identifies a historical group or a generic attribute). This second device especially strikes me as symptomatic of gender difference. It is difficult, to say the least, to imagine a chapter entitled "Heroism of a White Man" or "Man as Husband."

The prolific William Henry Davenport Adams favored the typological title. In *The Sunshine of Domestic Life*,[13] Adams extrapolates from his models the virtues they stand for, as for example: "Matronly Excellence. / The Story of Lady Vere"; "Mental Energy and Self-Reliance. / The Story of Elizabeth Inchbald"; "Fidelity to a Great Trust. / The Story of Flora MacDonald"; "Womanly Virtues in an Exalted Station. / The Crown and the Cross. / The Story of Lady Jane Grey"; "A Noble English Mother. / The Story of Mary, Countess of Pembroke." What is the difference between "matronly excellence" and "a noble English mother," and do these representatives not also stand for womanly virtues in an exalted station? Is Mary Herbert, Countess of Pembroke, Sir Philip Sidney's sister, not also a major literary patron, translator, and writer in her own right?

The rubrics of conduct pull toward abstraction, in the opposite direction of modern biography's drive toward specificity—and indeed, against the grain of the narratives so labeled. In the name of one ideal, Mrs. Steele's seven *Heroines of Sacred History* simply march down the title page: "Heroism of Miriam, / Heroism of Deborah, / Heroism of Ruth," and so on.[752] Collective modeling of more contemporary figures places individuals in context; thus the chapter titles in *Noble Women of Our Time*[468] "preposition" a well-known woman "among" or "with" the anonymous objects of her service, people exotic to the English upper classes: for example, "Miss de Broen among the Communists of Paris"; "Miss Carpenter among the Ragged Children of England and India"; "Mrs. Bowen Thompson with the Daughters of Syria." A comparable method encapsulates multiculturalism in such exotic titles as "Ma-Ta-Oka of Pow-Ha-Tan: The Girl of the Virginia Forests" (as E. S. Brooks[114] designates Pocahontas; see my chap. 5).

Typological titles in the early twentieth century came under the influence of comparative mythology and Germanic archetypalism. The Bishop of the Methodist Episcopal Church, Frank M. Bristol, orders his *Heroines of History*[112] under three commonly used categories: "Woman-Heroic in Mythology," "Woman-Heroic in Shakespeare," and "Woman-Heroic in the Bible." Within each part, most chapters begin with a similar hyphenation: "The Heroine-Mother: Thetis, Hecuba, Latona" or "The Heroine-Daughter: Miranda, Cordelia," repeating family roles. Bristol is certain that "the heroic element in woman's character . . . is one and the same virtue" everywhere (11). Well might he say so, given his fictitious samples. Yet presenters of actual "heroines of history" are just as inclined to erase differences in the name of archetypes. Gamaliel Bradford's *Daughters of Eve*[101] embellishes some French variations with one theme: "Eve in the Apple-Orchard: Ninon de Lenclos [*sic*]" or "Eve and Almighty God: Madame Guyon."

The second method, anonymous collective, more forcibly presses individuals into amalgamated service. It has a venerable tradition, at least as old as Plutarch's *Concerning the Virtues of Women* (first century A.D.), which, in a nineteenth-century American edition of *Plutarch's Morals* introduced by Ralph Waldo Emerson, includes numbered collective narratives: "Example 1. Of the Trojan Women"; "Example 2. Of the Phocian Women." In volumes that submerge biography in favor of the conventions of advice literature or of historiography, subjects may lurk in sentences and paragraphs, unnamed in a table of contents, and sometimes not even indexed. Adams relies on a blend of the anonymous collective with the typological, as in *Woman's Work and Worth*:[14] "Woman as Mother" or "Woman as the Heroine, Enthusiast, and Social Reformer." *Bible Types of Modern Women*[535] by the Scottish Rev. W. Mackintosh MacKay weaves biblical sources around collective characters in reprints of "Sunday-evening lectures," "popular and practical" (vii): "The Woman of Decision," "The Woman of No Importance," "The Factory Girl," and even "The Womanliness of Jesus." Compilers struggled to pin down variegated specimens of womanhood, yet they never abandoned the hope of a representative catalog.

Two competing midcentury volumes, Elizabeth Starling's *Noble Deeds of Woman*[751] and Jesse Clement's *Noble Deeds of American Women*,[182] crowd many anecdotes under headings for different virtues, frequently featuring anonymous groups. Starling's collection, published in London, spans roughly two millennia of Western history with a leaning toward modern France and England; approximately 225 narratives, sorted under "Maternal Affection" or other attributes, include anonymous examples of "The Humanity of a Negress" or "Admirable Conduct of the Ladies of America." A decade and a half later, Clement finds Starling's compendium wanting, however: "'Noble Deeds of Woman'... contains but three references to American women" (v); he will supply American types for "emulation" (v).[5] One of Clement's numerous anonymous chapters, "The Women of Wyoming" (142), also appears as part of a chapter in Ellet's *Women of the American Revolution*[259] (402–7; both presenters credit Miner's *History of Wyoming*).[6]

The introduction to *Noble Deeds of American Women*,[182] by Lydia Huntley Sigourney, is an epitome of midcentury American ideology in the spirit of Sarah Hale.[7] I would highlight Sigourney's citations of famous women and use of typological epithets. She cites ancient exceptions to history's "silence at the name of woman": the wife of Socrates, the mother of the Gracchi, Cleopatra, Boadicea. Against the background of pagan abuse of women (described in some detail), Sigourney hails Christianity and modern enlightenment as sponsors of increased historical agency for women (xiii–xv). She praises by epithet (not by name) women who have ascended to their "rest and reward": the "venerable moralist of Barley Wood" (if we don't remember the name of Hannah More's house, we can consult Sigourney's own biography of More, d. 1833); "that high souled apostle... in the plain garb of her order... among the convicts at Newgate" (Elizabeth Fry, d. 1845); the poetess of the "tuneful" "harp" who eschewed man's warlike fame in favor of "'words of home-born love,'" Felicia Hemans (d. 1835) (xvi). Sigourney's next allusion was transparent to her readers in 1851: "She, too, who sleeps beneath the hopia-tree in Burmah, whose courage and constancy no hero has transcended" but who has since been imitated by other missionary martyrs: Ann Hasseltine Judson (d. 1826), the fourth subject in Clement's collection (xvi). A living "Scandinavian maiden . . . compeer of the nightingale" is unmistakably Jenny Lind (xvi). Moral teacher, philanthropical reformer, poet, missionary, performer: five primary roles in the Victorian anthology of women, apotheosized in Sigourney's elevated typology. Because of the "deeds" structure, however, most of the subjects in the volume that Sigourney introduces are as obscure and nameless as the women of Wyoming.

Many collections develop elaborate taxonomies not for the heroism of a people in crisis but for solo celebrities of history. Samuel Mossman's *Gems of Womanhood*[589] may characterize dozens of others in the 1870 period.[8] I will unpack Mossman's "literary casket" (313), rich in famous subjects for my own readers. Mossman himself concedes the inexact match of his models with his headings, but he unites the assortment as a set of "diamonds of the purest water." "It must not be concluded . . . that the mine from whence the foregoing jewels were extracted is exhausted: there is abundance in store . . . of the GEMS OF WOMANHOOD" (313–14). The renewable supply is the priceless nature of womanhood itself, to be collected and displayed.[9] The headings and chapter subtitles, however, strive to differentiate and compare historic individuals in the standard vocational types.

The first of Mossman's eight headings, "Heroines in Times of Peril," subsumes:

1. JOAN OF ARC: The Maid of Orleans
2. OCTAVIA: Wife of Marc Antony
3. ZENOBIA: The Queen of Palmyra and the East
4. BOADICEA: Queen of the Ancient Britons

Already some patterns emerge. While many a heroine of history led in battle, each of these four was ultimately humbled, if not by ancient Romans then by the English and French hierarchies abetted by the Church of Rome. For Victorian Protestants, there remained an ambivalent fascination with things Catholic; in general, they were able to recast Joan as an evangelical in resistance to establishment or as a middle-class single woman with courage for leadership, while there might be an added aesthetic flirtation with Oxford Movement ritualism. Little remains of the fifteenth-century French peasant. The juxtapositions—Joan and Boadicea, for instance—suggest anachronistic disregard for the patriotic and ethnic loyalties for which these women fought. Thus the martyrdom of Joan held more fascination for the British than the story of the last queen and her

daughters defeated by the Romans (Joan rivals Nightingale for the most popular subject in my count). Zenobia, the prototype of Hawthorne's fiery woman
in *The Blithedale Romance,* enjoyed a revival in Harriet Hosmer's statue and
in countless schoolbooks and gift books; she was a great conquering empress
until she was led in the parade of captives through Rome (no one admired her
survival for many years thereafter). Octavia, the rival of Cleopatra, suffered a
Pyhrric victory, also in Rome: she survived both her husband and his mistress,
though she mourned Antony and her own son inconsolably: "She gave herself
up . . . to a terrible melancholy all the rest of her days" (33).

"Succourers in Days of Distress" is composed of rescuers rather than captives
or victims:

5. FLORA MACDONALD: The Deliverer of Prince Charles Stuart
6. MRS ELIZABETH FRY: The Reformer of Female Prison Discipline
7. GRACE DARLING: Who risked her Life in saving the Shipwrecked
8. AFRICAN WOMEN: Who succoured the Traveller, Mungo Park

The generic African women are the anomalies in this group, yet the three
celebrities also bear exceptional markings of nationality, sect, or class: a Scottish
clanswoman; a Quaker preacher; a lighthouse keeper's daughter. According to
Mossman,[589] European women emulate Florence Nightingale or the French
Sisters of Charity and Mercy because it suits women's God-given mission, for
the same reason that African women instinctively succor the traveler. Mungo
Park was "robbed, beaten, and left for dead by men, while poor negro [*sic*]
women took pity on him and saved his life" (95); Mossman's subject becomes
the explorer himself. I will feature below both Darling and MacDonald, great
celebrities of adventure in their day.

After an unusual selection under "Contributions to Literature and Art"—the
poet LEL; "the English Female Sculptor," "Mrs Anne Damer"; and Tarquinia
Molza, "who was made a Citizen of Rome for her great Learning"—Mossman's
series[589] turns to "Woman's Influence in the Political World," featuring Mme
de Staël, Jane, Duchess of Gordon, and the Duchess of Duras. Mossman contends that there has never been a real female politician, though women may
soon steer "the ship of the State," given the reforming "spirit abroad" (143).
Mossman indirectly answers the question of why British and American collections include so many Frenchwomen: "Almost all the celebrated French
women of the last three or four centuries have more or less influenced the
political world." Englishwomen of political inclinations always possess "minds
of a masculine character," whereas all Frenchwomen are "less feminine." Jane,
Duchess of Gordon, serves as "an example of this masculo-feminine class of
celebrities in history" (159). In effect, she was the Tory whip, and a social
leader as well, in the 1770s and 1780s. Mme de Staël provides "a type of the
highest excellence"; her international success with *Corinne* provoked Napoleon

to condemn her to exile, but she did not push too far into politics (144, 152). The Duchess of Duras, milder than her peers in this chapter, returned from exile to establish a liberal salon in Paris during the Restoration; as the pious author of *Christian Reflections,* she is as commendable as "the most celebrated English women" (174)—a "masculo-feminine" compliment indeed.

Still within an Anglo-French axis, "Woman's Influence in Society" comprises three comparable figures of influence in the political world:

15. MRS ELIZABETH MONTAGUE: Eminent for her Virtuous Influence on English Society
16. MADAME RECAMIER: Eminent for her Beauty and Power over Parisian Society
17. MARY, COUNTESS OF PEMBROKE: A Leader of English Society—time of Queen Elizabeth

Mossman[589] maintains that crowds of "superior men will listen with raptures to the conversation of some brilliant woman. There she sits supreme, a queen of society" (177).[10] Yet he suggests that socialites are redundant, even if politically distinguished; Mme Récamier, supreme beauty in France, was exiled by Napoleon, joining Mme de Staël (177–78, 187, 196).[11]

Avoiding the still smaller degree of narratability associated with "Woman's Influence in the Domestic Sphere," Mossman[589] lists there two famous writers of "the Domestic Affections," Mrs. Hemans and Mme de Sevigné, whose writings and lives little support the idea of a happy male-headed family under one roof. According to Mossman, de Sevigné, after two centuries, still compels the "admiration" of "writers on womanhood of all shades of opinion. More biographical sketches and memoirs of her life, sayings, and letters exist, than of any other French female celebrity." Yet Mossman seems to feel this story lacks a hook; "general excellence in mental refinement" seems undistinguished (224), rather like women's social influence. Hemans, like de Sevigné, was partly celebrated as a voice for relations among women.[12]

"Woman's Enduring Love and Filial Piety" might be a heading for many a narrative, but in Mossman[589] it presents:

20. LADY RACHEL RUSSELL: Whose Husband was beheaded on a false Charge of Treason in the Reign of Charles II
21. ELIZABETH OF SIBERIA: Daughter of an Exile, whose Freedom she obtained from the Czar of Russia

Here we encounter figures for what I call "petty treason," below. In their forays to prisons, their encounters with executions, their proximity to royal courts, these women might be located in what Mossman designates "Times of Peril" or "Days of Distress," yet the heading paints the customary moral of loving attachment rather than active courage.

Whereas most of the exemplars in Mossman's categories[589] assume the attribute of religious faith, the final category, "Woman's Devotion to Religion," features:

22. ANNE ASKEW: Who suffered Martyrdom, for Conscience' sake, in London—time of Henry VIII
23. MADAME GUYON: A French Religious Reformer and Poetess, persecuted and imprisoned—time of Louis XIV[13]

Undoubtedly, modern missionary women such as Ann Hasseltine Judson (see next chap.) conceived their roles in terms of these "saints" and became, in their turn, models for Anglo American Christian women who could readily imagine persecution on another continent.

Interchangeable feminine attributes seem to threaten any individual's claim to fame: the mineral-like abstraction contrasts with the woman's name and the clause that specifies subject, location, and association with a male persona of history. Though few collections match Mossman's elaborate outline, his unstable typecasting and his selection of subjects are characteristic. Many alternate subjects were waiting in the wings. Among those that I do not feature, Queen Elizabeth and Isabella of Castile outruled male monarchs, and Mme Roland and Abigail Adams sparred with the intellectuals in revolutionary times.[14] Mrs. Trimmer and Hannah More launched schools and wrote moral tales, and Mary Lyon and Emma Willard pioneered women's education in the United States. Dorothy Wordsworth and Meta Klopstock were the helpmeets of poets; Frances Ridley Havergal and Adelaide Procter were devout and irreproachable poets themselves. Angelica Kaufmann, Harriet Hosmer, and Rosa Bonheur each demonstrated that a woman could be a painter or sculptor (Edmonia Lewis, the African American sculptor, or Georgia O'Keefe or Frida Kahlo are likely to replace them since the early twentieth century). Jenny Lind, the poor girl discovered and transformed into "the Swedish Nightingale" much celebrated in the United States and Europe, metamorphosed into Marian Anderson in the twentieth century. The scientist has been modeled alternatively by Mary Somerville or Maria Mitchell, the New England astronomer, or in the twentieth century, Marie Curie. Laura Bridgman, the well-taught blind girl, vanishes with the advent of Helen Keller. While the story of each woman draws great interest to itself, the cumulative effect of immersing all of them in a sample of achievement may be even greater—and certainly more "representative"—than that of one woman in full-length detail.

Beneath the labels of type, what sorts of stories prevailed? I have noted the prominence of *vocation* and *deeds* in women's life narratives, with the emphasis on confirmed *prestige, influence,* and *religion.* These elements overpower expectations that women's lives are determined by the *body, love,* and *family.* Many collections emphasize extraordinary deeds of women, as in Starling's or Clement's anthologies of anecdotes. As proof that a woman's courage and strength are greater than a man's, Grace Darling's story was for a time supreme. The tale is almost entirely a nineteenth-century phenomenon as it flashed on the horizon in 1838 and largely disappeared after the first decades of the following century.[15] Darling no doubt needs to be reintroduced to most twenty-first-century readers, at least beyond Britain. The 1848 edition of Starling's *Noble Deeds of Woman*[751] includes a title-page vignette of the climactic event of Darling's brief tale, the rescue of survivors of a shipwreck, a narrative that serves several purposes at once. Starling devotes unusual space (twelve pages) to the lighthouse keeper's daughter from Northumberland (born 1815) in a section labeled "Humanity," under the title, "Instinctive Courage of Grace Darling." This placement interprets the story as an allegory of humanitarian aid rather than linking it to warlike feats cataloged under "Courage and Presence of Mind." The narrative serves to reconcile classes and genders within a strong nation; Darling's is "a name from the court to the cottage associated with one of the noblest acts of heroism which have done honour to the female sex," as Starling affirms (188–89). At the same time the tale satisfies the sort of fascination with disasters that keeps the sinking of the Titanic alive in popular imagination today.

Starling[751] quotes at length from an account by the respected reformer and writer William Howitt, who met Miss Darling in person (and in her craggy native setting) before her early death from tuberculosis. He affirms that there is "nothing masculine in her appearance" and nothing vulgar; rather, she is the "realization of his idea of Jeanie Deans" from Sir Walter Scott's *Heart of Midlothian* (190). (On previous pages Starling tells the life of Helen Walker, the original of Jeanie Deans, with an illustration from Scott's novel—the sisters embracing in prison—thus blurring fictional and historic heroines [52–54].) After such endorsement, Starling relates "the event which withdrew the name of Grace Darling from its hitherto humble obscurity, and called into action the whole energies of her mind and heart, in one momentary impulse of feeling" (190–91). In 1838, an unsound steamer traveling from Hull to Dundee wrecked on the rocks of the Farne Islands, splitting in two; half of the boat, with most of the upper-class passengers and the captain and his wife, was "instantly carried off through a tremendous current called the Pifa Gut, which is considered dangerous in good weather" (193). (Charlotte M. Yonge, in of *A Book of Golden Deeds*,[925] agrees with Starling that one gentleman saved himself by leaping into the sole lifeboat, in which he and a few of the crew escaped [434].) Five crew members and four passengers clung to the fore section of the boat throughout the night, expecting to be thrown into the sea at any minute. The two young children of a weaver's wife were "buffeted to death by the waves while she held them in her arms" (434).[925] The next day, the Darlings saw the wreck from their lighthouse a mile distant, and Grace, against the judgment of her father, insisted on rowing to the rescue: "even the stoutest of the male sex" feared "that terrible passage," "but what shall be said of the errand of mercy being undertaken and accomplished mainly through the strength of a female heart and arm?"

(194).[751] At great peril as the storm still raged, Grace and her father reached the shipwreck ("but for her excellent management" the boat "would have been dashed to pieces" [434][925]), and all the survivors were safely brought to the lighthouse, where they had to remain, with other rescue parties, for several days.

This heroic rescue "may be said to have wafted her name over all Europe"[751] (quoting Howitt). The lighthouse became a tourist attraction, and Grace Darling received many tributes, gifts, invitations from nobility, offers of marriage, and a substantial trust fund, none of which, according to Howitt, "produced in her mind any feeling but a sense of wonder and grateful pleasure."[751] The power of the story requires that Darling be of a transcendent goodness untouched by the desires of spectators, while her early death perfects the courageous sacrifice of the deed (196–200).[751];16 In her youth and feminine strength, she is a model to girls; in her humble origin, a model to working classes; in her maritime prowess and humanitarian sympathy, a model to the British. Portions of these volumes might almost be precursors of albums about the New York City fire fighters of September 11. Behind a popular representation, however hackneyed, the audience senses a genuine surplus of the best of human action, in which it could share.

Darling had many counterparts, American as well as British, who exhibited similar amazing agency, often in wild settings. Their tales metamorphosed into legends—or media events according to those times. Heads turned to gaze on these heroines but not in the streets or rooms of a (publishing) capital. Presenters shared with readers the vicarious satisfaction of *deeds* so well done that the heroine receives the *prestige* of a government pension, publicity, desirability— the "happily ever after" convention of this genre. In chapter 3, I will examine a set of less pivotal or death-defying narratives of eminent womanhood: the models of *vocation,* from prison reformers to missionaries. Ministering women sustain a performance of virtue for a lifetime rather than a peak experience; in part for that very reason—the need to tell the story of a lifetime—these subjects appear less frequently in more populous prosopographies that could be cataloged under the keywords "deeds" or "heroism." In this chapter, I pan through violent and luxuriant tales, placing ancient legends and more recent historical figures on the same footing. It would be a daunting task to trace the antecedents and versions of the stories that surface in Victorian collections, though some sources are conspicuous, such as the childhood reading of translations of Plutarch.[17] As later women reenact deeds in old legends, it seems as though the heroines were in communication and lending advice on how to play the part; more likely, narrative convention is shaping audience response and presenters' discourse in tandem.

Petty Treason; or, Prisoners in Drag

As opponents of patriarchy delight to point out, the murder of husband by wife (or master by servant) was long termed "petty treason." It hardly needs to be emphasized that the heroines of nineteenth-century prosopography are known for the opposite deed: for saving the life of a man himself condemned for an intended act of high treason. Someone has lost or will lose his head, but the woman takes salvific action. The theme, however extenuated, may be violence against the Father's law, but it is also the pleasure of appropriating that power. The misrule of age-old ballads and broadsides is re-presented with the dignity of history, the high rank and fine dress of romance, and a flavoring of burlesque. The doomed man is dressed as a woman or as a worker or foreigner; the rescuing woman is dressed as a man and substitutes herself for the condemned prisoner; "virtue" is redefined as skill in acting a masculine part.

Any wife of a condemned man might well look back to the model of Eponina, as differently embellished by Child in *Good Wives*[170] (286–88), Starling in *Noble Deeds*[751] (79–80), and Hale in *Woman's Record*[362] (99–100).[18] Eponina was the wife of Julius Sabinus, a leader who defied the imperial rule of Vespasian (ca. 70 C.E.). Defeated in a military campaign, Sabinus knew that "an immense reward [was] offered for his head,"[362] and he declared that he would burn himself alive in his own splendid house (or "an obscure cottage"[751]). Only two freedmen, faithful servants, knew that in fact the house burned without Sabinus, who had hidden himself in "a large cavern of white marble and granite, about fifteen miles from Rome," as Child puts it. Eponina, believing the report of her husband's death, became "frantic with grief" and seemed likely to starve herself to death. To avert this, the freedman Martial (or Martialis) hinted that Sabinus was in hiding. Eponina "continued to act all the exterior of grief,"[751] however, and visited her husband's womblike refuge only under cover of night. Child's version oddly states, "The delight, which her husband felt at seeing *him,* was mingled with anxiety and fear" (my emphasis). Who apprehends, who is apprehended? Who feels delight or grief? Who is on the point of death? Even the pronouns participate in the logic of substitution.

Thus began a double life for Eponina, who posed as a grieving Roman widow by day while enjoying an alibi for sexual pleasure and romance within marriage: "In the dead of night she visited Sabinus, and in his arms indulged the transports of her soul";[751] for months she "provid[ed] everything . . . for his comfort and amusement."[170] To explain long spells of living burial with her husband, she feigned visits to relatives or rubbed herself with "poisonous ointment" to simulate a "dropsy," in Hale's inventive version. Hale and Child agree that she bore children in the cave: twins, or two or three (Starling omits offspring, in spite of her more vivid account of the couple's intercourse).

At the end of nine years in this fertile underworld, the couple were finally detected and dragged before Vespasian. All three versions culminate in a scene in which Eponina dramatically throws herself at the emperor's feet, begging for mercy, especially through her children (a conventional presentation of the child before the ruler). Eponina delivers the only direct speech in all three accounts. This is Child's eloquent version: "Know, Vespasian . . . that in fulfilling my duty, and prolonging the days of your victim, I have enjoyed, in that dark cavern, years of happiness, which you, upon your splendid throne, will never know." Specifying that Sabinus and Eponina were beheaded, Child adds a coda, the grief-stricken death of the orphaned twins (sons) in a tower by the Tiber (perhaps the motif seeps in from the Princes in the Tower of London). Starling concludes with Plutarch's comment that divine vengeance destroyed Vespasian for this horrific murder of "the faithful" couple.

Elements of Eponina's story circulate in later tales. There is an epidemic of death sentences among the male family members of famous women. This induces the feminine paragons to usurp the father's or husband's active role, often in episodes of disguise, hiding, or defiance of authority.[19] It goes without saying that the heroines are unfailingly loyal to the men they attempt to rescue, and often they die in place of or with them.

In the early seventeenth century, a Dutch woman, Marie (or Mary) (de) Reige(r)sberg, wife of Hugo (or Hugh) Grotius had the chance to reinterpret the role of Eponina.[20] Again, the tale is variously reported in Child[170] (157–62), Starling[751] (128–29), and Hale[362] (335) in illustration of female ingenuity and daring devotion. Rather, the tale mocks men's law and learning. Starling is the most concise.

> When the celebrated Grotius was imprisoned in the castle of Louvestein, his wife Marie de Reigesberg followed him thither, to endeavour . . . to alleviate the miseries of a long captivity.
>
> Grotius was at that time occupied in writing the works which acquired for him so great a celebrity, and having occasion for a great number of books, he . . . obtained permission to borrow all that he should require. [He "who has a good wife, and is surrounded by good books, may defy the world"—Child.] He sent a large trunk for these books, into which he likewise put his own linen and that of his wife. When he had consulted these books and finished reading them, they were returned, and fresh ones brought in a similar manner.
>
> After about a year and a half . . . Marie, observing that the guards, weary of finding nothing in the trunk but books and linen, no longer took the pains to search it, persuaded Grotius to place himself in it instead of the books, having previously made some holes in the part where his head would lie to admit air. During two days before the execution of this project, she made him stay near the fire in an arm-chair, and she pretended to be much afflicted at her husband's indisposition. [She claimed "that she wished to send away a large load of books, because the prisoner was destroying his health with too much study"—Child.] On the day that the books were to be taken away, having put Grotius in the trunk, she drew the curtains of his bed very close, and requested the man who fetched away the box to do it as quietly as he could. With much difficulty he . . . carried it out, complaining bitterly of the heaviness of the burden. In this manner was Grotius conveyed to Gorcum, to the house of one of his friends, and from thence he went to Antwerp, disguised as a miller ["dressed like a mason, with trowel in hand"—Child]. . . . Marie had dressed herself in her husband's

clothes, and taken a seat by the fire . . . ; but when she thought her husband in
safety, she went herself to inform the guards of his escape, upbraiding them
with the little care they took of their prisoners. Ashamed to construe this
harmless contrivance into a crime, they permitted her to rejoin her husband.

The academic's wife who types and files index cards, without whom none of
this would have been possible, finds a worthy model in Mrs. Grotius. Child,
indeed, immerses the wife's story in a short biography of the husband.[21] Yet the
domestic trappings of linen and nursing care cut the matters of international
law down to size and give more credit to the wife. Hale's entry concludes by
quoting a biographer of Grotius to the effect that the scholar's beloved wife
perfected his works and prepared them for press, as well as steered his life
through all its "perils and perplexities."

In the popular biographical histories, such dramatic episodes often prove
men's need of women. Though the outcome may be tragic, the repetition suggests farce. The show is complete with the stage business of the trunk, cavern,
or other interior enclosure that permits escape from the outer prison, with the
help of the easily deceived guards; the feigned illness or grief; the cross-dressing
of gender and class; the imprisonment of the wife in the husband's stead. In this
vein, Child relates the narrative of the Countess of Nithsdale, whose husband
the earl "was condemned to be beheaded for his efforts to place the Pretender
on the British throne in 1715. . . . The day before the intended execution [the
countess] distributed money very freely among the jailers." Of a group of friends
visiting to wish him farewell, one "tall and robust lady" "affected to weep" as she
came in, and left behind her own clothes and departed, "perfectly calm," wearing
different clothes the countess gave her. Thus, the earl was able to "personate her,
and disguise his own features, by holding a handkerchief to his face," while the
countess had painted his eyebrows and cheeks and covered "his head with ar-
tificial hair." With "calmness and presence of mind," the countess followed her
husband out the door that the guard blandly opened. In the guard's hearing, the
countess urged "the pretended lady" to dispatch a servant with a petition to the
king, as though still fearing the impending execution. Friends then spirited
the earl away from the tower, and he slipped to France, disguised in "the livery
of the Venetian Ambassador," to end his days in Rome (302–3).[170]

Any reader might dream of a cause that would require such plotting and
such grace under fire. But this sort of test became almost commonplace for the
habitués of history, as Child, Starling, or Hale assembled them circa 1833–53.
The volumes never comment on the causes of these repeated narratives except
as testimony to the loving self-sacrifice of women. The context is almost always a
war. Mme Lavalette, a niece of Josephine, followed the fortunes of her husband,
Napoleon's aide-de-camp, who was imprisoned on that emperor's final defeat.
Unable to visit her husband, Mme Lavalette in time gave birth, alone, to a
son who died in a few hours. In a few weeks, learning of her husband's death
sentence, she sprang into action, petitioning for a royal pardon until only two

days remained. She commanded her husband to try her last hope, a plan of escape: she dressed him in her clothes, though she was slightly taller than he. "She charged him to hold his handkerchief to his eyes,—to walk slowly and wearily, as she had been accustomed to do,—to stoop at the door, to avoid breaking the plumes of his bonnet" (298).[170] The disguise succeeded, and he escaped by her sedan chair with their daughter. But in a few minutes the guards investigated and found their prisoner had become a woman, that is, Madame not Monsieur Lavalette. The freed M. Lavalette hid in a garret until he was able to escape to Belgium disguised as an English officer, while Mme Lavalette was held in prison for six weeks. This time the ending is not quite so gleeful. After six years of exile, he returned to find that those weeks in prison left her permanently subject to bouts of insanity. For the rest of her days, he tended her lovingly in their country retreat (293–301).[170]

Numerous heroines in nineteenth-century collections played prominent parts in armed conflict among factions within disputed territory, in large-scale civil wars. As Margaret R. Higonnet recalls, civil war historically has been analyzed as "a 'family' matter" of "fratricide," whereas its unexamined effect has been to reverse gender roles more compellingly even than conflicts with an external enemy.[22] History repeatedly generated the emergencies that required women to act and permitted the sort of action best performed in armor or military uniform. When the lives of family members were threatened, no one spoke of domestic duties. A reader of the popular biographies might have, however, detected an eagerness to playact scenes from historical romances and dramas. Those loyal to the Stuarts or other exiled rulers could draw their tactics from a history of such escapes. The story of Flora MacDonald (1722–90), who rescued "the Pretender," Prince Charles Stuart, during the events of the 1745 Rebellion, follows a familiar script from Jane Lane or Lady Nithsdale.

Mossman's set of *Gems*[589] includes the narrative of Flora MacDonald: after the Battle of Culloden, a reward of £30,000 was offered for the capture of the prince, and the English patrolled sea and land to find him. In humble dress, with one servant, he escaped as far as the Hebrides but soon found he was surrounded. Flora MacDonald, on a visit to relatives from her home in the Isle of Skye, entered into the plan to disguise him as "Betsy Burke, a young Irishwoman," who might accompany Flora and another servant under a pass from her own stepfather, a loyal Hanoverian (55). The prince was not easily dissuaded from hiding a pistol under his dress but seemed to enjoy the perilous playacting. They set sail at night for the Isle of Skye, and after several attempts eluded the patrols and landed. "Betsy Burke" was left to sit on their trunk on the beach, while Flora MacDonald paid a call on Lady Margaret MacDonald and entertained an officer of the crown there. The MacDonalds' estate agent, loyal to the Jacobite cause, escorted "Betsy Burke" on foot to Kingsburgh, though passersby and servants noted the oddity: "What long strides the jade takes! I daresay she's an Irishwoman, or else a man in woman's clothes," one remarked (58–60).[589]

The prince enjoyed the feast he was served in the house of Lady Kingsburgh. He remained dressed as a servant girl yet he was seated between two "gems of womanhood," his hostess and Flora MacDonald; later Betsy/Charles joined the gentlemen of the house in "a merry night by themselves" (60).[589] Realizing that word would be out, the conspirators dressed Charles as a Highlander: "All the ladies assisted in altering the feminine head dress of the Prince," saving a "souvenir" of his "long flowing hair"—at the time a sign of rank (61). After Flora parted with her gender-bending, class-crossing, interracial prince, he succeeded three months later in escaping to France, his hopes of restoration dashed. As Mossman opines, "No doubt it was for the best that an all-seeing Providence has blessed the nation with a female descendant of the House of Hanover, . . . obliterating entirely all wars and disputes of royal succession" (62). MacDonald herself was put under arrest on a ship anchored at Leith, a captivity that became more of a floating exhibit, swarmed by what now would be called fans. After two months, she was transferred to house arrest in London, where the celebrity was petted by the aristocracy. With a large fund raised in her honor, and several handsome marriage proposals declined, she retired once more to "her Highland home" (65) to write her memoirs and to begin a prosperous married life among her own people; thence to emigrate to America, where her husband fought among the loyalists of North Carolina; and finally to return to Scotland and raise five officers of the British army, fully reconciled to the House of Hanover. She was buried wrapped in the carefully preserved sheet on which Prince Charles had slept during his escape.[23] The attributes of masculine sovereignty appear to be matters of women's domestic management.

MacDonald's later American phase permits biographers to claim her as a heroine of that continent, as in Elizabeth Ellet's *Women of the American Revolution*.[259; 260]; 24 Ellet pursues not only the story of the prince's disguised escapade but the aftermath, in which Flora married and became mistress of the house that had sheltered the prince and that gave hospitality to Dr. Johnson and Boswell in 1773 (384). Highlanders had settled the Cape Fear region after the failure of the 1745 Rebellion, and the MacDonalds joined them in 1775. The Scots of the region rose to defend the crown in 1776. "Flora herself espoused the cause of the English monarch with the same spirit and enthusiasm she had shown thirty years before in the cause of the Prince she saved" (384), and was reported to mingle with the soldiers to whip up their courage. After defeat and imprisonment, her husband and others sailed for Scotland. Flora appears once again in a manly role, this time mounted on "the quarter-deck in the fiercest of the battle" with a French warship, herself wounded or suffering a broken arm, urging "the men to a more desperate conflict." But Ellet is certain that her "masculine courage" mixed with "thoroughly feminine" qualities (385–86). It is an exceptional heroine who features in rebellions thirty years and thousands of miles apart, first against and then for the same royal house.

Other wars or rebellions call forth the martial arts as well as the rescuing skills of wives, notably those whose memories defend the dead men. Many repeat Lucy Hutchinson's eloquent eulogistic words (Hale repeats verbatim part of Child's entry).[170; 362] In William Russell's synopsis,[692] the Hutchinsons are a fantasy of marital partnership heightened by the drama of the English Civil War.

> She was ... at her valiant husband's side, in the battle—the march—the hunted covert; and she never willingly left the side of Colonel Hutchinson at the memorable defense of Nottingham Castle, save when called to succour the dying and wounded of both parties. Lucy Hutchinson witnessed the triumph of the Parliamentarians with a sober, half-fearful joy—the execution of the King, whose death-warrant bore her husband's signature, with womanly sympathy and compassion; and when the terrible reaction came, when death in prison alone saved Colonel Hutchinson from death on the scaffold, she ... devoted herself not only to lighten and sanctify the last hours of the conscientious regicide, but to vindicate his memory by the graphic transcript of his life addressed to his children; which task accomplished, this true English maiden, wife, and mother passed from earth. (81)

The dignified pageantry of this life helps to preserve the name of one of the earliest women to write a full-length English biography. Her cause, moreover, was a source of later national pride, the ultimate defeat of absolute (Catholic-influenced) monarchy.

Women who serve the "right" side in a conflict tend to outlive those who champion the defeated or deplored parties; thus Royalists, Loyalists, or Confederate women have tended to be less honored in their own countries by later generations. Ultimately, the perspective of Victorian collections is Protestant, and very glad that William and Mary succeeded the Stuarts, that Prince Charlie took his (comical) flight, and that Victoria stabilized a Hanoverian succession. A measure of this tendency is the comparative preference of posterity for Hutchinson over a parallel example, Lady Fanshawe, wife of the Royalist Sir Richard. Fanshawe's story is sometimes spliced with Hutchinson's: in Starling,[751] they appear side by side, and in Mrs. Newton Crosland's *Memorable Women*[209] they share the same chapter. (Crosland's frontispiece, "Lady Fanshawe Visiting Her Husband in Prison," illustrates a passage from the lady's own memoir, a description of her predawn visits, lantern in hand, often soaked through with rain, to call to her husband outside his cell in Whitehall.) Child, who devotes some pages to both tales,[170] records the promise that the prisoner Charles I made to reward Mr. Fanshawe if he regained the throne, but "alas, the royal prisoner.... was beheaded at Whitehall. The famous Mrs. Hutchinson was at this eventful period suffering privations and perils nearly equal to those encountered by Mrs. Fanshawe. Colonel Hutchinson voted for the death of the king, while

Mr. Fanshawe would have given his own life to save him. The wife of each was zealous in the only politics which belong to woman—viz. loyalty to her husband." Like the recurring accounts of women's nursing the battle wounded of both armies (as Hutchinson did), this might suggest that a kind of feminine global resistance transcends local party; yet Child comments on the adverse effect for "the liberties of England" if the Fanshawe Royalist cause had triumphed (89).[170]

The narratives of both Hutchinson and Fanshawe dwell at length on the extraordinary companionship between high-born and comely husband and wife—all according to the memoirs composed by widows for their children. Lady Fanshawe succeeded in her petitions for her husband's release, and of course they were rewarded on the ascent of Charles II to the throne. En route, there were adventures: her house was attacked in her husband's absence, and she and a handful of servants fought to defend it. On a voyage with her husband, their ship was about to be attacked by a Turkish galley. She had been locked in the captain's cabin, but she caught the attention of a cabin boy, traded with him for his cap and coat, and joined her husband on deck, an indiscretion that she attributes to "the effect of the passion" she had for her husband. (Once again, a woman escapes captivity and joins battle, dressed as a man.) When the Turks retreated, dissuaded from fighting a well-armed ship, Sir Richard "snatched me up in his arms, saying, 'Good God! that love can make this change,'" both rebuking her for the risk and laughing at her boyish appearance (107).[751]; 25

These tales literalize the transferability of gender roles under the conditions of national misrule. The heroism of the partners does not diminish with defeat. There is the famous tragedy of Lady Russell, who avoided the corruption of the court of Charles II as a young widow before her second marriage. As Crosland puts it in *Memorable Women*,[209] without "admirable matrons who shrank from the pollution of the times" and devoted themselves to raising good children, "the nation must have sunk into a pit of infamy" (9–10). Lady Rachel's freely chosen second marriage, to Russell, was one of mature, intellectual devotion, praised in the same companionate terms lavished on the marriages of the Hutchinsons and the Fanshawes. Having denounced Charles's plot to reinstate a Catholic monarchy, Lord Russell was framed for conspiring to assassinate Charles, and no appeals for clemency availed. All narratives recount the trial scene at which Lady Russell demonstrated great fortitude, suppressing any show of grief (whereas the trial's "spectators . . . melted into tears" [494][362])—an interesting counterpart to the stories of pretended lamentations, from Eponina onward. When Lord Russell was granted a request for an assistant to record the proceedings, he publicly declared that his wife would be the best secretary (absent any other counsel, she sat in place of his lawyer, hence as a kind of Portia). He certainly did not overestimate her power as a writer, as much of the forty years that she lived after he was beheaded she employed in correspondence with her learned spiritual advisers, volumes of letters later published; these "established her fame in literature as one of the most elegant writers of her time" (495).[362]

A persistent parallel to the married role models who strove to rescue the condemned man took the form of the loving daughter, as with Margaret Roper (1505–44).[26] Darton's *Famous Girls*[220] displays a frontispiece, "Sir Thomas More taking his last leave of his daughter Margaret."[27] Darton confesses his love for Margaret Roper "because she was a true woman" (1). Much as we admire Margaret as scholar, sister, and wife, we must adore her as her father's "counsellor and confidant" (2). In Darton's hands she illustrates the rewards of learning (she can engage in Latin disquisitions with More and Erasmus), but largely she embellishes the great example of More's sacrifice for his beliefs (the father takes over as Darton's subject [16], as husbands tend to do in Child[170]). The famous scene of More's parting with his daughter (narrated in Dr. Knight's *Life of Erasmus*), a repeated tearful embrace, is said to have moved "officers and soldiers, as rocky as they were" (26–27).[220] In the sentimental tradition of *influence,* Roper, like Russell, affects all witnesses. Starling's account also culminates in the climactic scene before the execution, with Margaret's repeated impassioned embrace of the condemned prisoner in the midst of the crowd: "Even the guards melted into compassion at this affecting scene" (22).[751] "Tears flowed down the venerable cheeks of Sir Thomas" (23). This scene is the inverse of the father's parting with his daughter as she leaves for the mission field (a scene noted in chapter 3).

Like the widow, the bereaved daughter must tend the remains or the reputation, inverting the relative power of men and women in the family. Sir Thomas's head was exposed on London Bridge for two weeks and "would have been cast into the Thames, had it not been purchased by his daughter" (23).[751] Margaret was imprisoned for this defiance of the law but eventually allowed to escape to her family. When she died nine years later, "the head of her unfortunate parent was interred with her in her arms, according to some historians; as others say, deposited in a leaden box, and placed upon her coffin" (23). As Darton gruesomely pictures it, "The remains of this precious relic are said to have been since observed lying on what had once been her bosom" (27).[220] He concludes, "May we . . . imitate her example . . . amid a galaxy of eminent women, the brightest, as she is deservedly the most famous!" (28). Short of inducing one's father to die for conscience's sake, it is not quite clear how one is to imitate this "famous girl" except in the most general virtues. The tale recalls numerous noble daughters of fathers in Victorian fiction, including Margaret Hale in Gaskell's *North and South* and George Eliot's *Romola.* No one seems to blanch at Roper's posthumous embrace of the decapitated father.[28]

A cohort of historical heroines carries the physical succor of parents rather far, in the above manner, uniting *body* and *family* with *deeds.* Under "Filial Affection," Starling honors two unrelated Roman daughters who preserve the life of an imprisoned parent by breastfeeding (a deed mentioned in de Pizan).

Cimonus is saved by his daughter Xantippe, in whose voice the unattributed epigraph speaks:

> My child and father vital nurture crave,
> Parental, filial, fondness both would save;
> But if a nursling only one can live,
> I choose to save the life I cannot give. (19–20)[751]

The incestuous pietà as well as the infanticide that result from this choice to let her own baby die to save her milk for her father remain undescribed. Starling's accounts instead emphasize the celebrity that the Romans awarded the faithful daughters. Similarly, in the freezing winter of 1783, a young woman in New York resolved to sell her front teeth to support her aging parents, who were starving; the kind dentist refused "so uncommon a sacrifice" and paid her the money without taking the teeth (29).[751] During the French Revolution, Elizabeth Cazotte insisted on sharing imprisonment with her father and once threw herself under a rioter's ax raised to kill him (compare Pocahontas as she places herself in the way of the blow aimed at Captain John Smith). Even in the trial of Cazotte's father, her devotions moved sentiment in his favor, but she was unable to save him or to die with him (30–33).[751] "The heroism of Elizabeth Cazotte, which would not fail to excite the admiration and sympathy of her countrywomen, was imitated by many young persons," as Starling repeatedly illustrates (34–35, 37).

The deeds of filial sacrifice, according to Starling at least, almost always earn great reward in *prestige.* But what else is won through these tales? Why are the fathers or husbands in prison (or exile), condemned to death? Women in high ranks, of course, had family members who crossed swords with kings or took up arms in civil war. But I suggest an element of misrule, of inversion of hierarchy, in the forced passivity and enclosure of the lord and master—in a learned man lugged around like used books or dirty laundry, a man of fashion in drag, a prince dressed as an Irish servant woman and perched on a trunk on a beach, or, more ghoulish than ludicrous, a great man reduced to a token of the woman's loyal and brave venture, his skull like a saint's icon or his sheet her shroud.

The Judith School of Patriotic Gore

These rescuers of condemned loved ones are easy to celebrate. But what about women who themselves commit murder? The episodes of petty treason above play on castration anxiety, but other tales dramatize an execution as a woman's praiseworthy act. Many scholars have been quite taken with the sensationalism of late-nineteenth-century European cultures. What has been largely overlooked is the presence of stellar femmes fatales not only in melodrama, sensation fiction, and visual art but also in the very conduct literature of the respectable bourgeoisie. Ancient and biblical women could be valued for participation in sacred and national history and for their high crimes and misdemeanors. The woman in possession of a man's severed head belongs to a strange and persistent tradition that includes Margaret Roper, above, and the murderous scalper, Hannah Duston, heroine of an American captivity narrative, featured below. Vindicated violence seems to find its female epitome, however, in Judith, who slays the tyrant to free her people.

Judith might be one of the favorite biblical heroines, although she is not, in fact, in the Jewish or Protestant Bible. Her apocryphal book seems to be a romance modeled on Jael, who is "blessed above women" by Deborah, in the Book of Judges, for having lured Sisera to sleep in her tent and for having hammered a tent peg through his temple. Yet posterity has favored the more elaborate tale of Judith. Christine de Pizan, in *The Book of the City of Ladies* (1405), includes Judith alongside Esther as indications of God's intention "to save the human race through a woman" (143–44). Esther is chosen as good queen, as opposed to the willful Vashti, and acts through her uncle and her husband (though she later writes the judgment that decrees a reverse pogrom). Judith, in contrast, is a widow (a wealthy *feme sole*) who takes her own action and wields a sword. The Judith school of patriotic gore—she has her protégées—forms a significant if small portion of Victorian collections of women's lives, as it had since the early catalogs of women.[29]

In my pursuit of the figure of Judith, I will consider paintings along with the illustrations and texts of collective biographies. At the outset of her 1832 study of Shakespeare's heroines,[450] Anna Jameson offers the following menacing disclaimer about female genius. Among "all the distinguished women I can at this moment call to mind, I recollect but one who, in the exercise of a rare talent, belied her sex; but the moral qualities had been first perverted." Instead of listing her distinguished women here, Jameson names (in a footnote) only the unique transgressor: "Artemisia Gentileschi . . . painted one or two pictures . . . of which the subjects are the most vicious and barbarous conceivable. I remember one of these in the gallery of Florence, which I looked at once, but once, and wished then, as I do now, for the privilege of burning it to ashes" (11).[450] Jameson refers to *Judith Slaying Holofernes* (ca. 1620) at the Galleria degli Uffizi.[30]

Thus Jameson the pioneer art historian (who, as it happens, was like Gentileschi attached to her artist father) skirts the threat of female violence by imagining her own Inquisition, apparently purging unfeminine extremes from her collection of ahistorical heroines. Yet *Characteristics of Women*,[450] which I examine in detail in chapter 4, ends with a paean to Lady Macbeth, a devoted if pushy Scottish wife who happens to resemble Medea and Medusa. The themes of women's acts of murder, decapitation, and castration aptly if subtly frame Jameson's catalog of women. At the same time, these themes continue a chain of analogies with legendary battles with the beast by national heroes.[31] Ironically, Jameson's censure of Gentileschi and her Judith as epitomes of the "atrocious misdirection" of "genius" (quoted in Garrard, 295) also taps into a tradition that honors rather than censures the woman driven to vengeance.

Jameson would have known of the countless paintings in European galleries representing Judith, beautiful and wealthy widow from Bethulia, who to save her people from siege went with her maid Abra to the Assyrians' camp, and tempted the general Holofernes to a drunken supper in his tent, only to slice off his head with his sword. Tradition presents many interpretations of the figures, pre-op or post-op, within the tent or returning to Bethulia.[32] A history of representations of Judith and Holofernes is beyond my scope here. As Mary Garrard demonstrates in her magnificent book on Gentileschi, Gentileschi's reinterpretations of Judith stand out not for being more gruesome (compositions by Carravaggio and Gentileschi's father offer models) but for their portrayal of two similar women collaborating on a job to be done.[33]

Many interpreters of Gentileschi's paintings have known all too well, as Jameson evidently did, that in 1612 Gentileschi's father sued his friend, the artist Tassi, for having repeatedly raped his daughter, with the help of another man, in the father's house. Thus biographical readings, feminist or otherwise, of Gentileschi's Judith paintings tend to interpret them as outraged reaction to sexual abuse.[34] Early modern versions of Judith as robust savior comparable to David or Saint George (who in turn served as model saviors of Florence and Britain, respectively) were overridden by a centuries-long *querelle des femmes* in which each side argued, by exemplary extremes, the saint or the virago. Judith long held a respected place in English catalogs.[35] Heywood included Judith among his nine types in *The Exemplary Lives and Memorable Acts* (1640), as I noted in the introduction, and Nathaniel Crouch/Robert Burton in *Female Excellency* (in the year of bloodless revolution, 1688) sounded the theme of violent heroines, with one woodcut of Jael about to slay Sisera as Deborah smiles approval from among her armies and another of Judith with sword upon shoulder, stepping away from the tent in which Holofernes's corpse spews blood from the neck as she lowers the head into the sack the maidservant holds open. Burton would "incourage the reading the Life of this famous Heroine [Judith] not as a Fiction or Romance, but a Story full of Veracity. . . . Nothing Feminine must be expected in this Woman, all her Actions were manly and full of Generosity, and what was wanting in her Sex, was fully recompenced in her Virtue and Valour" (23).

The status of this legend depends on the civic motive for the woman's heinous deed. Among Victorians, as Jameson's aversion suggests, Judith lost most of her Renaissance luster.[36] After Jameson, Ruskin rejected the "millions of vile" Judiths in Florence (Garrard, 293–95), disparaging the painters who resorted "to the double show of an execution, and a pretty woman, . . . [while] hinting at previously ignoble sin."[37] He reserved admiration only for Botticelli's *Judith Returning to Bethulia* (1469–70), also in the Uffizi; here the scenes of battle appear like a frieze in the lower background.[38] A reproduction of this Botticelli is the sole illustration of the Judith story in *Heroines of the Bible in*

Art[845] by one of Jameson's later imitators, Clara Erskine Clement [Waters], who writes, "Botticelli has not resorted to the horrid details of murder—for Judith's act was nothing else" (339). But Botticelli's chaste rendering in this painting (he also painted a gruesome *Discovery of the Body of Holofernes* [1469–70; in the Uffizi]) rather elides the attractive mystery: What went on inside that tent?[39] Inside those heads, severed or not? Some in the nineteenth century continued to confront the macabre questions. In spite of Jamesonian disgust, it remained possible to celebrate Judith, perversely or righteously. Like any good legend, Judith's narrative allowed its use for many purposes; the name, the *fabula,* the assembled components (victim, bed, tent; head, bag, sword; maid and beautiful mistress transformed from seductress to assassin) provided rich material for arrangement and interpretation. Virginia Morris notes that the Victorians' image of Judith shifted to become the counterpart of Delilah or Salome.[40] The personal suffering or the political incitement disappear or become generalized in a figure for the menace that lurks in the repeated wrongs of woman.[41] Horror of the female mobs in France blended with the few well-publicized murder cases in a general unease about female violence, perhaps in response to the encroachments on patriarchal authority by middle-class European women. Bram Dijkstra's *Idols of Perversity* opens a gallery of examples of fever-pitch castration anxiety in Europe by the turn of the century, displayed not least in Gustav Klimt's *Judith I* (1901), exhibited as *Salome.*[42]

Yet the perverse versions, now better known, were outnumbered in the nineteenth century by the righteous ones. Most Victorian presenters cast Judith in the mold of Joan of Arc rather than of Salome. Some even manage to convert her into the heroine of a Victorian melodrama. Mrs. Steele, claiming Judith as an actual "character of Jewish history," relishes every moment imaginable in the tale: "an example of what woman may do if she will sacrifice her happiness for the good of her friends or country" (199–200).[752] Judith, in Steele's hands, is utterly good and feels appropriate qualms in advance: "Perchance he hath a wife. . . . Shall I make her the lonely widow that I am?" But thoughts of her people besieged in Bethulia stiffen her determination: "Crushing her woman's tenderness, she arose, firmly resolved to tread unshrinkingly the path she had chosen, which, even if it led through blood, would save her country, and the holy temple" (226).[752] Dialogue portrays Holofernes as Judith's wooer, whereas this woman plays the seducer's part: she "so excited the Assyrian by her beauty and wit, that he drank more than he had ever been accustomed, and Judith foresaw that he would be in a state fitting for her purpose" (228). Judith, with repeated invocations of the "Lord of Israel," severs the head, which she carries to her city as a token of her inviolate heroism ("and yet hath he not committed sin with me, to defile or shame me") and of the people's triumph: "Take this head and hang it upon the highest place of your walls" (229–31).

Throughout Steele's lushly detailed narrative, Judith performs in a spectacle that conquers onlookers: when she enters the Assyrian camp, "as she passed, every one looked on with wonder and admiration" (221); when she returns in triumph, her leader "beheld the heroic Judith . . . arrayed in magnificent attire, her countenance glowing, and her eyes flashing proudly . . . He thought the avenging Diety of the Israelites stood before him, and he fainted at her feet. When he revived, he kissed the hem of her robe" (231).[752] Among other satisfactions offered by this story, assuredly one is a female heterosexual fantasy that leaves her ecstatically glowing, him vanquished. Fittingly, Mrs. Steele, as I noted in chapter 1, commends reading stories from the Bible as a better alternative to the "novelty" and "empty husks" of popular "romance" (v–vi).

Striving toward moral historiography rather than religious romance, Emily Owen[615] expresses more concern than Steele about Judith's deed. With a conventional illustration of heroic Judith, severed head, and inquisitive maid, Owen's text on Judith frets at length about unjustifiable means to good ends and about thrill-seeking fables that aren't even real scripture (17–18).[43] Yet Judith's "stern self-sacrifice . . . for an elevated purpose" justifies her inclusion in "the record of famous women" (19). More sanguine, Harriet Beecher Stowe praises "Judith the Deliverer" in *Woman in Sacred History*, with its illustrations connoting the hot blood of the ancient Orient.[759] Just as the Judith legend shades into Salome, it verges on Delilah, a story with similar iconography and preoccupation with the man's head and symbolic castration (figs. 11 and 12). In the image in Stowe's collection, there is no sign of Samson but a lock of hair, no evidence of a deed but an overturned chair. Samson's defeat is more moral than physical, whereas Delilah's deed is personal rather than civic. Stowe takes a liberal, historical, and aesthetic view of the ancient texts: Judith's tale is as fanciful "as the Arabian Nights," a late "romance"; Judith herself is "glowingly alive on canvas," yet a true model of a woman, "poetess, prophetess, inspirer, leader" (159–66).

Others find that Judith sticks in their gorge: like Jael she plays her beauty for all it's worth, and she doesn't play fair. Mackay's *Bible Types of Modern Women*,[535] under the heading "The Woman of Public Spirit," criticizes hardhearted Deborah for praising Jael. True, "Sisera was a heartless villain," but Jael should have attacked like Charlotte Corday "in fair and open fight and given her life for her people." "But to welcome the man as a guest . . . to lull him to sleep with a smile, and then—then to . . . raise the hammer high to crash in the brains of the unconscious fugitive—this is not to be praised" (90–91). Owen, Steele, and Mackay include reprehensible models endorsed by religious history. Other collections mix categories of deeds or achievements almost indiscriminately, in the name of history—and the alphabet, as when Samuel Knapp[492] juxtaposes Judith with Ann H. Judson, the famous American missionary to Burma (278–83), or when H. G. Adams[5] groups Judith and the three successive Mrs. Judsons not far behind Anna Jameson—an ironic mixture of legendary with contemporary women of quite different fields of work (423–25, 410–12).

The most common typological link to Judith is Charlotte Corday, the Frenchwoman who assassinated Marat in 1793. Here, decapitation is the fate of the patriotic heroine. The exotic assassin may be as exemplary as the homegrown nurse, woman of letters, or missionary, with the requisite beauty, high purpose,

Fig. 11 *Delilah* by Louis Marie Baader, chromolithograph by Jehenne, from Harriet Beecher Stowe, *Woman in Sacred History* (1873).[759]

and undefiled attendance at scenes of violence. Thus, Euphemia Johnson Richmond seems to introduce Florence Nightingale, Harriet Beecher Stowe, and Mrs. Ann H. Judson to the more dubious heroines of the French Revolution.[673] According to Richmond, "the fair heads of Maria Antoinette, Madame Roland, and Charlotte Corday rolled from the executioner's block because woman had been false to her high and holy trust. . . . and bitterly did she atone for the prostitution of power of which her sisterhood had been guilty." The passage muddles who is guilty and whether the misdeed is treason or sexual license. Richmond

Fig. 12 *Judith* by Horace Vernet, chromolithograph by Jehenne, from Harriet Beecher Stowe, *Woman in Sacred History* (1873).[759]

probably intends to blame the Revolution on the savagery of the mass of French-women. Though Corday "was guilty of a crime at which humanity recoils, her motive was pure and her self-devotion heroic" (2:140–41).

Richmond[673] is one of many to remark that Corday chose Judith as role model. After she "pored over Plutarch's *Lives*," Corday turned to read the Apocrypha: "The history of Judith possessed a sort of fascination for her, and she marked with pencil the verse in which it is recorded that the Lord had gifted Judith with beauty for the deliverance of Israel" (2:142–43). In numerous collections, Charlotte Corday is cast as Judith redux. More commendable than

Judith or Jael, perhaps, the aristocratic French republican stabbed Marat in his bath as a means to end the bloodshed of the Revolution.[44] The above annotation of the verse on Judith's beauty notwithstanding, most versions portray her as unconscious of her beauty (indifferent to her suitors), inspired by zeal for her nation and by classical models of heroic sacrifice. Samuel Knapp[492] in 1836 notes that after Corday's execution "her portrait was in every print shop in England, and the United States; every museum had her image in wax. . . . All her biographers [acknowledged] that she was virtuous in her conduct, and lofty in her feelings. If Lucretia was right in sacrificing herself for her country, . . . if Brutus did a deed of glory by striking Caesar to the heart, this female patriot was not to be censured. . . . [Nevertheless] such deeds . . . are not to be imitated, and thank heaven" are rarely called for (152–53). Knapp includes a "life" of Judith as well but thinks to add a warning only to the modern example. Do not try this at home.

Corday's narrative shares several elements with Judith's: the beautiful, pure woman's deceptive admission to the private apartment, the powerful man wasted, his exposure in the bed or medicinal bath, her sharp weapon. But in Corday's narrative the beauty is lost on the tyrant, whose live-in mistress rushes to his aid. Corday wished to stage the assassination in public but changed her plan for a mass spectacle only when she found that Marat was too ill to attend the National Assembly.[45] She gained an audience with Marat not as a temptress but as an informer (though Judith similarly was admitted to the Assyrian camp as a kind of spy): Corday offered a list of names of Girondistes in her hometown—a list that after her death condemned them to theirs (she unwittingly becomes all the more a femme fatale). Richmond anticipates a painting of the encounter: "A strange picture did that narrow closet present. The monster, whose almost constant occupation had been the signing of the death-warrant . . . , reclining in fancied security while the avenging Nemesis stood before him, calmly, serenely beautiful, her white hand resting on the hilt of a concealed dagger." The slaying of the monster, so archetypal, seems self-fulfilling: the dagger was "buried in the heart which was meditating such dreadful deeds of blood"; syntactically, Corday's agency is buried in that of the dagger and Marat's heart.

Then the spectacle of the murderess begins: "A crowd gathered . . . struck dumb by the beautiful apparition" (2:144–45).[673] Representations of Corday in the collections offer no Caravaggiesque images of the act itself, no spurting blood, no accomplice. Like a saint, she gazes upward or afar (fig. 13). Every docudramatic detail is retold or shown—his head wrapped in cloth, the copies of Marat's incendiary journal, the map of France. In contrast, David's famous canvas restores Marat to a republican ideal, a Pietà without Madonna.

Corday prevails in the other movements of her story: her trial and execution (here she resembles Joan of Arc). *Four Frenchwomen*[238] sounds the conventional notes on the trial: "Like Judith of old, 'all marvelled at the beauty of her countenance.' The musical voice seemed to dominate the assembly,—the

Fig. 13 *Charlotte Corday after the Assassination of Marat* by Paul-Jacques-Aimé Baudry (1861), photogravure by Ludovic Baschet, from Charles F. Horne, ed., *Great Men and Famous Women*, 4 vols. (New York: Selmar Hess, 1894), vol. 3, facing 230.

criminal to sit in judgment on her judges" (21). Trowbridge's *Daughters of Eve*[812] reaffirms Corday's exotic feminine power: her "eyes were as calm as Asian lakes. . . . Like 'Judith, adorned with a marvellous beauty which the Lord had bestowed on her to deliver Israel'" (284).[46] Elements of the romance of Judith are further displaced in the execution, so that Corday's is the severed head held up for all to see (it is said to have blushed when an executioner slapped it). One Adam Lux or Luz, in the crowd at the guillotine, fell in love with the martyred beauty and sacrificed himself in defense of her honor.

Captivity and Interracial Crimes

The Judith school of female violence, exalted as resistance to tyranny, belongs to a large body of lore concerning women and war or women and interracial contact. Women were the captives, the booty, in millennia of warfare, a theme in many a classic narrative besides *The Iliad*. An ancient captivity narrative makes explicit the logic of decapitation as revenge for rape, itself an act of war or of contest for turf or wealth. Plutarch (first century A.D.) tells of Chiomara, wife of Ortiagon, seized by a Roman centurion in battle against the Galatians. The Roman "made use of his fortune soldier-like and defiled her." She offers a huge ransom, and for this he returns to trade her back to the Galatians. On a signal from her, one of her countrymen cuts off the Roman's head "while he was kissing and taking his leave of her" (appropriate symbolically but dangerous in practice). When she comes home and "casts down the head before" her husband, the husband exclaims, "O wife! thy fidelity is noble." In reply she boasts that "there is now but one man alive that hath ever lain with me." Plutarch cites an authority who met this woman in person and "admired her prudence and discretion"—her reputation intact (1:374). Thus might the violated femme fatale be approved as the patriotic and chaste wife. And thus the tellers of such tales exalt national standing through the superiority of "our" women.

The history of North America supplied classic martial encounters between women and Native Americans or opposing European armies, generating narratives of female heroism in captivity. Such tales have been a foundational generic hybrid in the New World, with continuing influence on narrative traditions at home and abroad ever since.[47] The genre draws on not only Christian confession and quest narrative but also romance conventions. Of numerous heroines of captivity, Hannah Duston (Dustin or Dustan) borrows the Judith precedent, and her story was early recognized as an antitype of Jael. Cotton Mather, in his 1697 sermon *Humiliations Follow'd with Deliverances,* praised the fact that one of the new chosen people could "imitate the Action of Jael upon Sisera."[48] Captivity narratives, popularly reproduced throughout the following centuries, underwent revision during the period of the female prosopographies in this study. According to Ann-Marie Weis, Jacksonian era redactors tried to accommodate violent women to domestic ideology.[49] John Greenleaf Whittier's "The Mother's Revenge," part of his *Legends of New England* (1831), and Nathaniel Hawthorne's "The Duston Family," in *The American Magazine of Useful and Entertaining Knowledge* (1836), in different ways censure or revile the murderous woman. Weis maintains that "antebellum writers . . . had difficulties finding acceptable Biblical or contemporary models to justify female brutality."[50]

Although some versions in the first half of the nineteenth century toned down the Medea-like deeds, I have found that many collective biographies framed acts of violence as feminine patriotic heroism. Samuel Knapp, writing as a contemporary of Whittier and Hawthorne, insists in 1834 that Duston "should be ranked among the heroines of antiquity" (179).[492] This comparison was a common strategy to explain how a good woman might commit a shocking deed: she must be a new imprint of a classical type.

Duston's tale is grisly enough, containing repeated acts of infanticide as well as genocide. The accounts complicate the Jael-Judith model by casting the husband in a dubious light (Jael's husband is absent; Judith is a widow). According to the brief notices in Knapp[492] and Clement,[182] on March 15, 1697, Indians attacked the Duston home in Haverhill, MA. The indecisive father fled in disarray with his older children to the garrison, but Mrs. Duston, bedridden with a newborn infant, was captured along with Mary Neff, the hired nurse. As they began the forced march back up the Merrimac River, an Indian seized Mrs. Duston's baby and "dashed its brains out against a tree. . . . This outrage nerved her soul for every enterprise. After this horrid outrage, . . . the agony of nature drank the tear-drop ere it fell. She looked to heaven with a silent prayer for succor and vengeance . . . the high resolve was formed in her mind, and swelled every pulse of her heart" (179).[492] The repetition here seems to make a slow-motion transition between a good Christian mother and the heroine of antiquity.[51]

Accounts differ as to what happened next: did Mrs. Duston, solo, wait till the captors slept and seize "one of their hatchets and [dispatch] ten of them in a moment, each with a single blow" (180)?[492] Or did she, the nurse, and an English boy who had long been captive, "each with a tomahawk, strike vigorously, and fleetly, and with division of labor," in the words that Clement quotes from Bancroft's "Hannah Dustin" (109)?[182] Why did she do what she did next? Again, versions differ. As she was about to flee, she "thought the people of Haverhill would consider her tale as the ravings of madness," so she "scalped the slain," which booty on return assisted her celebrity and earned her a reward of "fifty pounds" (180).[492] Or, once all but a child and one woman were slaughtered, "the love of glory next asserted its power; and the gun and tomahawk of the murderer of her infant, and a bag heaped full of scalps were choicely kept as trophies" (109, quoting Bancroft).[182] (The syntax downplays her act of scalping, which other records emphasize.) The tradition that Duston took the scalps as evidence covers for the probability that she was thinking of scalp bounty (or perhaps "glory"), though the law awarding payment for scalps had recently been repealed. If she was not actually paid for the scalps, everyone agrees that the Dustons received a substantial reward and that Mrs. Duston was widely celebrated at the time.[52] Mrs. Duston evidently returned to civilization and never did any further violence to sleeping heads.[53] But the tale is so narratable in part because of the possibility of a woman's sudden emulation of the violent uprising of the colonized or dispossessed. The deeds and their telling appear to be formulated in light of precedents, as readers become subjects and narrators of new incidents of captivity. Evidently, Hannah Duston knew Mary Rowlandson's celebrated narrative.[54]

Captivity narratives (which featured men as well as women) were adaptable to different uses at different stages of national development. The female survivors were heroines whether or not they committed any violent act; the proportion of violent resistance declined in the tales published after 1800.[55] John Frost issued an album of anecdotes of Western pioneer women that repeat many variations on captivity or encounter with the displaced Native Americans, without blinking from the point of view of the "pioneers," though at times with different configurations of racial alliances.[305; see also 256; 303; 340] Sometimes the subjects perform deeds of defense reminiscent of European history, such as "many instances of women successfully defending their homes in the absence of their husbands" (120).[305] When Mrs. Woods's husband was away one day in 1784, several Indians approached her Kentucky cabin, and one forced his way in. "A lame negro in the cabin instantly seized the savage.... The resolute black fellow held his antagonist so tightly that he could not use his knife. Mrs. Woods then seized an axe ... and, at the request of the negro, struck the savage upon the head" till "the brains of the Indian" splattered the cabin. The black man—probably her slave, though an ally against those who inhabit the same land but a different economy—wanted to "dispatch" in the same way the other Indians trying to force their way in, but rescuers shot one of the invaders to death and scared the others off. "Mrs. Woods behaved with the courage and devotion of a lioness defending her offspring. Had she not retained her presence of mind, and aided the efforts of the brave negro, a scene of massacre and desolation would have followed" (120–21).[305] Of course, she and her accomplices had killed two Native Americans. But if she is a lioness, her violence may be deemed natural self-defense (in this respect, nature and the classics offer similar justifications). The episode also belongs with Judith's tradition of defeating more powerful aliens, sword or hatchet in hand.

Though each tradition deserves full historical analysis—and increasingly scholars have offered it—a quick comparison suggests the shared conventions of early American captivity narratives, later Westerns, British and American novels, and the narratives of British women in the Empire.[56] In the imperial context (in India, Africa, Australia, and elsewhere), many British women reenacted the role of early American colonizers. For mid-Victorians, the Indian mutiny of 1857–59 was the paradigm of sexual and racial combat, meshing with available forms of captivity, sentimental, or gothic narrative. As Jenny Sharpe and Jane Robinson among others recently have argued, the actual or fabricated atrocities committed against British womanhood, particularly in the massacre at Cawnpore, increased the brutal British retaliation for the rebellion of some Indian troops.[57] The popular story of Miss Ulrica Wheeler translated her into "the Judith of Cawnpore" for fending off "sepoy" rapists.[58] According to the tale, a Sowar rescued or abducted her from the slaughter at the boats; in one account, she took a sword and sliced off the heads of every member of the abductor's household before throwing herself down a well; in another she defended herself with a pistol before cutting off her own head (fig. 14).[59] Closer to fact, the mixed-race daughter of General Wheeler continued to live in the region as a Muslim wife of her rescuer. But British womanhood, like saints of old, must prefer death to dishonor.[60] Other women became notable in the

Fig. 14 Miss Wheeler Defending Herself against the Sepoys at Cawnpore from Charles Ball's *History of the Indian Mutiny* (1858), reprinted in Jenny Sharpe, *Allegories of Empire* (Minneapolis: University of Minnesota Press, 1993), 84.

collections of biographies for having endured the Indian mutiny but without standing out for acts of violence. Thus Creighton honors Julia Selina Inglis, as I have noted.[207] Inglis belongs in the Mary Rowlandson category of captivity narrative—the survivor redeemed—whereas the Judith of Cawnpore is also the Hannah Duston of Cawnpore: the captive's revenge. Yet another variant of the melodramas of beset womanhood, assimilation, seldom appears in the prosopographies, though Mary Jemison's famous narrative of living for years with her Native American captors anticipates Ulrica Wheeler's secret survival.

The pre- or subtext of war against the "Indians," East or West, is the threat of sexual violation of European women; such motivation mixes with tropes of castration, defloration, decapitation, miscegenation, and genocide, all contained by an image of miraculous integrity: the upright individual against the wounded alien male and his hordes. With echoes of Judith or Corday, Miss Wheeler also resembles the battlefield nurses and social reformers in countless illustrations in anthologies after midcentury: an active female figure surrounded by darker, prostrate forms. Among its ideological motives, it may be iconographic revenge for all the female victims of Western art and historical narrative, prone or self-immolating, nude to the gaze between men (as in Gentileschi's recurrent images of Cleopatra or Susannah and the Elders). In female prosopographies, some subjects and presenters appear to conspire to behead the general, to render patriarchy impotent. Heroines of history were getting away with murder.

Over His Prone Body; or, Martial Arts

The stories of Eponina, Mrs. Grotius, Flora MacDonald, Judith, Charlotte Corday, Hannah Duston, and Ulrica Wheeler—and their ilk—erupt when two peoples or powers conflict. War is often the context, though the battlefield setting is not required. The heroine may rescue or attack one man or a small set of captors, rather than leading or confronting groups of men. Yet there were renowned examples of female heroism in war in a wide range of roles, from Joan of Arc, to the lady defending her castle, to the spy or the cross-dressing soldier, to Florence Nightingale. There is again a kind of international code of conduct whereby conjugal loyalty competes with patriotism, but patriotism may triumph. Unprotected "manly" heroines refuse to be seen as sexual targets or weaker bodies. If most of the tales put rape out of the question, they bring sexual harassment to the top of the agenda. Heroines of collective biography are renowned not only for moving mixed audiences to tears but also for quelling the hostile, sexualizing impulse of male hordes of all classes. My examples will move from the more direct military ventures, in this section, to the scenes in the next section in which the famous woman disciplines men to honor her education, expertise, and class, thereby gaining acceptance as a quasi-sacred leader and healer.

The American War of Independence brought forth numerous examples of women's courage as spies, rescuers, or combatants. Lady Harriet Ackland[170; 751] served as a loyal British heroine in North America at the same period as Flora MacDonald (235–39; 150–52, respectively). She bravely accompanied her husband Major Ackland to Canada in 1776 and endured all the hardships of the military campaign. When Major Ackland was wounded and captured, she insisted (Grace Darling ahead of her time) on rushing into the stormy night and taking an open boat down the river to the American camp; her companions were the British chaplain, her maid, and her husband's valet. The reception she received made it plain that this was indeed a "cousin's war"; a note from General Burgoyne to General Gates ensured that she was received like a guest for tea.[61] Major Ackland, who was later released, reciprocated the "generous treatment he had received" by aiding American "prisoners of distinction" held by the British. Later in England, having heard someone slander the American troops as cowards, he challenged the offender to a duel and died defending the honor of the American officers he had befriended (97–101).[260] Such tales exemplified an Anglo American upper class of honor. The man's captivity, as his wife came to his rescue, consolidated the manhood of gentlemen of both sides, which in turn became a theme in works paying tribute to the heroism of American women.

I have noted that the victorious cause generally has more lasting representation in the lists. The early Republic honored the female spies and soldiers who helped the cause of independence. Lydia Darragh was the Philadelphia Quaker wife, mother, and midwife who spied on the occupying British troops and passed behind British lines to warn Washington's army of a planned British attack in 1777 (89–92).[182]; 62 Elizabeth Ellet takes pains to distinguish a less famous heroine, Deborah Samson, from the maritime cross-dressers or the ballad heroines who follow a lover to war;[63] Samson "exhibited something of the same spirit" as Joan of Arc in fighting for her country (366).[260] A poor girl without education, "alone in the world," Samson was moved by "patriotism" to dress as a man and enlist as one Robert Shirtliffe (369–70). She survived being wounded twice, and twice experienced what it was to have a young woman fall in love with her. Discovering her secret, a doctor sent her to General Washington with a note that revealed her identity; Washington kindly discharged her from the service, later ensuring that she received a pension. Her ambiguous "career . . . cannot be commended as an example; but her exemplary conduct after the first step will go far to plead her excuse" (371–78).[64]

Other instances of women putting national interest before domestic affections or personal security were urgently repeated, as though to refute the slander that the sex was incapable of civic vision (as Romney Leigh charges in *Aurora Leigh*). Rebecca Motte, whose new mansion was occupied by the British in South Carolina, agreed to have it burned to the ground along with the enemy's stockpiles stored there, forcing the surrender of the garrison. Ellet regards the incident as a grand "subject for poetry," an example of a woman patriot "surrender[ing] . . . her own interest to the public service. I have stood upon the spot, and felt that it was indeed classic ground, and consecrated by memories which should thrill the heart of every American" (322–31).[260; see also 182, pp. 129–30] Motte's annihilation of her own home in the New World is the perfect inversion of the many performances by high-ranking European women in Amazonian defense of their estates in their husbands' absence. The Countess of Montfort defended her besieged city, leading her troops in battle, during the imprisonment of her husband circa 1341–42 [616; 751] much as the Countess of Arundel successfully defended Wardour Castle.[272; 751] Violent deeds can always be excused when the nation or home is under attack or when men have been rendered incapable. Such a heroine need not be noble or a regent. Jeanne (Jane or Joan) Hachette led women in battle to save Beauvais, earning the name of her typical weapon.[751; 847]

The Maid of Saragossa was once a renowned type of the woman warrior of common rather than high rank. In Elizabeth Starling's account, the Maid of Saragossa enacts another Joan of Arc in both story and image: white robed, hair flowing, she fired the cannon and inspired the troops like an abstract Liberty in the French Revolution (fig. 15). One Augustina (or Agostina) was celebrated by Byron in *Childe Harold's Pilgrimage* (lines 603–29; quoted in the epigraph to Starling's entry on this heroine): she "Stalks with Minerva's step where Mars might quake to tread" (line 611).[751] Starling's unnamed source is excerpted: "At the siege of Sarragossa [*sic*], in the year 1809," this young woman "of the lower class of people" came to the rescue of her city when the French had killed all the soldiers at one of the gates. As others "hesitated to re-man the guns," she "snatched a match from the hand of a dead artilleryman, and fired off a twenty-six pounder,—then jumping upon the gun, made a solemn vow never

Fig. 15 *The Maid of Saragossa* by J. Champagne, engraved by S. Hollyer, from D. W. Clark, *Portraits of Celebrated Women* (1863).[173]

to quit it alive during the siege." Her "daring intrepidity" inspired her "fellow-citizens . . . to fresh exertions" that repelled the assault. The short anecdote ends with a sign of its recycled nature (entirely within quotation marks), its anticipation of the sort of exhibit of lowly greatness that U.S. presidents repeat during televised State of the Union addresses: "For her heroism on this occasion, Augustina afterwards received the surname of 'Sarragossa,' a pension from the government, and the daily pay of an artilleryman; and, at the time Lord Byron was at Seville, the maid of Sarragossa walked daily on the Prado, decorated with medals and orders, by command of the Junta" (328–29).[751] The Maid of Saragossa shares the celebrity afterlife of Grace Darling and Flora MacDonald, while encouraging an orientalist fantasy of Spain.[65]

The American Jesse Clement seems to have enjoyed a surplus of warlike deeds à la Saragossa (including captivity narratives, as we have seen). One short entry, "Seneca Heroines," illustrates compulsory typology. With its multiple layers of citation—a "copy" of the "celebrated 'Lectures on the Iroquois'" by "Mr. Hosmer, the poet"—the short piece is worth quoting at length:

> In the celebrated battle between the French and Indians, which occurred near Victor, in the western part of New York, in 1687, five Seneca women took an active part in the bloody conflict.
>
> The memory of illustrious women who have watched in defence of altar and hearth, the deeds of the sterner sex, has been enshrined in song, and honored by the Historic Muse. Joan of Arc, and the dark-eyed maid of Saragossa . . . will be chivalric watch-words of France and Spain, but not less worthy of . . . poetic embalmment, were the *five* devoted heroines who followed their red lords to the battle-field near ancient Ganagarro. . . . Children of such wives could not be otherwise than valiant. Bring back your shield, or be brought upon it, was the Spartan mother's stern injunction to her son: but roused to a higher pitch of courage, the wild daughters of the Genesee stood in the perilous pass, and in the defence of their forest homes, turned not back from the spear, "the thunder of the captains, and the shouting." (244–45)

Clement stirs a heady diachronic intercultural brew of warrior maids, wives, and mothers. The heroic portrayal of Native American women occurs rarely, and almost always in anonymous groups. What is common is the typological framework endorsed by neoclassical reference.

Readers of Clement must have had numerous incentives to identify with one Esther Gaston, later Esther Walker (see 626–44),[260] who in 1770 rode on horseback with her sister-in-law toward the battlefield of Rocky Mount. "They soon met two or three cowardly men, hastening from the field of action. . . . Finding entreaties would not cause them to retrace their steps, [Esther] seized the gun from the hands of one of them, exclaiming, 'Give *us* your guns, then, and we will stand in your places.' The cowards, abashed, now wheeled, and, in company with the females, hurried on to face the cannon's mouth" (261–62). Perhaps Esther was chosen as protagonist over her anonymous sister-in-law in part because of her biblical namesake. Classical precedents also contributed to the scene, as in Plutarch's *Concerning the Virtues of Women*. For example, as the Persians under Cyrus retreated into their city pursued by the enemy, "the women ran out to meet them . . . plucking up their petticoats to their middle, saying, Ye vilest varlets among men, whither so fast? . . . The Persians blushing for shame . . . faced about, and renewing the fighting routed their enemies" (1st century A.D., 1:347).

The tales of the Senecan women, Spartan mothers, and Esther Gaston serve, among other things, to construct patriotic manhood through shame. They also diffuse a sense of indigenous greatness. Reiterations of daring rides as spies and messengers also counteract the similarly redundant captivity narratives, as testimonials to female agency, mobility, and invincible nationality rather than sexual vulnerability and susceptibility to going native. Thus, women's theft of the role of men works through some anxieties about the revolutionary upheavals from the 1770s through the 1840s.

The heroine on or near the battlefield is never far from Holofernes's shrouded bed, as the wounded soldier substitutes for the raped woman, that submerged story of all wars. It was a task of collective biographical histories to retrace national origins in the actual and legendary scenes of battle, as well as the common experience of the aftermath in which women preside over the dead as they have done over the newborn. The end of Esther Gaston's tale, significantly, converts her into a ministering woman: "While the strife was still raging, Esther and her companion busied themselves in dressing the wounded and quenching the thirst of the dying. Even their helpless enemies shared in their humane services." She aids "suffering humanity" in a church "converted . . . into a hospital"—women in charge where men have commanded the pulpit or the surgery (261–62).[182] Eyes readily turn to the woman who enters the contest between men that has dominated epic and historical drama. The outcome of such contests often is lamentable, as in the lays of the dying Indian, Highlander, or Anglo-Saxon.

As a history of England developed its racial genealogy, for example, many focused on 1066, when Harold, the last Saxon king, fell in the Battle of Hastings and the Norman yoke descended on the worthy shoulders of the British Isles. Harold fought William's troops to the death, beside his own standard (i.e., not hiding behind his lines), yet somehow his body was lost in the carnage. The search for the missing king is reenacted in an illustration in *Great Men and Famous Women* (fig. 16): "The king's body was found upon the field, recognized only by a former mistress, the fair Eadgyth Swanneshals ('Edith of the swan's neck')." An engraving portrays Edith, flanked by swarthy monks, searching the battlefield for Harold, amid reiterated prostrate male nudes, an empty helmet, and redundant phallic symbols: monoliths like the Washington monument pierced by jutting arrows and swords. Impertinently, one wonders what part of Harold the mistress is best qualified to recognize.[66] According to some, she found the body because of a tattoo "in old Saxon letters 'Edith,' and just below, in characters more fresh, 'England,' the new love that he had taken when duty bade."[67] England of course survives *because* of Harold's sacrifice, while loyal Edith survives his substitution of the nation for her.

Adventures in Nursing Administration

In the nineteenth century, the woman warrior was supposed to be a remote or bygone figure. Closer to home, a woman might stand in the aftermath and nurse the felled youth. With modern bureaucracies and warfare came a more definite role for the Esther Gastons or Ediths. The rise of the Lady with the

Fig. 16 *Edith Searching for the Body of Harold* by Alphonse de Neuville, engraved by J. Ettlin (?), from Charles F. Horne, ed., *Great Men and Famous Women*, 4 vols. (New York: Selmar Hess, 1894), vol. 3, facing 56.

Lamp, soon followed by Sister Dora of the Midlands and Clara Barton of the Red Cross and many other similar women, added new counterparts to Judith, Grace Darling, or La Saragossa, as well as the loyal rescuers of condemned men. I have elected to look closely at Clara Barton (1821–1912) and Sister Dora (1832–78), with passing reference to Elizabeth Blackwell and others, as representative of sanctified figures who dominated prone men in the name of modern administrative methods. Suitable in some ways for the saintly nurturing niche carved out by Florence Nightingale in the Crimean War of 1854–55, these figures also salvaged the wreckage of order in government, the military, medicine, and industry. The Sister of the Good Samaritans, Sister Dora, ran a hospital near Birmingham, England, that rescued body and soul of victims of industrial accidents beginning in 1865; and Clara Barton mastered statistics, institutional data, and supply management and, with others, flourished in battlefield and hospital settings in the Civil War of 1860–65.

The collective biographies published during or after the 1850s–60s move beyond the common legend of the angel of mercy; the women's service was systematic rather than miraculous, public as well as personal. At the same time, the models reinforce the class as well as gender difference between the woman leader and the people she disciplines and aids (sometimes her task is to civilize men of her own class). As I have said, these tales at times appear to overcome what we now term "sexual harassment."

Sister Dora was much beloved by the working people of Walsall just as she was a frequent subject of reverence in collective biographies for a middle-class audience. Dorothy Pattison (1832–78) met experiences in her work among the industrial poor near Birmingham that uncannily repeat details of Margaret Hale's experience in Gaskell's fictional Manchester in *North and South,* including the stoning during the riot; some features of the story recall *Jane Eyre* (and Charlotte Brontë's life) as well. This daughter of a Yorkshire clergyman became a "saint of these latter days," in Garnett's words in her chapter on Sister Dora in *True and Noble Women* (167).[270] Like an angel, she "brought the sunshine of human sympathy" to the smoke-darkened town of iron foundries and to the hospital wards (275).[887] As a teenager, she effectively ran away from home to nurse a dying woman (156–58),[207] and although she was "intensely eager to join Miss Nightingale's band of nurses for the Crimea," she chose the "life of hard work and poverty" as "a village schoolmistress" (277).[887] Rather like Jane Eyre disguised as Jane Elliott, "no one knew her here, and she lived alone in a small cottage, conducting the village school admirably" (171).[270] Against her father's wishes, she joined the Sisterhood of the Good Samaritans at Coatham (like Eliza Reed in *Jane Eyre,* perhaps?), where at first she was subjected to humiliating housemaid labor (172).[270; see also 207, pp. 159–60] As Gaskell's Margaret Hale in *North and South* finds in reduced circumstances, housework is "no bad outlet for superfluous energy" (278),[887] but her pride requires a sense that the work is voluntary. Sister Dora objects to the sisterhood's dictatorial rule, having chosen to join them, much as Margaret resists the limits on her actions as a lady while maintaining a sense of her inherent superiority of class.

Wilmot-Buxton claims of Sister Dora, "She was of too strong a nature to mould her character according to the bidding of others, . . . and had too masculine a force of both mind and body ever to settle down happily in a community of women" (278).[887] She sought liberty in a new servitude (after being forbidden to see her dying father [176]),[270] when she began to manage her own hospital. Like the heroine of an industrial novel, Sister Dora comes into conflict with the workers at first but discovers her gift of managing them better than the masters. According to Garnett, Sister Dora was the "last of the Sisters who met with persecution" (175); during the Murphy riots, a man threw a stone that hit her forehead, jeering her as a "Sister of Misery," but she later treated him gently when he came into the hospital with an injury, overcoming him with "good returned for evil" (175).[270]

Incidents in biographies of Sister Dora rely on physical and emotional intimacies with wounded or dying men. The men are victims of the frequent industrial accidents in the iron works. Some suffer fatal burns from being covered with molten lead. Others are dying of smallpox, as she faithfully tends them. One man begs, "'Sister, kiss me before I die.' She took him in her arms and kissed the poor disfigured face, promising she would never leave him while he lived" (280).[887] Such acts of temporary marriage seem to endow her with a saint's healing power. Yet like a good mother, she is playful; her "wonderful power over the men and boys" is partly due to her jokes, games, and reading as well as her class and beauty (161).[207] Garnett affirms that Sister Dora had a "bright face and lady's manner which not the roughest there dared to take a liberty with. . . . And . . . not only in the hospital was she an angel of mercy, but in every low alley and back slum" (184)—"where policemen dared not venture" (190). Like the ministering women that I discuss in chapter 3, Sister Dora is said to serve "as a beacon-light revealing Christ in the heathenism" (177).[270] Sister Dora's power (*influence*) relied on the disempowerment of workers hired for their physical strength; her success depended on laborious skill that endangered her class status. The bodies of the men were infantilized in her care, while those who recovered became her pupils in middle-class pastimes and manners (the hospital as a drawing room). She became a true model: "A sojourn in her hospital ward often sent a man out a reformed character" (281);[887] "she tried to mend her patients' morals as well as their limbs" (161).[207] Much of her effort was to save limbs from amputation, and in one case she took special care of a young man's "arm torn and twisted by a machine." The surgeon insisted the arm had to be amputated and angrily disavowed responsibility for the case when Sister Dora defied his diagnosis. Sister Dora's daily vigilance at last saved the man's arm. It was ever after "her arm," and the man was "nicknamed 'Sister's Arm'" (163).[207] Like "hands," the arm is a metonymy for the human component of the industrial machine, but in Sister's hospital, the part miraculously rejoins a whole body. There are many testimonials to her physical bonds with the grateful people, who claimed her lovingly as their own, while admiring "lady pupils" came to learn to be like her (165).[207] Long labor with the body at last reembodies her: she suffered secretly from cancer, and when she died a statue of her was erected, a sign of *prestige* that parallels both the statue of Mary Carpenter in Bristol cathedral and the statue of Nurse Cavell in Woolf's *The Years*— rare public monuments to women who were not queens.[68]

Veneration of an unmarried woman of a different order seems to teach men of all classes a way to substantiate their chivalry in public memorials.

When women encroach on fields of men's paid work, the respect is more grudging. Nursing accordingly was more readily open to middle-class women than advanced training as physicians. Elizabeth Blackwell carved out a path for women doctors that offered an interesting variation on the nurse's quasi-sacred maternal role, while it repeated some of the gender dynamics and bodily positioning of a battlefield. Blackwell, a frequent subject as a professional pioneer, serves as an example, briefly, of the sort of harassment that Clara Barton encountered from men of her own class when Barton invaded government bureaucracy. Blackwell, enrolled as the only female student in the medical college at Geneva, NY, came in danger of forfeiting the protective codes of her class and gender. She had entered this den of beasts as Sister Dora entered the streets of Birmingham, but she could not at first control the gaze on her, as an illustration in *Our Famous Women* suggests (fig. 17).[758] An autopsy of a male corpse is under way; the ministering doctors stand in the theater (one bearded, spectacled, lab-coated "Freud" seems to stare); the male students fill the benches; but in the foreground, a young lady stares at a paper on her arm, and all other eyes are on her averted glance. At first it might appear that Blackwell is conducting an experiment, but the text explains: someone in the rows of students has thrown a hostile note that landed on her sleeve. All depends on her complete control, as she continues to fix her attention on the notebook in which she writes, until, before the gaze of all, she shakes the offending note away unread. Throughout, she has kept her face impassive and her eyes down, as if the slightest sign of her own animation would identify her as a woman and, therefore, not a doctor in training (141–43).[758] Graphically, the illustration offers a fascinating alternative to the spectacle of Charcot's studies of female hysterics later in the century, as she is winning (by increments) her right to the gaze on the (male) patient's body. The harasser intercepts this professional inspection with his note, which turns all eyes on her instead of the corpse and which schools her self-consciousness as she must look at the message that labels her. Professional class status is also at stake in this move to embody the woman as well as the object of the examination. The body concerned in an anatomy lesson in that day was likely to be a pauper's corpse disinterred at night by a mob of (male) medical students.

Such an early trial bears repeating because Blackwell overcame it. Other women triumphed during the Civil War, which proliferated the sort of heroic narratives most in demand. In such tales, women gaze on prone and wounded men and command groups of men to respect a female in their midst. Abbot[1] subtitles his life of Clara Barton, "The American Florence Nightingale." *Vocation* and *influence* emerge early: just as Nightingale's story boasts the childhood anecdote of nursing the wounded dog, so the heroically named *Clarissa Harlowe* Barton's life features two years of devoted nursing of her severely ill brother.[622, pp. 61,66–67; 4, pp. 150–51] Barton repeatedly subdues both the working

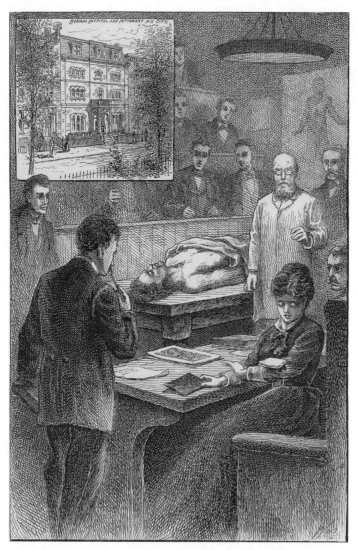

Fig. 17 *An Incident in the Student Life of Dr. Elizabeth Blackwell—an Actual Scene in the Operating-Room of a Medical College* by T. W. Williams, from Harriet Beecher Stowe et al., *Our Famous Women* (1884).[758]

and the managerial classes. She began as a New Jersey schoolteacher noted for bringing bullies to discipline. Later, appointed as head clerk in the U.S. Patent Office, a rare public office for a woman, she encountered a unified front of sexual harassment by the male clerks similar to that of Blackwell's fellow medical students, until "by reproof and by example [she] instilled . . . a new sense of honor" (156).[4]

The "Civil War created a new Clara Barton; . . . [she] became a national character" (294–95):[1] "The Angel of the Battlefield" and "Our Lady of the Red Cross"

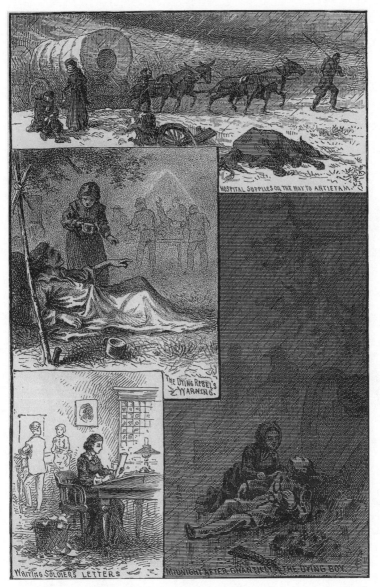

Fig. 18 *Scenes in the Life of Clara Barton* by T. W. Williams, from Harriet Beecher Stowe et al., *Our Famous Women* (1884).[758]

(77, 85).[622] In *Our Famous Women*, Larcom celebrates Barton's story with the aid of illustrations that mimic war photography or journalistic illustration (n.p. [between 104 and 105]) or illustrations for juvenile romances (n.p. [between 112 and 113]). (See figs. 18 and 19, respectively.) After managing the distribution of donated supplies to Union soldiers, she went as a kind of freelance nurse and supplier behind army lines, "a new profession" for women (164).[4] According to some, she encountered "rebellious drivers of her

Fig. 19 *Clara Barton Entering Strasburg with the German Army* by T. W. Williams, from Harriet Beecher Stowe et al., *Our Famous Women* (1884).[758]

army-wagons, who had little respect for . . . a woman in control," but she gradually formed them into her loyal team, "kinder and gentler every day," as she put it (73–75).[622] Like Sister Dora, she placed her body in danger, but she claimed to be "the best-protected woman in the United States" (77).[622]

After the war, she managed the agency that recovered records of the eighty thousand missing (78–81).[622] In 1869, she went to Europe for rest, only to nurse the wounded in the Franco-Prussian War. *Prestige* came to her: "Queen Victoria decorated her with her own hands" (298).[1] Years of campaigning succeeded in importing the Red Cross from Europe to the United States (167–68).[4] She retired as president of the Red Cross in 1904, under a cloud. In her words, "I have no mission. . . . But I have always had more work than I could do" (177).[4] Like other midcentury leaders, she had no self-worship, little sentiment about sisterhood or mission, but a daunting drive. Like Nightingale, her gift was administrative and material, whereas she became celebrated iconographically as a cross between Joan of Arc and a Madonna.

The force of compulsory typology shapes the above heroic narratives; names, dates, and details may change, but the patterns repeat. Petty treason, patriotic gore, captivity, martial arts, and nursing administration—my categorizations— are shorthand for some of the recurring motifs, tending to center on climactic episodes. Yet heroines such as Sister Dora and Clara Barton, though revered for life-long careers rather than gender-bending adventures, bear a kinship with the rescuers and assassins. In this sort of prosopography, women play the leading roles, turning not only the mobs and tribes and spectators but also the so-called leading men of history into extras on the scene. In chapter 3, the lurid lighting and physical action will be toned down, as scenes of war are left behind. But the biographies will continue to engage with prisons and hospitals, and courage still counts as the heroines carry their light into the dark zones of poverty and crime. The characteristic prop of the ministering woman is not the sword but the book. She is cast opposite not an individual male character (enemy or family member) but several groups of women or men of her class or those below it. Even more than the heroines that turn heads when heads roll, the ministering women realize their influence in moving all to tears—a sentimental power now widely recognized once more. Yet the precise forms of the ministering narratives offer unexpected ways to model feminine subjects and to enter the historical registries. Everywhere there were "grandmothers."

Chapter Three

How to Minister as a Woman

The Likes of Elizabeth Fry, Mary Carpenter, Dorothea Dix, and the Three Mrs. Judsons

In 1912, a Boston teacher of "college classes in English composition," Warren Dunham Foster, offered to supply the "need" for "short biographies...between two covers" "of such women as Florence Nightingale and Frances Willard." To be sure, there were lots of women's biographies already, but they "proved lacking in some essential"—some essential not named. Foster attests to a broad demand among teachers, librarians, education administrators, parents, and students for the very collection in the reader's hands. Women

> have founded or shaped so many of our institutions that modern
> society...is a woman-made society. Our penal system, by which
> wrong doers are reformed instead of flogged; our hospitals, with their
> life-saving care, and our nurses who prevent disease in the homes of
> the poor and aid physicians in the homes of the rich; our woman's
> colleges, where women are educated to be the peers of men, as well as
> the teachers of the young; our peace-time service of the Red Cross...;
> our riddance of negro slavery, once the menace of national honor; our
> temperance societies...; our fast-growing sentiment for woman
> suffrage...; our clubs in which women, escaped from the narrowness
> of the house, may both amuse and instruct themselves...and unite
> for social service; our settlements, trying to distribute the benefits of

civilization and recombine the classes in a true democracy—each of these things is . . . the work of women. (preface, n.p.)[4]

Heroines of Modern Progress, with a foreword by the head of the General Federation of Women's Clubs, Ellen M. Henrotin, solicits the collective pride of young American women, but it also hails the entire Anglophone middle class in "our" "modern society" (n.p.).[4] For many decades, "national honor" and social stability had been promoted by the philanthropy of women; a measure of "civilization" was the extent to which middle-class women exercised their right/duty to discipline/serve the young, the suffering, the socially other. The question of whether a lady could work ought finally to have been moot. After all, "woman has always been . . . in the labor-market and in industry," Henrotin observes. The volume claims agency for the leading women in the leading nations; in Henrotin's words, "The mere mother of the family" has become "the 'World Mother' of to-day" (n.p.).[4]; 1

In 1912, and indeed long before, trumpeting of women's public work sounded on all sides. The philanthropic World Mother on the verge of World War I may seem a menacing figure of Wagnerian proportions. Yet the claim that woman should become "a world-servant instead of a house-servant," made by Charlotte Perkins Gilman in 1898, may be traced back through the civilizing ambitions of many active American and British women in the nineteenth century.[2] A substantial record of "working women of the last half century" could be proudly cited in 1854, as Clara Lucas Balfour does in her book of that title. By 1868, she looks back on "working women of this century": "Not a single amelioration has occurred in our social system during the last seventy years, but woman has helped it forward" (9).[52] Such a panoramic history of progress guided and propelled by women had been on view well before the expansion of middle-class women's paid employment. In fact, much of the contribution of women honored in the collections of 1830–1940 would have been known as philanthropy: unpaid, voluntary work capitalizing on class advantages in education and social skills if not in property.

The biographical collections acknowledged few occupational distinctions as they constructed a great international collaboration in the progress of civilization. This synthesis depended in turn on a collaboration of all disciplinary institutions of which Michel Foucault himself would be proud.[3] Foucault stresses the sinister aspect of pervasive normalizing power, yet among Victorians the interconnection of various means of discipline appeared to signal the hope of social restoration and a special calling for middle-class women. Notably absent from Foucault's airless modernity are the spectacles of female intervention in the prisons of London, Yarmouth, and Bristol or of Massachusetts and New York circa 1810–70. By the 1820s, the proper sphere for middle-class women's work encompassed the range of institutions that would later become established as public (though at times privately owned), under bureaucratic regulation with specialized professional management. The biographical collections honor conglomerates of female vocation from writing to missionary work, not only disclaiming the separation of spheres but also assuming the permeability of fields before professional specialization.[4]

Licensed by women's "special" capacities for service and nurturing, internationally renowned and versatile careers became models of feminine ministry. These careers built on the "humanitarian narrative" that had emerged in Europe with the increasing establishment of the bourgeoisie in the eighteenth century, as the clergy's "pastoral power" increased in "secularization," in Foucault's terms.[5] The United States saw movements that paralleled those in Europe. From the first "female relief organizations founded" in the 1790s through the acceleration of women's careers after the Civil War, the effects of women's "voluntarism" extended through the arts and literature and from "new institutions and professions to institutional reform."[6] Between 1880 and 1920 in developed countries, varied "maternalist" movements evolved into welfare states: "Women's primary *private* responsibility" became "*public* policy."[7] Women's caring power or ministry served to re-form the discourses and institutions that shaped the modern Western subject and nation. Certainly, the biographers believed in the constructive power of reading biographies of "Woman the Pioneer of Progress" (the title of Balfour's introductory chapter): "Workers who received the wages of a glorious immortality" lead "us to follow in the path their feet have helped to smooth" (10).[52]

In this chapter, I seek neither to substantiate the practical effects of nineteenth-century women's ministry nor to recount the history of changing conditions for women's work. Rather, I trace the representations of such vocations in contemporary collective biographies, volumes that mimic the pedagogical methods of the ministering women themselves. If the typical scene for the heroic types in the last chapter showed the armed or uniformed woman standing above prone men, the scene here is often one of reading aloud to subordinated ranks of other women or conscripted groups of men. The teaching has a desired side effect, that of social consolidation, which in turn unites institutional functions. Thus, the middle-class woman worked in order that a prison might serve as a church, a school, and a kind of sweatshop; a ship or a missionary outpost might come to resemble a reformatory school, factory, or church; and during war, a church might literally become a hospital and serve the above instructive functions for the convalescents. All such kindred fields of women's activity became both institutionalized and domesticated as an extension of maternal instruction in the home. Most often what the lady read aloud was the Bible. As the model woman discursively formed the objects of her mission, the collective biographies repeated that rhetorical process. Literary vocations thus logically align with active social service in these collections. The prosopographies of Victorian women function as though they were scale models of reforming institutions.

There are too many ministering women in these volumes to be acknowledged here. I will concentrate on Elizabeth Fry at the outset because her type of pedagogical encounter presents a tableau of the biographical exchange carried out by the collections themselves. Fry's disciplinary method relied not only on surveillance but also on instruction in reading, which was franchised out to promising monitors, or teaching assistants. The scene of instruction was already familiar through Mrs. Trimmer, Anna Barbauld, Hannah More and countless Sunday schools and was reinforced by cheaply printed tracts as well as contemporary novels, but after Fry's initiative in 1817, the Lancasterian method of teaching through monitors united with penal reform and missions to laborers and emigrants, while women's special mission to women was incontrovertibly established.[8] In my "Pop Chart" (app. table A2), Elizabeth Fry stands as an exceptionally steady favorite across the decades (thirty-six appearances in general collections), second only to Joan of Arc, and only surpassed by the next most popular subject, Florence Nightingale, during the 1910–30 period.

Below, I select from the numerous successors to Fry who relied on similar methods, though with less permanent renown: Sarah Martin, the Yarmouth seamstress who educated prisoners between 1819 and 1843; the Anglican Catherine Marsh, who Christianized the three thousand navvies who arrived to rebuild the Crystal Palace at Sydenham in 1853; and Caroline Chisholm, who reproduced the educational institution on board emigrant ships, as Fry and her committees had begun to do, and who became a model to the Australian pioneer women whom she ushered into settled family life.[9] For a time, Martin's reputation outstripped a later member of the Fry contingent, the Bristol Unitarian Mary Carpenter—whose role as an international advocate for Ragged Schools (free schools for poor children), reformatories, and industrial schools developed around 1851—and the New Englander Dorothea Dix, who began in 1841 to modernize the treatment of the insane. These leaders formed influential committees, lobbied and addressed government bodies, and relied on their influence and renown for self-denying, hands-on aid to the suffering poor. Mother Theresa had a role well prepared for her. These models often align with Florence Nightingale as well as Sister Dora or Clara Barton, without the nurses' association with prone male bodies or war. My final models in this chapter belong to still another type of ministry, the foreign mission, that was less popular in general collections. I will feature the interlocking stories of the three wives of Adoniram Judson (1820s–50s). The American Baptist Ann Hasseltine Judson, first of the wives, appears fourteen times in the Pop Chart, comparable to Clara Barton (14) and Sister Dora (15), below Sarah Martin (20), but above Mary Carpenter (10). Judson's star had set, however, by 1910–30, at a time of widening secular careers and declining popularity of missionary zeal.

I reconstruct the popular versions of these women's missions as collected in books, rather than their actual histories. The volumes that represent these amateur experts mark the general shift of the model subjects after about 1850: down in rank and forward in history and political vision. A great transformation in the codes of women's work undoubtedly occurred, but the prosopographies suggest that the change involved matters outside the domain of economic history. Already in the mid-nineteenth century, observers could claim that women (that is, middle-class women) had entered the fields of work. Thus Harriet Martineau in her 1859 review essay, "Female Industry," declares: "Every woman who has force of character enough to conceive any rational enterprise of benevolence is sure to carry it through. . . . Mrs. Fry in Newgate, Florence Nightingale and Mrs. Bracebridge at Scutari; Miss Dix reforming lunatic asylums; Sarah Pellatt reclaiming the Californian gold-diggers from drink; Mary Carpenter among her young city Arabs: all these, and several more, are proofs that the field of action is open to women as well as men."[10] Instead of lasting proof that all women have escaped old restraints, such declarations suggest a constant need to repeat new affirmations of liberation for a select model class of women. The boasted careers, moreover, indicate the great demand for aid to outcast or destitute populations without addressing the causes of the heavy supply of those populations. Nevertheless, the excitement of these innovative careers must have been palpable to the original readers, as realms of significant action opened up.

Beacons Now Dimmed

Much has been written concerning the social work performed by middle-class European and American women during the nineteenth century—written in the framework of recent feminist, materialist, race, ethnic, and postcolonial studies. But a great deal more was written on this impressive if ambiguous theme before the rise of feminist historical recovery. Feminist studies have taken stock of particular forms of women's charity work in Britain and the United States and have revived such feminist pioneers as Elizabeth Cady Stanton, Susan B. Anthony, Bessie Rayner Parkes, and Barbara Bodichon.[11] Yet while the recuperation leaves many a missing person, it also underestimates not only how early and how thoroughly women organized expert social work but also how much contemporary commendation such work received.[12] These celebrations of eminent womanhood reach well beyond the ballads to Nightingale or Barton and emerge remarkably early in the century. I wish to question the absence of these models from many recent recuperations of Victorian culture.

Deborah Epstein Nord in *Walking the Victorian Streets* asserts, "In the final two decades of the nineteenth century . . . , the enterprise of British social investigation was joined by women." Until then, Nord claims, women had protested through the fiction they wrote, not through hard facts, while "men with professional authority" monopolized analyses of urban problems; from the 1890s, female "urban investigator[s]" inspected "not the street or the workplace but the home."[13] Nord's otherwise acute study overlooks a number of once-famous women (and their organized ladies' committees) whose philanthropic and reform efforts across the decades went well beyond the home visiting (à la *Bleak House* or *North and South*) that Nord mentions (208–11). The collective biographies show that Victorian presenters viewed literary achievement and practical reform as elements in the same project, that women reformers prowled the streets—mingling with working men as well as women outside the home—and that they claimed the investigative authority of statistics and governmental reports as early in the century as men. Traditional religious tropes cast their systematic practices as a heroic mission, as when Balfour lauds Elizabeth Fry, Miss Marsh, and others as "earnest spirits . . . working in the depths, probing the causes of evil, and letting in light on the dark places" (ix).[52]

Over the generations, the exciting aura of these women has vanished, replaced by the ludicrous and nasty images of Mrs. Jellyby and Mrs. Pardiggle in *Bleak House,* with their telescopic and myopic distortions of the charitable vision. But as late as 1935, Winifred Holtby in *Women and a Changing Civilisation* could praise the transgressive energies of the women who achieved so much more than missionary funds or distribution of tracts and soup, who in fact sponsored a range of causes at that time: Chartist, cooperative, abolitionist, married women's property, matrimonial causes, suffrage, temperance, and efforts to provide schooling and housing to the poor. "The philanthropists were breaking tabus—Elizabeth Fry, Sarah Martin, Louisa Twining who won the right of women to be appointed poor-law guardians, Mary Carpenter who opened the first Ragged School, Florence Nightingale and Josephine Butler, proved to men, and, still more significantly, to women, that both sexes had something to contribute to human welfare. . . . Charity was respectable—to do good to the poor a fashionable and even praiseworthy occupation. But it had unforeseen results."[14]

Though some recognition has returned to the once-famous women who instigated institutional reforms, their stardom has dimmed for several reasons. Most telling for my purposes are the reasons that lead scholars such as Nord, who are actively seeking examples of Victorian women in public, to overlook so many of the "heroines of progress," especially those who prevailed before the 1880s. First, feminist scholars have been overly reliant on the conceptual tool of separate spheres; second, some have focused too exclusively on literary history; and third, many today avoid the distasteful annals of philanthropy, the "cultural repertoire replete with condescending and distancing stereotypes" that, according to Judith Walkowitz, accompanied effective efforts to recognize and aid the poor.[15]

The first point, the concept of gendered spheres, is the most complex. It is true that many nineteenth-century voices proclaimed women's domestic destiny and that some women leaders themselves avoided publicity. As the influential feminist classics Florence Nightingale's *Cassandra* and Woolf's *A Room of One's Own* and *Three Guineas* testify, the education of girls of all classes was neglected until later decades of the century, and women of society found their time consumed in the unpaid work of maintaining the family status. Yet actual practices were much more varied and divergent from gender ideals. Feminist studies of nineteenth-century women's culture nevertheless remain attached to the sacrificial narratives of the unheard prophetess, Shakespeare's suicidal sister, the Angel in the House, and the "cult of true womanhood"—narratives that enhance the repression that exceptional women overcame.[16] Contemporary presenters of Victorian women's vocations seemed to be guided less by a rigid separation of spheres than by a fantasy of the feminine emissary across the classes and spheres. The eminent woman's life, in these collections, turns on her command over the working classes or the upper-class male guilds far more than on her "notable" virtues in the home. Of course, many commentators regarded the home as the workshop of nation-building; mothers formed the character of the Empire or Republican manhood.

An ideology of separate spheres was in any case quite moot beyond the middle class: working-class homes were cast as a kind of public space to be remodeled as schools, prisons, reformatories, hospitals. Harriet Martineau, again in "Female Industry," quotes at length Norris's *Minutes on Education* of 1855–56, urging the nation to educate working-class girls because,

> as the woman is, so will the home be; and as the home is, such, for good or for evil, will be the character of our population. . . . If we wish to arrest the growth of national vice, we must go to its real seminary, *the home.* . . . The more enlightened women of England must come forward and take the matter into their own hands, and do for our girls what Mrs. Fry did for our prisons, what Miss Carpenter has done for our reformatories, what Miss Nightingale and Miss Stanley are doing for our hospitals.[17]

The territories of the interior, like those of the globe, might be colonized through such a narrative of the "white woman's burden." Yet the "matter" that "enlightened women of England" "take . . . into their own hands" is as much the institutions controlled by elite men in the clerical, scientific, medical, educational, and government hierarchies as it is the poor girls and the moral character of the families they will raise.

The second tendency that may have distracted attention from the pioneer ministering women is the habit of basing cultural rates on the literary stock exchange. Feminist studies of the nineteenth century have been shaped by literary history. A range of causes for this bias toward the literary can be found in current as well as historical conditions. The earliest, and perhaps most pervasive, incursion of feminist discourse in the academy post-1970 came in literature departments, just as some of the earliest national anthologies of eminent women concentrated on literary achievements. The emphasis on writing and reading, while it obscures the many forms of success for which Victorian women were recognized, does accord with the pedagogical themes of women's ministry. Literacy was an essential benefit extended by the middle-class volunteers for social reform. More broadly, progress for different communities of women has historically correlated with the spread of education and publishing. The most likely means for self-made women who did not trade their persons on the stage or in society was through writing and teaching. The slow post-Enlightenment migration of sanctity from religious discourse to arts and letters contributed to the veneration of women writers. By the twentieth century, the heroines of bygone causes became obsolete, but a tradition of women writers continued to seem worth preserving—indeed, worth adding to. I noted in the introduction that models of piety tend to fade into obscurity faster than women of letters. Victorians, in fact, already held our own high estimation of women of letters. Charlotte Brontë (27) approaches Queen Victoria (29), as the fifth most popular subject in my chart of unspecialized collections. Female authorship was often cited as a measure of the progress of national civilization as well as of women. To this day, the women writers of a nation or ethnic group serve as harbingers of its emancipation or recognition.

Familiar to the point of going unnoticed, such focus on literary history as a measure of social power pervades the female collective biographies in the nineteenth century. Rufus Griswold, in *Prose Writers of America,* affirms that women on both sides of the Atlantic have achieved more "in the province of letters during the last fifty years than in the five previous centuries."[18] Many contemporary presenters regarded literary eminence, however, as merely one aspect of women's collective progress. Rather than the highest achievement, literary renown was justified as only one kind of contribution to human improvement. Millicent Garrett Fawcett reprinted her sketches from *The Mother's Companion* ("intended chiefly for working women and young people") in *Some Eminent Women of Our Times,*[282] honoring such writers as Joanna Baillie, Hannah More, Mary Lamb, and Harriet Martineau as evidence of "the remarkable development of literary activity among women." Fawcett nevertheless insists on the "equally remarkable activity in *spheres of work held to be peculiarly feminine. . . .* The names of Elizabeth Fry, Mary Carpenter, Sarah Martin, Agnes Jones, Florence Nightingale, and Sister Dora are a proof of this. I believe that we owe their achievements to *the same impulse* which in another kind of excellence has given us Jane Austen, Charlotte Brontë, and Elizabeth Browning" (v; my emphasis).

Fawcett, subordinating literature as one branch of women's social mission, also claims a socially constructive power for literature that ideological criticism has striven to reclaim from formalism in the past thirty years. For the Victorians, the urgent point was that women should not rest on their literary laurels; it was already commonplace that women might become celebrated as writers—of all sorts, not just poets or novelists. As Frances Power Cobbe affirms, "authoresses are already a guild, which . . . has met kindliest welcome"; Cobbe implies that stronger evidence lies in less encouraged zones of women's work.[19] Similarly, Clara Balfour, whose *Working Women of This Century*[52] I mentioned above, would shift more of the acclaim to the activists: woman must be not only an author but "the reformer in society" who particularly fulfills "her office as teacher of the young" (4, 6). Today, the imaginative writers in Fawcett's or Balfour's collections seem better preserved than the reformers or the authors of social science (e.g. Martineau or Carpenter). In Victorian group modeling, in contrast, the distinctions between fields of endeavor diminish; the writers *are* workers and reformers, and all subjects minister to the improvement of the audience.

Current perspectives may obscure ministering women not only because of these leaders' unexpectedly public action and their apparent irrelevance to our literary history today but also because of the third reason: they seem nearly irredeemable. Many of the famous women in the collections emerge from the (caricatured) Hannah More school, with heavy investments in Evangelical piety, didactic patronage of the poor, colored, or foreign, and a model of feminism hardly recognizable as such today.[20] Understandably, the most thoroughly buried of the Victorians' heroines are the foreign missionaries. The foreign campaigns appeared continuous with campaigns at home, however. The missionaries' travel into darkest zones writ large the journeys taken by the ministering women at home.

Deborah Cherry, elaborating on Gayatri Spivak's 1985 alignment of feminism and imperialism in the "'soul making'" projects of "the conversion of the heathen, the rescue of the fallen, the improvement of the uneducated," points, for example, to the Langham Place feminists, including Barbara Leigh Smith Bodichon and Bessie Rayner Parkes, who in the 1850s and 1860s took up the causes of women in Britain, Algeria, Australia, or Canada with comparable zeal.[21] Susan Zlotnick articulates the analogy between women's domestic and foreign service: "Maternal imperialists" exercised "the female moral authority of supervision and surveillance" over family members, the poor, and exotic populations.[22] The female missionary vocation specifically cited the abuse of women in the "Orient" or Africa as justification for Christian rescue—a mission compatible but not synonymous with imperialism. A missionary woman had a job: she found a *Bildung* or autobiographical script that expanded beyond the standard romance or vocation plots.[23] This vocation in turn reinscribed her advantages, as Western Christian woman, over the female objects of her mission. It is misleading to subordinate the female to the male missionaries, though they were usually sent as married complementary teams. Women missionaries, like pioneer settlers in various colonies, might rise to levels of administrative power that outshone their husbands (who were busy with their linguistics or theology); the women ran schools, hospitals, compounds, and conducted negotiations with regional governments and home societies. Education, health, and development aid, albeit with overt and hidden costs, was directed to women because of the women's missions.

The female missionaries flourished as biographical models from the 1820s through World War I, often as heroines to their own sects, but have only belatedly and equivocally been recuperated by feminist scholarship. Jane Addams the social worker remains a secure model for girls today, but Ann Hasseltine Judson and other heroines of sanctity such as Susannah Wesley and the Countess of Huntingdon drop out of sight in general selections in the early twentieth century (see table A2; this coincides with a proliferation of sectarian prosopographies of more recent Christian exemplars for an audience of believers). The missionaries participate in the same narrative of progress as the reformers and writers in these lists (the scene of reading the book recurs), but they also verge on the prison or battlefield like the heroic types in chapter 2, while their martyrdom accords with hagiography. The global unity of a female vocation to repair and redeem the world, from its arts to its institutions and its moral and spiritual character, seemed cause for unequivocal celebration in the prosopographies, well into the twentieth century. A challenge today is to reconstruct what Charlotte Brontë shares with Ann Hasseltine Judson, what Margaret Fuller has in common with Elizabeth Fry.

Defining the Domestic and Foreign Mission

The role of the ministering woman began to be codified and celebrated in the eighteenth century and was widely organized as a vocation by the mid-nineteenth century, earlier than is recognized in many accounts. This role depends on several historical developments: impoverished and displaced populations both in agricultural and urban settings, an Enlightenment investigative spirit joined with humanitarian principles and rejection of aristocratic license, and an Evangelical or dissenting Christian zeal. Philanthropists seem to invert the usual measures of success in life, though their work may be well rewarded. Thus Hannah More, often cited as a prototype, is most praised for her daring work "among the destitute young savages of Cheddar," though she could also be pictured as a self-made celebrity "surrounded by the great and gay" (66).[52] More's work (comparable to Mrs. Trimmer's schools at Brentford) is largely pedagogical and apparently benign enough: to instill "habits of order and decency. . . . reading, sewing, knitting, and committing to memory some plain primary doctrines" (66).[52] Yet her intervention met great resistance: a landowner warned her that bringing "religion into the country . . . made the poor lazy and useless." Some accused her of seeking personal gain from the school, while the poor parents believed a rumor that "the ladies would have a property in" the children they taught and "would ship them off to the Colonies!" (65–66). "However, her gentleness and presence of mind had their effect on the people, and . . . the moral improvement was so manifest that all scoffing and opposition was silenced" (66–67). The dynamic of instruction and conversion is established; the first step is to get the uncouth audience to listen to the Bible read aloud, preferably by the leading lady, but teachers might be delegated to extend the influence (68). In due course, male leaders would be induced to accept responsibility for the education of all classes.

However gentle the strategy, the ministering women become heroines bearing light into darkness, braving contact with the worst human depravity. Dorothea Dix, like a female Howard, "explored the realms of misery, sorrow, and woe throughout Europe, forgetting her ailments and her hardships," according to William Thayer.[24] The leaders transgress boundaries not just of gender and class but also often of the law, as well as the demarcations of race, religion, and civilization. Jesse Clement's *Noble Deeds of American Women*[182] lauds the early women philanthropists in New York City, lifting verbatim passages from Samuel Knapp's *Female Biography* (235–37; 264–67):[492] "Mrs. Hoffman, Mrs. Graham and their associates, often perambulated the districts of poverty and disease, from morning till night," bringing "consolation to many a despairing heart. They clambered to the highest and meanest garrets, and descended to the lowest, darkest and dankest cellars, to administer to the wants of the destitute, the sick, and the dying" (219).[182] Knapp's collection, nearly two decades earlier than Clement's, extols "these good Samaritans" at even greater length, likening them to "warriors arming for the battle field, philosophers who had made up their mind to die" or to the women "at the tomb of Jesus of Nazareth." Significantly, "they did not stop to . . . discover who professed to be an episcopalian, or a presbyterian, a baptist, a methodist" (266–67).[492] Though some ministering women met resistance from religious establishments, these "workers" gained more from claiming an international, united Christian women's front than from sectarian allegiance. The lasting role was that of a social rather than religious missionary who ventured across internal rather than international borders.

Throughout the nineteenth century, many voices declared that it was women's privilege and duty to minister in this overreaching way. Joseph Johnson[467] (1860) cites a range of examples of what he views as a united gendered mission: "Ministering is woman's vocation. Be her talents what they may—capable of sweeping the heavens, with Mrs. Somerville; leading armies, with Joan of Arc; limning the landscape and its objects, with Rosa Bonheur; mastering the subtleties of political economy, with Miss Martineau; interpreting the sublimities of Shakespear [*sic*], with Mrs. Siddons; ranging the field of politics and literature, with Madame de Staël; or circumnavigating the globe, with Ida Pfeiffer: yet, if she has not sympathy . . . she is wanting . . . the grace, the glory of woman" (1).[25] Faced with variety, Johnson hedges: "Woman's mission is best ascertained by a study of those who have fulfilled that mission well" (vi), that is, what women have done they should do. "Let every woman resolve to do what she can, and the opportunity to 'minister' . . . will be presented in the circle in which she moves" (13). Quoting Aimé-Martin, the source of Sarah Lewis's *Woman's Mission* (1839), Johnson's appeal to the glory of sympathy may seem out of date in 1860 (11). But his vision of careers open to talents begins to sound the call to action of collections twenty years later, which resonate with Margaret Fuller's challenge, "Let them be sea-captains, if you will."[26] Johnson might almost allow women to be sea captains if they will carry it out as a form of ministry. British women, Johnson proclaims in 1860, already have a noble tradition of activism: they "leave their homes of ease and elegance, and visit the cottages, cellars, and garrets" that are "denuded" by poverty or filled with "filth, crime, and disease," to transform "such places" into a bright national future (vii).

Johnson's depiction of ministering women reveals the class distinctions at stake; the move of visiting impoverished zones is only possible if you don't belong there. These deeds reinforce the status of both the agents and objects of charity. Yet the ministry also sought reconciliation of classes, unsettling the association of gentility, idleness, and unearned wealth. Johnson, in a different collection first published 1882, adjures the "desponding sister" to emulate "noble women doing noble work"; she may overcome "her own fatigues in the factory while ministering to her scholars" in "one of the many Sunday schools in Lancashire" (iv–v).[468] (Although Johnson elsewhere does offer a portrait of Sarah Martin the seamstress,[466] his subjects in *Noble Women of Our Time*, including Mary Carpenter and Sister Dora, never worked in factories.) Philanthropy rendered the upper-class woman a worker, the working-class woman a lady. Clara Balfour insists that "woman, if true to duty, must be a worker" (2),[52] as all classes must be "working classes." The "worker" who was able to assist other classes of worker, from governesses to prostitutes (4–5), invariably depended on the work of one or more servants; if she were a mother or household manager, such social service was in any case an overload.[27] A number of the celebrated reformers were unmarried and self-supporting but developed managerial careers out of their literacy (ministering women all seem to teach some form of school in their early years). Many of the prosopographical models narrate the class permeability of self-help: one might rise from need to ministry by determined effort. The role of caring power was a career open to talent, and many "redundant" middle-class women turned it to good purpose.[28]

Class differences were not to be lightly forfeited, however. Many placed a value on the privilege of choosing a vocation regardless of pay. Frances Power Cobbe, who attempted a domestic and ministerial partnership with Mary Carpenter and who herself gained some attention in the collective biographies,[e.g. 185; 488] touched on the distinction. She satirized the analogy between unmarried women and the objects of discipline or charity: "Transportation or starvation to all old maids! Poor old maids! Will not Reformatory, Union, or some other friends of the criminal, take their case in hand? They are too old for Miss Carpenter," who saved juvenile delinquents. Though Cobbe recognizes worthy working women in need of aid, her sympathies, like Mary Barfoot's in George Gissing's *The Odd Women*, center on the "higher class . . . of ladies" whose resources allow "the full exercise of their natural powers."[29] Most of the collective biographies share Cobbe's allegiance. Collective biographies in the 1840s and 1850s expect the model woman to work outside the home, decades before the expectation was widespread for most middle-class females (Sally Mitchell locates the shift between 1880 and 1905 in Britain).[30] Yet through the middle decades of the twentieth century, public work was often "unpaid work," for educated women black or white.[31]

At midcentury, campaigns to alter middle-class women's economic and educational prospects were prominent internationally.[32] Some educated British women shared in the developing models of the professions, which attempted to reconcile the ideals of Christian calling and aristocratic voluntarism—often termed "nobility"—with middle-class independence, integrity, and paid livelihood.[33] In the United States, there was a "postbellum explosion in women's organizing" and wage employment (about 300,000 white women entered the labor market) due not only to the "shortage of manpower caused by the war" but also to a transformation of middle-class white women's vocational expectations.[34] According to Carla Peterson, African American women of various classes as early as 1830 began to cultivate the discourse of "racial uplift," through preaching, lecturing, and writing, to form an ethnic public sphere.[35] The "noble" code of charity sustained its influence through the (segregated) club movements in the United States and the suffrage campaign in Britain. Because it was unsalaried, such work has been misconstrued as personal charity or a pastime, whereas for a number of decades it had quite official status and power.

Charlotte M. Yonge might almost serve as the fulcrum on which the scale finally tipped away from the unpaid domestic ideal for middle-class women. In *Womankind*,[[926]] Yonge adheres to old-fashioned manners, yet she insists that a woman should be "responsible to the one great Society" and find "a vocation" (7 [2d ed.]). "Care of the poor . . . is our bounden duty"; while some "are born nurses" and others may engage in "visiting, teaching, reading, . . . attending to clubs or libraries, &c. &c.—all must be regulated" and systematically shared by the ladies of a district (86–89). Yonge offers a glimpse of the changing significance of such "charity": "The mother who in her youth had to fight a battle to be allowed to minister to the poor, finds that her daughters view 'pottering about the cottages' as Mamma's dull notion of occupation, and talk the modern jargon about Sunday-schools being an infliction" (86). Yonge acknowledges an increase in women who "have a profession" but also makes an allowance that covers far more of the female population: a lady may turn to "money-making which is in a manner supplementary, whether used for personal or beneficent objects" (222). For decades before Yonge's typical concessions in the 1870s, Anglo American rhetoric concerning woman's mission had provided a window of opportunity for female activists. It was later, in the days of Octavia Hill, that women's unlicensed social work lost its standing in relation to the expertise and institutional controls of men.[36] Nevertheless, the versatile ministry of many international authorities from Fry to Barton remained models for young women into the twentieth century.

"She came . . . like a creature of another sphere": Elizabeth Fry

It would be difficult to find a more self-evident proof than Elizabeth Fry of the tautological principle that a woman's mission was the mission that she could perform well. Adams and Foster begin their list in *Heroines of Modern Progress* with Fry (among such peers as Nightingale and Barton). Mrs. Fry's story, the prototype of woman's progressive vocation, is so "familiar" that Balfour[52] need only sketch it in her introduction (Balfour's collection instead features Sarah Martin and the missionary Ann H. Judson):

> About fifty years ago there were 300 miserable neglected women at one time in our metropolitan prison; shut into two rooms, that were more like dens for wild beasts.... A kindly woman heard the appalling statement of their sin and misery, and she went to them unattended, unprotected. The story has been often told, never without awakening a new throb of emotion. She came, the good Elizabeth Fry! like a creature of another sphere, to these poor lost beings, and their turbulent spirits calmed before her gentle look.... What punishment never could have effected, sympathy brought at once—order, hope, reform followed. Senators, magistrates, rulers of all kinds proved the power for good that a weak woman ... beneficently wielded. (12–13)

Balfour is right to count on her readers' familiarity with the scene of Fry's visits among the women of Newgate: in illustration and text it ritually and emotionally recurred.[37] The story relies on the convention of the rescuing woman bearing light into darkness, like a virgin confronting a dragon, a Demeter/Persephone figure. It shares some of the motifs of the heroic types in "Heads Turn, Heads Roll," my previous chapter here, and could be reworked in that mold; very often, a volume will endorse Fry along with Florence Nightingale and sometimes Clara Barton or Sister Dora as well.[38] In the valiant spirit, Charles F. Dole in 1900 recalls "Elizabeth Frye [sic], who faced wild men [sic] in Newgate prison as serenely as soldiers ever went into battle.... There was Florence Nightingale, reorganising the forces of practical Christianity on fields of barbarous carnage."[39] By implication, armed men faced women with the greatest dread. The jailer, when Mrs. Fry first entered the gates in 1813, is said to have confessed that he "hardly dare venture unguarded where she meant to go.... When he urged her at least to leave her purse and watch in safe keeping, she replied calmly, 'I thank thee, I am not afraid' ... and went quietly on" (101).[270]; 40

The reality of her first encounters must have been rather different. According to June Rose, Fry first entered Newgate with another woman,[see also 207, p. 88; 589, p. 69] and left her watch behind with the keeper (Rose, 68–71). Adams and Foster,[4] in their story of Fry, reveal that she was indeed afraid but daring. Mary Sanderson, Fry's companion, described their first attempt four years later to begin the school for the convicted women: "I felt as if I were going into a den of wild beasts, and well recollect shuddering when the door was closed upon me, and I was locked in with such a herd" (17; also cited in Rose, 83). (Many retellings snap up Sanderson's image of beasts.) In fact, Fry had been in training for such encounters for a long time. As a young girl in Norfolk in 1799, Elizabeth Gurney cultivated her religious convictions by confronting dark enclosures: "I have been trying to overcome fear.... My method has been to stay *in the dark* of a night, to go into those rooms that are not inhabited" (Rose, 32). As Mrs. Fry, she regularly received poor women at her residence in London and visited them in their own haunts. Indeed, she found a kind of recreation in walking through the "seamier alleys of London" in search of cases of destitution, according to Rose (52).

Fry's first encounter with the women of Newgate is said to have been a revelation of horror, though perhaps she was as much on display for the prisoners as they for her. For some reason, almost four years passed after the first visit before she formed the plan that organized charity workers as much as it remodeled the raw incarcerated materials. The "herd" rapidly metamorphosed and individualized into near-replicas of the ladies of the committee who came to help them. In her journal—source of so many future iterations of the miracle—Fry marveled at the progress due to a shift from physical force to internalized discipline: "How have the spirits both of those in power and the poor afflicted prisoners appeared to be subjected" (18).[4] Mossman attests that "she threw a chastened spell over the prisoners, which even in one month worked almost a miraculous change on their conduct" (73).[589] Under the influence of Fry, as Adams and Foster explain, "our institutions for wrong-doers are now designed as moral hospitals" (28).[4] Fry "succeeded in changing . . . dungeons of depravity to comparative schools of discipline" (68).[589] The modeling switches from negative to positive: instead of places that converted novices in crime into hardened criminals, the women's prisons became reformatories.

As biographical subject, Fry exercises the themes of a woman's *religion, vocation, influence,* and *prestige* reconciled with *family.* Whereas many of the ministering women were unmarried, Elizabeth Gurney Fry (1780–1845) stands out as the Quaker wife of a London businessman and mother of eleven children. Like many women of her class and convictions, Elizabeth Gurney had formed and taught her own Sunday school in her youth (Rose, 32). According to type, she clashed with her own family and milieu in her effort to form a strict spiritual life. In 1806 she discovered a power to move her auditors to tears in reading religious texts aloud (Rose, 54). Fry likewise stunned meetings of male leaders with her inspirational outbursts. The Quaker religious community encouraged such channeling and called her as a minister. A typical short biography describes her power in the sentimental tradition: "If the tears she could draw, not only from unhappy women but from hardy sailors and stern gaolers, were any test of eloquence, hers could not be denied" (109).[270; see also 207] Not only did Fry convert a "disgrace to the British nation" (70)[589] into a system envied and emulated abroad, but she became a model as well of benevolent womanhood through her re-modeling of fallen women. Thus Sarah Hale in 1853 assumes it is impossible to overpraise Elizabeth Fry: "In all her domestic and social relations, she was equally exemplary"; she was "beloved and honoured in a degree which queens might envy; and women most renowned for genius might gladly lay down their crowns of laurel at her feet, and thank her for the glory she has conferred on the sex" (318).[362]; 41

The numerous popular accounts of Fry's life play down its compelling contradictions and place its climax at the beginning, in a grand intervention. The narratives cover for Fry's difficult personality—"her youthful obstinacy, became that finely tempered decision and firmness" in later life (69)[589] —by focusing on her ministering performances, while few retellings indicate any obstacles to her talents. She herself confessed, and a few biographers concede, her failure to discipline her children. Her personal relations were often conflicted or cold, and she suffered nervous ailments and depressions amid her chain of pregnancies, yet her extrafamilial role appears Madonna-like or maternal. The role is ascetic, yet the woman herself was handsome, elegant, formal. She reproached others for any indulgence, though she was a constant drinker and laudanum user under medical supervision and the encouragement of her family (Rose, 49–50, 73). She was known for the high white cap and plain clothes of her sect, but the materials were always of the finest: "The Quaker shawl of brown silk that she wore as a famous prison reformer was lined with ermine" (Rose, 35). Few celebrated women so successfully masked ambition as humanitarian self-sacrifice (and many presenters stress her effort to avoid fame). She addressed a Parliamentary committee on prison reform, well before the days when many women so testified on other issues, without raising controversy.[589, pp. 77–78; 270, p. 125] Generations of modeling derived from her: Florence Nightingale was "much impressed by meeting Elizabeth Fry," who guided her to the Institute at Kaiserwerth (128).[207] Sovereigns and officials of many countries are said to have welcomed Fry's visits to inspect their institutions and advise on reforms. At a public examination of London's schoolchildren, Fry delivered a report before Queen Charlotte, and the grandeur of the religious philanthropist seemed to humble the queen; it was a "scene...fit for...the greatest historical painter," a tableau of "royalty offering its meed of approval at the shrine of mercy and good works."[589, p. 75; 270, p. 118]

Fry's celebrity, however much it belies her actual life, seems to have registered the patent on a model of caring power that succeeded because it was so easy to copy. In effect she put into practice the narrative exchange of role modeling, as presenter and audiences together generated—and sometimes became—new subjects, taking turns in each part. Her approach developed from her observation of a school run by the Quaker Joseph Lancaster, who had devised a system for efficiently teaching poor children by supervising monitors of groups of twelve (Rose, 47–48). She adapted as well the plan of consensual self-government from the Quaker tradition, and her service on various committees guided her in organizing the ladies who helped her. Her own role of inspired reader was modeled to these volunteers, who multiplied her hours of charitable vigilance. Further, within the prison, eligible pupils were chosen as apprentice teachers, and the crowds were organized like army units under such monitors. Each pupil could rise to become a teacher of the younger or more ignorant. The first rule, adopted by vote of all the prisoners, was the appointment of a matron, paid at first by the committee and later by the Corporation of

London, who extended the relentless surveillance (to "superintend," to "over-look," and to "observe" and "keep an exact account of the work done by the women, and of their conduct" [Rose, 87–88]). Not least, the inmates were put to work: habits of self-improvement as well as sober attention would be reinforced by needlework, whereby the women convicts could earn money to sustain themselves when released to a new life.

The supervision and reform of character, the reading monitors, and the needlework were extended to the women who were transported to penal colonies, who might eventually model British womanhood in the empire.[42] Fry's ladies' committee first developed a way to prevent the usual riots as the women prisoners traveled to the ships by offering them rides in carriages with the ladies if they behaved. On board, the women were formed "into classes of twelve with a monitor to keep order," while some were prepared to read the Bible or teach a "school" (92–94).[207] Mrs. Fry and her friends provided, again, the materials for productive work during the long voyage. The needlework would allow each woman to be her own entrepreneur and keep her, at the same time, from sinking into ocean-going vices. When ready to sail, the crew and passengers assembled to repeat the "impressive and affecting" "scene" for which Fry was renowned. "The silence was profound, when Mrs. Fry opened her Bible, and in a clear, audible voice, read a portion from it." (This is the scene and caption of the frontispiece engraving in Mossman.[589]) Crews of other ships drew near to listen as well, as she knelt to pray for the mission. "Many of the women wept bitterly, all seemed touched," and they blessed Mrs. Fry with regret as she left them.[589, pp. 76–77; 207, pp. 92–94] Such testimonial scenes regularly recur in the many "lives" of Fry, who never missed an opportunity to remodel groups of men as well as women (as when in later life she promoted libraries for the Coast Guard[805, pp. 308–9; 207, p. 95]).

Reading Aloud, the Monitoring System, and Fry's Work: Sarah Martin, Catherine Marsh, and Caroline Chisholm

The secret of Elizabeth Fry's success may have been the paradigmatic scene in Newgate, repeated on shipboard. As pedagogical "contact zone," the scene depicted in the painting *Mrs. Fry Reading to the Prisoners in Newgate, 1816,* could serve as the emblem of Victorian women's ministry (fig. 20).[43] Mrs. Fry sits in the well-lit focal point of the painting, above the whitewashed floor and under a cross-pattern lantern that might have served as the model for Jesus' lantern in William Holman Hunt's *The Light of the World* (1851–53). Her Quaker garb, open palm, and hand on the sacred book (the latter propped over a white cloth that makes the plain table resemble an altar)—all do much to refer the viewer to the saints in art. On the far right, one woman gossips to another who holds a bottle of drink, and in the dark foreground two young boys fight over a playing card, ignoring a discarded broadside decorated with a hanged man: "Last Dying Speech and Confession. . . . " Between these

Fig. 20 Mrs. Fry Reading to the Prisoners in Newgate, 1816 by Jerry Barrett, engraved by T. Oldham Barlow, by permission of the Library of the Religious Society of Friends. Reprinted in June Rose, *Elizabeth Fry* (New York: St. Martin's Press, 1980). Engraved by Henrietta Mary Ada Ward, in Louise Creighton, *Some Famous Women* (1909), 93.[207] Detail, by a different hand, in Henry Ewart, ed., *True and Noble Women* (1889), 113.[270]

extremes, rows of women appear to listen, clasping their hands, folding their arms, gazing repentantly, weeping. Facing Fry, a pair of standing, barefoot women in timeless draperies mark a dark vertical opposite her bright space, setting apart the groups of prisoners from their genteel spectators on the left of the painting. The nearest woman in the embracing pair is bare-shouldered and downcast, like a penitential Magdalene, but the comforting companion holds a deck of cards behind their backs (tricking even Fry?). It is ambiguous whether Fry gazes heavenward or with patient sympathy at these two tough customers (who may be watching the fighting boys more than listening to Fry). Behind Fry stand two gentlemen in the doorway, one of whom is a portrait of Fry's brother, Joseph John Gurney. On the left, under open mullioned windows that cast bar like shadows on the back wall, fashionable ladies are seated, and other gentlemen and ladies stand, all with sad or pitying expressions (the witnesses appear to be portraits of well-known figures in philanthropy, Dorcas Coventry, Sir Thomas Fowell Buxton, Samuel Gurney, and others). Over the table that holds Fry's book—at which are seated several of the poor women, one nursing a child—a board is posted: "NOTICE is hereby given, / *That should any of the* Bibles, / Prayer Books, *or other* Printed / Books *which are deposited in the* / Ward, for the use of the Prisoners, / be injured, mutilated or defaced / every Prisoner in the Ward *where* / *such Offense may occur will* / *be held responsible, and be / subject to such punishment as / the* Keeper *may direct.*" The lettering style emphasizes the books, prisoners, and keeper, in an indelible logic.

Jerry Barrett's painting, variously reproduced, anachronistically combines elements of Fry's mission. The supply of books actually was implemented only after 1817, when the gentlemen at last came to see the effects of Fry's visits and to permit the founding of a school. The painting is symbolically accurate, in that Fry's readings were equally formative for the audience of her class, behind her, and for the class whom she faces to instruct. The pedagogical benevolence seems strangely reinforced by the notice, which anticipates that inmates will treat the books, provided as means for self-improvement, with hostility (as tools of their discipline) and which reminds all concerned that punishment is still the primary function of the prison. The simple human contact of Fry's spiritual ministry is similarly belied by the presence over her shoulder of the bewigged clerical gentleman, representative of established supervision of a Quaker woman minister.

It is crucial that the primary audience of the performance is female. I have noted the pattern of prison episodes in many of the narratives of famous women, yet such heroines usually sought to rescue beloved men. Sharing the pages with these rescuers are many models, inspired by the renown of Elizabeth Fry, who instead seek contact with female strangers. Not that the succor of prisoners was invented in 1817 or that the pathos of the woman bringing pity and aid to a fallen woman in prison had been unexploited in poetry, drama, biography, and fiction before then. The popular biographies included variations on the gendering of the encounter, as in the narratives of the Quaker philanthropists Isaac Hopper and his daughter Abby Hopper Gibbons. When Isaac Hopper began Sunday school in the Philadelphia prison in the late eighteenth century, the jailers and city fathers mounted a guard with cannon aimed at the prisoners, but the fearless "Friend Hopper" overawed his violent audience with his reading (318).[758] Hopper's daughter, as a married woman in New York, regularly visited the prison known as the Tombs to help the men as well as women; in an unusual illustration, she sits with a murderer condemned to death, ready to read to him the small tracts that she holds in her hand, his secular reading lying disregarded on the floor.[44] More commonly, however, the prison visit in these prosopographies is the didactic encounter between a woman philanthropist and incarcerated women.

The scene of reading would have been easy for many middle-class women to reenact. The methods of effective teaching, developing since the spread of Sunday schools à la More, seem adapted to later work in prisons, hospitals, the military, and the government office. In Fry's system of monitored instruction, as in role-model narrative, the intermediary or presenter joins in a mimetic circuit; many monitors no doubt learned to identify with teachers, and pupils might follow suit in their turn. Illustrations and narratives of other ministering women testify to the influence of Fry's performance. In Henry Ewart's *True and Noble Women*,[270] Mrs. Fry "Reading to the Prisoners in Newgate" (a detail of

Fig. 21 *Teaching in Yarmouth Workhouse* [*Sarah Martin*] by unidentified artist, from Henry Ewart, ed., *True and Noble Women* (1889), 147.[270]

the Barrett painting; 113) anticipates the same rites and relations that appear in another illustration in the volume, Sarah Martin "Teaching in Yarmouth Workhouse" (147): the seated lady turned toward her pupils on the right, with bonnet, book, indicative hands, clearly lit face, the more shadowy and unkempt group of women, a baby at nurse, scruffy boys in the right foreground (fig. 21).

As the orphaned daughter of a tradesman who earned her living as a seam-stress in Yarmouth, Sarah Martin (1791–1843) moved in an utterly different orbit than did Fry. Yet the resemblance between them begins when Martin teaches in a Sunday school and then in a workhouse. At a turning point in her narrative as in those of Fry, Dorothea Dix, and others, Sarah Martin deter-mined to brave a visit to the prison to help the inmates. Martin, like Fry, was first urged into the prison by the plight of a woman condemned for having harmed her own child.[45] Walter Scott's *The Heart of Midlothian* (1818) and George Eliot's representation of Dinah Morris's ministry to Hetty Sorrel in *Adam Bede* (1859) thus work from both the historical realities and the conventions of such encounters and help to perpetuate the popular drama of encounter between the ministering woman and the wronged sinner.[46] The illustration *Sarah Martin at the Door of Yarmouth Prison*[270] might show another Little Dorrit, a poor but honest and voluntary inmate incapable of the crimes caught within (fig. 22).

Fig. 22 *Sarah Martin at the Door of Yarmouth Prison* by unidentified artist ("W"?), from Henry Ewart, ed., *True and Noble Women* (1889) 151.[270]

Martin may have been a kind of folk heroine, but she gained considerable authority in spite of her poverty, almost as a hybrid of John Bunyan, Hannah More, and Elizabeth Fry.[47] The conventional formula of her success—a saintly life of service to the poor—nevertheless cannot disguise her enterprising activity. In other circumstances, she could have been a scholarly clergyman, a professional writer, or—with her ingenious nonprofit system of getting subscribers to pay for prison piecework that was then donated to clothe the poor—an entrepreneur in the textile industry. According to her own autobiographical narrative, she was always an avid reader, but in her teenage years was merely a consumer of such "trash" as novels, then Shakespeare and the British poets, all the while turning from the gospel "as from a reptile" (*Life of Sarah Martin,* 5–6). In spite of the secular influence of a local free-thinking gentleman, her mentor, she accepted revelation in 1810 and gradually learned to perfect the appropriate readerly susceptibility to (rather than scholarly study of) Scripture (8–11).

Literacy and the proper interpretation of the right texts, in other words, stand at the heart of her mission. Her audience—pupils and the readers of her own and other's narratives of her life—should help to stir more testimonial ripples rather than stop to identify with her or argue points of doctrine or text. As she recalls from her deathbed in 1843, she had to learn to put in their proper place the lives of exemplary people (such as the one she is reluctantly narrating of herself): "I have thought, as to the lives of persons whose writings, or other labours, have been most beneficial to their fellow creatures, that the success arose from the immediate power of the Holy Ghost . . . and I have thought it well, while setting a just value on the works of enlightened persons, to read them sparingly, . . . not as standards; and ever reserving a much larger portion of time . . . for the Bible" (*Life of Sarah Martin,* 11). Accordingly, much of the text of her own life consists of scriptural commentary and testimonials to the effects of grace on her dying acquaintances in the workhouse or prison. Once she had begun her assistance to the teachers in the workhouse and her double Sunday services with the prisoners, she also cultivated her writing of poetry, sermons, and meticulous journals and records of the progress of prisoners before and after release, anticipating prosopographical social science (110–32). The "outline of my life" only appeared posthumously, after she had "re-copied" an earlier account and edited out as far as possible any "egotistical appearance," so "that all the glory may be given to God"; the type, not the individual model, of self-reform and service to others is to be followed (36–37).

Fortunately, Martin fails to eradicate realist individuality from her story, which still suggests a sharp, sympathetic person of remarkable vitality and rhetorical power, capable of moving obdurate criminals and authorities alike. Her lasting influence, if not her interesting character, resonates in the short lives compiled for later readers. She became "the minister and pastor of this unpromising congregation" in the prison (153).[270] Her eloquence outshone the dry theology of clergymen "boy-bachelors" who oppose women's ministry, according to Sarah Hale (413).[362] She monitored the lives of those she schooled and befriended, while in turn she converted the drawing rooms of her friends and customers into complementary schools and workshops, teaching every hand to copy texts or to convert spare cloth into sewing projects for the prisoners, while she "would narrate some of the incidents" from the lives of the objects of their charity (267).[466] Martin herself became increasingly impoverished as she devoted more of her working days as a seamstress to the reform enterprise, but as word spread of her mission, support flowed in. Elizabeth Fry's British Ladies' Society gave annual support to the prison work of Sarah Martin in recognition of parallel missions.[360, p. 214; 467, p. 267] At length, Martin was persuaded to accept a small pension from the town. Narrators trace Martin's influence: "It was not logic that did it, but a luminous life" (159);[270] they tell of her saintly death: "Her joys were not of time" (268).[467] Hale quotes praise of Martin as the epitome of the model subject: "Such a life . . . should be included in collections of biography, and chronicled in the high places of history; men should be taught to estimate it as . . . entitled . . . to renown, and children associate the name of Sarah Martin with those of Howard, Buxton, Fry—the most benevolent of mankind" (414–15).[362] Yet while Martin flourished for a time with her ministering associates, by 1910–30 she no longer recurred in general collections.[48]

If the reading of sacred text in prison is a definitive scene, readers of the collections may sense at one remove the subduing power of scripture, as they may imagine themselves administering it. The fear of the rabble adds to the triumph when the threatening listeners respond instead with quiet assent. As in the Judith school, in the Fry school the woman's body is imperiled but only rarely by any sexual threat. Others whose work included an alarming mingling with the roughest classes were two somewhat less popular figures, Miss Marsh, a clergyman's daughter, and Caroline Chisholm, a yeoman's daughter, both portrayed in John Maw Darton's *Famous Girls*.[220] Like Martin, and like the missionary Judsons below, these models evaporate in the early twentieth-century general collections. They were heroines who brought order to two social upheavals of the mid-nineteenth century and served as spokeswomen and compilers of the hardships of the transient poor. Miss Marsh reformed the roving male laborers (or navvies) who built the railways in England, and Mrs. Chisholm provided supervision and protection to this class of worker (especially the females) when they emigrated (voluntarily or not) to the colonies. Marsh and Chisholm adapted the moral and pedagogical monitoring system, published representative narratives, and became examples to readers far and wide.

The story of Catherine Marsh, which is rather skeletal and rare in the prosopographies, is nevertheless richly iconographic, uniting the imperial prospects of the Great Exhibition with witness to the miracle of a Christian lady's influence.[49] As Darton tells it, in "1853, just after the successful closing of the 'Great Exhibition of the Industry of all Nations,' . . . so fruitful in love, in kindness, and mutual understanding between nations," the Crystal Palace was to be "permanently preserved . . . to minister to the enjoyment and instruction of the people" (220).[220] The project, with its grounds and branch railway, required an influx of about three thousand of "that strange, rough class, called 'navvies'—the very name almost conveying terror and alarm." At the village of Beckenham, Miss Marsh (her first name, Catherine, is scarcely mentioned) used the village pretext of visiting a sick man to get her foot in the door of the cottages, so like an urban slum. Her rank, gender, and performance of fearlessness warranted the worker's respect ("you will be very civil to me, I am sure"). Like Elizabeth Fry almost forty years before, Catherine Marsh conquered through manifestations of religion as well as good manners: "Then these great, rough men and this gentle woman knelt down to pray; . . . sobs burst from them; they were subdued, and gentle as little children" (222).[220] Leaving, she overhears one of the navvies reading the Bible aloud to the others—already her role has been modeled effectively.

Though her work closely resembled home visiting, Miss Marsh relied on bureaucratic and business methods. She controlled an invasion of urban vice into rural England with a combination of Bible classes and an informal system of franchise and export (with detailed records). Her Sunday evening classes became an institution that reformed the workers and produced those who would teach and model in turn (220–23).[220] As they went forth "to work on continental railways, or to emigrate to America, Canada, or Australia" (243),[220] they disseminated her instruction and popularized her bestselling didactic tales about workmen like themselves; hundreds of the men returned to thank her or bring testimonials or donations for the cause (243–46). Thus citizens of empire were mass produced under the auspices of the Crystal Palace and the exhibition of modern industry. Catherine Marsh became a biographer, presenting models of Christian manhood with *Memorials of Captain Hedley Vicars, Ninety-seventh Regiment* (1856, abridged by the American Tract Society in the 1890s), a biography of her father (1868), and narratives of the workmen she had known: *English Hearts and English Hands; or, The Railway and the Trenches* (1858) and *A Light for the Line; or, The Story of Thomas Ward, a Railway Workman* (1859).

Caroline Chisholm is best remembered for her work in Australia as "the girl emigrants' fairy godmother" (a subtitle in one version of her life),[444] though she played her philanthropic part in India and England as well. Lives provide only a hazy origin; her father encouraged her to form opinions on political issues of the day, and she early absorbed "tales of distant lands, and the advantages to be gained in them" (62).[253] In her own words, we have the childhood vocational anecdote (as when Nightingale nursed the wounded dog): "My first attempt at colonisation was carried out in a wash-hand basin before I was seven years old. I made boats of broad beans; . . . removed families . . . located them in the bed quilt, and sent the boats, filled with wheat, back to their friends" (62).[253] Appropriately, as "a woman of the world" (192)[444] she married a

Captain Archibald Chisholm and departed for Madras. Many activist women found India to be rich in the need for humanitarian reforms (Nightingale and Carpenter would later discover this); here Chisholm founded the Female School of Industry for the Daughters of European Soldiers, instilling the arts of house-keeping, bookkeeping, and charity: "The girls trained in [this 'Home'] were eagerly sought for as housekeepers, and as wives for non-commissioned officers" (253).[220] Irvine notes Chisholm's "gift for detail" (191),[444] and Dark suggests that "waste, whether of human life, of human labour, or of bar-ley [in the school's stores], was abhorrent to her" (63).[253] Interestingly, for both Irvine (191)[444] and Dark (61),[253] this passion for practical management relates directly to Chisholm's visions both of colonization and of women's rights.

When Captain Chisholm was sent on sick leave to Australia, Mrs. Chisholm exerted herself on behalf of emigrants. Darton pictures Chisholm as bring-ing order to "a heterogeneous mass of human beings" including "broken up families," and "friendless females" who were "prey" to procurers "for the vilest purposes" (254–55).[220] Chisholm saw that girls of "respectable" character were left to find their way in Sydney and to sleep "under rocks in the Domain at night" (69).[253] In her own words, the case of "a poor girl suffering distress and losing her reputation in consequence" weighed on her conscience; she prayed for God's "blessing" on her work (69).[253] Thus, as the Mrs. Fry of the Antipodes, this married mother of numerous children was called to action by her faith and by a particular wronged woman's need. She petitioned Governor Gipps, who recalled his surprise to find her young, pretty, and practical rather than old and Evangelical (70).[253] History paints the governor as the figurehead of es-tablished interests resisting the forces of right. But Chisholm did not wait for history; she mustered "the power of the press" (195)[444] as well as the sympa-thies of Lady Gipps. Eventually the governor gave Chisholm a shed to shelter the women, warning her that no government funds would be provided.

In order to guarantee her rescue campaign, she had to sleep in the shelter herself; on the terrifying first night she kept as many as thirteen rats at bay by feeding them her bread. Refusing "to be outgeneralled [sic] by rats" (72),[253] she persevered even when it became necessary to send her children away to protect them from disease in the crowded shelter. She began to manage an elaborate employment agency with contracts "in triplicate" and "committees in the country centres" to place women where they were needed as servants or wives (73);[253] she always investigated the character of the prospective masters or husbands. When the city-bred women refused to be sent into the bush, Chisholm escorted them herself. "Thus began those epic journeys" celebrated in *Punch*: "'It was a second Moses, in bonnet and in shawl.'" Her "strange pilgrimages" became "a kind of legend to the country folk," many of whom fed and sheltered the large parties for free (73–74).[253] In this phase she also became an Isabella Bird, a pioneer European woman enduring long, perilous travels in wild country.

Her fixed idea was to reunite families or to create new ones, in a sense exporting British domesticity. As significantly, she was a transporter of model narratives. When she and her family embarked for England in 1846 after public tributes from some of the eleven thousand people she had assisted, she took with her the oral histories that she had collected from emigrants: "These were to be their own voices speaking to their own people at home" (76).[253] Without editing to correct style, she recorded details that would identify the speaker to those who knew them—and that would serve in place of identification papers or fingerprints. *Voluntary Information from the People of New South Wales* consists of the briefest autobiographical statements, numbered and dated; this prosopography was to encourage others to follow the example of the model emigrants and to gain official assistance for reuniting families. As in Australia, in England Chisholm gradually overcame resistance and gained the support of influential members of society. Like Fry, she redesigned the conditions on the emigrant ships, reported to the House of Lords, and led a vanguard of ladies' committees. Emigrant ships became continuous with Fry's and Martin's prison Sunday schools, with careful registry and identification, monitored classes, paid sewing "work," and a safe reception to further surveillance onshore.[50] Chisholm returned to Australia in 1854 as an international "personage" praised by British newspapers and Australian legislators (81).[253] Now her mission became to provide family life to the "diggers" in the Australian gold rush and to secure homes and land that would improve Australia's agriculture. On a final return to England, she was granted a pension. As a fairy godmother or a Moses, and in the name of domestic ideology, she acted all the parts of a cabinet-level administrator of an emigration and naturalization service while sustaining her personal influence on the objects of her care. Apparently her tactics were just the combination of grassroots and paternalistic—or maternalist—that worked at that time.

Light upon Darkness: Experts on Discipline and Care

Fry's successors not only reform character through reading and modeling middle-class domestic economy, but they also reform institutions through new tools of knowledge and management, as charity evolves into the welfare state. Catherine Marsh's testimonials, Sarah Martin's records of prisoners, and Caroline Chisholm's prosopography of emigrants are different versions of the documentary basis for reforming the poor. Mary Carpenter and Dorothea Dix went even further in the direction of sociological investigation to support new laws for social outcasts, in the mode that Nord recognizes later in the century. As Sarah Knowles Bolton wrote of Dix, "She dared, and entered, and observed closely" (247).[97] The ministering woman's daring venture into dark precincts, celebrated in mythic terms, permitted intervention in a wide range of causes hardly assumed to be a lady's business at that time. Dr. Martineau's inscription on Mary Carpenter's monument in Bristol Cathedral praises this preprofessional nonspecialization: she "led the way to a national system / of moral rescue and preventive discipline. / . . . No human ill escaped her pity."[185, p. 83; 731, p. 318]

Ladies had long visited the homes of the poor, of course. Now, in their own and others' accounts, the ministering women heroically descend into dark zones inhabited by what Mary Carpenter called "the perishing and dangerous classes"; they appease the drunken, blasphemous, violent beast, and ascend to win the keys to the kingdom, that is, the support of powerful men. Elizabeth Gaskell's Margaret Hale in *North and South* (1854–55) exercises such power of appeasement in the scene after the factory girl Bessy Higgins has died and the father Nicholas Higgins tries to seek comfort in drink. Margaret bars his exit from the house, and he threatens to "strike" her with the "violence" he has already used on his surviving daughter. "But she never moved a feature—never took her deep, serious eyes off him. . . . If she had stirred hand or foot, he would have thrust her aside," but he is "daunted and awed by her severe calm" and finally "acknowledged her power. . . . half-conquered, half-resenting."[51] Margaret sometimes miscalculates the protection she possesses in her class and gender, but the biographical paragons rarely fail to use these status codes to bring out the better selves of the men and women they encounter.

The difference between cottage visiting and the errands of Elizabeth Fry or Mary Carpenter is not simply one of scale—hundreds of women and children have been forced into Newgate's two rooms, for example—but also of what we could call generic convention; these precincts might be the "homes" of gothic or sensation fiction. Mary Carpenter's deeds present her as a "bright ensample of virtue" like Longfellow's "lady with a lamp" (319);[731] she was "perfectly devoid of fear, and would traverse alone, and at nights, courts into which policemen only went by twos" (289). Another biographer writes of Carpenter that "controlling her repugnance, she . . . [took] positive delight in forcing herself into visiting the worst houses of all. . . . Like Sister Dora, too, she won the regard of the very vilest by her utter unselfishness, devotion, and lack of any sign of loathing or fear" (58).[185] Dorothea Dix, comparably, dared to probe the nightmare places where human beings were "confined . . . in *cages, closets, cellars, stalls, pens; chained, naked, beaten with rods* and *lashed* into obedience," bringing with her human pity and aid and the light of public scrutiny.[52] Neither Carpenter nor Dix performed spectacles of spiritual influence like Fry's scenes in Newgate, though they happily employed public measures for reform. Warm solidarity with other ministering women seems to have failed in the narratives of Carpenter and Dix, while Dix positively resisted her own celebrity. Thus in spite of the short collected lives and the full-length biography each received, it became difficult to preserve the name, scene, iconographic image of these leaders, admired and effective as they were in their day.

How might the narratives romanticize the administrative woman, as Fry's biographers had done? Mary Carpenter (1807–77) was hardly romantic material.[53] The eldest daughter of a Unitarian minister who ran a boys' school in Bristol, Carpenter was educated in the classics and sciences with the boys (Dr. Martineau was also one of her father's pupils [200–201]).[270] As a young teacher and schoolmistress herself, she took an interest in the abolition movement in the United States (287)[731] and gained her lifelong commitments to "destitute children" and to the condition of India through the visits of foreign Unitarians to her family's home (280–81).[731] Having formed such committees of women as the "Ministry to the Poor, or Domestic Mission," Carpenter established in 1846 a Ragged School (282, 288).[731] In 1849, she published *Ragged Schools, Their Principles and Modes of Operation, by a Worker* (292)— a telling alternative byline to "a Lady." Her 1851 book *Reformatory Schools for the Children of the Perishing and Dangerous Classes, and for Juvenile Offenders* drew on international comparative statistics to argue that almost all children might be reformed by "judicious control and training" and that current penal systems trained criminals rather than producing "useful members of society" (295–96).[731] Eventually, three levels of schooling for working-class and poor children, from the voluntary to the involuntary, were instituted according to Carpenter's plans. By the mid-1860s, much of her energy turned to the causes of women's education and prison reform in India. In her four trips to India between 1866 and 1875, she gained trust and political influence there, in part because she came with "no proselytising objects, and treat[ed] them as friends and equals," in her words (307).[270]

While Carpenter was a kind of Hannah More of schools and an Elizabeth Fry of the penal system, she was also an Octavia Hill of housing, and, like Dorothea Dix and others, she compiled statistics, inspected institutions, and promoted legislation according to the newer methods. Even her turn to interest in India was shared with Caroline Chisholm and Florence Nightingale. By 1857, she was addressing the National Association for the Promotion of Social Sciences (like other mid-Victorian women activists), and in 1860 she spoke to "the statistical section of the British Association for the Advancement of Science, from which she had been debarred as a woman in 1836."[54] When Carpenter toured the United States in 1873 a woman journalist observed: "It was her *knowledge* that gave her power" (314–16).[731] Yet she is a lady with a lamp, in many versions. Like Sister Dora, she subdues wild people of the streets. "Men and women lost to all sense of shame . . . slunk away abashed when she appeared; guilty lads hung their heads lest they should see the look of reproachful woe in her eyes" (58).[185] Her ability to melt the hardened children in the Kingswood Reformatory School is attributed to her "*motherliness* . . . her gentle care . . . and her noble example" (69).[185] The children whom she rescued were to become good "not by force, but example" (70).[185]

The example, indeed, was designed to shape good men and women of her own class and above, as well. Frances Power Cobbe, encouraged by their mutual friend Lady Byron to join Carpenter in her work, writes of her first encounter in 1858 with the famous woman, who gave an impression of "a high and strong *Resolution,* which made her whole path much like that of a plough in a

well-drawn furrow, which... gently pushes aside into little ridges all intervening people and things."[55] Rosamond Davenport Hill, a pioneer woman in
politics, wrote a short biography of Mary Carpenter that is almost a family
memoir, as her father Matthew D. Hill in 1851 became a powerful supporter of
Carpenter's campaign for reformatory schools (209),[270] and she and her sisters
collaborated in the work.[56] Rosamond Hill acknowledges the flaws in the great
reformer, whose "gravity" and "indomitable perseverance" could seem "hard
and unsympathetic" to those who did not know her well (202).[270] The younger
women gradually guided Carpenter into a more public and feminist political
role, and in 1877, Carpenter joined Cobbe in promoting women's suffrage while
she supported the causes of "the Higher Education of Women, the Temperance
cause, and the repeal of the Contagious Diseases Acts" (316).[731][57] As Ruth
Watts writes, "She was held as a role model by the Englishwomen's Review
especially because of her work in India and her particular 'imperial role' for
women."[58] Her stature was international and reached the highest ranks. Before
her second trip to India in 1868, her prestige was confirmed in an audience
with Queen Victoria, who inscribed a copy of the Highland journal to her.
Princess Alice (Princess Louis of Hesse) summoned Carpenter to Darmstadt
(with her friend Florence Davenport Hill, Rosamond's sister) for a conference
on women's work.[59] The princess wrote to Carpenter, "I would like all to know
and share my admiration for such a benevolent and useful life as yours.... Your
example will ever incite me to try and do better" (313).[731] It is a repetition of
the historic tableau of Queen Charlotte paying homage to Elizabeth Fry.

Carpenter's narrative, then, is powerful in a network of subject-forming
models, across spheres and classes. Crucial to the tale of the light-bearing
champion is her capacity to overawe both the brutal poor and the heartless
powerful. The lady's calm, unflinching gaze when she herself is imperiled, her
insistence on moral rectitude (often focused on temperance and the concepts
of female purity and private property), combined with her forthright respect
for individuals who have only known inhumane usage, seem rapidly to induce
grateful obedience from even the hardest cases. The career of Dorothea Dix
(1802–87), overlapping with the ministry of Carpenter in some ways yet rarely
appearing in the same volume, exhibits less of the saintly aura. Largely, she
was a lobbyist rather than a preacher, teacher, or nurse; legislators across the
United States and abroad granted the lands, funds, and laws she required. Dix's
daily actions were even harder to cast in traditional feminine roles than those
of Carpenter. In 1890, Francis Tiffany published the first full-length biography
of Dix, wondering why "the present generation know little or nothing of so
remarkable a story," that of a Protestant "St. Theresa."[60] Dix had absolutely
refused "to permit anything to be written of her" and declined the invitation
of Sarah Hale, back in 1851, to be noted in Woman's Record (Tiffany, iii–v);
Hale's critical article on Dix thus appears to be an "unauthorized" biography
(862–64).[362] Indeed, Dix seems to have feared that her own example would
be infectious; girls ought to be urged into happy domestic pursuits rather than

"undertake some work of a similar kind" (Tiffany, viii). Like Mary Carpenter, Dorothea Lynde Dix was an unmarried polyglot with a scientific avocation, who began as teacher and schoolmistress and became an international authority on carceral reform. Unlike most of the famous philanthropists, her early life was poor, her family broken, and she ran away to live with her grandparents. Her drive to support her mother and brothers and to make her mark on the world, inspired by the example of others, overcame resistance and strove against the limitations on what any one person could do.

Though opposed to serving as a model, Dix evidently relied on precedents for her own self-development. In a letter to her grandmother, Dix wrote to plead for the "good to the poor, the miserable, the idle, and the ignorant, which would follow your giving me permission to use the barn chamber for a schoolroom.... You have read Hannah More's life. You approve of her labors for the most degraded of England's paupers; why not ... let *me* rescue some of America's miserable children from vice and guilt?" (242–43).[97; see also 791, pp. 64–65] Beginning her life of active service on the tireless plan of a Carpenter, Dix ran a household and two schools while continuing her own education. As Gladys Brooks wrote of Dix in a collective biography in 1957, "the days flew by and the nights, with the smallest modicum of sleep."[61] In 1841, as though inspired by Fry or Martin, Dix made a visit to teach Sunday school to women in the East Cambridge House of Correction and soon discovered the torture and neglect of insane inmates; "the vision came to Dorothea of other Black Holes of Calcutta where human beings were held in hopelessness" (Brooks, 26).

At age thirty-nine, she "had begun her life-work," as Bolton puts it (246),[97] a labor of fifty years to reform the treatment of the insane. Many accounts repeat her shocking reports of bodily torture and her interviews with complacent keepers.[97, pp. 247–51; 59, pp. 142–50; 791, pp. 72–76] Eventually, all the states, and later Britain and the Continent, from France to Scandinavia to Turkey, yielded to her undeniable evidence of atrocities. In each state, she would establish herself in an alcove or room near the chambers and allow legislators to pay court to her as at a salon. One doctor who knew her wrote, "What a heroine she is!.... Over the whole breadth and length of the land are her footsteps, and where she steps flowers of the richest odor of humanity are sprouting and blooming as on an angel's path" (255).[97] If many statesmen were swayed by this visitation of the goddess Flora, others were irritated, much as Florence Nightingale had provoked the British Home Secretary by exposing the incompetence of the military in the Crimea. Sir George Grey in the House of Commons found it shameful that the British reform of the treatment of the insane was forced on them by Dix, a "foreigner, and that foreigner a woman, and that woman a dissenter" (quoted on 260);[97] others declared that "searching out misdeeds was unbecoming in a woman!" (249).[97]

In later life, Dix undertook reforms such as providing lifeboats, rescue facilities, and libraries in life-saving stations along the North American coast (257–58),[97] as though emulating the later life of Elizabeth Fry. In 1861, she gave warning of a plot to capture railroad lines and besiege Washington, D.C.; the defense of the capital and of the president-elect's life was "really due to the sagacity, courage, and patriotism of Miss Dix," another Lydia Darragh, perhaps.[79 1, pp. 84–85; 97, p. 262] During the Civil War, she was appointed superintendent of women nurses by the secretary of war, in an intersection with the narrative of Clara Barton. In spite of her immense administrative responsibilities, she could be cast in the Nightingale role in some of the short lives: "Administering, with her own hands, physical comforts to the suffering, and soothing the troubled spirits of the invalid or dying soldiers with a low voice, musical and attractive, and always burdened with words of heartfelt sympathy and religious consolation."[62] Mary A. Livermore, herself cast as a Civil War heroine, recalled of Dix, "Her fortune, time, and strength were laid on the altar of her country in its hour of trial" (265).[97]; [63] The government offered a public tribute and monetary reward, but she preferred a pair of flags (86).[792] Having deferred *love* and *family*, Dix chose to make her final home in one of the hospitals that she founded: "'For half a century she had had no home, but had been in every fibre of her being a public character. The asylums were her children. . . . The natural order of family'" would be for them to care for her in the end (unknown source quoted on 87).[792]

On Martyrdom and Self-Help

The lives of missionary women, like those of the penal reformers, share the honors of spreading the light of civilization. I round out my group portrait in this chapter with the most extraordinary proof of the power of exemplary biography to model lives, as it is the epitome of mutual multibiography. The lives of Ann Hasseltine Judson, Sarah Boardman Judson, and Emily Chubbuck Judson intertwine rhetorically, much as they share serial marriage to Adoniram Judson. In this role modeling, a member of the audience reads the life of a subject whose career was to model audiences: to convert foreigners and inspire her peers at home to similar missions. The reader then turns biographer of another woman in the same mold as the first subject, and this reader-presenter in her turn rises to become one of the series of lauded subjects. This is a form of self-help hagiography, with all the appeal of martyrdom. Middle- and working-class girls in Britain and the United States, reading the biographies of missionary women, were moved to choose that calling, and often to marry a man who called them, though it seemed he led her to a foreign grave. *Love* and *family* curiously fuse with *religion, vocation,* and *deeds,* culminating in suffering of the *body* and *death.* The missionaries seldom receive the *prestige* of government recognition but often attain a certain celebrity among the faithful and readily enjoy confirmation of their *influence.*

Among the very first in this line, Ann Hasseltine married Adoniram Judson and voyaged with him as a Baptist missionary to Burma, where among her many feats she rescued her husband from prison and met an early death.

Lydia Huntley Sigourney, introducing *Noble Deeds of American Women*[182] at midcentury, assumes everyone knows the woman "who sleeps beneath the hopia-tree in Burmah" and affirms Mrs. Judson's effectiveness as a prototype: "How rapidly has she been followed in the same self denying path, by others who 'counted not their lives dear unto them,' if they might bear to the perishing heathen the name and love of a Redeemer" (xvi). It was not long before Sarah Hall Boardman, widowed on her own Eastern mission, followed that path and married the now-renowned Judson to carry on the missionary work, only to die in her turn. Judson, seeking in the United States a biographer for Sarah the second wife, found the young writer Emily Chubbuck, who was known pseudonymously as Fanny Forester. Having long admired the first Mrs. Judson and dreamed of missionary sacrifice, Chubbuck dropped her career as a secular writer to become the third Mrs. Judson in the mission field. Eventually her writing talent was turned to sacred account when she published the life of the second Mrs. Judson.

The wife's expected martyrdom did not come this third time. It was Mr. Judson who died in the field, whereas Mrs. Judson survived a short time after returning to the United States. The deaths sanctify the vocation and add to the proselytizing effect of the narratives. Elegy, epitaph, and the tropes that shape prosopographies guide the representations of this self-immolating family. In one popular illustration, there is the ever-emblematic hopia tree; an image of St. Helena, where the second Mrs. Judson is buried like Napoleon; an image of the ocean waves that, presumably, absorb Mr. Judson's remains; and the graveyard in Hamilton, NY, in which the much younger Emily Judson is buried—all hallowed spots.[64]

The three Mrs. Judsons were featured, separately or together, in many collections of female biography published between about 1830 and 1900.[65] As Linda Peterson explains, the contemporary flurry of tributes to women missionaries provides the context for the strange courtship of Jane Eyre by St. John Rivers.[66] Recall that St. John has commanded Jane to study "Hindoostanee" and to marry him so that she can serve as his missionary counterpart. Jane's mind races ahead to the end of this "glorious" calling: she thinks, "if I go to India, I go to premature death." She finds herself willing to "throw all on the altar—... the entire victim," but not as St. John's wife.[67] Readers today applaud when Jane refuses to settle for a loveless marriage, and most will be relieved not to follow our heroine through this imperialist project. But it seems foreign to twenty-first-century readers that Jane should not decline the deadly job outright. She, like Brontë and her contemporary readers, may have been under the sway of the tales of noble careers in the mission field.[68] Arabella Stuart Willson, in a book popularly known as *The Lives of the Three Mrs. Judsons*,[886] sheds light on what might have drawn Jane to such a high-risk vocation: "The missionary enterprise opens to women a sphere of activity, usefulness, and distinction, not ... to be found elsewhere." Besides skills in linguistics and personnel management, the woman missionary may "exhibit" "Christian heroism" in defiance of "appalling dangers, and even death in its most dreadful forms" (iii).[886] (See also Brumberg, *Mission for Life,* 80; Peterson, *Women's Autobiography,* 95.) At the same time, "women missionaries also viewed their work as promoting the cause of—and improving career opportunities for—Western women," as Peterson puts it (*Women's Autobiography,* 94). Undoubtedly, missionary work beat school teaching or working as a governess for narratability.[69]

Peterson claims that "women missionaries and their memoirists developed a new form of Victorian life writing, one that represented women taking heroic action, women engaged in serious work outside the home" (97). Yet "heroic action" and public ministry pervade women's life narratives in the nineteenth-century collections. Female missionary narratives thus shared common tropes rather than inventing them. Missionaries' lives, devoted to transforming the alien converts, were promoted at the same time as role models for the domestic audience, like other ministering women. Conversion is only a more dramatic form of the narrative interaction among presenters, subjects, and audience. Thus the three short-lived Mrs. Judsons minimize the distance between action, representation, and emulation. The end of this role-modeling chain, the last of the wives, displays the effect most visibly.

Emily Chubbuck's autobiography portrays her search for a heroic role, especially in death. As a little factory girl in 1828, she avidly read forbidden novels and "[imagined] my favorite character going on, on—but it would always end in *death.* Of what avail, then, [were] beauty . . . wealth and honor?" (quoted on 297).[173] Later, in a cheap Baptist newspaper she glanced at "the words: 'Little Maria lies by the side of her fond mother.'" Recognizing that it was Adoniram Judson's letter narrating the famed death of his wife Ann Judson and their daughter, she read on, and imagined the "glory" of the lonely missionary widower. "After this I had my romantic dreams of mission life . . . and though they, like the others, ended in death, somehow death in such an employment came pleasantly" (297–98).[173] Hagiography then offered the ventures and self-fulfilled closure of romance, yet the protagonist might be as staunchly dedicated as a Hannah More or an Elizabeth Fry.

What would a mission entail, to a reader of the life and death of the first wife, Ann Hasseltine Judson? A true original or ur-text, she was "the first American woman who resolved to leave friends and country to carry the Gospel of Christ to the heathen," in a day—1812, about the time Fry was venturing into Newgate—when the "great enterprise" was thwarted and opposed (57).[173] Avid followers at home contributed funds and read the latest epistolary installment in Ann Judson's development as teacher, translator, writer, and even preacher alongside her husband. Returning to the States in 1823 for her health, Mrs. Judson was much in demand as a speaker. Her celebrity blossomed during the British war with Burma in 1824–25, in which she reenacted the political prison dramas of Lady Fanshawe, Lady Russell, Madame Roland, and other much-anthologized heroines of the English Civil War or the French Revolution. Suspecting Adoniram Judson of being a British spy, the Burmese government threw him "into the death-prison." Mrs. Judson remained steadfast: "Her activity, invention and resources. . . . display her character in glowing colors" (335).[331] For months she petitioned for the release of her husband and other European prisoners, dispensed bribes and flattery at the court, preserved valuables from plunder—including Mr. Judson's life work, the Burmese Bible—and generally served as "ministering angel" (337)[331] to feed, protect, and comfort the tortured prisoners. When Mr. Judson was forced on a brutal march to another town, she followed with her small family and camped in a storage room, where she gave birth to a daughter before nearly dying of a fever herself. As she lay ill and unable to nurse her baby, the imprisoned husband and father was temporarily released to carry the baby through the village in search of a wet nurse. Mr. Judson was ultimately freed after further torments, and Mrs. Judson assisted as diplomat and translator during peace negotiations with the British, but she never recovered sound health. This outline only hints at the richness of the tale, a hard act to follow. Nevertheless, or therefore, it solicited many to try to follow it.

The representation of the three Mrs. Judsons forms fascinating patterns. A considerable biographical industry immediately began converting these lives into effective emblems. James D. Knowles, with his *Memoir of Mrs. Ann H. Judson* (1829), helped to initiate the effect of this new martyr. In 1833, Lydia Maria Child included "Mrs. Judson, Wife of Adoniram Judson," in her popular *Good Wives*,[170] a year before it would become necessary to note which Mrs. Judson. Sarah Hall, a school teacher and emerging poet, had read the narratives of the Burmese mission and heard Ann Judson speak during her visit to the States in 1823. She married the missionary George D. Boardman in 1825 and arrived with him in time to attend the burial of the child Maria Judson beside her mother under the hopia tree. When Mr. Boardman died in 1831, Sarah continued a solo administration in the mission field until she married Judson in 1834. When her health declined, Mr. Judson reluctantly and belatedly accompanied her homeward; she died at sea in 1845 and was buried at St. Helena. Besides her emblematic gravesite, Sarah Boardman Judson left few traces—no genuine portraits and few narratable incidents. Though granted some vivid short biographies of her own, she often appears as the somewhat generic second term in the Judson series. One biographer of Sarah suggests the problem of fair representation in the crowded mission field: "Perhaps it might appear invidious to sketch the life of any one of those amiable heroines of the cross, when the lives of all are so full of true courage and faith" (107).[37] Sarah Hale's *Woman's Record* of 1853 included Ann and Sarah Judson (367–69)[362] side by side (the then-living third wife appeared in the appendix [709–12]). Hale wrote, "If this second Mrs. Judson was less distinguished than her predecessor for strength of mind and the power of concentrating her energies, . . . yet she was not inferior in loveliness of character" (369).[362]; 70

Emily Chubbuck was prepared for her vocation by the lives before her. The factory girl became a teacher and then a writer, making a breakthrough in 1844 as "Fanny Forester." Twice-widowed Adoniram Judson, temporarily returned from Burma, took an interest first in Fanny Forester's work: "A lady who writes so well, ought to write better," that is, on serious subjects. He engaged her to write the biography of his second wife and, in due course, engaged her to become the third Mrs. Judson and go with him to Burma.[71] Here was a heroic way to end in death: the famous twenty-nine-year-old writer was "pluming her wings for a higher flight," as Clark puts it, "but the crown was laid aside for the cross and the grave" (311).[173] Marriage extinguished Fanny Forester, but the new Mrs. Judson published an effective tribute to Sarah Boardman Judson in 1848 that eventually sold more than thirty thousand copies (Brumberg, 138). At last it was Mr. Judson's turn: he died after only four years of his third marriage, and the widow soon returned to the United States, too ill to continue the mission alone. Until her own death four years later, the business of her life became the preservation of his biographical heritage.

Though some present a trio of equal martyrs, many tributes perceive a degeneration from the inspired to the workmanlike to the derivative. More celebrated than Sarah, Emily is necessarily less sanctified than Ann, as a model not of service but of literary fame in antebellum America. The public was sorely tried when asked to accept a third Mrs. Judson: Evangelicals criticized Mr. Judson for infatuation with a worldly woman and for neglect of his first wives' sacred memories, whereas others criticized the zeal that led people to die in the mission field (Brumberg, 132–37). At thrice, the tragedy becomes farce. The last of the series, moreover, predicts that this type would be edged out later in the century by more of Fanny Forester's ilk: self-made women of letters likely to survive a mission or a husband.

Illustrations as well as texts suggest the mutual modeling among these exemplary women. Goodrich's *World Famous Women* or *Women of Beauty and Heroism*[331] presents a typical gallery; the nineteen names include warrior queens (such as Zenobia), martyred queens (such as Mary Queen of Scots), exotic patriots such as Joan of Arc, Pocahontas, and the Maid of Saragossa (fig. 15), Charlotte Brontë, Queen Victoria, and Ann Judson.[72] All represent uncommon agency, and most attest to an experience of racial contact zones, though none besides Judson are the sort of ministering women I bring forward in this chapter. Inevitably, the models rival yet mimic each other. Goodrich promotes Judson with national pride: "The American reader will hardly need to be told . . . that his country has never produced her superior." Evidently, Britain has: "The world has read with more emotion of the philanthropy of Florence Nightingale than of the martyrdom of Anne Hasseltine; she who nursed Caucasians at Scutari will be ever more familiarly famous than she who ransomed Malays at Rangoon" (350–52)—a prophecy fulfilled. The portrait of Ann H. Judson (painted by J. B. Wandesforde and engraved by Halpin [fig. 23]), reappears in another "holiday and gift-book" (iv), the Reverend D. W. Clark's *Portraits of Celebrated Women*,[173] which expands on Goodrich. In Clark, Judson is joined by her counterpart of Scutari, a near twin (also painted by Wandesforde; also

Fig. 23 *Ann Hasseltine Judson* by J. B. Wandesforde, engraved by F. Halpin, from D. W. Clark,
Portraits of Celebrated Women.[173] Reprinted in Joan Jacobs Brumberg, *Mission for Life*
(New York: Free Press/Macmillan, 1980), n.p.

in *Eminent Women of the Age*[630] [fig. 8]). Neither image is a likeness, nor do
these give any indication that the originals led active rather than contemplative
lives. Here, both Ann Judson and Nightingale are commissioned to represent literacy and piety in an exotic clime (foreign fanes and foliage, the
romantic touch of the flower). Clark includes the third wife, "the Missionary Poet," no rival for the first, to judge only by appearances: Emily Judson
(fig. 24).[73]

Male artists and engravers at midcentury embellish the images of delicate
flowers wilting in a hostile climate. The portraits may promise tranquility or
authority as well as refinement, belying harsh conditions or the actual pain of
martyred death. The verbal text tends to be less idealized, revealing feats of ex-
ecutive strength in the short careers. While the conventions of romance color

Fig. 24 *Emily C. Judson (Fanny Forester)* by F. E. Jones, in D. W. Clark, *Portraits of Celebrated Women* (1863).[173]

both the marriage and the death of the missionary heroine, the two events are too hard to tell apart: marriage literally spells the heroine's end. Many biographies exalt the missionary heroine's choice of delayed suicide, in the recurring scene of the daughter's departure from her family, a ghoulish variation on the exchange of women. Whatever the benefits of good biographical models, one doesn't want one's daughter to *be* a Joan of Arc or a Mrs. Judson. When Adoniram Judson first proposed, he asked Ann Hasseltine's father if he would consent to the marriage in the likelihood that she would face "degradation, insult, persecution, and perhaps violent death." The pious father consented (Brumberg, 23). As Sarah Hall Boardman left her parents' home for the last time, they grieved to lose their daughter. She urged, "Say, father, that you are willing I should go." "Yes, my child, I am willing" (296).[97] Journalists censured Emily Chubbuck's union with Judson as "another case of *infatuation* for an untimely death.... The wholesale sacrifice of life" should be outlawed (quoted in Brumberg, 41). One of the surviving widow's last publications was a volume to counter such prejudice against women's missionary work.

Jane Eyre, severe on all foreign forms of female sacrifice, might have risked death to join a celebrated Anglo American sisterhood. To many it seemed the missionary wife committed a kind of sati like the Indian widow (as Jane's own thoughts suggest), but the volunteers saw it as a special calling to lessen the suffering and subjection of heathen women (Brumberg, 81–83).[74] Charlotte Brontë, with her own short and sanctified life, soon entered the lists with the Judsons. The novelist, however, has long outlived the missionaries in the prosopographies; indeed, Brontë rates twenty-seven places in my Pop Chart samples (peaking in the 1880–1900 period), above Madame de Staël and below Queen Victoria (app. table A2). Sarah Knowles Bolton, in *Famous Types of Womanhood*,[97] was one of the last of the popular hagiographers of the Mrs. Judsons. Bolton prophesies mistakenly (in 1892) that Dr. Adoniram Judson "will live in history, forever associated with the three women who . . . will always be an inspiration to the womanhood of America" (274–75).

The collective biographies of women reconsidered here suggest that the emergence of women into civic activity and leadership should be dated earlier than the rise of the "New Woman." They show that professional vocations were commended in mythic as well as pragmatic terms, well before large numbers of middle-class women found paid work outside the home. Gradually, the status for women as well as men might be redefined by productivity and compensation. Feminists at the end of the nineteenth century disparaged domestic women as primitive parasites.[75] In 1910, Emily James Putnam indicted "the lady" as an archaic, "dangerous element of society" uniquely unproductive and self-serving.[76] Idle ladies, as much as unschooled or diseased indigents and immigrants, could be characterized as dangerous and doomed classes. Any middle-class girl should learn how to earn her keep.[77]

Female prosopographies and self-help of all kinds adapted to the new expectations. In the 1927 *Girls Who Did*,[286] the girl reader is invited to peruse nineteen "stories of real girls," now successful working women, in order to choose her own career.[78] The models are women who "did," but not in the heterosexualized sense of Grant Allen's 1895 New Woman novel *The Woman Who Did;* they belong more with Allen's *The Type-Writer Girl* of 1894.[79] Paid work becomes the sign of a generation's liberation. As an advice writer of 1942 imagines the change, "Whistler's mother sat with her hands folded idly in her lap. . . . She was passive; she was . . . completely removed from the business of her world. . . . In her place today sits the girl working at the typewriter. . . . active, not passive . . . finding herself through work."[80] As usual, the new active woman feels a peculiar need to conceive of previous generations of inert nonentities. For a century before 1942, women activists had been inspecting, managing, and reforming every corner of their world, though only belatedly in the guise of clerks or businesswomen.

Victorian collective biographies reshaped the shared standards of a middle-class British or American woman's life. The short exemplary lives imply that there were hordes of women like these models who bravely bore the beacon into the dark streets and rooms of poverty and vice; who endured the gore of surgery or the battlefield, the curses and jeers of common or genteel men, even the desolation and fevers of the jungle; who by performing courage and faith overcame the brawling impulses of the mass; who by teaching the discipline of reading and mutual instruction modeled their ministry in turn; who moved powerful men of their own class to institute their reforms; and who galvanized all classes to mutual sympathy and improvement. Among the immediate effects, these volumes may have modeled daydream heroism for feminine middle-class subjects while justifying discriminations and national agendas. Cumulatively, however, such narratives transformed expectations for the work that women might do.

Chapter Four

The Lessons of the Medusa

Anna Jameson and Mutual Multibiography

Anna Brownell Murphy Jameson (1794–1860), celebrated in Victorian biographical collections, might serve as a liaison between the heroic types and the ministering women of the preceding chapters. Her works presented queens, martyrs, and literary heroines, while her life intersected with those of eminent women of literature and the arts, as well as with a younger generation of feminist activists. She was, indeed, a pioneer feminist prosopographer whose writings and reception reveal much about the history of representation of women's lives. In 1832, Jameson introduced the work that would confirm her reputation, *Characteristics of Women,* with a dialogue on the question of women's standing in history and culture.[1] Alda, the heroine of the dialogue, as charming in her way as Woolf's Mary Beton in *A Room of One's Own* a century later, prefers to "illustrate certain positions by examples, and leave my readers to deduce the moral themselves" (xiii).[450] Alda's interlocutor, Medon, seems to hold traditional misogynist views of women's capacities, but Alda affirms "that women have achieved enough to silence [those angry common-places] for ever." At this point Jameson's footnote offers a miniature catalog of women's triumphs: "In our own time, Madame de Staël, Mrs. Somerville, Harriet Martineau, Mrs. Marcet; we need not go back to the Rolands and Agnesi, nor even to our own Lucy Hutchinson" (xxxiv).[450] As is the custom with citations of famous women, the list appears offhand;

any among countless names would do. But somehow this bounty of achievement has never silenced the *querelle des femmes*. In Jameson's day, as in Christine de Pizan's, it did not go without saying that women might be great or might contribute their cultural capital to the wealth of nations—specifically, to "our" nation, though the examples themselves might be French or Italian.[2]

Yet *Characteristics of Women,* later known as *Shakespeare's Heroines,* suggests that there is cause to mistrust historical examples as means of giving women their due. Initiating a form of feminist criticism, Jameson challenges masculinist historiography: "Women are illustrious in history, not from what they have been in themselves, but generally in proportion to the mischief they have done or caused" (xviii).[450] Since the annals caricature a woman as either "angel" or "fury" or both (xviii–xix),[450] Jameson turns instead to literary heroines. Shakespeare—and all the better that it should be the greatest of British writers—presents a far more flexible and realistic range of female character, by Jameson's lights, than written history. Jameson was by no means the first to laud Shakespeare's feminine insight, and she contributes to a considerable line of typologies of feminine characteristics, as we have seen. *Shakespeare's Heroines* might be the first full-length example, however, of feminist literary criticism.

In a career of presenting diverse models of feminine historicity, Jameson resoundingly disproved her own commonplace, that history lacks positive records of women. I wish to reexamine Jameson as a compiler of historical narratives of and for women. Her contradictory representation of individuals within an anti-individualist countertradition offers an instructive model for feminist archeological work. Her recuperative biographical practice should be viewed in the context of the reception of Jameson herself and within a network of mutual representation that sanctioned Victorian women of letters. Jameson affords a closer look at a presenter, after focusing on venturesome or dedicated subjects. The models in her studies of Shakespeare and of early Italian art personify the potential of feminist biographical representation. I offer access to her remarkable works as antecedents of some forms of feminist criticism. Anna Jameson's comprehensive oeuvre was devoted to a vindication of the achievements of woman. She participated in an internecine citational practice within circles of middle-class women in Britain and North America during her lifetime and beyond; such mutual biographical recognition provides the proper context in which to reassess Jameson's works. Jameson herself is undergoing a restoration within a network of influential Victorian women of letters. She was one of the first women ever to attain international recognition as a critic, and for a period she prevailed as an authority on both the woman question and Christian art.[3] After one foray into fiction, *The Diary of an Ennuyée* (1826)—and true to her later hybrid forms, this was a travel journal studded with art criticism— "Mrs. Jameson" found her niche and for more than thirty years supplied the English-reading public with such works as *Shakespeare's Heroines* and *Sacred and Legendary Art,*[456] running through recurrent editions.

In spite of her increasingly outspoken criticism of the subjection of women, Jameson remained thoroughly respectable and unchallenged in her pedagogical service, though rivals from Ruskin to Martineau disparaged her.[4] Her rhetoric tends to the prosopoetic, reanimating absent, often martyred spirits. Formally, she favors the compilation of fragments; her readers would have recognized her designs as those of travelogue, Menippean satire, apologia, the humanist essay or confession, encyclopedias of useful knowledge, gift annuals, monthly magazines, and museum catalogs. Her persona as the leader of a self-taught sisterhood curiously enhanced the authority of her criticism and scholarship, while her collective representations of women not only helped to expand the repertoire of women's biography but also compiled an aggregate resistance to historical canons. Jameson's varied oeuvre becomes coherent when viewed as a range of contributions to a prosopography of women, anticipating later feminist criticism. Yet Jameson both represented and suffered the limitations, even the policing function, of public recognition of heroines of culture within this idiom.

Characteristics of a Woman Critic

Anna Jameson modeled a quest for Anglo American middle-class women—in person and in publications. She was one of the first celebrity intellectuals, yet her current obscurity accords with the neglect of most records of women. Jameson contributed to a number of genres that were inviting to women writers in her day, but the narrowing definition of literary genres has since worked against her: she was neither novelist nor poet, nor did she produce monographic history or biography. Further, Jameson modeled her own narrative persona as sisterly instructor, a type ill-adapted to survive into the twentieth century. And finally, her tragicomic fate was spelled in part by her biographical construction by other women writers; the network of recognition that she helped to weave ensnared her.

First the question of genre: as I noted in the introduction, Jameson contributed to several ongoing categories of collective biography: the glamour album, *Memoirs of the Beauties of the Court of Charles II* (1833)[452]; the lives of women with ties to great men, *Memoirs of the Loves of the Poets* (1829)[455]; and studies of queens, *Memoirs of Celebrated Female Sovereigns* (1831).[453] Models of royalty and celebrated beauty or muse-like power in different ways belie the universal domestic destiny of woman, as do the holy women featured in her later work.[5] In literary criticism, *Characteristics of Women* was an innovation, followed by Mary Cowden Clarke's and Fanny Kemble's studies of Shakespeare, that helped to build a pulpit for Julia Kavanagh, Margaret Oliphant, and other critics later in the century and that was eventually echoed in images-of-women criticism since the 1970s. Jameson also kept pace in the 1840s with ambitious historiography intended for general readers by such historical biographers as Agnes and Elizabeth Strickland, Louisa Stuart Costello,

Mary Ann Everett Green Wood, and Elizabeth Ellet. Jameson's comparable project built on years of study in galleries in England and Europe and followed several guidebooks of her own, including essays first published in the *Penny Magazine* in 1841 and collected as *Memoirs of Italian Painters* (1845).[6] *Sacred and Legendary Art*[456] was a great success in the new line of popular art history (Alexis François Rio had shown the way), and she added to it a series of related studies, *Legends of the Monastic Orders* (1850), *Legends of the Madonna* (1852),[451] and *The History of Our Lord, as Exemplified in Works of Art* (1864), completed after her death by Lady Eastlake.[7] Jameson also contributed significantly to the genre of women's personal narratives and travels, emulating above all Madame de Staël.[8] In this plethora of works, Jameson covers most of the territory, apart from poetry and drama, available to a woman of letters in her day.

To later readers, Jameson's works can appear veiled in excessive humility, as in her prefatory expressions of a "timidity almost painful" and of ambitions no greater than those of a "mere compiler." Yet even in an early and especially apologetic volume, *Memoirs of the Loves of the Poets* (1829),[455] she asserted that "it is for women I write" and proceeded to judge canonical writers and their societies according to their veneration for good women (Greeks and Romans fare very poorly [22, vii]). Her position indeed dissents from scholarly objectivity, appealing rather to an authority of experience that at the same time admits its own construction. There would be, she asserted, "less egotism in simply expressing, . . . what I thought and felt," since "no one has a right to clothe . . . opinions" as though they were "universal" (viii). In every publication, in various modes of address, Jameson plays the leader of a feminine audience striving together toward cultural attainment, though at times it is difficult to distinguish her from more sublime figures offering lessons rather alien to the salon. The instructive quest in Jameson's work is always a collaborative journey beyond domestic boundaries. All her works are particularly addressed to women readers on matters pertinent to the woman question, while they chart an educational trajectory beyond the traditions mapped by men.[9]

Gerardine Macpherson suggests a biographical source for the persona of sisterly leader that presides in Jameson's works.[10] From the time that Anna's father, an Irish painter, brought her and her mother to England, leaving two younger sisters temporarily behind in Dublin, she seems to have felt "chosen" for "great adventure." Macpherson describes Anna "as the leader of the little troop" of sisters (two more were born in England). She "evidently exercised her power with . . . unquestioned and beneficent despotism." Macpherson recounts childhood episodes, such as the plan to pursue their parents who were traveling in Scotland, which have the elements of Jameson's later modeling: a display of learning beyond her years or her sex; a desire to penetrate forbidden zones; a need to narrate what she has discovered and to prompt other domestic inmates to action (*Memoirs*, 4–23).[11]

Jameson's works depend on an audience prepared to emulate this persona of head girl, senior acolyte. The dialogue that begins *Characteristics of Women* stages the rhetorical challenge faced by a woman writing about women's cultural roles to a resistant male audience. Alda's first words are: "You will not listen to me?" Medon, with "mock airs of gallantry" (ix–x),[450] suspects Alda of having "written a book to maintain the superiority of your sex over ours." Alda refuses to claim such "superiority, or speculat[e] on the rights of women"; such views are "quite out of date" (xi). Rather, she speaks from experience and observation: "The condition of women in society . . . is false in itself, and injurious to them, . . . the education of women . . . is founded in mistaken principles." Alda proposes to argue through biographical narratives, leaving "readers to deduce the moral themselves" (xii–xiii).[12] Like Mary Beton's elusive fish of thought in *A Room of One's Own*, Alda's moral is "a very deep one, which those who seek will find" (xl). Such indirection, coupled with Alda's discriminating critical skills, helps to remodel Medon and his cohort within Alda's audience: "I am now prepared to listen in earnest," he concludes (xl).[13]

Alda, an ingénue fearlessly reaching for the fruits of knowledge, also introduces *Visits and Sketches at Home and Abroad* (1834),[458] which Medon at first mistakes for a feminine cliché, another "'*Sentimental Travels in Germany*' on hot-pressed paper." But Alda earnestly defends her compendium of dialogues, travels in Munich, Nuremburg, and Dresden, and "sketches" on English subjects (v–vi). Alda demonstrates that the feminine medium can not only influence but instruct as well, and Medon assents: "If nations . . . learn to love and sympathize with each other, it will be through the medium of you women" (17–19).[14] Alda as tour guide and docent is kin to the more complex medium of the fascinating *Winter Studies and Summer Rambles in Canada* (1838),[459] who tracks down demographics and regional history and advises about the roads from Toronto and the writings of Schiller but who turns in a moment to sibylline effusion. Her "journalising," addressed to her beloved friend Ottilie von Goethe, vacillates between diversion and instruction, but she presents both aims as efforts to lend purpose to her suffering sojourn. "Before the languid heart gasp and flutter itself to death . . . let us see what can be done," and so she undertakes to translate Eckerman's *Conversations with Goethe*: "something to try my strength,—and force and fix my attention" and the strength and attention of her readers as well.[15]

Far from pastimes, such winter studies rescue women who share this narrator's position, who have been raised in a hothouse only to "pass their lives in the arctic zone" when the supposed "destiny" of happy marriage and motherhood fails—bitter words from Jameson in icebound Toronto, on the verge of a formalized separation from her husband.[16] She makes a broad claim for female agency in a world where chivalrous protection fails: "The more paths opened to us, the less fear that we should go astray" (118–20).[17] Vigorous as her intellectual exercise has been, Jameson gains daring and independence in her summer rambles: "Westward Ho!" (359). Sojourning among Europeanized Native Americans, she represents herself as though in precolonial contact, hurtling down the Sault Ste. Marie in a canoe, a sensation of "giddy, breathless, delicious excitement." As "the first European female who had ever performed it," she is embraced as an honorary Chippewa and renamed "the woman of the bright foam" in their language (461–62).

Incongruous as it might seem for Mrs. Jameson to model the European woman leaping rapids and going native, it is characteristic of her more scholarly escapades as well to culminate in thrilling dislocations. In the scholarly *Sacred and Legendary Art,* she introduces herself as the scout: "Like a child that has sprung on a little way before its playmates, and caught a glimpse through an opening portal of some varied Eden within . . . ; and . . . runs back and catches its companions by the hand and hurries them forwards . . . ; even so it is with me:—I am on the outside, not the inside, of the door I open" (1:38).[456] These words hover above a delicate drawing of a winged angel of indeterminate sex, playing on a bagpipe ("After Gaudenzio Ferrari, at Saronno"). The figure is not intended as a self-portrait, but it does designate Jameson's presence as skillful, hands-on witness while it adds to the collective personality of the work.[18] What could have been received as a flirtation with popery had paid off, yet in *Legends of the Madonna* (1852)[451] she still warns of the risks of exploring Catholic history: "I have had to ascend most perilous heights, to dive into terribly obscure depths"; together "*we* must take the higher ground, perilous though it may be" in order to survey Madonna legends across epochs and cultures (xvi, xviii; my emphasis).[451] The introductory persona of venturesome but self-deprecating sister was crucial to the acceptance of Jameson's works, belying her revisionary power.

Though Jameson's scholarly works promise readers cultural literacy more than self-help, the power of example is a coveted by-product. Her instruction parallels that of inspirational readers such as Fry and education reformers such as More, with the difference that she primarily serves women of her own class. Her role as a woman addressing a female audience and redistributing the wealth of art may have prevented her later canonization as a sage in what Dorothy Mermin calls "the arena of high-prestige nonfictional prose."[19] Yet Jameson's contemporaries positively welcomed her incursions compared to the barricades erected by twentieth-century literary history. The woman who could be recalled as simply "the great Victorian popularizer of early Christian art" was at one time Ruskin's senior competitor.[20] She modeled a pre-Arnoldian function of criticism, before a much-noted professionalization excluded from aesthetic authority those who tended to be figured either as commodities or as consumers.[21] On the other side of this divide, it may be difficult to recognize the power of criticism addressed to the amateur reader, of biography unabashedly didactic or socially constructive. Her critical habits were the respected norm in her day. Narrative study of Shakespeare's characters was taken seriously throughout the eighteenth and nineteenth centuries.[22] Jameson also rode a wave of enthusiasm for early Christian art in the wake of the Tractarian movement. According to Mrs. Steuart Erskine in 1916, Jameson's books remained popular, outlasting "many more pretentious essays in criticism."[23] But between the 1920s and 1980s, Jameson sank almost completely below the horizon, gaining only occasional references in Shakespeare studies, art history, or Canadian studies.[24] Any resurrection of Jameson in recent decades has been due to her role as woman writer, most often focused on *Winter Studies,* claimed as a founding text of Canadian literature, or her lectures in support of Victorian vocational feminism.[25] Yet as though she does not meet the implicit criteria of our own model lists, she gets small mention in feminist studies of Victorian culture.[26]

Though Jameson is hardly the predecessor that leaps to mind for feminist critics today, she developed feminist positions that seem very close to home. She denounces "the universal bruise, the putrefying sore" of the sexual double standard and exploitation of women in every country (364–65).[459] Her studies anticipate familiar kinds of feminist writing, from "images of women" to gynocriticism to feminist social history, folklore, and even comparative religion: in *Legends of the Madonna,*[451] she notes the appropriation of ancient forms of "the mother-Goddess" in Christian Madonna worship and unearths a redeeming heritage in European folk traditions, a faith in a "prevailing . . . feminine character of beneficence, purity, and power" (xvii–xix).[27] Progressively more feminist in each of her works, as Judith Johnston has shown, Jameson draws on both Wollstonecraft's rationalist arguments for equal education and a Romantic "difference" feminism that circulated alongside the conservative discourse of woman's mission in the 1830s and 1840s. The question of political rights for women seemed moot, but she worked to educate middle-class women to pursue a "vocation . . . for social progress" (23).[457] Like other Victorian architects of woman's "mission," Jameson maintained that women could manage social reform like housekeeping "on a larger scale" (29–33).[457] In the process, Jamesonian sisters would collaborate in the public work of men in a sort of universalized middle class.

Meanwhile, Jameson served as a missionary of high culture, offering literate women the "unpaid-for" education that Woolf traced in brief "lives" of Victorian reforming women in *Three Guineas* (78). Yet Jameson's promotion of middle-class women's rights and opportunities combined with a more sweeping cultural critique and an exaltation of feminine self-immolating power. Her critical performance can be startling, verging on the blasphemous "confusion of boundaries" of a cyborg or the Medusa, strangely at odds with her apparent aim of reproducing women as exemplary individuals.[28] The idea of selflessness may build to utopian visions of precapitalist communities of women and of nonpatriarchal folk culture.[29] While Jameson promoted her persona as a role model, an exception leading others toward distinctions of taste and rare knowledge, her representations of characteristics of women provide far more than a female appendix to history as the biographies of great men.

The sort of feminist scholarship that recovers exemplary women is often presumed to depend on a naive faith in autonomous identity or transparent representation. Jameson recuperates a biographical heritage for women, however, that is neither consistently individualistic nor simply realist, certainly not essentially sexed as female. She gives name, face, and animation to an intersubjective, compiled history of women: a prosopography in my terms. Eschewing the attempt at a universal monographic history, she recuperates contested legends and overlapping typologies in order to model the interpretative skills of the amateur as well as the historical power of exemplary women. The hope is that an audience response—reawakened sympathies and competencies to "read" historical representations—will also reconstruct female subjectivity or "characteristics of women." The exemplary feminist scholar herself participates in the search for the coveted moment in which a representative woman may be transposed from object to subject of historical discourse, from outsider to insider in the traditions.

Mutual Multibiography

Where does this assiduous presenter of female prosopographies belong in the recovered traditions of women writers? I have suggested that the form of series of life narratives underlies many contributions to feminist discourse. While the biographical bent of much feminist criticism is no secret, the clustering of such representations in groups deserves more remark. Certainly, argument by examples shapes the rhetoric of many contributions to women's studies, whether or not a publication is structured on narratives of named individuals. Moreover, literary anthologies, with their short lives of the contributors, have been a much-handled tool of intervention on women's behalf. Landmarks of academic feminist criticism similarly exhibit eminent women writers through a sequence of chapters. Ellen Moers's *Literary Women* (like other classics of feminist literary criticism) incorporates formal characteristics of collective biography. Moers picked out patterns in the carpet of women's biographical traditions hidden since the nineteenth century. Within a few pages of discussion of the myth of de Staël's *Corinne,* she interweaves a coterie of women, analogous to a male literary movement. As I shall show, the relations among these women of letters were actually full of bias and tension and had lasting effect on their reputations. The cast of characters in Moers's drama includes the "Yankee Corinna," Margaret Fuller (177); the "English Corinne," Anna Jameson; and Fanny Kemble and Elizabeth Barrett Browning, both Jameson's friends who longed to win poetic laurels in Italy (187–88). Beyond these, the circles extended to Harriet Martineau, friend of Charlotte Brontë who overlapped with Jameson and Fuller in America; and Margaret Oliphant, who later offered acerbic comments on Martineau, on Charlotte Brontë (with her Corinne-like Vashti in *Villette*), and on the whole vain performance of literary heroism and citations of famous women. In unraveling the serial biographical recognition, the intercalated mutual reference among these women, I am acutely aware that like Moers I will create a crowded effect that is nevertheless partial and exclusive. As in literary canon building for centuries, the critic is impelled, I admit, by the Higher Gossip.[30]

My civic purpose in reconstructing this attenuated coterie is to illustrate the effect of collective life narratives of women of letters, who as subjects, presenters, and audience mutually shape women's cultural agency. It is an old girl network that long precedes second-wave feminist commitments, and that exposes the limitations of the obligatory memorialization and recovery of "our" role models.[31] As invested as each woman necessarily was in customs of certifying women's cultural achievements, Jameson, Oliphant, and others sometimes suggest that any list of examples is supererogatory, even as they list examples—they waive a catalog by sketching its outline. At the same time, they reflexively censure contenders for the scarce positions in such catalogs. Such mutual criticism, albeit similar to the contention among any cultural authorities, is symptomatic of the handicaps placed on the public endeavors of women at that time. Anna Jameson, while not the first, was the most prominent to familiarize a British reading public with German culture and with early Italian art, ahead of her friend Carlyle and her sometime associate Ruskin. Yet the networking and competition among the Victorian (male) sages produced more lasting rewards than that among Jameson and her female peers and disciples.

I begin this anecdotal multibiography at the intersection of North American travel, a crucial location for claiming a role for women as cultural critics and as negotiators at the point of racial contact. Anna Jameson is often recalled as a sort of international mentor; her *Winter Studies and Summer Rambles in Canada* [459] is often grouped with the travels of two sisters of those biographers of queens, Agnes and Elisabeth Strickland: Catherine Parr Traill's *The Backwoods of Canada* (1836), and Susanna Moodie's *Roughing It in the Bush* (1852).[32] More celebrated even in their day than Traill or Moodie were the famous travelers Jameson and her friends or acquaintances Fanny Kemble, Harriet Martineau, and Margaret Fuller. Fanny Kemble, the young actress friend to whom Anna Jameson dedicated *Characteristics of Women* in 1832, took a starring tour of the Eastern seaboard in that year before marrying a slaveholder, and she met Harriet Martineau during the latter's visit to the United States in 1834–36. Kemble's early and late memoirs and her *Residence on a Georgian Plantation* dispute Martineau's observations about the South, though Kemble was also an ardent abolitionist.[33] In late 1836, Anna Jameson visited Canada for several months, during which time she read advance excerpts of Martineau's *Society in America.* Jameson's *Winter Studies* notes that Martineau's comments on America bespeak "a good woman" who has written in "a tone . . . of high principle and high feeling . . . which has added to my admiration of her" (251).[459]

Margaret Fuller, who met Martineau in Boston in 1835 but missed Jameson's brief sojourn there, had her own ambitions to join this growing generic circle. Fuller wrote an impassioned letter to Jameson asking for details of Goethe's life for a biography Fuller was writing (Jameson did not reply). Fuller's own travel memoir, *Summer on the Lakes,* emulating Jameson's journey westward, cites Jameson's materials on Ojibwa folklore, which were based on Jameson's "adoption" by an extended family of Native American women and European missionary men, the Johnsons and Schoolcrafts.[34] "Mrs. Jameson made such good use of her brief visit to these regions, as leaves great cause to regret that she did not stay longer and go farther" (191). Fuller's *Woman in the Nineteenth Century* (1844), which consists in large part of a quilt of "the shining names of famous women" (296), repeatedly refers to Anna Jameson.

Fuller relies on the rhetoric of prosopography to establish the claims of woman "to take her turn in the full pulsation" of human progress (252). Men have been eager to honor exceptional women: "In any age a Semiramis, an Elizabeth of England, a Catharine of Russia [*sic*], makes her place good" even if she is rather "bad" herself (note the Carlylean conversion of names into kinds [266]). Fuller confronts an oversupply of female eminence: "I could swell the catalogue of instances far beyond the reader's patience" (275)—and Fuller's text continues for more than a hundred pages, or three-quarters of the whole, surveying such examples as Mary Wollstonecraft (284), George Sand (284), and Anna Jameson (319–20). Fuller notes that Dr. Channing was persuaded to campaign for justice for women by "the progress of Harriet Martineau through this country, . . . and the visit of Mrs. Jameson," who exhibited "dignified courage . . . in taking up the defence of her sex" (308). Fuller writes, "Mrs. Jameson is a sentimentalist . . . but she is full of talent. . . . Her opinions . . . are sometimes inconsistent." Fuller praises above all her willingness to decry prostitution, a topic most women fear to touch (319). Jameson finally met Fuller in Rome but referred to her only a few times in letters and memoirs.[35]

In their auto/biographies as in their travel writings, Jameson, Martineau, Fuller, and Oliphant took care to regulate each other's performances. As cultural arbiters and ambassadors, these women seem to have had an incentive to belittle any one woman's efforts. Martineau is the harshest judge of her fellow women writers (with Oliphant a close second). The intertextual relation between Martineau and Fuller is as tangled as any among these eminent women. In the *Autobiography* (1877) Martineau writes, "In Margaret Fuller's Memoirs there is a letter which she declared she sent to me, after copying it into her common-place book . . . a condemnatory criticism of my 'Society in America'" for its abolitionism. Martineau denies that this was the same letter as the one she received. "I wish she had mentioned it to me when my guest some years afterwards, or that my reply had appeared with her criticism."[36] The dead memoirist, Fuller, should not control the dialogue. Martineau's own posthumous last word in turn provoked an apologia for the predeceased woman of genius. In *Our Famous Women,* Kate Sanborn pays tribute to Fuller, typologically, as Sappho, "this modern Hypatia, this Yankee Corinne, this feminine Socrates, and nineteenth-century Sybil," "an Oriental priestess" in "Puritan" "straight jacket" (295, 299, 297).[758] Sanborn reprints a recommendation from Elizabeth Cranch, who applies to Fuller what Elizabeth Barrett Browning said of George Sand, "Thou large-brained woman, and large-hearted man" (301). Although Sanborn sympathetically recounts Fuller's struggles to attain her ideal of eloquence even when Carlyle would not let a word in edgewise (311), Sanborn also transcribes the attack on Fuller in Martineau's *Autobiography* (omitting Martineau's objection to Fuller's obnoxious letter). Thus Martineau, repeated in Sanborn: "While Margaret Fuller and her adult pupils sat 'gorgeously dressed,' . . . fancying themselves the elect of the earth," others were devoting themselves to saving the Republic. Worse than Fuller's "metaphysical idealism" was her mockery of practical advocates like Martineau. The "mischief" might have been "spared," Martineau suggests, if Fuller could have married someone early in the United States rather than in Italy; "It is the most grievous loss . . . , the deferring of Margaret Fuller's married life so long." Sanborn with good reason comments that Martineau gave "every one a black eye as she passed them" (311–12).

Martineau certainly took effective aim at Jameson. A posthumous decline in Jameson's reputation was given a shove by Martineau's 1861 obituary of Jameson, reprinted in her *Biographical Sketches*.[37] Martineau places Jameson in a rearguard and attributes her peculiar "views of life and love" to a "desolate wedded life" (115). The study of Shakespeare's heroines, though "charming," conveys "no philosophy" or substance (116). Naturally Jameson was lionized in America, "where the characteristics of women" are all the rage "and sentiment flourishes." Jameson, "with her Irish vehemence," gushed about German and Italian art and English literature, whereupon she "rushed into a wild Indian life." Her Canadian travel memoir marked a downturn to explicit feminist grievance (117). If Jameson had not been so hungry for attention, she might have been a great reformer, while her art criticism was a useful popularization. Later generations will now and then recall that there was once a "fervent, unreasoning, generous, accomplished Mrs. Jameson among the lights of the time" (119). Martineau was prescient; this is the Jameson that has prevailed until recently.

Martineau's slighting of practically everyone derives in part from an awareness that a canon of women is always in the works, always at the margins of a canon of men. Certainly her jabs at Jameson suggest such an awareness. In her *Autobiography* she lists Jameson among several examples of literary women whose "palpable vanities may . . . discredit the pursuits of other women," even counterbalancing the "really able women," Joanna Baillie, Mary Somerville, Elizabeth Barrett Browning. True, the odd vanities of a few conspicuous women of letters do less harm than the widespread vanities of men of letters because "the time is not yet arrived when national interests" depend on the "dignity of individual women of genius" (1:265–66). On the contrary, that time had long since arrived, according to many midcentury compilers.

According to Martineau, excessive emotion, desire for adulation, and the female fate of marriage mar the careers of Jameson and Fuller. But this was not always Martineau's formula. Apart from objections to the heart hunger in Charlotte Brontë's novels, Martineau exalts the novelist: "In her high vocation she had, in addition to the deep intuitions of a gifted woman, the strength of a man, the patience of a hero, and the conscientiousness of a saint" (*Biographical*

Sketches, 45).[38] This echo of Barrett Browning's praise of Sand—later repeated, we have seen, in Sanborn's praise of Fuller—anticipates Virginia Woolf's praise of Brontë's sister Emily for androgynous disregard of social constraints. Martineau similarly praises Charlotte Brontë for avoiding the feminine foible, "regard to opinion, to appreciation, to applause" (*Biographical Sketches,* 46).

Any one thread leads to many others in these interwoven lives. As in published volumes of biographies, the same subject appears in antithetical guises or associations, while actions or characterizations migrate from one person to another. Thus Margaret Oliphant creates an image of Charlotte Brontë that resembles Martineau's views of Jameson and Fuller: talent misfired and strangely celebrated; unhealthy preoccupation with the grievances of the sex. In the coauthored collection *Women Novelists of Queen Victoria's Reign,* Oliphant writes of Brontë's works that they are marred by the "philosophy of life . . . of a schoolgirl, . . . the haste and passion of a mind self-centred and working in the narrowest orbit" (5).[607] The professional promoter of her own career or the vainglorious performer; the reclusive genius or the naive sentimentalist—the optional roles seem perilous. And as both Martineau and Oliphant suggest, the parade of women of genius may have little effect, either on "national interests" or the status of women in general.

Martineau and Oliphant, though they shared ambivalence about Jameson as person and as mode of feminist argument, each enabled the production of the only life of Jameson published before the twentieth century (there have been only two since). *Memoirs of the Life of Anna Jameson* was composed by Gerardine Macpherson, Jameson's niece, who figured prominently in the Roman expatriate community that had included Margaret Fuller, Harriet Hosmer, Elizabeth Barrett Browning, and in the younger generation, Margaret Oliphant. In her preface, Macpherson remarks on the family's reluctance to share the troubled private life of the great art historian and advocate of women. At last she decided a biography was needed to counteract *The Autobiography of Harriet Martineau,* "in which my aunt . . . is made the subject of various depreciatory animadversions."[39] In direct contradiction of Martineau's "posthumous malice," Macpherson notes that Martineau's correspondence with Jameson was mutually admiring and cordial (*Memoirs,* ix–x). Indeed, Martineau even appears as an involuntary coauthor of the memoir of Jameson, as Macpherson transcribes lengthy correspondence and narrates amicable visits between the two women. With some asperity, Macpherson observes that "Miss Martineau's disapproval of the publication of letters is well known," yet as "Miss Martineau's representatives have not themselves respected" this "wish" (the *Autobiography* includes correspondence), Macpherson reproduces the epistolary exchange, within a friendly "literary circle," concerning Martineau's cure by mesmerism (205–9).

The preface to *Memoirs of the Life of Anna Jameson* is followed by a glowing memorial to Macpherson herself, who "has not lived to see it through the press" (xiii). It was Margaret Oliphant who stepped in to do the final rites of her friend and her friend's aunt. After a brief eulogy, Oliphant notes that Macpherson had to be persuaded to preserve her aunt's many appreciative comments on her niece, which the "modesty of [Jameson's] biographer" would have deleted. Macpherson, again, had been a youthful collaborator on illustrations of saints' legends and artists' lives but was unwilling to step forward as autobiographer as well as biographer (*Memoirs,* xiii–xvii, 228–35). Thus a chain of life narratives adds links made of the varied materials that may be published of women. In turn, Oliphant's own autobiography underwent a radical amputation by amanuenses anxious to preserve privacy and to shape a formally flexible text into an account of fortitude under a series of bereavements.[40]

I suggest that such invidious mutual constructions and highly edited posthumous records result from the fact that the boundaries between subjects, presenters, and audience seemed especially permeable in contemporary representation of women's roles, whereas the barrier to the masculine tradition seemed nearly impenetrable. Each woman could readily move from the role of admiring reader to biographer to the subject of others' tributes, knowing how muffled the chorus of praise for famous women became in the vast hall of fame. Willy-nilly, they would be grouped together in constrained comparison. A single life alters chameleon-like in new settings, serving different comparative functions.

If not for the unreliability of mutual censure and recognition, we might find a certain justice in the ways that Martineau's last words on Jameson were subjected to emendation. Martineau was at times paired with Jameson in contemporary accounts. Thus, in *A New Spirit of the Age,* an 1844 anthology of living models who were female as well as male, the convention of diptychs of feminine types serves for a chapter, "Harriet Martineau and Mrs. Jameson." Both win praise for advancing the cause of women. "The one represents the intellect of the question, the other the feeling; one brings to it an acute abstract comprehension, the other all the sympathies of a woman."[41] This antithetical pair met again nearly fifty years later, when Margaret Oliphant assembled her canon-building study, *The Victorian Age of English Literature,* and saw to it that many women of letters were recognized.[42] Here Jameson appears not as the unhappily married vain celebrity or feminist reformer, but as the author of an ambitious series on religious art: "The books are beautiful books, full of entertainment as well as instruction. . . . Not even Mr. Ruskin has made them out of date" (2:529). Oliphant's Martineau, in contrast, is the author of a *History of the Thirty Years' Peace* (1850), which has an "enervating" tone of "preachment" (1:183–84). Jameson's date in fact was about to expire, although the Victorian coterie of women of letters was perpetuated in some form throughout the twentieth century. Jameson herself is a rare subject (she surfaces in encyclopedic volumes[5; 362] and collections of writers or feminist pioneers[372; 621]), as is Oliphant, a cultural mediator of the other end of the century whose troubled family life reached print only belatedly.[306; 674] Fuller and Martineau, in contrast, had highly narratable lives (Fuller appears in at least seventeen compilations; Martineau in nineteen).[43] In such juxtaposed images, the women of letters—serving as audience, subjects, and presenters of role model narratives—shaped a vocabulary for women's careers. Through comparisons and mutual assessments, biography becomes *ad feminam* critique of the woman's public achievement.

In her own lifetime Jameson had been one of a horde of women of letters (including Fuller and Martineau) admitted to Sarah Hale's *Woman's Record*,[362] which echoes some of the terms in which Fuller and Martineau criticized the art historian. According to Hale, Jameson "has a deep sense of the dignity of her own sex; she seeks to elevate woman"; but some of her works have pernicious effects. *Memoirs of Celebrated Female Sovereigns* was based on the "wrong principle, namely, the *inferiority* of the female sex to the male"; Jameson exalts "*reason* as the highest human attribute," whereas Christians know that that honor goes instead to "*moral goodness*"—that specialty of woman and "the highest perfection of human nature" (706–7).[362] Worse perhaps are Jameson's later works, which "mislead . . . young readers" to regard "marriage a slavery, a sin, or a sorrow" because Jameson's own marriage was a calamity. Just as Martineau had done to Jameson and Fuller, Hale reads Jameson's work biographically while censuring her for forming her opinions autobiographically, that is, for projecting her individual conditions onto those of the sex in general: "Had she been fortunate (like Mrs. Howitt)" in married companionship "she would have been a shining light in the onward movement of Christian civilization . . . instead of . . . deifying the worship of the Beautiful in Art." The role of the presenter of roles must be closely supervised; Jameson's critique of marriage but apparent fealty to "man's philosophy" (706–9)[362] strike Hale as out of step with the vanguard, defined by the superior moral spirit of Anglo-Saxon Christian women. Jameson had in fact changed her views since *Celebrated Female Sovereigns* to join with the feminism if not the Evangelicalism of the day.

The gallery of noteworthy womanhood could display adversaries as though they were photographs of the same figure in different tempers. Yet the same life was capable of very different construction. One of Jameson's protégées, Bessie Rayner Parkes, collected her own biographical journalism as an album of women, *Vignettes* (1866),[621] in which Jameson shines as a brilliant art critic whose feminist activism was her crowning achievement rather than the defect Hale takes it to be. Parkes pays tribute to Jameson as "a great and good character," a "most valuable life to the social interests of England" and one that was internationally mourned (441–42).[621] Parkes describes the excitement of touring ancient Roman scenes with Jameson and reading the art there like "plain writing" to her imagination (446) or, on another occasion, witnessing Jameson's elderly participation in the 1857 Social Science Meeting at Bradford as others would later describe sighting George Eliot at an afternoon concert (447–48).

This is largely the same Jameson, though somewhat faded to later taste, who gains admittance to Ray Strachey's 1928 collective biographical history of British women's movements: "Mrs Jameson was . . . the idol of thousands of young ladies. Her books on pictures, on Shakespeare's heroines, . . . were exactly what the period admired, and with their elegant culture and their earnest feelings, and their sentimental philosophy, they had penetrated even into the most conventional homes. When she, therefore, came forward as the champion of the new cause the effect was prodigious" (89–90).[761] Yet Strachey has a later feminist's incentive to distance and typecast the old school. True, Jameson's feminist broadcasts—the published lectures *Sisters of Charity* and *The Communion of Labour* of 1855 and 1856—were made possible by grants she had earned as an authority on canonical fine arts. But it is also true that the admiration for the books on art and literature owed much to the interwoven message against the subjection of women. Nevertheless, if Jameson had become identified with the feminine powers modeled within her texts, she might easily have been cast as monstrous, gaining the sort of bad public relations that gave headaches to posthumous biographers of Margaret Fuller. Jameson preserved a benign image through a disarming authorial persona.

Characteristics of Women

Though Jameson may not seem to be lacking in our disciplinary pantheons today, her expansive models of feminine subjectivity provide a welcome antidote to some forms of canon or tradition building. Let me illustrate her practice more fully, albeit briefly. In Jameson's two most consulted and reprinted works, the studies of Shakespeare's heroines and of sacred art, she attempts a fundamental revision of the characteristics of women. If "women need in these times *character* beyond everything else," as Jameson affirmed (119),[459] she was also prepared to uphold the astounding "modifications of which the female character is susceptible" (xiii).[450] Conscientious study of canonical drama and painting seems to cover for alchemical experiments that simultaneously reflect on the reforms and revolutions that coincided with their respective publication, in 1832 and 1848.

Both *Characteristics of Women* and *Sacred and Legendary Art* obviously capitalize on the prestige of their subject matter. Jameson could rely on widespread assent to her view of Shakespeare as a divine and infallible source: "If it be in nature, why should it not be in Shakespeare?" (86);[450] more particularly, he could be exalted as "the POET OF WOMANKIND" (182, 190).[455]; 44 Similarly, she could count on respect for European art and Christian themes, though Catholicism itself was still controversial in Britain in 1848. Powerful icons endorsed by history nevertheless become, in Jameson's collections, means of restoring an apocryphal countermemory that inverts if it does not level hierarchy. By the standards of this other tradition, a woman's "qualities" are more valuable than her "attainments" (xxxiv),[450] the "poetry" of religion is superior to its dogma, and popular moral recognition of art is superior to "mere connoisseurship" (1:2–3, 10).[456] As part of a long modern trend toward privileging affective interiority, Jameson finds an audience well prepared to mirror her unorthodox response to treasures of culture. At the same time her work resists any attempt to decontextualize art or to disenfranchise the audience.

As though the order of things were still intact, both biographical compilations display a clear catalog structure. *Characteristics of Women* begins with "Characters of Intellect" (Portia, Isabella, Beatrice, Rosalind), then "Characters of Passion and Imagination" (Juliet, Helena, Perdita, Viola, Ophelia, Miranda), followed by "Characters of Affections" (Hermione, Desdemona, Imogen, Cordelia), and finally, "Historical Characters" (Cleopatra, Octavia, Volumnia, Constance of Bretagne, Queen Elinor [known as Eleanor of Aquitaine], Blanche of Castile, Margaret of Anjou, Katherine of Arragon [*sic*], and Lady Macbeth).[45] The first heroine might be the best: Portia, at least, was the favorite Shakespeare heroine of Jameson's lifelong friend, Fanny Kemble, to whom Jameson dedicated the book.[46] Lady Macbeth, coming last, is surely Portia's base opposite: "a fierce, cruel woman, brandishing a couple of daggers, and inciting her husband to butcher a poor old king" (288–89),[450] as Jameson parodies the popular view of her. The very assortment of heroines into types—like the later taxonomies such as *Gems of Womanhood*[589]—may suggest that female character must specialize in order to excel. Yet Jameson's characterizations deviate from the projected typecasting. *Sacred and Legendary Art* likewise presents a hierarchical table of types; sections resemble the spheres in medieval cosmology: "On Angels and Archangels," "The Four Evangelists," "The Twelve Apostles," and on down, in the second volume, through "The Patron Saints of Christendom," "The Virgin Patronesses," to various historically identified martyrs, hermit saints, and warrior saints. There are lists of "Emblems and Attributes," the symbolism of colors, and the names of the Archangels along with Jameson's woodcuts of works of art. Yet order resides in tension with excess; a scholar's footnotes and indexes gloss spectacular tales.

Both volumes whet an appetite for knowledge that they then chasten, challenging the narrow definition of an identity or life behind a given name. Rather than consulting the volumes as dictionaries, the reader is asked to read from beginning to end, while also immersing herself in multiple associations among a host of interrelated names. *Characteristics of Women* might enhance knowledge and appreciation of Shakespeare, but more urgently it should open vistas of female psychology to serious study. "The riddle which history presented I found solved in the pages of Shakespeare": women not as extreme types, the "fury of discord" versus "the angel of benevolence," but as "complete individuals" yet susceptible to analysis as "real people" are not (xviii–xx).[450] Just as Shakespeare and his heroines become pretexts for contemplating feminine effects, the codes of early Christian art merely initiate the lessons of *The Poetry of Sacred and Legendary Art,* as it was first titled. The collection is not what it resembles, a "mere manual of reference, or . . . catalogue"; it should be read as a "narrative" inviting "the fancy" to flow (1:vii–viii).[456] Reading with a kind of negative capability, one might revel in other appetites than the epistemophilic, other powers than the appropriative.

Both collections offer glimpses of an archive of feminine characteristics that not only instigate collaborative reading but also gainsay masculinist interpretation. Opening the Shakespeare gallery with "Characters of Intellect," Jameson affirms that "the intellect of woman bears the same relation to that of man as her physical organization—it is inferior in power, and different in kind. . . . In women . . . talent . . . is in a much greater degree modified by the sympathies and moral qualities" (11).[450] What need for superiority in large-motor functions in the realm of aesthetic response? Performing herself as a "character of intellect," perhaps, she is authorized to correct "signal mistakes" of "men of genius." Schlegel is denounced for describing Portia as "clever" (at least in translation): "What an epithet to apply to this heavenly compound of talent, feeling, wisdom, beauty, and gentleness!" Jameson attributes Hazlitt's dislike of Portia to "his predilection for servant-maids" (12–13)—turning the biographical weapon back on the biographical critic, perhaps. In addition to more reasoned debates with such critics as Dr. Johnson, "Professor Richardson," Goethe, and Coleridge, Jameson exploits her assured allusions to European literature and art. At times, she rivals Shakespeare as redactor, as in her lengthy biography of Constance of Bretagne (229–47). Jameson serves as a curator who has brought out of storage many neglected or misinterpreted models.

These models may be presented as realist-humanist individuals. Such is Jameson's tactic for reawakening her reader's interest in Saint Gregory Nazianzen "as a boy educated between a tender mother, . . . and a lovely and saintly sister!" (1:340)[456]—a model perhaps for Olive Schreiner's domesticated Gregory Nazianzen Rose. Yet on closer inspection both heroines and saints elude realist identification. Though she claims of Shakespeare's heroines as she would of saints that "we seem to have known them previously" (70),[450] she does not simply literalize her models as real people; recognition, rather, is composed of collective characteristics.

Thus under the heading "Characters of Passion," the heroines are arranged in a sequence "to rise, in the scale of ideality and simplicity, from Juliet to Miranda"; having said this, Jameson turns to an autobiographical impression of an evening view above Florence:

> A transparent vapour or exhalation, . . . as rich as the pomegranate flower . . .
> rolled through the valley, and the very earth seemed to pant with warm life
> beneath its rosy veil. . . . The faint perfume of trees and flowers, and now and
> then a strain of music . . . completed the intoxication of the senses. But . . .
> immediately above this scene hung the soft crescent moon—alone . . . : and as
> that sweet moon to the glowing landscape beneath it, such is the character of
> Miranda compared to that of Juliet. (131–32)[450]

The synaesthetic intoxication of a Juliet-Persephone seems far more alluring than the chaste Miranda-Diana, in spite of the latter's ascendancy in the "scale." The surreal effect here is quite at odds with any attempt to "realize" a character.

Thus there might be limitless seductive series of likenesses-in-contrast: "The wit of Portia is like attar of roses, rich and concentrated; that of Rosalind, like cotton dipped in aromatic vinegar; the wit of Beatrice is like sal-volatile, and that of Isabel like the incense wafted to heaven" (12–13).[450] So much for essential womanhood. By convention fluid and elusive, femininity also customarily does not set its own economies of difference, as Luce Irigaray has discerned.[47] The sequence of similes tests the mimetic limit as it invites the reader to sample yet again each woman's indescribable wit in unending pursuit of the differences among them.

Jameson similarly assorts iconography, rare facts, and lore under the disputed names of saints. In the manner of Scott, the Grimms, or Andrew Lang, she recuperates oral traditions, depicting a rather Gothic scene of populist resistance to (Catholic) patriarchy. During "the 'Dark Ages'" only the legends, "in which the tenderness, the chastity, the heroism of woman, played a conspicuous part," supported women and the common people against vile tyranny. The tide of popular faith was too strong for orthodoxy and "reversed the outward order" of Church and state power. Early painters could depend on "certain associations and certain sympathies in the minds of the spectators" (1:2–10).[456] In more recent times, the common property of faith had been reified as art objects torn "from their consecrated localities" and accumulated by the church and aristocracies and, more recently, the wealthy middle classes. The gentleman's classical education contributed to a "general ignorance" of "the subjects of Mediaeval Art" (1:8), while an art history that consisted in naming artists and schools or ideal forms belied the original meaning of indigenous works. Scholarly commodification must yield to an irrepressible faith in a legend such as Saint Ursula's—a sort of role model fest as the saint's martyrdom was instantly emulated by eleven thousand virgins—a legend "especially delightful to the women." The multiple versions of the tale and paintings of Ursula yield a sense more of the capacity to signify than of a singular identity. The name, the core *fabula*, and key attributes flourish in each generation's desire for variations on them (2:501–16).

While thus challenging singular identity, Jameson's collections seek to model character, albeit in ways far from practical. If the compilation of Shakespeare's heroines is intended to have a ripple effect on her audience, it is scarcely meant to induce literal emulation, any more than hagiography is a guide to everyday living. Jameson the learned venturer leads her peers not only through their lessons but also toward powers of horror, the menace of Medusa. She compiled with a vengeance. In these collections the witty survivors are outnumbered by the saintly victims and vengeful furies. But I would suggest that the latter are shadow representations of the daylight models of wise and sensible companions and that both together enhance the powers gained for all types of womanhood in the Jamesonian catalog. The forthright heroines at the Portia end of the spectrum solicit the martyrs and viragos at other extremes, much as the heroines of the Judith school consort with ministering women in the

Victorian prosopographies displayed above. In Jameson's poetic prose, the effect may dislodge the symbolic order; in de Lauretis's terms, "the woman, fixed in the position of icon, spectacle, or image" also stands outside the frame.[48]

Jameson rhetorically demands, "That Magdalene, weeping amid her hair, who once spoke comfort to the soul of the fallen sinner—that Sebastian arrow-pierced, whose upward ardent glance spoke of courage and hope to the tyrant-ridden serf . . . can they speak to *us* of nothing save . . . correct drawing and gorgeous colour?" (1:10).[456] The spectacle of sacrifice may suggest extraordinary recursive power. Take Desdemona: "To see her fluttering like a cherub in the talons of a fiend!" Yet she "is not weak; . . . the mere presence of goodness and affection implies . . . power without consciousness, power without effort" (156–57). In *Winter Studies,* Jameson had satirized Coleridge's claim that Ophelia or Desdemona would be a man's choice for a wife, as though "the perfection of a woman's character is to be *characterless*" (119).[459] As models for real women, self-effaced martyrs won't do; as icons of feminine power, they serve Jameson well. Indeed, Jameson exploits the distance between contemporary models of real women and the hagiographical or legendary extreme. Canonized saints seldom figure in collective biographies published in the nineteenth century, works with varied commitments to self-help history (and Protestantism). Jameson seems to be mixing a headier brew, scaling, as she said, "perilous heights."

The female critic would appear not only to participate in the objectification of Ophelia as mortality effect—"like the exhalation of the violet, dying even upon the sense it charms—like the snowflake, dissolved in air," and so on (111)—as, perhaps, Poe's quintessential poetic topic, the death of a beautiful woman. Jameson also supplements this objectification with another narrative in which the heroine and her elusive qualities are the subjects. Such is the potential suggested in Slavoj Žižek's spectacle of the saint in a moment of hysterical resistance to "interpellation" as "pure object."[49] Similarly, Kristeva suggests that the saint's performance of abjection might rend the "veil of death" in which Western art and religion have shrouded the "oriental nothingness" of the maternal body.[50] In this manner, Jameson witnesses the jouissance of Raphael's *Madonna of San Sisto:* "an abstraction of power, purity, and love, poised on the empurpled air," gazing with "her slightly dilated, sibylline eyes, quite through the universe," foreseeing her son's sacrifice—"the visionary sword that was to reach her heart" through the baby "now resting" on her. In this elaborated ekphrasis, Mary may not seem quite the benign model of Victorian motherhood (xlii).[451] Jameson writes elsewhere of having seen this painting face-to-face in Dresden: "like the mystic Isis behind her veil"; to describe it is "like measuring the infinite, and sounding the unfathomable."[51] In other words, art and poetry epiphanically approach the immortal, as they memorialize absence and loss. Yet Jameson's prosopography reanimates as well.

Perhaps Jameson's favorite sacred heroine, Mary Magdalene, unites the sexual vulnerability and omnipotence of Desdemona and the Madonna with Portia's talent for debate among men. The "matter" of Mary Magdalene consumes an entire section of the first volume of *Sacred and Legendary Art*, right after "The Doctors of the Church," who themselves could not shake "the fast hold which the Magdalene had taken of the affections of the people." The historical woman (or women) so named has generated, over the centuries, a kind of metamodel for other legends, throwing "her mantle over all" female saints and all penitents (1:343–44).[456] The magdalen, of course, was being revived as a role model for Victorian prostitutes, but Jameson's version of the folk tale also resembles the career of a learned lady, the companion of public men, in contrast to the worldly domestic, Martha. Jameson alludes to a modern incarnation of the magdalen, an unnamed famous woman who died giving a "solemn warning . . . and whose starry crown may be seen on high even now, amid the constellations of Genius."[52] The stellar genius or the luxuriating sinner are both exalted in this legend, kin perhaps to the hysteric or witch in diverting bodily suffering into an insurgent craft.[53] In a sense the Magdalene is undead. Her story defies the law: "Poets have sung, and moralists and sages have taught, that for the frail woman there was nothing left but to die" (1:393–94).[456] But this survivor models female cultural authority rivaling the fathers.

Jameson recuperates Shakespearean "Historical Characters" less readily than she honors martyrs. Historical agents nevertheless may be presented as chain reactions of other figures of female power rather than as great individuals. Cleopatra becomes an oriental mystery as disturbing as "one of her country's hieroglyphics"; her "qualities . . . shift, and change, . . . like the colours in a peacock's train" (193)[450] or like an "antique arabesque" (214)—rather different from the Cleopatra represented by Mary Cowden Clarke, for example (fig. 2). Even Lady Macbeth, "though so supremely wicked" (305), remains magnificent as a force field of likenesses and differences. She compares favorably with the "atrocious" Clytemnestra or the relentless Electra; her "gothic grandeur" contrasts with Medea's classical "refinement of cruelty" (306–8).[450] This difference in turn can only be registered by the contrast between da Vinci's painting of Medusa "and the Medusa of the Greek gems and bas-reliefs":

> In the painting, the horror of the subject is at once exalted and softened. . . . We gaze, until . . . the serpent hair seems to stir and glitter . . . and the head itself, in all its ghastliness and brightness, appears to rise from the canvas with the glare of reality. In the Medusa of sculpture. . . . every feature is chiselled into the most regular and faultless perfection; and amid the gorgon terrors there rests a marbly, fixed, supernatural grace, which . . . stands before us a presence, a power, and an enchantment![450, p. 308; cf. 459, p. 162]

Unlike Hélène Cixous's Medusa, or even Walter Pater's smiling Mona Lisa, this supernatural figure is not quite amused. This model for mythic female vengeance is a daunting final image in a work that has promised to serve the cause of woman through examples. In a subtler way, even the saints convey a similar threat to return the gaze. "Our puritanical ancestors chopped off the heads of Madonnas and Saints . . . *now,* are these rejected and outraged shapes of beauty coming back to us, or are we not rather going back to them?" (1:6).[456]

Jameson's images of heroic or holy women coerce like the return of the repressed. The spectator is to behold "the transfigured woman," a synchronous revelation of all art, all sacred symbols, "the end and consummation of all things" (xlii).[451] Like some more recent feminist critics, Jameson appears to urge readers "to look at the Medusa straight on," to perceive the proscribed power and beauty in "the history of all women," as Cixous puts it.[54] Yet even in ecstasy, this figure keeps her head, teaching the lessons that must restore the history of her sisters—a particular, not universal, history. The most important lessons, finally, might be skills in interpretation, as Lady Macbeth consists of a regress of performances across many styles and ages.

In her influential manifesto "The Laugh of the Medusa," Cixous prophesied that when "the repressed of culture" becomes the subject of a "new history," it will dissolve the "phallogocentric" order that equates woman with death and "Lack" (349, 353–54). It is an avowedly utopian dream of a common language that would undo the deadly myth for which Medusa stands. Cixous's feminine prosopography, with its mix of poststructuralism and Romantic neoclassicism, ventures into anonymity, becoming tributary to a "limitlessly changing ensemble" (359). As many have since pointed out, Cixous cites few women, favoring a mythic or unwritten history that features Medusa, Dido, Cleopatra, or Marguerite Duras and Colette.[55] Cixous builds a collective history for women, as so many have done, on a founding fiction of their past obliteration, adhering to the same gender ideology that dictates women's historical marginalization in the first place. The laugh of the Medusa may simply clinch the commonplace of women's historical nothingness. Jameson, instead, is also willing to instruct us to the contrary. Her instructions should be heard as part of a chorus of collections of heroines of history, rising to a crescendo through the Victorian period.

Jameson contributed to self-help history, a prosopography for Anglo American middle-class women in the middle of the nineteenth century. While the project of reassembling a women's history has expanded, a prescription of historical progress tends to demote or erase earlier contributions, as I have suggested. Anna Jameson's studies and her reception illustrate the paradoxical effects of canonical revision and recuperation. Jameson's example(s) demonstrate(s) the subject-modeling power of life narrative when audience and presenter collaborate in interpreting the transformative subject. The serpent hair of the painting comes alive, the model returns the gaze, escapes the frame, and consorts with multitudes in an unattributed but glorious tradition. Like many recent feminist scholars, Jameson sought to supplant the stereotypes with her own models "to show . . . how much of what is most fair, most excellent, most sublime among the productions of human genius, has been owing to [women's] influence, direct or indirect; and [to] call up the spirits of the dead,—those who from their silent urns still rule the pulses of our hearts—to bear witness to this truth" (1).[455]; 56 This rather ambiguous statement of purpose is characteristic of Anna Jameson's recuperative work.

To honor women's "fair . . . influence" and to summon the overpowering spirits of women past are not quite the same project. Anna Jameson served as a collaborative contributor to an ever-revised catalog of irrepressible heroines and also as an erudite woman of the bright foam and, still further, as an instructive and bonneted Medusa. Let us now praise once-famous women—the extreme heroic types and the good working models. Or, let us dissolve the panegyric of heroines in quite a different medium, the hagiographical and elegiac. These contrasting strains in Jameson's writings have been interdependent impulses of women's biographical history for centuries. Those who rely on such representational apparatus should bear in mind that the collective record absorbs all but a few names into an unregistered mass forgotten by successive generations. Jameson never set out to disappear into a ghostly, maternal past, among the unvisited tombs of feminist criticism. As her writings regain some of the consideration they deserve, perhaps she and her subjects will rouse sensational recognitions.

Chapter Five

The World's Fair Women; or, Racial Progress in the Nineteenth Century

Prosopographers of women eagerly retell the story of a great submerged force: wronged, abandoned, suppressed, forgotten, but now to be released. This rescue fantasy accords with proverbial gender dualisms in which the Other is the negative pole. Yet as the dualisms play out, the feminine may be both spirit and matter, eternal and time bound, the forsaken side of the moon and the restorative dawn. The gendered mythic history enchanted even advocates of cultural progress for women—even those who recognized different degrees of oppression among women (due to slavery, prostitution, exploited labor, colonization). For Anna Jameson as for Virginia Woolf and others in this tradition, the elegy for a universal feminine may be as compelling as the particular recognition of foremothers. It is not uncommon to find presenters depicting women as the ahistorical sex, even as they place Western upper-class women in the vanguard of a history that leaves most traditional cultures in the dust.[1] For presenters in the latter half of the nineteenth century, the gendering of history became more emphatically racial as well, as though to claim culture rather than nature for some white women were to place the rest of the world's population outside the zone of civilization. "By the degree of [woman's] influence and measured by her position, the comparative civilization of the greatest empires has been rightly guaged," as William Ricketts Cooper put it in 1875 (5).[198] In 1907,

Edward B. Pollard, a George Washington University professor who advocated both eugenics and women's suffrage, asserted, "The relative position which woman occupies in any country is an index to the civilization which that country enjoys" (4:vii).[899]; 2

Catalogs of exemplary Western women often unite praise with invidious comparison: other races or cultures lag behind because their women languish in obscurity. In this chapter I turn from portraying individual subjects, types, and presenters of female prosopographies in a European-American tradition to drawing out the master narratives of universal gender, national progress, and racial difference. Subjects in female collective biographies may appear to be so many snapshots of universal woman in her different phases or tempers, supporting a racist geohistory. In contrast, they may illustrate a documented history of women, suggesting that nurture more than nature has limited women's accomplishments in less advanced cultural conditions. Elements of the "scientific" racism of late-century eugenics, combined with claims for the innate superiority of women, appear in collections as early as the 1830s. Sarah Hale's midcentury encyclopedia, with its global vision of triumphal Anglo-Saxon Christian womanhood, provides a prime example. In answer to a competition among nations, *The Dictionary of National Biography* and eugenicist prosopographies build Anglo American bulwarks of cultural achievement in the 1890s–1920s. This was also a period of consolidating recognition of women by state and nation, reinforcing segregation and orientalist imperialism, as an examination of the representations of women associated with the World's Columbian Exposition of 1893 will reveal. The early anthologies of African American female biographies appeared in direct contradiction of the World's *Fair* Women. Like the models of ministry featured in chapter 3, the honorees in representations of club movements, black or white, gained their distinction through the abjection of others in need of help.

Clearly feminism, racism, and orientalism have been interdependent in the nation building and imperial projects of Britain and the United States. Feminists have long believed "that white women have a special responsibility to undo racism, given the benefits they have derived from it and given the deliberate and unwitting ways in which they have abetted it," in the recent words of Samina Najmi and Rajini Srikanth.[3] It was more in a spirit of empathetic identification than of confessed guilt that many women adopted the moral missions of abolition and reform, justified by master narratives that are repugnant today. The "causes" of relatively privileged women and of peoples of other classes, races, and nations were in fact at odds in many unacknowledged ways. The boasts of Western female progress that slander other cultures are one symptom of this incompatibility of causes. Certainly these structures of competition among relatively marginal groups are familiar by now. It remains fascinating to retrace the complex and unpredictable ways that gendered racial discourses might be deployed, early in the nineteenth century as well as late.

Anglo-Saxon Girls, Race Women

As the longstanding association and rivalry between feminist and civil rights movements indicates, the discourses of gender, racial, and national difference have been mutually constitutive in the modern West. Accordingly, printed prosopographies of the female sex not only began as national collective histories but also quickly developed into diagrams of racial hierarchy. When George Ballard compiled his *Memoirs of Several Ladies of Great Britain* in 1752, Britons had begun to forge the nation, as Linda Colley puts it.[4] By the early decades of the nineteenth century, collective pride in the status of Anglo American women often relied on disparagement of caricatured European atheists, pagans, "Orientals," savages, or others outside the pale. The American Samuel Griswold Goodrich asks, in 1844, "Shall we, in Christian countries, who make it our boast that we have elevated woman to free companionship with man, still look backward, return to the selfish philosophy of the Turk, shut woman up in the harem, and gloss over our despotism by quotations from the Swiss Diogenes?" (i.e., Rousseau [6]).[332] The self-improving exemplification in prefaces frequently relies on such compliments to the advanced historical condition of the reader, at times with reminders that she now enjoys privileges denied to members of any other race or religion or to her foremothers. "Your world is more friendly toward you than it was toward your grandmother when she was a girl," Elsie Egermeier assures girl readers in 1930 (v).[251] The constructed community, "we" or "you," forms a feminist history of progress, yet often at the expense of immigrants, workers, the less "advanced."

Though the rhetoric commending historical women often depended on the denigration of other races or cultures, it also relied on controlled integration or contact. In the introduction, I pointed out the presence of tokens of diversity in the lists. Not only the familiar Pocahontas but the occasional Sojourner Truth joins in to illustrate the united colors of woman. National differences often figure in much the same way as race, so that the modern Russian or Asian, the ancient Greek or Egyptian, the Jewess of the Bible all assist in a kind of warm-hearted, pre-Disney exoticism, complete with sexy illustrations. More explicitly, the collections honor examples that appear the reverse of xenophobic or racist. Anglo American prosopographies feature a large proportion of narratives of interracial contact, from the travels of Lady Mary Wortley Montagu, Mary Kingsley, and Anna Jameson to the missionary work of Mrs. Wilkinson and the Mrs. Judsons or the abolitionism of Lucretia Mott, Harriet Beecher Stowe, and Lydia Maria Child. Often the rise of social-scientific intervention generates model careers. Some, like Mary Carpenter, moved from reforming the "street Arabs" in Britain to the causes of the indigent and indigenous of Asia or the Middle East. Others, such as Frances Willard and Jane Addams, later moderated the increasingly heterogeneous working classes. The humanitarian tales may dream of overcoming boundaries of difference. Thus Willis J. Abbot, endorsing the racist cultural rankings of empire, romanticizes Helen Hunt

Jackson's research among the Native Americans: "She won their confidence—no easy thing with the American aborigine—and in many villages they called her 'queen.'" He notes Jackson's burial on a Colorado mountaintop, "lonely as the grave of some chieftain of that red race she served so well" (414–15).[1] Social ministry, budding social science, and investigative reporting authorized the interloper; Jackson served on a commission concerning California Indians and published a study and a novel to sway the public much as Stowe wrote *Uncle Tom's Cabin* (404–5).[488]

Undoubtedly, the subjection of other races and classes helped to authorize middle-class European women's vocations, as the biographies of ministering women attest. The ways that abolitionism in Britain and the United States helped to spark organized movements for women's rights have been well documented. Louise Michele Newman traces "social evolutionary theories" from the 1870s onward that "equated advanced civilizations with white racial superiority, and anchored both of these in sexual difference"; "the country's obsessions with 'Americanizing' the immigrant and 'uplifting' the Negro" provided a pretext for "a more powerful public role for elite, white women as civilization-workers."[5] For British women as well, aggressive imperialism in the latter half of the century recast feminine influence in evolutionary terms. At least since Gayatri Spivak's key 1985 essay "Three Women's Texts and a Critique of Imperialism," critics have examined the coordination between narratives of middle-class European women's self-development (as in *Jane Eyre*) and "imperialism and its territorial and subject-constituting project."[6] Yet colonized and colonizing women, as well as those less directly participating in imperialism, transmit and receive differential signals according to different codes. Sarah Mills and others began in the 1990s to retrace the complex conditions and relations of European women travelers and settlers in different colonial contexts, beyond nostalgic tributes to "eccentric" women who defied Victorian rules, on the one hand, and "symbolic" representations of female purity "as a moral justificatory power for the empire" on the other.[7] More recent studies such as Stephen Heathorn's *For Home, Country, and Race* have focused on imperialism at home in Britain, observing the construction of gendered and classed subjects of a global hierarchy through education and popular reading.[8] Malini Johar Schueller traces the North American "orientalisms" that contended with "internal colonization of Native Americans and African Americans" and with unstable comparative models of gendered nations and empires, preceding actual imperial expansion of the United States.[9]

The prosopographies of women often subscribe to a racist global history that had evolved since the beginnings of European exploration—well before the infusion of Darwinian evolutionary theory. The intersections of feminism and eugenics were only a further development, in the last decade or so of the nineteenth century, of notions widely held in the first decades. British and American authorities adapted German Romantic theories of race and culture to explain their nations' growing prosperity (and their subjection of indigenous or immigrant peoples) in terms of a Teutonic and Anglo-Saxon superiority; Reginald Horsman notes the racial themes of international relations circa 1850.[10] As Douglas A. Lorimer shows, a number of antebellum abolitionists subscribed to racial theories of progress, often confusing "race and culture" or associating "anatomical" with "mental and social traits" in inconsistent ways.[11] As the United States struggled over its union, it elaborated different developmental narratives of Native Americans and African Americans within the plan for Anglo-Saxon progress and nation-building.[12] These narratives stretched and twisted to accommodate the palliative role of ministering women, at times conceived as an international and interracial solidarity among all women. The usual axiom is that the best races have the most exalted women.

A vivid example of the hierarchy of races and classes according to the status of women appears in the editor's introduction to a collaboration, *True and Noble Women*:

> Whether women or men have done most to advance human progress, would be a foolish question. We might as well ask which is the most useful half of a pair of scissors. . . . But . . . women have not always been equally respected or valued. Among savage races women are made to do the hardest work. . . . Also among those classes and races of civilized society which are least removed from barbarism, the same unequal distribution of life's burdens may be noticed. In many portions of Europe, and in some parts of our own country as well, the woman may be seen bending her back to the heaviest tasks. (13–14)[270]

The most "cultivated" communities realize the injustice and "bad economy" of using the weaker sex for the hardest labor: "It is like using a watch to knock tacks into a board" (14). In contrast, "too many races. . . . went to the other extreme, and treated [women] as pets and toys. . . . Nearly all the Eastern nations, with one notable exception [the Jews] . . . shut up their women. . . . There can be no doubt that the decay and degeneracy which has overtaken the Turks, and to a lesser extent the Arabs and Hindoos, is largely owing to their irrational treatment of women" (15). Ewart, the editor, devotes some space to an account of the evolving dignity of Jewish and then Christian women, before concluding: "The following pages show that the modern Church and the British race can illustrate, not less strikingly than in ancient times, the pure lustre given to woman's nature by exalted faith" (18). Ewart's common-sense economics (illustrated through everyday tools) and his confident racial hierarchy prepare the way for a remarkably homogeneous list, including Elizabeth Fry, Sarah Martin, Sister Dora, Mary Carpenter, and Caroline Chisholm (British ministering women featured in my previous chapters).

Many examples of such timelines of merit surface in my bibliography, taking on more "scientific" authority in later decades. As Anne McClintock has shown, in "colonial discourse . . . movement through space becomes analogous to movement" through a history of civilization.[13] Accordingly, contemporary primitive races and unregenerate classes fuse feminine essences of the past, whereas advanced peoples distinguish individual women who lead the vanguard of change. The invidious cultural comparisons were not always to the home advantage, especially in antebellum American prosopographies that sensed British and European superiority.

Samuel Knapp, in a lengthy introduction to *Female Biography*,[492] reverses the usual strategy of deploring the subjection of women in ancient times and non-Christian nations; he registers the importance of women in every context, as he synthesizes biographical records in Hebrew, Greek, Latin, English, French, Italian, and Arabic. Presuming that the sexes are equal within their separate spheres, Knapp justifies a program for female education "sufficiently masculine" in its depth and extent, especially in biography and history (x). Great cultures had flourished with enfranchised women: "The Jewish history abounds in instances of female distinction" (iii); Roman law, education, and customs protected "the rights of women"; the Koran and classic Arab culture honored women and fostered their genius (iv); and even the Winnebagoes assigned their women "important offices" (v–vi).[14] Like Anna Jameson and later Ruskin, Knapp cites the "high and heroic female conduct" in Shakespearean and other drama (vi). All this was intended to guide the development of the new republic, and Knapp would provide the sourcebook of great women that America needed. Much of Knapp's career was devoted to constituting Americans ("Author of Lectures on American Literature, Advice in the Pursuits of Literature, American Biography" and a well-known history of the United States), yet he cannot fill a volume with American women. The young nation has fewer "distinguished female scholars and writers" than England, yet "it must be remembered, that our population . . . is as yet sparse, and . . . the best books, were difficult to be obtained" (vii). Knapp would educate "young ladies in our schools and at home" through an international sample of models (x).[15]

With a similar motive thirty years later, Henry Watson, in *Heroic Women of History*,[847] lays out an American program of gender modeling "to set before the women of America examples for imitation. . . . In no country upon earth is the sex so generally respected and so deferentially consulted." "Our society possesses the cream of the days of chivalry, with much more enlightenment" than old Europe. Just as men have "been made great and heroic by Plutarch's 'Lives,'" let women read "'Heroic Women' . . . and our wives, mothers, sisters, and daughters will become more renowned for resolution, fortitude, and self-sacrifice than the Spartan females were of old" (5–6). Heroism is transhistorical; the best nation—a collective (of men) that possesses the most advanced women ("our wives")—will adhere to and outdo classical models. Phebe Hanaford a generation later confirms Watson's prediction of the triumph of American women: they have "been a marvel to many in the Old World," enjoying a cultivation and "freedom which the women of European nations have never enjoyed, and of which those of Asiatic peoples never dreamed" (5).[376]

An international selection of subjects and an ideology of universal gender mask the national agendas of many collections. Yet nationally exclusive publications did at times appear, sooner in Britain than in the United States. Twelve years after Knapp's eclectic *Female Biography* for American schoolgirls, the Reverend Thomas Timpson, minister of Union Chapel in Lewisham, developed *British Female Biography* (1846)[806] for the comparable British audience. Timpson had already gathered lives of women of the New Testament (1834),[807] followed by lives of women missionaries (1841)[808]—reconfirming that cross-cultural modeling was part of the mission of female prosopographies. Timpson's British catalog is designed "to secure the benefit of his" six daughters and to be "useful to Christian families, and adapted for schools" and "SUNDAY READING" (iii–iv). The examples must be very British and irreproachably pious, according to the Gibbons-Jerment model, to increase the material as well as spiritual dower of the Timpson daughters; in consequence, most of the subjects are obscure. The frontispiece of a grandmotherly Hannah More presides over a series that might be More's own progeny: sixty-five subjects arranged like a female chain of being, under such banners as "British Queens," "British Female Martyrs," "British Learned Ladies." The spirit of the collection is epitomized by Jane Taylor's poem "To Madame de Staël," beginning, "Oh, woman, greatly gifted! why / Wert thou not gifted from on high?" (244).[806] Any young middle-class British reader might identify with one Miss Gray (1741–92), benefactor of the clergy and of the Society for Promoting Religious Knowledge among the Poor in Edinburgh, who gave a prize for the best theological essay ("many of her works of mercy will be made known only in the great day of the Lord" [291]). A Scotswoman secures her place in the order that excludes Frenchwomen and that serves the poor.

At midcentury, the promotion of national standing and "improvement" of the populace turned to various encyclopedic projects, from the Great Exhibition of 1851 to female prosopographies such as Sarah Hale's *Woman's Record*.[362]; 16 Though much less heralded than London's international collection of arts and industries, Hale's publication in 1853 of a synthesis of all national traditions of women should be recognized as an analogous project. Hale attempted nothing less than a "perfect Cyclopedia" to demonstrate "the true mission" and achievements of woman, a predigital database. While not nationalist in Timpson's manner, *Woman's Record* does rely on a narrative of racial progress that appoints American women to lead Anglo-Saxon "maternal imperialism"—in its way, a contemporary claim that sisterhood is powerful.[17] Resembling a reference work in its plain binding, alphabetical columns (with excerpts of the subjects' writings), 230 modest wood-engraved portraits, and various appendixes, *Woman's Record; or, Sketches of All Distinguished Women from the Creation to A.D. 1868; Arranged in Four Eras* contains "about *two thousand six hundred names*" (almost a thousand pages) in the third edition (ix), intended "to give WOMAN her true Saxon *name*" (vii). Hale's sample necessarily is skewed to serve this prophetic goal: fewer than two hundred of her subjects "are from heathen nations, yet these constitute at this moment nearly three-fourths of the inhabitants of the globe, and for the first four thousand years, with the single exception of the Jewish people, were the world" (ix). Readers may object to omissions and to the preponderance of celebrities; "millions of the sex whose names were never known beyond the circles of their own home influences, have been as worthy of commendation." Yet most of the missing women have not been commendable because they have not been rescued by the Bible, which is "the only guarantee of woman's rights, and the only expositor of her duties" (viii–x).

Americanists know Hale as a notorious antiabolitionist and opponent of women's rights. Yet as Nina Baym has suggested, Hale can be seen "either as a profound conservative or equally as a progressive liberal." Baym calls *Woman's Record* "a work of history rather than a collection of biographies," whereas it is clearly both, for important reasons: because it wishes "to restructure world history *as* the history of women."[18] Hale would promote a radical pro-woman program through middle-class liberal means; she approves advances in married women's property rights, women's education, and access to the professions, as well as the boom in women's cultural prominence: "Within the last fifty years more books have been written by women and about women than all put forth in the preceding five thousand eight hundred years of the world," and all these women writers find representation in Hale's volume (vii).[362; 19]

Hale's highest types are contemporary women writers and missionaries, who provide "examples for the young, and encouragement" for the aspiring, exerting greater influence than exemplars from history (563).[362] As Baym argues, Hale demolishes her own model of separate spheres when she intervenes in theology and politics by commending "the woman missionary" as the true Christian type and "the United States . . . as the premier Anglo-Saxon nation" for fostering that type.[20] Hundreds of missionaries surface only in appended lists according to denomination (their memories reside "with their own families and in the hearts of those they have served" [905]):[362] by name, maiden name, husband's name, birthplace, "Field of Labour," and "When Sent" (fields run from Syria to "Choctaws" to India to "Ojibwas" to West Africa, and onward, blending all different "fields" in one mission). Hale reserves individual treatment for women who are writers rather than missionaries.

"The Anglo-Saxon race . . . will soon rule the world—the only people who have the true light. . . . In this galaxy of living feminine genius, there is not a single ray from the wide horizon of heathendom," where women, "shrouded in . . . ignorance," leave men in the "gross darkness of idolatry and sin." In Europe, too, because "the feminine mind is considered *inferior* to the masculine," their "gifted daughters" become mere "romance-writers, public singers, dancers, artists" rather than moral guides (563–64).[362] Hope lies in the thirty million Anglo-Saxons "living on a little island in the stormy Northern Ocean," who "hold the mastery of mind over Europe and Asia" because of the true Christian influence of women (564). Although "the Old Saxon stock is yet superior to the New in that brilliancy of feminine genius" (as Knapp had conceded twenty years earlier), the United States will soon rule "the destiny of the world," largely because of the greater influence of American women (564). Thus, in an appendix, "Young Writers and Others," Hale, in the manner of eugenic proso-pographers fifty years later, measures by alphabetical list the "developement of female genius" in various nations (823) and finds that America wins, hav-ing "the most numerous band of female poets and teachers" who excel in "good books for children and youth," of far greater benefit than "a great work on philosophy" (823). Benefactresses, whose "exertions of talent are of higher worth than . . . literary genius" (859), must nevertheless accord with the plan for Anglo-Saxon progress.

The principles of this plan, and thus Hale's comparative judgments on no-table women and their different lines of service, can be puzzling. Hale asserts that "the most distinguished exponent of the remarkable progress of the Anglo-Saxons . . . is Laura Bridgman," producing an illustration of that star disabled pupil, prototype of Helen Keller, in her black spectacles (564, 592–97).[362] The two recent biographies of Bridgman notwithstanding, such bathos may be a lesson in the transience of historical eminence, as well as an indication of Hale's obtuse reading of history.[21] Hale's admiration for the disabled Bridgman de-rives from her promotion of male-sponsored education for women rather than from any liberal agenda. By Hale's established lights, reforms often encourage evils (as foundling hospitals increase the rate of illegitimacy). Dorothea Dix, in Hale's view, misdirected her "disinterested zeal" toward aiding the insane when the millions of immigrant children receive no schooling (863–64). Lydia Maria Child had "generous sympathies," but her abolitionism, based on ignorance of the true scheme for the races, "wasted" her "soul's wealth." Jesus never engaged in "political questions" (619–20). Child should have quietly labored to "establish schools in Liberia—preparing and sending out free coloured emigrants, who must there become teachers and exemplars to thousands and millions of the poor black heathen" (620).

Hale's melodramatic global narrative places American women's develop-ment at the heart of progress and yields remarkably "particular" history, a catalog of local, realist, personal detail. "Mrs. Hale" presents herself in the fron-tispiece and in an autobiographical entry as one of the grand succession of "examples . . . advancing the moral progress of society."[362]; [22] The encyclope-dist is first the reader of other biographers and other subjects' writings and, then, in turn, their critic and biographer; many of her pages consist of excerpts from the publications of her subjects.[23] In some respects Hale models the role of later feminist presenters of a female tradition. Englishwomen of achievement may be respected but in their too-cerebral line; Mary Somerville is "the most learned lady of the age" (789). Home-grown Lydia Huntley Sigourney, however, speaks for truly feminine Christian morality, a spirit greater than reason. British critics have attempted to disparage Sigourney's genius by accusing her of imi-tating Mrs. Hemans, yet Sigourney's works are "esteemed by English Christians as the most useful of their class." She is a "truly American poetess" (782). The doctor Elizabeth Blackwell, whose life spanned Britain, the United States and Europe, earns Hale's patriotic admiration: "the spirit of adventure never had a more gentle and tranquil lodgment in woman's nature" (585). An international network of mutual recognition begins to weave, as her subjects themselves engaged in the practice of compiling lives of eminent women; Mary Howitt, who assisted Hale in preparing the *Record,* receives warm praise in it (699–702).

Encyclopedic zeal clashes with exclusive prejudices and failures of attention or resources. Thus a "Mrs. Gaskill," born "Miss Stromkin," author of "Mary Barton," appears among "Young Writers and Others" in the first edition (844)[362]— mistaking Elizabeth Stevenson Gaskell (a more correct entry is added in the 3d ed. [1870], 844). In the unindexed "List of the Living Not Found in the 4th Era," Hale offers a short entry on "George Eliot," "now Mrs. Lewes . . . daughter of a dissenting minister" (901). In spite of such errors, Hale may be a fairly reliable if opinionated reference on many other women of renown in Victorian collections, including Elizabeth Fry, Hannah More ("among the best benefactors of mankind," whose "writings . . . are . . . probably more read in America than England" [444]), and Sarah Martin, the seamstress-philanthropist: "Whilst great and good men, unknown to her, were inquiring and disputing . . . here was a poor woman who was actually herself personally accomplishing" the goals (412).

For all its disturbing mix of racism, xenophobia, and personal censure of women who differed from her views and ideals, *Woman's Record* compelled emulation, as least in the form of further collective biographies. While Hale continued to expand and reissue *Woman's Record,* Henry Gardiner Adams began his own derivative *Cyclopaedia of Female Biography* (1857).[5] Adams includes an entry on Hale, based on her autobiographical article in *Godey's Lady's Book* in 1850 (360–62). Adams's *Cyclopaedia* presents for English readers the valuable essence of a "complete record of womanly excellence and ability"; "the task of its compilation must have been one of great labour and research; far more indeed than the present Editor can claim credit for;—his work having been chiefly that of condensation from a large and costly volume," *Woman's Record,* which took Hale three years, "itself a striking example of female ability in authorship" (iii).[5] (The publisher's notice in the 3d ed. of *Woman's Record* cites as "proof that the contents of this book are highly valued" the fact that an editor in London "confesses his obligations to the American work and has judged it worthy to be placed before his own countrywomen," quoting Adams's preface directly.) Some of Adams's excerpts of Hale are those she herself lifted from such sources as Knapp's *Female Biography.*[492] The same biographical currency is later banked in Sophia Goodrich Ashton's *The Girlhood of Celebrated Women* (1877),[37] though this collection of far fewer but longer life narratives eschews alphabetical order (without focusing on the girlhood promised in the title). (A smaller selection of Hale's pieces—with scant overlap in the material that Ashton later reproduced—appeared as *Lessons from Women's Lives.*[360]) Both Adams and Ashton at times copy verbatim from Hale, at times cut or splice from other sources. Clearly the discourse is international public property at midcentury.

By the later nineteenth century, further imperialist exploration and war had added jingoism and muscle to Hale's geographical models of race and gender. E. S. Brooks's *Historic Girls*[114] might appear multicultural, with chapters such as "Zenobia of Palmyra: The Girl of the Syrian Desert," "Woo of Hwang-Ho: The Girl of the Yellow River," "Elizabeth of Tudor: The Girl of the Hertford Manor," and "Ma-Ta-Oka of Pow-Ha-Tan: The Girl of the Virginia Forests [Pocahontas]," but the effect is both to essentialize the model as a native of her land ("of" lends a poetico-archaic tone) and to homogenize a "never-changing girl-nature" on the model of what might be expected of Anglo American middle-class daughters (iv). In 1900, Charles D. Michael, "Author of 'Well Done!,' 'Heroes All!,' 'Success,' Etc.," produced for Partridge—a London house with a large children's list—*Heroines: True Tales of Brave Women: A Book for British Girls,*[570] a colorful, illustrated book (inclining toward stormy sea rescues and battlefields). On the cover stands Joan of Arc facing a giant crown of laurels, her full armor peeping through her full-length skirt.[24] Whereas Knapp met the need for self-improving educational materials, Timpson addressed readers accustomed to Hannah More's pedagogy, and Hale supported a growing market for women writers, Michael's collection a half century later competes with the fiction in Partridge's Girl's Imperial Library or the Red Mountain series.[25] Characteristic of Michael's twenty-four adventure-story biographies is "A Missionary Heroine," a short life of Ann Hasseltine Judson (81)—a subject also honored in Knapp's and Hale's collections. Michael includes stories of wives who fought in Indian rebellions or the Boer War or who assisted in converting Zulus to Christianity.

The epigraph and the conclusion of Michael's preface both consist of a stanza by Charles Kingsley that recurred in other collections:[e.g., 114]

> Be good, sweet maid, and let who will be clever;
> Do noble deeds, not dream them all day long;
> And so make life, death, and that vast forever
> One grand, sweet song.

This imperative is a touch equivocal, since doing noble deeds might create all sorts of disharmony and might even entail cleverness.[26] The sort of tension in Hale's modeling of educated women writers (are they good writers, by English standards, or good women, by American?) became aggravated in later decades, as action rather than quiet service became the ideal. Michael assures us that women are "more heroic by nature than men" and will often show more "fortitude" than men.[570] (Joseph Johnson agrees [13].)[468] Michael's stories are designed "to impress upon the minds of British girls the real nobility of heroic womanhood" (7). Yet Michael cautions, as Darton had done decades before, "opportunities for heroism lie always in the path of duty" (8). Like Timpson,

Michael commends some nearly unremarkable women on behalf of a composite model of female Britishness.

An American counterpart to Michael's gung-ho stories is again international and transhistorical: *Heroines That Every Child Should Know* (1915),[527] part of Doubleday's series of what every child should know. (Whereas Hale, Adams, and Ashton had compiled without thought of copyright, this early-twentieth-century collection acknowledges the permissions of several major publishers.) The intertwined themes of Hamilton Mabie's introduction to this book are the heroism of the obscure and racial progress, with a new note of masculinist manifest destiny: in the "three centuries" of settling this continent, "the skirmish line of civilisation has moved steadily forward from the Atlantic to the Pacific.... There have been more heroines than heroes in the long warfare of the race against foes within and without." Women, as courageous as men "from the days of Esther, Judith and Antigone," now "outrank the men ... who have led splendid charges in full view of the world, who have achieved miracles of material construction in canal or railroad, or the reclaiming of barbarous lands to the uses of civilization" (viii–x). Women's heroism evidently borrows its grandeur from conquest and engineering, in this vision; the biographies themselves may be a technology of racial progress. As Reginald Horsman explains, "Americans were able to see new meaning in their drive to the Pacific and Asia" when they mapped German philological theories of language and race onto their history, "as the most vital and energetic of Aryan peoples."[27] And of course the most advanced peoples honored and fostered the advancement of their women.

Not uncommonly, the biographical histories of women lodge three contradictory principles: woman is a universal, ahistorical element; history is the biographies of innumerable women; and the status and achievements of women are the measure of a race's level of civilization. In a collaborative series published in Philadelphia in 1907–8, *Woman: In All Ages and in All Countries,*[899] the ten unnumbered volumes by a range of American male professors offer four thousand and more pages of learned speculation, narrative social history, comparative anthropology, and short lives grouped by nation and epoch, beginning with *Greek Women* and ending with *Women of America.*[28] "G.C.L.," in his general introduction to the series, expounds the thesis that women have quietly guided "the greatest and most enduring effects" of history. "Were true justice done ... the world itself ... could hardly contain the statues which would be reared to women" (1:xix).[899]; 29 John A. Burgan's introduction to the last volume, *Women of America,* confirms: "The history of nations is ... largely that of woman" (10:vii).[899]; 30 Not incidentally, this master narrative gives other races little hope of ever catching up. Edward B. Pollard, in "Women of the Backward Races of the East," the last chapter of *Oriental Women,* presumes that the "advance of the world's civilization from crude savagery to high culture" may be observed in conditions today (4:341). He suggests that the "Australians" (i.e., aborigines) may present a "picture of a previous condition of the Caucasian race" (343). Similarly, "the Orient reveals many stages yet to be achieved"; in the East, "woman is the slave of man" (viii). *Woman: In All Ages and in All Countries,* in other words, supports current eugenics and orientalist anthropology, in accordance with the wisdom of H. Rider Haggard.[31]

The gallant scholars of the early twentieth century supplement racial geohistory with a tour through the progress of woman, writing as though overqualified for this highbrow potboiler. Pierce Butler of Tulane, for example, in *Women of Medieval France,*[899] presumes that "the lives of historic women" provide gossip, "ancillary to history" (ix). He places his volume, nevertheless, in a long exemplifying tradition that proves "the essential nobility of the feminine character" (357), the tradition, that is, of Christine de Pizan, whose life he narrates along with those of Joan of Arc and other early Frenchwomen. The volumes document many individuals and historical differences among women, even against a background theme of feminine anonymity and marginalization. The volumes visually reinforce the imperial uses of a certain form of essentialist feminism. Each volume is identically bound in purple moiré cloth stamped in gold, its front cover bordered with a pattern of peacock feathers and nosegays linked in a large gold chain. This border surrounds a cruciform woman standing on the charted globe, her feet above Europe as Asia fades to her left and Africa recedes underneath her. Thus beauty and vanity, captivity, sexuality, an idealized transcendent virtue, and imperial domination are all stamped together. (The naked, loosely coifed woman has no distinguishing cultural or racial characteristics, though her ampleness would become outmoded in our times.) The frontispieces depict slightly more individualized women (the only illustration in each volume). All these women are fair skinned, regardless of the exotic setting (there is no volume on African women). Much of that skin is exposed; these women are exhibits of beauty, whether leering at the viewer or gazing upward in piety, with the exception of a muscular group of Teutonic women.

Not all global compendiums reduce women to typecast indicators of the level of civilization, however. A less scholarly contemporary prosopography, *Woman, Her Position, Influence, and Achievement throughout the Civilized World,*[488] includes a few anonymous, exotic/erotic images like the above—"A Roman Boudoir" (142), "Mohammedan Woman" (173)—and generalizes about "Woman from the Time of Christ to the Fall of Rome," for example. Nevertheless, this collaborative album of *Woman* largely concerns the biographical record of numerous eminent individuals, some still living, with composite photographic portraits, such as the page of five middle-aged dignitaries, Frances Power Cobbe, Julia Ward Howe, Adelaide Procter, Harriet Beecher Stowe, and Mary A. Livermore (419). The heavy volume of seven "books" includes Pundita Ramabai Sarasvati, "Educated Hindu Defender of Child-Widows" (460–61)[also featured in 156; 163; 279; 486] and Tsze Hsi An, "The Famous Empress Dowager of China" (462–63),[also featured in 373; 712] as well as the renowned Pocahontas (265; sixteen entries in my Pop Chart [table A2]), all unpictured. Otherwise the named subjects of recent eras are the usual European or Anglo American notables, some of whom help other races. The international mission of female prosopography circa 1900 might range, then, through the conventions of juvenile adventure fiction to evolutionary sociology to contemporary documented biography, always reinforcing a hierarchy for woman in all ages and in all countries.

Encyclopedias and Eugenic Prosopography

Few observers have put much serious store in the above varieties of self-help history, though the matters of social evolution, race, and international competition appeared urgent enough as the nineteenth century ended. Many voices called for a British or American codification of biography to match those of other nations, while most critics dismissed popular prosopography. The only biographical collections that have commanded much critical attention are the encyclopedic projects epitomized by the *Dictionary of National Biography,* arising at the same time as statistical prosopographies supported by eugenic theory. Biographical dictionaries, indeed, proliferated in the later nineteenth century at a time of consolidating nationalism, challenged imperialism, and diversifying claims to citizenship and histories of one's own, as in the souvenirs of women of 1893 that I examine below. The height of the British Empire seemed to call for the fulfillment of a longstanding British dream of an inclusive prosopography.

During World War I, Waldo H. Dunn, apparently the first British or American professor of English to attempt a lengthy study of biography, reiterated R. C. Christie's 1884 reproach that the English had failed to produce a universal biographical dictionary to rival the French.[32] The progress of European nations might be measured by the rise of their collective biographies: from fifteenth-century beginnings in Spain and Italy to the sixteenth- and seventeenth-century encyclopedias and dictionaries in Latin and French that prepared the way for the Abbé l'Advocat's pioneering "general biographical dictionary" (contemporaneous with Ballard's compilation of British women of letters, in 1752, as Dunn does not observe); followed by the emergence of biography in the late eighteenth century in Germany and in the twentieth century in Russia.[33] Dunn seems patently competitive, in a manner reminiscent of Mr. Ramsay's alphabetical efforts in *To the Lighthouse,* when he recalls the first attempt at an "English general biographical dictionary," before the French *Biographie Universelle* and *Nouvelle Biographie Générale* that dominated the middle of the nineteenth century. The English project, Dunn recalls, "was undertaken by the Society for the Diffusion of Universal Knowledge, and progressed (1842–4) through the letter A in four volumes, when, owing to lack of adequate support, it was discontinued."[34] Dunn's substitution of "Universal" in the title of the Society for the Diffusion of *Useful* Knowledge (SDUK) is telling. Sarah Hale might attempt a universal biographical record of "woman" as late as 1853, but George Long and his supporters had quailed before the alphabet of man's achievement; the project was perhaps too universal to be useful. Swedish, Dutch, Austrian, Belgian, and German national collections appeared in the later nineteenth century before the British succeeded in launching a *Dictionary of National Biography* (*DNB*) in 1885.[35] The *DNB* advertised aims that were much less "diffusive" than those of the SDUK: determined to succeed in a monumental definition project not unlike Johnson's dictionary, it began with a proposed list of subjects and a model entry ("Addison") circulated among readers of prestigious journals, the *Cornhill* and the *Athenaeum*.[36]

Leslie Stephen's *DNB*, like the English postage stamp, appears to have waived the need to spell out its country of origin. Its questionable selection has been a theme since its inception. Gillian Fenwick finds that women represented about 3.5 percent of the subjects in the *DNB*'s first series (1885–1901), a rate that increased to 4 percent through 1985 (18), and reached 11.8 percent in the 1981–85 supplement alone (21).[37] From the beginning, a few women participated as contributors, though they wrote primarily on male subjects; through 1901, forty-five of the 696 contributors were women, and only six of the female contributors "qualified for admission to the *DNB*" themselves (Fenwick, 8). Trev Broughton, elaborating on Fenwick's findings, remarks that the business-like "homosocial" enterprise of the *DNB*, a training ground for future historians, nevertheless accommodated a surprising number of female contributors (some perhaps ghosting behind male names).[38] In the past generation, the push toward inclusiveness has been ever stronger, yet such redress for past inequities as the *Missing Persons* companion to the *DNB* reproduces the pattern of selective recognition.

International emulation of encyclopedic projects continued in the twentieth century. *The Dictionary of American Biography*, begun in 1928 as though to claim the United States as a rising empire, patterned itself on the *DNB*.[39] It is quite old news that these works neglected women and overrepresented European men of the middle and upper classes; corrections came hot on their heels. The register of living American achievement that approaches inclusiveness, *Who's Who*, first published in 1899, was followed by *Who's Who of the Colored Race* (1915) and *Who's Who in Colored America* (1927–50), also including women. Just as George Eliot might earn a volume in John Morley's English Men of Letters series with few objections, an occasional queen or French *salonnière* and a selection of people of color were featured in national or universal dictionaries without much fanfare. Gender, class, or nationality is only remarked as a principle of selection in the "minority" cases; there is the "universal," and then there is the specialized collection. The standardizing national records arguably strive to restore order during an onslaught of popular biographical collections. National scope and international rivalry could effectively screen out most women from the general dictionaries, in spite of the ready conjunction of women's biographies with the narrative of national development in contemporary all-female collections. In later editions of reference works, women might be introduced in supplements or in encyclopedias of their own.[40]

Early twentieth-century prosopographers recognized the useful knowledge diffused in the many reference works as potential data for their own socio-biological interpretations. Thus an American researcher, Cora Sutton Castle, drawing on the eugenic social science of Francis Galton and J. McKenn Cattell, produced *A Statistical Study of Eminent Women* in 1913.[41] Castle notes that Galton, in his pioneering "statistical study of distinguished men," defines "'an eminent man'" as having "'achieved a position'" comparable to "'one person in each 4,000'" (1). Accordingly, Castle adopts the "objective method" of Cattell's *Statistical Study of Eminent Men* (1903) by combing six encyclopedias and retaining "every woman named in any three out of the six." Disappointed in reaching her goal of a list of a thousand, Castle could only sustain 868 eminent women in all of history, once the twenty-three biblical characters were elimi-nated. Castle then arranged the women "in order of merit" as determined by "the number of lines" they earned in her reference sources (standardized by the average length in each source [2–3]).[42] Castle concedes some difficulty in determining merit for women, whose renown may be inborn or given (through beauty, rank, marriage, calamity), or indeed may be ill-gotten (1). She almost gives the game away when she admits that different biographical references would have yielded different results (23). The point, however, is to produce a credible "catalogue of the distinguished" that ranks a few great women (1).

Scholars were willing to engage in such quantitative absurdity for serious aims: to measure progress and national superiority in terms of race and gen-der. (Even today the eugenicist method of encyclopedia measuring seems to Charles Murray a reliable way to identify the 4,002 best artists and scientists of history.)[43] Castle is able to expand the concept of historic womanhood as she charts activities across centuries and nations. Though 868 seems a pal-try number of women to survive from hundreds of generations, Castle's list, headed by Mary Stuart, Joan of Arc, Queen Victoria, Queen Elizabeth, George Sand, Madame de Staël, becomes increasingly eccentric as eminence decreases through fifteen fine-type pages. The subjects "achieved fame in twenty-nine different lines of activity, but 38.8 per cent.[*sic*] of the total group were writers" (40–47, 87). Nevertheless, the highest eminence goes to women who worked in the standard elite line: "It has been as sovereigns, politicians, mothers, and mistresses that women have acquired the greatest distinction" (87). Traditional family roles have not been incompatible with career for these women, as Castle indirectly affirms: "The 142 unmarried eminent women can not be said to have won greater eminence than those who married; their average length of life was not longer" (88). Longevity, a preoccupation of prosopographers, raises an encouraging national observation: "American women of ability live on the average 2.8 years longer than Scotch women, 3.5 years longer than German women, 6.4 years longer than English women, and 7.9 years longer than the eminent women of France." No longer need America defer to Europe on the score of female achievement, as Knapp had allowed in the 1830s and Hale begrudgingly admitted in the 1850s. Granted that life expectancies have improved over centuries, and "we are a young nation," the difference, Castle insists, "reflects credit on the physical vigor of the American people as well as upon our hygienic and sanitary conditions and the skill of American physicians and surgeons." This rare expression of opinion is immediately followed by the implacable statement: "62 of the eminent women suffered violent or unnatural deaths" (89). Perhaps on average it is not a bad plan to become an eminent woman in America.

This may be the science of eugenics self-destructing. Yet a mania for positivist record keeping in the 1890s–1920s assisted in legitimizing the social ambitions of various communities and identities. Castle's definition of eminent women tacitly supports a national literary and historical canon around daughters and sons of New England. Her academic study shares such aims with some popular collective biographies of the day. Many have continued to long for objective measures for honor rolls and canons, as Charles Murray's *Human Accomplishment* attests. (My own Pop Chart [table A2], and the enumeration that this project provokes, can seem like throwbacks to Castle's generation in spite of my best efforts.) Encyclopedias of national biography mounted a sort of civil defense against the onslaught of biographical records from within as well as international prosopographies from without. Once again, the status of the participants—subjects, presenters, audience—helps to determine the lasting status of the texts. The encyclopedias, while obviously not considered literature, claimed greater cultural capital than the popular compilations of short biographies of women. *Who's Who in Colored America* of 1927 perished, *The Dictionary of American Biography* of 1928 endured, though their aims and designs overlap.

The World's Fair Women and African American Women of Distinction

A logical extension of the aim of exhaustive representation in encyclopedic or prosopographical studies is the demand for supplements for those left out. If the stage of civilization of any race could be measured by the stature of its women, a race could raise its reputation by exhibiting its most honorable females. Accordingly, circa 1893, prosopographies of African American women were published almost as appendixes to the great catalogs of the World's Columbian Exposition in Chicago. This event, as formative in its way as the Great Exhibition of 1851 in London, has increasingly invited readings as a performance of the social, political, and commercial state of an industrial empire and as a site that mapped mass culture for the coming century. In its planning and staging, the Columbian Exposition confirmed the racism of post-Reconstruction North America, while it afforded an extraordinary platform for contemporary women's movements. The many features of the Woman's Building and the Congress of Women suggest intriguing patterns in collective representation. Most important here are the published female prosopographies generated by the occasion: 1893 was the first year since 1854 in which the annual production reached thirty-seven, a number only exceeded again in 1900. The multibio-graphical collaborations that flurried in the early 1890s figure the middle-class woman as the heroine of the progress of the races, while these volumes pit each state and region against the other in boasting of their women. In that era, many presenters acknowledged contemporary political issues such as temperance or suffrage, bracketing segregation as a variety of regionalism. Communities were asked to think globally by celebrating locally.

The African American collections, to which I turn in a moment, should be viewed in the context of the fair's exclusive representations. According to Hazel V. Carby, the World's Columbian Exposition so notably barred women of color that it motivated the foundation of the National Association of Colored Women three years later.[44] African Americans were repeatedly denied participation in the commissions and boards that designed the fair, and by 1892 it had become "clear that the 1893 fair was white America's show."[45] Ida B. Wells and Frederick Douglass jointly raised funds for a pamphlet to protest the representation in the imperial White City—as well as the economic exploitation and lynchings at that time—with the telling title, *The Reason Why the Colored American Is Not in the World's Columbian Exposition.* Contemporary racism and the racist practices of the exposition are well documented, supporting the view that people of color were absent from the fair except on exhibit or as custodial staff, whereas Christopher Robert Reed documents many details of "diasporan" and African participation.[46] This is a classic instance of some actual participants in the pageant of history becoming invisible. The fact that some representations did infiltrate the dominant prosopography fails to tell the truth of exclusivity, which is remembered as total absence.

In this context, several African American women's collective biographies emerged as supplements to contemporary volumes of tacit or trumpeted white-ness. In many respects, the "colored" counterparts relied on rhetorical and for-mal conventions already established; they engaged in the same sort of mutual representation, whereby audience, subjects, and presenters exchange places. Similarly, the role of male presenter recurs in these female prosopographies as in others. The enterprises of recognition of black middle-class women, well beyond the more familiar zone of the Harlem Renaissance, would richly reward more study than they have yet received or than I can devote to them here. Some recent publications in African American studies have begun to recover these records in partial ways. From a bibliographical point of view, it may look like a coincidence that two biographical collections of African American women, each presented by a black male doctor, appeared in 1893: Dr. Monroe A. Majors's *Noted Negro Women: Their Triumphs and Activities*[542] and Dr. Lawson A. Scruggs's *Women of Distinction.*[706] Brief lives in magazines and newspapers (and tributes circulating on the lecture circuit) evidently predated these ency-clopedic projects, and men were not quite pioneers in this community-building zone. Neither Majors nor Scruggs takes note of Susan Elizabeth Frazier's 1892 article "Some Afro-American Women of Mark."[47] But both Scruggs and

Majors include a biography of Susie I. Lankford Shorter, who appears to be the first "woman of African descent" to compile a "collective biography of Afro-American women," *The Heroines of African Methodism* (1891).[717; 48] There are other signs of women's head start in this effort. Scruggs thanks Mrs. N. F. Mossell in his preface (vi)[706] and includes her biography. Majors not only includes a biography of Gertrude Mossell but also reprints a sample of her journalism, "Our Women in Missions," from *Ringwood's Illustrated Magazine* (131–33);[542] this magazine in turn is advertised on an endpaper of Scruggs's collection.[49]

The mission of giving credit to African American women in the manner of white women's prosopographies had been gathering momentum. In the article reprinted in Majors, Mossell responds to an editorial: "Have we no Clara Bartons in our Race.... From the times of Joan of Arc down to Clara Barton...each race and era has been blessed" with "noble women to rise from their ranks...opening the way for multitudes" (131).[542] This journalistic sketch of Mossell's full-length volume[588] calls for a complement to the catalogs that are felt to lack the proper faces and voices. In her own collection, Mossell acknowledges: "The men of the race, in most instances, have been generous, doing all in their power to allow the women of the race to rise with them. 'Woman's Work in America,' by Anna Nathan Myer [*sic*], garners up the grain from the harvest field of labor of our Anglo-American [*sic*] sisters. I would do for the women of my race...this work that has been so ably done for our more favored sisters by another and abler pen" (10).[588; 50] Like other collections of the 1890s, Mossell's encompasses missionaries, teachers, church- and clubwomen, businesswomen, and performers as well as literati. Generously might the likenesses be drawn, in a wide net of mutual recognition.

Mossell's compensatory design—to do for the women of her race what had been done for the Anglo Americans—might seem based on a puzzling claim, that white women had been fully recognized for their work, but it makes sense in light of the frenzy of recognition in the 1890s, as seen both in the biographical collections that I examine and in concentrated efforts surrounding the World's Fair. The honor rolls for women of color make no loud protests, though many appeals since 1889 to win African American participation in the fair had been rebuffed. No mention of the World's Fair appears in Majors's book, published as though on the very site, in Chicago in 1893. Dr. M. A. Majors of Chicago served as "a vice president on the committee planning Colored American Day" in the White City.[51] As though translating the motto of the fair that boasted to the world of the triumph of American civilization, one of Majors's epigraphs reads in small capitals: "The highest mark of our prosperity, and the strongest proofs of Negro capacity to master the sciences and fine arts, are evinced by the advanced positions to which Negro women have attained." Between the covers is a prosopographical exhibit of that advanced position— and a missing element in the Woman's Building of the Columbian Exposition. Majors's three other epigraphs are variations on one theme of contemporary racial and gender theory: "The criterion for Negro civilization is the intelligence, purity and high motives of its women." The introduction, a commendation of Majors himself by the president of Paul Quinn College in Waco, Texas, Majors's hometown, promotes the "epic" pride and progress of the race, with standard *apology* and *exemplification*: there are "hundreds of . . . no less . . . noble exemplars of our possibilities and queens in our homes" (v–vi);[542] "many a . . . darling daughter will catch the inspiration of womanly attainments" (viii). The Ruskinian chivalry links this collection to countless others in this period— and to the representation of Mrs. Palmer or Queen Isabella at the fair, noted below.

The provocation of the years before and during the World's Columbian Exposition surfaces more directly in Mossell's 1894 collection. Choosing to put the criticism of the fair into positive terms—praise of the (unacknowledged) achievements of the race—Mossell honors the service of "five experienced refined and cultivated women upon the World's Fair State Committees" (21–22).[588] She also makes note of the efforts of "the Woman's Loyal Union of Brooklyn and New York, and the Colored Woman's League, of Washington, DC," in "collecting of statistics and facts showing the moral, intellectual, industrial, and social growth and attainments of Afro-Americans" (32). Mossell relates, too, at some length, the story of the "martyr editor" of Memphis, Ida B. Wells, her lecture tours in England to generate antilynching support, and her publication of *The Reason Why* ("for distribution at the World's Fair" [32–38]). Another essay in Mossell's collection, "Our Afro-American Representatives at the World's Fair," presents a group biographical sketch, largely in quotation marks, of the prominent African Americans, male and female, who against all odds participated in organizing the fair (104–14).

In some ways, the most public protest by African Americans during the fair is itself a prosopography, a sustained effort to correct a distorted collective representation. *The Reason Why,* rushed to publication in Chicago in 1893, seeks in prose (with preface translated into French and German) to signify what is missing, "the exhibit of the progress made by a race in 25 years of freedom as against 250 years of slavery" (3). I. Garland Penn provides a miniature of the sort of comprehensive compilation to be desired ("The Progress of the Afro-American since Emancipation," 44–64), listing statistics of population, institutions founded, patents won, and achievements in a range of professions including literature (Phillis Wheatley without fail) and the arts (various artists are named, including Edmonia Lewis). Penn quotes at length both Anna Julia Cooper's *A Voice from the South,* "the ablest book yet written by a Negro," in praise of the Tuskegee Institute (55–56), and Antonin Dvořák in praise of the rich resource of "Negro melodies" (62–64). F. L. Barnett, in his essay "The Reason Why," sums up the view that prevails today: "Theoretically open to all Americans, the Exposition practically is, literally and figuratively, a 'White City,' in the building of which the Colored American was allowed no helping hand, and in its glorious success he has no share" (79–80).

Reed's evidence in *"All the World Is Here!"* notwithstanding, the rhetoric of the exposition overwhelmingly favored an Anglo-Saxon script of progress and union for the states as a global empire, at the direct and indirect expense of any racial inclusiveness. August 25, 1893, was set aside as "Colored People's Day," adding insult to the injury of refusing any but menial jobs to African Americans (there were two who served as clerks [Barnett, "The Reason Why," 80]). Some contemporary African Americans rejected the terms of segregated supplemental access. There had been analogous objections to the Board of Lady Managers' plan for "a separate building for a separate exhibit of women's work," but the Woman's Building, designed by Sophia Hayden, became one of the most popular sites at the fair.[52] One of the aggravations was the exclusion of African American women from the commission's Lady Managers and from delegations to the World's Congress of Representative Women. The famous educator and elocutionist Hallie Q. Brown had refused the terms on which she was asked to serve as the sole liaison for "the women of her race."[53]

The hopes for prosopographical representation were high surrounding the fair. Great forces rallied to represent every constituency, and much attention centered on the events of the World's Congress. According to Hazel Carby, six African American women addressed the Congress, May 15–21, 1893: Frances Harper, Fannie Barrier Williams, Anna Julia Cooper, Fannie Jackson Coppin, Sarah J. Early, and Hallie Q. Brown.[54] These addresses at the main congress sessions do not appear in the vast prosopographical memorial, *The Congress of Women, Held in the Woman's Building, World's Columbian Exposition*,[245] edited by Mary Kavanaugh Oldham Eagle, organizer of the series of separate, smaller sessions held in the building itself.[55]

Eagle's printed museum helps to characterize the aims and designs of the "colored" annexes to it. *The Congress of Women* is saturated with signals of contemporary modeling of woman's civic and global service. The introduction to this 824-page fund-raising album testifies to the great effort, within the few months before publication, to obtain "complete representation in this volume of each contributor to the Congress" (13).[245] One looks in vain for any personified representation of the 8 million citizens of African descent in the United States at that time. "Thirty states and twenty nations" (14), numerous professions, and many religious affiliations are represented in this exclusively white collection. Its global ambitions to give face, name, and voice to a cohort of powerful womanhood lend themselves to various formal devices of collective biographical representation: numerous panels of clustered portraits; the varied articles (indexed by title and by author), almost all adorned at the beginning with the author's photograph and at the bottom of the first page with a small-print biography; many essays in the form of group or individual biographies, such as Mrs. Caroline Fuller Fairbanks, "Some English Women of the Eighteenth Century" (503–7) or Miss Ida M. Street's "George Eliot" (286–92). Anglo American women were known for their mission to ameliorate other peoples and to bring sociological understanding to intercultural power relations.

Accordingly, contributors report on such missionary encounters, as in Mrs. Caroline G. Reed's "Historic Women of Egypt" (240–42), based on living in Egypt in 1891–92, Mrs. Amelia L. Howard's first-person testimony, "Moorish Women as I Found Them" (463–68), and Mrs. Amelia S. Quinton's "The Woman's National Indian Association" (71–73).

The single-sex catalog seeks global representation and acknowledges racial and cultural difference. All the more glaring then is the absence of African American women as contributors and subjects. The near-absence of any reference to Americans of African descent throughout this volume, like the omission of African Americans from the U.S. Capitol, could be the result of pressure to unite the white middle classes of all sections.[56] Clues to this appear in the several articles that raise voices on behalf of Southern women (there are no designated collective descriptions of the unmarked group that dominates the congress, Northern "Anglo-Saxon" women secure in their cultural capital). Thus, Mrs. S. C. Trueheart's "Women of the South" euphemistically portrays slavery: the "Anglo-Saxon women of the South" before 1861 could not have been idle, as charged, because they had to keep "others busy in useful tasks. About them were those who must be taught to work, must not be permitted to suffer, must not know the sordid pain of poverty" (805).[245] Southern womanhood had been conservative, undeveloped, asleep before the Civil War.[57] "Awake now to affairs that affect the good of the race, they realized that a better way to establish the home, as well as preserve it, is to rid the country of the great evils, dark and threatening, that confront it" (806–7). Without specifying those dark evils, Trueheart suggests that Southern women after emancipation had turned against vice and drunkenness, as when she praises the effort to teach temperance to "a school of negro children" (807).

"The good of the race" seemingly requires a union of white women of all zones under "Our Queen," Mrs. Palmer (817)[245] of the ephemeral "palace in the White City" (824).[58] As extensions of the exposition, *The Congress of Women* and other printed pantheons of the leading contemporary women served like souvenir programs commemorating the daily performances of women in public. Thus, what might be called a book of civic beauty, *A Souvenir of World's Fair Women*,[405] punningly gathers a "flower-garden" of the "fair" at the Columbian Exposition: "The most prominent, or most beautiful women" among the Board of Lady Managers and the wives of prominent officials, with once again, Mrs. Bertha M. Honoré Palmer leading the way.[59]

The collective biographies published in 1893–94 and thereafter sought to complement the segregated prosopographies generated by the encyclopedic Columbian memorials. A new era of recognition among educated North American women of color seemed to dawn in response: a mutual multibiography similar to that among Victorian women writers. Readers might readily become subjects and presenters in turn. Monroe Majors lauds Mrs. Mossell as "one of the leading women of a struggling race, whose brightest hope is that it can bring forth just such women." An "eminent writer," she "has acted as agent and canvasser to several race publications, and has a well-stocked library of Negro literature of her own" (129–30).[542] In Mossell's own collection, it is not inappropriate to list herself as Sarah Hale does in hers. Among instances of female invention ("Afro-American women" may be "too poor to secure patents"), Mossell acknowledges that "Mrs. N. F. Mossell, of Phila., has invented a camping table and portable kitchen" (25).[588] In her turn she celebrates "the noble work being done by Miss Hallie Quinn Brown," among other "Women in Missions" (133).[542] Brown, according to Mossell, is "among the finest elocutionists of the United States," one of those who "not only [delight] the millions of the common people, but receiv[e] marked tokens of appreciation from the crowned heads of the European nations" (22). Brown, who was honored in both Majors's and Scruggs's collections, eventually compiled a collaborative collective biography, *Homespun Heroines* (1926),[120] and added *Our Women* in 1940.[121] Brown herself appears in the frontispiece of *Homespun Heroines* as the "Hon. President of the N.A.C.W."—the organization sparked by the fair, according to Carby. Yet Brown fails to recall the preeminent Mrs. Mossell, writer (and inventor), who has dropped out of sight across the twentieth century. Omissions are endemic to the genre, yet celebrations are severely short in African American history.

Turn-of-the-century African American female collective biographies seek rhetorical parity with other contemporary catalogs of women. The very titles of some works could "pass," since whiteness has gone unmarked. The title of Scruggs's collection, *Women of Distinction*,[706] is indistinguishable from dozens of others, primarily white, published in the United States in the 1890s and probably has been cataloged at times without awareness of its contents.[60] Most likely there are more collections around the turn of the century than remain visible in library records, and some whose titles quietly integrate the Eurocentric collections of women—often but not always the goal at that time. Thus, Benjamin Brawley puts forth *Women of Achievement* (1919)[108] without a segregating signal. Hallie Q. Brown's title, *Homespun Heroines and Other Women of Distinction* (1926),[120] provides no clue apart from the folksy "homespun" and the wide celebrity of Brown herself. In many details, the rhetorical apparatus of the African American female prosopographies corresponds with contemporary all-female collections of unmarked race.

Like other collective female biographies in this period, the African American catalogs often invite collaborative presentation as well as mixtures of genre (frequently they serve as literary anthologies), while their subjects may include acquaintances and family, the historical and the living, the obscure and the famous. Majors's notices range from eight-page studies to paragraphs to simple lists; an appendix includes Mattie E. Dover's prosopographical essay, "Woman as Educator," which identifies Georgia Green Majors, the wife of the compiler, as one among many teachers (336). Scruggs, incorporating entries of three-to-eight pages written by at least fourteen contributors including Ida B. Wells, likewise intersperses feature essays, such as "Influence of Negro Women in the Home," and lists his late wife, "Miss" Lucie Johnson Scruggs (231).

Nevertheless, each volume remains mute as to the existence of the rival compiler's wife. Mossell's essay, "The Work of the Afro-American Woman," names "Mrs. Majors, Mrs. Scruggs" among many others who have helped "in literary lines" (16).[588] The intimacy of reference is standard practice, as when Brown includes portraits of her mother and aunt (xxvii–xxviii, 71–80, 81–83).[120] The discourse of the World's Fair Women likewise concerns the mutual mirroring of a small if cosmopolitan cohort.

The tables of contents of the volumes by Majors, Scruggs, and Mossell suggest no scarcity of models for African American girls in 1893, a plentiful store from which to draw some representatives for the World's Congress. The triumph of a massive European-American women's annex to an American global museum encouraged further catalogs. Journalistic advocacy for African Americans, as for women of any group, often took the form of group biographies.[61] The collections circa 1893 acknowledged notables still eminent, in some cases re-eminent, in lists of black womanhood today: Frances E. W. Harper, Ida B. Wells, Sojourner Truth, and Phillis Wheatley; only Scruggs includes Harriet Tubman. The collections also celebrate the lasting importance of Charlotte Forten Grimké, Fannie Jackson Coppin, Edmonia Lewis, Anna Julia Cooper, and Josephine Turpin Washington (who is credited with the introduction to Scruggs[706] and the foreword to Brown[105]), among many others less familiar today. The disappearance of Mossell from Brown's later collection suggests, however, the unreliability of these records as preservative media. Predictably, many prosopographies in the modes of racial-uplift or Black Pride or even African American studies have limited themselves to the handful of names that stand for the female half of "the race." So, for instance, women are only two members of Edwin R. Embree's *Thirteen against the Odds* (1944), representing, and providing models of success to, the 13 million African Americans at that time.[62]

The typological representation of a vast population through a small portion of models follows other restrictive patterns that are shared by African American as well as white collections. The favorite models during the era of clubwomen, as today, were middle-class women of letters. It is a standard prosopographical claim for ethnic groups: the anthology of authors.[63] To modify Majors's epigraph, The criterion for African American or women's culture is the talent, ambition, and success of its writers. This principle has been indispensable to African American studies, which has done most to restore a heritage of novelists and poets, while biography lurks on the margins of the literary. For literary canon-construction, there is no better store than that Home Depot, the Schomburg Library of Nineteenth-Century Black Women Writers, a series of thirty volumes, plus a supplement of ten. In 1988, as I noted, the series reprinted both Mossell's[588] and Brown's[120] collections. As general editor, Henry Louis Gates Jr. outdoes Majors or Scruggs in mustering collaborative tributes. He self-reflectively reincarnates W. E. B. DuBois as proponent of a new talented tenth, writing a sophisticated prosopography, *Thirteen Ways of Looking at a*

Black Man, and paying tribute to his ancestor in fulfilling DuBois's planned encyclopedia of Africa.[64] Yet he has also served as a kind of corporate sponsor of African American women writers.

The Schomburg Library editions gather great stores under a series of volumes with a uniform format (not unlike *Woman: In All Ages and In All Countries*[899] above). Each Schomburg volume carries the "Foreword: In Her Own Write" by Gates, narrating "the birth of the African-American literary tradition" through Phillis Wheatley, followed by other introductory business. But in pride of place, the dedication to Gates's own mother, Pauline Augusta Coleman Gates, a woman who, as Michele Wallace and Susan Fraiman have observed, plays both a dominant and subordinate role in Gates's autobiographical writings.[65] This is more than an echo of the support of model women by Dr. Majors, who dedicates his collection to the "achievements and activities," the "unspotted lives" of "our sisters," or by Dr. Scruggs, with a similar dedication to the "mothers and daughters" past and present who "establish[ed] unimpeachable character in the womanhood of the race." The Schomburg series itself becomes a prosopographical exhibit, a figuration of the absences of other canons as well as the contingencies of this one.

Not unlike the World's Congress of Women publications, the Schomburg Library contains collections within collections and copes with difficulties of categorization and selection. The set includes anthologies (e.g., four volumes of *Collected Black Women's Poetry*) and a large portion of collective life narratives: *Six Women's Slave Narratives, Spiritual Narratives, Collected Black Women's Narratives,* and *Two Biographies by African-American Women,* in addition to Mossell's and Brown's compilations. The Schomburg series culminates in Jean Fagin Yellin and Cynthia D. Bond's *The Pen Is Ours,* an exhaustive bibliography that, as noted above, expands Yellin's list published in 1982 in *All the Women Are White, All the Blacks Are Men, but Some of Us Are Brave.* The bibliography is a major achievement, though like any it has its limitations as new works continue to be discovered, not least Gates's recent recovery of the manuscript novel, *The Bondwoman's Narrative* by Hannah Crafts.[66]

Any restorative researcher must be humbled by the elusiveness of traces due to pseudonyms, the notorious changeability of women's names, the racial indifference of most names, the lack of records of most publishing houses—not to mention the lost records of the poor, uprooted, illiterate, and stigmatized. The anthologist Joan R. Sherman, for example, in 1974 construed two women, Molly E. Lambert (African American) and Mary Eliza (Perrine) Tucker Lambert (white), as a single poet, with the result that the Schomburg series reprinted two of the white woman's books (ed. Sherman) in 1988; Ann A. Shockley established the white woman's authorship in that year. Yellin and Bond's tasks included returning to oblivion not only the white Tucker but several other women falsely believed to have been black, even as they added more names to their list.[67] It is a fascinating indeterminacy within a determined purpose: the list gathers women writers of one race only.

My point, of course, is not to pity a handful of excluded white women writers but, rather, to call attention to the interpretative framework in biographical recovery. The segregated, all-female collections, whether Anglo or African American, presume an identifiable sex and race. As always, there are costs in affirming separate traditions for social categories. It may be true, as Walter Benn Michaels argues, that "the modern concept of culture is not . . . a critique of racism; it is a form of racism."[68] If we segregate our honor rolls according to the marks of social difference—race, gender, class, nationality—we must deploy the terms that made compensation necessary by first drawing distinctions. Although the renewed recognition may be worth the risk of reinforced difference, no one should imagine that such recognition can avoid excluding others as it defines its own selective tradition or that it can be completed once and for all. The Schomburg series has the aura of a "first," yet like all the intervening compilations it derives from the 1890s multibiographies of black women, which have received remarkably little attention. Ida B. Wells's works of protest inevitably regained prominence sooner than the albums of praise for middle-class role models. The paragons of 1893, white or black, appear too "advanced" for deeds, too well bred to fight or cause a scandal. But that appearance is largely the distortion of an uplifting exposition. Suffragists, revolutionaries, New Women of various kinds—including, under greater constraints, women of color—were already astir, providing subjects for later collective tributes. The obliteration of the collective biographies of African American women, and the obscurity of all but a few of their subjects, is only a more extreme case of the fate of the contemporary female prosopographies that sampled several nationalities in the name of a civilization led by Anglo-Saxon Christian middle-class women. Some of the race women are better known today than most of the women of the fair. I have suggested that this discourse generally represents Who Is Not Who. Its (apologetic) omissions as well as its exemplary representative selections are alike necessary to a prosopoetic practice of memorializing loss. Such publications invite corrections of their partiality through further disproportionate lists. Representations of "our" women have assisted in reinforcing the racial narratives of history that continue to plague the world today. Yet as self-help history, the prosopographies seem infinitely better than the alternative, an absence of models for women's development in any social, national, or racial categories.

The existence of such records directly contradicts the histories of the genre of biography that I examine in the next chapter. In spite of the international rhetoric of the World's Fair, its effects seem to have vanished twenty-five years later in Bloomsbury, when Virginia Woolf wrote longingly of the anonymous mothers lost to history. A Room of One's Own, published just a few years after Homespun Heroines (1926),[120] stands both outside and inside the racist history of civilization that placed women and other races in the primitive past. Woolf's prosopographies trace the lives of nineteenth-century English women writers as a metonymy for "woman." Woolf's narrator suggests that it is in the nature of being "a woman" not to try "to make an Englishwoman" out of "even a very fine negress" (*A Room of One's Own,* 50). The slippery terms of identity and of honor in this claim produce the sort of vertigo that the nude World Mother ought to feel, standing on the globe on that series of purple volumes, *Woman: In All Ages and All Countries*.[899] It was nevertheless possible, in 1929 as in 1893, for presenters to gather more than "very fine" material, to establish instead names, personas, and life narratives in a heritage of "other women of distinction."

Chapter Six

Writing Women's Lives, Revisited

Virginia Woolf and the Missing Canons of Biography

The years between 1890 and 1930 generated many encyclopedic catalogs of imagined communities, supposedly exhaustive yet carefully
selected for race, nationality, gender, class, or other valued traits.
Narratives of the history of biography, largely defined by the modernists, have included one such prosopography, the *Dictionary of National Biography (DNB)*, but not its less monumental counterparts, *The
Congress of Women*,[245] *Noted Negro Women*,[542] or *Woman: In All
Ages and All Countries*.[899] It is not surprising that the "companion"
or reference work for the dominant cultural tradition should continue
to be consulted. But even those who seek other traditions tend to look
right past the existing self-help histories, preferring collective elegy,
a poetics of dispossession. As Carolyn Steedman put it some time
ago, "A sense of that which is lost . . . has been one of the most powerful rhetorical devices of modern women's history."[1] Thus both the
standard definitions of the genre of biography and the conventions
of feminist recuperation contribute to the neglect of most women's
biographies.

  Virginia Woolf, the great elegiac poet of women's unrecorded lives,
charged that women, "all but absent from history" (*A Room of One's
Own* [*ROO*], 43), lurk only "in their husband's biographies" (*Three
Guineas* [*TG*], 77). Why did she ignore the hundreds of female prosopographies? There are many possible reasons. As one of the few female

biographers, subjects, or critics to have a role in mainstream stories of biography, she shared in contemporary criticism that devalued popular, didactic, collective lives of those who are not in the male literary elite. Most presenters of female biographical collections appear almost as anonymous as the audience, while the texts may seem to be interchangeable and inelegant means of keeping certain subjects' names and stories in currency. Even the most definitive life tends to have a very brief shelf life, as later generations need new versions of the past. (Biographers are hardly more willing to give Froude the last word on Carlyle, for example, than historians are likely to leave the French Revolution to Carlyle.) Collections, with their inevitably dated lists, seem particularly perishable, while the bulk of published lives of women have appeared in transient collective forms. Though the modernist aesthetic favored the idea of spontaneous impressions, it could also take the very long, monumental view of cultural traditions.

Woolf could be highly skeptical about monuments and heroes. Not simply a champion of modernist aesthetics, she also clearly espoused biography's tradition of ethical influence. Her lament for the lost records of woman was rhetorically designed as a feminist rallying cry. She reserved praise largely for sources of ulterior energy or inspiration, and she might wrongly have assumed that popular collections honored famous monuments to virtue. At the same time, she participated in collective biography herself. Lives of women pervade Woolf's pioneering works of feminist cultural criticism: *A Room of One's Own* and *Three Guineas* may both be read as prosopographies.

A sketch of Woolf's relation to the many biographical collections surging around early twentieth-century London will help to correct the imbalance in the histories and criticism of life writing. Definitions of genre have political and ethical implications, as I have suggested. I shall attend to the standard narratives of biography, both in and around Bloomsbury and more recently in academia. Critics seem haunted by the failings or losses of biography, much as Woolf seeks a spectral archive, imagining that there is somewhere an intact recognition of great men. As I argued in chapter 1, criticism of biography focuses both on problems of representation (the genre is "handmaiden of both history and literature") and on the ethical relations among biographers, subjects, and audience.[2] Feminist researchers seeking critical ways to think back through foremothers need to rethink the history of life writing as well.

The ironies of recognition—how can we call up lists of the truly anonymous, why must we always repeat the summons?—do not discourage me from an effort in which I participate. Woolf, a triumphant biographical subject who is now perhaps the most compelling type of the woman writer, restimulated the historical recuperation of women, and she revitalized legends of feminine heroism that have been productive for generations of feminists. The alarming fact is that far from being unrecognized, the lives of competing constituents saturate every possible mode of representation. To lend what Woolf calls "sentence" and "sequence" (*ROO,* 81) to this inassimilable infinity of stories, critics as well as presenters have turned to selective traditions of representative lives. No matter how some critics have striven to undo the misrecognition that biography has suffered, it refuses to be the reserve of the few great men of letters but descends into the traffic of the streets as a useful collective practice shaping subjects within national histories.

Woolf in the Well-Lit Corridors of History

The critical tradition that resists self-help history or popular prosopography developed with literary modernism in Britain. Woolf, daughter of the *DNB*, helped to steer that tradition and is often featured as the author of the pivotal essay "The New Biography." This 1927 piece praises the fictional technique that captures "personality" but that avoids the Victorians' prolix tributes to paragons.[3] She shares with Harold Nicolson, Edmund Gosse, Lytton Strachey, and their successors an ironic distance from the heroic subject and a preference for fine-tuned aperçus rather than good deeds.[4] In other words, she places biography on the side of literature rather than history and would minimize the ethical function. Yet any familiarity with Woolf's practice and orientation as an essayist shows a more complicated view of biography as a historical medium rich in the ethical potential of restoring or reforming personality. She famously and repeatedly raises objections to the traditional erasure of subordinate subjects. Her many writings imagine a lively tradition of collective biographical history, the common life.[5] As generations of feminist critics have argued, her fiction moves subtly along an ethical axis, as in her satire of imperialism in the "life" of Orlando or her insistence on what might be called the epistemological justice of attention to marginal characters such as Lily Briscoe or Septimus Smith. Her "Journal of the Mistress Joan Martyn," her reviews of publications of early modern diaries and letters, and many other writings suggest that she wished to look behind the towering great men to the feminine past—the origins that her male counterparts sought to escape. As the exhortations in *A Room of One's Own* reveal, Woolf maintained that the dispossessed need role models as well as material support; the young women in her audience are to begin to write a history of women and to prepare the way for future Judith Shakespeares. In feminist studies, Woolf authorizes countless projects of recovery and reassessment that regard life writing as a contribution to historiography and the ethics of recognition.

In the field of biography studies, Woolf nevertheless diverts attention from the masculinist definition of the genre or, rather, she leaves it intact because it appears so unassailable. Living in an "age of biography," she claims that "biography is too much about great men" (*ROO*, 53, 108–9). When literary history demands broad-shouldered classics, women's lives quail. "There were the biographies: Johnson and Goethe and Carlyle and Sterne and Cowper and Shelley and Voltaire and Browning and many others" (*ROO*, 86)—a daunting, unpunctuated canon, unencumbered by first names and implicitly occupying two or three volumes each. Brief, collected biographies would have little hope of breaking into the linked elbows of "the biographies." Undoubtedly, this masculine canon has overshadowed the majority of lives, but it is a list that already ends elliptically in "many others." Feminist critics continue to overstate the coherence and hegemony of masculine life writing to make way for feminine alternatives.

Woolf's writings suggest that she derived her fascination with biography from full-length solo lives. She hardly made a habit of reading collective biographies addressed to the female common reader.[6] Given the low status of many of the publications, it would perhaps be more surprising if Woolf had, in fact, cited Eric S. Robertson's *English Poetesses* (1883)[679] or Elbert Hubbard's *Little Journeys to the Homes of Famous Women* (1897)[425] as authorities on Christina Rossetti or Jane Austen. Sets of short biographical studies nevertheless were a modernist craze, and apart from *Roger Fry, Orlando,* and *Flush,* Woolf's own biographical writings appeared serially or in essay collections. Further, she speaks a highly developed vocabulary of historical examples of womanhood that exceeds the individual biographies of women then available.

In both *A Room of One's Own* and *Three Guineas* she expresses desire to know the women of the past, primarily of the middle class, though "it is much to be regretted that no lives of maids . . . are to be found in the *Dictionary of National Biography*" (*TG,* 166). These manifestos in different ways rely on conventions of auto/biography (the first-person travel or literary essay; the letter) and devote many of their pages to series of biographical vignettes of women, the sort of prosopographical "supplement to history" that Woolf tentatively solicits from the college women of the future. *Three Guineas* compiles the life narrative of a "collective 'us,'" as Georgia Johnston has observed, yet its documented sources are numerous separate biographies of women, apart from four collections: Ray Strachey's *The Cause*[761] (a biographical history of the British women's movement [see *ROO,* 20]), Margaret Llewelyn Davies's collection of working women's testimonies, *Life as We Have Known It* (published, with Woolf's introduction, by Hogarth in 1931), George Ballard's 1752 *Memoirs of Several Ladies of Great Britain,* the great-granddaddy of Victorian collective biographies of women, and of course *The Dictionary of National Biography.*[7] Woolf's manifestos appeal to a collective endeavor to construct a nearly anonymous or legendary female biographical history, under the names, perhaps, of Mrs. Seton or Judith Shakespeare or the Society of Outsiders. In support of this common biographical history, she names women whose memory was largely preserved in biographical albums. Collections and single biographies available in Woolf's day had honored each of the women writers who have a role in chapter 4 of *A Room of One's Own,* including Aphra Behn, Fanny Burney, Jane Austen, and Florence Nightingale (featured in her friend Lytton Strachey's prosopographical *Eminent Victorians*). So enterprising had the biographical compilers been in "think[ing] back through our mothers" (*ROO,* 76) that early twentieth-century collections amply represented the Victorian reformers alluded to in chapter 6 of *A Room of One's Own* and in *Three Guineas,* including Emily Davies, Anne Clough, Josephine Butler, and Mary Kingsley (*TG*, 76–77). Most of the women featured in Woolf's own multivolume, largely biographical essays were kept in contemporary currency in collections of biographies published between 1880 and 1930 alone: there were the perennial favorites including the Brontës, George Eliot, Mme de Sévigné, and Elizabeth Barrett Browning, as well as the less popular Duchess of Newcastle, Hester Thrale, Dorothy Wordsworth, Jane Carlyle, Mary Russell Mitford, Maria Edgeworth, Laetitia Pilkington, Ellen Terry, Lady Hester Stanhope, Joanna Baillie, Sappho, and George Sand.[8] Collective biography itself might have been granted higher stature, as a form that included the achievements not only of Johnson, Hazlitt, Carlyle, Pater, or Beerbohm but also of Agnes Strickland, Anna Jameson, Harriet Martineau, Margaret Oliphant, Charlotte M. Yonge, Bessie Rayner Parkes, not to mention numerous "lesser" men of letters from William Howitt to William Henry Davenport Adams to Francis Birrell and Philip Guedalla. As I noted in the introduction, the late nineteenth century saw a variety of collections with literary and aesthetic pretensions suitable to the day.

In spite of her resounding defense of "thinking in common" (*ROO*, 65), Woolf seems oblivious to her own immersion in a collective biographical tradition. Most prominently, there were Leslie Stephen's *DNB* and his collections of largely biographical essays, such as *Men, Books, and Mountains,* and Strachey's *Eminent Victorians,* or Harold Nicolson's *Some People,* the volume that Woolf reviewed in her essay "The New Biography." Less well-recognized, Woolf's aunt (actually, the sister of her father's first wife), Anne Thackeray Ritchie, published *A Book of Sybils* (1883),[674] a reprint of essays from the *Cornhill Magazine* (a prestigious journal then edited by Leslie Stephen, that was later to publish several reviews by Virginia Stephen in 1908). Ritchie's collection is dedicated to Margaret Oliphant, with studies of "Mrs. Barbauld, Mrs. Opie, Miss Edgeworth, and Miss Austen." At the other end of Woolf's life, the Hogarth Press in 1937 began a series of short volumes known as World-Makers and World-Shakers, in an attempt, in Leonard's words, to "explain history" to "young people" "through the lives of great men and women." The second of four books actually published was *Joan of Arc* by Vita Sackville-West—the one female subject in this series being one of the most popular subjects in all collective female biographies in English.[9] Sackville-West also contributed an Orlando-esque portrait of Aphra Behn to a collection produced by Woolf's friend Francis Birrell, *Six Brilliant English Women* (1930).[81] The Duckworth house, which published Woolf's first two novels, published collections of women, including *Historic Nuns* (1899)[620] by the mid-Victorian feminist Bessie Rayner Parkes, who had become Mme Belloc (mother of Hilaire).[10]

Besides being a common publishing venture known in Bloomsbury and elsewhere, collective biographies were associated with the campaign for women's suffrage. In 1889, Millicent Garrett Fawcett published *Some Eminent Women of Our Times.*[282]; [11] In 1909, Edith Craig produced Cicely Hamilton's *A Pageant of Great Women,*[373] an honor roll performed by eminent Edwardian women: the list included learned women (from Hypatia to Mme Curie), artists (including Sappho and Rosa Bonheur), saintly women (featuring Elizabeth Fry and Catherine of Siena), heroic women (including Charlotte Corday), rulers (including Victoria, of course), and warriors (from Joan of Arc to Florence Nightingale).[12] Yet canons of great women continued to be proposed without any explicit agenda for women's rights and very often with a high proportion of women of letters. Woolf could expect her audience to be familiar with such figures as Eliza Carter, "the valiant old woman who tied a bell to her bedstead in order that she might wake early and learn Greek" (*ROO*, 65–66), through worthy sources such as *Famous Blue Stockings* (264).[683] In alluding to the ballad of four Marys in *A Room,* Woolf also referred to a fashion for collective biographies with a medievalist device of plural names, such as *Four Margarets* (1929).[775]; 13

Woolf inadvertently encouraged later feminist scholars in the view that a female tradition had been lost, as Magaret Ezell has suggested.[14] The recognition of women that surrounded Woolf in the 1920s and 1930s must have seemed irrelevant to the enterprise of building a literary city of women. The belief that women's lives utterly languished has a corollary—that certain biographies of men of genius remain fixed for all time. Compensatory prosopographies tend to posit an ideal complete personified history elsewhere; this supports a standard before-and-after story of suppression and liberation. Recall that Woolf equivocates on the absences within tradition. She lures readers into "those almost unlit corridors of history," where the "generations of women" are only "dimly" recorded.[15] Yet in *Three Guineas* she invites a thorough reading of biography, "that witness which anyone who can read English can consult on the shelves of any public library"—a record, she suggests, that includes "the lives of the poor, of the obscure, of the uneducated" (*TG,* 24–25). In context, she refers to unprivileged men who covet a university education. But why imagine that men's biography and history are intact and transparent and women's a jumble of shards? Any library in her day would have included lives of women, in reference books and a multitude of collections—certainly few of the poor and uneducated but well beyond a handful of celebrated women.

Woolf perhaps prefers to continue the search for something more precious. Here is a key passage in *A Room of One's Own,* in which Woolf calls for female prosopography ("a mass of information" on the patterns in women's lives in the past) to supplement the standard histories. It is worth quoting at length because of its oscillation between the named and the discounted and because of the stated gap between what we have and what is desired. She begins by searching for "the Elizabethan woman. . . . History scarcely mentions her."

> Occasionally an individual woman is mentioned, an Elizabeth, or a Mary; a
> queen or a great lady. But by no possible means could middle-class women with
> nothing but brains and character at their command have taken part in any one

of the great movements which . . . constitute the historian's view of the past. Nor shall we find her in any collection of anecdotes. Aubrey hardly mentions her. She never writes her own life and scarcely keeps a diary. . . . What one wants, I thought . . . is a mass of information; at what age did she marry; how many children had she as a rule. . . . All these facts lie somewhere, presumably, in parish registers and account books; the life of the average Elizabethan woman must be scattered about somewhere, could one collect it and make a book of it. It would be ambitious beyond my daring, I thought, looking about the shelves for books that were not there, to suggest to the students of those famous colleges that they should re-write history, though I own that it often seems a little queer as it is, unreal, lop-sided; but why should they not add a supplement to history? calling it, of course, by some inconspicuous name so that women might figure there without impropriety? For one often catches a glimpse of them in the lives of the great, whisking away into the background, concealing, I sometimes think, a wink, a laugh, perhaps a tear. And, after all, we have lives enough of Jane Austen; it scarcely seems necessary to consider again the influence of the tragedies of Joanna Baillie upon the poetry of Edgar Allan Poe; as for myself, I should not mind if the homes and haunts of Mary Russell Mitford were closed to the public for a century at least. But what I find deplorable . . . is that nothing is known about women before the eighteenth century. (44–45)

"That is an awkward break, I thought"—as Woolf writes of Jane Eyre's meditation on the roof of Thornfield (*ROO*, 69). True enough, the majority of illiterate Elizabethan women were little known in 1929. Yet is there no Anne Askew or Margaret Roper, or no woman of the seventeenth century, no Lucy Hutchinson, no Lady Rachel Russell? Since the time of Dr. Johnson and Mary Astell (Woolf later refers to Ballard's record of Astell in *Three Guineas* [25, 153n.21]), earlier Englishwomen of middling as well as high ranks had been repeatedly honored—honored we might say in droves—for their part in historical movements such as the Civil War or penal, educational, or religious reform. Are the glimpses we wish to catch only of women writers? *A Room of One's Own*, like the mode of feminist study that has followed Woolf, seeks to represent the history of women through exemplary women writers, a literary focus that is shared by many earlier collective biographies of women. When do we have too much biographical history? Apparently, we have more than enough biography and lop-sided history of all sorts of men and a redundancy of some kinds of female biography. Woolf especially slams the door on middle-class women writers of the eighteenth and early nineteenth century who won great praise from men.

Mary Russell Mitford is a significant ghost author to incarcerate in her own home: the famous writer of what might be called topographical essays, *Our Village*, who gave to her friend Elizabeth Barrett Browning the pet dog who became the star of Woolf's parodic biography, *Flush*. Mitford, who figures in at least eight all-female collections,[6; 8; 125; 175; 195; 372; 433; 554] helped to promote the "homes and haunts" genre—a form of popular literary biography fused with travels that fostered literary England and a transatlantic English-speaking union. As Deidre Lynch has noted, *A Room of One's Own* precludes a certain kind of literary history: the textual pilgrimage to the woman author in the house.[16] Yet Woolf herself participated in that sort of parabiographical criticism cum travel memoir, from her first published piece, "Haworth, November 1904," to a satiric review in 1920 of *Mary Russell Mitford and Her Surroundings*. In the latter she implies that, like all well-read contemporaries, she is far too familiar with biographies of famous British women of brains and character and, at the same time, that there is a shortage of female representative subjects.[17]

The overstatement of simultaneous plenitude and dearth—a truly Woolfian motif—seems conditioned, in part, by her experience of reviewing numerous single biographies of women writers and, in part, by the sense of competition for the limited number of slots available for more recent Judith Shakespeares who were not anonymously buried at the crossroads. Beyond such self-reflection, however, Woolf is a poet of prosopography, desiring the unspeakable names of the dead. The lady writing at the window should be anonymous, according to her various ghostly appearances in Woolf's writings; Miss Mitford is entirely renowned, familiar, and at home. The ample supply of women's lives that was at Woolf's fingertips appeared too substantially personal (like women writers who expose their anger) or too domesticated by common recognition. The desired history of women consists of elusive traces, departed beings to whom one attributes bodies and passions but not, in Woolf's imagining, registered names.

To Woolf, it seems, the lost biography is much more desirable than the one ready to hand. This is according to custom: champions of different groups are compelled to call up again and again the lists always under erasure. There is, at least, an uncanny anticipation of *A Room of One's Own* in a collection published in London and New York in 1880, *Six Life Studies of Famous Women* by Matilda Betham-Edwards.[75]; [18] The neglected exemplars—Fernan Caballero (Spanish novelist), Alexandrine Tinné (African explorer), Caroline Herschel (astronomer), Marie Pape-Carpantier (education reformer), Elizabeth Carter (scholar), Matilda Betham (the compiler's aunt, a writer and artist, early compiler of women's lives)—arouse a "keen regret" for the missing, the "glorious women of all ages and countries" to whom "history has been indeed unjust"— thus Betham-Edwards sounding highly Woolfian (viii). "Here and there [sic] imperious queen or saintly devotee has won recognition.... We know something about Louise of Savoy, Anne of Brittany, Margaret of Parma; from earliest childhood we have been taught to admire Joan of Arc, Elizabeth of Hungary, and Saint Theresa. But there are heroic women of another type of whom we would fain know something also; fireside heroines whose lives are more in sympathy with our own" (ix). Betham-Edwards continues with a list of famous names that sidestep ordinary heroism: "The Aspasias and Cleopatras of antiquity, the Elizabeths of England and Isabellas of Castile do not fairly represent them.

Nor do the Joans of Arc or the Saint Theresas." These Carlylean plurals are followed by a few snapshots of "intermediate notabilities . . . worthy of a biographer," such as Sarah Fielding (ix–xii). In effect, Betham-Edwards, like Woolf and many others, reiterates a ghostly catalog of women from the books that elude recognition. A hypostatized plenitude of one sort of archive, great men or great women, heightens the desire for the perfect encyclopedia of nonentities, those anonymous complements to one's own bid for humanity. The facade of this hall of fame is always under scaffolding, while some Mrs. McNab or Mrs. Bast tends the house of civilization.

Life Narratives of Biography

Where does Woolf's feminist prosopography belong in the tradition of criticism of biography? The professional studies of biography are much more alike than the warehouse full of books on the novel or the shipping container bulging with studies of autobiography. From Boswell's *Life of Johnson* to Edel's *Henry James*, the history of the genre has been written largely as a colloquy in an Augustan coffeehouse among a few (male) authors and their scribes, with polite bows to a few women as foils or muses: as Woolf observes, "every Johnson has his Thrale" (*ROO*, 87).[19] In 1892, for example, George Saintsbury charged the critic of biography to appreciate great conjunctions of biographer and subject—"Boswell's *Johnson,* Moore's *Byron,* Lockhart's *Scott,* Carlyle's *Sterling* . . . and . . . Trevelyan's *Macaulay.*"[20] The art of biography consists in "fixing the attention of the reader on the character of the subject" in a closed circle of mutual reference: "To any really good literary judge the thing was certain beforehand."[21] The pattern of a homosocial series of mimetic pairs is remarkably durable: A. O. J. Cockshut structures *Truth to Life* (1974) on the bonds between "Stanley's Arnold," "Trevelyan's Macaulay," "Froude's Carlyle," "Morley's Gladstone," and "Ward's Newman."[22] Disconcertingly, William Epstein's 1987 poststructuralist analysis of biography deliberately limits its sample to "the four English biographers whom *everyone* seems to have read": Walton, Johnson, Boswell, Strachey. Notably, three of Epstein's figures wrote collective biographies. Critics have been caught in a detective plot with the wrong clues, searching for monumental equivalents to the timeless epic or novel certified by a great elective affinity between two writers. As Trev Broughton observes, "There is a certain circularity in the attribution of great Lives to great subjects, since the marks of greatness have a tendency to migrate between the two."[23] I would add that the accolades migrate to and from the audience as well; suitable conditions for great biography require a homosocial exchange of likenesses. Matters are not altered radically by the insertion of Diane Middlebrook's Anne Sexton; it is still a highly literary, exclusive exchange. The episode of "The New Biography" slightly displaces the great man and introduces Woolf without serious interruption of the traditional sequence. Prosopographies of modernist life writing assemble the usual suspects. For example, Ruth Hoberman's

Modernizing Lives begins with a list: "Lytton Strachey, Geoffrey Scott, David Cecil, Percy Lubbock, A. J. A. Symons, Virginia Woolf, E. M. Forster, and Harold Nicolson . . . an apparently motley crew who are, collectively, the subject of this study."[24] Not motley enough, perhaps.

Woolf in fact diverges so much from "the Stracheyan Revolution" that her presence ought to shatter the New Critical narratives of the genre. Altogether her oeuvre embarrasses the notion of pure biography that Harold Nicolson put forward. Nevertheless, she began to serve as the Woman in Biography well before she was revived by feminists who were inspired by her splendid performance as auto/biographical subject in Quentin Bell's *Virginia Woolf* and the editions of her diaries and letters. Most later-twentieth-century narratives of the life of biography include her, as author of "The New Biography," *Flush,* and *Orlando,* the definitive "mock biography."[25] Book-length studies of biography afford only a limited number of female participants (biographers or critics), who tend to be discarded after a time; Woolf has the distinction of lasting. John A. Garraty's *The Nature of Biography* (1957) acknowledges a range of female biographers such as Katharine Anthony, Catherine Drinker Bowen, Louise Hall Tharp, and Madeleine B. Stern.[26] Woolf is joined by Margaret Oliphant, Marchette Chute, Iris Origo, and Hester W. Chapman among forty-seven critics in James L. Clifford's *Biography as an Art* (1962) and by Elizabeth Porter Gould, Elizabeth Drew, and Iris Origo in David Novarr's collection of forty-nine critical essays on the genre, *The Lines of Life* (1986).[27] As so often happens, the designation of one eminent woman eventually diminishes the recognition of many, much as Gaskell's *Life of Charlotte Brontë* is a placeholder for so many lives of women by women.

I sketched, in chapter 1, the current standing of biography in epistemological and ethical terms; the critical history that submerges female collective biography concerns me here. Until the later nineteenth century, most concurred that biography was an instructive, character-forming medium of history (i.e. fact). Late Victorians began to arrange a marriage of biography with belles lettres (i.e. fiction), leaving the household of useful biographies behind.[28] Biography came to be judged wanting, under the code that devalued the rhetorical, as the practices of literature became more professionalized.[29] Simultaneously, the professionalization of positivist historiography demoted the long tradition of "particular history," of Plutarchan biographical collections, deeming narratives of individual lives to be woefully subjective.[30] Since the early twentieth century, charges often have focused on three kinds of abuse committed by the presenter: faults of representation, including distortion or excess of fact (i.e. bad history) or lack of vision, form or style (i.e. bad literature); ethical violations against the subject (theft, slander); and designs on the reader (preaching, pandering, gulling). Sometimes, the motives or the quality of the audience take the blame: readers are voyeurs or celebrity hunters—uncritical, ignorant, or susceptible. The positive qualities sought in excellent biographies may have been less readily stated, but they center on attributes of the subject: admirable deeds, public service, vocational self-development, and participation in national history—aspects of many notable women's lives.

The standard of life writing favored autonomous agency as well, which both collective publication and construction of the reader might seem to mitigate. Relying on metaphors of the stages of a human life, many critics write a kind of biography of biography, expecting it to mature into the individuality and interiority of the modern subject. It is a masculine, middle-class story of triumphant recognition, but it is followed by failed promise, Prufrockian dissipation. Back in 1832, Thomas Carlyle marveled that a genre that affords "unspeakable delight" should so often fail: "few genuinely-good *Biographies* have yet been accumulated in Literature."[31] Critics try to uphold the genre as disinterested art representing universals of human nature, but their tropes betray the instructive purposes—historical, ethical—that they expect biography to serve: formation of a nationally representative subjectivity. Indeed, biography (in spite of its private, feminine tendencies) is looked to as a hero of national epic. Carlyle's lament about the inferiority of biographies expresses envy of other traditions: "How comes it that in England we have simply one good biography, this Boswell's *Johnson;* and of good, indifferent, or even bad attempts at biography, fewer than any civilised people?"[32] In this spirit, later students of the form describe "the slow rise, and the gradual maturing, of the criticism of biography" and the "retarded evolution" of English biography itself, lamenting great biographies unborn.[33] Novarr's collection *The Lines of Life* traces the ritual calls for the missing rigorous study of the genre up through the inauguration of the journal *Biography* in 1978 and Leon Edel's keynote address at the Biographical Research Center at the University of Hawaii in 1981.[34] Yet recent critics echo Carlyle's reproach that such a popular (and nationally significant) form should be managed so haphazardly.[35] According to Novarr, biography's "critics . . . merely play ring-around-the-rosies; they rarely wrestle or stand on each other's shoulders."[36] Standing on each other's shoulders and playing ring around the rosies: perhaps the gendering formulas repeat themselves.

Criticism of biography may be forgiven an appearance of amateurism, given the impossibility of its custodial task. The accelerated production of biographies in the later Victorian period, and the more recent proliferation of individual lives of women, of everyone, demand extreme measures to impose any order on them. The few academics who stake part of their careers on writing a book about biography inevitably discard most of the mass of lives, too many for one person to read. Ready to hand they have found a standard account of the genre's development set down at the turn of the twentieth century. This modernist literary history now appears to have been an extreme effort to exclude most popular forms and to resist the competition of women in the literary marketplace. Assessments of biography in recent decades, more open to a range of subjects, actually take the form of collected autobiographical essays by biographers, who write as survivors of a sort of posthumous transference.[37] After introductory generalizations about the genre, these essays expand on the details of one subject's life and the biographer's struggles to design the text (worthy matters in themselves), not on questions of literary history. Critical and historical studies of life writing (rather than reviews or testimonies of biographers) studiously ignore collective biographies of women, as they invent an unfinished bildungsroman for biography as a form held back by sentiment and convention.

Accounts of biography trouble over its birth. Albert Britt, who before World War II taught a course on biography in the English department of Knox College, deems the genre an "art . . . as old as memory, coeval with articulate speech, yet difficult to define and trace historically."[38] With acknowledgments of the roots of life writing in panegyric, Christian hagiography, classical and Renaissance encomia, most studies trace the modern genre of biography, rather tautologically, from usage of the term itself by such men of letters as Dryden and Addison.[39] Most accounts agree that biography in its infancy required the exchange of moral precepts. Continuing practices of popular biography are often said to characterize more primitive, earlier stages, with the usual alignment of maturity and masculinity. Edmund Gosse, for example, called in 1901 for a new scribal hero: "Some young man of ambition and energy, looking about for a subject on which to exercise his pen, might do worse than devote himself to the History of Biography in England. It is, I believe, a virgin theme."[40] According to Gosse, Izaak Walton might be the first notable English biographer for his observational skill, were it not that "his aim was pre-eminently edification." In a rare assignment of credit to a female biographer, Gosse allows that Lucy "Hutcheson" "adds to English biography the element of a precise and even sequence of events" in her quaint tribute to her husband (199–200; *Hutchinson* was a favored subject in nineteenth-century women's collections). Gosse's history continues: "The last remarkable biography in the old, dim manner . . . was Dr. Johnson's 'Life of Savage.'" Abruptly, biography was born anew in Boswell's *Life of Johnson* in 1791 (202–3).

Linda Wagner-Martin is one of many critics who pan quickly to a Boswellian point of origin for "modern biography in the English-speaking world." What Boswell began remains unaccounted for since, according to Wagner-Martin, in the ensuing century and more "*biography* meant stories about the lives of prominent male subjects, written with an emphasis on the external . . . events of their lives, praising . . . rather than questioning their characters"—a curious consequence of the intimate chronicle of Dr. Johnson's quotidian peculiarities.[41] Yet the Boswellian birth is also a climax: biography "after 1791, had reached maturity."[42] If so, the subsequent life course of biography must be construed as a decline and dotage; Victorians failed "to reproduce the Boswell formula."[43] Part of the formula undoubtedly was the role of professional men of letters as neither "hacks" nor dependents of patrons.[44] As Michael McKeon puts it, "The emergence of the novel and the transformation of biography in the seventeenth and eighteenth centuries profoundly express the modern discovery of . . . the autonomous subject."[45] The most honored biographies model the hero as man of letters.

If the triple birth of the individual, the man of letters, and modern biography was so auspicious, the custom of Victorian biography appears to have stunted its growth, if it did not commit outright child murder. The modernists' "New Biography," a sort of rebirth after formulaic eulogy, provides a fine turn in the plot of the genre. The Victorians, the story goes, were a nation of undertakers, indulging in mortuary pomp. The modernists slew their elders not only to clear the way for their own biographical ventures but also to improve the international reputation of English biography. Concerning Victorian biography, Strachey in his preface to *Eminent Victorians* (1918) deplores the fact that the English "have never had, like the French, a great biographical tradition."[46] Writing a life has been delegated to "the journeymen of letters," whereas it is as delicate an art as living itself. He dismisses "those two fat volumes . . . with their ill-digested masses of material, their slipshod style, their tone of tedious panegyric, their lamentable lack of selection. . . . They are as familiar as the *cortège* of the undertaker, and wear the same air of slow, funereal barbarism" (10). Strachey's terms of disgust ("fat," "ill-digested") characterize a *body* of life writing that attends on death.

While funereal themes have adhered to biography since ancient times, Strachey also may have been recalling Edmund Gosse's opening conceit in "The Custom of Biography" (1901): "Various nations have diverse ways of building the tombs of their prophets. The Americans endow institutions . . . and give them the names of the deceased. The French . . . fill the squares of their country towns with bronze statues. We in England bury our dead under the monstrous catafalque of two volumes (crown octavo), and go forth refreshed. . . . The custom has now grown into a [national] institution." Quoting at length a "foreign writer" who mocks English indiscriminate tributes, Gosse deplores the shelves of biographies that "mak[e] this portion of the library a sort of solemn Kensal Green" (195) or, elsewhere, "a dust-heap . . . devoted to oblivion" (205). (In more than one sense, collective biographical history is indeed devoted to oblivion.) With little to say about the few nineteenth-century works that "have afforded English readers pleasure of a very high kind, and have taken a permanent place in history," Gosse heaps scorn on amateur or doting biographers ("the worst is the Widow" [204–5]).[47] Happy in their witticisms, Gosse and Strachey invite their audience into an Olympic coterie, above mortal, effeminate Philistines.

In a 1927 contribution to the Hogarth Lectures on Literature series published by the Woolfs, Harold Nicolson praised Gosse and Strachey for their courage in breaking with Victorianism, which "only died in 1921"; in 1911, Sir Sidney Lee still sustained the "nineteenth-century spirit."[48] Evidently, the old laudatory mode is a blot on the British literary escutcheon. Nicolson considers the period "between 1838 and 1882, between the date of Lockhart's *Scott* and that of Froude's *Carlyle*"—notably, a high point of Englishwomen's literary achievement—to be a relapse into the "old, unworthy origins of English biography," the "impure," hagiographical tradition.[49] Whereas Gaskell's *Charlotte Brontë* is "an excellent sentimental novel," Nicolson dismisses it along with the (unidentified) hundreds of singular and collective biographies that preceded Froude, Gosse, Strachey, and the "pure" modern biographers.[50]

Plainly, the modernists claim biography as a branch of literature and reproach ethical excesses. The narratives should delight but should aim for moderation between veneration and satire.[51] Biographies, in any case, should have nothing in common with community rituals such as funerals, nor with the sentiments or sensations of *le corps moyen*. Such views evidently would have encouraged Woolf in her disregard of most existing biographical records of women. Yet in spite of the consensus that modernism purified biography of such promiscuous dealings, it is curiously difficult to distinguish between Victorian and modernist behavior in this field (as in other cultural matters).[52] Albeit with different narrative means and different models of the subject, the modernist plan for biography continued to strive to capture and commend great personality. Moreover, the modernist practice leaned toward collective biography, just as Victorians had issued collections as commonly as two-volume catafalques.[53] The sketch of personality advocated by Woolf (in "The New Biography"), by Philip Guedalla, and by the "psychographer" Gamaliel Bradford, as well as by Strachey, produced volumes resembling impressionist portrait galleries.[54] The prestige of the subjects, presenter, audience, and their social milieu guided the lasting reputation as much as the quality of the works themselves. Lytton Strachey's *Eminent Victorians* of 1918 remains vastly more notable than Gamaliel Bradford's *Portraits of Women* of 1916,[103] though Bradford's urbane "psychographs," modeled on Sainte-Beuve, resemble Strachey's own magazine pieces on Mme du Deffand and others.[55] A psychological imperative entailed a reinvention of the form of brief parallel lives: a gemlike, Paterian program of *Imaginary Portraits* or a Proustian history of sensation. Though knocking down public-monument biography might clear space for many ordinary lives, the requirement of refined psychological fidelity and aesthetic precision generally kept Mrs. Grundy or Mrs. Brown out of the picture.[56] "The New Biography" scarcely heralds a shift to social history and recognition of women, working classes, and others. A large part of the Victorian tradition that the modernists spurn is remarkably open to the self-improving workman, the provincial spinster with her Ragged School. Modernist critics consigned collective biographies of women and other self-help history to the impure dust heap.

Misadventures of Life Narrative in Academe

It is easy enough to see where the literary histories of biography went wrong. Critics expect the iconic text, whereas biographies are transient and serial. Critics seek masculine models of individuality, whereas life narrative is inherently collective and readily associated with the feminine: private life, the everyday, personal relations, the mortal body. Arguably, modern biography, like the novel, constructs the bourgeois subject as feminine, in what Carolyn Steedman calls the "historical romance" "of getting closer," of feeling the "delightful weight of detail, littleness, and interiority."[57] It may also be agreed that life narratives of women, along with representations of interpersonal immanence rather than of autonomous transcendence, now flourish if they don't actually dominate in academic studies. Perhaps it is not so obvious, however, that studies of life narrative rely on a dubious before-and-after story. The gender dualism that aligns male auto/biography with linear coherence and female auto/biography with rupture and recurrence has distorted expectations for both bodies of works. While this book should make untenable the notion that women's lives went largely unwritten until the twentieth century, it may be harder to dispel the prevailing account of the past dominance of the monologic public man.

Here it is helpful to recall the marginalization of studies of life narrative during the second half of the twentieth century before the successes of (Woolfian) feminist studies. Before World War II, there were courses and even academic departments devoted to lives of great men. Yet in the later heyday of American higher education, biography was placed off limits by arbiters of various methods. Scholars strove to distance themselves from hero worship or from psychoanalytic reductiveness, or they resisted biography as too individualistic an approach to historical or cultural developments. (Art history may be one of the last holdouts, with its lives of the painters—perhaps because of the value of authentication in the art market.) Particularly in literary studies, biography was proscribed by both New Critics and poststructuralists. Successive generations of formalist literary theories, armed with the "intentional fallacy" or the "death of the author," militated against biographical studies.

The various theoretical objections to biography developed alongside the diversifying access to higher education for women and minorities—social elements missing from the narrow canon of lives. As Nancy Miller, Cheryl Walker, Valerie Ross, and other feminist critics have argued, attempts to render biography irrelevant simultaneously exclude marginal life narratives.[58] Yet while auto/biography has been important at each stage of feminist studies, it is risky to defend the personal in antitheoretical terms. The modernist homosocial tradition of biography itself persisted as though in proud imperviousness to theory.[59] Some academic feminist biographers have become uneasy in an antitheory alliance in which biography may figure, in Elisabeth Young-Bruehl's words, as "a kind of retrograde genre for people who had not properly problematized the notion of 'the self,' or 'identity.'"[60] Diane Wood Middlebrook employs remarkably similar terms for a genre suspected of nostalgia for home, of retrogression toward ancestry: "Biography . . . would seem to be a bastion of humanism safe from encroachment by the spirit of postmodernism."[61] In historiography, "the new social history" was met with objections that it returned to discredited biographical approaches in order to recuperate upper-class white

European women.[62] However resisted by various theoretical positions, biography perches like those ubiquitous pigeons on the sills of the humanities building, and it soars through Amazon.com.[63] In every branch of the humanities it is now common to pursue documentary recognition of multitudes of historically excluded predecessors.

Few today would wittingly approach life narratives as unmediated experience. Feminists expose the myth of the autonomous individual and celebrate the funeral rites for the masculine author.[64] Yet many accounts have missed the inherent collectivity and rhetorical commitments of all life writing and have overstated both the oppressive coherence of the old auto/biography and the liberating indeterminacy of the new. Many an informed academic may assemble syllabi, conference programs, or the contents of essay collections or anthologies on a foundation of identity politics as crude as any corporate ad campaign: the picture looks better with an assortment of types.[65] The very disciplines that teach skepticism about representation have been themselves constructed on prosopographies: genealogies of proponents of ideas, methods, schools that resemble, in turn, literary traditions and national histories.[66] Above all, feminist criticism has also retained a desire for the great self-expressive subject. What Carla Kaplan calls "a feminist *politics of voice*" has governed most "recuperative" studies of women's texts, whereby the writing of an autobiographical work such as Harriet Jacobs's *Incidents in the Life of a Slave Girl* becomes a triumph of "textual agency" equivalent to socially "subversive 'acts.'"[67]

Woolfian ethics of recuperation tend to support highly selective reconstructions of tradition (we have too much of Mary Russell Mitford) and to seek to amplify the voice of "Anon." Theoretically aware of the textual invention of the subject, the researcher nevertheless desires originating, unmediated agency, perhaps resenting having another person in the way—a biographer, say, or the white woman editor of the black former slave woman's text, or anyone else whose function resembles the researcher's. Feminist critics in the 1980s, often drawing on Woolf's authority, sought to recapture *auto*biography from masculine self-definition. This recovery might be justified even within a sophisticated model of representation. In 1982 Janet Varner Gunn was among the first American feminist critics of autobiography to emphasize the discursive construction of "the self who speaks, who lives in time. . . . It is by means of language (*graphie*) that self . . . achieves and acknowledges its *bios*."[68] An understandable preference for such a model of contextualized, relational subjectivity seemed to entail a caricature of all previous life writing as a self-enclosed exercise in "*auto*." In 1988, to take another comparatively early example, Shari Benstock swept aside "the tradition of autobiographical writings in Western culture" in order to rediscover female life writing: "The confessions of an Augustine or a Rousseau . . . do not admit internal cracks and disjunctures, rifts and ruptures. The whole thrust of such works is to seal up and cover over gaps in memory, dislocations in time and space, insecurities, hesitations, and blind spots."[69] Though the alliteration and parataxis here would suggest a translation from contemporary French poststructuralism, Benstock may not have been reading her de Man, who exposed the "de-facement" in the European canon of autobiography.[70]

The desired life writing is imagined as everything the canonical model of creative agency is not. Thus Sidonie Smith characterizes the modern subject: "unique, unitary, unencumbered, the self escapes all forms of embodiment" and any "constitutive affiliations." The old subject elicits a grandiose style (as in Shari Benstock's description above): "imperial interpreter, provocateur of totalization, the essential self is likewise a 'free' agent, exercising self-determination over meaning, personal destiny, and desire."[71] Smith would be quick to insist that this impregnable subject is legendary, yet she, like most recent observers, would locate it in history: a necessary invention for developing capitalist democracies, and one that is particularly invidious against women and those associated with the irrational and embodied.[72] An imaginary construct can of course have palpable effects, one of which is to mislead later observers into taking the legend as the truth for all social and discursive practices. The universalized (masculine) individual seemed real enough, in any case, to Virginia Woolf and others in the twentieth century who went on record as its opponents. My quarrel with Smith's account comes when the "hard core at the center" of the normative subject hardens further into the supposed fact of "traditional autobiography" as "an official account for the community." A monologic discourse takes the blame. Then, not a moment too soon, the "colorful, the nonidentical, the carnivalesque" arrives with its "'mess and clutter.'"[73]

Many feminist studies of life writing celebrate that sort of carnival. Influenced by theorists of gender difference such as Chodorow, Gilligan, and Irigaray, many critics expect women's texts to offer liberating fragmentation and multiplicity. Thus Susan Stanford Friedman insists that the requirements for women's life narrative reverse those of traditional autobiography: instead of autonomy, women's lives serve "*identification, interdependence, and community,*" and for that reason female autobiography has appeared invisible in studies of autobiography by James Olney, Georges Gusdorf, and others.[74] Obviously I concur with such an objection to exclusive literary history—I, too, am a recuperative researcher dwelling on mutual multibiography. A small deck of "great" life narrative has been stacked in favor of a few apparently isolated European men.[75] It is simply too tempting, however, to overstate the prevalence of a straight model of individualist life narrative. An alternative feminine style, or a utopian disruption of master narratives, dubious as a strategy for social reparation, seems even more so when held up to the "mess and clutter" of actual narrative practices, including the many all-male or mixed prosopographies. Feminist criticism of autobiography, a crucial recent development, inadvertently "helped to keep the old Gusdorf model in place . . . by attacking it," according to John Paul Eakin.[76] A less dualistic account of evolving forms of life writing would recognize the "rifts and ruptures" within traditional biography and autobiography.

All is not symmetrical and smoothly plastered on the classic facade of sub-jectivity. Biographies have been popular reading because they are shared busi-ness. Agreeing with the feminist principle that "*all* identity is relational," Eakin draws on Vincent Descombes's depiction of the Cartesian subject as already split between the bodily person and the speaking subject, in Descartes's dou-bled use of the pronoun "I."[77] A proponent of heroic lives such as Emerson may nevertheless recognize the discursive constructions of prosopographies— as Emerson significantly puts it, "The Uses of Great Men." When he praises great men in Carlylean plurals—"the Werners, Von Buchs, and Beaumonts"— he anticipates that their greatness "will pulverize" over time.[78] His own list has blurred like the lichened names carved around the cornices of Victorian buildings. But Emerson understands that names may be interchangeable in the mask-making serialization of types. His great men are representative fragments of "the genius of humanity . . . the real subject whose biography is written in our annals. We must infer much, and supply many chasms in the record. The history of the universe is symptomatic, and life is mnemonical. No man, in all the procession of famous men, is. . . . that essence we were looking for; but is an exhibition . . . of new possibilities." We should outgrow idolatry of individuals as, collectively, we are "multiplied by our proxies."[79]

Granted that Emerson demotes the individual in the name of a universal humanity. But it is time to look again at such cracks in the facade of hero wor-ship, such concessions to mutable, contingent, discursive subject positions, well before modernist iconoclasts tossed aside the Victorians' "lives" or post-modernists deconstructed the subject. Romantics and Victorians had often avoided monumental biography in favor of memorial impressions or medita-tions on their own contradictions. As David Amigoni notes, Carlyle recognized "the hero as a component in a rhetorical transaction," not a fulfilled being in splendid isolation.[80] Martin Danahay similarly finds in the sages "a deeply divided and conflicted subjectivity" that strains to disavow their interdepen-dence with and dependence on "a feminized other" (not least, on the labor of women and workers) to support the illusion that the man of letters works alone.[81]

I have no interest in underestimating the effects on traditional life writing of an ideology of autonomous individualism or of the constitution of European literate men as the standard of humanity. Emerson, with only a nervous glance toward the poor "Paddies" or Irish immigrant laborers, does not happen to drop the names of Martha Washington or Abigail Adams, Queen Elizabeth or Hannah More—names readily available in midcentury New England.[82] Like most who wish to view history on the panoramic scale, Emerson sees only the biographies of a very few great men. Women and "minor" men, like dots in color graphics, tend to become invisible from a distance. But this harmful illusion, corrected as much as possible by recognition of the missing lives, should not be attributed to some essential difference in the gendered forms of writing. The absence of lives of the obscure and of women from the panorama of history does not mean that all public men's lives were declarations of independence, nor indeed, that there were no records beyond the male elite.

It does not go without saying that the desire to recover the stories of subalterns has an ethical motive. It may be theoretically questionable to attribute both direct self-expression and subversive intersubjectivity to all women's contributions to the "minor" forms of memoir, diary, letter, oral narrative, collections, or autobiography in general. But it is also fair to say that Emerson and others denied those Irish laborers a podium. The preference for autobiography over biography in academic studies today derives in part, I believe, from an ethical objection to the power of the biographer or presenter.[83] The recent revival of ethical criticism could help to promote recognition of the rhetorical commitments of all life writing and, perhaps, correct for a simplified history of representation that views textual mediation as avoidable interference.[84] Histories of biography or autobiography would no longer suppose that the full-length individual narrative had been not only an ideal but also the prevailing reality and would no longer find it surprising that women served as subjects or biographers. Recognition of new lives, whether in first-person or third-person form, need not rely on a caricature of previously recognized lives. Advocates of marginal subjects might eschew romanticizing or colonizing exploitation, resisting both the view that women and people of color experience an interpersonality and textual jazziness closed off to the privileged and that they inhabit a feminine, ahistorical sphere. The supplement to exclusive prosopographies might not reinforce the structure and principles of dominant national histories. So, at least, I like to hope. Still I am influenced by the model of Virginia Woolf, who so often rediscovered hidden, intertwined lives of women.

In the same year that Woolf published "The New Biography," she wrote "Two Women," reviewing separate biographies of Emily Davies and Lady Augusta Stanley. This brief essay appears to prepare for some passages of *A Room of One's Own*. It begins with a prosopographical vision that readers of this study will find off kilter in a familiar way:

> Up to the beginning of the nineteenth century the distinguished woman had almost invariably been an aristocrat. . . . From the huge middle class few women rose to eminence. . . . There they remain, even in the early part of the nineteenth century, a vast body, living, marrying, bearing children in dull obscurity until at last we begin to wonder whether there was something in their condition itself—in the age at which they married, the number of children they bore, the privacy they lacked, the incomes they had not . . . which so affected them that though the middle class is the great reservoir from which we draw our distinguished men it has thrown up singularly few women to set beside them.[85]

Obscurity was true enough for the vast majority of members of the middle class, male or female, yet from the eighteenth century a remarkable series of middle-class women had been, for some time, distinguished. As is customary in such essays, Woolf relies on citations of famous women and scenes of autobiographical dispossession. She quotes Charlotte Yonge and Queen Victoria against equality or rights for women and describes the conditions that depressed the talents of young ladies and drove them to religion or, as Florence Nightingale said, to "perpetual day-dreaming" (420). Woolf names a few exceptions: Harriet Martineau who, when her family lost "gentility," was allowed to write uninterrupted and Barbara Leigh Smith, Elizabeth Garrett, and Emily Davies, whose families permitted unexpected careers. Disliking to rely on feminine wiles to get their way, these leaders of "the army of the unemployed" consulted among women. "Mrs Gurney . . . pointed out that 'Miss Marsh's success among the navvies' had been mainly won by these means. . . . It was agreed therefore that charm was to be employed" (420–21). The editor's notes to this essay identify the many distinguished middle-class women to whom Woolf refers but concede "Miss Marsh, unidentified" (425n.15). Miss Marsh, now obscure, was once featured in collective biographies[24; 220; 465; 892] and recognized for her own popular writings (see my chap. 3). She succeeded as a model to the poorest working men and to women of her class and above, though her reforming aims were quite remote from the feminist promotion of higher education and professions for women that Woolf wants to recover.

Such failure of records to sustain the once-distinguished might have suggested to Woolf the gaps in her own history of women. Her charming vignette of two contrasting Victorian women models ways to overcome class and gender prejudice: careful selection of previous examples and collaboration in a collective biographical history. The life of one woman is permeated with others, and pioneers rediscover predecessors. The modern collector of women's lives catches clusters rather than individual lives in her net. She yearns for "a vast body, living, marrying, bearing children in dull obscurity," buried in the past. She imagines a union of Davies and Stanley, "the middle-class woman and the court lady," giving birth to "some astonishing phoenix of the future" that combines "courage" and "charm" (419, 424). Such a phoenix (in *A Room of One's Own* she is named Judith Shakespeare) would rise from the ashes of hundreds of collective biographies of women published well before the advent of the activists in the later nineteenth century.

Chapter Seven

Our Queen Victoria

Feminist Prosopography

In the summer, in London, 2001 seemed like a very big year for Queen Victoria. In July, the museums and academic halls in South Kensington reverberated with the exhibits, lectures, and performances of a large international conference, "Locating the Victorians," on the 150th anniversary of the Great Exhibition and the centenary of Queen Victoria's death. The assembled Victorianists talked of many things besides Victoria.[1] Yet Victoria's presence was everywhere: throughout the Victorian Vision exhibit at the Victoria and Albert Museum, on the covers of new biographies, and on the museum's posters featuring the queen holding a red mobile phone.[2] This royally sponsored conference formed part of a conjunction of events and publications throughout the year and the preceding decade.[3] The jubilees in the last decades of Victoria's life and the ceremonies of international mourning that followed her death might seem to have said goodbye to all that, but in many ways the queen who lent her name to the age before "the American century" still holds sway. According to the usual response to turning points of the calendar, a new fin de siècle urged us to rediscover the many forms of Victoria that defined the close of the nineteenth century for so much of the world.[4]

Of course there is more than historical periodization at stake in the revival of Victorianism and of the queen herself. Contemporary issues concerning feminism, feminist scholarship, and questions of agency and gender seem implicated in the matter of Victoria and the Victorians. In many ways we are recovering *our* Queen Victoria; something about Victoria solicits a first-person plural—specifically rather than universally applied.[5] Laurie Langbauer, in "Queen Victoria and Me," draws out the associations among Victoria's "royal 'we,'" her publicized private life, and anomalous agency as female monarch, on the one hand, and the peculiar location of successful feminist academics on the other. Not coincidentally, according to Langbauer, in the 1990s feminist scholars turned both to recovery of Victoria and to reflection on feminism's history through "the personal essay."[6]

Such a link between the queen and feminists' self-referential scholarship today may seem a stretch, but I couldn't agree more. Indeed, I had developed a related argument in papers or presentations given on several occasions in 1997 and 1999, and Langbauer's essay generously responds to essays, including mine, in the 1997 collection, *Remaking Queen Victoria,* edited by Margaret Homans and Adrienne Munich.[7] I mention my own varied participation in the revival of Queen Victoria neither to claim precedence nor to shoulder into the lists of academic life narratives.[8] Rather, I find that "the Victoria question" is neither private nor public but inextricably both. Queen Victoria has repeatedly brought about a certain unwilled coauthorship, the sort of conjunction among women of letters that Fuller, Martineau, Oliphant, and Jameson strove to resist. Without idealizing sisterhood or collegiality in general, I would like to remind myself and others to value the times when each other's work seems too close for comfort— when someone else says what we mean or meant to say. Ordinarily, (hints of) intimacies are reserved for the first-person genre of "acknowledgments," but we could try it more often, without losing face, in the scholarship proper. We could think of it as the friction of collective activity. Representations of Victoria—a figure, perhaps, for the supreme ruler "alone," as she described herself, or for the great autonomous subject as *feme sole*—actually dissolve identity in multiple collective constructions. Victoria gathers together many aspects of female prosopography as I have defined it, and she provides me with questions—particularly concerning agency, recovery, and the privileging of literature—to address to feminist Victorian studies. In this concluding chapter, I trace through Victoria a genealogy that calls into question my role as presenter of *How to Make It as a Woman.*

I shall examine the figure of Queen Victoria both in collective biographies and in recent feminist scholarship. In the midst of longstanding efforts to define the Victorian period, Victoria herself has "been hidden in plain view for a hundred years," as Margaret Homans and Adrienne Munich put it in *Remaking Queen Victoria.*[9] While North American and British feminist studies have dwelt among Victorian ways since the 1970s, the queen herself has recently commanded critical attention that might seem, like so many features of Victoria's public performance, anachronistic and out of proportion. She has become the persona of Victorian literature and culture much as Dave Thomas is of the restaurant chain Wendy's.[10] Yet that excess, like our obeisance to the arbitrary power of the calendar, seems to be the very stuff of imagined community and ideological construction and, thus, worth watching in action. Why more than a few English professors in the United States in the late twentieth century, trained in feminist literary history, criticism, and theory, became quite literally Victorianists seems to call for analysis by some omniscient prosopographer.

Prosopographical Victoria

Victoria gives name and face to haunting ways of life. She seems to raise the topics of female agency, subjection, and sexual repression. No feminist herself, she exercised a power that inspired feminists in her day.[11] Yet she personi-fied preliberated woman during the century following her death. Like other famous historical figures, she is reduced to a few quotations, representative traits, and reported actions, which are read literally as signs of the existence of a coherent subject. In this manner, Victoria appears in *Great Women Paper Dolls*: young, pretty, in 1840s fashion with coronation accessories, standing beside ambivalent text: "WAS *THIS* GREAT WOMAN *THE* ARCH-VILLAIN?" The title is followed by the famous quotations: Victoria's censure of "this mad, wicked folly of 'Woman's Rights'" and her assertion that women are unfit to govern. "Queen Victoria's life belied her sentiments however. . . . Just how strong-willed she was can be seen, alas, in the success of the foisting of her opinions upon the world." After quoting Florence Nightingale on the sorry state of woman in the nineteenth century (evidently Victoria's fault), the text concludes: "If your favorite Great Woman isn't in this book, please don't dismay [*sic*]. Look for her in Bellerophon's soon-to-appear Great Infamous Women." Yet an epi-graph, under a cutout for the imperial state crown, exclaims "*What nerve! What muscle! What energy!*—Disraeli about Queen Victoria."[12] Victoria, great in this pedagogical context because of her strength, is un-great for her antifeminism; she seems to erase "your favorite Great Woman," as she stood in the way of Victorian women themselves. The paper doll context illustrates well the collab-orative and intersubjective mode of all historical biography: as though applying Carlyle's "clothes philosophy," a child attributes roles to the cutout according to the presenters' cues for respect or censure; such manipulation is counteracted by the opposite pull of celebrity, which grants a powerful, unique historical identity to the subject.

Victoria eludes the judgment of her contemporaries as well as twentieth-century and recent observers, who seem at a loss whether to praise or reproach, whether to deem her responsible for or irrelevant to the history of her era. She gives name and face to a collective heritage, much as Darwin, Marx, and Freud preside over the diffusion of their ideas or spirits. Yet is she not more of a replica than an originator of what she stands for? In another respect, as sovereign she fits into the traditional designs of folklore, tragedy, and epic, in which the note-worthy person wears the badge of high rank. Victoria nevertheless serves a kind of antiheroic veneration in contemporary prosopographies and in more recent feminist studies. Victorian collective biographies often compared her interchangeably with notable women of her day or immersed her in generic roles. *Peerless Women* portrays Victoria as another Nightingale to wounded soldiers in the Royal Victoria Hospital, founded under her "motherly" care in 1856 (12–13); Britain's "national troubles" (such as industrial disasters) were always eased by "messages . . . from [Victoria's] true and tender woman's heart," "queen and mother of her people"—as though she were the type for Sister Dora (19; on Nightingale, 151–64; on Dora, 28–53).[185] Virginia Tatnall Peacock, in her preface (dated from Paris, June 22, 1900) to *Famous American Belles of the Nineteenth Century,* celebrates the "charm" and "power of a queenly personality" and looks forward to twentieth-century avatars to rule the "empire" of beauty (ix).[635]; 13 What does a living, reigning queen do for female prosopography in her day?

If Victoria had not existed, we would not have had to invent her: the collective biographies found many examples of sovereign femininity. Women of different walks of life became "noble" or "queens."[14] John Ruskin was neither the first nor the last to urge that women model themselves as queens or women of the highest feudal ranks.[15] One Charles F. Dole, in *Noble Womanhood* (1900), an advice book for American women, constructs a *"noble . . . ideal"* of woman adapted to a democracy that strives "to lift and educate all men and women to the level which feudal society assigned to the class or caste of the nobles."[16] At heart, nobility is an Anglo-Saxon Christian principle of gender balance— "May our boys be pure and our girls brave!" (20–21)—and noblesse oblige: "The English noble class in all periods of their history, from Runnymede to Queen Victoria, have devoted themselves to public service" (25–26).[17] We have seen that, in various contexts, model subjects become "queens": Helen Hunt Jackson, Frances Willard, and social leaders such as Bertha Palmer or Madame Récamier.

A large majority of collections of women's lives include at least one queen. Prosopographies entirely of queens have a strong claim to be historiography rather than self-help—queens seldom model exemplary character—yet lives of female sovereigns do participate in the construction of middle-class feminine subjects. The representation of Queen Victoria in collective biographies of women exemplifies the ironies of representative status. In a series, the queen is like women who are unlike other women; she is also a paragon of her sex and nation. Victoria is one of a kind, preeminent, the very *type* of Anglo-Saxon progress, maternal rule, the empire of duty; yet her distinction blends in with the multiple subjects associated in a volume. Perhaps she can still help to arm us against individualist heroic historiography.

As a woman "conceived, born, and bred. . . . to mount to the summits of greatness," Victoria is perhaps most readily imagined alone.[18] Alone was a quality she frequently attributed to herself in her journals, whether as a declaration of independence or bereavement, from her accession to her widowhood.[19] Yet as the representative of a nation whose women were encouraged to emulate queenliness, Victoria could scarcely claim to stand alone; her public life and the proliferation of "lives" of her ran the risk of dissolving the difference between her and her middle-class female subjects.[20] Well-known biographies of Victoria have established the commonplace that she was the quintessential sovereign yet the archetypal middle-class Englishwoman. Indeed, her power as a representative figure derives from the conjunction of differences, as in Stanley Weintraub's tally of contradictions: "Victoria was pleasant and unpleasant, selfish and selfless, democratic and dictatorial, . . . queenly yet middle-class at heart. . . . She contained multitudes."[21]

Queen Victoria's appearances in collective biographies exhibit fascinating intersections of narratives of class, gender, and empire. Synecdoche of multitudes, she both shapes her audience and is shaped by the company she keeps: according to the volumes' different forms, contents, and ideological orientations. I will examine several ways that Victoria's story stands apart from those of queens as well as of eminent commoners, particularly in her unwavering goodness and in her claim to coincide with the spirit of her age without losing her middle-class integrity. When the queen is immersed in a diverse assembly of renowned and obscure women through the ages, when she presides at the end of a gallery of English queens, or when she sets the stage for strong-minded *Victorian* women, her narrative takes on the coloring appropriate to different habitats, yet the story always stands out in its simplicity, felicity, predestined historical prominence, and in some perspectives, its lack of distinct achievement.

Queen Victoria appears in over thirty collective biographies of women and lends her name to at least seven titles, from the mid-nineteenth century to the 1930s, often with emphasis on her function as a role model to women of her race and nation.[22] Frank Goodrich, in *Women of Beauty and Heroism*, praises "an exemplary mother of a family, who. . . . not only furnishes a model for all queens . . . , but . . . sets before every woman in her kingdom a pattern which . . . they may safely and honorably follow" (385, 376, 386).[331] A quarter century later, William Henry Davenport Adams, in his *Celebrated English-women of the Victorian Era*,[6] praises Victoria's "nobly useful life" in similar terms, elaborating the characteristics that she models: "a character which all English girls may well do their best to imitate, and a life which, in their lowlier spheres, they may rightly attempt to follow. Her moral courage, her fortitude, her industry, her elevation of aim, and her tenacity of purpose—these are qualities which they may successfully cultivate, even if they cannot hope to equal their Queen in perspicuity, in soundness of judgment, in breadth of intellectual sympathy, and in artistic feeling. They may take the woman as their exemplar, though they cannot approach the Queen" (1:86). The British Adams may be more of a royalist than the American Goodrich, yet the latter insists that Americans have "a more profound and abiding respect for Victoria than perhaps for any other living person. A practical people, we recognize and appreciate the value of her example to rulers and the ruled" (387).[331]; 23 Thus although Adams places the queen at a higher remove from her emulous female subjects, both presenters locate Victoria in the rhetorical exchange of role modeling.

The mimetic iteration among subject, presenter, and audience depends, in the first place, on certain shared attributes, usually those of sex and race or nationality, if not class (notice that common English girls may emulate the queen). The differences among the participants are also salient, such as the undisputed distinction of being the only contemporary Englishwoman who is also a reigning monarch (her daughters become foreign consorts). At times, collections insist that the modeling has an imperial and racial dimension. Louise Creighton concludes her life of Victoria, the ultimate subject (as well as the frontispiece) in *Some Famous Women*: "People in all the wide lands which made up the British Empire felt that she was the outward sign of the unity of the Empire. They venerated her for her long and blameless life, devoted to duty. In far distant lands, black and savage people honoured the great white Queen and trusted her justice" (190).[207] She might be the capital or period in an imperial sentence, a figure for woman at the World's Fair of 1893 or in contemporary eugenic prosopographies. In texts that seem caught between the democratizing tendencies of self-help and the closed kinship rules of *Who's Who* or Debrett's, representations of Victoria epitomize a productive ambivalence.

The Nell Gwyn Problem

The tales of women who have a history are retold because they wander from the foregone paths and fenced properties. Many women of record have crossed gender barriers with a mobility that transgresses class codes as well. It is hardly surprising that Victorian or post-Victorian presenters of conspicuous women feel they have some explaining to do. What is more remarkable is that Victoria and her true peers in these volumes, contemporary middle-class women of letters or of ministry, evade the Nell Gwyn problem. The significance of this problem is best indicated by examining Willis J. Abbot's *Notable Women of History* (1913)[1] in some detail. Subtitled *The Lives of Women Who in All Ages, All Lands and in All Womanly Occupations Have Won Fame and Put Their Imprint on the World's History* (echoing the 1907–8 encyclopedic *Woman: In All Ages and in All Countries*,[899] discussed in chap. 5), the volume presents Victoria among seventy women illustrating the inevitable "upward and onward movement of womankind" (1–4).[1] Such complacency does not resolve a presenter's difficulties when exemplary women have moved upward and onward in ways that should not be followed. Abbot responds to improper deviations with what might serve as the caption for most pre-nineteenth-century examples: "Other times, other manners." Take for instance Nell Gwyn: "If in this day of a more superficial, or, it may be actual, morality, a girl could come from the slums of New York, proceed through the stages of street peddler, orange girl in the theatre, be an inmate of a brothel and finally wind up as the mistress of a king, and possibly his wife, the world would stand aghast." According to the conventions of his day—when there was a renewed fashion for scandalous biography—Abbot cannot condone but does admire Nell Gwyn as the toast of great literary men (328). In his preface, she is the antithesis of a pure American heroine, Martha Washington, though both contribute to "the composite picture of the eternal woman" (3). In his table of contents Abbot groups Nell Gwyn with several more respectable "Women of the Footlights" and sets Martha Washington apart with Dolly Madison and Joan of Arc as three "Women Who Stand Alone"—Victoria being placed not "alone" with these three, but among "Many Queens and Some Martyrs." The inclusion of twelve "Women of Wit and Pleasure" (e.g. Ninon de l'Enclos, "A Typical Parisian Parasite") suggests that the Nell Gwyn phenomenon is far from rare. Indeed, some collections are entirely dedicated to historically remote adulteresses. Yet very few women whose life spans overlapped with Victoria's could succeed at Nell Gwyn's metamorphosis and be included in the lists of commendable biography.

Victoria cohabits with Nell Gwyn not only in Abbot's early-twentieth-century collection but also in Goodrich's *Women of Beauty and Heroism* of 1859, introduced above. Goodrich first notes that Anna Jameson and other biographers of Nell Gwyn have always begun with an apology but then notes that the orange girl who became an actress and mistress to Charles II remains, in Anna Jameson's words, "the idol of popular tradition" (235).[331] Unlike other courtesans, her virtue improved with age. Again quoting Jameson: "The course of her life, which had begun in the puddle and sink of obscurity and profligacy, as it flowed, refined" (236).[331] Her transposition from the gutter to the palace, withal her unspoiled English playfulness and geniality, made her a popular favorite, especially in contrast with Charles's other mistress, a humorless, French Catholic noblewoman: "She was an English girl—a Protestant—of humble origin, and . . . was both a beauty and a wit" (242). It is clear that, like Victoria, Nell Gwyn serves as national model but in a far different, self-made cast. That collective character ultimately makes up for errant ways through good works—by later women. Goodrich points out that Nell is an indirect ancestor of Angela Burdett-Coutts, "the richest private woman in the world, and the most munificent benefactress of modern times" (252).[24]

Some Victorian models seem to require no polishing. Victoria, Florence Nightingale, Ann Hasseltine Judson, Charlotte Brontë, and their like never appear to cross class or gender ("moral") boundaries as do so many of their predecessors in history. Among chaste women who remain within their class, Victoria assumes a lasting, prominent place in the records with exceptional ease. Among regnant queens, moreover, she is unique for retaining her status as moral model. In spite of her long reign, Victoria's story is rather short and straightforward, from birth to accession to marriage, motherhood, and widowhood; the granddaughter and niece of kings avoids both the perils and the career opportunities of a Nell Gwyn. Such brevity may signal virtue: Lady Jane Grey sets a strict standard for the blameless queen, executed days into her reign. Brevity or simplicity is not, however, the greatest attraction in female prosopography. Even Victoria's admirer, Frank Goodrich, seems comparatively unimpressed: "That Alexandrina Victoria should ever have ascended the

English throne is, perhaps, the only remarkable event in her life" (376). Victoria seems to abdicate from a plot conflict. Yet certain crossings of boundaries in Victoria's story do call for explanation. Instead of asking how a common woman became great or how a deviation became historically representative, the questions should be: How did a woman come to inherit the throne? How did a German mother give birth to an English girl, and the Hanoverian line yield yet another English monarch? After the fact, she is supposed to have been born to be the best example of both English sovereign and woman, though biographies focus on the strangely static yet cataclysmic moment in which she became both. The questions answered, more than sixty years of tableaux ensue (the costume changes to deep mourning almost halfway through).

For Victoria, the Nell Gwyn problem of social mobility is moot, as she never had to stir to attain her sovereignty. It was a short journey, indeed, from girl to queen: "I got out of bed and went into my sitting-room (only in my dressing-gown) and *alone,* and saw" the messengers bearing news that the king had died, "and consequently that I am *Queen."* The annunciation scene is replayed in most collected biographies.[25] The detail of her dressing gown (some add that her hair was down) focuses the vulnerability of an ordinary girl meeting several men in a private room and heightens the contrast with the grandeur of a transfer of regal state. Victoria and her witnesses collaborate in sanctifying her feminine embodiment as a kind of discipline for her subjects rather than a monstrous transgression of sovereignty.[26] Biographers recall a magic transformation of innocent girl into queen: "A Royal Idyll indeed! . . . like a fairytale . . . we heard it first at our mother's knee," as Rosa Nouchette Carey puts it (28).[143];[27] Victoria's most heroic achievement is to remain an authentic English lady in settings and situations indeed suited to fairytales. She was placed on the throne by genealogical fate—or according to Thayer, by "Providence . . . for divine reasons" (262),[792] not by her ability to captivate a king; in this, she not only transcends the Nell Gwyn problem but the several problems of the biographies of queens as well.

The Bad Queen / Good Queen Model

Victoria takes a prominent position in anthologies of queens or royal women. As she produced so many of the royal mates of Europe, she assumes the role of progenitor—at the head, for example, of *The Sovereign Ladies of Europe,*[100] edited by the Countess A. von Bothmer (1899)—though not all the ruling women are close relations. The virtues that Samuel Smiles would instill in the working men of England apparently had been anticipated by the Duchess of Kent as early as 1819, in a curious inversion of the moral standing of the classes. Von Bothmer writes, "The Empress of Russia," daughter of Victoria's daughter Alice, "grew up with very English ideas" because of her intimacy with her grandmother (43), though she married into a people of "Oriental traits," "half-barbaric, half-childish" (58).[28] Similarly, "The Empress Frederick," or "Vicky," Victoria's eldest daughter, imbibed Albert's enlightened ideas and learned "military nursing" from Florence Nightingale (79).[100] The regimen of "severe mental discipline" in Princess Vicky's education, a repetition of the strict moral schooling of her mother, contrasts with the "all-round indulgence and cotton-wool" treatment of the young of "the middle classes," according to von Bothmer (80). Thayer similarly lauds the "poverty," "industry," "self-help," and orderly routine of Queen Victoria's upbringing (265–74),[792] source of continuing guidance to her children and her people. Victoria's sense of duty, deliberately etched in childhood, in turn is printed on the royal houses of Europe as they generate new ruling subjects, while the middle classes lapse into leisured license.

In spite of apparent family bonds with other royal women, Victoria (with her expertise in middle-class values) appears less at home in this diachronic elite than among contemporaries of ordinary rank. In all varieties of collection, queens either were very very good or they were horrid—the same queen's biography becoming either saintly or villainous in different volumes. Willis J. Abbot spells out the typical alternatives: "Catherine of Russia was an unspeakable libertine; Victoria a wife and a mother without blemish. But as queens they were equally great," equally sponsoring the expansion of empire (3).[1] A rarity among queens, Victoria never appears as the bad queen. Rather than exemplifying the temptations of wealth and power or the vulnerability of her sex, Victoria demonstrates judicious discipline and domestic virtue.

The encyclopedic *Woman's Record* by Sarah Hale, with its commitment to female moral superiority and racial progress, venerates queens on principle but Victoria above all. Even the "odious" African queen Anna Zinga (1582–1663), who feigned conversion to Christianity, is said to have had "better dispositions than any king of her race" (560–61).[362] But Queen Victoria serves a special purpose in the vanguard of Christian womanhood: "the best sovereign . . . , morally speaking, that ever sat on England's throne," a sign of Anglo-Saxon fitness to rule "the destiny of the world" (806, 563–64).[29] Yet according to two of the many writers in Hale's volume, Anna Jameson and Agnes Strickland, queens have offered an unflattering sample of womankind (Hale suggests they have at least been better than kings, who "have usually been very poor specimens of humanity" [799][362]). I noted in chapter 1 Jameson's harsh opinion of the masculine and wayward Queen Christina of Sweden; similarly, Jameson asserts that Catherine II was warped by her "one overmastering passion—ambition," which should have devoted itself "to shining in a drawing-room" (2:5–6, 214).[453] In Strickland's account many an English queen was likewise corrupted by unfeminine power: Isabella, wife of Edward II, became "a vindictive political agitator, and finally branded her once-honoured name with the foul stains of adultery, treason, and murder" (91).[764] Thus the two writers who did most to awaken biographical interest in queens during the nineteenth century encouraged readers to relish stories of queens' catastrophic defiance of standards of feminine conduct (Strickland does have exemplary favorites in her roster). The young woman who came to England's throne in 1837—too late to be featured in Strickland's *Lives of the Queens of England, from the Norman Conquest to the Reign of Queen Anne* (1840–48)[763] or Anna Jameson's *Memoirs of Celebrated Female Sovereigns* (1832)[453]—promised to obey those standards perhaps too well, her virtue nigh on unnarratable.

Portraiture of Victoria, whether in anthologies of mixed rank or of queens only, submitted to several pressures: not only did judgments of queens gravitate to saint-virago extremes, but, as I have suggested, the judgment of manners and morals became more strict in the more contemporary biographies. Thus, like Nell Gwyn the courtesan who has become part of the spirit of her age, many earlier models have been whitewashed by history. Another pattern in sequential modeling, however, aligns history with teleology and equates the later with the better. In collections of English queens where Victoria takes the ultimate position, history's linear plot suggests that she is best or most advanced, though not actually higher ranked than her fellow "subjects." The age demanded that the living or recent queen of England be the good queen, sponsor of Britain's deserving domination of the world. All the better that Victoria made discipline appear voluntary; the biographies repeat her performative utterance, "I will be good."[143, pp. 21, 33; 791, p. 277]

Victoria's story stands apart among the queens of England for its good fortune and its compatibility with a national narrative happily remembered. She can appear as an anticlimactic, ubiquitous influence at the end of a series of violent or woeful tales. Many of Victoria's royal predecessors in Britain had to flee their husband's enemies or friends and forfeit their children; they were relatively powerless genetic vessels except in instances of regency or military leadership such as Margaret of Anjou's. Most often foreign born, they were frequently viewed as alien to their people. Agnes Strickland finds a source of romance and civilizing influence in the stories of exotic royal brides: "Our Queens . . . have been brought from foreign climes to plant the flowers and refinements of a more polished state of society in our own."[763]; 30 But such a Victorian conception of the proper role for a queen scarcely accords with the treatment, for example, of Anne of Bohemia and Isabella of Valois as pawns in attempts at royal endogamy and territorial consolidation or with the English attacks on the "foreign influence" of Johanna of Navarre.[31] Yet while some biographers (especially during World War I) stress Victoria's German derivation—"the English crown . . . was 'made in Germany,'" and Albert was part of a "German invasion" (200, 204)[1]—most accept her English birth and lavish praise on the Duchess of Kent and Baroness Lehzen as her excellent role models and on Albert as her Prince Charming (425).[630]

A pair of volumes, *The Queens of England*[764] published in New York in 1851 and *Biographical Sketches of the Queens of England*[424] published in London in 1851, with additional portraits in 1868, illustrate Victoria's privileged placement yet diminished allure in an unromantic age. Each is a massive book for display or for prize presentation, conspicuously illustrated to serve as a *Royal Book of Beauty* (the 1868 subtitle[424]). In *Queens*,[764] twenty-eight full-page engravings accompany as many biographies adapted "from Agnes Strickland" (the latest queens were silently added where the Strickland series ended). *Biographical Sketches,* edited by Mary Howitt, includes twelve more biographies and three more images interspersed with the engraved series of full-busted, wistful or imposing antique beauties (there is no acknowledgment of the earlier collection).

The New York and London versions both end with nearly the same biography and the same illustration of Victoria (fig. 25): the young, fresh-faced queen on her semidomestic throne, a miniature of Albert on her right forearm, smiling without command at the viewer. In the New York collection,[764] the

Fig. 25 Queen Victoria by Sir William Ross, R.A., engraved by F. Bacon, in Agnes Strickland and Elisabeth Strickland, *Queens of England* (1851),[764] and Mary Howitt, ed., *Biographical Sketches* (1868).[424]

Fig. 26 Matilda of Scotland by J. W. Wright, engraved by W. H. Mote, frontispiece in Agnes Strickland and Elisabeth Strickland, *Queens of England* (1851);[764] also a figure in Mary Howitt, ed., *Biographical Sketches* (1868).[424]

frontispiece displays a girlish folk heroine, Matilda of Scotland, who offers drink and buns as though illustrating the Old English derivation of "lady" as "bread maker" (hlæfdige) (fig. 26). Sweet, trusting Matilda might be the native sister of Pocahontas, perhaps easing colonization through her ready welcome (fig. 4). The frontispiece of Mary Howitt's London edition in 1868[424] replaces Matilda with a daunting, classical bust of Victoria (fig. 27). Images of sculptures are rare in the collective biographies; while many illustrations copy paintings, an engraving of a sculpture heightens the sense that a valuable work of figural art, not a person, is being represented.[32] Howitt's roster of queens thus begins with an imperial abstraction and ends with a domestic young woman, both named Queen Victoria. Howitt's volume also includes a third image of Victoria, a smaller oval portrait in imperial robes and crown, sternly staring to the reader's right. All three unmatched images of the queen are out of keeping with "the Royal Book of Beauty" sequence, which appears to sympathize with a reader's desire for fashion tips as well as history (the biographies devote paragraphs to sumptuary description, as the engravings detail textiles). *The Queens of England* announces the aims of the series of queens in both volumes: to "portray equally the grandeur of the queen, the attachments of the wife, the affection of the mother, and the charms and the infirmities of the woman" (4).[764] The last words alert us that these models, beautified and almost beatified in the engravings if not in the text, cannot always be made good.

The reader should have the luxury of browsing through all of these portraits, but a few will give a taste. Notably, these could not be likenesses of actual women in the remoter past, though a few were evidently copied from contemporary portraits. The series of subjects becomes sparse after the seventeenth century, leaping from the wife of Charles I to the wife of George II to Victoria. The styles of representation in any period, and the Victorian artists' preferences, overwhelm individual features. Victoria, though the first British sovereign of the age of photography, remains open to a fantastical range of

Fig. 27 Queen Victoria (classical bust) by J. Durham, frontispiece in Mary Howitt, ed., *Biographical Sketches* (1868).[424]

depiction, like other living subjects in midcentury collections. The English queens take on a family resemblance to each other and to the heroines in similarly designed contemporary collections, such as Goodrich's *Women of Beauty and Heroism* [331] and Mary Cowden Clarke's *World-Noted Women* [174]— as illustrated in the latter's Cleopatra, Joan of Arc, Pocahontas, and Florence Nightingale (figs. 2–5).

Victoria's predecessors portray extremes of suffering and vice, heightened by contrasts. Queen Elizabeth (fig. 1) is certainly the least charming. As an equestrian figure—and hence like a ruling man according to pictorial convention (though the difficult horse is not shown)—she comes closest of any queen in these collections to appearing with a sword (like Judith or Joan). Her nose and the positioning of her arms correspond with the Cleopatra in Clarke [174]— also a powerful and warlike queen regnant, whose love story perhaps softens her image (fig. 2). Elizabeth's sister, sometimes portrayed as "Bloody Mary," would appear to be all that a good woman should be, a saint gazing heavenward (fig. 28); "that horrible persecution of the Protestants, which has stained her name to all futurity" should be blamed on Parliament and the maneuvers of her Spanish husband Philip as she lay dying (286–87). [764] Howitt concurs: the "vicissitudes" of Queen Mary's life serve as "extenuation for" her "faults" (349). [424] Conversely, Elizabeth's "harsh trials" during Mary's reign failed to teach a lesson to "the unfeminine mind of the energetic princess; and when, in her turn, she obtained the power of persecuting and oppressing, she manifested to another Mary a far greater extent of hate and cruelty than she herself had ever experienced" (290). [764] Elizabeth, Howitt declares, was a "treacherous" old "wanton," stiffly "dancing . . . and ogling striplings. . . . She was all that even the least rigid man would most abhor to detect in wife, sister, or mother" (389). [424]; 33

Though the contrasts of Elizabeth with the two Marys suggest that the bad queen type serves to reinforce the prohibition on female agency and desire, it is by no means true that all strong queens are censured in these collections. In *Biographical Sketches* Catherine of Aragon, for example, is rated as high as the best English queens (fig. 29). Her "queenly dignity" and "womanly piety" daunted "her most deadly enemies. Her masculine abilities, and her lofty and assured temperament, set at defiance all the arts of her savage husband." Catherine, well-educated and popular, resisted Henry VIII's efforts to erase their marriage and endured her dismissal to obscurity during his second marriage, to Ann Boleyn. Catherine is said to have gained, as Victoria later did, her nation's "deepest sentiments of respect and affection" (271). [424] Like a powerful abbess, Catherine also resembles a Victorian ministering heroine intent on doing good, holding a book like an iconic attribute. In spite of the jewels, I see a Dorothea Brooke, a beauty set off by plain dress, unself-consciously on the lookout for useful knowledge. Eleanor of Provence, in contrast, is more characteristic of the youthful queens in the collections, a Rosamond Vincy: her gaze averted to her own image, delicately gesturing, in bejeweled, skin-tight dress; while she

Fig. 28 *Queen Mary I* by A. Bouvier, engraved by W. H. Egleton, in Agnes Strickland and Elisabeth Strickland, *Queens of England* (1851),[764] and Mary Howitt, ed., *Biographical Sketches* (1868).[424]

might be an emblem of vanity, she has almost enough hair to be a magdalen (fig. 30). Known as "La Belle," Eleanor is said to have written a "fine Provençal romance" that commended her as bride to Henry III, but she became "the most unpopular queen that ever presided over the court of England" (65–66).[764] She owned "nine guirlands, or chaplets, for her hair, formed of gold filagree and clusters of colored precious stones"; one of these costly chaplets is pictured in the model's hair (67). Her personal vanity, greed, and despotic ambitions seem to have ensured her ill repute.

Necessarily last in both chronological collections of English queens appears the more prosaic life of Victoria. Its static quality could be due to the fact that

Fig. 29 *Catherine of Arragon: Queen of Henry 8th* by Frederick Newenham, engraved by J. W. Knight, in Agnes Strickland and Elisabeth Strickland, *Queens of England* (1851),[764] and Mary Howitt, ed., *Biographical Sketches* (1868).[424]

the original Strickland series omitted Victoria, and a less gifted writer took her life in hand, but the blandness is also an effect of Victoria's proximity. The text, closely corresponding in both volumes, acknowledges its superfluity yet inevitability: "The name of Victoria is on every lip, and imprinted on the heart of each of her subjects, yet would the memoirs of English royalty be incomplete, without a brief outline of the life of the reigning sovereign."[424, p. 511; 764, p. 337] Outline it is, listing travels and assassination attempts and recalling how the public rejoiced at her accession and felt for her at the births of her children and, in Howitt's longer account of 1868, how they grieved at the death of her husband. Howitt's last paragraph seals the series of queens in the whole

Fig. 30 Eleanor of Provence by J. W. Wright, engraved by B. Eyles, in Agnes Strickland and Elisabeth Strickland, *Queens of England* (1851),[764] and Mary Howitt, ed., *Biographical Sketches* (1868).[424]

volume with a rather characterless encomium: "Queen Victoria presents the noblest example of domestic purity and social propriety. She has always been ready to second the plans of sound reform . . . ; and with the blessings of cheap bread, of literature, commerce, . . . her reign is . . . one of the most beneficently great, in the English annals" (516).[424] Both the 1851 and 1868 biographies end with a ritual tribute to the generic Queen of England in the volumes' preceding series of portraits. The 1868 version, hinting at the lapse in Victoria's popularity with her prolonged mourning, is more fulsome: "Her subjects throughout the world hail with joy and delight her reappearance in public. 'THE QUEEN! GOD BLESS HER!' resounds on all sides as echo to the national prayer: 'GOD SAVE THE

QUEEN!'" (516).[424]; 34 The surplus of three images of Victoria in 1868, like the repeated national declamations of her generic title echoed round the world, suggest that she has become more elusive yet more ubiquitous over time and the expansion of the empire. Born and trained for her oxymoronic role as feminine ruler, Victoria more easily conforms to prevailing gender differences of the industrialized middle classes than the many queens plucked young from foreign courts or the native queens untutored in family life.

Victoria as the Spirit of the Age

A queen, like other monarchs, is expected to stamp her imprint on the period of her reign. Victoria may figure as one among many examples of the age or as the presiding spirit. Frequently, this much-reproduced regal figure fills the frontispiece, as she served on postage stamps and coins.35 Often in mixed-rank selections she comes first or last. Prominently as she may be figured, however, she can appear comparatively characterless. Goodrich, in *Women of Beauty and Heroism,* disparages the "form and routine" of the English sovereign's duties, easily performed by any queen as well as a king (384–85).[331] Thus the latest monarch fails in her prosopoetic role:

> Queens are not what they were. Time was when the history of her Majesty was a history of her kingdom. He who reads the history of Isabella, reads the history of Castile and Aragon. . . . The daughters of royal houses have seen their best days; there will never be another Maria Theresa. . . . The British constitution permits the queen to be virtuous, amiable and charitable; it does not allow her to be sagacious, learned or acute; she may be good, she cannot be great. . . . Victoria and her reign are two very distinct themes. The one falls within the province of Mrs. Jameson; the other within that of Macaulay. (375–76)

Goodrich concludes his biography of this good woman by asserting that Americans can "heartily concur" in the British anthem, "GOD SAVE THE QUEEN!" (388)—as though sharing in the chorus of Strickland and Howitt. But evidently his denials of Victoria's political and historical relevance, which continue for several more sentences, carry an urgent animus. Not incidentally, his diatribe divides the biographical history of women (Mrs. Jameson's province, and indeed Goodrich's in this collection) from history proper by Macaulay and his ilk.

It was not unusual, however, to deny a queen credit for the authorship of her reign. Biographies of queens who reigned before Victoria observe a discrepancy between the character of the sovereign and her times. Willis J. Abbot, for example, sets Queen Anne at odds with her day: "After all Anne was commonplace. Her era was glorious; . . . but . . . she was [not] in any sense the animating force" (96).[1] Elizabeth's "success and glory were probably as much the effect of chance as of talent . . . the sources of the public prosperity will be found more in her vices than in her virtues" (405). Notably, Victoria's consistency with the norms of her middle-class subjects, not her outstanding leadership, seems to be the "animating force" of her age; even as some biographers deny her direct credit for industrial, imperial, or intellectual progress, they regard these as sponsored by the benevolent female sovereign.

Victoria comes first in William Henry Davenport Adams's two-volume *Celebrated Englishwomen of the Victorian Era* (1881),[6] which I cited for its designation of Victoria as model for English girls; she is followed by Harriet Martineau, Charlotte Brontë, Mary Russell Mitford, Mary Somerville, Sara Coleridge, Mary Carpenter, Adelaide Anne Procter, George Eliot, and, finally, Jane Welsh Carlyle. Within her own biography Victoria is undoubtedly supreme, yet her effects are diffused by Adams's desire to convert a gentle-hearted English wife and mother into the spirit of the age. As though her narratable life ceased with Albert's death two decades before, this biography shifts midway to become a portrait of the era.[36]

Adams traces what might be called the global reproductive capacities and indirect economic and political effects of the eponymous heroine of the period: "We already speak . . . of 'the Victorian age'" (1:25–26).[6] "Cabinets come and go, but the Queen remains, and by her presence guards against any sudden arrest of the wheels of government" (1:69). The calm repository of British memory, she also personifies the benevolent dominion over India and Ireland. As feminine inertia, she has ensured "the peace, prosperity, and contentment of the empire," which in turn ensure progress in the railway system, the telegraph, the post office, and other measurable improvements during her reign (1:83, 73–78). Adams concludes with a paean to the "intensity and universality" of Victoria's popularity, at its height in 1881 (the final stages of her reign [1:80–86]). Henry C. Ewart, writing a few years later, marvels at the unprecedented "rapid and beneficent progress" between 1837 and 1888. "The United Kingdom, with its Colonies and Dependencies, includes about one-fifth of the entire globe," and railways, steamships, and the telegraph and post reduce distances while education and religion advance. "It may be said with truth that the progress . . . must have gone on, no matter who sat on the throne; but it would be unjust not to recognize the close influence which the Crown has . . . exercised" (22–24).[270; 37] Louise Creighton, in *Some Famous Women* eight years after Victoria's death, similarly affirms the queen's popularity in the later years, associated with her jubilees: "she was the outward sign of the unity of the Empire" (190).[207]

Willis J. Abbot attributes national prosperity and preeminence to female rule, though I noted above how little credit he gives Anne and Elizabeth for the glory of their own eras: "During the three most glorious epochs of English history the crown was worn by a woman" (197).[1] Abbot repeatedly stresses the expansion of empire while Victoria anchored her nation: "During the calm reign of the British sovereign the national red was far-flung over the map of the world" (3). Victoria, "The Most Splendid Monarch of the Nineteenth Century, 1819–1902 [*sic*]" as the subtitle of her biography in Abbot has it, might be the genius of technology conquering the world. "When she was crowned it took months for her Foreign Office to communicate with her most distant posses-sions. When she died the news was flashed over mountains and under oceans to the very antipodes in a few seconds" (198).[38] Victoria influenced a worldwide advance in humanitarian principles as well as communications: "Mankind pro-gressed in brotherly love. . . . Child labor was regulated . . . ; women were no longer permitted to work in mines; the negro, however savage, was free wher-ever the British flag waved; her ships were the chief factors in suppressing the African slave trade on the high seas and her influence was thrown on the side of the anti-slavery forces in our own war between the states" (198).[39] Victoria, in Abbot's hands, assumes the agency of the entire British government, which is then personified as a liberal reformer granting freedom to savages instead of as a contentious set of institutions that helped enforce British dominion (and for a time attempted to support the slaveholding states). Though Abbot em-phasizes Victoria's imperial might, he also capitalizes on the view of woman as the weaker sex. The "fundamental fact that [Victoria] was a woman" eased the progress of democracy.[40] Abbot implies that a dominion so mild and self-disciplined insinuated itself into every corner of the world (202–3). In closing, Abbot affirms Victoria's effective fusion of national destiny with an exemplary female life: "All London, all England, was draped in the purple hue fixed upon for mourning, but all the world sincerely mourned . . . a good queen, a good wife and a good mother" (206).

So representative that she is hard to distinguish, Victoria is ultimately far from alone, a spectacle witnessed by all the world. She is the *prosopon*—as well as the color code—of the British Empire, a figure for collective history. In such programmatic modeling, the queen appears as though in a stereoscope that pairs the close-up of a domestic middle-class woman with the outline of a global force. Curiously, Abbot, Adams, Hale, and others exalt Victoria as model to the world, yet never consider what might happen if this spirit of the age succeeded in modeling an audience equal to itself. The British queen can be commended not just to English girls, or women, or her nation but also to any spectator across the globe as a model for self-improvement, even by presenters who appear dedicated to immutable racial or class hierarchies. Yet we can observe in volumes such as Abbot's, supportive of women's and civil rights as well as Western imperialism, that the fiction of a universal passport to eminence is easily reconciled with a conservative agenda. Though volumes that present women of many ranks appear to promise more options for social transformation, they present their own codes of exceptionalism and trickle-down majesty.

A True Middle-Class Heroine

As the spirit of her age, Queen Victoria can serve as a mere backdrop for women who make a name for themselves. Indeed, in collections that require documented life works, Victoria's only ticket for admission is her royalty. In most cases Victorian notable women meet the same standards of domestic virtue, accomplishments, and learning as Victoria. A queen, in contrast, rarely strives to achieve such standards and never exceeds them as many subjects in the collections do. Although a woman's reign is said to encourage the expectation of female achievement in wider fields of endeavor, Victoria herself hardly led the way. Thus, presenters often appear to recommend her as a model to reproduce the run-of-the-mill. According to Carey, Victoria's daily schedule as a young queen exhibited "that untiring industry and remarkable aptitude for business that was to set such a noble example to her subjects" (33, 43).[143] Thayer recommends Victoria's lifelong regimen of simple "diet, dress, and exercise," "punctuality and promptness," use of every precious moment, and "frugality and economy." These practices were carefully instilled by her mother as though by a living advice manual with the ideal malleable audience (268–70).[792] Creighton attributes Victoria's influence to her goodness rather "than to any special gifts or talents. . . . she was always true to the best that she knew, and it is this that makes her an example for us all" (192).[207] Whether the queen is most constrained to follow her subjects' example or the other way around is never quite resolved, however.

One of the eccentricities for which Victoria was both revered and reproached was her preference for plain clothes. Many anecdotes tell of commoners, especially Scots country folk, who mistook the queen for an ordinary person because she wore none of the marks of rank; as Adrienne Munich argues, these tales underline Victoria's virtue and her intimacy with the people, but they suggest that "the highest woman in the land appears indistinguishable from the lowest."[41] Euphemia Richmond relates a series of episodes illustrative of Victoria's goodness as a mother and her sensitivity to the needs of servants, culminating in a longer incident proving "the kindness and condescension of the royal lady," which has prevented "insurrection" during her reign and lulled "the old Scottish hatred of the English usurpers" (2:247).[673]; 42 Richmond savors the tale of "an ancient dame who had walked a long distance" to see Victoria at a levee in Edinburgh. When after great difficulty the Scotswoman stands in the audience in the anteroom, a door opens only to show:

> so many magnificently dressed high-born dames that the poor old lady cried out in despair, "They are all queens."
>
> She was directed to look for one plainly dressed lady, whose only ornament was a rose worn in her hair. Just at this moment the crowd separated and revealed the fair young queen in her simple loveliness, and the old creature . . . cried out with a shrill voice, "I see her, I see her, the bonny queen. . . . now I can gang back to my mountain hame and dee."
>
> If a bomb shell had burst . . . it would not have caused greater consternation than that aged-bowed [sic] figure craning her neck over the threshold and clasping her withered hands in ecstasy. . . . Victoria hastened to her side, and . . . led her to a sofa and seated herself by her side, conversing so kindly and

familiarly that the aged face beamed with delight. . . . The next day the youthful queen might have been seen in a humble cottage . . . sitting upon a wooden stool eating oatmeal porridge and talking familiarly with her humble friends. (2:246–47)

In this tale, parallel scenes of familiar conversation align sofa and stool, the assembly rooms and the cottage. Ruskin would approve that all the ladies are "queens," but Victoria alone among them has the privilege of not looking like a queen and of causing a sensation by eating porridge. Victoria's sterling worth is proven by her act of condescension, which also perhaps averts the revolutionary explosion that the above passage half imagines. But royal youth condescending to peasant age is one thing and dowdiness another; as an old queen, the unfashionable monarch seemed less bonny.

The tales of class transcendence are shared within a wide-ranging literate public. Though Scottish folk revere her legend, it is an international middle class that Victoria's biographies aim to model. Other subjects outweigh the queen on the dual scales of domestic virtue and intellectual achievement or public service. Adams's *Celebrated Englishwomen*[6] is particularly instructive, as it cuts the queen down to size. Adams warmly praises her and figures her as a historical guidepost at the beginning of the first volume and of several of the biographies: "Queen Victoria had been eighteen years on the throne when Mary Russell Mitford closed her useful and honourable career" (1:189).[6] She may become an incident in contemporary memoirs, as in Charlotte Brontë's recollection of seeing Queen Victoria in a carriage on the Rue Royale in Brussels: "She looked a little stout, vivacious lady, very plainly dressed; not much dignity or pretension about her" (1:154).

Biographical realism, in Adams's collection as in others, further contributes to the image of the queen as a plain middle-class woman. Adams observes Victoria as closely as he does his other subjects: "In stature her Majesty is below the average height, and of late years has shown a decided tendency to *embonpoint*; but . . . she has the air of command natural to her lofty station, with the refinement of bearing that comes from high culture. . . . Deep furrows, traced by affliction, experience, and meditation, mark the thoughtful face. Altogether, one who saw the Queen without knowing who she was, would look at her again and again, as at a woman of strong character, of high position, and accustomed to great responsibilities" (1:67). What at first appears unmajestic—a short, fat woman—is read more carefully as an authentication of upper-class excellence that would command attention regardless of the rank of queen. Such scrutiny of the qualities of a revered global influence invites closer comparison with other high-minded women of her day. She meets their highest standards in domestic matters, yet in other respects she fails to measure up.

Victoria's own biography in Adams's collection, the second longest after George Eliot's, seems to exhaust the representative qualities of Victoria's domestic life: "The Queen to perfect husband was perfect wife" (1:39). She has "set her family a noble example," reproducing her own excellence in children and grandchildren (1:62–66). Eyewitness accounts of marital interludes lead to glimpses of the many elaborate shrines to Albert (1:42, 50–56). Adams condones the widowed queen's prolonged absence from the public (lessening by 1881) because "the nation . . . gain[s] by the lofty example she has set of conjugal devotion" (1:60–61). But more than family devotion is required for entree to this collection, and in instances of sufficient achievement such a standard of piety may even be waived.

All Adams's exemplars besides Victoria have committed themselves to action or authorship, and some even verge on the Nell Gwyn problem of unchastity. Adams seems compelled to acknowledge defective models. Harriet Martineau—"the first notable Englishwoman of the nineteenth century," a "pioneer" (1:89)—exemplifies more strongly than the queen "the highest development of the intellect of women," a characteristic of the Victorian age (2:86–7). Adams has misgivings about this woman of intellectual enterprise, however. In contrast with Victoria's soothing influence, Martineau's career is "typical of the unrest and feverishness of the nineteenth century" (1:88)—a symptom also of Charlotte Brontë, though the latter is a true genius, "a practical and sensible Yorkshire woman," and pious Christian (1:156, 123). No "woman of genius," Martineau succeeded through "a colossal self-confidence" and ambition (1:89, 92), rather like a bad queen. Among Martineau's errors are her atheism and her desire to set the terms of social visiting: "She should have accepted the homage paid to her [as literary celebrity] . . . instead of insisting on being brought down to the level of ordinary womanhood" (1:107). Adams seems uncertain of the terms on which to base his disapproval of this irritating eminence.

Adams encounters a nearer repetition of the Nell Gwyn problem in his biography of George Eliot, who exceeds Charlotte Brontë in artistic achievement but falls far short of Victoria's and Brontë's examples of virtue. Victoria is unnamed in nearly one hundred pages on Eliot, as though the two models occupy separate worlds due to the novelist's unforgivable breach of conduct, her "so-called marriage." Adams supposes that Eliot's novels stress "the sanctity of domestic ties" to counteract "the injurious effect" of "laxity . . . on the part of individuals [Eliot and Lewes] so conspicuous by their genius and general elevation of character" (2:108). The works themselves become the proper role model when the woman threatens to encourage pernicious behavior. When the standard of cultural achievement is invoked, Eliot ranks supreme and Victoria sinks below the horizon.

Each distinctive subject has her excuse for being an exception: some public confirmation of her deviation from the norm. Such confirmation is then wrought backward to the birth or nature of these heroines, who are said to be as chosen and removed from common service as Queen Victoria. Genius should exempt Charlotte Brontë from "arbitrary social conditions"; Adams sees Brontë's labor as a governess as a debasement of almost sacred powers, as though "the waters of Niagara are expended in turning a petty millwheel"

(1:141). More platitudinously, Thayer stresses the childhood promise of his subjects, yet advises his readers to follow their examples of hard work. "The maxim 'self-made or never made' has been applied to men only. It is just as true of women. Those only who overcome difficulties, and make themselves a name in spite of privations . . . are known in history," Thayer writes in introducing Frances Power Cobbe, who showed no early inclination to learning (116).[792] "Even Jenny Lind, who Mendelssohn said was endowed with the richest vocal powers of any artist he had ever met, consecrated herself to the work of improving her gift" (204). The most fortunate examples encounter circumstances that concur in their exceptional nature, the equivalent of being chosen for coronation. Thus James Parton sees a providential design in Florence Nightingale's life: "Inheriting from nature a striking and beneficent talent, she was able . . . , finally, to exercise it on the grandest scale in the sight of all mankind" (11).[630]

The Lady with the Lamp has been aligned frequently with the queen; the two models, often appearing in the same collection, share the function of codifying Victorian femininity.[43] A glance at this preeminent Victorian lady suggests not only how readily Victoria was outdone by enterprising female subjects but also why anthologized biographies of Victoria tend to swerve from narration of a particular life to congratulations either on the queen's extraordinary ordinariness or on her benign worldwide effects. In short, Victoria has done too little alone; solitary yet surrounded, her every action has the air of being pre-scripted. Though Nightingale's model career was similarly constrained by proprieties and myths, it was indisputably also self-made and helped directly to initiate other women's careers.

Lady and queen both figure in *Eminent Women of the Age,* in sketches by the editor, Parton.[630] Florence Nightingale adorns the title page (a detail of fig. 8) and leads the way in an untitled first section, whereas Victoria's biography is set alone in its own category, between "The Woman's Rights Movement and Its Champions in the United States," and "Eminent Women of the Drama." The presenter quotes uncritically the popular imagery of Nightingale as heroine and saint of the Crimean War. He mentions signs of *prestige,* Victoria's gift to her of a cross, and the visit Nightingale paid to Balmoral, "receiving the homage of the royal family." Homage is due from the queen to this practical world leader who became an effective model for the American women who nursed soldiers during the Civil War (29–37). The contributor's portrayal of Victoria is considerably less devout, mixed with satire of the historical fiction of monarchy and with novelistic insights into the emotions of the bride and wife (422–23). Like Carey, Thornton-Cook, and other biographers, the biographer in *Eminent Women*[630] offers glimpses of the woman beneath the surface by strategically excerpting the "trifles" of her own memoirs. "Her Highland Diary . . . exhibits to us the picture of a happy family, always delighted to escape from the trammelling etiquette and absurd splendors" to find "pleasures which are accessible to most of mankind" (436–37). Whatever else Nightingale's story may be, it is not cozy; the royal family's escape from court to hearth is a small venture compared to

Nightingale's campaign to reorganize the apparatus of the empire (albeit from an invalid's couch in later years).

In each of the biographies I have discussed, Victoria is one in a series of women chosen to represent that curious contradiction, a woman so unlike other women that it is remarkable that she is just like other women. The demand for such role models requires an unstable blend of intimacy and distance, likeness and singularity. Queen Victoria perfected an image of herself as middle class and regal, alone yet containing multitudes. Collective biographies often recruit her into service because of this representative versatility, for different ends. In general, alongside contemporary commoners Victoria is used to encourage aspiration; her own qualities blend into the background of the age, allowing leaders such as Florence Nightingale to shine forth more brightly. Among famous women of all ages, Victoria stands out for the simplicity of her quest, the refined compass of her actions and principles. As the culmination of a series of queens, Victoria is most certain of preeminence by every standard except the demands of historical romance; here she may solicit in the audience a self-congratulatory fantasy of high hereditary rank and nationhood.

As good queen or spirit of the age, as a woman unstained by an episodic quest, Victoria might seem the perfect model of historic womanhood. Yet she is by no means omnipresent in collective biographies of women from the 1840s to 1940s. Her virtues and her good fortune may detract from her narratability, just as the world's collaboration in recognizing her public role may erase peculiar details that enliven brief or lengthy biographies. Female prosopography, building on comparative distinctions among subjects, pulls together a normative womanhood. As many feminist theorists now recognize, however, not all universalizing moves are alike; some are the precondition for social transformation on behalf of the posited category.[44] At the margins of these British and American collective biographies of women one always detects a vast archive, the annals of European men's history compelled to ingest more representatives of the category of womanhood. Victoria assists the genre in chipping away at the undervaluation of such women's contribution to history, at the supposition that fame and virtue, history and happiness, are incompatible or unattainable for women, even at the shibboleths of race and nation, of birth and rank, of identity as isolated self-determination. It is collective, even collaborative biographical history, and it has been one strategy for empowering the women who could obtain but not get in such books.

Victoria in Feminist Literary Histories

If such is the composite portrait of Victoria in the collective biographies during her day and after, what has become of the queen in feminist discourse of the past quarter century? I have suggested that Victoria helps to figure three crucial issues in this discourse: agency, recovery, and what I will call literary tropism. Of all nineteenth-century women, Victoria the monarch might seem to have had least trouble in claiming agency; of all historic women, Victoria might be among those least in need of recuperation, never having been obscured. Further, Victoria might seem to have little to do with the female literary traditions that have preoccupied so much of feminist work in the academy. Yet lately, "our" Queen Victoria has proven to be an occasion for addressing these questions. When feminist literary critics such as Adrienne Munich, Margaret Homans, and Gail Turley Houston devote years to writing full-length studies of a woman who was neither a feminist nor a professional writer, something is up.

Persistently, the reconstructions of Queen Victoria emphasize her multiplicity and self-contradiction, in part to authorize yet more representations of her. As Gail Turley Houston adds in introducing *Royalties*, third in line after Munich's *Queen Victoria's Secrets* and Homans's *Royal Representations*, Victoria's "complexity" affords "room for many to study this fascinating monarch" (ix).[45] The queen's reign is the prevailing paradox, in these feminist studies as in the Victorian collective biographies. "To function simultaneously as wife, mother, and queen fitted no Victorian conventions," according to Munich (20), yet her name and image were used to reinforce those very conventions (see Homans, 2–4; Houston, 6–17), as well as to perpetuate British monarchy (Munich, 11). A kind of collective megalomania projected many replicas of queenship, whether in the form of models of queenly middle-class women or in literary invention (Munich, 194; Homans, 68–69).[46] The proliferation of Victorias ought to dispel the desire for a unique original, a model subject. To suggest that these monographs are rivals would be to claim that someone could copyright the Victorian age. Instead, we can recognize customs of self-help history persisting in sophisticated feminist studies today.

In Virginia Woolf's *Orlando* the Victorian age, immersed in a Ruskinian storm cloud, produces a "fecundity" of "ill-assorted objects," "crystal palaces, bassinettes, military helmets, memorial wreaths" "piled higgledy-piggledy . . . where the statue of Queen Victoria now stands."[47] In many ways this is the Victoria that Munich, Homans, and Houston exhibit: the queen as commodity maven (Houston, 55–56), Victoria herself as collectible. The various crystallized images include the young mother leaning on Prince Albert's arm as sponsor of industry and arts; the spider-like widow overindulging in death; the admiring fan of famous authors, herself a rival author; the donor of the Bible, "the secret of [Britain's] greatness," to the African chief (Munich, 144–45); the conspicuous home-and-mausoleum decorator (tartan carpets at Balmoral! [Munich, 46]) who eschewed a crown and scorned fashion.

In the midst of the dazzling array, the puzzle of Victoria remains, centering on the question of her agency: Is she an autonomous subject or a cultural construction? In her introduction, "The Queen's Agency," Homans recognizes a persistent "antithesis" in feminist studies of historical women, between claims of "self-determination" and "social construction" (xxxiv). Homans, like Munich, places Victoria's public performances as constructed yet grants Victoria and other women a degree of autonomy or agency within such construction (xxxiii–vi). The very project of feminist studies indeed seems to require a double thesis of feminine repression and female agency; such is the double pretext of biographical recuperation. Homans writes, "I am in part performing one of the humbler tasks of feminist literary history, that of honoring, and in many cases of recovering from oblivion, the woman author's subjectivity, signature, and agency" (xxxvi). Here again are the women, all but absent from biography and history—missing from the shelves, as Woolf and others have lamented.

In this tradition, the feminist re-searchers set out to counteract a perceived underestimation of Victoria: "Victoria herself suffers, not just the overshadowing of her own monumental artistry but the complete obliteration of her person. . . . We use the word 'Victorian' without thinking about Queen Victoria" (Homans, 227).[48] Yet in what oblivion has Victoria languished?[49] *Royal Representations* and *Queen Victoria's Secrets* perceive the queen to be deprived of authority like many a forgotten woman writer, over fifteen years after a groundbreaking feminist-Victorianist study to which both volumes acknowledge a debt, Nina Auerbach's *Woman and the Demon,* in which Victoria is a presiding spirit.[50] Published in 1982, at the turning point in feminist studies from "victimization" to a "celebrat[ion of] women's powers" in Homans's words (xxxiv), *Woman and the Demon* anticipates many later feminist inquiries. Not only does Auerbach provide blueprints for studying the queens in Carroll, Ruskin, Haggard, Rossetti, and the like, she might almost be summarizing the major themes of Munich and Homans as well (setting aside Auerbach's emphasis on Victoria's modeling for single women such as Florence Nightingale). Here is Auerbach: "Ironically, Queen Victoria, that panoply of family happiness and stubborn adversary of female independence, could not help but shed her aura upon single women. Her long and early widowhood that drowned out the memory of her marriage, her relentlessly spreading figure and commensurately increasing empire, her obstinate longevity which engorged generations of men and the collective shocks of history, lent an epic quality to the lives of single women" (119–20). This précis does not obviate the achievements of the recent full-length studies, which focus on Victoria as text and author rather than as pretext or mascot who "could not help but shed her aura." No one can claim proprietorship of Victoria. But the belated claims of Victoria's neglect—like the laments for the women buried in biographical history—seem more customary than accurate. Scarcely a work of Victorian literary or cultural studies published in the 1980s–90s omits a few indexed references to Queen Victoria, particularly if empire joins gender, class, and race as categories of analysis.[51]

It is true that the queen has been difficult to pose as feminist heroine, and hence it has taken decades to reach the point of current studies of Victoria herself. Nor does a right-minded scholar redress any significant wrong by restoring recognition to a celebrated sovereign. Yet this most archetypal of famous women (a queen regnant) emerges in feminist histories only as the lady who vanishes. A clue lies in Homans's concession concerning the effort of recovery, which she calls a "humbler task." Why the apology for what has after all been the driving motive of much transformative critical work? Perhaps recuperation resembles housework, always to be done again. It may also be accused of nostalgia, the heroics of rescue, or at least an undertheorized representationalism. Further, historical feminist studies recover figures that provoke great cultural anxiety: the older woman, mother, or spinster (Munich, 104–26) or the woman in the generational past. Victoria perhaps allows a recovered sensation of heroine worship because she is an ironic role model.

Certainly Victoria gives a name to a desired agency. Langbauer suggests this as the source of feminist scholars' attraction to Victoria: "If there is *any* room for agency at all, Victoria as queen represents one of those liminal sites in which we might hope to find it" (221). Victoria may then serve us as an exempt or "aggrandized agency," in Amanda Anderson's terms; in some feminist studies, exceptional women (analogues to the critic herself) are granted self-reflexive detachment from the "ideological formations" that otherwise constrain contemporary subjects.[52] Such exemption offers an inviting alternative to the views of privileged Victorian women as either hapless victims or unwitting delegates of hegemonic power. Victoria is a particularly useful aggrandized agent because we find it hard to identify with her except in a mediated way; she isn't going to mentor us, she would not like us much, and we're not at all sure we like her. Yet Victoria may have proven altogether too compelling, as a figure for the age that has consumed more than its share of feminist studies—with a curious literary bias.

Without considering the collective female biographies of the period, Homans, Houston, and Munich figure Victoria as model woman of the age and as sponsor of Victorian literature. For the most part, the agency recuperated by these professors of English, women's studies, and art history is that of authorship. Why has so much of feminist discourse across centuries concerned women writers? The answers may be too complex to pursue here, though pertinent enough to a study of biographical collections, many of which feature women writers. For an observer in Woolf's position, women's literary history remade history altogether, and many feminists continue to share this view: "Towards the end of the eighteenth century a change came about . . . of greater importance than the Crusades or the Wars of the Roses. The middle-class woman began to write" (*ROO*, 65). The change still radiates through the work of women writers of other origins than the British middle class. The effects have made it too easy to mistake studies of writings by or about certain kinds of women for studies of the conditions of all women. This overemphasis on literary enfranchisement especially concerns me here because it has contributed to the neglect of female collective biographies. A history of women read through the novel—even with the addition of conduct literature, poetry, or literary anthologies—is narrower, more capitulating, than one that would encompass biographical collections of many kinds of exemplary women. Literary periodization and cultural history more generally tend to be gendered and "genred," that is, narrowly defining the social roles and literary forms that remain in view.[53] Whenever monarchs personify such periods, canons magnetically cluster around their image, perhaps never so intensely as in the "Elizabethan" and the "Victorian." With her plainclothes sentiment and fusion of vocation and marriage plots, Victoria seems to epitomize an age of classic realist fiction; her genre, from our perspective, appears to be the novel. A renewed interest in Victoria, then, seems to evolve from a longstanding emphasis, in feminist discourse, on Victorian women novelists.

Most are now familiar with the challenges that have been brought to feminist criticism's preoccupation with nineteenth-century women novelists. Elaine Showalter noted in 1977 that "women's literary history has suffered from an extreme form of . . . 'residual Great Traditionalism,' which has reduced and condensed . . . English women novelists to a tiny band of the 'great.'"[54] What we might call Greenwich time has been reset from a variety of longitudes, postcolonial and French poststructuralist among them. In 1985, Toril Moi characterized "Anglo-American" feminist criticism as a deluded search for "a *real* woman hidden behind the patriarchal textual facade."[55] Today, not only the class and racial exclusivity but also the phallogocentric and heteronormative conventions of the classic realist novel seem thoroughly called into question.[56] But for reasons that may not bear much investigation, critics now relish studying what they deplore: the conservative monitor queen, for example. I see no sign that the early fixation on Woolf's gender-and-genre club of "the four great women novelists" has dwindled, though it is now immersed in crowds of other studies.[57]

In spite of the demand for social history, literary sociology, and cultural studies, female prosopography has substituted the biographies of a few renowned women of letters for the feminist cultural histories of entire epochs. Victorians invoked the queen, as we do, to give name and face to a collective history of women. Yet Victorian prosopographies tend to be more inclusive in some ways than feminist literary histories that reconstruct the period. Victorian gatekeepers anticipated our habit of eponymous periodization, and they compiled biographical anthologies in the queen's name. Queen Victoria could appear as a writer manqué.[58] That the queen might have been one of the novelists of her own era, the novelist Rosa Nouchette Carey[143] considers a great point in Victoria's favor: slightly misquoting *The Private Life of the Queen* by One of Her Majesty's Servants (168), Carey suggests "'that if the Queen had been destined to write in lieu of ruling, she must have left a great mark on the literature of the country'" (76; cf. Houston, 61). Of course, recent studies make much of the fact that she did write and did place her stamp on Victorian literature. Victoria readily claims authorship, it seems: a multiauthored collection, *Queen Victoria and Other Excellent Women* (1903),[655] is cataloged in the British Library under her name (it includes a short life of the late Victoria by James Macaulay).

The queen would have left her mark on the literary period whether or not she published her bestselling journals. Victoria was associated with the triumph of women writers in her age, as implied in a title such as *Queens of Literature of the Victorian Period*[414] (Houston, 79). Some accounts of new modes of women's work paid tribute to the monarch's leadership, as when nurses and reformers are said to be "following in their Ruler's footsteps" in *Pioneer Women in Victoria's Reign* (159–60).[652] Other compilations of women's work were strictly literary and seem to attribute an organic collective authorship to the queen. *Women Novelists of Queen Victoria's Reign* collects biographical "appreciations" by women novelists: Margaret Oliphant demoting the overrated Brontës; Eliza Lynn Linton crowning Eliot with laurels; Edna Lyall sugaring Gaskell with "love and gratitude" (117).[607] Beyond this the numerous subjects and biographers in *Women Novelists* would shatter our tiny canon: Who now discusses Mrs. Stretton or Mrs. Marshall? Here is Adeline Sergeant on Mrs. Caroline Crowe, not Queen Victoria: "She left a mark upon the age in which she lived, and she helped . . . to mould the women of England after higher ideals." "Those who consider the development of women to be one of the distinguishing features of Queen Victoria's reign should not forget that they owe deep gratitude to writers like Mrs. Crowe," who championed women's rights before there was a newsworthy women's movement. Sergeant paraphrases George Eliot on this modern Saint Theresa: "It is owing to the labours of those who . . . lie in forgotten graves, that things are well with us here and now" (160).[607] Perhaps tributes to the Mrs. Crowes and Adeline Sergeants will prepare the way for a Judith Shakespeare.

Just as the queen gives a kind of bodily shape to the entire century, a very few women represent the sex when they must compete with men for "the highest place in literature." For example, Margaret Oliphant published a golden jubilee assessment titled "The Literature of the Last Fifty Years," which uncannily anticipated the "major writers" selected by Anglo American Victorianists after World War II. She includes "the greatest Woman-poet whom England has known," Barrett Browning, and "the great female writer of the Victorian period," indeed the only woman to ever attain literary greatness, George Eliot. With low expectations for women writers in general, Oliphant hustles the Brontës and Gaskell to the back with the minor men. Her "Majesty of England" provides a pretext for a brief survey "of those writers who will hereafter be known in universal history as of the age of Victoria. It is pleasant . . . that so many of the greatest periods in our literary history should coincide with the reigns of female sovereigns."[59] In Oliphant's two-volume textbook, *The Victorian Age in English Literature* (1892), her scope is neither strictly Victorian nor strictly English. She includes Romantics, Scottish and Irish writers in many genres, and an impressive range of women, from poets such as Felicia Hemans and novelists such as Mary Elizabeth Braddon, to the thriving prose writers Mary Howitt, Harriet Martineau, Julia Kavanagh, Frances Power Cobbe, and Geraldine Jewsbury—writers busily being revived by countless literary descendants of Margaret Oliphant today.

Feminist recuperation of female agency has been preoccupied with a small cohort of Victorian women of letters and lately with the queen as author and guiding spirit of Victorian literature. The map could readily be redrawn from another location, but this is a perspective like that of Steinberg's cartoon of the United States as seen from Manhattan.[60] With Laurie Langbauer I would press the question of what "cultural work attention to Victoria is doing for feminist scholarship and literary studies right now" (213).

Ends and Origins: Inventing Ourselves

Virginia Woolf's *A Room of One's Own*, "the Great Mother of all feminist critical texts," as Sandra Gilbert and Susan Gubar call it, helped to shape the prosopography of literary women when feminist literary criticism was comparatively new as a recognized field (xxviii). Gilbert and Gubar's classic of 1979, *The Madwoman in the Attic,* forcefully promoted the Woolfian canon without much notice of Victoria, yet twenty years later the second edition seems all the more "Victorian." Fittingly, Gilbert and Gubar delivered a keynote at the "Victoria Redressed" conference at the University of California, Santa Cruz, in 1999, which consisted of parts of their new introduction to the "millennial" edition of *Madwoman.* Diane Sadoff, asked to wind up the conference, noted the prevailing theme of changing generations of feminist scholarship. It was as though recuperation of Victoria and the Victorian period—the topic of the conference—inevitably elicited a history of twenty years of feminist studies. The published introduction to the revised edition of *Madwoman* (2000) accounts for the limited pantheon of early feminist criticism in ways that I recognize as implicating me—and hundreds of others at work in the field since 1979.[61]

Gilbert and Gubar wonder that they, two scholars trained in eighteenth- and twentieth-century studies, should have migrated to "that fascinatingly problematic heart of the nineteenth century known as the Victorian period": "There were clearly reasons why, like so many of feminist criticism's other newly born women, we focused our earliest intellectual energies on the nineteenth century. For one thing, most of the major texts that we now understood to have constituted us as *female* readers were in fact nineteenth-century texts. . . . The syllabus that became the basis for *The Madwoman* probably reflected a canon that lived in the mind of just about every *femme moyenne intellectuelle* who spent her girlhood avidly devouring the classics of the female imagination" (xxvii). This presents a modeling community among the writers (Gilbert and Gubar name Austen, Shelley, and Dickinson, as well as Eliot and the Brontës), their heroines, the readers, and the critics, a zone of mutual representation. The passage immediately becomes a list of acknowledgments of fellow feminists, historians, and critics, who at that epoch turned the mirror on the texts and times that had formed their subjectivities. Next, Gilbert and Gubar hastily list a range of texts and writers that had already been "excavate[d]" or "resurrect[ed]."

> But we sensed that the most powerful and empowering forces acting on our
> female imaginations and those of many other women readers and writers were
> nevertheless those four horsewomen of at least one kind of novelistic

Apocalypse: Jane Austen, Charlotte Brontë, Emily Brontë, and George Eliot. And because we sensed, too, that the great women poets who were these writers' contemporaries or descendants—notably Elizabeth Barrett Browning, Emily Dickinson, and Christina Rossetti—both shared in and were shaped by the particular, often duplicitous sensibility that inhabited those novelists, we experienced these poets, too, as powerful in a richly significant female literary tradition. (xxviii)

This familiar model of literary tradition combines the Romantic expressive theory of art, the Victorian privileging of impressionist receptivity, and the self-help discourse of identification and empowerment. The newly invented discipline, feminist criticism, might be an imagined community establishing its ancestry after the fact: "Female literary history . . . is shaped very differently from male literary history" (xxviii). As I have noted, critics of academic feminist studies in the past twenty-five years have raised many objections to such a jubilee tribute to the few Victorian women novelists.[62] The passage above immediately segues into the supplements to the short list, as new genealogies always challenge the founders: not only the poets—who evidently share the powerful sensibility of the four novelists—but also earlier or less renowned writers of various genres (xxvii–xxix).[63] This increasingly substantial tradition (often represented by citations of a list of more or less renowned names) nevertheless remains lacking: "It plainly didn't feel comparable in weight and strength to the mainstream tradition . . . [though] it offered possibilities of place and precedent—offered a perhaps invisibly thickening critical mass of literary *femininity*—to aspiring women of letters" (xxx). (I will return to that ominous "thickening . . . *femininity*" in a moment.) The paragraph concludes with the example of Elizabeth Barrett Browning's claim that she could find no "grandmothers," even as she admitted that predecessors abounded. Once again, women's history is prosopographical, naming its missing, threading its few pearls to the main strand, with detachable pendants.

Gilbert and Gubar perform a dual apologia in tandem scenes of autobiographical dispossession like those I noted in chapter 1. While many in my generation would find this performance engaging though not of course omniscient, many emerging feminist scholars (at least my students as well as the graduate students in the audience at the Dickens Project conference in Santa Cruz) seem to reject it as a nostalgic rearguard defense against subsequent critiques: "Bliss *was* it to be alive in that time, at that place!" (xx). The new introduction does telescope important later developments beyond the literature of Anglophone white women. "Short of admiring the sophistication" of readings within "new historicism, queer theory, postcolonialism, African-American studies, cultural studies, and poststructuralism," they ask, "what can we possibly say about them? Most obviously, they demonstrate that feminist criticism in nineteenth-century studies functions as a microcosm of English in particular, the humanities in general" (xxxix). Gilbert and Gubar seem at a loss that is also their gain: there are too many complex new schools to encompass, which only reconfirms the productivity of the original work that spawned so many descendants and provoked so many attacks. It is quite possible, on the contrary, that the militant young have no inclination to think back through their mothers. Having become iconic personae of feminist criticism, Gilbert and Gubar came under attack for "sins that in those early days we knew not of—essentialism, racism, heterosexism, phallologocentrism—accused, sometimes shrilly, by sister feminists, and, sometimes patronizingly, by male quasi-feminists" (xxv). Inevitably, they bristle when recalling how it felt to be cast as "establishment puppets" (xxv)—their predicament resembling that of successful intellectual women in the nineteenth century. It would be worse still to be hidden in plain view like Queen Victoria herself, or indeed like many of the women in Victorian prosopographies.

Coda

Perhaps I have needed the queen's agency in order to narrate an auto/biographical story—to create the persona that authored *How to Make It as a Woman.* It is a stripped-down story that suggests how little is done through critical work alone. Beginning a Ph.D. program in 1981, I studied nineteenth-century British literature for years without much thought of the queen. In the first year of that program at Princeton, I remember tacitly declining a general invitation from the director of graduate studies to participate in the program in women's studies, though I had been active in women's groups at Bennington and Cornell, because I sensed that feminism was not seen as serious or competitive work at Princeton. Within the following three years, I was participating in an interdepartmental graduate colloquium in feminist studies as Sandra Gilbert and Elaine Showalter arrived on campus. Already ABD when they came, I never took a course with either of them, though I remember a very encouraging office visit with Sandra, as well as an encounter with Elaine on the pavement near Firestone Library in which I, visibly pregnant, enjoyed her supportive humor about my stigma. Yet though Showalter's articles and chapters on Eliot and Woolf helped to shape my dissertation as much as did *The Madwoman in the Attic,* I knew it would be unwise to become her disciple (as a few other students willingly did). I never wanted to be anyone's disciple. The publications of the pioneering feminist critics were my practical mentors as I moved to my assistant professorship, where I had been hired to teach feminist criticism and theory, though I would be doing so almost self-taught. (By that time I had become Jewish, married, a mother. Was this due to the influence of my role models, the times, the prosopography of our field? Or, as I prefer to believe, a matter of sequences of choices that I made?)

Christine de Pizan in her study, Woolf in the British Library figure as the woman in the scene of autobiographical dispossession, wishing a heritage into existence—the feminist re-searcher today is one in a crowd, one who has arrived very late. Our work, rewarded for originality, is also valued according to how much it knits together strands of the current discourse and then unravels and attributes them in the notes. The temptation to consign predecessors to swift oblivion has been strong indeed, in the urgency to keep pace with professional progress. (*The Madwoman in the Attic,* adapting Bloom's "anxiety of influence," understood the profession's competitive agon very well.) Yet there is a strong taboo against admitting the affective investments we bring to "the field." Like life narrative in general and role modeling in particular, our careers are driven by the triangulation of desire. The worst fear may be to be left out—the excluded third term, perhaps. But there is danger as well in being caught in the act of allegiance. To acknowledge my affiliation with Gilbert and Gubar and Showalter and others of the Anglo American female-literary-tradition school strikes me as akin to admitting that I am attached to my mother. Not rigorous. Old-fashioned. "Seventies." Stuck in recovery, as a book on centuries of recovery projects must be. Biography in general carries the burden of emotional attachment, abject hero worship.

I urge us to revise the progressive narratives that are imposed on feminist studies as on women's history. Reading itself is impossible without identification; feminist studies inevitably involve recuperation as well as critique. The turn to memoir in the past decade seems to me an effort both to cleave to the notion of autonomous self-directed careers and to dissolve that model. Culture inhabits us; our narratives require coauthorship. I have been induced to wait on Queen Victoria far more than I ever intended. Margaret Homans and Adrienne Munich's invitation to contribute to their collection of essays on Queen Victoria gave me a useful name and face to personify the traditions of collective female biography that I recently had begun to study.[64]

Meanwhile, I published an article on Camille Paglia's *Sexual Personae* (a macabre prosopography, though I had not yet developed my usage of the term), in which I argued that Paglia inverted and darkly parodied feminist goddess worship.[65] In light of Paglia's self-advertisement as a potential member of the Judith school of female violence, I wrote of having witnessed a scene in the Commons of Bennington College: the Amazonian Nietzschean professor "ass kicking" a male student and harrying him out of the building. Imagine my fascination to read Elaine Showalter's most recent book, *Inventing Herself,* a rich auto/biographical prosopography, in which she tells the story (entirely familiar to me) of the Gail Thain Parker presidency of Bennington and Paglia's cameo appearance in it, followed by a full-length portrait of Paglia.[66]

Showalter makes no secret of her own investments: "My choices among those who both preached and lived their freedom reflect my own situation as a literary critic and sixties feminist activist.... I have put some of my own history into this book" (17). Echoing Carolyn Heilbrun's autobiographical reflections and argument in *Writing a Woman's Life* (17–19), Showalter unwittingly chimes with the material I have revived in this study: "Reclaiming our feminist icons is a necessary step in our collective memoir." For her, making it as a woman paradoxically entails emulating predecessors who dared to go it alone: collective progress, inspired by recovery and praise, is to be driven by heedless self-determination (or aggrandized agency). "As we come to the end of a century in which women have made enormous gains, we still lack a sense of the feminist past. Other groups have celebrated their heroic figures, but women have no national holidays, no days of celebration for the births or deaths of our great heroines.... We need to know about the patterns in our own intellectual tradition, to engage and to debate with the choices made by women whose restless, adventurous, and iconic lives make them our heroines, our sisters, our contemporaries" (19). Showalter reiterates the tropes of most presenters' prefaces, as she specifies the plenitude of female subjects that she does not include: "This is not a book about Madame Curie. Nor will you find Eleanor Roosevelt ... Jane Addams, Harriet Tubman, Susan B. Anthony.... " These commended "role models ... practiced self-denial" rather than living the revolution that Showalter personally favors (16–17). It is a scene of autobiographical disinheritance but with the common variation of naming a long list of all-too-available models. Other people have an intact history (Woolf: "There were the biographies, Johnson and Goethe and Carlyle ..."). Indeed, we have rather too much of one kind of representative (Woolf, again: "After all, we have lives enough of Jane Austen"). "I never met a feminist when I was growing up. I never even met a 'career girl'" (17)—Showalter, sounding like Paule Marshall or Carolyn Heilbrun or others I have mentioned, recalling her childhood dearth of role models.

Showalter's narrative gifts are considerable, and her biographical syntheses of mutually influential lives are energetic and acute. I delight to see that the form of collective female biography thrives. But surely it should become harder to lament the missing tradition, faced with the heaps of lives from "our" past. What Showalter's narratives prove is that, rather than "inventing herself," each of the women copied, borrowed, shared, or opposed her selves with those of others. Accordingly, Susan Sontag learns through Simone de Beauvoir to recognize herself as one of a "small band of women of genius" and then moves in to replace Mary McCarthy (225–27).

Showalter's series of interlinked role model biographies follows the logic of incarnation to be found in female prosopographies. She begins by overlaying Princess Diana as a kind of transparency on Mary Wollstonecraft's life story (13–14), calls Margaret Fuller the American Wollstonecraft (41) and Mary McCarthy "the Dark Lady of New York," "Zenobia on the Hudson" (177–86), and offers typological subtitles in the Victorian or modern manner: "Hannah Arendt: Pallas Athene" (186). Seamlessly, the aspiring presenter joins the sequence in her portrayal of her wish to "apply for the job" of "Dark Lady" at *Partisan Review* (271), her partnerships with women colleagues, and her knack for being in "the right place at the right time to do the right thing by women."[67] Bliss was it to be alive—but: "The glare of living as a feminist icon, and navigating the treacherous waters of hostility, rivalry, and competition, had become ex-hausting for many of those who had attempted to play a public role" (301). The model famous women abruptly step aside to retake control of representation in "other modes of writing," including autobiography or memoir (301).

Here one begins to sink into that thickening femininity that the female pub-lic intellectual dreads more than anything. Showalter writes that she "stopped writing essays on feminist criticism in 1989; they had outlived their useful-ness, like the cat we got for the children, who hung on, hungry, demanding, and querulous, long after the children had grown up" (301). Old feminism is an excess of misplaced, primitive need for ersatz family intimacy (the very night-mare image of what happens if you acknowledge affiliation with this "school"). As though of necessity, the next chapter or stage in Showalter's collective his-tory/autobiography is Camille Paglia, and waves of antifeminism ensue. Some-thing of the whining cat that won't die does seem to be writ large in Paglia's caricature of woman as lurid swamp of mindless, impulsive repetition, as well as in Paglia's vituperation against Susan Sontag and any well-known female rival. However much Showalter admires (from a critical distance) Paglia's un-censored egomania, she makes it plain that "Paglia was not . . . alone, isolated, or peculiar" in the 1990s (316). Though individuality is still her fetish, Showalter tells stories of generations, not of one individual after another who "invents herself." It is critical and intelligent panegyric, and more books like it would be welcome—indeed there have been many.

Reading Showalter, I asked myself about my own relation to the models in this book. At times, as I wrote, I wondered whether I was doing justice to the women who lived and died, who became pretexts for the self-help histories. My subjects are the texts; with an occasional "identifying" twinge, I deal with the equivalent of photographs of statues, not people. As sets of representations, the prosopographies allow a kind of antiheroic admiration. Victoria serves me well as a model subject because she has been so thoroughly represented by others and yet it is safely impossible for me to identify with her in any sustained way. She garners my respect and attention, yes, but rivalrous desire, no (although a full-length biographer of the queen would probably enter into a contract with her as a once-living person). Immersion in the biographies rather than the finite lives allows me to perceive the amusing or frustrating or generative patterns, the ideological commitments and rhetorical aims. In contrast, Showalter is writing a collective auto/biography in which the airwaves of emulation and rivalry are broadcasting at full bandwidth.

While Showalter's personal history without a doubt belongs in an updated version of "Our Famous Women," memoir has much less place in my book. For one thing, the center of gravity of *How to Make It as a Woman* is the nineteenth century, and for another, I was never in the right place at the right time with the founders of U.S. feminist discourse—unless we count the Com-mons at Bennington. Yet while third-person address is the appropriate default mode for this study, my engagement as presenter is probably only a degree less manifest than Showalter's. I suspect that I have been writing my own genealogy where it appeared to be missing. It seems no coincidence that I was raised by two ex-Mormons, descendants of mutual improvers and genealogists. At one point during the project I realized that my mother, father, and I were all simultaneously writing books that could be associated with self-help.[68] It may not have been a liberating recognition but it was certainly an amusing one, and something of a relief, to sense that the purpose was not mine alone—as when one has been temporarily lost on a solitary walk in the woods, only to find that some tendency of the right "lead" has provided a circular path back to the group. I feel little of the absence of responsive models or ancestry that so many writers describe; I could be said to have more than enough. Like other second-generation feminist critics (a few generations have already ensued), I face rather the oversupply of originating work and models of success since the 1970s, even as the history of the field is being fast forgotten, its initiatives abandoned or diverted into different compelling projects.

I would not turn back the clock if I could. The genealogy that I recover is more historical than personal, the collective biographical history of some kinds of women; it is symptomatic of times that I would not want to relive. I have not offered new models of development for women in the twenty-first century. I have joined many in the search through the shelves and have offered new ways to see the books that are there. For now, we can look forward to the discovery of prosopographies that enliven as much as they commemorate a collective biographical history. These names and narratives crop up in curious sets in every medium, whetting our imitative desires. We need not go alone into remote archives to retrieve them.

Introduction

1. De Pizan drew on Ovid and revised Boccaccio (de Pizan 1405, xxxviii) yet included recent Christian models among those of "pagan Antiquity" (xxxvii).

2. Sybil Oldfield, *Collective Biography of Women in Britain, 1550–1900* (London: Mansell, 1999). I had written my critique of Virginia Woolf's and Carolyn Heilbrun's assertions of the absence of women's history and biography before I obtained a copy of Oldfield's introduction (1–2), which begins with Woolf's *A Room of One's Own* (1929; reprint, New York: Harcourt, 1981) and continues to Heilbrun's *Writing a Woman's Life* (New York: Ballantine, 1988)—the sort of confirmation that should be welcomed, as I suggest in chap. 7. I include some British works in Oldfield's time period that she omitted; my international all-female bibliography covers a different historical span. *A Room of One's Own* is henceforth cited parenthetically in the text as *ROO*.

3. An Anglo American axis may seem narrow in light of global studies but beyond the scope of most Americanist or Victorian studies. See Lawrence Buell, "Circling the Spheres: A Dialogue," *American Literature* 70 (1998): 465–90; Fred M. Leventhal and Roland Quinault, eds., *Anglo-American Attitudes* (Aldershot: Ashgate, 2000); Paul Giles, *Transatlantic Insurrections* (Philadelphia: University of Pennsylvania Press, 2001). As primarily a Victorianist, I am less versed in American examples than I might wish.

4. James Agee's *Let Us Now Praise Famous Men* (Boston: Houghton Mifflin, 1941) brilliantly revises the ancient conventions of prosopography (group biographical history), but this move was not his invention. Compensatory collective life narratives of women, workers, provincial groups, and others at the margin have existed almost as long as canons of powerful men.

5. O. E. Fuller, ed., *Brave Men and Women* (Ypsilanti, MI: J. C. Fuller, 1884).

6. Studies such as Sara Alpern et al., eds., *The Challenge of Feminist Biography* (Urbana: University of Illinois Press, 1992), primarily consist of memoirs by feminist biographers of women. Alpern et al. collaborated after "periods of intense . . . growth," working on separate biographies. "By sharing . . . that experience with others, we hoped to bring an important chapter of our lives to a formal close" (1). See also Teresa Iles, ed., *All Sides of the Subject* (New York: Teachers College, Columbia, 1992). Feminist studies have favored autobiography over biography, e.g., Susan Groag Bell and Marilyn Yalom, eds., *Revealing Lives* (Albany: State University of New York Press, 1990). Exceptions include Linda Wagner-Martin, *Telling Women's Lives* (New Brunswick, NJ: Rutgers University Press, 1994); Elisabeth Young-Bruehl, *Subject to Biography* (Cambridge, MA: Harvard University Press, 1998); Paula R. Backscheider, *Reflections on Biography* (Oxford: Oxford University Press, 1999); Judy Long, *Telling Women's Lives* (New York: New York University Press, 1999); Laura Marcus, *Auto/Biographical Discourses* (Manchester: University of Manchester Press, 1994).

7. Recent collections nearly coincide with those published fifty or a hundred years ago, e.g., Cokie Roberts, *Founding Mothers: The Women Who Raised Our Nation* (New York: HarperCollins, 2004); Francine Prose, *The Lives of the Muses* (New York: HarperCollins, 2002); Elizabeth D. Leonard, *All the Daring of a Soldier* (New York: Norton, 1999); Susan Ware, *Letter to the World* (New York: Norton, 1998). Jennifer S. Uglow's *The Lunar Men* (New York: Farrar, Straus & Giroux, 2002) stands for many studies of male associations.

8. Reliance on representative multibiography takes many forms, from the video *Great American Indian Heroes* for grades four through nine (Mahwah, NJ: Troll Associates, 1986)—and comparable materials supplied by Social Studies School Service, Culver City, CA—to memoirs by Native American alumni of Dartmouth College in Andrew Garrod and Colleen Larimore, eds., *First Person, First Peoples* (Ithaca, NY: Cornell University Press, 1997).

9. Long, *Telling Women's Lives,* 101. Long herself argues for a "partnership of subject, narrator, and reader," but like others she downplays audience in her interpretation (3).

10. Backscheider, *Reflections on Biography,* 226.

11. Exceptions include the contributions to Claudia Nelson and Lynne Vallone, eds., *The Girl's Own* (Athens: University of Georgia Press, 1994); Nina Baym, *American Women Writers and the Work of History, 1790–1860* (New Brunswick, NJ: Rutgers University Press, 1995); Kate Flint, *The Woman Reader, 1837–1914* (Oxford: Clarendon Press, 1993); Harriet Guest, *Small Change* (Chicago: University of Chicago Press, 2000), esp. chap. 7; Pamela Corpron Parker, "Good Women, Good Works: Victorian Philanthropy and Women's Biography," *Trinity: The Cresset* 59 (1996): 17–21.

12. Nancy Armstrong, *Desire and Domestic Fiction* (New York: Oxford University Press, 1987). Long-influential feminist studies of nineteenth-century fiction and conduct literature include Judith Lowder Newton, *Women, Power, and Subversion* (New York: Methuen, 1985); and Mary Poovey, *Uneven Developments* (Chicago: University of Chicago Press, 1988). Increasingly, this duet (novels and conduct literature) has played out in terms of class or empire: e.g., Elizabeth Langland, *Nobody's Angels* (Ithaca, NY: Cornell University Press, 1995); and Susan Meyer, *Imperialism at Home* (Ithaca, NY: Cornell University Press, 1996). Postcolonial and poststructuralist theories and semiotics have enhanced histories of the novel, as in Deidre Lynch and William B. Warner, eds., *Cultural Institutions of the Novel* (Durham, NC: Duke University Press, 1996). Franco Moretti aligns "the novel and the geo-political reality of the nation-state" (*Atlas of the European Novel, 1800–1900* [London: Verso, 1998], 16–17). Few take note of contemporary nonfiction models of women.

13. Patricia Yeager warns of the dangers of "positing . . . female powerlessness," yet Yeager like many critics listens for "emancipatory," "subversive multivoicedness" in women's writing (*Honey-Mad Women* [New York: Columbia University Press, 1988], 36).

14. *ROO,* 26–27. I honor here a tradition of feminist critical essays impersonating Woolf the scholar, as in Domna C. Stanton's "Autogynography: Is the Subject Different?": "What did that ghostly absence mean, I asked, looking as did Mary Beton, at 'the blank spaces' on those shelves?" (in *The Female Autograph,* ed. Domna C. Stanton [Chicago: University of Chicago Press, 1987], 4). Susan Gubar performed another "Mary Beton" in "A Feminism of One's Own," Keynote Address, Twelfth Annual Eighteenth- and Nineteenth-Century British Women Writers Conference, University of Georgia, March 27, 2004.

15. Brenda R. Silver, ed., *Virginia Woolf's Reading Notebooks* (Princeton, NJ: Princeton University Press, 1983) provides no index entry for de Pizan. The index of Rosalind Brown-Grant's *Christine de Pizan and the Moral Defense of Women* (Cambridge: Cambridge University Press, 1999) indicates no reference to Woolf. Margaret J. M. Ezell, *Writing Women's Literary History* (Baltimore: Johns Hopkins University Press, 1993); further citations in the text. On de Pizan and other early catalogs of women, see Glenda McLeod, *Virtue and Venom* (Ann Arbor: University of Michigan Press, 1991), esp. chap. 5.

16. Ezell notes that Sandra M. Gilbert and Susan Gubar's *Norton Anthology of Literature by Women* (New York: Norton, 1985) does respect the "'independent bourgeoise Christine de Pisan,'" who is beyond Woolf's ken; these later feminists overlook "isolated aristocrats" (41–45, 49–50). Jennifer Summit follows Ezell in questioning the neglect of many women writers as "history's

shadowy ghosts" (*Lost Property* [Chicago: University of Chicago Press, 2000], 4–5). See Summit's chap. 2, "The *City of Ladies* in the Library of Gentlemen: Christine de Pizan in England, 1450–1526," 61–107.

17. Linda H. Peterson, *Traditions of Victorian Women's Autobiography* (Charlottesville: University Press of Virginia, 1999), identifies Arabella Mary Stuart Willson as Arabella W. Stuart.

18. Long, *Telling Women's Lives,* 1–2. Gianna Pomata asks, concerning new textbooks of women's history: Is the silence being broken "for the first time. . . . ? Is the commonplace [that] women have been generally excluded from historiographic memory, really true?" ("History, Particular and Universal," *Feminist Studies* 19 [1993]: 10).

19. Marilyn Booth, "The Egyptian Lives of Jeanne D'Arc," in *Remaking Women,* ed. Lila Abu-Lughod (Princeton, NJ: Princeton University Press, 1998), 172–73. See Booth's extraordinary article, "'May Her Likes Be Multiplied': 'Famous Women' Biography and Gendered Prescription in Egypt, 1892–1935," *Signs* 22 (1997): 827–90. These articles form part of Booth's *May Her Likes Be Multiplied* (Berkeley: University of California Press, 2001). Egyptian magazines in the early twentieth century took note of de Pizan's defense of women (62–63).

20. Brian Maidment, "Popular Exemplary Biography in the Nineteenth Century: Edwin Paxton Hood and His Books," *Prose Studies* 7 (1984): 148–67, accounts for the "uses" of lives of male artisans by men (ignoring comparable female collections). Maidment notes that in the 1860s and 1870s volumes appeared in "gift book or prize book" design ("multicoloured decorated or pictorial cloth covers, large formats, gold edges, and gothic lettering") sponsored by "Sunday School, chapel, or cultural club" (153–54). The trend is in place at least by 1857.[174]

21. I make no attempt in this study to measure actual reader response. Apart from publisher's blurbs, contemporary comments are extremely rare and personal narratives seldom mention a particular collection. Peter Rabinowitz, in *Before Reading* (Ithaca, NY: Cornell University Press, 1987), distinguishes the "authorial audience" rhetorically constructed by the text from the "actual audience" (20–46). Fiction also solicits a "narrative audience" that believes the events narrated (93–96). In some ways, readers of these biographical collections are both authorial and narrative audience—relying on habits of reading both history and fiction. Liz Stanley, in "Process in Feminist Biography and Feminist Epistemology," in *All Sides of the Subject,* ed. Iles, 109–25, recalls: "When I was a very little girl and my Mum was getting me off to sleep, I would read haltingly aloud . . . the lives of kings, queens, and famous men and women from my small store of books" (110)—those books being left unnamed. Robert Darnton, "What Is the History of Books?" in *The Book History Reader,* ed. David Finkelstein and Alistair McCleery (London: Routledge, 2002), 9–26, describes the continuing mystery of reading (20–22). Kate Flint notes that "mention[s] of books of advice themselves are relatively rare" (*Woman Reader,* 206); in discussing identification and role modeling, Flint examines three collective "didactic biographies" (36–38). Response may at times be recorded through mutual references or role switching among female presenters, subjects, and readers (see chap. 4 in this book).

22. The networks of mutual notice weave closely. Julia Ward Howe published a biography of Margaret Fuller (1889); Howe's daughters, Laura E. Richards and Maude Howe Elliott, won the 1917 Pulitzer for biography for *Julia Ward Howe* (Wagner-Martin, *Telling Women's Lives,* 2). See discussion of Stowe et al.,[758] pp. 58–61.

23. Dr. Howe plays a role in the lives of several female subjects, as the famous instructor of the blind Laura Bridgman who "also contributed signally to the aid of Dorothea Dix." In 1914, the statue—resembling a saint holding an antique lamp—was unveiled with some praise of Dr. Howe as an early influence (240–43).[862]

24. Whiting,[862] warning against "indiscriminate praise" in biography, avers "the simple truth" that Willard "'was of the angelic order'" (189–90). Jennie Chappell, while also hagiographical, offers a more detailed, persuasive portrait of Willard as a lively, generous, tolerant, courageous person (13–52)[162]—not at all today's stereotype of temperance activists. Chappell notes the elective affinity of Willard and Lady Henry Somerset; a mutual friend wrote that "'they were made for each other'" (48). Lady Henry sought Willard in Evanston after reading her memoir of a deceased sister (47–48); their "close and tender friendship" lasted until Willard's death (48); "they loved one another as sisters" (52), spending summers together.

25. Suzanne M. Marilley, in "Frances Willard and the Feminism of Fear," *Feminist Studies* 19 (1993): 123–46, delineates Willard's mobilization of nearly 200,000 diverse members of the Woman's Christian Temperance Union (WCTU) by the late 1890s in part by exploiting the ideology of motherhood and feminine moral superiority (123, 126–27, 131). Jennie Chappell notes that Willard was dubbed "the 'Uncrowned Queen' of the United States" and was celebrated in Britain from the 1890s (49).[162] Louise Michele Newman, in *White Women's Rights* (New York: Oxford University Press, 1999), recognizes the racism in Willard's concept of "a white life"; Willard conflicted with Ida B. Wells over the matter of lynchings (66–69). Contemporaries venerated Willard; her statue was erected in Washington in 1905 (Newman gives the date as 1906; 67).

26. *Harriet Hosmer Standing on a Ladder with Statue of Thomas Hart Benton,* Schlesinger Library, Radcliffe Institute, Harvard University. See the cover of Julia Markus, *Across an Untried Sea* (New York: Knopf, 2000), which recuperates Charlotte Cushman, Hosmer, Geraldine Jewsbury and Jane Carlyle, among other women, a number of them lesbian, sojourning in Italy.

27. The slippage among repetitions of subjects in prosopography bears some analogy to the concept of *différance.* Judith Butler claims that the Lacanian Law of the Father "is not deterministic" if a reiteration of a category of difference permits "multiple identifications," opening up "gaps and fissures" in the naturalized facade (*Gender Trouble* [New York: Routledge, 1990], 67, and *Bodies That Matter* [New York: Routledge, 1993], 10).

28. In 1927, Harold Nicolson repeated the *OED*'s definition of biography as "the history of the lives of individual men as a branch of literature" (*The Development of English Biography* [London: Hogarth, 1927], 157). Collectivity and historiography lurk in the very definition that claims to emphasize individualism and literature.

29. Gerda Lerner, "Placing Women in History: A 1975 Perspective," in *Liberating Women's History,* ed. Berenice A. Carroll (Urbana: University of Illinois Press, 1976), 357. Lawrence Stone, "Prosopography," *Daedalus* 100 (winter 1971): 57–59, warns of prosopographical generalizations based on skewed samples of elites whose records are intact.

30. Stephen Watson Fullom, *The History of Woman,* 3d ed., rev. (London and New York: Routledge, 1855), 379. Fullom's text begins with a badly drawn frontispiece of Florence Nightingale and concludes with a short prose sketch of Nightingale (still in "the East") and a tribute to Queen Victoria (405–7). In between, many pages consist of short biographies.

31. Elise Boulding, *The Underside of History,* rev. ed., 2 vols. (Newbury Park, CA: Sage, 1992), 2:157. *A History of Women in the West,* edited by Pauline Schmitt Pantel, begins in ancient times with "goddesses" and "such 'divinized abstractions' as Renown" (trans. Arthur Goldhammer [Cambridge, MA: Belknap Press, 1992], 6, 26–27).

32. Newman, *White Women's Rights,* 66–69, 116–17.

33. Stone, "Prosopography," 46. See Donald J. Winslow, "Glossary of Terms in Life-Writing, Part I," *Biography* 1, no. 1 (1978): 75. The *OED* offers sixteenth-century usage of "prosopography" (*obs.*) as "a description of the person or personal appearance." Stone hoped prosopography would "form the missing connection between political . . . and social history," institutions and biography (73).

34. Paul Sturges, "Collective Biography in the 1980s," *Biography* 6, no. 4 (1983): 319–22. Laura Marcus, *Auto/Biographical Discourses,* 58–64, discusses prosopography in the context of Galton's and Havelock Ellis's ethnographies of genius. Annette Wheeler Cafarelli, in *Prose in the Age of Poets* (Philadelphia: University of Pennsylvania Press, 1990), dismisses the merely "prosopographic or alphabetically encyclopedic" in favor of collections that make an art and an "ideological program" of "subjective sequencing" (5). I too eschew the encyclopedic but regard prosopography as ideological sequencing of subjects.

35. Linda Colley, *Lewis Namier* (New York: St. Martin's, 1989), 72–78.

36. The journal *Medieval Prosopography* has been published in Kalamazoo since 1980. Research centers in Athens, Paris, Rome, and elsewhere in Europe and the United States continue to issue such works as John D. Grainger, *Aitolian Prosopographical Studies* (Leiden: Brill, 2000);

K. S. B. Keats-Rohan, ed., *Domesday People: A Prosopography of Persons Occurring in English Documents, 1066–1166* (Rochester, NY: Boydell, 1999).

37. Thanks to Robert Holton for making this point on a panel that I organized at the Narrative Conference at Rice University in March 2001. Pierre Bourdieu, in *Distinction,* trans. Richard Nice (Cambridge, MA: Harvard University Press, 1984), measures taste in relation to life patterns through statistical ethnographic research that is not "naively empiricist" (503). Without using the term "prosopography," *Distinction* offers anonymous biographical vignettes, including many individuals portrayed in photographs. I find that neither sociologists nor historians in the United States commonly use the term.

38. Raymond Williams, *The Long Revolution* (New York: Harper & Row, 1961), 49, quoted in Robert Lanning, *The National Album: Collective Biography and the Formation of the Canadian Middle Class,* Carleton Library Series 186 (Ottawa: Carleton University Press, 1996), 20. Lanning offers a rare consideration of collective biography in a national context. Like other emerging nations, Canada produced female prosopography, e.g., Byrne Hope Sanders, *Canadian Portraits: Famous Women* (Toronto: Clark, Irwin, 1958), biographies of Emily Carr, Cora Hind, Dr. Augusta Stowe Gullen, Emily Murphy: an artist/writer, an editor/agricultural expert, a doctor, and a judge/politician.

39. Benedict Anderson, *Imagined Communities,* rev. ed. (London: Verso, 1991), 194–206, xiv.

40. Ibid., 195, 204–5.

41. Mary Evans, *Missing Persons* (London: Routledge, 1999), 137.

42. Paul de Man construes prosopopoeia as "the fiction of an apostrophe to an absent, deceased, or voiceless entity," based on "the etymology . . . *prosopon poien,* to confer a mask or a face *(prosopon)*" ("Hypogram and Inscription: Michael Riffaterre's Poetics of Reading," *Diacritics* 11 [1981]: 17–35, reprinted in *Resistance to Theory* [Minneapolis, 1986], 44, 47, and "Autobiography as De-facement," *MLN: Comparative Literature* 94 [December 1979]: 926). Michael Riffaterre, responding to de Man, insists that prosopopoeia "must not be confused with personification" and has little tie to referentiality but is a "figure of figurality" ("Prosopopeia," [*sic*] *Yale French Studies* 69 [1985]: 113, 108, 123). See J. Hillis Miller, "Prosopopoeia and *Praeterita,*" in *Nineteenth-Century Lives,* ed. Laurence S. Lockridge, John Maynard, and Donald D. Stone (Cambridge: Cambridge University Press, 1989), 125–39. A related trope is "apostrophe": "the direct address of an absent, dead, or inanimate being by a first-person speaker" (Barbara Johnson, "Apostrophe, Animation, Abortion," in *Feminisms,* ed. Robyn R. Warhol and Diane Price Herndl, rev. ed. [New Brunswick, NJ: Rutgers University Press, 1997], 694–707).

43. Diana Robin, "Cassandra Fedele's *Epistolae* (1488–1521): Biography as Ef-facement," in *The Rhetorics of Life-Writing in Early Modern Europe,* ed. Thomas F. Mayer and D. R. Woolf (Ann Arbor: University of Michigan Press, 1995), 187–204, makes this de Manian point: "*Prosopopeia,* maskmaking, as the ancient Greeks called biography. . . . is clearly privative and disfiguring as well" as "constitutive" (187).

44. Anna Makolkin, *Name, Hero, Icon: Semiotics of Nationalism through Heroic Biography* (Berlin: Mouton de Gruyter, 1992), 18.

45. *Lingua Franca,* in its tenth anniversary issue, displayed a cartoon poster of Rafael's *The School of Athens,* replacing the faces of famous philosophers with caricatures of currently renowned critics.

46. Joseph Bartscherer composes an ongoing work of installation art, *Obituary,* that consists of a collection of all the issues of the *New York Times* since January 1990 that display an obituary on the front page. These papers (more than three hundred of them) are arranged in series of six on horizontal planes of Plexiglas four inches above the floor. Arthur C. Danto likens the exhibit to "a cemetery" (*Obituary,* exhibition catalog, Davis Museum and Cultural Center, Wellesley College, Wellesley, MA, September 4–December 30, 2001). According to Lucy Flint-Gohlke, curator (in conversation, February 2002), the accumulation of the piece necessarily slowed after September 11, 2001; the *Times* front page repeatedly has been crowded with war news, and obituaries of unknowns fill inner pages.

47. Jean Baudrillard claims it is "invariably *oneself* that one collects" ("The System of Collecting," in *The Cultures of Collecting*, ed. John Elsner and Roger Cardinal [Cambridge, MA: Harvard University Press, 1994], 12). As James Clifford has argued, the Western practice of collecting is a search for an authentic "possessive self [and] culture" (*Routes* [Cambridge, MA: Harvard University Press, 1997], 20). Leah Price, in *The Anthology and the Rise of the Novel* (Cambridge: Cambridge University Press, 2000), associates the practices of the collection with those of the novel.

48. Erving Goffman, *Stigma* (Englewood Cliffs, NJ: Prentice-Hall, 1963), 26.

49. On the Modern Library's list of the twentieth century's best novels, see "Comment," *Women's Review of Books* 15 (September 1998): 7; James Wood, "Bookdumb," *New Republic* (August 17 and 24, 1998): 14; Louis Menand, "Novels We Love," *New Yorker* 74 (August 3, 1998): 4–5; and many others. John Guillory ("Canon, Syllabus, List: A Note on the Pedagogic Imaginary," *Transition* 52 [1991]: 36–54) writes that "the canon is preeminently a list of *authors*" (37).

50. Baudrlllard, "The System of Collectıng," ın *Cultures of Collecting*, ed. Elsner and Cardinal, 23.

51. Marjorie Garber, *Symptoms of Culture* (New York: Routledge, 1998), 42.

52. Tricia Lootens, *Lost Saints* (Charlottesville: University Press of Virginia, 1996), 5.

53. In 1901, to compete with pantheons in Rome and Paris, Munich's Temple of Fame, and Westminster Abbey, the Hall of Fame was dedicated at New York University. Although an art nouveau image of Lady Fame rules on the cover of *The Illustrated Story of the Hall of Fame* (ed. Louis Albert Banks [New York: Christian Herald, 1902]), no woman was among the twenty-nine "elect" (and only three of a hundred judges were women); of 234 nominees, only nine were women. "A list of America's most eligible women" supplements the volume (398–409). The colonnade, designed by Stanford White, displayed tablets representing each great man; after 1920, a series of statues was added to what is now part of Bronx Community College.

54. Negro History Week, founded in 1926 by Carter G. Woodson, became Black History Month (February because of Lincoln's and Douglass's birthdays) in 1976. A National Women's History Week (in March to overlap with International Women's Day) was initiated in 1978, gaining congressional approval in 1981, followed by Women's History Month in 1987. George William Douglas, *The American Book of Days* (New York: Wilson, 1937), includes such tributes as Frances E. Willard Day.

55. Caryl Churchill, *Top Girls* (London: Methuen, 1982).

56. The book accompanying Chicago's exhibition nicely fits the subgenre of prosopographies of women: Judy Chicago, *The Dinner Party: A Symbol of Our Heritage*, designed by Sheila Levrant de Bretteville (Garden City, NY: Anchor Press/Doubleday, 1979). Robert Harbison, in *Eccentric Spaces* (New York: Knopf, 1977), notes that museum catalogs express the desire to include everything, always apologizing for some omission (154). "Museums, by arranging history spatially, . . . experiment with various sequences of remembering" (142). "Like the dictionary a museum cannot be enjoyed passively," given the equidistant, exhaustive offerings (145–55).

57. Tony Hendra's *Brotherhood* (New York: American Express/Sterling, 2001), a memorial volume for the New York City firefighters, includes images of sidewalk shrines and the adorned firehouses, portraits of the dead, and series of names along the foot of the page.

58. In an unprecedented "mobilization," 143 writers and numerous staff produced 1,910 portraits, as documented in the album *Portraits: 9/11/01*, foreword Howell Raines, introduction Janny Scott (New York: Times Books/Henry Holt, 2002). *Portraits* alphabetizes the sets of lives (through February 3) that originally appeared in daily batches in the order of completion (facts confirmed, family consulted). Though the immensity of the volume adds weight to the loss, there is a yearbook effect, whereas the newspaper pages are more like obituaries. Photographs of street memorials, funeral services, and desolated family members contrast with the cheerful "characters," who seem alive or brought to life in the book (208–9). This revivification was intentional: Christine Kay decided "that these profiles must be about life . . . snapshots, not obituaries" (557). Typical titles in the paper: "Life as a Joy Ride," "Stealing Quiet Moments," and "Brooklyn Kid Does Good" ("The Victims: Finding Excitement in the Big City, on a Harley and on the Golf Green," *New York Times*, November 5, 2001, B9). See <www.nytimes.com/portraits>.

This daily feature, begun September 15 as "Among the Missing," ended January 1, 2002, though the newspaper's staff (reporters of all ranks contributed) continued to reconstruct the lost lives. Mark Singer, "The Grief Desk," in "The Talk of the Town," *New Yorker* (January 14, 2002), 30–31. Nancy K. Miller, "Brief Lives" (paper presented at the "Anecdotal Theory" session, Modern Language Association meeting, New York, December 28, 2002). My thanks to Nancy Miller for sharing ideas about these collective memorials and for a copy of her paper.

59. The reading of the proper name on the marker establishes a specular relation between the living and the dead, as de Man suggests in his essay on Wordsworth's *Essays upon Epitaphs* (de Man, "Autobiography"). Lin set the "two walls . . . so that one pointed to the Lincoln Memorial and the other pointed to the Washington Monument." Conceived as a boundary between "two worlds, one we are a part of and one we cannot enter," the memorial is designed for contiguity or displacement rather than identity: "To find one name, chances are you will see the others close by, and you will see yourself reflected through them" in the polished black granite (Maya Lin, "Making the Memorial," *New York Review of Books* 47, no. 17 [November 2, 2000]: 33–35). Lauren Berlant, discussing the Vietnam Memorial, traces "contact with the monumental nation" as a search for intact subjectivity (*The Queen of America Goes to Washington City* [Durham, NC: Duke University Press, 1997], 25–35).

60. Vivien Green Fryd observes that the iconography of the Rotunda was selected (between 1815 and 1860) to narrate "the early course of North American empire" through "the subjugation of the indigenous peoples," while barring reference to those of African descent to evade the antebellum conflict over slavery (*Art and Empire* [New Haven, CT: Yale University Press, 1992], 1, 177).

61. Relocation of *Portrait Monument to Lucretia Mott, Elizabeth Cady Stanton, and Susan B. Anthony* (May 12, 1997), Architect of the U.S. Capitol, http://www.aoc.gov/currproj/suffmove.htm. In the Rotunda, statues are of white male individuals, apart from a powerful bronze bust of Martin Luther King Jr., confronting the eight-ton block of partially unpolished marble with three ladies jutting out of it. In the Hall of Statuary (begun in 1864), each state is represented by a statue, of which five represent women (Mother Joseph/Esther Pariseau, Esther Morris, Jeannette Rankin, Florence Sabin, and Frances E. Willard), and two are non-European: King Kamehameha of Hawaii and Sequoyah, the Cherokee linguist and leader. Johnson presented individual busts of Mott, Stanton, and Anthony (along with one of Dr. Caroline Winslow, "a feminist homeopathic physician") at the World's Columbian Exposition in 1893. See Jeanne Madeline Weimann, *The Fair Women,* introduction by Anita Miller (Chicago: Academy, 1981), 289–94. The dedication of the three-headed statue, "called 'Ladies in a Bathtub' by some," occurred on February 15, 1921, Susan B. Anthony's birthday (294).

62. Willie van Peer analyzes the process thus: "The number of literary works increases continually over time," while all "literate cultures are constantly engaged in selection" of the "skewed subset" that "they will preserve, distribute, teach, and cherish" ("Two Laws of Literary History: Growth and Predictability in Canon Formation," *Mosaic* 30 [1997]: 121–24).

63. Joanna Russ, "Anomalousness" (1983), reprinted in *Feminisms,* ed. Warhol and Herndl, 98–99.

64. Boswell's *Johnson,* according to Felicity Nussbaum, strains in competition with Hester Thrale, whose marginalization is crucial to the formation of this new center, the man of letters (*The Autobiographical Subject* [Baltimore: Johns Hopkins University Press, 1989], 122–23).

65. See Cafarelli, *Prose in the Age of Poets,* 113–50. Cafarelli views Johnson's *Lives of the Poets* as a prototype for a mode of literary criticism and critical biography that was neglected in favor of full-length fact-finding biography such as Boswell's *Johnson* (1–29).

66. Exact counts of male, female, collective, or individual biographies would be nearly impossible to obtain. Proportions can be estimated from publisher's catalogs in endpapers, though these notices appear to be most common among publishers of popular and juvenile series. Of the approximately 613 books advertised in S. W. Partridge's catalog appended to Michael,[570] approximately 103 are biographies. Juvenile publishing allowed fiction to be historical or biographical and history and biography to be fictionalized. Thus, *True Stories of Brave Deeds; or, What Boys and Girls Can Do* by Mabel Bowler belongs on the One Shilling

Reward Books list with a "story," *Dick's Desertion: A Boy's Adventures in Canadian Forests* by Marjorie L. C. Pickthall (21). Partridge offers fifty-five individual biographies of men but only five of women: Queen Victoria (twice), Queen Alexandra, Florence Nightingale, and Helen Keller. Collective biographies of men (with a few women)—about 37 publications—tend to be grouped by occupation, e.g., F. M. Holmes's *Great Works by Great Men: The Story of Famous Engineers.* Approximately seven works group women only. The catalog sorts books for girls from books for boys, but the salient category is price, in descending order through the catalog. In catalogs printed in twenty-one collections between 1848 and 1900, there are usually from three to six times as many male as female biographies, usually more single than collective male, and more collective than single female.

67. Most biographical collections aim at a common-denominator reader and are straightforward in narration and in "moral" (Reed Whittemore, *Pure Lives* [Baltimore: Johns Hopkins University Press, 1988], 54).

68. On collective biography, see Donald C. Yelton, *Brief American Lives* (Metuchen, NJ: Scarecrow, 1978).

69. Sturges, "Collective Biography in the 1980s," traces "national biographical collections" from the seventeenth century through the later twentieth (316–17). Contributions to a national canon of lives may presuppose that these worthies would warrant full-length treatment instead of the "skeleton," "miniature," or "Spartan" version permitted en masse, according to Sidney Lee, "Principles of Biography," in *Elizabethan and Other Essays* (1929), 55–57, reprinted in Ira Bruce Nadel, *Victorian Biography* (New York: Garland, 1986), n.p.

70. Mayer and Woolf, introduction to *The Rhetorics of Life-Writing*, 1–3, 13–17. Waldo H. Dunn, *English Biography* (London: Dent, 1916), surveys many collective biographical projects in Europe from the seventeenth century forward.

71. Whittemore, *Pure Lives*, 2.

72. Margot Peters, "Group Biography: Challenges and Methods," in *New Directions in Biography*, ed. Anthony M. Friedson (Honolulu: Biographical Research Center, 1981), 41–51.

73. William Hazlitt, *Lectures on the English Poets and the Spirit of the Age*, introduction by Catherine MacDonald Maclean (London: Everyman, 1967). On a similar contemporary work, Henry Cockburn's *Memorials of His Time* (recollections of educated Edinburgh), see Mark Salber Phillips, *Society and Sentiment* (Princeton, NJ: Princeton University Press, 2000), 309–20.

74. Richard Henry Horne, ed., *A New Spirit of the Age* (New York: Harper & Brothers, 1845). See Ezell, *Writing Women's Literary History*, 89.

75. Hazlitt, *Lectures on the English Poets*, 146–48.

76. William Howitt, *Homes and Haunts of the Most Eminent British Poets*, 2 vols. (London: R. Bentley, 1847; New York: Harper, 1847).

77. Edward Bulwer-Lytton represents various political and intellectual positions through satiric types (*England and the English* [London: Bentley, 1833]). Vernon Louis Parrington suggests, in chapters such as "John Dickinson—the Mind of the American Whig" or "Samuel Adams—the Mind of the American Democrat," that there were neither women nor unlettered or working men in the colonies and early republic (*The Colonial Mind, 1620–1800*, in *Main Currents of American Thought*, 3 vols. [New York: Harcourt, Brace, 1927], 1:xiii–xiv).

78. Leonard Russell, ed., *English Wits* (London: Hutchinson, 1940); reprinted through 1953.

79. Richard D. Altick, *The Scholar Adventurers* (New York: Macmillan, 1950). "Many of the men and women who teach English in our colleges and universities . . . have adventures which are as exciting as any that have ever been told of . . . the research scientists" (1). Altick celebrates the "fraternal" spirit of the annual Modern Language Association (MLA) convention: "Nine-tenths of the papers read . . . should have remained unread"; "most seasoned MLA-ers travel long distances each Christmas season for the sake of renewing old friendships, trading scholarly and academic gossip"; "the most uninhibited . . . gatherings at MLA are those in the bedrooms of the members . . . where a medieval scholar is playing host to a Whitman specialist, a Shakespearean, and a Miltonist (all sprawled on the single bed), a Meredithian (in the armchair)" (9–10). Any

suggestion that these (gender-unspecified) specialists are doing anything other than talking and drinking remains for us to surmise.

80. For example, Esther Pohl Lovejoy, *Women Doctors of the World* (New York: Macmillan, 1954); Elizabeth Jenkins, *Ten Fascinating Women* (London: Odhams, 1955); Byrne Hope Sanders, *Canadian Portraits: Carr, Hind, Gullen, Murphy: Famous Women* (Toronto: Clarke, Irwin, 1958); Sylvia G. L. Dannett, *Profiles of Negro Womanhood*, 2 vols., Negro Heritage Library (New York: Lads, 1964–66); Emily Douglas, *Remember the Ladies* (New York: Putnam, 1966); and Felicia Warburg Roosevelt, *Doers and Dowagers* (Garden City, NJ: Doubleday, 1975).

81. For example, Andrew Ewart, *The World's Most Wicked Women* (London: Odhams, 1964); David Plante, *Difficult Women: Jean Rhys, Sonia Orwell, Germaine Greer* (New York: Dutton, 1984).

82. For instance, Diane Johnson, *The True History of the First Mrs. Meredith and Other Lesser Lives* (New York: Knopf, 1972); Jan Marsh, *The Pre-Raphaelite Sisterhood* (London: Quartet; New York: St. Martin's, 1985); on women in different educational contexts, Ellen Condliff Lagemann, *A Generation of Women* (Cambridge, MA: Harvard University Press, 1979); Susan J. Leonardi, *Dangerous by Degrees* (New Brunswick, NJ: Rutgers University Press, 1989).

83. Phyllis Rose, *Parallel Lives* (New York: Vintage, 1984), 5; Henry Louis Gates Jr., *Thirteen Ways of Looking at a Black Man* (New York: Vintage, 1997), xvii. See also Whitney Chadwick and Isabelle de Courtivron, eds., *Significant Others* (London: Thames & Hudson, 1993), among other biographical studies of collaboration.

84. Heilbrun, *Writing a Woman's Life*, 26. Heilbrun's *Women's Lives* (Toronto: University of Toronto Press, 1999), reprinting Alexander Lectures at the University of Toronto, focuses on recent memoirs against a background of transformation: "Until just the day before yesterday, all narratives and plots were modelled upon and identified with the linear pattern of male sexuality" (33).

85. Carolyn Heilbrun, *When Men Were the Only Models We Had* (Philadelphia: University of Pennsylvania Press, 2002). Heilbrun's cultural histories for a general audience tell a strong but misleading story. Her suicide on October 9, 2003, the chosen ending of her career and life, has been difficult for many to accept. I return to Heilbrun in later discussion.

86. On working-class auto/biography, see Regenia Gagnier, *Subjectivities* (New York: Oxford University Press, 1991); Julia Swindells, *Victorian Writing and Working Women* (Cambridge: Polity, 1985). Most consideration of nineteenth-century women's life writing concentrates on middle-class women's autobiographies: Mary Jean Corbett, *Representing Femininity* (New York: Oxford University Press, 1992); Valerie Sanders, *The Private Lives of Victorian Women* (New York: Harvester Wheatsheaf, 1989); Linda Peterson, *Victorian Women's Autobiography*.

And among studies, too numerous to mention, of slave narratives and minority autobiographies in the United States and elsewhere, see William L. Andrews, *To Tell a Free Story* (Urbana: University of Illinois Press, 1986), and Andrews, ed., *African American Autobiography* (Englewood Cliffs, NJ: Prentice Hall, 1993); Valerie Smith, *Self-Discovery and Authority in Afro-American Narrative* (Cambridge, MA: Harvard University Press, 1987); Kari J. Winter, *Subjects of Slavery, Agents of Change: Women and Power in Gothic Novels and Slave Narratives, 1790–1865* (Athens, GA: University of Georgia Press, 1992); Audrey A. Fisch, "'Repetitious accounts so piteous and harrowing': The Ideological Work of American Slave Narratives in England," *Journal of Victorian Culture* 1 (1996): 16–34; James R. Payne, ed., *Multicultural Autobiography* (Knoxville: University of Tennessee Press, 1992); Jan Welsh Hokenson, "Intercultural Autobiography," *Auto/Biography Studies: a/b* 10 (1995): 92–113.

87. In addition to those noted above, see Alison Donnell and Pauline Polkey, eds., *Representing Lives* (Basingstoke: Macmillan Press; New York: St. Martin's, 2000).

88. Linda Peterson, *Victorian Autobiography* (New Haven, CT: Yale University Press, 1986); James Eli Adams, *Dandies and Desert Saints* (Ithaca, NY: Cornell University Press, 1995); Martin Danahay, *A Community of One* (Albany: State University of New York Press, 1993); David Amigoni, *Victorian Biography* (New York: Harvester Wheatsheaf, 1993); Trev Lynn Broughton, *Men of Letters, Writing Lives* (London: Routledge, 1999).

89. William Epstein, *Recognizing Biography* (Philadelphia: University of Pennsylvania Press, 1987); Mary Rheil and David Suchoff, eds., *The Seductions of Biography* (New York: Routledge, 1996).

90. Wagner-Martin registers some women's biographies by women before 1970: "Had critics noticed what women biographers wrote about their subjects—even during the nineteenth century—the so-called revolution in biography might have come earlier" (*Telling Women's Lives*, 1–4). Alpern et al., in *The Challenge of Feminist Biography*, locate a new golden age: "Nearly two hundred biographies of women have been written since 1970"; "biography, once a 'men's club,' has been radically changed" (5). "The androcentric tradition of autobiography was untroubled by gender until 1980" (Long, *Telling Women's Lives*, 18). Long perceives the ample recognition of women "in every age" and the process of erasure: "the social production of obscurity" (106). "If women's writing until the last decade has been secretive, . . . readers have been no less unable to read or understand women's hidden stories," claimed Heilbrun in 1985 ("Women's Autobiographical Writings: New Forms," *Prose Studies* 8 [1985]: 14–28, reprinted in *Women and Autobiography*, ed. Martine Watson Brownley and Allison B. Kimmich [Wilmington, DE: Scholarly Resources, 1999], 23).

91. Oldfield, *Collective Biography of Women*, 1–2. Oldfield's indexes of categories and subjects, as well as the excerpts, annotations, and illustrations, make this a rich source.

92. Flint, *The Woman Reader*, 38–39, 88.

93. On the history of the book, see Cathy N. Davidson, "Introduction: Toward a History of Books and Readers," in *Reading in America*, ed. Cathy N. Davidson (Baltimore: Johns Hopkins University Press, 1989), 1–9; and Robert Darton, "What Is the History of Books?" (1982), reprinted in *Reading in America*, 27–52. Among studies of the literary marketplace, see Richard D. Altick, *The English Common Reader* (Chicago: University of Chicago Press, 1957); Cathy N. Davidson, *Revolution and the Word* (New York: Oxford University Press, 1986); John O. Jordan and Robert L. Patten, eds., *Literature in the Marketplace* (Cambridge: Cambridge University Press, 1995). Michael Warner examines the function of reading in constituting an imagined public sphere in eighteenth-century America (*The Letters of the Republic* [Cambridge, MA: Harvard University Press, 1990], xiii).

94. Nina Baym, *American Women Writers*, and *Feminism and American Literary History* (New Brunswick, NJ: Rutgers University Press, 1992), esp. chap. 7; Martha Vicinus, *Independent Women* (London: Virago, 1985), and "Models for Public Life: Biographies of 'Noble Women' for Girls," in *The Girl's Own*, ed. Nelson and Valone, 52–70; Sally Mitchell, *The Fallen Angel* (Bowling Green, OH: Bowling Green University Popular Press, 1981); Flint, *The Woman Reader*. Further studies of women in the literary marketplace include Summit, *Lost Property*; Susan Coultrap-McQuin, *Doing Literary Business* (Chapel Hill: University of North Carolina Press, 1990); Gaye Tuchman, with Nina E. Fortin, *Edging Women Out* (New Haven, CT: Yale University Press, 1989); Catherine Gallagher, *Nobody's Story* (Berkeley: University of California Press, 1994); Paula McDowell, *The Women of Grub Street* (Oxford: Clarendon Press, 1998).

95. I share Martha Woodmansee's critique of the Kantian aesthetic theories that overturned "millennia" of measuring the arts *"instrumentally*, in terms of their success (or failure) in serving . . . broad human purposes" (*The Author, Art, and the Market* [New York: Columbia University Press, 1994], 12). The conception of the author evolved with increasing middle-class demand for reading material but "the requisite legal, economic, and political arrangements and institutions . . . to support the large number of writers" emerged slowly after the early 1800s (42, 50–53). Only after about 1880 do I find scattered acknowledgments of permissions to borrow biographies from other publishers; some earlier compilers mention in a preface the authors or titles from which they borrow.

96. Cafarelli, *Prose in the Age of Poets*, 6–7.

97. See J. S. Bratton, *The Impact of Victorian Children's Fiction* (London: Croom Helm, 1981); Claudia Nelson, *Boys Will Be Girls* (New Brunswick, NJ: Rutgers University Press, 1991); Flint, *The Woman Reader*.

98. The Barthesian concept of the "zero-degree" reader minimally educated to read the text—as constructed by the text—forfeits historical context for the sake of structuralist principle.

Yet I share Makolkin's model of the interpellative function of biography: "The national bond between the subject, biographer, and biographee is particularly significant in a heroic biography which is primarily a panegyric to the national hero of a given group" (*Name, Hero, Icon,* 17).

99. For ancient Chinese collections of women, see Sherry J. Mou, *Presence and Presentation: Women in the Chinese Literati Tradition* (New York: St. Martin's, 1999); and Oldfield, *Collective Biography of Women,* 1; for medieval lives based on classical models, Ruth Morse, "Medieval Biography: History as a Branch of Literature," *Modern Language Review* 80 (1985): 257–68; for humanist catalogs, James Michael Weiss, "The Harvest of German Humanism: Melchior Adam's Collective Biographies as Cultural History," in *The Harvest of Humanism in Central Europe,* ed. Manfred P. Fleischer (Saint Louis: Concordia, 1992), 341–50; and for series modeled on classic Arabic collections, M. Booth, *May Her Likes Be Multiplied.*

100. Geraldine DeLuca refers to biography in general but immediately welcomes the correction to the existing records by "feminist scholars . . . search[ing] in earnest for their foremothers" ("Lives and Half-Lives," *Children's Literature in Education* 17, no. 4 [1986]: 242).

101. Karen A. Winstead, in *Virgin Martyrs,* attests to the continuing popularity of virgin martyrs in "conduct books written by and for laypeople" (Ithaca, NY: Cornell University Press, 1997), 12. See the flourishing feminist studies of medieval materials, including Jane Tibbetts Schulenburg, "Saints' Lives as a Source for the History of Women, 500–1100," in *Medieval Women and the Sources of Medieval History,* ed. Joel T. Rosenthal (Athens: University of Georgia Press, 1990), 285–320; Thomas J. Heffernan, *Sacred Biography* (New York: Oxford University Press, 1988).

102. Christopher Lasch, "The Comedy of Love and the *Querelle des Femmes,*" in his *Women and the Common Life,* ed. Elisabeth Lasch-Quinn (New York: Norton, 1997), repudiates an anachronistic feminist reading of de Pizan and other advocates of women (4–9).

103. Mary D. Garrard, *Artemisia Gentileschi* (Princeton, NJ: Princeton University Press, 1989), 141–79. On the analogies drawn in early modern biographies, see Sheila ffolliott, "Exemplarity and Gender: Three Lives of Queen Catherine de' Medici," in *The Rhetorics of Life-Writing,* ed. Mayer and Woolf, 321–40.

104. Antonia Fraser, *The Warrior Queens* (New York: Knopf, 1989), is an entertaining example, with some critical distance on the typecasting. A tradition of feminine or feminist Jungian archetypal criticism begins with Helen Diner's *Mothers and Amazons,* ed. and trans. John Philip Lundin (New York: Julian Press, 1965); and Dorothy Dinnerstein's *The Mermaid and the Minotaur* (London: Souvenir, 1978), but remains eccentric to academic feminism. See Carol Hanbery MacKay, *Creative Negativity* (Stanford, CA: Stanford University Press, 2001).

105. The pre-1830 collections of female biographies cited in this discussion by author, title, and date appear chronologically in pt. 1 of the bibliography.

106. Thomas Heywood's *The Exemplary Lives* of 1640 continues the typological pattern of nine but focuses on the lives of eminent women in a providential world history instead of mythology (his subjects: Deborah, Judith, Esther, Bunduca/Boodicia/ Boudicea/Voadica/ Boundvica, Penthisilaea, Artemisia, Elpheda, Queen Margaret [wife of Henry VI], and Queen Elizabeth).

107. Diane Bornstein, in *The Feminist Controversy of the Renaissance* (Delmar, NY: Scholar's Facsimiles and Reprints, 1980), v–xii, notes that "even the profeminist works contain some antifeminism" (xii). Heywood's is of course a belated instance of a Renaissance form, as in Sir Thomas Elyot's *Defense of Good Women* (1545) or English translations of Agrippa's *De nobilitate et praecellentia foeminei sexus* (Cologne, 1532). A universal history of woman still seems to be a goal, as in Ruth Ashby and Deborah Gore Ohrn, eds., *Herstory* (New York: Viking/Penguin, 1995).

108. On Fuller, see Ruth Perry, introduction to *Memoirs of Several Ladies of Great Britain* by George Ballard, ed. Ruth Perry (Detroit: Wayne State University Press, 1985), 28–29. Both John Aubrey, in *Brief Lives* (1667–96), and Samuel Clark, in *Lives of Sundry Eminent Persons in this Later Age* (1683), also include female subjects.

109. Burton writes that after doing "The History of the Nine Worthies" he decided "to try whether I could not find out as many Renowned Women in History" (1687, n.p.). He warns that he can't "justify self-homicide, of which some of my Heroines were guilty . . . however I hope none

will make that a President [*sic*], since so many worthy Things may be observed in their Lives and Actions, both for Information and Delight" (n.p.).

110. Oldfield, *Collective Biography of Women*; Perry, introduction to *Memoirs of Several Ladies* by Ballard; Summit, *Lost Property*, 109–61.

111. Natalie Zemon Davis, "Gender and Genre: Women as Historical Writers, 1400–1820," in *Beyond Their Sex,* ed. Patricia H. Labalme (New York: New York University Press, 1980), 153–82; Bonnie G. Smith, *The Gender of History* (Cambridge, MA: Harvard University Press, 1998). On Victorian women's nonfiction writing, see Rohan Amanda Maitzen, "This Feminine Preserve," *Victorian Studies* 38 (1995): 371–93, part of her *Gender, Genre, and Victorian Historical Writing* (New York: Garland, 1998); and Nicole Tonkovich, *Domesticity with a Difference* (Jackson: University Press of Mississippi, 1997). Miriam Elizabeth Burstein takes stock of eighteenth- and nineteenth-century histories of women as well as collective biographical histories by women, in "'The Reduced Pretensions of the Historic Muse': Agnes Strickland and the Commerce of Women's History," *Journal of Narrative Technique* 28 (1998): 219–42, "From Good Looks to Good Thoughts: Popular Women's History and the Invention of Modernity, ca. 1830–1870," *Modern Philology* 97 (1999): 46–75, and *Narrating Women's History in Britain, 1770–1902* (Burlington, VT: Ashgate, 2004), which includes the *Modern Philology* article.

112. Davis, "Gender and Genre," 156–57. Davis notes that Ballard's *Memoirs of Several Ladies* (1752) included only one historian, the Duchess of Newcastle. Self-consciously repeating Woolf's recuperative moves with a twist, Davis acknowledges Christine de Pisan, Catherine Macaulay, Mme de Staël and a handful of other early female historians. See Natalie Zemon Davis, *Women on the Margins* (Cambridge, MA: Harvard University Press, 1995), a prosopography of "varied lives, but produced within a common field" (203).

113. Baym, *American Women Writers,* 1–10.

114. There were histories of women that did not take the form of series of biographies, e.g., William Alexander, *The History of Women,* 2 vols. (Dublin: Price, Cross, 1779); Lydia Maria Child, *The History and Condition of Women,* 2 vols. (Boston: Allen, 1835); Fullom's *The History of Woman,* cited above; and in the twentieth century a proliferation, including Walter Lionel George, *The Story of Woman* (New York: Harper, 1925); Winifred Holtby, *Women and a Changing Civilisation* (London: Longmans, Green, 1935); and national histories, more or less biographical, e.g., Inez Haynes Irwin, *Angels and Amazons;*[443] Elisabeth Anthony Dexter, *Colonial Women of Affairs* (Boston: Houghton Mifflin, 1924), and *Career Women of America, 1776–1840* (Boston: Houghton Mifflin, 1950; reprint, Clifton, NJ: Kelley, 1972). By now the history of women is too large a field to compass.

115. Maitzen, "This Feminine Preserve," 371–93.

116. Cathy N. Davidson, in *Revolution and the Word,* observes that "the book business in the early national period was strikingly small and localized" before "mechanized printing," "new methods of transporting books," and "increased urbanization" in "the second quarter of the nineteenth century" and after (16).

117. I would not want to reduce the differences between or within the gender codes of Britain and the United States. Sarah Lewis's *Woman's Mission* (1839) and Sarah Ellis's series of advice books beginning with *The Women of England* (1839) are often cited as sources for the Victorian code of womanly influence. Barbara Welter in effect coined the byword of second-wave studies of nineteenth-century gender ideology in the United States ("The Cult of True Womanhood, 1820–1860," *American Quarterly* 18 [summer 1966]: 151–75; see Coultrap-McQuin, *Doing Literary Business,* 10–12. Comparatively few studies attempt to bridge the conditions of women's cultures in Britain and the United States.

Among many accounts of the trend toward conspicuous leisure time among women, Woodmansee contributes a perspective on the German literary marketplace (*The Author, Art, and the Market,* 22).

118. Simon Eliot has traced similar patterns in book publication in Britain during the nineteenth century: a transition in the 1840s to much increased production that peaked around 1851–53; a plateau in the 1860s; "by 1879 the rate was probably about thirty-five percentage points above a 1855–59 baseline"; another surge in the 1890s; and then, between 1912 and 1914,

book publication "rose to its climax . . . at around 284 percentage points above its 1855–59 baseline" ("Some Trends in British Book Production, 1800–1919," in *Literature in the Marketplace,* ed. Jordan and Patten, 28–33). Eliot details the changes in record keeping that make any patterns shaky. Here and elsewhere he summarizes innovations that produced a surge in book publishing between 1830 and 1855: "The Foudrinier machine (1800s on), steam-driven presses (1814 on), case binding (mid- to late 1820s on), the gradual reduction and final abolition of the 'taxes on knowledge' and the evolution of the railway system (1830s on)" ("Some Patterns and Trends in British Publishing, 1800–1919," *Occasional Papers* 8 [London: Bibliographical Society, 1994], 107).

119. *Portraits of Celebrated Women,*[173] engraved by American artists, is offered "as a holiday and gift-book, no less than a volume for general reading" (iii–iv). With the spread of elementary education and religious and social missionary societies, presenters began to resemble textbook committees today. See Bratton, *The Impact of Victorian Children's Fiction,* 13–18; Edward G. Salmon, "What Girls Read," *Nineteenth Century* 20 (1886): 515–29.

120. Sybil Oldfield estimates that "a quarter of the collective biographies of women 1850–1900 were explicitly aimed at the girl reader" (*Collective Biography of Women,* 3).

121. Miriam Burstein notes John Millar's *The Origin of the Distinction of Ranks* (1779), "which connected the progress of woman's social position to the development of civilization more generally" ("From Good Looks," 50; see her *Narrating Women's History,* chap. 1). Francis Augustus Cox, in *Female Scripture Biography* (1817), continues the eighteenth-century "periodization" of women's history through Christianity (Burstein, "From Good Looks," 55–56).

122. Linda H. Peterson, "'Women in Print Culture': A Review Essay," *South Atlantic Review* 62 (1997): 121–30, in reference to Patricia Okker, *Our Sister Editors* (Athens: University of Georgia Press, 1995).

123. I suspect that we have lost hundreds of pamphlets (sometimes in sets) featuring short lives of female missionaries, at home or abroad. The tiny format of these drab publications, classed with ephemeral print matter, lends to their being wadded together in the Bodleian or British Libraries.

124. In the period of intensified international registers of women surrounding the World's Columbian Exposition (1893), a translation from the German of Henry Zirndorf's *Some Jewish Women* appeared.[930]

125. "Some of the most dramatic cases of self sacrifice and devotion on American soil were cases of Jewish women during the colonization of South America, Mexico and this country and during the wars for our independence and the abolition of slavery" (*The Part Taken by Women in American History,* 631).[516]

126. Wearily if "cheerfully," an aging Mary Hays compiled her *Memoirs of Queens* (1821), from Agrippina the Younger to Zoe ("fourth wife of the emperor Leo VI" [479]), to promote the enlightenment-feminist precept of a single human standard of morality and achievement (v–vi). Mary Roberts's *Select Female Biography* (1821) is a common form of renewal of Ballard. See Ezell's *Writing Women's Literary History:* "Between 1675 and 1875, there were at least twenty-five biographical encyclopedias and anthologies" on English women writers (68).

127. Baym has charted a parallel transition in publications by North American women, who came to insist not on the parity of the sexes but, rather, on the difference between historical women and "prominent men of the past" (*American Women Writers,* 215, 1–45; *Feminism,* 105–19).

128. Miriam Burstein, in "'The Reduced Pretensions of the Historic Muse,'" traces the Strickland sisters' success and the reviewers' increasing intolerance for the sentimental-partisan form of women's history with the rise of professionalized empirical standards. Scott E. Casper, "An Uneasy Marriage of Sentiment and Scholarship: Elizabeth F. Ellet and the Domestic Origins of American Women's History," *Journal of Women's History* 4 (1992): 10–35, traces a similar decline in the standing of the American counterpart to the Stricklands.

129. See Susan Avery Phinney Conrad, *Perish the Thought* (New York: Oxford University Press, 1976), 105–13; Baym, *American Women Writers,* 224–27.

130. Child's collection under its aliases chimes in with similar contemporaneous works: *Lives of Celebrated Women*,[184] *Memoirs of Celebrated Women of All Countries*,[474] and *Lives of Celebrated Women*.[332]

131. Sophia Goodrich Ashton's publishers seem to have cobbled together several pieces (not written with a focus on childhood) and labeled them *The Girlhood of Celebrated Women: Women of Worth and the Mothers of the Bible*.[37] William Henry Davenport Adams gave the concept a try, with *Child-Life and Girlhood of Remarkable Women*.[8] Kent Carr, a prolific children's writer, relied on an audience for *Girls Who Were Famous Queens*,[144] which appears to be a reissue of *Love Stories of Royal Girlhood* (1913).

132. Staal's illustrations are engraved by William Holl, W. H. Mote, and others, as well as Francis Holl.

133. See the updated Cleopatra in *Superwomen*, 136.[788]

134. *Women of Beauty and Heroism* (1859)—or *World-Famous Women* (1858)—reappears in 1891 with an added chapter on Cleopatra, who replaces Semiramis as frontispiece; Victoria and Charlotte Brontë trade places. Others serve more than Cleopatra the purposes of sexual allure and exoticism; thus in Goodrich's volumes, Nell Gwynn might illustrate the Song of Solomon or pastoral verse, her bared bosom like fawns among lillies or the sheep in the meadow behind her, while the girlish Pocahontas entirely bares one breast as she leans on a mossy rock in the woods of Virginia.

135. The list of portraits in *World-Noted Women* does not trouble to give accurate credit; Catherine II Empress of Russia, who does not resemble Pocahontas or Nightingale in features, like Nightingale stands in a triangle of drapery upheld by her folded arms in a design by the Staal and Mote team (though from a different original artist), yet the list claims that Catherine was engraved by Cook (other portraits are similarly misattributed).

136. The latter is an improvised design of a lady standing to read in the corner of heavy stone walls, attended by three women and a girl, one barefoot, another seated on a basket; a broken bottle on the pavement (most images of Mrs. Fry emphasize the format of an assembly).

137. Johnson includes *Catherine Macaulay in Her Father's Library* (see frontispiece in Oldfield's *Collective Biography*) and *Ida Pfeiffer Confronting the Two French Soldiers.* The Austrian Ida Pfeiffer (1791–1858), famous world traveler, as a tomboyish child and would-be soldier is said to have told Napoleon's conquering soldiers what she thought of them. She recalls that she earnestly wished to murder Napoleon herself; Johnson quickly reminds the reader not to assume that Pfeiffer's heart lacked "principles of common Christianity" just because of her patriotic exuberance.

138. The anthology of miscellaneous papers delivered at the World's Columbian Exposition in 1893, *The Congress of Women*,[245] functions in many ways as prosopography, with portraits and biographies of the Board of Lady Managers and other participants.

139. Amelia J. Calver's *Every-Day Biography* (New York: Fowler & Wells, 1889), e.g., offers a selection of very short biographies of men and women for each day of the year. If it happens to be May 19, you could open the volume and find Sir George Prevost, English general; John Wilson (the critic "Christopher North" for *Blackwood's*); and Anna Jameson, "an earnest laborer for the mental development of the women of England, . . . the most celebrated female art critic of this century" (126). The early sociologist Auguste Comte redesigned the Catholic Holy Year as the Positivist Calendar of Great Men, with a Festival of Holy Women for the extra day in leap years (*Catechism for the New Religion* [1858], reprinted in *The New Calendar of Great Men*, ed. Frederic Harrison [New York, 1892]; Comte, *Auguste Comte and Positivism*, ed. Gertrud Lenzer [New York: Harper & Row, 1975], 472–73). Web sites today offer lists of celebrity birthdays.

140. Carrie Chapman Catt, ed., *Woman's Century Calendar* (New York: National American Suffrage Assoc., 1899). The phrase recurs; see Tina Schwager and Michele Schuerger, *Gutsy Girls: Young Women Who Dare* (Minneapolis: Free Spirit, 1999).

141. Jane Legget's *Local Heroines: A Women's History Gazetteer of England, Scotland and Wales* (London: Pandora, 1988), perfectly illustrates the spatial axis of veneration in modern pilgrimages. Legget hints that localities should study the history of their women and set up a shrine to promote tourism (xv–xvi).

142. On Ellet, see Ann Douglas, *The Feminization of American Culture* (New York: Avon, 1977), 221.

143. The subtitle of one work from the latter period drives home the wish to project a universal history: *The Lives of Women Who in All Ages, All Lands and in All Womanly Occupations Have Won Fame and Put Their Imprint on the World's History.*[1]

144. The year 1928 was a good one (at least thirty-four collective biographies of women were published). Many volumes that year located women in the history of a place.

145. H. E. Marshall, *Boy-Kings and Girl-Queens* (New York: Stokes, 1914), 7.

146. Some biographies of queens and kings were imported, but others appear homegrown. Annie F. Bush, *Memoirs of the Queens of France*[138] appeared in London in 1843 and Philadelphia in 1847; Lydia Hoyt Farmer, *The Girls' Book of Famous Queens*[276] was published in New York in 1887, London, 1927; Rosalie Kaufman abridged Strickland's *The Queens of Scotland*[765] for a Boston issue in 1886–87.

147. See *The Ladies of the White House,*[410] *Our National Government . . . with Sketches of the Presidents and Their Wives,*[515] *Wives of the Prime Ministers, 1844–1906,*[507] *Our Presidents and Their Mothers.*[374]

148. Anderson, *Imagined Communities,* 195, xiv.

149. Lives of the unsaints have ranged from *The Lives and Amours of Queens and Royal Mistresses, with Some Intrigues of Popes . . .* (1727) to Bleackley's *Ladies Fair and Frail* (1909),[89] Trowbridge's series of historical scandals published 1906–11,[811–13] and Gribble's *Queens of Crime* (1932).[346] Sidney Dark's books included *Twelve Bad Men* and *Twelve More Ladies: Good, Bad and Indifferent* (1932).[219] See also William Henry Davenport Adams, *Wrecked Lives; or, Men Who Have Failed* (cited in Richard Altick, *Lives and Letters* [New York: Knopf, 1966], 89n); Rogers, *Gallant Ladies* (1928);[681] von Gleichen-Russwurm, *The World's Lure* (1927).[326] Some commended daring innovators, e.g., *Five Queer Women* (1912).[464] Frances Bickley embraces *King's Favourites* of both sexes, a rare acknowledgment that sexual politics could include homosocial bonds (London: Methuen, 1910).

150. Other collections of actresses are Izard[446] and Gilder.[322] Two Englishmen set themselves up as experts on actresses (as well as on women of court in certain periods): Hugh Noel Williams[869; 871] and Lewis Melville [i.e., Lewis S. Benjamin].[561; 563]

151. Jean Adams, Margaret Kimball, and Jeanette Faton, *Heroines of the Sky* (Garden City, NY: Doubleday, Doran, 1942); Esther Pohl Lovejoy, *Women Doctors of the World* (New York: Macmillan, 1954).

152. Out of eighteen biographical chapters in John W. Cromwell's *The Negro in American History* (1914), four are dedicated to women: Phillis Wheatley, Sojourner Truth, Blanche Kelso Bruce, and Fanny M. Jackson Coppin.

153. Jean Fagan Yellin makes note of the sole African Americans in Hanaford's collection (renamed *Daughters of America*),[376] Mary Peake and Charlotte Ray ("Afro-American Women, 1800–1910: Excerpts from a Working Bibliography," in *All the Women Are White, All the Blacks Are Men, But Some of Us Are Brave,* ed. Gloria T. Hull, Patricia Bell-Scott, and Barbara Smith (Old Westbury, NY: Feminist Press, 1982), 221–333. Hanaford's list encompasses a remarkable range, from "Women in Heathenism" to "Women Inventors," and she names many heroines of this study, including presenters Child, Hale, Stowe, Sigourney, and herself, Phebe A. Hanford, among "Women Preachers."

154. Elizabeth Leonard, in *All the Daring of a Soldier,* traces some of the celebrated adventurers of the Civil War.

155. The imaginary portraits parody literary biography, as in the epistolary tale of James's marriage to "Muriel Agatha, eldest daughter of the Earl of Bilton," ending in Henry's telegram to William announcing that he has fled to Dijon, abandoning bride, "luggage all similar connotations Dover" in order to achieve "identity of simplification" (183–90).

156. P. David Marshall, in *Celebrity and Power* (Minneapolis: University of Minnesota Press, 1997), follows Hans Robert Jauss in outlining stages in audience response to exemplary biographies: "active participation"; the recognition of the hero as "exemplary for a particular

community"; "solidarity" or placing oneself "in the position of the hero"; and an "emancipation" through an abstracted "aestheticized relation to the hero" (69).

157. Daré [Frances Stanley Serrano], *Lovely Ladies* (Garden City, NY: Doubleday, Doran, 1929), 71.

Chapter One

1. Thomas Salter, *Mirrhor mete,* sig. Bii, subscript 1, as quoted in Kate Flint, *The Woman Reader, 1837–1914* (Oxford: Clarendon Press, 1993), 23. Thomas Fuller explained his aims in the *History of the Worthies of England* (1662): to praise God, "to preserve the memories of the dead . . . to present examples to the living . . . to entertain the reader with delight: and . . . to procure some honest profit," reprinted in James L. Clifford, ed., *Biography as an Art* (New York: Oxford University Press, 1962), 9.

2. Reed Whittemore, in *Pure Lives* (Baltimore: Johns Hopkins University Press, 1988), associates biography with "primitive purification rites" to accommodate the individual to the group imperative (4).

3. Key formulations of this model are René Girard, *Deceit, Desire, and the Novel,* trans. Yvonne Freccero (Baltimore: Johns Hopkins University Press, 1976); and Peter Brooks, *Reading for the Plot* (1984; reprint, Cambridge, MA: Harvard University Press, 1992).

4. Patricia Meyer Spacks, *Gossip* (Chicago: University of Chicago Press, 1986), redeems the triangulated personal exchange of gossip, which, like the identification that I refer to below, has been devalued as a female cultural practice. Life narrative, especially when collected, resembles the "para-social interaction" among "hosts, guests, and audience members" according to conventional roles on TV talk shows, as described by Janice Peck ("The Mediated Talking Cure: Therapeutic Framing of Autobiography in TV Talk Shows," in *Getting a Life: Everyday Uses of Autobiography,* ed. Sidonie Smith and Julia Watson [Minneapolis: University of Minnesota Press, 1996], 134–55), which produces an "'intimacy at a distance'" that "is enhanced with technical and representational codes," such as homey sets and frequent close-ups (137–38).

5. Cathy N. Davidson ("The Life and Times of *Charlotte Temple,*" in *Reading in America,* ed. Cathy N. Davidson [Baltimore: Johns Hopkins University Press, 1989], 157–79) surveys the vituperation against the novel: "metaphors of serpents, slavery, seduction, and satanic possession . . . dramatize[d] the ostensibly sinister powers of the insidious but increasingly popular literary form" (161).

6. Franco Moretti (in *Atlas of the European Novel, 1800–1900* [London: Verso, 1998]) offers a spatial method of reading the European novel: "The nation-state . . . found the novel. And viceversa: the novel found the nation-state" (16–17; ellipses in original). See Cathy N. Davidson on the novel's threat to upper-class male control of education and culture (*Revolution and the Word* [New York: Oxford University Press, 1986], 13, 10). Although Davidson discusses "an adult self-help book" (6–10), George Fisher's *The Instructor* (1727), and a few other examples of prose nonfiction, she favors the novel as presumably more democratic and accessible to female readers' control (72–74).

7. One good attempt at an explanation occurs in Tania Modleski's *Loving with a Vengeance* (New York: Methuen, 1984), which examines the "disappearing act" of the woman reader of romances, whose "substitution of the 'I'" or "identification with the heroine" offers a temporary disruption of the specular economy. Thus identification, at least in this form of mass culture, may be an attempt to "stop being seen," to become the "surveyor" (56–58).

8. Scott E. Casper, "An Uneasy Marriage of Sentiment and Scholarship," *Journal of Women's History* 4 (1992): 10–11.

9. Henry Fielding, *Joseph Andrews,* ed. Paul A. Scanlon (Peterborough: Broadview, 2001), 59.

10. All life narrative is didactic or exemplary to the extent that it performs the imitation or re-presentation of a life, a mimetic act that the reader emulates in turn by reconstructing the narrative, perhaps even consciously shaping his or her own life narrative along that model. In this view, Augustine's *Confessions* is quite literally a "self-duplicating machine," as Martin Danahay puts it (*Community of One* [Albany: State University of New York Press, 1993], 39–40).

11. Johnson, "*Rambler* No. 60," in *Samuel Johnson's Literary Criticism,* ed. R. D. Stock (Lincoln: University of Nebraska Press, 1974), 40–41. Johnson understood that written lives both shape and lead out or educe every rank of reader. See Richard Altick, *Lives and Letters* (New York: Knopf, 1966), 47.

12. Altick, *Lives and Letters,* 88–90, notes that "the universal justification of biography was its didactic usefulness." Alan Rauch canvasses the nineteenth-century popularization of "knowledge" by Craik, the Society for the Diffusion of Useful Knowledge, and various encyclopedic projects, all as instruments of civilization and "moral growth" (*Useful Knowledge* [Durham, NC: Duke University Press, 2001], 24). Reed Whittemore, in *Pure Lives,* notes a high point of the didactic biographical tradition in the establishment, in 1920, of a department of biography at Carleton College, run by a former missionary (7).

13. John Edward Bruce, ed., *Short Biographical Sketches of Eminent Negro Men and Women* (Yonkers, NY: Gazette Press, 1910). Bruce included such eminent women as Phillis Wheatley and Ida B. Wells in a proportion of about one in ten—a standard shortchanging of women in mixed company.

14. Mary-Ellen Kulkin, *Her Way: Biographies of Women for Young People* (Chicago: American Library Assoc., 1976), xxi–xxii, xvii. Kulkin advises librarians not to be "guilty of elitist and snobbish ideas" by denigrating popular or celebrity biographies (xix). Yet some series of biographies of famous paragons risk teaching the child reader "that he or she . . . [is] doomed to mediocrity" (xix). "Children, as well as adults, tend to believe what they read in a book. . . . The book's permanency and bold print gives it an air of authenticity and authoritativeness" (xviii). Kulkin's warning labels call for "wise librarians, teachers, and parents" to administer the proper doses of esteem and self-esteem to children, suggesting that too much biography (an entire series of lives, e.g.) is worse than the disease (xix–xx).

15. George Jerment, ed., *Memoirs of Eminently Pious Women,* by Thomas Gibbons, 2 vols. (London: Ogle, 1804). See annotation under Jerment (1804); further citations will appear parenthetically as Gibbons and Jerment (1804) in the text.

16. The biographies by Kendrick often lose track of the narrative, and like those originally in Child's collection, allow confusion as to which person is the protagonist. For instance, a pious eighteenth-century writer, Miss Elizabeth Singer, is suddenly referred to as Mrs. Rowe (a well-known personage) after a page and a half of "Avarice we abhor. . . . Detraction we despise"(126); Mrs. Rowe, we learn, enjoys an intimate domestic life with a younger sister, but herself falls mortally ill, to the grief of her nursing sister; "Mrs. Rowe recovered," but the sister "was herself destined to be the first victim" (128). Only later do we gather how Miss Singer became Mrs. Rowe in 1710 (129); later still, after her long widowhood and a sermon on never losing one's temper, we are informed that "Mrs. Rowe's health had always been excellent" due to her "calmness" and "temperance"—the mortal illness now forgotten (135). In some of the biographies by Child, the husband's life subsumes that of the wife: though the life of Catherine de Bora, wife of Martin Luther, begins by claiming that "*his* biography forms a part of the world's history" and hardly needs repeating (249), it goes on for seven pages before Catherine is mentioned, and Luther is decidedly the subject of all the remaining paragraphs, even those recording his opinion of her, with perhaps the exception of the penultimate paragraph: "Catherine, the widow of Luther, survived him nearly seven years, and died at Torgau in 1552" (262).

17. Pierre Bourdieu, *Outline of a Theory of Practice,* quoted in William Epstein, *Recognizing Biography* (Philadelphia: University of Pennsylvania Press, 1987), 85. See K. Anthony Appiah, introduction to *The Seductions of Biography,* ed. Mary Rhiel and David Suchoff (New York: Routledge, 1996), 9–11.

18. Martin Kreiswirth ("Trusting the Tale: The Narrativist Turn in the Human Sciences," *New Literary History* 23 [1992]: 629–57), offers a comprehensive consideration of the effects in many disciplines of the replacement of "*argument* and *explanation*" with "*narrative,* or . . . *story*" (637). Jens Brockmeier and Donal Carbaugh, in their introduction to *Narrative and Identity,* ed. Jens Brockmeier and Donal Carbaugh (Amsterdam: John Benjamins, 2001), 1–22, confirm continuing consequences of the "narrative turn" in the sciences: "Narrative is a central hinge between culture and mind"; "the study of life narratives is . . . a laboratory of possibilities for human identity

construction" (8–10). Howard Gardner envisions a survival of the fittest among narratives as among genes: "The 'memes'—a culture's version of genes—called stories compete . . . and only the most robust stand a chance of gaining ascendancy" (Gardner, with Emma Laskin, *Leading Minds: An Anatomy of Leadership* [New York: Basic/HarperCollins, 1995], 14). *Leading Minds* is in part a prosopography of leadership, featuring nine lives including Margaret Mead, Eleanor Roosevelt, Margaret Thatcher, and Martin Luther King Jr.

19. Among the works in this vein that I have found suggestive are Jerome Bruner, *Actual Minds, Possible Worlds* (Cambridge, MA: Harvard University Press, 1986); Robert Coles, *The Call of Stories* (Boston: Houghton Mifflin, 1989); David Novitz, "Art, Narrative, and Human Nature," *Philosophy and Literature* 13 (1989): 57–74; Dan McAdams, *The Stories We Live By: Personal Myths and the Making of the Self* (New York: Morrow, 1993); Charlotte Linde, *Life Stories* (New York: Oxford University Press, 1993); Sherry Turkle, *Life on the Screen* (New York: Simon & Schuster, 1995); David B. Morris, "Narrative, Ethics, and Pain: Thinking *With* Stories," *Narrative* 9 (2001): 55 77; and Peter Brooks and Paul Gewirtz, eds., *Law's Stories: Narrative and Rhetoric in the Law* (New Haven, CT: Yale University Press, 1996).

20. Brockmeier and Carbaugh, introduction to *Narrative and Identity*, 9.

21. Ruth-Ellen Boetcher Joeres and Barbara Laslett, "Personal Narratives: A Selection of Recent Works," *Signs* 18 (1993): 389–91; Camilla Stivers, "Reflections on the Role of Personal Narrative in Social Science," *Signs* 18 (1993): 408–25; and Sidonie Smith, "Who's Talking/Who's Talking Back? The Subject of Personal Narrative," *Signs* 18 (1993): 392–407.

22. Suzanne W. Hull, *Chaste, Silent, and Obedient: English Books for Women, 1475–1640* (San Marino, CA: Huntington, 1982), writes: "Men wrote almost all the women's books printed before 1640" (16).

23. Exceptions include some widely recognized arbiters of opinion: Lydia Huntley Sigourney, *Examples*;[718] Harriet Martineau, *Biographical Sketches* (New York: Hurst, 1868; London: Macmillan, 1869); Margaret Oliphant, *The Victorian Age of English Literature*, 2 vols. (New York: Tait, 1892).

24. Miriam Elizabeth Burstein, "'The Reduced Pretensions of the Historic Muse': Agnes Strickland and the Commerce of Women's History," *Journal of Narrative Technique* 28 (1998): 224.

25. Pamela Corpron Parker, "Good Women, Good Works: Victorian Philanthropy and Women's Biography," *Trinity: The Cresset* 59 (1996): 17–21. Burstein, in "The Reduced Pretensions of the Historic Muse," "finds that any given author of a 'Lives of Eminent Women' . . . has also written devotional works, fiction, poetry, popular science, textbooks, literary appreciations, or art criticism" (220). In "From Good Looks to Good Thoughts: Popular Women's History and the Invention of Modernity, ca. 1830–70," *Modern Philology* 97 (1999): 46–75, Burstein emphasizes the strategy in these women's biographical histories of "inverting the political historian's priorities by making Christian virtue . . . the prime mover in national life," thereby uplifting the homogeneous uneventfulness of "pattern" lives that propel the "progress of morality" (53, 65).

26. On the attraction and risk of women's collaboration, see the double issue of *Tulsa Studies in Women's Literature* in 1994–95. Janice Doane and Devon Hodges in "Writing from the Trenches: Women's Work and Collaborative Writing," concede that women should not forfeit "the agency and status that comes [*sic*] with being an author and 'origin'" (*Tulsa Studies in Women's Literature* 14 [1995]: 53). In practice, feminist criticism of life narrative has remained attached to Romantic expressive models: the ideal of the author or genius. Holly Laird, *Women Co-Authors* (Urbana: University of Illinois Press, 2000); Bette London, *Writing Double* (Ithaca, NY: Cornell University Press, 1999).

27. The "woman as physician" category included Mrs. Clemence S. Lozier, M.D. (then still living), who united her mother's folk medicine learned from the Native Americans of Virginia with her husband's and her own medical training (tacitly without benefit of degree) and, in turn, served as a mentor to other women and men pursuing medical learning.

28. One contributor expresses hope that postbellum American "public sentiment . . . accords to woman the right to enter any field of literature or art" with training equal to "her brothers"

(Rev. E. B. Huntington, 272);[630] another celebrates the first graduations of women from medical colleges (Rev. H. B. Elliot, 513–15).

29. Julia Ward Howe was the subject of a biography by her daughters Maude Howe Elliott and Laura E. Richards that won the 1917 Pulitzer (Linda Wagner-Martin, *Telling Women's Lives* [New Brunswick, NJ: Rutgers University Press, 1994], 2).

30. Woolf, *A Room of One's Own* (1929; reprint, New York: Harcourt, 1981), 50, credits Pericles with this dictum. Edward B. Pollard quotes Plutarch's citation of Thucydides on the principle that "the very name of a good woman ought to be retired"(4:119).[899]

31. Jenkins intends only mild criticism of Wordsworth, "the pure and simple-minded, though almost too unworldly" poet. "Above mortality" alludes to the epigraph from Felicia Hemans on the title page, in which Fame allegorically offers an inebriating drink simulating transcendence of mortality. The address to his male friend (dated from Auburn, NY, August 1851) is a rarity; usually a presenter claims community with the female (and male) anonymous audience. Jenkins's aim has been to "present pictures" in the "spirit" and not "the letter of history." He has no "particular plan" of selection in the list; some are "classic," some early modern or eighteenth century, and all but Joan of Arc and Mme Roland were recognized European rulers or consorts (v–vi).[461]

32. Sarah Stickney Ellis, *The Women of England* (London: Fisher, 1839), urges her "countrywomen" to "a fresh exercise of moral power . . . to win back to the homes of England, the boasted felicity" (n.p.). The "*moral characteristics*" of a country determine its "station, either high or low, in the scale of nations," and women govern domestic morals (9).

33. Like Sarah Hale in the following year, Julia Kavanagh attempts a historical synthesis, grouping hundreds of subjects under four periods. She offers an unusual alphabetical list, "Authors and Works Consulted," with close to a hundred sources, many notable for female prosopography.

34. The preface states that these were "originally written for a periodical which I was engaged in editing," that is, the *English Woman's Journal,* printed by Emily Faithfull's all-female Victoria Press (collaborative enterprises begun in 1857 and in place by 1860). Bessie Rayner Parkes distinguishes among her sources and subjects, being herself responsible for putting some of them in English circulation. Her pieces on Mme Luce, Mme Pape-Carpantier, and Mrs Jameson are "strictly original"; the two former personally gave her notes. Those on Mme Swetchine, La Soeur Rosalie, Harriot K. Hunt, Mme de Lamartine, and Bianca Milesi Mojon were "translated and abridged." The life of Mojon was privately printed, then translated in an "American periodical"; Parkes did more research in Paris to produce her own version. On "Governor Winthrop's Wife," Miss Cornelia Knight, Miss Bosanquet, and Mrs. Delany, she wrote "biographical reviews cast into the shape of a short story," based on well-known books (v–vi).

35. Others similarly attributed Christian progress to women's influence. The Reverend Thomas Timpson[806] refers to Dr. Fuller concerning the first two exemplars in Timpson's collection: "Bertha and Ethelburga, queens of Ethelbert and Edwin, who occasioned and expedited the conversion of their husbands' kingdoms" (4–5).

36. Beaufort's chapter concludes with an image of the "Tudor Rose (White and Red), from the gates of the Chapel of Henry VII" (her son [70]).

37. The biography of Lady Russell concludes: "Three of the chief families of England, the houses of Devonshire, Bedford, and Rutland, look back to this pure, warm-hearted woman and her murdered husband as their common ancestors" (84).

38. The specificity and venom of this history of Louisa Harrington suggest that Mrs. Pilkington had no fear of suit for libel. The corruption of Louisa originated in a match between "Eastern magnificence, and Hibernian pride" (1–2), that is, a man who won a fortune in India and a poor Irish noblewoman. Mary Pilkington (1766–1839), not to be confused with Laetitia Pilkington of the scandalous memoirs, published animal stories and moral tales for children, including *Biography for Boys* (1799) and *A Mirror for the Female Sex* (1798).

39. Mary Hays (1760–1843) read *A Vindication* in 1792 and became a close friend of Wollstonecraft and Godwin (Janet Todd, ed., *A Dictionary of British and American Women Writers 1660–1800* [Totowa, NJ: Rowman & Littlefield, 1987], 156–57).

40. This phrase pops up as a second title heading the biography of Semiramis. Hewitt's collection may have been a cobbling job similar to Ellen Clayton's, but it was published under the title *Heroines of History* in 1852 and *Lives of Illustrious Women of All Ages* in 1860.[403]

41. Richard D. Altick, in *The Cowden Clarkes* (London: Oxford University Press, 1948), notes that Mary Cowden Clarke produced a series of studies of the heroines of such authors as Chaucer and Spenser, The Woman of the Writers (1851–53), for the *Ladies' Companion* (149–50). With compliments for her research, narrative skill, and didactic restraint, Altick calls *World-Noted Women* "a favourable example of mid-nineteenth-century parlour literature" (150–51). Clarke includes contributions by Grace Greenwood (Sara Jane Lippincott) of Philadelphia (on Joan of Arc) and Mrs. Robert Balmanno of New York (on Pocahontas).

42. Yopie Prins, in *Victorian Sappho* (Princeton, NJ: Princeton University Press, 1999), examines *World-Noted Women* with its frontispiece of Sappho and short biography of the poet, both presenting a "lyric figure" on the verge of "dying for postcrity" (184 86).

43. See Anna Jameson, "Zenobia, Queen of Palmyra," reprinted in Charles F. Horne, ed., *Great Men and Famous Women* (New York: S. Hess, 1894), 3:26–30. Jameson has high praise for this cultivated intellectual woman of beauty and valor.

44. On the Froude/Carlyle controversy, see Trev Lynn Broughton, *Men of Letters, Writing Lives* (London: Routledge, 1999), 83–112. Edmund Gosse, in "The Ethics of Biography," *The Cosmopolitan* 35 (July 1903): 317–23 (reprinted in *Biography as an Art*, ed. Clifford, 113–19), suggests that "the majority, whose curiosity is to be entertained," will always clash with the minority committed to protecting the subject; the biographer should set out "to be as indiscreet as possible within the boundaries of good taste and kind feeling" (113–14). Gosse also writes of the "moral significance" of the material of an individual's life (117). Exposing secrets thus is also an ethics of biography. See James C. Johnston, *Biography: The Literature of Personality*, introduction by Gamaliel Bradford (New York: Century, 1927), on intrusive modern readers (7), on "questions of ethics" in biographical representation (16), and in praise of the ancient tradition of collective biography (39–42).

45. As Herbert Tucker has reminded me, as early as the 1873 conclusion to *The Renaissance,* Walter Pater had offered intensity of aesthetic attention as a form of "success in life." Ruth Hoberman (*Modernizing Lives: Experiments in English Biography, 1918–1939* [Carbondale: Southern Illinois University Press, 1987]) writes: "From Strachey on, biography is aestheticized and psychologized" (13).

46. David Novarr (ed., *The Lines of Life* [West Lafayette, IN: Purdue University Press, 1986]) offers a synopsis of Gosse's views on biography, particularly the entry in *Encyclopedia Britannica,* 11th ed. (1910–11), in which Gosse emphasizes the art of personality (Novarr, 15–18). Gosse's modern judgment against old impure biography influenced Harold Nicolson (18); for Gosse, "biography is not a philosophical treatise, a polemical pamphlet, or a portion of a chronicle," and the old biography was too "'moral' or 'religious'" and too "historical" (17). Reed Whittemore quotes Gosse in order to disagree with him (*Pure Lives*, 2).

47. The Society for the Diffusion of Useful Knowledge (SDUK) published *The Penny Cyclopedia* (London, 1833–43). On the model of German "conversations-lexicons," there was a nineteenth-century boom in *Information for the People*, as one 1857 title promised (Robert Lewis Collison, *Encyclopaedias: Their History throughout the Ages*, 2d ed. [New York: Hafner, 1966], 185, 188). See Alan Rauch, *Useful Knowledge*, 24. The structure might be thematic rather than alphabetical, as Tom McArthur notes in *Worlds of Reference: Lexicography, Learning, and Language from the Clay Tablet to the Computer* (Cambridge: Cambridge University Press, 1986), 155–60. J. S. Bratton stresses the production of reward books, including biographies, for pupils in the English Sunday and National schools (*The Impact of Victorian Children's Fiction* [London: Croom Helm, 1981], 11–22). Publishers competed for approval of texts for the Board schools founded by the 1870 Education Act. By the 1890s the London School Board selection committee were rejecting tracts and old-fashioned moral tales in favor of "literature" (novels by Gaskell or Brontë), yet also approved *Great Explorers* and *Eminent Women* (Bratton, 191–96).

48. Altick, *Lives and Letters*, 77–78, 87–88.

49. Although Altick acknowledges that Victorian literary biography "served some of the same purposes" as the common fare that "catered to the era's hunger for 'useful knowledge,'" he exempts the literary variety from the crudest appetites (*Lives and Letters*, 87, 91).

50. Albert Britt, *The Great Biographers* (New York: Whittlesey/McGraw Hill, 1936), 9–10, 21.

51. Paula R. Backscheider, in *Reflections on Biography* (Oxford: Oxford University Press, 1999), makes a similar point (18–20). Altick praises the inspiration of the best examples of twentieth-century literary biography (*Lives and Letters*, xiii, 91, 87).

52. Fred Kaplan, *Dickens: A Biography* (New York: Morrow, 1988); Juliet Barker, *The Brontës: A Life in Letters* (New York: Overlook Press, 1998); Germaine Greer, *The Obstacle Race* (New York: Farrar Straus Giroux, 1979); Elizabeth Longford, *Eminent Victorian Women* (London: Weidenfeld & Nicolson, 1981).

53. John Guillory, *Cultural Capital* (Chicago: University of Chicago Press, 1993), 76–77. Martha Woodmansee, in *The Author, Art, and the Market* (New York: Columbia University Press, 1994), writes of an "aversion to rhetoric" in the rise of Kantian aesthetics (5) and carefully traces a history of "the interests in disinterestedness" (11–29).

54. Wagner-Martin, *Telling Women's Lives*, 133. Liz Stanley ("Process in Feminist Biography," in *All Sides of the Subject*, ed. Teresa Iles [New York: Teachers College, Columbia, 1992]) writes of being expected to like Hannah Cullwick if she were to write a "proper" feminist biography of her (109).

55. Lawrence Quirk's biography of Cher (1991) is "a kind of soft pornography" that commodifies the subject. Quirk evidently relies on a rags-to-riches formula that pervades many more artful or psychologically realist biographies (Wagner-Martin, *Telling Women's Lives*, 152–53).

56. Stanley Fish, "Just Published: Minutiae without Meaning," *New York Times*, September 7, 1999, A19, col. 1; see "Stanley Fish Inveighs against Biographies While Recruiting and Promoting Biographers in His Own Department," *Chronicle of Higher Education*, September 24, 1999, Research and Publishing A22. If Fish is doing a Plato or a Carlyle, banning poetry or fiction from the republic, why permit politics and wrestling as brazen performances? Character- and muscle-building activities, like biography, were once commended for the citizenry.

57. As Jay Parini notes, "Biographers have a contract with their readers to deliver the facts to the best of their ability," but they also need a narrative or "mythos" to shape and give life to the material. Parini counters Fish's accusation that biographers lie: "Why expect a biographer to adhere to narrative strictures [i.e., objectivity] . . . that no storyteller could expect to follow?" ("Biography Can Escape the Tyranny of Facts," *Chronicle of Higher Education*, February 4, 2000, A72).

58. The controversy over Edmund Morris's *Dutch* is characteristic: as Morris creates imaginary scenes with Ronald Reagan and himself as character, the contract breaks, and it's a novel, not a biography (*Dutch: A Memoir of Ronald Reagan* [New York: Random House, 1999]).

59. Janet Malcolm, "The Silent Woman—I," *New Yorker* 69 (August 23 and 30, 1993), 86. This article formed part of Malcolm's *The Silent Woman: Sylvia Plath and Ted Hughes* (New York: A. A. Knopf/Random House, 1994). Malcolm had earlier entered the fray on the ethics of biographical representation in *The Journalist and the Murderer* (New York: Vintage Books, 1990) and *In the Freud Archives* (New York: Knopf, 1984).

60. John Paul Eakin, *How Our Lives Become Stories* (Ithaca, NY: Cornell University Press, 1999), 172–74; Daphne Patai, "Ethical Problems of Personal Narratives, or, Who Should Eat the Last Piece of Cake?" *International Journal of Oral History* 8 (1987): 21, quoted in Eakin, 174.

61. Malcolm's image of "tiptoeing down the corridor" ("The Silent Woman," 86) brings to mind Max Beerbohm's famous caricature of Henry James kneeling outside a hotel bedroom door, intensely deciphering a pair of men's boots beside a pair of women's shoes: "Mr. Henry James," image HD 802 [ca. 1904?] Ashmolean Museum, Oxford; reprinted in *Beerbohm's Literary Caricatures*, ed. J. G. Riewald (London: Allen Lane, 1977), 225.

62. In 1995, Jean Bethke Elshtain deplored "the collapse of a distinction between public and private," "the unraveling of democratic civil society," and the rise of individualist identity politics

(*Democracy on Trial* [New York: Basic Books, 1995], 38, 41–43, 77). Charles Taylor warns against an overemphasis on commensurate recognition, which can produce "homogenizing demand for recognition of equal worth" and an opposing separatism, without a grounds for comparing the relative worth of different cultures (*Multiculturalism and "The Politics of Recognition": An Essay by Charles Taylor*, ed. Amy Gutman, with commentary by Amy Gutman, Steven C. Rockefeller, Michael Walzer, and Susan Wolf [Princeton, NJ: Princeton University Press, 1992], 64, 72–73). Examining Charles Taylor's essay "The Politics of Recognition," Linda Nicholson argues that multiculturalism must not only make claims of "worth" for marginalized groups, but question "the process by which judgments of worth have and can be made" (*The Play of Reason* [Ithaca, NY: Cornell University Press, 1999], 142). Like Elshtain (*Democracy*, 41), Taylor seeks to reconstitute a "we" that raises concerns for those seeking to extend recognition (Nicholson, 137).

63. Richard Sennett, *The Fall of Public Man* (New York: Knopf, 1977), 223.

64. From the very different position of queer cultural studies, Lauren Berlant in 1997 challenges a shell-game substitution of the personal for the political: in *The Queen of America Goes to Washington City* (Durham, NC: Duke University Press, 1997), she deplores a turn in the United States to the infantilized, traumatized subject, and "the use of intimacy crises as . . . a distraction from 'real' politics" (9, 67). Arthur M. Schlesinger Jr., in *The Disuniting of America* ([Knoxville, TN]: Whittle Direct Books, 1991), seems to present a balanced review of the representation of ethnicities in American history, noting that "ethnic enclaves . . . developed a compensatory literature" of model Irish or model Jews for "tribal celebrations," but on assimilation, they became staunch defenders of Anglo American canons (25–26). Schlesinger's balance tilts, however: "Self-styled 'multiculturalists' are very often ethnocentric separatists who see little in the Western heritage beyond Western crimes" (72). Compare Gertrude Himmelfarb, *One Nation, Two Cultures* (New York: Knopf, 1999), 36. It is possible to be a "unifier" without being a conservative humanist, however. Some feminist historical scholars have challenged the model of separate spheres, which can obscure the different constructions of women's actual "mobility and access," including the work of a majority of black women in others' homes, as You-me Park and Gayle Wald put it in "Native Daughters in the Promised Land," *American Literature* 70 (1998): 612, 614. At the same time, a collapse of the spheres model might lose the focus of still-needed feminist inquiry, as Cathy N. Davidson warns in "Preface: No More Separate Spheres!" in "No More Separate Spheres!" ed. Cathy N. Davidson, special issue, *American Literature* 70 (1998): 449.

65. James Monaco, *Celebrity* (New York: Delta, 1978), 6, quoted in Joshua Gamson, *Claims to Fame: Celebrity in Contemporary America* (Berkeley: University of California Press, 1994), 8–9. Jean Baudrillard develops an entire inverted metaphysics of "simulacra," an endless, "hyperreal" substitution of signifiers, of images that murder "their own model as the Byzantine icons could murder the divine identity" ("Simulacra and Simulations," in *Selected Writings*, ed. Mark Poster [Stanford, CA: Stanford University Press, 1988], 167, 170). Baudrillard himself punctures the notion that a revolution separates "the grievous and heroic Age of Production from the euphoric Age of Consumption." The work ethic and consumer gratification remain within the same economy ("Consumer Society," in *Selected Writings*, ed. Poster, 50). As P. David Marshall notes, Daniel Boorstin anticipated Baudrillard on illusory substitutions (*Celebrity and Power* [Minneapolis: University of Minnesota Press, 1997], 11). Boorstin, in *The Image*, wrote: "The celebrity . . . is the human pseudo-event. . . . The hero was distinguished by his achievement; the celebrity by his image or trademark" (47, 57, 61, quoted in Gamson, *Claims to Fame*, 57). The downfall is usually dated to the era in which Richard Ohmann locates the development of mass culture in the United States, 1885–1900 (*Selling Culture* [London: Verso, 1996], 10–23).

66. Maxine F. Singer, "Heroines and Role Models," *Science* 253 (July 19, 1991): 249, an editorial based on the address at Barnard College, May 14, 1991. Gamson (*Claims to Fame*, 29–34) identifies the "paradox of egalitarian distinction" in the representation of American heroes (31). Marshall notes that consumer capitalism has repositioned "the mass" as the audience and defined "social identity in terms of consumption" (*Celebrity and Power*, 63). On the shift from heroism, character, and fame to twentieth-century celebrity, see also Leo Braudy, *The Frenzy of Renown* (New York: Oxford University Press, 1986).

67. Gertrude Himmelfarb, *On Looking into the Abyss* (New York: Knopf, 1994), 27–34. Carlyle's philosophy of clothes in *Sartor Resartus* might seem to initiate a valet's perspective on the public personage, and that text's multiplicity of voices hardly encourages a monologic hero worship. Thanks to Herbert Tucker for pointing out the oddity of Himmelfarb's invocation of Carlyle.

68. Taylor, *Multiculturalism*, 25.

69. Judith Hilkey, *Character Is Capital: Success Manuals and Manhood in Gilded Age America* (Chapel Hill: University of North Carolina Press, 1997).

70. Like the American women writers of sentimental literature in Marianne Noble's account, the participants in role model self-help may be "exploiting a culturally overdetermined form of self-expression for the pleasures and powers . . . derived from it"; "masochism in sentimental fiction cannot be univocally celebrated as an empowering rhetorical device, though, for it is also both symptom and agent of the ideological manipulation of female desire" (Noble, *The Masochistic Pleasures of Sentimental Literature* [Princeton, NJ: Princeton University Press, 2000], 5–6).

71. Contributors to a special issue of *Women's Studies in Communication* in 1995 faced the anomaly: "The genre's roots stem from white Protestant heterosexual male ideology" (Victoria Leto DeFrancisco, "Helping Ourselves: An Introduction," *Women's Studies in Communication* 18 [1995]: 107–10). Yet "women account for 75%–85% of total sales of self-help books" today (Maureen Ebben, "Off the Shelf Salvation: A Feminist Critique of Self-Help," *Women's Studies in Communication* 18 [1995]: 111–22).

72. Hilkey, *Character Is Capital,* 3–9. As she notes, many of the manuals emphasized biographical heroes in text and illustration (33–43). The celebrated self-help entrepreneur Stephen R. Covey counsels the cultivation of principles of "enduring, permanent value," a return to "the *Character Ethic* as the foundation of success," after a 1920s swerve to "the *Personality Ethic*" of "quick-fix influence techniques" (*The Seven Habits of Highly Effective People* [New York: Fireside/Simon & Schuster, 1989], 35, 18–19).

73. Tim Dean, "Sex and Syncope," *Raritan* 15 (1996): 64. Bernice Fisher recalls her deep resentment of role models in the women's movement, which urged "us to look *up* to 'special women'" in a "psychological version of the American dream" that masked "material conditions" with an "ideology of individual success" ("Wandering in the Wilderness: The Search for Women Role Models," *Signs* 13 [1988]: 212–13).

74. According to Mary Ann Doane, women watching movies and reading romances are cast as incapable of maintaining appropriate adult distance (*The Desire to Desire: The Woman's Film of the 1940s* [Bloomington: Indiana University Press, 1987], 13–19, 32–33).

75. Carla Kaplan describes Judith Kegan Gardiner's defense of identification, which should not be regarded as "feminism's cardinal sin," as Kaplan puts it: "Reading is pretty much unthinkable without different forms of identification" (*The Erotics of Talk* [New York: Oxford University Press, 1996], 45). Kaplan describes the "archeological imperative" on 25.

76. Victoria Glendenning, "Lies and Silences," in *The Troubled Face of Biography,* ed. Eric Homberger and John Charmley (New York: St. Martin's, 1988), 61, quoted in Joe Law and Linda K. Hughes, "'And What Have *You* Done?': Victorian Biography Today," in *Biographical Passages,* ed. Joe Law and Linda K. Hughes (Columbia: University of Missouri Press, 2000), 13.

77. Max Weber, in *The Protestant Ethic and the Spirit of Capitalism,* trans. Talcott Parsons (New York: Scribner, 1958), famously linked the rise of modern capitalism to a Protestant ascetic imperative: a social ethic of "one's duty in a calling" (54); a utilitarianism and "strict avoidance of all spontaneous enjoyment of life" (52–53), as exemplified in Benjamin Franklin's *Autobiography.* Wendy Simonds, in *Women and Self-Help Culture* (New Brunswick, NJ: Rutgers University Press, 1992), records that one reader "said that she considered biographies to be self-help"; others "see the activity of reading self-help books as a serious and self-reflective activity. . . . Despite the plenitude of case-study 'characters' . . . with whom readers can (and do) identify, this identification does not result in a detachment from reality the way it can in fiction" (47).

78. Brian Maidment, "Popular Exemplary Biography in the Nineteenth Century: Edwin Paxton Hood and His Books," *Prose Studies* 7 (1984): 154–57.

79. Gertrude Himmelfarb, *The De-Moralization of Society* (New York: Vintage, 1996), 165; Samuel Smiles, *Self-Help* (1859; reprint, London: John Murray, 1958); Alexander Tyrrell, "Class Consciousness in Early Victorian Britain: Samuel Smiles, Leeds Politics, and the Self-Help Creed," *Journal of British Studies* 9 (1970): 102–25, esp. 118. As a Unitarian, Smiles was an associate of Hamer Stansfeld, who showed Smiles his correspondence with the American Unitarian William Ellery Channing and who helped to import the Unitarian-derived ideas of Emerson, including the term "self-help" (Alexander Tyrrell, review of *Samuel Smiles and the Construction of Victorian Values*, by Adrian Jarvis, *Victorian Studies* 41 [1998]: 536–38).

80. Smiles had been the editor of the Radical *Leeds Times*, and he continued to support working-class radicalism and cooperative movements well beyond the first version of *Self-Help* as a public lecture to the Leeds Mutual Improvement Society in 1845 (Tyrrell, "Class Consciousness," 116); he took the side of the more grassroots Improvement Societies rather than the patronage of the Mechanics' Institutes (119). Anne Baltz Rodrick ("The Importance of Being an Earnest Improver: Class, Caste, and *Self-Help* in Mid-Victorian England," *Victorian Literature and Culture* 29 [2001]: 39–50) similarly emphasizes the "mutual improvement" themes of *Self-Help*, reading Smiles's "growing emphasis on individual, rather than cooperative, effort" as a reaction to the failures of earlier cooperative movements (47–48n.1, citing R. J. Morris, "Samuel Smiles and the Genesis of Self-Help," *History Journal* 24 [1981]: 91–94).

81. Smiles, 18; chap. 1, quoted in Rodrick, "The Importance of Being an Earnest Improver," 40. With few exceptions, *Self-Help* is peopled by Englishmen—not simply out of nationalist pride but also because of the concentration of industrial development from the previous century in Midlands textiles.

The phrase "Everyman's Carlyle" is from Himmelfarb, *De-Moralization*, 167. Other Himmelfarbian heroes include Dickens and Lionel Trilling (*On Looking into the Abyss*, ix–xi, 27–49). The Victorians themselves seemed to endorse Margaret Thatcher's campaign of privatization and demolition of the welfare state: in 1986, "Sir Keith Joseph, Mrs. Thatcher's mentor, brought out an edition of [Samuel Smiles's] *Self-Help* to encourage the entrepreneur"; Smiles, according to Sir Ian Gilmour, became "the Victorian hero of Thatcherism" (Tyrrell, "Review," 536–38).

82. I have no interest in defending Smiles's program as an answer to the needs of the actual workers of the day. The "steps" to success are one size fits all and universalizing (*Self-Help* was translated into Japanese); different rules turn out to be variations on one theme, maximal profit on time and money (Smiles, e.g., 269–89). Smiles wished to define the "'True Gentleman' [as] essentially classless," as Robin Gilmour notes in *The Idea of the Gentleman in the Victorian Novel* (London: Allen & Unwin, 1981), 99–100.

83. Examples of the rare mention of women in *Self-Help* include de Tocqueville's assertion of the value of a "noble-minded" wife in "elevat[ing] the character of her husband" (56–57), the story of Lady Peel (70), Heilmann's wife (90), and Flaxman's wife (187–90), the latter a figure in Child's *Good Wives*. The inventor Arkwright's unnamed wife, growing "impatient at what she conceived to be a wanton waste of time and money," destroyed the early models of the spinning machine as "the cause of the family privations" (64). Arkwright, after separating from his wife, soon had to flee a mob of machine-breaking workers likewise threatened with privation by the invention (64–66).

84. Simonds, *Women and Self-Help Culture*, 63–65.

85. Roger Woolger and Jennifer Barker Woolger, *The Goddess Within* (New York: Fawcett Columbine/Ballantine, 1989). Clarissa Pinkola Estes's *Women Who Run with the Wolves* (New York: Ballantine, 1992) similarly offers typological models with a claim to timeless transcendence.

86. Weber, "Class, Status, Party," in *From Max Weber: Essays in Sociology*, trans. and ed. H. H. Gerth and C. Wright Mills (1946; reprint, New York: Oxford University Press, 1973), 188–90.

87. Dr. Harry Edwards, "The Athlete as Role Model: Relic of America's Sports Past?" *Sport* (November 1994), 32; Daniel Seligman, "Exemplarism," *Fortune* 123 (June 17, 1991): 135. In business contexts, role models may be rival companies or national industries (the Japanese as role models), consciously disliked. Human resources discourse weighs role modeling in terms of career more than character. According to one study, gender is not the most important determinant in the choice of role model by employees in public administration; the model's

perceived performance or success means more than whether he or she shares the same sex as the aspirant (Mansour Javidan et al., "Superior and Subordinate Gender and the Acceptance of Superiors as Role Models," *Human Relations* 48 [1995]: 1271–84).

88. On roles and society as theater, see Sennett, *The Fall of Public Man,* 28–41.

89. Bahktin/Volosinov define any utterance as a rhetorical interaction engaging "three participants; a sender, a listener . . . and the hero . . . or the topic" (Amigoni, *Victorian Biography,* 43–44). Thus the subject of the narrative is also a "configuration of signs" (43).

90. Margo Jefferson, "Woman as Icon: Disturbing, Inspiring," *New York Times,* December 15, 1996, C15. See the entire issue, "Heroine-Worship," *New York Times Magazine,* November 24, 1996. An ad in *Time* (October 5, 1998) shows a long-haired, perhaps Hispanic-looking teenage girl with rollerblades over her shoulder, above a picture of Toni Morrison on the cover of *Time;* the large type reads: "The Time Education Program took Andrea de Niemeyer from Rollerblades to Role Models," while the text below explains: "The TIME EDUCATION PROGRAM introduces students like Andrea de Niemeyer to people who inspire, and whom they'll want to emulate. Politicians. Scientists. Thinkers" (n.p.). "The Lives They Lived: An Annual Issue," *New York Times Magazine,* January 7, 2001, presents an illustrated prosopography memorializing eminent people who died in 2000, with articles by "distinguished writers" who were somehow connected to the subjects. Not using the term "role models," the issue nevertheless affirms that "lives well lived provide rich fodder for all imaginations" (7); it features ads for A&E's Biography that are full-page portraits of Walter Mathau, Charles Schultz, and Loretta Young (all died in 2000). (This is a series of annual collective eulogies, e.g., January 4, 1998, and December 30, 2001.)

91. Smith and Watson, introduction to *Getting a Life,* ed. Smith and Watson, 7.

92. Geraldine DeLuca, "Lives and Half-Lives: Biographies of Women for Young Adults," *Children's Literature in Education* 17 (1986): 214–52, notes: "Publishers for young adults have shifted their attention from queens, nurses, and ballerinas to women who stepped out of their traditional roles" (242). "Strides," by the Women's Sports Foundation, "Every Girl Should Have One," features photographs of Wilma Rudolph, Babe Didrickson Zaharias, Billie Jean King, and Donna de Varona (*Women's Sports and Fitness* 8 [June 1986]: 54).

93. Gayle Jo Carter, "The New Face of a Role Model," *USA Weekend,* June 18–20, 1999, 6–7. A picture of Mia Hamm scoring her 108th international goal is captioned: "You goal, girl! . . . Her role models? Chris Evert, Wayne Gretzky, Jackie Joyner-Kersee and Michael Jordan, for 'the way they carried themselves on and off their respective fields of play'" (6). Three years earlier, the same magazine displayed Madonna as Evita on the cover, over the boxed text: "Arguing Family Values with Madonna: 'I'm a very good role model,' the new mom declares in a contentious, revealing conversation" (Jonathan Alter, "'I Don't Want to Be the Material Girl,'" *USA Weekend,* December 13–15, 1996, 6–7).

94. See the March 2000 issue of *Hadassah Magazine* (vol. 81), titled "Emulating Esther: Jewish Heroines," with several articles that help to perpetuate biblical women as models (4, 18, 37; see also vol. 80 [November 1998]). Penguin Putnam's catalog "Women's Studies Books for Courses 2000" features many auto/biographical and prosopographical works, such as Sheila Rowbotham's *A Century of Women,* Joyce Johnson's *Minor Characters: A Beat Memoir* (2000), and Michele Serros's humorous *How to Be a Chicana Role Model* (2000). See Jo Napolitano, "Two-Inch Latino Role Models, for Good or Ill," *New York Times,* May 1, 2003, B1, 5, on popular tiny plastic figurines modeling stereotypes of "urban Mexican-Americans."

95. The 2001 catalog (*Celebrating Women of Courage and Vision* [Windsor, CA: National Women's History Project, 2001], 23, 34–35) of the Women's History Project ("a nonprofit organization since 1980"), on a page titled "Role Models," lists *Girls Who Rocked the World,* volumes 1 and 2: "These books tell the stories of real girls, past and present, who achieved amazing feats and changed history before age 20!" Also listed are the series Cool Careers for Girls in computers, sport, and engineering. Pages under the heading "Women Make History" advertise such books as Gail Meyer Rolka's *100 Women Who Shaped World History* (San Mateo, CA: Bluewood, 1994) or Vicki Léon's *Uppity Women of Medieval Times* (Berkeley: Conari, 1997). Another regular item in such catalogs is Toyomi Igus et al., *Great Women in the Struggle,* Book of Black Heroes, vol. 2 (East Orange, NJ: Just Us Books, 1997). Apart from the merchandising of

mugs, tee-shirts, and posters, such catalogs repeat the formulas of prosopographies a hundred years earlier. Some models are American, some global, some are grouped by historic period or occupation, some are more diversified.

96. "We were subjected to The Maria Syndrome, which equated Latinas with the sacrificing *Virgen Maria*, purity and motherhood, or *Maria de Magdalena*, the prostitute" (Nicholasa Mohr, foreword to *¡Latinas! Women of Achievement*, ed. Diane Telgen and Jim Kamp [Detroit: Visible Ink, 1996], xiii–xiv). *¡Latinas!* was advertised in the 1999 catalog for Women's History Project, 31.

97. Telgen and Kamp, eds., *¡Latinas!* 109, xiv. *¡Latinas!* is a selected reprinting from *Notable Hispanic American Women*, ed. Diane Telgen and Jim Kamp (Detroit: Gale Research, 1993), a library reference work. See also Nicolás Kanellos, ed., *The Hispanic Almanac: From Columbus to Corporate America* (Detroit: Gale Research, 1993).

98. Marshall, *Celebrity and Power*, 11.

99. Michael P. Rewa, *Reborn as Meaning* (Washington, DC: University Press of America, 1963), xiii, 1.

100. Reprinted in the *Daily Progress* (Charlottesville, VA), April 11, 1996, A1, A8. The journalist is predictably silent on the fact that Mayor Saunders, like Secretary Brown, is black. The photographs have no such reticence as to the racial pertinence of this story, documenting the grief of "prominent black Americans" Stevie Wonder and Wynton Marsalis (A1, A8).

101. Jan Farrington, "Lighting the Way: Role Models and Mentors," *Career World* 2/4 (199?): 8–14, explains, "A role model is someone we use as a 'pattern' for our lives," perhaps from afar, while "a mentor has come to mean an experienced adult who befriends, encourages, and helps 'show the ropes' to a younger, less experienced person." Farrington's example is Marian Wright Edelman, who became both role model and mentor to Hillary Rodham Clinton (8–9). Tavis Smiley writes, "We're simply not replacing our great African-American heroes and she-roes fast enough. Where is the next Thurgood Marshall, . . . the next Barbara Jordan . . . ? . . . Black leaders also must heed the call to make the word 'mentor' into more of a verb than a noun" ("Requiem for a Dream," *USA Weekend*, January 11–13, 2002, 24).

102. Wollstonecraft, *A Vindication of the Rights of Men . . . and A Vindication of the Rights of Woman*, ed. D. L. Macdonald and Kathleen Scherf (Peterborough: Broadview, 1997), 169. Further citations in the text.

103. Fittingly, all Wollstonecraft's named models reveal a fatal flaw in their renown: martyrs for love, the butt of popular satire (Macaulay's late marriage), the paragon of evil (Catherine the Great's murder of her husband), or the queer impostor (the cross-dressing Charles de Beaumont, Chevalier d'Eon, was legally declared a woman in 1777 [*A Vindication*, 197n.1]).

104. For Margaret Oliphant's appeal for women's economic equality, see "The Grievances of Women," in *Criminals, Idiots, Women, and Minors*, ed. Susan Hamilton (Peterborough: Broadview, 1995), 231–44; quote on 234.

105. Barbara Taylor, "Mother-Haters and Other Rebels," *London Review of Books*, January 3, 2002, reviewing Elaine Showalter's female prosopography, *Inventing Herself* (London: Picador, 2001), cites Wollstonecraft on "the example of a few women" in terms quite similar to mine (3). On Showalter's book, see my chap. 7, 278–81.

106. John Stuart Mill, *The Subjection of Women* (New York: Appleton, 1870). Citations will follow in the text.

107. Frances Power Cobbe, "What Shall We Do with Our Old Maids?" *Fraser's Magazine* (November 1862), reprinted in *Criminals, Idiots, Women, and Minors*, ed. Hamilton, 85–107; quote on 96. Further citations in the text.

108. In *A Room of One's Own*, Woolf famously writes that "Chloe likes Olivia, and they share a laboratory" (84). If the fact of lesbian relations remained comparatively submerged until recently, by 1920 women had for decades been invited to follow mathematicians, chemists, physicists, astronomers—Emilie du Chatelet, Marie Lavoisier, Mary Somerville, Caroline Herschel, Maria Mitchell, and, in due course, Marie Curie—and work in a laboratory.

109. John Ruskin, *"Sesame and Lilies," "The Two Paths" and "The King of the Golden River"* (London: Dent; New York: Dutton, 1928), 59; further citations appear in the text.

110. Winifred Holtby, in *Women and a Changing Civilization* (1935; reprint, Chicago: Academy, 1978), countered women's "inferiority complex" with famous examples: "When a woman believes enough in her own mission to be ruthless—a Mrs. Siddons, a Florence Nightingale, a Mrs. Pankhurst—then, indeed, something happens. . . . When an Amy Johnson breaks aviation records, when a Madame Curie discovers radium, an Ethel Smyth composes a Mass, a Frances Perkin controls perhaps the most difficult government department in the American New Deal—then it becomes a trifle harder for young girls to tell themselves: 'It doesn't matter. I'm only a woman'" (105).

111. Sekou Molefi Baako, as quoted in Darrel E. Owens, "Teaching Black History," *Central Florida Family* (Web magazine), September 23, 1998, on a discontinued site owned by the Disney Corp. at Family.com. One of two epigraphs summarizes the imperative, aimed at parents, to teach the biographical heritage: "If a race has no history, . . . [it] stands in danger of being exterminated" (Carter G. Woodson). Many sites on the Web provide role model biographies for Black History Month.

112. Mary-Ellen Kulkin, *Her Way: Biographies of Women for Young People* (Chicago: American Library Association, 1976), xv.

113. Paule Marshall, "The Making of a Writer," in *Reena and Other Stories* (Old Westbury, NY: Feminist Press, 1983), 11, quoted in Gregory S. Jay, *American Literature and the Culture Wars* (Ithaca, NY: Cornell University Press, 1997), 19.

114. Carolyn G. Heilbrun, *Writing a Woman's Life* (New York: Ballantine, 1988), 26–27.

115. Alice Walker, *In Search of Our Mothers' Gardens* (New York: Harper, 1983), 238–40.

116. Cornel West, *Race Matters* (Boston: Beacon Press, 1993), 35.

117. Louise Bernikow, *The American Women's Almanac* (New York: Berkley, 1997), ix–x.

Chapter Two

1. *The Letters of Elizabeth Barrett Browning*, ed. Frederic G. Kenyon (London, 1897), 1:231, quoted in Angela Leighton, *Elizabeth Barrett Browning*, Key Women Writers (Bloomington: Indiana University Press, 1986), 11.

2. *The Letters of Elizabeth Barrett Browning to Mary Russell Mitford*, ed. Meredith B. Raymond and Mary Rose Sullivan, 3 vols. (Winfield, KS: Wedgestone, 1983), 2:425, quoted in Angela Leighton, *Victorian Women Poets: Writing against the Heart* (Charlottesville: University Press of Virginia, 1992), 42. Barrett Browning evinced qualified admiration for predecessors who were constrained by the gendered coding of women's writing.

3. The formula, e.g., transforms Peter Cooper (1791–1883) into a reincarnation of "Barzillai, of sacred history . . . a type of our American philanthropist" (O. E. Fuller, ed., *Brave Men and Women* [Ypsilanti, MI: J. C. Fuller, 1884], 351).

4. Antonia Fraser, *The Warrior Queens* (New York: Knopf, 1989), 10–11.

5. Jesse Clement's apology is standard: "Although something like two hundred [out of 480] of these pages are in our own language, we deserve but little credit for originality, and would prefer to be regarded as an unpretending compiler" (v–vi)—an interesting corrective to the view that it was Victorian women, rather than men, who modestly veiled their appearances in print.

6. Charles Miner, *History of Wyoming* (Philadelphia: J. Crissy, 1845).

7. Lydia Huntley Sigourney (1791–1865) was herself the author of *Examples from the Eighteenth and Nineteenth Centuries*,[718] which includes seven women out of seventeen lives, and of *Great and Good Women*.[720] Among the notices of her in collections is "The Lesson of a Useful and Beautiful Life," in *Brave Men and Women*, ed. Fuller (483–89).

Elizabeth Starling, in 1835, insisted that woman may add to her domestic obligations "the sublime virtue of patriotism": "In extraordinary times, as are those in which we live, her integrity, fortitude, courage, and presence of mind, may be frequently called forth" (iii–iv). In contrast, Sigourney, in 1851, seems to be reining in abolitionists and Seneca Falls feminists: woman's "patriotism is, to labor in the sanctuary of the home, . . . to form and train a race that shall bless their country" (xx–xxi).

8. Gall & Inglis issued *Gems of Womanhood* with a frontispiece of the scene in which Mme de Staël asks Napoleon, "Whom do you think the greatest woman, dead or alive?" His reply: "Her, madam, who has born the most sons" (147).[589] Thanks to Lillian Nayder, I own a copy of a later nearly exact reprint, with the simplified subtitle *Of Various Ages and Nations*; the identical preface with the original 1870 date deleted; the frontispiece moved to de Staël's biography; and Elizabeth Fry's moved into its place (the "4 Coloured Steel Engravings" remain the same, though uncolored in my copy). This reprint boasts the sort of colored and decorated cloth cover that is common for British children's books by the 1890s—inexplicably, there is a scene with a castle and fortress town beside a mountain lake, a rowboat in the foreground. Is it a reference to travels in the European picturesque? To the "romantic chateau . . . of Coppet, overlooking Lake Leman," de Staël's residence in exile (152), or the Duchess of Gordon's Castle in the Highlands (164–65)? Its spine bears the seal "The Lorne Series." On the inside front cover, a printed plate has been pasted: "Mount Zion Pleasant / Sunday Afternoon Class, / Wolverhampton. / Half Yearly Prize / Received by / Mr. John Lane [holograph] / For Regular Attendance. / Price Lewis, President. / W. H. Chambers, Hon. Sec. / April, 1894." (The plate has been numbered by hand 621.) The floral decorations of the plate include a small boy in boots and jacket waving his cap overhead. Evidently, gems of womanhood were intended to reward a boy for good behavior in Sunday school.

9. Samuel Mossman (unwittingly?) places European women's contribution to "the advancement of civilisation" in a context of colonial diamond industries with their slave or near-slave labor conditions. Indian diamonds had been coveted for ages; Brazilian supplies had slowed by the mid-nineteenth century, but there was a rush after 1870–71 in South Africa and the Congo, soon exploited by the monopoly of De Beers (cofounded by Cecil Rhodes). Pure white women would thus be the high-priced product of racist imperialism, yet the metaphorical gems are said to serve "suffering humanity" (313).[589]

10. Mossman has in mind *Queens of Society* [797] and quotes it at length regarding Montague (182).[589]

11. Bloomsbury shared a fascination with beauty, wit, and social standing as commodities. Thus, Lytton Strachey's *Biographical Essays* displays Mme du Deffand and Mary Berry, hostesses of the old regimes. This posthumously constructed multibiography compiles pieces first published in such journals as the *Nation and Athenaeum* between 1904 and 1931. It includes female subjects familiar in Victorian collections: Lady Mary Wortley Montagu, Mlle de Lespinasse, Lady Hester Stanhope, Mme de Lieven, and Sarah Bernhardt. Virginia Woolf's Mrs. Dalloway is a sort of descendant of Elizabeth Montague with a hint of the Duchess of Gordon. Lady Bruton, the backroom politician, stands in for centuries of Duchesses of Gordon; Richard Dalloway intends to write a history of Lady Bruton's family. This pattern in *Mrs. Dalloway* adds a layer of reference to women's history for the common reader. *Three Guineas* acknowledges: "If we . . . run over the memoirs of a century and a half we can hardly deny that there have been women who have influenced politics. The famous Duchess of Devonshire, Lady Palmerston, Lady Melbourne, Madame de Lieven, Lady Holland, Lady Ashburton" (13).

12. LEL's "Stanzas on the Death of Mrs. Hemans" (1835) is an instance. Angela Leighton and Margaret Reynolds, eds., *Victorian Women Poets: An Anthology* (Oxford: Blackwell, 1995), in their introductions and headnotes, trace a network of mutual reference among nineteenth-century British women poets (xxv–xl; on Hemans, 1–3).

13. Guyon offers instruction in self-chastening that seems to be repeated in the story of Esther Summerson in *Bleak House*: an extraordinary beauty as a young wife and mother, she was horribly disfigured by smallpox and expressed great relief to be freed of the body's burden. As a wealthy widow, she espoused Christ and traveled on a mission that was characterized as a heretical Protestantism of sanctification through faith. Crowds of workers and women flocked to hear her preach. She was repeatedly imprisoned but was also befriended by Mme de Maintenon (wife of the king), Mme de Miramion, the Duchesse de Chevreuse, and other eminent Frenchwomen and men. Mary Dyer, in addition to Askew and Guyon, is a religious martyr, a New England Quaker executed in 1638.

14. Most accounts of Mme Roland in the collective biographies emphasize her purity, her sage counsel to her husband, and her courage in prison, eliding any affairs. Sainte-Beuve, in his 1845

collection translated in 1868,[697] portrays his French subjects in the light of modern historiography (the theme is very much the development of a true France), with excerpts from their own writings and from letters, and narration of the events in which they participated. He disputes some of Mme Roland's judgments but asks, "Could she herself, had she been a man, have become the good genius of patriotism, the savior of the land?" (111). Sainte-Beuve calls attention to a "romance" with Bancal and a grand passion with an unknown man (116–18); he suggests that Mme de Staël regarded Mme Roland as a rival in political stature (119).

15. Grace Darling's narrative arises in at least fifteen collections, including Starling,[751] Yonge,[925] Mossman,[589] and Hale.[362] Ida Lewis Wilson is called America's Grace Darling in O. E. Fuller's *Brave Men and Women* (Ypsilanti, MI: J. C. Fuller, 1884), 447.

16. Starling catalogs many martyrs. Immediately after narrating the last words of Mme Roland, under the heading "Fortitude"—"Oh, Liberty! how many crimes are committed in thy name!"—Starling inserts a sort of memorial to the unknown martyrs: the "innumerable instances of fortitude displayed by the female martyrs" include "revolting . . . details of unparalleled cruelty and superstition" that should be suppressed. The repetition would have no benefit "in the present enlightened state of society," in which persecutions won't recur (289).[751]

17. Mrs. Richmond names Plutarch's *Lives* in Mme Roland's and Charlotte Corday's reading lists (2:110, 142).[673] Chantal Thomas ("Heroism in the Feminine: The Examples of Charlotte Corday and Madame Roland," in *The French Revolution, 1789–1989*, ed. Sandy Petrey [Lubbock: Texas Tech University Press, 1989], 67–82) observes that both Corday and Roland avidly read Plutarch for models of "republican fervor" and virile heroism (70–71). Hannah More also relished Plutarch.

18. These accounts vary enough to suggest diverse sources that ultimately derive from Plutarch's *Moralia*. I will use the past tense in the following composites of the past tense versions and avoid the clutter of page references. Historical facts seem to have been of no concern for presenters or readers. Eponina or Empona is absent from Boccaccio (1361–75), de Pizan (1405), and Chaucer (1372–86) as well as from most dictionaries of the classics, but she appears in Plutarch's twenty-fifth "Dialogue on Love." Her renown in modern Europe appears to derive from several Italian theatrical and musical productions: Giuseppe Bartoli wrote a tragedy, *Epponina*, performed in Turin in 1767. In 1781, Giuseppe Sarti presented an opera, *Giulio Sabino* (i.e., on Julius Sabinus, Eponina's husband), performed in German as well in 1791; it had its debut in London (English and Italian libretto) in 1788. Sarti also produced *Epponina: ein Shauspiel*, in Berlin in 1803. Angelo Tarchi's opera *Giulio Sabino* opened in Turin in 1790. Jean Delisle de Sales (1741–1816) wrote *Éponine, ou de la République* (1791; reprint, Paris: Diffusion les Belles Lettres, 1990), not a retelling of this legend but a dramatic disquisition on the constitution—perhaps a source for the character's name in *Les Misérables*. Child notes that the story "furnished a subject to many tragic poets"; "a painting representing the interview with Vespasian, received a prize from the National Institute of France" (288).[170]

19. A list of the examples of such rescuers suggests the frequency of this kind of tale, as in 1850–70 general collections: Lady Russell (14), Lucy Hutchinson (13), Ann Hasseltine Judson (8), Margaret Roper (7), Lady Fanshawe (5), Flora MacDonald (5), Mme Lavalette (5), Jane or Jeanne Montfort (4), Gertrude van der Wart (4), Lady Ackland (3), Mlle Desmoulins (2), Marie de Reigesberg (Mrs. Grotius; 2), Mme de Lafayette (2), Jane Lane (2; rescuer of Charles II), Lady Nithsdale (2), Elizabeth of Siberia (1).

20. Grotius, born Huig de Groot (1583–1645), Dutch jurist and historian, married Maria van Reigersberch in 1608. He was an apologist for imperial free trade (on behalf of the Dutch East India Co.) and for the ancient independence and sovereignty of Holland. Prince Maurice of Nassau arrested him in 1618 to repress an independence movement; imprisoned for life in Loevestein Castle, "Grotius escaped in a book chest brought in by his wife and a servant and went to France" (*Encyclopedia of World Biography*, ed. Paula K. Byers, 2d ed., 17 vols. [Detroit: Gale Research, 1998]).

21. Child's entry continues well past the prison escape through the couple's sojourn in France and Mrs. Grotius's travels to pave the way for him to return to Holland (he became for a time the French ambassador for the itinerant Queen Christina of Sweden).

22. Political upheaval at "home" raises the possibility of sexual upheaval: "Civil war serves as emblem and catalyst of change in the social prescription of sexual roles" (Margaret R. Higgonet, "Civil Wars and Sexual Territories," in *Arms and the Woman,* ed. Helen M. Cooper, Adrienne Auslander Munich, and Susan Merrill Squier [Chapel Hill: University of North Carolina Press, 1989], 80–82).

23. Starling also conveys the tale of "The Devoted Loyalty of Mrs. Jane Lane" (413–25),[751] a much less common subject, extracted from *Tales of Female Heroism.*[591] Charles II, in flight in 1651 after his defeat in the battle of Worcester, was variously disguised as a servant and a farmer's son. Royalist families arranged for him to escort Jane Lane as she visited a friend near Bristol, from whence he hoped to take ship for France. In the Restoration, she was handsomely rewarded. In these tales, the descriptions linger on the cutting of the king's fashionable long hair, his rustic costume, and the royal hands stained with walnut juice (414),[170] as well as his comic errors in impersonating common people. Lane may have served the ultimate victor, but English history then defeated the profligate (French-Catholic-leaning) Stuarts.

24. Ellet's chap. 32, "Flora M'Donald," begins by quoting William Henry Foote's *Sketches of North Carolina* (New York: Carter, 1846): "Massachusetts has her Lady Arabella, Virginia her Pocahontas, North Carolina her Flora M'Donald" (379). Lady Arabella Johnson and her husband Isaac Johnson arrived at Salem in 1630. These founding parents survived less than a year in the new world (241–42).[170]

25. Mme de Lafayette, according to Child, like Lady Fanshawe and Mrs. Hutchinson, illustrates endurance associated with political upheaval: a tale of the French Revolution that included a hero of the American. Mme de Lafayette was in prison in Paris under Robbespierre, while General Lafayette was imprisoned by Austria. As soon as she was freed, she traveled to Vienna and sought her husband's release; instead, she was only allowed to join him, with her two daughters, in prison. Her health declined, but she refused to endure another separation from her husband. After Bonaparte negotiated their release, she never fully recovered and died in 1807. "All the world know that the venerable patriarch still survives, at La Grange, surrounded by affectionate children and grandchildren" (292).[170]

26. Jennifer S. Uglow, ed., *The International Dictionary of Women's Biography* (New York: Continuum, 1982), offers this and more of Margaret Roper: "Noted for her learning in Greek, Latin, philosophy, astronomy, mathematics and music. . . . She was a staunch defender and supporter of her father during his imprisonment in the Tower of London and was briefly imprisoned herself. After his execution she recovered his head, although this was forbidden by law, and it is buried in St Dunstan's Church, Canterbury."

27. Later editions, which add to the contents the queen, princess of Wales, and Princess Louisa, replace this frontispiece with an image of the princess of Wales, her baby on her back; the engraving of Margaret and father, both in dark robes, surrounded by helmeted soldiers and the populace, in style similar to the illustrations of George Eliot's *Romola,* is printed after the introduction.

28. See also Clayton's *Notable Women*[178] on Margaret Roper, "The Devoted Daughter," followed by a portrait of Lucy Hutchinson, "The Perfect Wife." The head of Sir Thomas plays a role here too: "In 1835, when the chancel of the church was being repaired, the Roper vault was opened, and several persons . . . saw the skull in its leaden box, which was shaped something like a bee-hive . . . , and which was placed in a square recess in the wall" (24). Clayton's frontispiece of "Florence Nightingale on her nocturnal rounds" finds a visual echo in an image of Elizabeth Fry's "Ministry of Love": an upright woman bearing lamp or book among prostrate sufferers. "Lucy Hutchinson aiding the wounded soldiers," in spite of seventeenth-century costume and a crowded composition, repeats the scene.

29. Judith, although not her counterparts Jael or Salome, appears with some frequency as a model in collections of women's biography from the period. On the resonant story of Jael's slaying of Sisera, no one has written more brilliantly than Mieke Bal (*Murder and Difference: Gender, Genre, and Scholarship on Sisera's Death,* trans. Matthew Gumpert [Bloomington: Indiana University Press, 1988]).

30. To view an image of this painting, see Carol Gerten-Jackson, "CGFA" (Carol Gerten's Fine Art—a Virtual Art Museum), http://cgfa.sunsite.dk/g/p-agentileschi2.htm.

31. This chain of associations is reinforced by Gentileschi herself in the gorgon's head on Judith's sword pommel and the image of David or Saint George on the brooch in the heroine's hair, in *Judith with Her Maidservant* (ca. 1613–14), in Palazzo Pitti, Florence (Mary D. Garrard, *Artemisia Gentileschi* [Princeton, NJ: Princeton University Press, 1989], 318–19); further citations to Garrard in the text.

32. Judith is ethereal or voluptuous, embodied virtue or the artist's mistress; Holofernes's features are brutish or those of the artist himself; the maid, sometimes absent, is often old or at times African or Asian.

33. Images of paintings by Gentileschi (1593–1652) are readily available on Web sites. *Judith with Her Maidservant,* 1613–14, Palazzo Pitti; *Judith and Her Maidservant with the Head of Holofernes,* ca. 1625, Institute of Arts, Detroit. See Tracy Marks, "Artemisia's Artistry," 1999, http://www.webwinds.com/artemisia/art.htm. Roland Barthes ("Two Women," in *Mot pour mot/Word for Word,* by Barthes, Eva Menzio, and Lea Lublin [Paris: Yvon Lambert, 1979]) calls it an "act of genius" to have "two women joined in the same undertaking" in the painting, though he is mistaken that Artemisia Gentileschi originated this. He notes that the women might be raping the general or "slaughtering a pig," preparing "viands" for a "dining couch" (11).

34. Agnes Merlet wrote and directed the film *Artemisia* (1998), inspired by Gentileschi's painting *Judith Beheading Holofernes* and by admiration for the artist as "a strong, passionate young woman, who defied society to become a recognized artist." "She refused to be a victim and we can recognize her as a true heroine" ("Director's Note," *"Artemisia,"* posted on the Miramax Web site in 1998).

35. Antonia Fraser retrieves the fact that Aethelflaed, Lady or Queen of the Mercians (ca. 870–918) was probably the subject of the Old English poem *Judith* (*Warrior Queens,* 154).

36. Thanks to Janna Henrichsen, who in correspondence "Re: Patriotic Murderesses" on VICTORIA@LISTSERV.INDIANA.EDU (VICTORIA-L) mailing list (June 10, 1998) referred me to J. R. Herbert's *Judith and Holofernes* of 1863 (Walker Art Gallery, Liverpool), a rare depiction of Judith before the deed.

37. John Ruskin, *Mornings in Florence* (New York, 1877), 53, quoted in Elizabeth Philpot, "Judith and Holofernes," in *Translating Religious Texts,* ed. David Jasper (New York: St. Martin's, 1993), 83.

38. To view an image of *Judith Returning to Bethulia,* see C. S. Straughan, "Images of Women in Western Art," Ithaca College, http://www.ithaca.edu/faculty/cstraughan/imagesofwomen/judith.htm.

39. For Botticelli's *Discovery of the Body of Holofernes,* see "Olga's Gallery," http://www.abcgallery.com/B/botticelli/botticelli3.html.

40. Virginia Morris, *Double Jeopardy: Women Who Kill in Victorian Fiction* (Lexington: University Press of Kentucky, 1990), 11–13, 24.

41. Thanks to Sheldon Goldfarb for pointing out (VICTORIA-L, June 9, 1998) that Thackeray's *Catherine* (1839) compares the real murderess Catherine Hayes to Judith through two references to Judith and Holofernes. In classic realist fiction in English, the other woman—Thackeray's Becky Sharp, Eliot's Mme Laure, Dickens's Mlle Hortense, e.g.—becomes an incarnation of Procne and Philomela, Clytemnestra, or Judith. In *Dombey and Son,* Phiz's illustration of a scene between Carker and Edith Dombey (she has fended him off with a knife) displays a shadowy painting of Judith about to slay the sleeping Holofernes. See Morris, *Double Jeopardy,* 61, reprinting the Phiz illustration without remarking the analogy to Judith (62–63).

42. This famous image encrusts a modern woman in an almost two-dimensional decorative screen of ancient symbolism; she is gazing in vampiric satisfaction, clutching a dark head at her hip. The painting emphasizes "Salome's" murderous, heated sexuality rather than patriotic resistance (Bram Dijkstra, *Idols of Perversity* [New York: Oxford University Press, 1986], 386–92; Philpot, "Judith and Holofernes," 94–95).

43. In the illustration in Owens, Judith stands like a caryatid or a baseball hero with a head in one hand, sword in the other, her timid maid peering over her shoulder. The presence of maid and head suggests a visual pun on maidenhead, in an English-speaking context.

44. Numerous operas and dramas featured Judith or Charlotte Corday. See François Ponsard's *Charlotte Corday: A Tragedy* (1850), published in French for "use in schools," with introduction and notes by Arthur R. Ropes, Pitt Press Series (Cambridge: Cambridge University Press, 1892). In act 2, Charlotte speaks: "La Bible décide / Qu'il est, dans certains cas, permis d'être homicide. / Chez tout autre, forfait, chez Judith c'est vertu. / —Fantôme de Judith, que me demandes-tu? / Pourquoi me montres-tu, d'une main, ton épée? / Pourquoi tiens-tu, de l'autre, une tête coupée?" Charlotte sees a vision of her predecessor: "The Bible determines that in some cases it is permissible to commit murder. What is a crime in all others, in Judith is a virtue. Phantom of Judith, what dost thou ask of me? Why dost thou show me your sword in one hand, why dost thou hold a severed head in the other?" (act 2, scene 2, lines 1053–58; my translation).

45. Thomas, "Heroism in the Feminine," 70–71.

46. Lamartine assessed in the Revolutionary heroine "that desperate state of mind, which is the suicide of happiness, not for the profit of glory or ambition, like Madame Roland, but for the profit of liberty and humanity like Judith" (quoted in Trowbridge, 260[812]).

47. Nancy Armstrong, "Captivity and Cultural Capital in the English Novel," *Novel* 31 (1998): 373–98, examines the influence of captivity narratives on subsequent English fiction (376). Susan Jeffords, in "Rape and the New World Order," *Cultural Critique* 19 (1991): 203–15, claims that the captivity narrative's interdependent triad of "villain, victim, protector" is a classic American scenario, visible today in film and international relations (207). Rajini Srikanth ("Ventriloquism in the Captivity Narrative," in *White Women in Racialized Spaces,* ed. Samina Najmi and Rajini Srikanth [Albany: State University of New York Press, 2002], 85–103) considers the captive as a "participant-observer" (88) adopting the position of the racially other to critique European American patriarchy (86–87). See Richard Slotkin, *Regeneration through Violence* (1973; reprint, New York: HarperPerennial, 1996).

48. Ann-Marie Weis, "The Murderous Mother and the Solicitous Father: Violence, Jacksonian Family Values, and Hannah Duston's Captivity," *American Studies International* 36 (1998): 46–65. Edward M. Griffin, "Women in Trouble: The Predicament of Captivity and the Narratives of Mary Rowlandson, Mary Jemison, and Hannah Dustan," in *Fur eine offene Literaturwissenschaft: Erkundungen und Eroprobungen am Beispiel US-amerikanischer Texte/Opening up Literary Criticism: Essays on American Prose and Poetry,* ed. Leo Truchlar (Salzburg: Neugebauer, 1986), 41–51, also notes Mather's praise, repeated in *Magnalia Christi Americana* (1702), and the subsequent versions of the tale by Thoreau and Hawthorne (44–47).

49. Weis, "The Murderous Mother," notes nine books from 1829 to 1837 featuring Duston's tale and, altogether, twenty-nine versions (46, 62n.1), but she mentions no collective biographies. June Namias (*White Captives* [Chapel Hill: University of North Carolina Press, 1993], cited in Srikanth, "Ventriloquism in the Captivity Narrative," 91) identifies phases in women's captivity narratives according to type: survivor (colonial era), Amazon (revolutionary period), and frail flower (westward expansion, 1820–70). I find that the earlier types survived in collective biographies published during westward expansion.

50. Weis, "The Murderous Mother," 46–48. Whittier omits the captive English boy and he demotes Mary Neff to a servant girl (Weis, 51–52) to heighten Hannah's bloodthirsty, inhuman powers. Hawthorne includes vivid empathy with the Native Americans and imaginary violent revenge on Hannah Duston (50–60).

51. Knapp's language imitates (without direct quotation) Whittier's in "The Mother's Revenge," as quoted in Weis, "The Murderous Mother," 51. Weis shows that illustrations and tales in the 1830s focus on the father rescuing the children, omitting Hannah Duston and the murderous scene (59); she had become a devouring child slayer, not the Judith of her people.

52. Weis, "The Murderous Mother," 56n.27.

53. According to Weis, Duston had a "violent family history": her father had been fined for beating her younger sister, who was years later hanged for infanticide or (what was equally a

capital offense in 1693) concealing the death of her illegitimate stillborn twins. Infanticide runs through every stage of the history ("The Murderous Mother," 48).

54. Griffin, "Women in Trouble," 47. "Mrs. Jordan's Captivity, Narrated by Herself" tells of being captured and forced to be the passive witness to the torture and burning alive of her family until, the captors having drunk themselves "stupid and senseless," she reflects, "with one of their tomahawks I might with ease have dispatched them all, but my only desire was to flee from them as quick as possible," on which escape she journeys homeward with the help of "an Indian of the Shawanese" (294–98).[305] Mrs. Jordan makes Mrs. Duston's heroism appear gratuitous. Clement's somewhat debunking entry on Duston includes a lengthy note mentioning other heroines of captivity narratives (a common practice in *Noble Deeds*[182]). Clement includes "The Captivity of Mrs. Rowlandson," 299–302.

55. Melvin J. Thorne, "Fainters and Fighters," *Midwest Quarterly* 23 (1982): 426–36.

56. Armstrong, "Captivity and Cultural Capital," 373–98.

57. The Mutiny created its own grudgingly admired warrior queen, the Rani of Jhansi. See Fraser, *Warrior Queens*, 272–96. Cicely Hamilton's *Pageant*[373] in 1910 includes the "Ranee."

58. Jenny Sharpe, *Allegories of Empire: The Figure of Woman in the Colonial Text* (Minneapolis: University of Minnesota Press, 1993), 71.

59. Jane Robinson, *Angels of Albion: Women of the Indian Mutiny* (London: Viking, 1996), 131–34. See illustration in Sharpe, *Allegories of Empire* (84), and Karen Chase and Michael Levenson, *The Spectacle of Intimacy* (Princeton, NJ: Princeton University Press, 2000), 198.

60. Robinson, *Angels of Albion*, 131–35.

61. See Kevin P. Phillips, *The Cousins' Wars* (New York: Basic, 1999); and Eliga H. Gould, "The American Revolution in Britain's Imperial Identity," in *Anglo-American Attitudes*, ed. Fred M. Leventhal and Roland Quinault (Aldershot: Ashgate, 2000), 23–37. National entities were formed through the designation of prisoners of war: deeming the American colonies part of Britain, the British had to treat colonist soldiers as rebel Englishmen; once they adopted the "customary rights of war" for citizens of "a foreign state," sovereign independence was anticipated (24, 29–31).

62. The story came into circulation in the *American Quarterly Review* in 1827, based on purported testimony of the heroine herself, though Darragh had died in 1789. Ellet's narrative (in the manner of historical fiction) cites the above article, "letters written at the time," and "many persons in Philadelphia, who heard it from their parents" (114–20).[260] See Elizabeth D. Leonard, *All the Daring of a Soldier* (New York: Norton, 1999), on Lydia Darragh, a founding mother (21–25).

63. Daniel A Cohen, ed., *The Female Marine and Related Works* (Amherst: University of Massachusetts Press, 1997), traces more than a hundred "Anglo-American Female Warrior ballads," some fictional, some like Deborah Sampson Gannett's historical (8–9).

64. Elizabeth Martin dressed as a soldier and intercepted British dispatches in South Carolina (combining Samson and Darragh); or, according to another account, she played the Mother of the Gracchi, declaring that she wished she had fifty instead of seven sons to devote to the Revolutionary cause (178–79),[182] while it was her daughters-in-law who dressed as soldiers to ambush British messengers (176–77).

65. See Charles Swain, "Maid of Saragossa" (*Poems* [Boston: Whittemore, Niles & Hall, 1857]). An upper-class warrior wife, Constance de Cezelli, a Frenchwoman, took command of Leucates in defense against the Spanish when her husband was thrown in prison in 1590; she appeared "upon the walls with a pike in her hand, encouraging the garrison by her example." The enemy tried to "intimidate her by threatening to put her husband to death," but she did not yield, even when they "strangled him." In reward, Henry the Fourth commissioned her as governor of the town, "which she held for twenty-seven years" (316–17).[751]

66. Harold, "the last of the native English kings" for only forty weeks, maintained "thoroughly English" ways against the eleventh-century French influence ("Harold, King of England," in Charles F. Horne, ed., *Great Men and Famous Women* [New York: Selmar Hess, 1894], 3: 54–56).

67. "Harold the Last Saxon King of England," in *Brave Men and Women*, ed. Fuller (347–50).

68. Images of the statue of Sister Dora recur, as in, e.g., Chappell[160] and Cochrane.[185]

Chapter Three

1. Ellen Martin Henrotin, wife of a Chicago banker and close friend of Bertha Palmer (the president of the Board of Lady Managers of the 1893 Columbian Exposition), appears in the comprehensive prosopography *The Congress of Women*:[245] her photograph and a brief biography (she was born in Maine and educated in Europe) accompany her article, "The Financial Independence of Women" (348–53). "Why in the nineteenth century, in this land of plenty . . . [woman] and her little children should be pushing into this struggle for existence . . . is a sociological question. . . . and the next question is, How to improve her economic and financial condition so that life may be made at least worth living" (348–49).

2. Charlotte Perkins Gilman, *Women and Economics: A Study of the Economic Relation between Men and Women as a Factor in Social Evolution*, ed. Carl N. Degler (New York: Harper & Row, 1966), 331–32, 268–69.

3. "'Discipline'" is a "type of power . . . a technology [that]. . . . may be taken over either by 'specialized' institutions (the penitentiaries or 'houses of correction' of the nineteenth century), or by institutions that use it as an essential instrument for a particular end (schools, hospitals), or by pre-existing authorities," such as the family, or by disciplinary organizations such as state bureaucracies or the military, or overarching disciplinary "apparatuses" such as the police (Michel Foucault, *Discipline and Punish*, trans. Alan Sheridan [New York: Vintage, 1979], 215–16). A graphic demonstration of overlapping discipline can be viewed today at the site of the old Gaol in Hobart, Tasmania. Old Trinity Church has become Penitentiary Chapel Historic Site, owned by the National Trust: a massive edifice that resembles a church on the outside indeed contains what was the chapel, with two separate interior slopes of pews, resembling bleachers, for convicts and settlers. Beneath the steeply inclined floors of the chapel, solitary confinement cells were stacked in rows of shrinking sizes, like cross-sections of aqueducts. The chapel was just one corner of a massive penal complex to shelter, feed, and retrain in various menial labors the men, women, and children dispatched to the colony, and those at worship above would be well aware of those in penance below. The building became the Tasmanian Supreme Court, and in addition to impressive Victorian chambers it housed the gallows (with small balcony for witnesses) used into the mid-twentieth century.

4. Household and social duties or wage labor may be mentioned but never serve as the warrant for inclusion. Adams and Foster's largely American catalog includes Elizabeth Fry; the founder of Mount Holyoke, Mary Lyon; Elizabeth Cady Stanton; Harriet Beecher Stowe; Florence Nightingale; Clara Barton; the founder of the first women's club so called, Julia Ward Howe; two temperance campaigners, Frances E. Willard and J. Ellen Foster; and Jane Addams, with a chronological outline and an index. These lives intersect. Nightingale was influenced by Elizabeth Fry (128)[207] and by Julia Ward's husband Samuel Howe, founder of schools for the blind. Dr. Howe, who taught the blind Laura Bridgman (made famous by Dickens's *American Notes*), certified Dorothea Dix's first campaign to improve treatment of the insane (72–73).[291] J. Ellen Foster (1840–1910), the least renowned subject, was a politician, lawyer, and temperance campaigner. Balfour's more Evangelical and now more obscure subjects are Mrs. Trimmer, Mrs. Hannah More, Mrs. Barbauld, Elizabeth Smith, Charlotte Elizabeth, Mrs. Sherman, Mrs. Mary Lundie Duncan, Sarah Martin, Mrs. Ann H. Judson, Hannah Kilham, and Charlotte Brontë.

5. On the emergence of the humanitarian narrative, see Thomas W. Laqueur, "Bodies, Details, and the Humanitarian Narrative," in *The New Cultural History*, ed. Lynn Hunt (Berkeley: University of California Press, 1989), 176–77, cited in Mike Sanders, "Manufacturing Accident: Industrialism and the Worker's Body in Early Victorian Fiction," *Victorian Literature and Culture* 28 (2000): 313–14.

Annemieke van Drenth and Francisca de Haan discuss Foucault's concept of "pastoral power" in *The Rise of Caring Power: Elizabeth Fry and Josephine Butler in Britain and the Netherlands* (Amsterdam: Amsterdam University Press, 1999), 14–16.

6. Kathleen D. McCarthy, ed., *Lady Bountiful Revisited: Women, Philanthropy, and Power* (New Brunswick, NJ: Rutgers University Press, 1990), 1–17, and *Women's Culture: American Philanthropy and Art, 1830–1930* (Chicago: University of Chicago Press, 1991), ix–8. Jesse Clement portrays "A Modern Dorcas," Mrs. Isabella Graham (1742–1814), Scottish immigrant

widow and philanthropist in New York City, who was the first director of the society "for the relief of poor widows" founded in 1797 (213–17).[182] Clement's next biography is that of Mrs. Sarah Hoffman, cofounder of the society (218–22).

7. Seth Koven and Sonya Michel, eds., *Mothers of a New World* (New York: Routledge, 1993), 10–11, 2. The contributors to *Mothers of a New World* offer substantial studies of the varied national contexts for these movements.

8. The Religious Tract Society was instituted in 1799. Balfour notes that Hannah More and her sister Martha contributed to the "new product of literature," invented to counteract "noxious principles . . . imported from France" (76–77).[52] Balfour dislikes More's Tory, High Church counsel of "quiet submission" in these tracts: "If such a contentment . . . had been characteristic of the sisters More, they would all have passed through life as humble women in the hamlet of Fishponds" (77–78).

On specific developments in education, see Mary Hilton and Pam Hirsch, eds., *Practical Visionaries: Women, Education and Social Progress, 1790–1930* (Harlow: Longman/Pearson, 2000); on Lancasterian method, 57–58; Jane Martin, *Women and the Politics of Schooling in Victorian and Edwardian England* (London: Leicester University Press, 1999); and Wayne J. Urban and Jennings L. Wagoner Jr., *American Education: A History* (Boston: McGraw Hill, 2000). Elisabeth Anthony Dexter's *Career Women of America, 1776–1840* (Boston: Houghton Mifflin, 1950; reprint, Clifton, NJ: Kelley, 1972) includes a chapter on women as teachers (1–28).

9. Catherine Marsh's work with men finds a counterpart in several less celebrated figures, such as "Sarah Robinson, the Soldier's Friend," featured alongside Nightingale, Fry, Martin, Sister Dora, Carpenter, Octavia Hill, and numerous women writers in Cochrane.[186]

10. Harriet Martineau, "Female Industry," *Edinburgh Review* (April 1859), reprinted in *Criminals, Idiots, Women, and Minors,* ed. Susan Hamilton (Peterborough: Broadview, 1995), 29–70, quote in text on 68.

11. For example, Lori D. Ginzberg, *Women and the Work of Benevolence: Morality, Politics, and Class in the Nineteenth-Century United States* (New Haven, CT: Yale University Press, 1990); Martha Vicinus, *Independent Women* (London: Virago, 1985); Hilton and Hirsch, eds., *Practical Visionaries.*

12. Perhaps because of a kind of G-rating, certain exemplars rarely appear, e.g., Josephine Butler (aid of prostitutes and the campaign against the Contagious Diseases Act) and Annie Besant (birth control, radicalism, theosophy).

13. Deborah Epstein Nord, *Walking the Victorian Streets* (Ithaca, NY: Cornell University Press, 1995), 207; further citations appear in the text.

14. Winifred Holtby, *Women* (Chicago: Cassandra/Academy, 1978), 44–46. A prosopography produced by the Australian women's movement[253] significantly cites Holtby on the rise of philanthropic reform during the nineteenth century, suggesting an international solidarity across the generations. The reference occurs in Eleanor Dark's biography of Caroline Chisholm (61).

15. Judith R. Walkowitz, *City of Dreadful Delight* (Chicago: University of Chicago Press, 1992), 56.

16. Mary Poovey, *Uneven Developments* (Chicago: University of Chicago Press, 1988); and Mary P. Ryan, *Women in Public* (Baltimore: Johns Hopkins University Press, 1990) were among the first influential feminist studies to complicate the model of the separate spheres. Nina Baym (*American Women Writers* [New Brunswick, NJ: Rutgers University Press, 1995]) similarly challenges "present-day preoccupations" that overstate the separation of spheres (4–6).

17. Martineau, "Female Industry," in *Criminals, Idiots, Women, and Minors,* ed. Hamilton, 69–70.

18. Griswold, quoted in Balfour (3).[52] Griswold echoes Sarah Hale in *Woman's Record*: "Within the last fifty years more books have been written by women and about women than all put forth in the preceding five thousand eight hundred years of the world" (vii).

19. Frances Power Cobbe, "What Shall We Do with Our Old Maids?" (1862), in *Criminals, Idiots, Women, and Minors,* ed. Hamilton, 258.

20. More's life compares with Elizabeth Fry's in several collections at midcentury.[174; 236; 465; 479; 923]

21. Deborah Cherry, "Shuttling and Soul Making: Tracing the Links between Algeria and Egalitarian Feminism in the 1850s," in *The Victorians and Race,* ed. Shearer West (Aldershot: Scolar, 1996), 157–58. See also Reina Lewis, "Women and Orientalism: Gendering the Racialized Gaze," in *Victorians and Race,* ed. West, 180–93.

22. "By imagining themselves as moral missionaries not only to their husbands and children, but to the 'ignorant' working classes and the 'benighted' natives of the empire, Victorian women could use, as Mary Poovey contends, the conservative rhetoric of a woman's domestic mission to underwrite their excursions into the public sphere" (Susan Zlotnick, "Jane Eyre, Anna Leonowens, and the White Woman's Burden: Governesses, Missionaries, and the Maternal Imperialists in Mid-Victorian Britain," *Victorians Institute Journal* 24 [1996]: 27–56).

23. Linda H. Peterson, *Traditions of Victorian Women's Autobiography* (Charlottesville: University Press of Virginia, 1999), 92–95.

24. Thayer applies Edmund Burke's eulogy of Howard to Dix: "He has visited all Europe, not to survey the sumptuousness of palaces . . . but to dive into the depths of dungeons; to plunge into the infection of hospitals . . . and to compare and collate the distresses of all men in all countries. . . . It was a voyage of discovery, a circumnavigation of charity" (83–84).[792] Compare: "Among all the most distinguished female benefactors of our country and of mankind, the pre-eminence must certainly be yielded to the late Mrs. Fry . . . 'THE FEMALE HOWARD!'" (296).[806]

25. Joseph Johnson (b. 1822) is author of *Living in Earnest, Living to Purpose,* and *Self-Effort* (in a series for men advertised by Nelson under the latter title). Johnson credits Lydia Sellon and other women who early discovered "female usefulness in ministering" (1, 253).[467] Johnson's frontispiece features Grace Darling and Charlotte Brontë, while his introductory chapter offers citational lists, one of which winds up: "Madame du Châtelet introduced the discoveries of Newton into France, and Mrs. Somerville the discoveries of Laplace into England; Hannah More taught morals to Europe and the world; while Grace Darling, by one act of womanly sympathy, earned for herself undying fame" (6).

26. The prosopography of New England activists, *Our Famous Women,*[758] quotes Margaret Fuller's famous challenge: "Nature . . . sends women into battle, . . . she enables the man . . . to nourish his infant. . . . Presently she will make a female Newton. . . . But if you ask me, what offices [women] may fill, I reply—any. . . . Let them be sea-captains, if you will" (134–35). Mary A. Livermore, the Bostonian orator, is said "to make feminine sympathy tell with masculine force," in the words of Elizabeth Stuart Phelps, herself also a subject in *Our Famous Women* (399).

27. Margaret Oliphant points to the heavy duties of all women below "duchesses" and "millionaires," from housekeeping and domestic manufacture to childcare to assisting in the family's business (including the church or school). The "mass of working women" gain nothing from ideals of feminine influence and get no "standing-ground" of their own for the work "which is 'never done'" ("The Grievances of Women," reprinted in *Criminals, Idiots, Women, and Minors,* ed. Hamilton, 235–36). Winifred Holtby, in *Women in a Changing Civilisation* (1935), understands the double shift for women in two-career couples: "While Carlyle was shutting himself up in his sound-proof room, and sacrificing his wife to his dyspeptic or creative agonies, Mrs. Gaskell was writing her novels at the end of a dining-room table, among a constant whirl of children, servants, draughts and callers" (104).

28. The ideal of married motherhood eluded a "surplus" of middle-class women as early as the 1830s in America and markedly in the 1851 census in Britain. Elizabeth K. Helsinger, Robin Lauterbach Sheets, and William Veeder, eds., *The Woman Question,* 3 vols. (Manchester: Manchester University Press, 1983), 2:134–35. Martha Vicinus thoroughly mapped the changes for the single Victorian woman. The number of positions for middle-class educated workers (teachers, clerks, civil servants, etc.) doubled between 1861 and 1911, and the share of these occupied by women increased to 16.4 percent (*Independent Women,* 5).

29. Cobbe, "What Shall We Do with Our Old Maids?" in *Criminals, Idiots, Women, and Minors,* ed. Hamilton, 92–94.

30. Christopher Keep, "The Cultural Work of the Type-Writer Girl," *Victorian Studies* 40 (1997): 403–7.

Sally Mitchell describes the delayed expansion of paid white-collar work for women and the shift in the expectations for most middle-class women: "Girl's Culture: At Work," in *The Girl's Own*, ed. Claudia Nelson and Lynne Vallone (Athens: University of Georgia Press, 1994), 243–58, esp. 243. Further substantiation of the changing expectations for women's work by the end of the nineteenth century appears in Patricia Marks, *Bicycles, Bangs, and Bloomers* (Lexington: University Press of Kentucky, 1990), 55–89.

31. Stephanie J. Shaw, *What a Woman Ought to Be and to Do: Black Professional Women during the Jim Crow Era* (Chicago: University of Chicago Press, 1996), 136–39. Just as employment history for women below the middle class differs from the narrative of progress suggested in the prosopographies of women published during the period, the story alters greatly among women of color. Jacqueline Jones, *Labor of Love, Labor of Sorrow: Black Women, Work, and the Family from Slavery to the Present* (New York: Basic, 1985), 6–8.

32. Key events in both countries changed the context: the founding of Oberlin College (coeducational) in 1833 and Mount Holyoke Seminary in 1837 and, in Britain, the Governesses' Benevolent Institution (1841), Queens College (1848), Bedford College (1849), and after long campaigns, the establishment of women's colleges at Cambridge University by 1870; the Womens' Rights Convention in Seneca Falls in 1848, and the petition for female suffrage during the passage of the Second Reform Bill in Parliament in 1867 (Helsinger et al., *The Woman Question*, 2:40–41); the American Paulina Wright Davis's international feminist journal *Una* (1853; Bonnie S. Anderson, *Joyous Greetings: The First International Women's Movement* [Oxford: Oxford University, 2000], 192–95), and Anna Jameson's published lectures, *Sisters of Charity* and *The Communion of Labour* in 1855, which helped to encourage a bolder generation, including Barbara Leigh Smith Bodichon, who published *Women and Work* in 1856, and who with Bessie Rayner Parkes and others in the "Langham Place" group launched the Society for Promoting the Employment of Women, the *English Woman's Journal* in 1858, and Emily Faithfull's Victoria Press in 1860. See Anderson (196–206) on these and other efforts in publishing and reform campaigns.

33. According to Robin Gilmour, young men recruited "to run the Empire" relinquished the "traditional connection between gentility and idleness" (*The Idea of the Gentleman in the Victorian Novel* [London: Allen & Unwin, 1981], 98). The rise of professions for men assimilated competition with "the 'service ideal' . . . of preindustrial aristocracy" and the "candor and probity of the traditional middle class" (John Kucich, *The Power of Lies* [Ithaca, NY: Cornell University Press, 1994], 164).

34. Louise Michele Newman, *White Women's Rights* (New York: Oxford University Press, 1999), 26–28. Frances B. Cogan in 1989 helped to complicate the model of the antebellum "Cult of True Womanhood" gender ideology; contemporary modeling in all genres of writing also encouraged robust and practical "Real Womanhood" (*All-American Girl* [Athens: University of Georgia Press, 1989], 1–21).

35. Carla Peterson, *Doers of the Word* (New York: Oxford University Press, 1995), 3–23.

36. Male professionalization often rose up in resistance to female encroachments, as did white middle-class credentialing organizations against black (Shaw, *What a Woman Ought to Be*, 135–37, 213). The late-Victorian social-working women "often enjoyed less prestige among middle-class male philanthropists than among the working people" (Walkowitz, *City of Dreadful Delight*, 59, 54, 65). It is common to focus on the expansion of women's opportunities in the early twentieth century, e.g., with the passage of the Sex Disqualification Removal Act in Britain in 1919. But there is no linear progress in the history of women's work, as in the later twentieth century the range of occupations returns to the gender integration found in Europe in the late middle ages and early modern times. See Sheila Lewenhak, *Women and Work* (New York: St. Martin's, 1980), 105–15; Elise Boulding, *The Underside of History* (Newbury Park, CA: Sage, 1992), 2:67–79.

37. See June Rose, *Elizabeth Fry* (New York: St. Martin's, 1980), 82–83; further citations of this biography appear in the text. Scenes of Fry reading to convicts, emigrants, and sailors provide the frontispieces and narratives in at least two collections.[589; 692] A psychological study by Jonathan

Haidt measures the physical response to examples of caring power, the emotion of "elevation" that leads people "to do good deeds or become better people" (Eric Swensen, "Award-winning U Va Professor Seeks to Elevate Psychology," *Daily Progress* [Charlottesville, VA], June 4, 2001, B1–2).

38. Fry shares a number of volumes with Nightingale alone[173; 178; 467; 615; 776] and with Nightingale in combination with others: with Barton,[4; 419] with Sister Dora,[185] and with Barton and Sister Dora both.[207] In another volume,[373] Fry joins the high-heroic company of Corday, MacDonald, Darling, Nightingale, and the Maid of Saragossa.

39. Charles F. Dole, *Noble Womanhood* (Boston: Caldwell, [1909]), 35. Dole also lists Lucretia Mott and Harriet Beecher Stowe.

40. The French American Stephen Grellet, a Quaker, brought Fry to visit Newgate, having been disturbed to see the drunken mobs outside the prison the night before hangings, as well as the terrible conditions in the women's prison. Fry, with Anna Buxton, visited the women's yard for the first time in 1813, bringing donations of baby clothes. Four years later, Fry developed a plan to institute a school and a work program for the women of Newgate, whose conditions had physically improved since her first visits (Rose, 84–87). Repeated consultations with authorities brought reluctant permission to attempt the scheme; within a few weeks, the Lord Mayor, sheriffs, and aldermen visited to observe the effects: "This 'hell on earth' where only a few months ago abandoned and shameless women affronted their eyes now appeared more like 'a well-regulated family'" (Rose, 89). In the brief Victorian biographies, the transformation becomes a loaves-and-fishes multiplication of one lady's reading a Bible aloud into many "good" readers.

41. Amusingly, Hale does find a flaw in Fry as a writer ("it was not her mission to write books" [318]); the vast majority of modern women in *Woman's Record* practice writing among their accomplishments.

42. Joseph Gurney wrote a memoir of his sister's campaigns in which he praised this branch of her work (quoted on 295–96).[806] Since 1818, "a sub-committee of ladies for visiting the convict-ships" had provided "about *ten thousand* female convicts" with a Bible and material for needlework sufficient to occupy a voyage of four months (306).[806]

43. The term is Mary Louise Pratt's (*Imperial Eyes* [New York: Routledge, 1992]). The oil painting by Jerry Barrett (1824–1906), *Elizabeth Fry Reading to the Prisoners in Newgate in the Year 1816* (ca. 1860), engraved by T. Oldham Barlow, appears in Rose's biography. As engraved by Henrietta Mary Ada Ward (1832–1924), it appears in Creighton (93),[207] with a detail, by another hand, in Ewart (113).[270]

44. Mrs. Gibbons worked for many causes: "Education of women, . . . the amelioration of punishments, the establishment of ragged schools, the relief of the sufferers of Kansas, Hungarian liberty, and the victims of Austrian despotism . . . sixty years of self-sacrificing labor in scenes and among people offending every instinct of taste or morals" (Lucia Gilbert Runkle, 336).[758] The family has a penchant for confronting violent masses: during the Draft Riots the mob attacks their house (Mrs. Gibbons and her daughter are absent working in the Union hospitals).

45. According to Sarah Martin's own account, she visited a woman sentenced "for having cruelly beaten her child" (*A Brief Sketch of the Life of the Late Sarah Martin, of Great Yarmouth* [London: Religious Tract Society, n.d.], 14); further citations of *Life of Sarah Martin* appear parenthetically in the text. This drab little tract intermixes letters, reports, journals, sermons, and biography with Martin's autobiography. (My copy—"A New Edition, with Additions"—is signed "Hannah Bowler, Alton Manor Farm, Wirksworth," without date.) Autobiographer and biographer fuse; e.g., "I went with [T. B.] to the shop, chose, and paid for [the trousers]" concludes one paragraph, and the next begins without typographical distinction, "The unwearied zeal of Miss Martin in collecting her subscriptions is remarkable" (132).

46. Christine L. Krueger, *The Reader's Repentance* (Chicago: University of Chicago Press, 1992), examines the sources of *Adam Bede* in popular Methodism and the ministry of Eliot's aunt, as well as actual cases of infanticide. Fry's journal associates the beginning of her Newgate project with her repeated visits to "a poor creature who murdered her baby," whose execution disturbed her deeply (Rose, 81). See Christine L. Krueger, "Literary Defenses and Medical Prosecutions: Representing Infanticide in Nineteenth-Century Britain," *Victorian Studies* 40 (1997): 271–94.

47. Martin appears in twenty unspecialized collections before 1901; she shares some volumes with both More (whose Pop Chart [table A2] total is twenty-six) and Fry (total thirty-six).[178; 236; 924]

48. Martin appears in 1861 with Fry and Nightingale,[615] in 1868 with Anne Hasseltine Judson,[816] and through the 1880s in general collections alongside Fry, Sister Dora, Mary Carpenter, and Caroline Chisholm[270] or with Fry and Catherine Marsh.[5]

49. Marsh appears three times each in the 1850–70 and 1880–1900 samples, joined by Fry, Nightingale, and More,[467] by Fry and Martin,[14] and by Nightingale.[24]

50. She formed the Family Colonisation Loan Society serving those who could provide "certificates of good character" and "persistent thrift and industry" (Dark, 79).[253] In her home and in lodgings that she arranged, friendless young women received instruction in "the principles of self-supporting emigration," what to bring, to expect, to hope for (instruction included the display of a model of a berth on board [80]).[253] By the time the gold rush made any recruitment of emigrants superfluous, her model of ship conditions had become the standard.

51. Elizabeth Gaskell, *North and South* (New York: Oxford University Press, 1998), 220. Later, as an independent woman in London, Margaret briefly takes up work among the poor, which suggests she has studied at the school of Fry and Carpenter (416–17).

52. The seven general collections of 1880–1900 and two in 1910–30 that feature Mary Carpenter are exclusively British prosopographies; her cohort is Fry, Nightingale, Martin, and Sister Dora[185; 282] or Chisholm instead of Nightingale in that lineup.[270] Though Dix was well known in her day, her renown appears to have remained largely North American and moderate (four volumes in the 1880–1900 and one in the 1910–30 samples); the general collections that include her are all published in the United States. They link her to Ann Hasseltine Judson[97; 182] or to Clara Barton and Elizabeth Fry[419; 792] among various model American women.
The quoted passage is from Dix's first memorial to the Massachusetts State Legislature, quoted in Francis Tiffany, *Life of Dorothea Lynde Dix* (1890; reprint, Boston: Houghton Mifflin, 1918), 76.

53. J. Estlin Carpenter published *The Life and Work of Mary Carpenter* in 1879 (2d ed. [London: Macmillan, 1881; reprint, Montclair, NJ: Patterson Smith, 1974]), reproducing correspondence and journals by the subject. I focus on the narratives in Ewart[270] and Smith,[731] with reference to Cochrane.[185] Both Ewart and Cochrane head their lists with Queen Victoria and include several models of social work.

54. Ruth Watts, *Gender, Power, and the Unitarians in England, 1760–1860* (London: Longman, 1998), 48–49.

55. Frances Power Cobbe, "Personal Recollections of Mary Carpenter," quoted in J. E. Carpenter, *Mary Carpenter* (1974), 199. Cobbe "went to reside with Miss Carpenter in the Red Lodge House, to be company for her in her home and a help to her in her Reformatory and Ragged School work," according to Jeanie Cochrane in her life of Cobbe (201).[185] Cobbe, who would be described as a lesbian today, shared Carpenter's sense of being authorized to take on many humane causes.[185, p. 202; 731, pp. 287, 298, 301] Eventually, Carpenter's strict regimen, driven activity, and incomprehension of common human foibles (as opposed to "actual *vice*") may have impaired Cobbe's health and certainly led to her departure in 1859 (Cobbe, quoted in J. E. Carpenter, *Mary Carpenter*, 201, 209).

56. Rosamond Davenport Hill was elected in 1879 to the London School Board as a Progressive member (Jane Martin, *Women and the Politics of Schooling in Victorian and Edwardian England* [London: Leicester University Press, 1999], 84–85).

57. On Carpenter's promotion of women's suffrage, see Ruth Watts, *Gender, Power*, 49.

58. Ibid., 49.

59. In Ewart's collection,[270] Princess Alice is the second subject, after Victoria, and before otherwise middle-class examples.

60. Tiffany, *Life of Dorothea Lynde Dix*, iii; further references appear parenthetically in the text. Later as Dix traveled alone in remote regions of the United States, she was up at dawn and rarely slept more than a few hours, "conducting these campaigns" in person and in writing (114, 126).

61. Gladys Brooks, *Three Wise Virgins* (New York: Dutton, 1957), 16; the subjects are Dix, Elizabeth Palmer Peabody, and Catharine Maria Sedgwick. Further references appear in the text. Dix, friend of the Channings, visited England in 1836–37, staying with wealthy Unitarians in Liverpool. Reforming circles were in steady communication; William Ellery Channing regularly corresponded with Dr. Carpenter, and leaders of the Boston Ministry to the Poor who visited the Carpenters in 1833 and 1838 greatly infuenced Carpenter's plans (E. J. Carpenter, *Mary Carpenter*, 34–39), but I find no record of an encounter between Carpenter and Dix. The continuing reputation of Fry or the rising reputation of Martin might have supplemented the written model of Hannah More through this trip.

62. Benson J. Lossing, *Pictorial Field Book of the Civil War,* quoted in Bolton (265).[97]

63. Mary A. Livermore's "representative" life (appearing three times in the 1880–1900 and two times in the 1910–30 samples) overlaps with those of Dix, Barton, and numerous other "army women" (Phelps, 386, 395);[758] Bolton features Livermore in her biography of Dix (263–64).[97] Descended from Welsh preachers, Livermore became one of the top-paid lecturers in the United States (Phelps, 411),[758] campaigning for suffrage and temperance. The wife of a Unitarian minister in Boston, mother of three, newspaper editor, during the Civil War she combined "home, commissary, and hospital service," running the Northwestern branch of the U.S. Sanitary Commission (397).[758] Dix consulted Dr. Howe after her first prison visit (245–46),[97] thus linking her to another subject, Julia Ward Howe.[758]

64. Joan Jacobs Brumberg, *Mission for Life* (New York: Free Press/Macmillan, 1980), reproduces this image. I am indebted to Brumberg's biography of the family, which also serves as a history of American evangelical missions. Further citations appear in the text.

Anglo American readers knowing nothing of Burmese botany or etymology could accept the emblematic construction of the hopia tree as "the tree of hope."

65. To these many collections[5; 37; 170; 249; 376; 386; 492; 643] could be added others mentioned here.

66. Peterson, *Traditions of Victorian Women's Autobiography,* 92–108; further citations of this study appear in the text. James D. Knowles published *Memoir of Mrs. Ann Judson* as early as 1829. Emily Chubbuck Judson's biography of Sarah Boardman Judson (d. 1845) appeared in 1848, but the narratives of the first two wives circulated broadly at the time of the publication of *Jane Eyre,* as in John Dowling, *The Judson Offering,* a "commemorative volume" including elegiac poetry, published in 1846 (Brumberg, *Mission for Life,* 16–17).

67. *Jane Eyre,* ed. Richard J. Dunn, Norton Critical Edition, 2d ed. (New York: Norton, 1987), 356.

68. Mary Ellis Gibson draws a connection between *Jane Eyre* and the early-nineteenth-century missionary biographies of Henry Martyn, in which the "Victorian evangelicalism [that] legitimated Victorian imperialism" produces narratives that unite "violence and romance" as well as "domestic morality" ("Henry Martyn and England's Christian Empire: Rereading *Jane Eyre* through Missionary Biography," *Victorian Literature and Culture* 27 [1999]: 421). Gibson cites many critics who regard Martyn as a model for St. John Rivers (433), particularly in his renunciation of the woman he loved, Lydia Grenfell, and his early "martyrdom" (death from disease [424]). Like Patrick Brontë, Martyn was a provincial who matriculated at Saint John's, Cambridge, under Wesleyan evangelical auspices (422).

69. Resisting all this, Jane "chooses woman's mission at home," "rehabilitating the colonizer," Rochester, as Peterson observes, borrowing Deirdre David's terms (*Women's Autobiography,* 96–97). On the interaction of women's domestic and foreign missions, and the lines of work available to middle-class women, see Zlotnick, "Jane Eyre, Anna Leonowens, and the White Woman's Burden," 27–56.

70. The Pop Chart (app. table A2) finds Ann H. Judson eight times in 1850–70 and six times in 1880–1900, including twice with Sarah Judson and once with Emily. Hale's 1853 notice of Ann Judson reappears in condensed form in Adams's 1857 *Cyclopaedia,* with acknowledgment (423–24),[5] but Adams in 1869 can also include Emily C. Judson (424–25) and Sarah B. Judson (425),[5] in alphabetical order. *Girlhood of Celebrated Women,*[37] in part another sampler of Hale, portrays only the second wife: "The Teacher in the Wilds: Sarah Boardman Judson" (106–38)

concentrates on *Mrs. Boardman,* in details and substance showing no derivation from Hale or Adams.

71. See Brumberg, *Mission for Life,* 130–31. Brumberg cites Asahel Clark Kendrick, *The Life and Letters of Mrs. Emily C. Judson* (New York, 1861), as the source for passages that I find to be identical in Clark, *Portraits of Celebrated Women.*[173] The latter acknowledges various sources for its chapters but not Kendrick for Emily Judson.

72. Goodrich[331] was retitled and repackaged as late as 1891 with the addition of Cleopatra. The illustrations tend to be identical with those in Clark.[173]

73. The age of the daguerrotype affords less latitude for romance, as another of Clark's portraits suggests: Mrs. Ann Wilkins, whose long missionary career in Africa began in 1837 (in the era of the second Mrs. Judson). Wilkins resembles one of my own staunch-jawed Mormon ancestors who went West instead of East for reasons of religious zeal in the middle decades of the nineteenth century. Like Clark, Balfour's *Working Women*[52] also skips the second wife, including Ann Judson—and Charlotte Brontë—and the widowed Emily who "survives to be a true mother to [Mr. Judson's] children" (328).

74. Rajini Srikanth ("Ventriloquence in the Captivity Narrative," in *White Women in Racialized Spaces,* ed. Samina Najmi and Rajini Srikanth [Albany: State University of New York Press, 2002]) examines an 1833 collection, *Sketches of the Lives of Distinguished Females,*[26] with its frontispieces: a portrait of Ann Judson and an illustration, "Burning of a Widow in India." Without noting that this anonymous collection was later attributed to Judson herself, Srikanth detects the link between the white woman's mission and the "exotic" and "sensational" display of female vicitimization, but Srikanth doesn't spell out the element of captivity narrative in the Judson narrative (90–91).

75. Gilman, *Women and Economics,* 331–32, 268–69. American Nationalists, British Fabians, Olive Schreiner's *Woman and Labour* (1911), and the writings of George Bernard Shaw, among other groups and texts, encouraged the association of marriage with prostitution, with the corollary that decency was linked to self-support. Notwithstanding the ridicule of old maids, there had long been a place of honor in biographical collections for the unmarried woman who earned a living and supported an extended family.

76. Emily James Putnam, *The Lady* (New York: Sturgis & Walton, 1910), xiii–xix. Especially in later chapters, this historical review of "The Greek Lady," "The Lady of the Castle," "The Lady of the Salon," "The Lady of the Slave States," etc., consists of biographical notices, with portraits, supporting an argument about class and gender prejudice.

77. Such was the advice of Mrs. George Curnock, *A Girl in Her Teens, and What She Ought to Know* (London: Cassell, 1907), 110, quoted in Sally Mitchell, "Girl's Culture," in *The Girl's Own,* ed. Nelson and Vallone, 243.

78. In the afterword, Mary Van Kleeck, head of the Women's Bureau in the U.S. Department of Labor during World War I, urges "you" to "eliminate the *either or*" of marriage or career (306). The range of occupations is remarkable: director of nurses in a city hospital, librarian, secretary to the chairman of the board in a banking firm, gardening expert, head of the department of sciences in a high school, hotel dietitian, judge in a New York state court, photographer, physics professor, sculptor, director of a cultural center, and concert musician, among others. Only Ethel Barrymore and Peggy Hoyt, among those portrayed in *Girls Who Did,* were famous then or now; Inez Haynes Irwin, the only writer in the group, went on to publish *Angels and Amazons,*[443] a prosopography of women's occupations that acknowledges "Negroes," working classes, trade unions, and other matters beyond the purview of *Girls Who Did.*

79. Keep, "The Cultural Work of the Type-Writer Girl," 407–9. A 1929 self-help book addressed to fashion magazine readers offers advice on pleasure-seeking self-grooming and on work: "Woman has come into her own! One finds her clacking away at a typewriter or sitting with the board of directors; managing a restaurant, tearoom, or bookshop; in the newspaper and advertising office" (Daré [Daré Frances Stanley Serrano], *Lovely Ladies* [New York: Doubleday, 1929], 500). Daré cites Olive Schreiner (334–41). "Marriage is a profession" (342) and "a partnership" (347); a woman should expect to work before marriage and after motherhood.

80. Aimée Buchanan's *The Lady Means Business: How to Reach the Top in the Business World—the Career Woman's Own Machiavelli* (New York: Simon & Schuster, 1942), ix. Sections carry titles such as "Discrimination against Women . . . The Real Reason: Businessman's Phobia, or Fear of Matriarchy," "Remember That the Boss Is Chiefly Interested in Himself" (290), and "Avoid Being Exploited" (288), with extensive appendixes on pay discrimination and job sources. A businesswoman needs to manage her "personality" but this is no synonym for "charm." "There will be no discussion here of the values of blonde or brunette hair, a good figure, the correct mannerisms" (250–51).

Chapter Four

1. *Characteristics of Women*[450] includes the introductory dialogue that I cite in the text (ix–xl). Otherwise, parenthetical citations will be to Dutton's *Shakespeare's Heroines* (1901?), one of many later editions that omit the dialogue.

2. Maria Agnesi (1718–99) was an Italian mathematician, a professor at the University of Bologna, and a hospital administrator. Besides "Mrs. Marcet," the other names are widely circulated in Victorian biographies.

3. Until Judith Johnston's *Anna Jameson: Victorian, Feminist, Woman of Letters* (Aldershot: Scolar, 1997), the only full-length biography was Clara Thomas's *Love and Work Enough: The Life of Anna Jameson* (Toronto: University of Toronto Press, 1967). Attention to Jameson has increased in recent Victorian studies, e.g., Tricia Lootens, *Lost Saints: Silence, Gender, and Victorian Literary Canonization* (Charlottesville: University Press of Virginia, 1996); Anne E. Russell, "'History and Real Life': Anna Jameson, *Shakespeare's Heroines*, and Victorian Women," *Victorian Review* 17 (1991): 35–49; Alison Booth, "The Lessons of the Medusa: Anna Jameson and Collective Biographies of Women," *Victorian Studies* 42 (1999–2000): 257–88, on which this chapter is based; Kimberly VanEsveld Adams, *Our Lady of Victorian Feminism* (Athens: Ohio University Press, 2001), and others cited below. Michele Martinez, "Reinventing the Art of Romance: Anna Jameson's *Visits and Sketches*," British Women Writers Conference, University of Georgia, March 27, 2004.

4. Jameson deftly handled her separation from her husband and her social connections. Lady Byron, Ottilie von Goethe, Fanny Kemble, Elizabeth Barrett Browning, and Catharine Sedgwick were her friends; the first three were embroiled in scandals of divorce or unwed motherhood. Thackeray and others helped place her on Her Majesty's Pension List in 1851. Gerardine Macpherson, *Memoirs of the Life of Anna Jameson* (Boston: Roberts, 1878), 190–91, 265–67, 275–77; Johnston, *Anna Jameson*, 2–8.

5. See Lootens, *Lost Saints,* on saints as models for Victorian literary careers (3–9); on Jameson's contribution to "Saint Shakespeare" and his heroines, see her chap. 3.

6. Thomas, *Love and Work Enough,* 165–66.

7. *Sacred and Legendary Art* was too capacious for quick reference, and imitators provided more compact guides, e.g. Waters,[845; 846] Tabor,[780] and Estelle M. Hurll, *The Madonna in Art* (1897; Boston: L. C. Page, 1901).

8. Ellen Moers, *Literary Women* (1977; reprint, New York: Oxford University Press, 1985), 122–26, 187–88, 294–95; further citations appear in the text.

9. On Jameson and the woman question, see Bina Friewald, "'Femininely Speaking': Anna Jameson's *Winter Studies and Summer Rambles in Canada*," in *A Mazing Space: Writing Canadian Women Writing*, ed. Shirley Neuman and Smaro Kamboureli (Edmonton: Longspoon, 1986), 61–73; Dorothy Mermin, *Godiva's Ride: Women of Letters in England, 1830–1880* (Bloomington: Indiana University Press, 1993), 97.

10. Macpherson, *Memoirs;* further citations appear parenthetically in the text.

11. Anna Jameson, *Commonplace Book,* 104–31;[449] Thomas, *Love and Work Enough,* 3–11.

12. On this dialogue, see Marlon B. Ross, *The Contours of Masculine Desire* (New York: Oxford University Press, 1989), 260–66.

13. See Johnston, *Anna Jameson,* 79–81.

14. When Medon blames "the thirty years' war" on the Helen of Heidelberg, Elizabeth of Bohemia, Alda defends Elizabeth as a creature of her education and circumstances. "For how many ages will you men exclaim against the mischiefs and miseries caused by the influence of women; ... yet taking no thought how to make that influence a means of good" (65–66).

15. Anna Jameson, *Winter Studies and Summer Rambles in Canada,* afterword by Clara Thomas (Toronto: McClelland and Stewart, 1990), 102–3; parenthetical citations to this edition follow. See Johnston on the conjunction of German-English "translation" with Canadian cross-cultural encounters in *Winter Studies* (*Anna Jameson,* 127–46). Jameson writes of biography as a difficult art that captures only some facets of character as "viewed through the mind of another" (*Winter Studies,* 104).

16. Helen M. Buss, *Mapping Our Selves: Canadian Women's Autobiography in English* (Montreal: McGill-Queen's University Press, 1993), 97–98.

17. Thomas M. F. Gerry, "'I Am Translated': Anna Jameson's Sketches and *Winter Studies and Summer Rambles in Canada,*" *Journal of Canadian Studies* 25 (1990–91): 34–49.

18. Jameson's handiness as an illustrator adds to the authority and the attraction of the volumes. In the preface, she writes, "The little sketches and woodcuts are trifling as illustrations, and can only assist the memory and the fancy. ... Those who take an interest ... can easily illustrate the book for themselves." She imagines a sort of hypertextual portfolio of these images and "the hundreds of others ... not cited," arranged by subject rather than "schools, or styles, or dates," as a means to higher contemplation (ix).[456] The preface to the 3d ed. (1857) notes that the copper etchings "have been newly etched on steel" and "twelve new woodcuts have been introduced" (n.p.). Macpherson accompanied her during the Italian sojourn shared with the newly wed Brownings: "I was my aunt's assistant in her important work, ... to trace, to draw, to note" (*Memoirs,* 230–34).

19. Mermin, *Godiva's Ride,* 95; on Anna Jameson, xiii–v, 97–100, and elsewhere.

20. Hugh Witemeyer, *George Eliot and the Visual Arts* (New Haven, CT: Yale University Press, 1979), 18. Ruskin exploited team advantage against Jameson, as when he recalls discussions of art between men, with Jameson tagging along: she "was absolutely without knowledge or instinct of painting (and had no sharpness of insight ...)," but she strove to be agreeable (*Praeterita, the Works of John Ruskin,* ed. E. T. Cook and Alexander Wedderburn, 39 vols. [New York: Longmans, Green, 1902–12], 35:373–74, quoted in Thomas, *Love and Work Enough,* 214). David A. Ludley cites Ruskin's comparison of Jameson to his father's servant and traces Jameson's influence ("Anna Jameson and D. G. Rossetti: His Use of Her Histories," *Woman's Art Journal* 12 [1991–92]: 29–33). On Ruskin's use of Shakespeare's heroines, see Nina Auerbach, *Woman and the Demon* (Cambridge, MA: Harvard University Press, 1982), 209–13. On Hawthorne's and Henry James's mixed responses to Jameson, see Thomas, *Love and Work Enough,* 176, 213, 218; and Randall Stewart, *Nathaniel Hawthorne: A Biography* (New Haven, CT: Yale University Press, 1948), 197.

21. Rita Felski, *The Gender of Modernity* (Cambridge, MA: Harvard University Press, 1995), 63–64, 80–81.

22. For more on narrative study of Shakespeare's characters, see Christy Desmet, "'Intercepting the Dew-Drop': Female Readers and Readings in Anna Jameson's Shakespeare Criticism," in *Women's Re-Visions of Shakespeare,* ed. Marianne Novy (Urbana: University of Illinois Press, 1990), 41–57; Brian Vickers, "The Emergence of Character Criticism, 1774–1800," *Shakespeare Survey,* vol. 34, ed. Stanley Wells (Cambridge: Cambridge University Press, 1981), 11–21.

23. Mrs. Steuart Erskine, *Anna Jameson: Letters and Friendships (1812–60)* (New York: Dutton, 1916), 9–11.

24. Among studies of Shakespeare's female characters by women, I find a rare reference to Jameson, in Irene G. Dash, *Wooing, Wedding, and Power* (New York: Columbia University Press, 1981), 135. L. C. Knights deplores "that kind of interest in Shakespeare that is represented at certain levels by Mrs. Jameson's *Shakespeare's Heroines* and Mary Cowden Clarke's *Girlhood of Shakespeare's Heroines*" ("How Many Children Had Lady Macbeth?" in *Modern Shakespearean Criticism,* ed. Alvin B. Kernan [New York: Harcourt Brace Jovanovich, 1970], 45–76). A. C. Bradley, whom Knights attacks, has the temerity to cite Jameson three times (*Shakespearean*

Tragedy [Greenwich, CT: Fawcett, n.d.], 139, 171, 314). See Desmet, "Intercepting the Dew-Drop." On Jameson's role in art history, see Ludley, "Anna Jameson and D. G. Rossetti," 29; and Clara Thomas, "Anna Jameson: Art Historian and Critic," *Woman's Art Journal* 1 (spring/summer 1980): 20–22, as well as Adele M. Holcomb, "Anna Jameson on Women Artists," *Woman's Art Journal* 8 (1987–88): 15–24.

25. Margaret Atwood, introduction to *Roughing It in the Bush,* by Susanna Moodie (London: Virago, 1986), vii–xiv. Friewald, "Femininely Speaking." Lisa Vargo, "An 'Enlargement of *Home*': Anna Jameson and the Representation of Nationalism," *Victorian Review* 24 (1998): 53–68, traces Jameson's critical redefinition of nation through domesticity in *Winter Studies,* in the manner of Wollstonecraft's 1796 volume, *Short Residence in Sweden, Norway, and Denmark* (56). Jameson signed the "Petition for the Married Women's Property Act" in 1856 and sponsored the Langham Place group, with their Society for the Promotion of Employment for Women, as well as Bessie Parkes and Barbara Leigh Smith's *English Woman's Journal*; see Carol Bauer and Lawrence Ritt, *Free and Ennobled: Source Readings in the Development of Victorian Feminism* (Oxford: Pergamon, 1979), 172–74; Thomas, *Love and Work Enough,* 209–10; Candida Ann Lacey, *Barbara Leigh Smith Bodichon and the Langham Place Group* (New York: Routledge & Kegan Paul, 1987), 1–14; and my *Greatness Engendered* (Ithaca, NY: Cornell University Press, 1992), 30, 36–38, 155.

26. Elaine Showalter's "Representing Ophelia" (in *Shakespeare and the Question of Theory,* ed. Patricia Parker and Geoffrey Hartman [New York: Methuen, 1985], 77–94) makes no mention of Jameson but discusses Clarke's *The Girlhood of Shakespeare's Heroines,* because "unlike other Victorian moralizing and didactic studies of the female characters of Shakespeare's plays, Clarke's was specifically addressed to the wrongs of women" (87). Jameson's was precisely so addressed.

27. Evidence of Jameson's gynocriticism can be seen in the way she posits separate female traditions: "You must change the physical organization of the race of women before we produce a Rubens or a Michael Angelo. Then, on the other hand, I fancy, no *man* could paint like Louisa Sharpe, any more than write like Mrs. Hemans" (364–65).[458] Painting or writing like a woman can be policed by women, as in her censure of Artemisia Gentileschi (11),[450] noted in chap. 2 above. See Holcomb, "Anna Jameson on Women Artists."

28. On the figures of cyborg and Medusa, see Donna Haraway, "A Manifesto for Cyborgs," reprinted in *Feminisms/Postmodernisms,* ed. Linda J. Nicholson (New York: Routledge, 1990), 190–233; Hélène Cixous, "The Laugh of the Medusa," trans. Keith Cohen and Paula Cohen, reprinted in *Feminisms,* ed. Robyn R. Warhol and Diane Price Herndl, rev. ed. (New Brunswick, NJ: Rutgers University Press, 1997), 347–62. See Jay Clayton, "Concealed Circuits: Frankenstein's Monster, Replicants, and Cyborgs" (*Charles Dickens in Cyberspace* [Oxford: Oxford University Press, 2003]), including discussion of Cixous's Medusa (124–45).

29. Engels was not the first to associate sexual and class hierarchy with private property, of course, nor were Carlyle and Ruskin the only influential Victorians to invoke medieval culture as antidote to industrial capitalism. A true "sister of charity" worked "for love" rather than "for money," according to Jameson (Lacey, *Barbara Leigh Smith,* 62).

30. As Patricia Meyer Spacks writes in *Gossip* (Chicago: University of Chicago Press, 1986), "biography can involve . . . delight in the *process* of finding out," similar to gossip (100); biography, like gossip, establishes "common experience" among narrator, audience, and subject(s) (118–19).

31. Susan Hamilton's collection *Criminals, Idiots, Women, and Minors* (Peterborough: Broadview, 1995) is appropriate here; indirectly repeating the form of Victorian collective biographies, Hamilton reprints works by Jameson, Martineau, and Oliphant, Frances Power Cobbe, Eliza Lynn Linton, Helen Taylor, Millicent Garrett Fawcett, and Mona Caird, each with a biographical note. Andrea Broomfield and Sally Mitchell produced a similar anthology, *Prose by Victorian Women* (New York: Garland, 1996), with a longer list of writers that overlaps with Hamilton's, essays on diverse subjects, and greater emphasis on biography and career.

32. Leslie Monkman, "Primitivism and a Parasol: Anna Jameson's Indians," *Essays in Canadian Writing* 29 (1984): 85–95; Mermin, *Godiva's Ride,* 96–97, 99–100; Buss, *Mapping Our Selves,* 86–102; Lorraine M. York, "'Sublime Desolation': European Art and Jameson's Perceptions of Canada," *Mosaic* 19 (1986): 43–56.

33. Alison Booth, "From Miranda to Prospero: The Works of Fanny Kemble," *Victorian Studies* 38 (winter 1995): 227–54.

34. Fuller, *Summer on the Lakes, in 1843,* reprinted in *The Essential Margaret Fuller,* ed. Jeffrey Steele (New Brunswick, NJ: Rutgers University Press, 1992), 88, and *Woman in the Nineteenth Century* (1844), reprinted in *Essential Margaret Fuller,* ed. Steele. Page references to these works appear parenthetically in the text.

35. I am indebted for some of these mutual reflections to Adams's *Our Lady of Victorian Feminism.* She notes that Jameson resisted the younger woman's request for information for a work on Goethe and that her fleeting references to Fuller show signs of criticism for her excesses of style (17–19). Jameson seems to respond to Fuller's *Woman in the Nineteenth Century* in her *Legends of the Madonna* (57).[451]

36. *Harriet Martineau's Autobiography,* with memorials by Maria Weston Chapman, 3 vols. (London: Smith, Elder, 1877), 1:380–84, 517; further parenthetical citations to this edition in the text.

37. Harriet Martineau, *Biographical Sketches* (New York: Leypoldt & Holt, 1869). Parenthetical page references to this edition appear in the text.

38. Because Fuller eschewed the self-effacing persona of Jameson's prefaces while continuing her Romantic vein of impassioned and impressionistic cultural criticism, she was easy to ridicule; Martineau, with her ear trumpet, her atheism, and her mesmerism, could certainly be satirized as well. The design of Fuller's life could also be compared to that of Mary Wollstonecraft. Nevertheless, Fuller and Martineau made it into numerous collections (see below), whereas to my knowledge Wollstonecraft appears in only three lists in my bibliography, after 1830.[195; 264; 554]

39. Macpherson could also have been motivated to write "a true and genuine account" of her misrepresented aunt (ix–x) by Martineau's obituary notice, examined above.

40. *The Autobiography of Margaret Oliphant,* ed. and intro. Elisabeth Jay (Oxford: Oxford University Press, 1990), 8–10.

41. R. H. Horne, ed., *A New Spirit of the Age* (New York: Harper & Brothers, 1845), 236. Horne's contributor anticipates a long career for Jameson and an early death for Martineau—known to be ill, before mesmerism; yet Martineau was the survivor.

42. Margaret Oliphant, *The Victorian Age of English Literature,* 2 vols. (New York: Tait, 1892). Citations appear parenthetically in the text.

43. See table A2 on their appearance in nonspecialized collections: Fuller, 16; Martineau, 13. Both appear in Abbot;[1] Bolton includes them in her "famous books"[97; 98] (Martineau and Fuller, respectively). Martineau also appears in Darton.[220] *Daughters of Genius* [624] asks: "As reformers and world-improvers, what men have surpassed the single-eyed and courageous devotion of such women as Miss Martineau?" (3). Martineau was the updated "bluestocking," as when she joins Hannah More, e.g., in Fawcett.[282]

44. Marianne Novy, introduction to *Women's Re-Visions of Shakespeare,* ed. Novy, 1–15; Lootens, *Lost Saints,* 77–115.

45. Jerome McGann has pointed out to me the resemblance of these categories to Wordsworth's divisions of his collected poems from 1815 on. Another precedent might be Joanna Baillie's plays on the passions. See Lootens, *Lost Saints,* 95–104.

46. Leota S. Driver, *Fanny Kemble* (1933; reprint, New York: Negro University Press, 1969), 31, 42.

47. Luce Irigaray, *This Sex Which Is Not One,* trans. Catherine Porter with Carolyn Burke (Ithaca, NY: Cornell University Press, 1985), 109–10, 192–97.

48. Teresa de Lauretis, *Alice Doesn't* (Bloomington: Indiana University Press, 1984), 44, 113.

49. Slavoj Žižek, *The Sublime Object of Ideology* (London: Verso, 1989), 113–16.

50. Julia Kristeva, "Stabat Mater," in *The Kristeva Reader,* ed. Toril Moi (New York: Columbia University Press, 1986), 177, and "Motherhood according to Giovanni Bellini," in *Desire in Language: A Semiotic Approach to Literature and Art,* ed. Leon S. Roudiez, trans. Thomas Gora, Alice Jardine, and Leon S. Roudiez (New York: Columbia University Press, 1980), 240.

51. Anna Jameson, *Visits and Sketches* (1834), reissued as *Sketches of Art* (349–50).[458] Freud's Dora shares Jameson's fascination with the Madonna (*Sistine*, not *San Sisto*). Hélène Cixous and Catherine Clément, *The Newly-Born Woman,* trans. Besty Wing (Minneapolis: University of Minnesota Press, 1986), 154–55. A scene in Jameson's *Sketches* anticipates the opening of *Daniel Deronda:* in a gambling hall at Spa, a young baroness on the verge of damnation, surrounded by skeletal hags—"often, since that time, her face has risen upon my day and night dreams like a horrid supernatural mask," says Alda (38–41).

52. Judith Johnston elicits the contemporary associations Jameson found in the character of Mary Magdalene. Jameson's readers were much intrigued by this mysterious allusion at the end of volume 1 (Johnston, *Anna Jameson,* 197–99).

53. Cixous and Clément, *The Newly-Born Woman,* 3–57.

54. Cixous, "The Laugh of the Medusa," 355, 352; further citations appear in the text.

55. Toril Moi, *Sexual/Textual Politics* (London: Methuen, 1985), 108–16.

56. See Johnston, *Anna Jameson,* 51–54.

Chapter Five

1. On women as the ahistorical sex, Elizabeth Ellet,[259; 260] e.g., laments that "political history says but little" of women; in their secluded sphere, they seldom take part in "sufficient incident" to highlight their character (v–vii). Nevertheless, Ellet insists that the story of the American Revolution cannot be told without the women: "Patriotic mothers nursed the infancy of freedom" (10). Ellet appears along with Lydia Maria Child and others in an early feminist recovery by Susan Avery Phinney Conrad, *Perish the Thought* (Secaucus, NJ: Citadel, 1978), 116–22. On Ellet, see Nina Baym, *American Women Writers and the Work of History, 1790–1860* (New Brunswick, NJ: Rutgers University Press, 1995), 233–39.

2. Pollard's addresses to the Baptist Ministers of Philadelphia were published as *The Rights of the Unborn Race* (Philadelphia: American Baptist Publishing Society, 1914), and *Women, Home and Government* (New York: National Woman Suffrage Publishing Co., [1915]).

3. Samina Najmi and Rajini Srikanth, introduction to *White Women in Racialized Spaces,* ed. Samina Najmi and Rajini Srikanth (Albany: State University of New York Press, 2002), 1–26.

4. Linda Colley, *Britons: Forging the Nation, 1703–1837* (New Haven, CT: Yale University Press, 1992).

5. Louise Michele Newman, *White Women's Rights* (New York: Oxford University Press, 1999), 29, 52.

6. Gayatri Spivak, "Three Women's Texts," reprinted in *Feminisms,* ed. Robyn R. Warhol and Diane Price Herndl, rev. ed. (New Brunswick, NJ: Rutgers University Press, 1997), 901. For extensions of Spivak's challenge to feminist readings of *Jane Eyre,* see Jenny Sharpe, *Allegories of Empire: The Figure of Woman in the Colonial Text* (Minneapolis: University of Minnesota Press, 1993), 27–55; and Deirdre David, *Women, Empire, and Victorian Writing* (Ithaca, NY: Cornell University Press, 1995), 77–117.

7. Sarah Mills, "Knowledge, Gender, and Empire," in *Writing Women and Space,* ed. Alison Blunt and Gillian Rose (New York: Guilford, 1994), 37–39. In *Discourses of Difference* (London: Routledge, 1991), Mills offers an astute historical study of gendered conventions of travel writing as a genre.

8. Stephen Heathorn quotes Alice Ravenhill of the Yorkshire County Council, who wrote in favor of "domestic science" as a subject for girls in 1903: "Good homes are the basis of the highest and most fruitful civilization; to secure them for the British Empire depends on her women, her schools, and her educational zeal" (Ravenhill, "Hygiene and Household Economics in Education," quoted in Heathorn, *For Home, Country, and Race* [Toronto: University of Toronto Press, 2000], 169–70).

9. Malini Johar Schueller, *U.S. Orientalisms* (Ann Arbor: University of Michigan Press, 1998), 1–21.

10. Reginald Horsman, *Race and Manifest Destiny* (Cambridge, MA: Harvard University Press, 1981), 62–70, 114–15, 189–90. See the introduction by Shearer West, ed., *The Victorians and Race* (Aldershot: Scolar, 1996), 1–11; and Douglas A. Lorimer, "Race, Science and Culture," in *The Victorians and Race*, ed. West, 12–33, on the views of Thomas Arnold and Robert Knox: "Anglo-Saxon racism and . . . advocacy of the rights of persons of colour were not necessarily contradictory" at the time (17).

11. Douglas A. Lorimer, "Race, Science and Culture," in *The Victorians and Race*, ed. West, 15–17, 20–21.

12. Priscilla Wald, "Terms of Assimilation," in *Cultures of United States Imperialism*, ed. Amy Kaplan and Donald Pease (Durham, NC: Duke University Press, 1993), 59–63. As Wald puts it in *Constituting Americans* (Durham, NC: Duke University Press, 1995), "belief in the nation as a coherent entity, posits the collective subject, the 'we' whose self-consciousness in turn confirms the nation" (196).

13. Anne McClintock, *Imperial Leather* (New York: Routledge, 1995), 9. McClintock's work is key to the understanding of race, gender, and class as mutually constitutive, as "articulated categories" (7), in the context of imperialism.

14. William Cooper, in an 1875 lecture to a Working Men's Institute in Leighton Buzzard, suggests that the ancient East was more progressive than contemporary Asia or the Middle East. Contrary to earlier views, "the records of ancient history not only afford us many examples of illustrious empresses, sole and regnant, but they also show that in certain flourishing states the royal succession ran in a female line . . . for many centuries" (9).[198] "Think of woman as she is in our own happy, virtuous, and queen-governed England, and not as she now exists as a mere instrument of sensation, a living article of furniture" in India, Egypt, or Turkey (10).

15. Samuel Griswold Goodrich, in *Lives of Celebrated Women*,[332] contributed to the mythology of the United States in his sentimental tale (based on biographies by Catherine Sedgwick and Washington Irving) of Lucretia and Margaret Davidson, sister poets homegrown in Vermont, whose "angelic purity and beauty of soul" and precocious genius inevitably brought early death (9–48). National pride early relied on a collection of women writers.

16. Sarah Hale edited *Godey's Lady's Book* from 1837–77; it had 150,000 subscribers by 1861. Isabelle Lehuu, "Sentimental Figures: Reading *Godey's Lady's Book* in Antebellum America," in *The Culture of Sentiment*, ed. Shirley Samuels (New York: Oxford University Press, 1992), 73–91, argues that the sentimental mode of the illustrated magazine had "transformative force . . . [as] a public event" (74).

17. On the narrative of racial progress, see Susan Zlotnick, "Jane Eyre, Anna Leonowens, and the White Woman's Burden," *Victorians Institute Journal* 24 (1996): 27–56; Lori D. Ginzberg, *Women and the Work of Benevolence* (New Haven, CT: Yale University Press, 1990).

18. Nina Baym, in "Onward Christian Women: Sarah J. Hale's History of the World," *New England Quarterly* 63 (1990): 249–70, notes that Hale's collection includes less than a handful of women of color and no Asians but that it achieved a "polyvocality" through excerpts of many women's texts (251–52).

19. *Godey's Lady's Book* warmly received Ellet's *Women of the American Revolution* for preserving woman's influence at the heart of history (Scott E. Casper, "An Uneasy Marriage of Sentiment and Scholarship: Elizabeth F. Ellet and the Domestic Origins of American Women's History," *Journal of Women's History* 4 [1992]: 21).

20. Baym, "Onward Christian Women," 260–61.

21. Ernest Freeberg, *The Education of Laura Bridgman* (Cambridge, MA: Harvard University Press, 2001); Elisabeth Gitter, *The Imprisoned Guest: Samuel Howe and Laura Bridgman, the Original Deaf-Blind Girl* (New York: Farrar, Straus & Giroux, 2001).

22. "As author of this work" she "may hope that her name will not be considered out of place" (686–87);[362] the transcription of a notice from "the Lady's Book" is followed by a first-person account "respecting the influences which have, probably, caused me to become the Chronicler of my own sex." Discovery of a book by a woman (*The Mysteries of Udolpho*) aroused her desire to "promote the reputation of my own sex, and do something for my own country" (686–87). See

Nicole Tonkovich, *Domesticity with a Difference* (Jackson: University Press of Mississippi, 1997), on Hale (26–35) and on her successive autobiographical records (32–33).

23. Among many women writers, Hale honors Joanna Baillie (with excerpts from her play *De Montfort* [which produces the subject Jane de Montfort for later biographies], 575)[362] and Frederika Bremer. Hale praises Agnes Strickland, "Whose graceful pen has made the dead queens of England objects of deep interest to the living world" (798); see chap. 7.

24. The frontispiece of *Heroines*[570] reveals a Native American running toward our left, a baby and a rifle in his arms, at the cabin behind him a European woman screaming, her arms thrown wide as though shielding her husband, who stands behind her in the doorway with his hatchet. This image and the caption, "The Indian darted from the cottage," based on a single phrase in a story in the collection, "An Ontario Romance," suggests the perils of the contact zone, but the story, of Scots pioneers in the 1810s, rather demonstrates native resourcefulness, expertise, and good will: the man borrows the baby in a last-ditch effort to get the settlers to follow him to a much better location for their farm (this man had previously saved Mrs. M'Dougal's life when she lost her way in the forest).

25. *A Girl's Battle* by Lillias Campbell Davidson, in the Girls' Imperial Library series, cost two shillings and six pence, as did W. M. Graydon's *Lost in the Slave Land*, one of the many Red Mountain books (Partridge's catalog, 4–5, in Michael).[570] Evidently, girls read boys' adventure stories, which outnumbered the girls' books; books soliciting male as well as female readers tended to be more explicitly located in geography and history.

26. *Clever Girls of Our Time Who Became Famous Women* (1862) recommends cleverness (3),[466] but Anna Jameson, three decades earlier, had detected a demeaning and deceptive quality in the term (*Winter Studies*, 13).

27. Horsman, *Race and Manifest Destiny*, 5.

28. The books themselves bear no volume numbers, but cataloging identifies an order resembling relative levels of civilization in the project's view: Greek, Roman, early Christian, "Oriental" women; women of medieval France, of "Romance" countries, and modern France; "Teutonic," English, and American women. Women even of modern France or Germany remain "behind." In 1907–8, no comparable commercial venture in universal male prosopography would have been attempted: "Man: In All Ages and in All Countries" would never have been so conveniently short of evidence in so many regions and eras or so readily associated with the primitive.

29. G.C.L. echoes the usual view: "The typical woman, as she is seen in the pages of history, is either very good or very bad" (1:vii).[899]

30. The volumes do strive for recognition of distinct cultures that "each lead a rounded existence" (4:343). They can be inclusive. "Women of America" refers to Central and South American women as well as "aboriginal" or Native Americans. *Women of England* includes a chapter on "The Women of Scotland and Ireland," no separate recognition of Wales. Bartlett Burleigh James's preface—after a voluptuous frontispiece of Lady Godiva—celebrates "the influence of woman upon . . . that race which has come to be known as English . . . at the apex of modern civilization, whose women, clasping hands throughout the British Empire, form a splendid chain of hope for womankind" (9:vii).

31. See McClintock, *Imperial Leather*, 1–4, 232–57, on Henry Rider Haggard.

32. R. C. Christie, "Biographical Dictionaries," *Quarterly Review* 157, no. 313 (January 1884): 187–230, reprinted in *Victorian Biography*, ed. Ira Bruce Nadel (New York: Garland, 1986), n.p. (Christie, 188). Christie reproves the *Biographie Universelle*'s surplus of minor French generals and politicians and the solecisms in its entries on English subjects (218–19). James L. Clifford, ed., *Biography as an Art* (New York: Oxford University Press, 1962), places Stanfield's 1813 book as the first full-length study of biography in English (xiv).

33. Waldo H. Dunn, *English Biography* (London: Dent, 1916), 249–50. Dunn's chapter "A Comparative View" seems much indebted to Christie's 1884 article (cited above), but Dunn's sole reference states that Christie's "suggestive article" is "marred by many errors of fact" (245n.1).

34. Ibid., 247–48.

35. Christie, in "Biographical Dictionaries," recognizes various biographical dictionaries of the early and late nineteenth century but regrets that most include only "men of eminence." Christie does not mean to plead for inclusion of women, or even to correct class bias, but to register historical agents who are not famous (203–4).

36. Gillian Fenwick, *Women and the Dictionary of National Biography* (Aldershot: Scolar, 1994); further references to Fenwick appear parenthetically. See Ira Bruce Nadel, *Biography* (New York: St. Martin's, 1984), 47–51.

37. Of "28,201 subjects, 998 . . . were separate articles on women" (Fenwick, 6).

38. The tasks of "collecting, collating, . . . digesting and editing" could be cast as feminine yet at the same time as professional contributions to the nation (Trev Lynn Broughton, *Men of Letters, Writing Lives* [London: Routledge, 1999], 34–36).

39. The international interdependence of these omnivorous dictionaries is illustrated by the fact that some contributors to *Appleton's Cyclopedia* invented subjects and biographies for them by mixing ingredients from French and other European collections (John Blythe Dobson, "The Spurious Articles in *Appleton's Cyclopedia of American Biography*," *Biography* 16, no. 4 [1993]: 387–408).

40. Only in supplement four of the *Dictionary of American Biography* was there as many as 5.1 percent women among the subjects; Edward T. James, one of the editors of the supplements to the *DAB*, issued a separate dictionary, *Notable American Women*, 3 vols. (Cambridge, MA: Harvard University Press, Belknap Press, 1971), noted in Donald C. Yelton, *Brief American Lives* (Metuchen, NJ: Scarecrow, 1978), 51–55. The struggle with categories is illustrated by a series of "living" biography, forerunner of *Who's Who. The Men of the Time* (Clinton Hall, NY: Redfield, 1852), also published in London in 1852, appeared in a revised edition in 1856 (ed. Alaric Alexander Watts), with an addition of one hundred "Women of the Time"; the 3d ed. (ed. Watts, 1859) announced on the title page "Also biographical sketches of celebrated Women of the Time"; the 10th ed. (ed. Thompson Cooper, 1879) was entitled *Men of the Time: A Dictionary of Contemporaries containing Biographical Notices of Eminent Characters of Both Sexes* and continued to be published in London and New York under that title and with various editors until Victor Plarr edited the 13th ed. in 1891: *Men and Women of the Time: A Dictionary of Contemporaries.* I am grateful to Michael Wolff for informative correspondence about these editions.

41. Cora Sutton Castle, *A Statistical Study of Eminent Women*, vol. 27 of *Archives of Psychology*, ed. R. S. Woodworth, Columbia Contributions to Philosophy and Psychology 22, no. 1 (New York: Science Press, 1913); further parenthetical citations appear in the text.

42. Castle notes various precedents, including Havelock Ellis's "Study of British Genius," *Popular Science Monthly* (February–September 1901), which derived subjects (975 men, 55 women) from the *DNB*, and other studies that relied on *Men of the Time* or *Who's Who* for data (3). Castle acknowledges Amanda Carolyn Northrop's "The Successful Women of America" in *Popular Science Monthly* (January 1904), based on the "954 women culled from the 1902 edition of 'Who's Who'" (3).

43. Charles Murray, *Human Accomplishment* (New York: HarperCollins, 2003).

44. Hazel Carby, *Reconstructing Womanhood* (New York: Oxford University Press, 1987), 3–6, 96.

45. Robert W. Rydell, "Editor's Introduction: 'Contend, Contend!'" in Ida B. Wells et al., *The Reason Why the Colored American Is Not in the World's Columbian Exposition*, ed. Robert W. Rydell (Urbana: University of Illinois Press, 1999), xxiv.

46. Christopher Robert Reed, *"All the World Is Here!": The Black Presence at the White City* (Bloomington: Indiana University Press, 2000), 3.

47. Susan Elizabeth Frazier, "Some Afro-American Women of Mark," *A. M. E. Church Review* 8 (April 1892): 378–86, according to the tireless Jean Fagin Yellin's "Afro-American Women, 1800–1910: Excerpts from a Working Bibliography," first published in *All the Women Are White, All the Blacks Are Men, But Some of Us Are Brave*, ed. Gloria T. Hull, Patricia Bell Scott, and Barbara Smith (Old Westbury, NY: Feminist Press, 1982), 227. Gertrude Mossell, *The Work of the*

Afro-American Woman,[588] lists Frazier (16); Hallie Q. Brown, ed., *Homespun Heroines,*[120] presents a short life of Frazier (222–24). Both Mossell's and Brown's works were reprinted in the Schomburg Library by Oxford University Press in 1988; references to these reprints, by item number, appear parenthetically.

48. Mossell (16)[588] and Brown (205–7)[120] include Shorter in their biographical collections. Randall K. Burkett refers to Shorter's work and other early prosopographies of black women in his introduction to the Schomburg Library reprint of Brown's *Homespun Heroines* (xxxii–iv).[120]

49. Majors, Scruggs, and Mossell include among their subjects the editor of the magazine, Julia Ringwood Coston. Jean Yellin and Cynthia Bond were "unable to locate a copy of *Ringwood's Afro-American Journal of Fashion,* which she established in 1892" (*The Pen Is Ours* [New York: Oxford University Press, 1991], 9). The latter bibliography extends the one that Yellin published in 1982.

50. Annie Nathan Meyer is one of several women in *The Congress of Women* [245] whose bio states the following: "In religious faith she is a Jewess." Meyer contributed "Woman's Place in Letters," an amusing piece refuting common critical truisms about "sex in literature," i.e., gender difference in writing (135–37).[245] Meyer would later, as president of Barnard College, provide the scholarship that allowed Zora Neale Hurston to attend Barnard.

51. Reed, *"All the World Is Here!"* xiv, 4.

52. The Isabella Association formed to campaign on behalf of Isabella of Castile as codiscoverer of America with Columbus; they frequently clashed with Bertha Honoré Palmer's Board of Lady Managers, not least on the question of representation of women of color in the work of the fair. The Isabellas commissioned the statue of Queen Isabella by Harriet Hosmer, "who did not believe in segregating women's art" (Jeanne Madeline Weimann, *The Fair Women* [Chicago: Academy, 1981], 39, 55, 65, 110–24, 148–56, 277). Anna Jameson advised Hosmer on her famous sculptures of Zenobia and Queen Isabella, with their specific messages to contemporary feminists (Kimberly VanEsveld Adams, *Our Lady of Victorian Feminism* [Athens: Ohio University Press, 2001], 102–10).

53. Weimann, *The Fair Women,* 116–20. Barnett, in "The Reason Why," details Brown's interaction with the Board of Lady Managers (in Wells et al., *The Reason Why,* 71–73).

54. Carby, *Reconstructing Womanhood,* 5. See Newman, *White Women's Rights,* 7, 188n.17. Harper, Cooper, Coppin, and Brown figure prominently in the collective biographies of black women that emerged in that era.

55. Weimann, *The Fair Women,* 545–47.

56. For more on the omission of African Americans from the U.S. Capitol, see Vivian Green Fryd, *Art and Empire* (New Haven, CT: Yale University Press, 1992), 1, 177.

57. Benedict Anderson discusses the trope of "awakening from sleep" in European nationalisms of 1815–50 (*Imagined Community* [London: Verso, 1983], 194–95).

58. Adams, in *Our Lady of Victorian Feminism,* explores the competing references to queenship at the World's Columbian Exposition (102–9). The statue of Isabella overwhelmed the homemade things that Queen Victoria donated for exhibit (Weimann, *The Fair Women,* 270–71).

59. The Congress of Women culminated in the unveiling (with speeches) of a commissioned portrait of Mrs. Palmer, full-length in the manner of Sargent (816–19), and Palmer's speeches open and close the months of proceedings.

60. Burkett identifies a tradition of African American collective biographies (introduction to *Homespun Heroines* [120] by Brown, xxxii–iv). My bibliography includes fourteen all-female African American collections, published either in 1891–94 or 1919–33,[108; 120; 136; 216; 227; 228; 329; 390; 542; 588; 665; 706; 717; 796] another that includes men,[375] and three specifying women (i.e., primarily whites) in Africa,[512; 618; 711] as well as intermittent mention of the European missionary or traveler in Africa (e.g., Mary Kingsley).

61. For example, Ellen Tarry's column "Negroes of Note" in the *Birmingham Truth,* 1927–29, as noted in *Harlem Renaissance and Beyond,* ed. Lorraine Elena Roses and Ruth Elizabeth Randolph (Cambridge, MA: Harvard University Press, 1990), 304–5. Note the photographic "Men

of the Month," *Crisis* 33 (January 1927): 147, reproduced in Daylanne K. English, "Selecting the Harlem Renaissance," *Critical Inquiry* 25 (summer 1999): 813.

62. Edwin R. Embree, *Thirteen against the Odds* (New York: Viking, 1944).

63. Slight variations on biographical collections of women writers include Roses and Randolph, eds., *Harlem Renaissance and Beyond;* Roger Streitmatter, *Raising Her Voice* (Lexington: University Press of Kentucky, 1994); Marcia Y. Riggs, ed., *Can I Get a Witness?* (Maryknoll, NY: Orbis Books, 1997).

64. Henry Louis Gates Jr., *Thirteen Ways of Looking at a Black Man* (New York: Vintage, 1997)—possibly echoing Embree's title but obviously alluding to Wallace Stevens's poem, "Thirteen Ways of Looking at a Blackbird." See "Planet Africa: Black History on Disk," Circuits, *New York Times,* January 21, 1999, announcing *Encarta Africana,* the "Digital Diaspora," with a photograph of Gates in front of a bust of Du Bois as though in illustration of compulsory typology.

65. Michele Wallace, "Negative Images," in *The Cultural Studies Reader,* ed. Simon During (New York: Routledge, 1993), 128–31. Susan Fraiman, *Cool Men and the Second Sex* (New York: Columbia University Press, 2003). See Henry Louis Gates Jr., "Where My Mother's Voice Led Me," *NewYork Times,* OP-ED, May 9, 2004, 4:13.

66. Hannah Crafts, *The Bondwoman's Narrative,* ed. Henry Louis Gates Jr. (New York: Warner, 2002).

67. Yellin and Bond, *The Pen Is Ours,* 9–11, 14–15n.5.

68. Walter Benn Michaels, "Race into Culture," *Critical Inquiry* 18 (summer 1992), reprinted in *Identities,* ed. Kwame Anthony Appiah and Henry Louis Gates Jr. (Chicago: University of Chicago Press, 1995), 60.

Chapter Six

1. Carolyn Steedman, "Women's Biography and Autobiography: Forms of History, Histories of Form," in *From My Guy to Sci-Fi: Genre and Women's Writing in the Postmodern World,* ed. Helen Carr (London: Pandora, 1989), 104. Steedman regards a public woman as a contradiction of gender convention; thus "the nineteenth-century heroine of biography . . . remains an exceptional figure" (104–5).

2. The quote is taken from Waldo H. Dunn, *English Biography* (London: Dent, 1916), 1. William Epstein registers history and literature as opposing loyalities of biography (*Recognizing Biography* [Philadelphia: University of Pennsylvania Press, 1987], 7).

3. Woolf, "The New Biography," review of *Some People* by Harold Nicolson, *New York Herald Tribune,* October 30, 1927, reprinted in *The Essays of Virginia Woolf,* ed. Andrew McNeillie (London: Hogarth, 1994), 4:473–80. Further citations in the text.

4. This model of subjectivity adapts more to the managerial or intellectual than to the empire-building tasks being offered to sons of Britain's educated men—Bernard, that is, not Percival, in *The Waves.*

5. See my *Greatness Engendered* (Ithaca, NY: Cornell University Press, 1992).

6. Perhaps the household at Hyde Park Gate owned copies of Betham-Edwards's *Six Life Studies of Famous Women* [75] or others of the dozens of collections of Woolf's childhood years. Though the Stephen family had strong credentials in British literary and artistic circles, their heritage included as well prominent families of Evangelical reform; the mores of the latter dominated Victorian and Edwardian collective biographies of women, whereas the former gained upper hand in Bloomsbury.

7. Georgia Johnston, "Women's Voice: *Three Guineas* as Autobiography," in *Virginia Woolf: Themes and Variations,* ed. Vara Neverow-Turk and Mark Hussey (New York: Pace University Press, 1993), 322.

8. Woolf includes later Victorian campaigners who had not made it into many collections by the 1920s and 1930s—Josephine Butler, Anne Clough, Emily Davies—but she neglects many favorites of standard Victorian, Edwardian, and Georgian collections, including the more nonliterary or the pious: Harriet Martineau, Hannah More, Joan of Arc. Woolf had no time for

most missionaries to the poor, Mary Carpenter, Elizabeth Fry, Sister Dora, etc., though she favored Octavia Hill with notice. A few other names prominent in Woolf's essays and manifestos appear infrequently in collections of 1830–1940: Lady Winchelsea, Margaret Oliphant, Elizabeth Gaskell, and Mary Wollstonecraft. Sophia Jex-Blake is not a figure in the anthologies, and curiously, neither Christina Rossetti nor Aphra Behn (favored by Woolf) crops up frequently. Behn and Wollstonecraft could equally be banned from most collections for their sexual transgressions.

9. On Sackville-West as author of *Joan of Arc,* see Ruth Hoberman, *Modernizing Lives: Experiments in English Biography, 1918–1939* (Carbondale: Southern Illinois University Press, 1987), 3; Leonard Woolf, *The Journey Not the Arrival Matters* (New York: Harcourt Brace & World, 1969), 98–99.

10. Duckworth also published Brailsford's *Quaker Women.*[105]

11. Fawcett was president of the National Union of Women's Suffrage Societies and one-time opponent of Woolf's uncle Fitzjames Stephen (Hermione Lee, *Virginia Woolf* [New York: Knopf, 1997], 62). In 1931, Woolf and Ethel Smyth appeared at a meeting of the London and National Society for Women's Service in a hall named in honor of Millicent Fawcett; among the invited guests were Vita, Vanessa, and Cicely Hamilton (Lee, 590). Woolf later donated books, "especially biographies," to the Millicent Fawcett Library (Lee, 593).

12. See Barbara Green, *Spectacular Confessions* (New York: St. Martin's, 1997), 75–78. Whether Woolf attended or read the pageant when published by the Suffrage Shop in 1910 she was active in the adult suffrage movement for a brief time in 1910. She was acquainted with the actress Edy Craig, at whose theater Vita Sackville-West held a reading of her poem *The Land* in 1932 (Lee, *Virginia Woolf,* 623).

13. In London in 1928–29 alone there were several collections: Tabor's *Four Margarets*[775] and Thornton-Cook's *Royal Elizabeths*[803] and *Royal Marys,*[804] which followed Humphrey's *The Story of the Elizabeths*[431] and Harvey's *The Six Maries.*[387] These in turn echoed earlier studies of Marthas,[638] Marys,[639] and Elizabeths,[755] usually with more devotional than courtly connotation. In *Three Guineas,* Woolf could also have taken note of *Seven Women against the World,*[328] which commended revolutionaries from Charlotte Corday and Flora Tristan to Emma Goldman and Rosa Luxemburg.

14. Margaret J. M. Ezell, *Writing Women's Literary History* (Baltimore: Johns Hopkins University Press, 1993), 39–65; Catherine Sandbach-Dahlström, "'Que scais-je?': Virginia Woolf and the Essay as Feminist Critique," in *Virginia Woolf and the Essay,* ed. Beth Carole Rosenberg and Jeanne Dubino (New York: St. Martin's, 1997), 275–93.

15. Woolf, "Women and Fiction," in *Collected Essays,* 4 vols. (New York: Harcourt, 1967), 2:141.

16. Deidre Lynch, "Homes and Haunts: Austen's and Mitford's English Idylls," *PMLA* 155 (2000): 1103–8.

17. Woolf's review essay asks why Miss Hill wrote the book. The answer takes the form of citations of famous women, and at the same time it removes those it names, as in the scenes of disinheritance. First,

> Miss Mitford was a lady; . . . the stock of female characters who lend themselves to biographical treatment by their own sex is, for one reason or another, running short. For instance, little is known of Sappho, and that little is not wholly to her credit. Lady Jane Grey has merit, but is undeniably obscure. Of George Sand, the more we know the less we approve. George Eliot was led into evil ways which not all her philosophy can excuse. The Brontës, however highly we rate their genius, lacked that indefinable something which marks the lady; Harriet Martineau was an atheist; Mrs Browning was a married woman; Jane Austen, Fanny Burney, and Maria Edgeworth have been done already; so that, what with one thing and another, Mary Russell Mitford is the only woman left. ("Outlines I: Miss Mitford," an essay in *The Common Reader* [1925], based on two reviews; reprinted in *The Essays of Virginia Woolf,* ed. McNeillie, 4:193–94)

18. The preface affirms that "ordinary readers, and especially young readers . . . read short biographies, or none at all." It includes Matilda Betham, "the friend of the Southeys, Coleridge,

and Charles and Mary Lamb, and herself the first biographer in our language of celebrated women" (v–viii). Back in 1804, Betham compiled *A Biographical Dictionary of the Celebrated Women of Every Age and Country,* yet she was at least fifty years too late to be first (if we discount the seventeenth-century catalogs). Family pride aside, no one had thought to trace a canon of such works.

19. Richard Altick, *Lives and Letters* (New York: Knopf, 1966); Richard Ellmann, *Literary Biography* (Oxford: Clarendon Press, 1971); Ira Bruce Nadel, *Biography* (New York: St. Martin's, 1984); and David Amigoni, *Victorian Biography* (New York: Harvester Wheatsheaf, 1993) all appear preoccupied with an almost exclusively male biographical canon. In 1990, B. L. Reid collected a lifetime of biographical essays on male writers (*Necessary Lives* [Columbia: University of Missouri Press, 1990]).

20. George Saintsbury, "Some Great Biographies," *Macmillan's Magazine* 66 (June 1892): 97.

21. Ibid., 99–102. Saintsbury is typical of a late Victorian impressionist critic, relying on the lo-and-behold mode: "I have nothing more to say but to repeat that I for my part know no book of the kind equal to this" (103). Compare twentieth-century pronouncements on the art of biography in John A. Garraty, *The Nature of Biography* (New York: Knopf, 1957); Jeffrey Meyers, ed., *The Craft of Literary Biography* (New York: Shocken, 1985); and William Zinsser, ed., *Extraordinary Lives* (New York: American Heritage, 1986). Paula R. Backscheider writes, "Biography is an art" (*Reflections on Biography* [Oxford: Oxford University Press, 1999], 121). P. N. Furbank disagrees: "Biography is a craft, not an art" ("The Craftlike Nature of Biography," in *Biographical Passages,* ed. Joe Law and Linda K. Hughes [Columbia: University of Missouri Press, 2000], 18). Albert Britt (*The Great Biographers* [New York: Whittlesey, 1936]) marked epochs in the development of biography by movements ("The Dawn of the Renaissance") or by names: "Johnson and Boswell," "Scott and Brontë." The protagonists of this story may be biographers, autobiographers, or subjects of biography. Britt notes contemporaries Gamaliel Bradford and Philip Guedalla (187–97, 209–18), who favor short collective studies, some of women; postwar studies of biography tend to drop Bradford and Guedalla.

22. A. O. J. Cockshut, *Truth to Life* (New York: Harcourt, 1974), 11. Anticipating later perspectives, Cockshut's company is more diverse than Saintsbury's, accommodating Samuel Smiles, Margaret Oliphant, W. H. Davenport Adams, and, as a subject, Grace Darling (87). Daniel Aaron's collection *Studies in Biography* (Cambridge, MA: Harvard University Press, 1978) sustains the Victorian conviction that the biographical ideal is the elusive encounter of two great men: "Great biographies like Froude's *Thomas Carlyle* are rare, because such happy conjunctions of writer and subject are rare" (v). Aaron seems to find in biography a refuge for eccentricity out of reach of materialism and theory. A few of Aaron's contributors depart from the standard line: James Clifford on non-Western ethnobiography (41–56); Jean Strouse on Alice James (113–29).

23. Trev Lynn Broughton, *Men of Letters, Writing Lives* (London: Routledge, 1999), 9; her capitalization.

24. Hoberman, *Modernizing Lives,* 1. Like most academic books, Hoberman's presents snapshots of the right colloquium or salon: the book begins with a foreword by Cockshut and an epigraph from James L. Clifford.

25. Donald J. Winslow, "Glossary of Terms in Life-Writing, Part II," *Biography* 1, no. 2 (1978): 68.

26. Garraty, *The Nature of Biography* (New York: Knopf, 1957), 134, 144–45.

27. Like Harold Nicolson, Woolf lends two pieces to Novarr's anthology. The scant presence of female critics of biography may be fairly representative of the comparative absence of women from the circles that John Gross describes in *The Rise and Fall of the Man of Letters* (London: Weidenfeld & Nicolson, 1969). Gross's one reference to Frances Power Cobbe as the butt of Arnold's antiphilistinism (55) does not quite make up for the lack of many thriving women of letters in the period. He does acknowledge modernists such as Edith Sitwell, Katherine Mansfield, and of course Woolf. See Carol T. Christ, "'The Hero as Man of Letters': Masculinity and Victorian Nonfiction Prose," *Victorian Sages and Cultural Discourse,* ed. Thais E. Morgan (New Brunswick, NJ: Rutgers University Press, 1990), 21–22.

28. Woolf's terms for the factual and fictional, concrete and imaginative elements essential to biography are "granite and rainbow" ("The New Biography," 478). I discuss the grounds for criticism of biography in chap. 1, 73–77.

29. Raymond Williams, *Marxism and Literature* (Oxford: Oxford University Press, 1977), 149, quoted in Amigoni, *Victorian Biography*, 18–19. Later Victorian biographical writing sought to "discipline the distinction between 'literature' and 'history,'" due to a "politically motivated" distrust of "rhetoric" (Amigoni, 20). On such professionalization, see Gerald Graff, *Professing Literature* (Chicago: University of Chicago Press, 1987), 55–64; Gross, *The Man of Letters*; John Guillory, *Cultural Capital* (Chicago: University of Chicago Press, 1993).

30. Gianna Pomata, "History, Particular and Universal," *Feminist Studies* 19 (1993): 15–16, 25–26.

31. Thomas Carlyle, "Biography," *Fraser's Magazine* 5, no. 27 (April 1832): 253–60, reprinted in *Victorian Biography*, ed. Nadel, n.p.; 253, 260.

32. Carlyle, "Biography," 260.

33. On the gradual maturation of biography criticism, see James L. Clifford, ed., *Biography as an Art* (New York: Oxford University Press, 1962), xx. The phrase "retarded evolution" is from Dunn, *English Biography*, 1. Quoting Carlyle at length, Dunn suggests that the sage's lament concerning the dearth of good English biography augured a blooming: "During the last half of the nineteenth century, no language surpassed the English in the importance and number of biographies written and published" (250–51).

34. David Novarr, ed., *The Lines of Life* (West Lafayette, IN: Purdue University Press, 1986), xi–xv.

35. Backscheider calls biography "the least studied and understood of the major literary genres," though it is the last of them "to be read by a very wide cross-section of people" (*Reflections on Biography*, xiii–iv). See Jay Parini, "Biography Can Escape the Tyranny of Facts," *Chronicle of Higher Education*, February 4, 2000, A72.

36. Novarr, *Lines of Life*, xiv. Clifford, ed. (*Biography as an Art*), reproaches early biographers for having little curiosity about the demands of their art and overestimating "the value of praising great men" (xi).

37. For example, Jeffrey Meyers, in *The Craft of Literary Biography* (New York: Schocken, 1985), collected essays by authors of biographies published between 1976 and 1983, all on eminent men (of the three female contributors, Lyndall Gordon and Elizabeth Longford were then or later became well-known biographers of women). Zinsser, in *Extraordinary Lives,* collected essays by biographers (one woman out of six) on "the art and craft of American biography" (two women as subjects). Gail Porter Mandell's *Life into Art* (Fayetteville: University of Arkansas Press, 1991) created a somewhat different atmosphere in her interviews with seven biographers, including Phyllis Rose and Elisabeth Young-Bruehl. Some of their subjects are Asian, and Arnold Rampersad is among the company, while the spirit remains highly literary. As noted, collections of feminist studies of life writing often consist of testimonies by biographers of women. Teresa Iles, ed., *All Sides of the Subject* (New York: Teachers College, Columbia, 1992), combines such auto/biography (essays sketch biographer and subject): Judith Jordan's "Telling Choices in the Life of Isabella Bird" becomes in part a brief biography of Bird (80–89).

38. Britt, *The Great Biographers,* 3–5. Margaret Oliphant, in "The Ethics of Biography" (1883), concurs: "The art of biography is one of the oldest in the world," a mode of "primitive story-telling" that governs Homeric, biblical, and other collections of foundational lives (in *Victorian Biography,* ed. Nadel, 76–77).

39. Michael P. Rewa, *Reborn as Meaning* (Washington, DC: University Press of America, 1963); Thomas J. Heffernan, *Sacred Biography* (New York: Oxford University Press, 1988); Donald Stauffer, *English Biography before 1700* (Cambridge, MA: Harvard University Press, 1930); Donald J. Winslow, "Glossary of Terms, Part I," *Biography* 1, no. 1 (1978): 65–66.

40. Gosse, "The Custom of Biography," *Anglo-Saxon Review* 8 (March 1901): 196. Citations appear henceforth in the text. Gosse is unusual in dating the birth of English biography to 1557 "in the shape of a little masterpiece," George Cavendish's *Life of Cardinal Wolsey,* "born full-grown"; like Boswell or Walpole, Cavendish saw his subject "clearly and saw him whole"

(196–98). (Most critics of biography have followed an Arnoldian practice, searching for touchstones.)

41. Linda Wagner-Martin, *Telling Women's Lives* (New Brunswick, NJ: Rutgers University Press, 1994), 1. Wagner-Martin devotes a few pages to group biographies (124–27) and to family or coterie memoirs (94–110, 127–33). Yet she ignores the main form of proto-feminist female biography by women; the "new biography" of her subtitle is consciously feminist individual biography that portrays the daily lives, sexual appetites, and private sufferings of women (11–13).

42. Garraty, *The Nature of Biography*, 96.

43. Cockshut, *Truth to Life*, 13, 16–17.

44. As Felicity Nussbaum shows, Boswell's own ambivalence about competing ideologies of the self and reworkings of "classical heroic models" in his journals help to shape the *Life of Johnson* (*The Autobiographical Subject* [Baltimore: Johns Hopkins University Press, 1989], 103–4, 117–20). Altick associates biography with the rise of the man of letters, in *Lives and Letters,* 5–11. The term "hacks" is from Gosse, "The Custom of Biography," 202–3.

45. Michael McKeon, "Writer as Hero: Novelistic Prefigurations and the Emergence of Literary Biography," in *Contesting the Subject,* ed. William H. Epstein (West Lafayette, IN: Purdue University Press, 1991), 17. Garraty, *The Nature of Biography*, 76–77.

46. Lytton Strachey, *Eminent Victorians* (1918; reprint, Harmondsworth: Penguin, 1986), 10. Parenthetical citations follow.

47. Harold Nicolson makes a similar point about family biographers in "The Practice of Biography," *American Scholar* 23, no. 2 (spring 1954): 152.

48. Harold Nicolson, *The Development of English Biography* (London: Hogarth, 1927), 144–45. The endpaper advertisement lists Virginia Woolf's *Phases of Fiction* as "in preparation" in the series.

49. Ibid., 9–13, 125. Nicolson nevertheless credits the Victorians with creating a large audience for biographies and establishing "the professional biographer," as well as developing "'biography for students'—a form of history" realized in the excellent *Dictionary of National Biography* and John Morley's English Men of Letters (*Development,* 126–27). See, on Nicolson, Amigoni, *Victorian Biography,* 14–15.

50. Nicolson, *Development,* 128. Nicolson reads like a parody of literary-historical narratives, as, disconcertingly, he admits: "I have throughout adopted the convention of speaking (as if I believed in such things) of 'influences,' and 'innovators,' of 'reactionaries' and of 'pioneers'" (132).

51. Nicolson warns successors of Strachey that "irony . . . is a dangerous tincture"; the hardworking "biographer must be fortified by a fundamental respect" for his subject ("Practice," 156). Gosse similarly advises against "biography as a form of revenge" ("Custom," 207–8).

52. Hoberman, *Modernizing Lives,* 11.

53. Nadel, in *Biography,* claims that Gosse, Charles Whibley, Strachey, and others "extended the movement towards brief lives originating in nineteenth-century biographical dictionaries and collective lives" (62–66).

54. Woolf, "The New Biography"; Garraty, *The Nature of Biography*, 121–51; Bradford, xi–xii.[102]

55. Bradford's portraits are copyrighted from 1912 onward in such journals as the *North American Review,* and Lytton Strachey published on du Deffand (1913), Mlle de Lespinasse (1906), Horace Walpole (1904), and others in the *Edinburgh Review,* the *Athenaeum,* and the *Independent Review* and elsewhere—collected in *Biographical Essays* (New York: Harvest/HBJ, n.d.).

56. As Woolf famously argued regarding modern fiction in "Mr Bennett and Mrs Brown" (1924), something more than realist detail was required for the effect of living individuality (in *The Essays of Virginia Woolf,* ed. McNeillie, 3:384–89).

57. Steedman, "Women's Biography and Autobiography," 103.

58. Nancy Miller, *Subject to Change* (New York: Columbia University Press, 1988); Cheryl Walker, "Persona Criticism and the Death of the Author," in *Contesting the Subject,* ed. Epstein

(109–21); Valerie Ross, "Too Close to Home: Repressing Biography, Instituting Authority," in *Contesting the Subject,* ed. Epstein, 135–65.

59. James L. Clifford wrote in 1970 (when theory was making ominous inroads in English departments), "life-writing is the last major discipline uncorrupted by criticism" (*From Puzzles to Portraits* [Chapel Hill: University of North Carolina Press, 1970], 102).

60. Elisabeth Young-Bruehl, *Subject to Biography* (Cambridge, MA: Harvard University Press, 1998), 7.

61. Diane Wood Middlebrook, "Postmodernism and the Biographer," in *Revealing Lives,* ed. Susan Groag Bell and Marilyn Yalom (Albany: State University of New York Press, 1990), 155.

62. Sara Alpern et al., eds., *The Challenge of Feminist Biography* (Urbana: University of Illinois Press, 1992), 4.

63. David Bromwich cautions, "whether or not we deal with biography, biography may be dealing with us" ("The Uses of Biography," *Yale Review* 73 [1984]: 161). Stanley Fish declares that "it makes no sense to urge a return to biography, since biography is not something from which we can swerve" ("Biography and Intention," in *Contesting the Subject,* ed. Epstein, 15). Biography may be both too personal and political for New Critics and poststructuralists (Valerie Ross, "Too Close to Home," in *Contesting the Subject,* ed. Epstein, 136–37). See Mary Rheil and David Suchoff, introduction to *The Seductions of Biography,* ed. Mary Rheil and David Suchoff (New York: Routledge, 1996), 1–5.

64. Backscheider, with an epigraph from Lytton Strachey, affirms that "the most invisible person in a biography is the most powerful—the author" (*Reflections on Biography,* 3). As William H. Epstein writes, "'recognizing the biographical subject' authorized the virtual disappearance of the biographer, except as a scribe or amanuensis" (*Recognizing Biography,* 80). Just as there is no "unmediated" fact in a life, the narrative is "underwritten by . . . cultural institutions" (32).

65. With the most inclusive intentions, we may reduce individual representatives of a "different" culture to interchangeability in what Uma Narayan calls the "Package Picture of Cultures," which homogenizes any one culture in order to acknowledge differences among cultures ("Undoing the 'Package Picture' of Cultures," *Signs* 25 [2000]: 1083–86).

On identity politics in relation to ad campaigns, see Wendy Somerson, "A Corporate Multicultural Universe: Replacing the Nation-State with *Men in Black,*" *Narrative* 7 (1999): 213–34.

66. Amigoni notes this practice in literary and historical studies (*Victorian Biography,* 2, 20–21). Young-Bruehl calls for "*Lives of the Philosophers* . . . to rediscover the historical and individual developmental sources of philosophy. . . . thinking—presented in life-story-telling—as a way of relatedness to others." She notes the biographical studies of philosophers by Karl Jaspers and Hannah Arendt (*Subject to Biography,* 10–11).

67. Carla Kaplan, *The Erotics of Talk* (New York: Oxford University Press, 1996), 12, 45, 53.

68. Janet Varner Gunn, *Autobiography: Toward a Poetics of Experience* (Philadelphia: University of Pennsylvania Press, 1982), 7–9.

69. Shari Benstock, "Authorizing the Autobiographical," in *The Private Self,* ed. Shari Benstock (Chapel Hill: University of North Carolina Press, 1988), 20.

70. Paul de Man, "Autobiography as De-Facement," *MLN: Comparative Literature* 94 (1979): 919–30.

71. Sidonie Smith, *Subjectivity, Identity, and the Body* (Bloomington: Indiana University Press, 1993), 6, 8.

72. Ibid., 9–12. Smith cites Peter Stallybrass and Allon White (*The Politics and Poetics of Transgression* [Ithaca, NY: Cornell University Press, 1986], 199) to the effect that the rational, autonomous subject is interpenetrated with the other "voices" that it repudiates; as Smith puts it, "In return for this evacuation of 'color' [or] . . . self-regulation, the democratic self can claim equal access to the universally human" (*Subjectivity,* 9).

73. Smith, *Subjectivity,* 19–20. The terms "mess" and "clutter" derive from Stallybrass and White (*Politics and Poetics,* 199).

74. Friedman, "Women's Autobiographical Selves: Theory and Practice," in *The Private Self,* ed. Benstock, 37–38.

75. James Olney's magnificent study, *Memory and Narrative* (Chicago: University of Chicago Press, 1998) gives Augustine, Rousseau, and Becket the thorough attention they deserve. He adds a miscellany of contemporary life writing that includes women. Each of his trio, however, becomes an immortalized representative of an entire phase of Western subjectivity; and when has a woman been able to attain that stature?

76. John Paul Eakin, *How Our Lives Become Stories* (Ithaca, NY: Cornell University Press, 1999), 48–49.

77. Ibid., 43, 46–47, 6–7.

78. Ralph Waldo Emerson, "The Uses of Great Men," in *Representative Men,* ed. Pamela Schirmeister (New York: Marsilio, 1995), 9.

79. Ibid., 23, 9.

80. Amigoni, *Victorian Biography,* 45.

81. Martin Danahay, *Community of One* (Albany: State University of New York Press, 1993), 135, 3.

82. Emerson, "Great Men," 22.

83. Studies of collaborative autobiography or autoethnography comprehend the discursive mediation and ethical perils. See Caroline B. Brettell, "Blurred Genres and Blended Voices," in *Auto/Ethnography,* ed. Deborah E. Reed-Danahay (Oxford: Berg, 1997), 223–46. See Camilla Stivers, "Reflections on the Role of Personal Narrative in Social Science," *Signs* 18 (1993): 408–25. *Interpreting Women's Lives* by the Personal Narratives Group (Bloomington: Indiana University Press, 1989) set out the issues of the new use of women's autobiography in literary, sociological, and anthropological studies. See Sidonie Smith, "Who's Talking/Who's Talking Back?" on "other's" claims to subjectivity and the interviewer/editor's control (*Signs* 18 [1993]: 392–407); and Doris Sommer, "Taking a Life: Hot Pursuit and Cold Rewards in a Mexican Testimonial Novel," in *The Seductions of Biography,* ed. Rhiel and Suchoff, 147–72. G. Thomas Couser, "Making, Taking, and Faking Lives," *Style* 32 (1998): 334–50, writes: "Ethical issues may be particularly acute in collaborative autobiography," between "solo autobiography, in which the writer, the narrator, and the subject (or protagonist) . . . share the same name" and "biography, in which the writer and narrator are one person, while the subject is someone else" (334). See G. Thomas Couser, *Vulnerable Subjects: Ethics and Life Writing* (Ithaca, NY: Cornell University Press, 2003). I would argue that collaborative life writing and biography raise similar role-splitting ethical problems.

84. Furbank suggests that "the right model for the biographer might be a trainer." Yet the biographer writes "about himself or herself . . . trying out a new personality"; therefore it is best to write only a few biographies in one's life, to avoid "promiscuity" ("The Craftlike Nature of Biography," 21–22). Liz Stanley warns against the biographer's being "god" who shines a "spotlight" on one individual ("Process in Feminist Biography and Feminist Epistemology," in *All Sides of the Subject,* ed. Iles, 109–25).

A useful review of the recent revival of ethical criticism appears in Jil Larson, *Ethics and Narrative in the English Novel, 1880–1914* (Cambridge: Cambridge University Press, 2001), 1–19. The field of ethical criticism rapidly expands. See the special issue, "Ethics and Literary Study," introduction by Lawrence Buell, *PMLA* 114 (1999): 7–19. Buell, in "Circling the Spheres: A Dialogue," *American Literature* (Special Issue: "No More Separate Spheres!") 70 (1998): 465–90, suggests that "'ethics' has become a positive conjure word," though one of Buell's personae warns that the "ethical turn" may be a "retreat from politics" and ideology (473–74). In a 1998 issue of *Style* on the debates of ethical criticism, Marshall W. Gregory, in "Ethical Criticism: What It Is and Why It Matters," advocates a humanist ethical criticism "because who we become matters" (215); but he anticipates a patronizing poststructuralist attack on his position (208–9). Charles Altieri defends "lyrical ethics and literary experience" (his title) because he is "angry and frustrated" with current ethical critics such as Martha Nussbaum and Wayne Booth for their apparent wish to dampen "attentive pleasure" (272–73). In the concluding essay, "Why Ethical Criticism Can Never Be Simple," Booth acknowledges that "entire critical schools" have avoided dealing with "the power of stories" as "moral teachers"; he calls for a pluralist criticism responsive to differing genres and intentions (354–55).

85. Virginia Woolf, "Two Women," in *The Essays of Virginia Woolf,* ed. McNeillie, 4:419–26; further references appear parenthetically.

Chapter Seven

1. "Victoria Herself" claimed only two sessions, as one of the shortest of twenty-two thematic "strands." On the whole, technology, science, history, and the study of institutions and disciplines dominated literature, yet elements of prosopography infiltrated most sessions. Thus a characteristic session, "Transport," began with Di Drummond's "The Lives of the Great Railway Engineers and the Acceptance of Technology in Victorian Britain." The "Mirror Images" strand largely concerned auto/biography. Many paper titles named Victorian individuals or groups, while others focused on biographical histories of Victorians (e.g., William Lubenow, "Lytton Strachey's *Eminent Victorians*").

2. It is not, of course, Victoria's hand. Yvonne Ward pointed out to me in conversation at the International Autobiography and Biography Conference in Melbourne, July 15–19, 2002, that the hand pictured was that of a young model, out of keeping with the image of Victoria in old age. Among the new biographies are Lynn Vallone, *Becoming Victoria* (New Haven, CT: Yale University Press, 2001); Elizabeth Longford, *Queen Victoria* (Stroud, Gloucestershire: Sutton, 1999). At least four other biographies of Victoria were published in 1999.

3. Hosted by the Science Museum, "Locating the Victorians" was supported by the British Academy and the Royal Commission for the Exhibition of 1851. Associated conferences were held in 2001 at CUNY and UC Santa Cruz. John Kucich and Dianne F. Sadoff edited *Victorian Afterlife: Postmodern Culture Rewrites the Nineteenth Century* (Minneapolis: University of Minnesota Press, 2000), an important study of recent recapitulations of Victorian culture.

4. In the 1990s there was a spate of studies of fins-de-siècle, including Elaine Showalter, *Sexual Anarchy* (New York: Viking, 1990); Elaine Scarry, ed., *Fins-de-Siècle: English Poetry in 1590, 1690, 1790, 1890, 1990* (Baltimore: Johns Hopkins University Press, 1995); and Joan DeJean, *Ancients against Moderns* (Chicago: University of Chicago Press, 1997).

5. Carolyn Heilbrun writes vividly of her male models' characterization of an assumed interpretative community that excluded women: "When Trilling said 'we' he meant men like himself. . . . I never was part of 'we'" (*When Men Were the Only Models We Had* [Philadelphia: University of Pennsylvania Press, 2002], 8). My feminist training has taught me to be wary of "we," except when it clearly designates an immediate audience.

6. Langbauer, "Queen Victoria and Me," in *Victorian Afterlife,* ed. Kucich and Sadoff, 212, 214.

7. Langbauer organized a panel discussion, "Why Do Victorian Narrative?" at the Narrative Conference, April 4, 1997, University of Florida, for which I formulated some of the points that I later shaped into a paper, "But Why Always the Victorian Novelists? Periodization in Women's Literary Histories," delivered at the South Atlantic Modern Language Association convention in Atlanta in November 1997. This paper evolved into the talk I presented at the "Victoria Redressed" conference at University of California, Santa Cruz, for the Dickens Project, August 5–8, 1999. Later in this chapter I adapt parts of my review essay, "Millennial Victoria," *Victorian Literature and Culture* 29 (2001): 159–70.

8. The personal voice is risky in academic writing not because it violates scholarly objectivity but because it exposes competition and disempowering affect, admiration and envy included. The "I" seems most suited to a star who has influenced a generation; the personal voice presumes an audience interested in a recognized career author. As Langbauer writes, "Autobiography and personal confession are possible to such an extent within feminist scholarship right now because a whole generation of women scholars have achieved the economic security and professional recognition . . . that give them the protection to explore such forms" (214).

9. Margaret Homans and Adrienne Munich, introduction, *Remaking Queen Victoria,* ed. Margaret Homans and Adrienne Munich (Cambridge: Cambridge University Press, 1997), 1.

10. Of Dave Thomas, in a very different context, it was said after he died on January 8, 2002, "He was loved throughout the Wendy's family as a perfect example of how really good guys can finish first" ("Wendy's Founder Passes Away," March 15, 2002, wendys.com [discontinued]). At http://www.wendys.com/dave/flash.html, many images and short quotations emphasize Thomas's

"humble beginnings," "old-fashioned," simple values of hard work and self-help, and triumph as an American "folk hero." The site is commercial role-model biography: his success can be franchised.

11. Victoria's conservatism (resistance to Chartism, objections to female suffrage) seems overridden by the perception that she democratized her nation and performed female leadership—a process of national "feminization," according to Gail Turley Houston (*Royalties* [Charlottesville: University Press of Virginia, 1999], 64–65; further references will appear in the text).

12. *Great Women Paper Dolls* (Santa Barbara, CA: Bellerophon Books, 1994), n.p. The series of dolls resembles the 1850s books of beauty and heroism by Clarke or Goodrich spliced with Sarah Bolton's posthumous early twentieth-century list: Sappho, Cleopatra, Queen Boudicca, Theodora, Lady Murasaki, Eleanor of Aquitaine, Joan of Arc, Vittoria Colonna, Pocahontas, Mme de Pompadour, Amelia Earhart, Susan B. Anthony, Florence Nightingale, Sarah Bernhardt, Beatrix Potter, Mme Curie, Anna Pavlova, Bessie Smith, and Golda Meir. The last page features Charlotte Corday, from *Infamous Women Paper Dolls*. Victoria as archvillain seems to invite a contemporary girl to read about aggressors: Corday appears to say "Never shall any man be my master!"

13. The "preeminent" belles of "the century now drawing to its close . . . belong . . . to the history of their country." Peacock, like biographers of Victoria, stresses the technological change that occurs in her subjects' lifetimes; it wasn't easy to be a belle before the day of the telegraph or railroad (vii–viii).[635]

14. There was an outburst of "noble deeds" at midcentury (Clement[182] and Starling[751]) and a fashion for the "noble" surged after 1880, primarily with a missionary connotation. A few samples: *Noble Dames of Ancient Story*;[250] several titles by William Henry Davenport Adams, e.g., *Stories of the Lives of Noble Women*;[12] medieval-style titles such as *The Book of Noble Englishwomen*;[125] and two books entitled *A Book of Noble Women*.[140; 887] In a Christian context, Jennie Chappell relied heavily on the noble epithet, as in *Four Noble Women and Their Work*,[160] and she contributed to a study of religious women, *The King's Daughters*,[486] i.e., servants of Jesus. In the 1880s, Ewart edited *True and Noble Women*,[270] and Johnson compiled *Noble Women of Our Time*.[468] *Noble Womanhood*[730] shares its title with Dole's *Noble Womanhood* (Boston: Caldwell, 1909), below.

"Queen" is more likely to be used in its literal sense than "noble." As a metaphor, it often refers to predecessors of "stars"—the performers or society leaders of questionable sexual reputation: e.g., *Queens of Song*,[179] *Comedy Queens of the Georgian Era*,[307] and *Queens of the French Stage*.[872] The much-consumed *The Queens of Society*[797] leads to the more lurid *Queens of Crime*.[346] But allied with the above connotation of regnant beauties are more respectful uses, as in *The Queens of American Society*,[257] conferring manners and refinements on the New World; *Queens of Literature of the Victorian Era*,[414] suggesting the reign of women of letters; and as in "nobility" above, religious stature: *Queens of the Bible*[196] and *Uncrowned Queens*.[728]

15. On Ruskin's reconstruction of queenliness as middle-class in "Of Queen's Gardens," see Margaret Homans, *Royal Representations* (Chicago: University of Chicago Press, 1998), 67–72. References to Homans will appear parenthetically in the text. See also Sharon Aronofsky Weltman, "'Be no more housewives, but queens': Queen Victoria and Ruskin's Domestic Mythology," in *Remaking Queen Victoria*, ed. Homans and Munich, 105–22. Weltman argues that Ruskin promoted the Queen as a model of public service: "Queenship is conceived as housewifery on an Olympian scale" (112). This essay forms part of Weltman, *Ruskin's Mythic Queen* (Athens: Ohio University Press, 1998), 103–23.

16. Charles F. Dole, *Noble Womanhood* (Boston: Caldwell, [1909]), 19–20. The cover of this small book (copyright 1900 L.C. Page & Co.) is decorated like a Christmas card: holly, a golden bell tipped to reveal inside its bowl an evening scene of a church in snow. Parenthetical references appear in the text.

17. Dole's brief chapters cite a few great women such as Dorothea Dix. In "Virtue Knows No Sex," he follows citational convention, naming Fry, Lucretia Mott, Nightingale, and Stowe ([35]; see quotation in chap. 3 above, 148). The status of woman serves as the measure of "human advancement and civilisation" (11).

18. The quote about Victoria's predestined encounter with the summits of greatness is from Edith Sitwell, *Victoria of England* (Boston: Houghton Mifflin, 1936), 115.

19. Giles St Aubyn, *Queen Victoria: A Portrait* (London: Sinclair-Stevenson, 1991), 65, 362. Louise Creighton, in *Some Famous Women*,[207] herself repeats the word that Victoria's journal reiterates: "She who had been so carefully guarded by mother and governess had now to act alone. . . . She went to [her first Council] quite alone" (176).

20. In 1995 Elizabeth Langland read Victoria as the epitome of the queenliness urged on middle-class Englishwomen by Patmore, Ruskin, and others (*Nobody's Angels* [Ithaca, NY: Cornell University Press, 1995], 68–79).

21. Stanley Weintraub, *Victoria: An Intimate Biography* (New York: Dutton, 1987), xii; Langland, *Nobody's Angels,* 62–63; Lytton Strachey, *Queen Victoria* (New York: Harcourt Brace Jovanovich, 1921), 415–16.

22. Adrienne Munich states that, by 1901, "Victoria's legend joined other legendary women . . . in popular compendia of the ten best of a category" (*Queen Victoria's Secrets* [New York: Columbia University Press, 1996], 210; further references to this study appear parenthetically). In fact, Victoria broke into such biographical honor rolls in the early decades of her reign. In my Pop Chart (table A2) she appears twenty-nine times in general collections in the three periods, behind only Joan of Arc, Elizabeth Fry, and Florence Nightingale, and just above Charlotte Brontë. The Pop Chart counts necessarily omit the representation of Victoria in specialized collections, e.g., of queens or Victorians.

23. William Thayer[792] expresses admiration for Victoria. "Of our Republic we say, 'How much it owes to the mothers of Washington and Lincoln!' and the English say, 'How much we owe to the mother of our Queen!'" (262). Victoria, in old age, has "endeared herself . . . to her own people and to all mankind" (287).

24. Goodrich twice quotes Peter Cunningham to the effect that the freehold house given to Nell Gwyn by Charles II was later "tenanted by the Society for the Propagation of the Gospel in Foreign Parts" (236, 242), thus further associating Gwyn with piety and charity, as well as with one of Goodrich's favorite subjects in the volume, Ann Hasseltine Judson.

25. For example, Adams, *Celebrated Englishwomen* (1:6),[6] Carey, *Twelve Notable Good Women of the XIXth Century* (28–29),[143] Abbot (201–2),[1] and Mary Howitt, ed., *Biographical Sketches of the Queens of England* (513).[424] Susan P. Casteras, "The Wise Child and Her 'Offspring': Some Changing Faces of Queen Victoria," in *Remaking Queen Victoria,* ed. Homans and Munich, offers an illuminating reading of paintings of the "annunciation" scene for this "secular Madonna" (195–98).

26. Victoria exposes, like Elizabeth I, an inherent "plasticity of gender in the field of sovereignty," which according to Louise Olga Fradenburg is due to sovereignty's drive toward both "exemplarity" and exclusive "difference" from the common body ("Introduction: Rethinking Queenship," in *Women and Sovereignty,* ed. Louise Olga Fradenburg, vol. 7 of *Cosmos: The Yearbook of the Traditional Cosmological Society* [Edinburgh: Edinburgh University Press, 1992], 1–3).

27. Elsie Egermeier[251] tells the story of "The Little Princess Who Became a Great Queen": "'Little Dwina,' the princess of our story, is not a make-believe somebody of fairyland lore, but a real person" (70).

28. A presenter of rank, von Bothmer offers a privileged travel narrative as well as guidebook, with numerous photographs of royal rooms, gardens, and families. Characteristic passages testify: "In the private treasury at Moscow I have seen, each on its pillar of marble, the marvellous crowns of Russia" (60). The English monarchy seems both warmer and more secure: it appears "impossible" for the Russian czars to have "any intimate acquaintance with this affectionate Russian people, and many times the free, happy life at Balmoral must have filled the young Tzaritza with longings that it were possible for her to talk to the subjects. . . . Never can they love her as the English love their Queen, for she is too far off" (64).

29. Hale's Victoria,[362] the epitome of "the reign of feeling and intellect, of industry and peace," becomes a static emblem of feminine rule, leaning on her husband's arm at the Crystal Palace (809). See Homans, *Royal Representations,* xxv, 6.

30. As quoted in Hale (799).[362]

31. Elsie Prentys Thornton-Cook, *Her Majesty* (New York: Dutton, 1927), 85–96, 100–103.

32. Photographs of full-length statues do appear, more frequently in later highly illustrated volumes intended to convey a sense of locale. A bust of Harriet Beecher Stowe, photographed, serves as frontispiece in *Heroines of Modern Progress*,[4] a volume that offers head-and-shoulder photographs of contemporaries in all their idiosyncrasy. *Women Who Have Ennobled Life*[862] features a frontispiece photograph of a 1914 bas-relief of Julia Ward Howe by Cyrus E. Dallin; the statue of Florence Nightingale (mentioned in my introduction) appears in Howe's biography, which is introduced with a drawing of "a photograph taken in middle age" (facing 234).

33. See Lady Antonia Fraser, *Mary Queen of Scots and the Historians*, Royal Stuart Papers, 7 (London: Royal Stuart Society, 1974), on the conventions of interpretation of Mary: the "Scarlet Woman," "The Martyr Queen," "the 'Dynastic' issue," and the "Femme Fatale" (1); the centuries-old inverse relation of the reputations of Elizabeth I and Mary Queen of Scots in which defense of one is attack on the other (11–12).

34. *Queens of England* concludes, "GOD SAVE OUR GRACIOUS QUEEN!" (341).[764] The specter of a debauched and bedecked Elizabeth I or other transgressive queen helps construct Victoria's thorough goodness. The scandal of her attachment to her Scottish servant John Brown does not appear on Howitt's soft-focus screen in 1868, though journals had blown it up in 1866–67 (St Aubyn, *Queen Victoria*, 360–62); if collective biographies mention Brown at all, they present Victoria's benign condescension to a faithful servant (Thornton-Cook, *Her Majesty*, 370–71). This was the closest glimpse of the flipside of a queen's card: the class-crossing "quean," in Howitt's punning term for Elizabeth (404).[424]

35. Victoria serves as frontispiece in, e.g., Ewart[270] (an older Victoria in profile with a veil flowing down her back, reading), Creighton[207] (a young Victoria, holding a letter in her lap and gazing outward, chin propped on hand), Carey[143] (contemporary photograph of seated empress), Thornton-Cook, *Her Majesty* (formal, royally crowned full-length portrait by Winterhalter, 1859); von Bothmer[100] (*The Queen in State Robes* [engraved from a drawing by A. E. Chalon] standing on steps, leaning on ermine draped over a classical balustrade—an illustration also in Abbot[1]).

36. Stephen Heathorn finds a shift in English schoolbooks in the representation of Victoria from model of domestic virtue in the 1850s to Saxon sovereign of the world at the end of the century (*For Home, Country, and Race* [Toronto: University of Toronto Press, 2000], 58, 82–84).

37. By "the Crown," Ewart[270] means "the Royal Family," and he gives Albert much credit for the initiative to progress that was the Great Exhibition (24).

38. Thornton-Cook makes a similar point (*Her Majesty*, 372).

39. Abbot details Albert and Victoria's softening of Lord Palmerston's ultimatum concerning the incident on the British steamer Trent: "The influence of the royal couple undoubtedly averted war" with the Union in 1861 (205).[1]

40. Parton, in *Eminent Women of the Age*, suggests that her "chief service" to her country may have been to postpone revolutionary protests against the "costly pageant" of monarchy (438).[630]

41. Munich, *Queen Victoria's Secrets*, 58–60; further references appear parenthetically.

42. Daniel Siegel has an article forthcoming in *Victorian Literature and Culture* on the evolving codes of condescension.

43. Mary Poovey, *Uneven Developments* (Chicago: University of Chicago Press, 1988), 171. See Richmond (vol. 2),[673] Creighton,[207] Carey,[143] and Thayer.[792]

44. Susan Bordo, *Unbearable Weight* (Berkeley: University of California Press, 1993), 222–25.

45. Munich and Houston cite articles by Homans that form parts of *Royal Representations*, whereas Homans's and Houston's later books refer extensively to *Queen Victoria's Secrets*. All three works build on the collection coedited by Homans and Munich, *Remaking Queen Victoria*, to which Houston was a contributor.

46. Langbauer concurs (regarding the collective megalomania), as I read after writing the previous sentence: "The idea that feminist scholars personally identify with Queen Victoria . . . sounds literally mad (the Victorians incarcerated madwomen who believed themselves to be Victoria)" (216).

47. Woolf, *Orlando* (1928; reprint, New York: Harcourt Brace, 1956), 227–32.

48. As Homans and Munich remark in *Remaking Queen Victoria,* "the term 'Victorian' is not likely to bring the Queen herself to mind" (1); as Elizabeth Langland confirms, "Victorian" has been applied to "movements, behaviors, and beliefs that extend beyond England's borders" and have only tangential relation to Victoria herself ("Nation and Nationality: Queen Victoria in the Developing Narrative of Englishness," in *Remaking Queen Victoria,* ed. Homans and Munich, 22–23). Compare Munich (2). Victoria having become ubiquitous once more, Houston perhaps serves less as rescuer; "the author is not dead, and neither is the queen" (*Royalties,* 5).

49. As Langbauer puts it in her own discussion of Homans's and Munich's works, "such critics might seem hard at work applying the standard feminist methodology of recovery to the woman in all of time who would seem least to warrant it: Queen Victoria, absent from history?" (212).

50. Nina Auerbach, *Woman and the Demon* (Cambridge, MA: Harvard University Press, 1982), 2. Citations will appear parenthetically in the text.

51. For example, Patrick Brantlinger, *Fictions of State: Culture and Credit in Britain, 1694–1994* (Ithaca, NY: Cornell University Press, 1996); and Jenny Sharpe, *Allegories of Empire: The Figure of Woman in the Colonial Text* (Minneapolis: University of Minnesota Press, 1993). Deirdre David's *Rule Britannia* (Ithaca, NY: Cornell University Press, 1995) features illustrations of Victoria (including on the paperback cover) that appear in either Homans or Munich and offers more sustained vignettes of the queen than in most studies primarily focused on novels. Langland's *Nobody's Angels* devotes an entire chapter to "England's Domestic Queen and Her Queenly Domestic Other." Langland refers to Munich and Homans's emerging projects (*Nobody's Angels,* 63n.1), and Homans and Houston acknowledge Langland (Homans, esp. xxxiii–iv; Houston, *Royalties,* 2). Houston's *Royalties* is cited in Homans (xxix, 246n.19, 262n.23). Among many recent biographies, Dorothy Thompson's *Queen Victoria* (New York: Pantheon, 1990) seems to have furnished most for a feminist reading of the Queen. Kimberly VanEsveld Adams, *Our Lady of Victorian Feminism* (Athens: Ohio University Press, 2001), and Sharon Aronofsky Weltman, *Ruskin's Mythic Queen,* in different ways contribute significantly to the current figuration of Victorian queenship.

52. Amanda Anderson, "The Temptations of Aggrandized Agency: Feminist Histories and the Horizon of Modernity," *Victorian Studies* 43 (2000): 52.

53. On the drive to "carve up" or periodize literary history, see Susan J. Wolfson, "Our Puny Boundaries," *PMLA* 116 (2001): 1432–41.

54. Elaine Showalter, *A Literature of Their Own* (Princeton, NJ: Princeton University Press, 1977), 6–7. Showalter, resistant heir to Woolf in so-called Anglo American feminist criticism, notes that "many of the original gynocritical theories of women's writing were based primarily on nineteenth-century English women's texts." Classics of feminist criticism, however nuanced and responsible, have appeared less relevant to the concerns of black, lesbian, and working class women and others not represented in canonical Victorian novels ("A Criticism of Our Own," 1989, reprinted in *Feminisms,* ed. Robyn R. Warhol and Diane Price Herndl, rev. ed. [New Brunswick, NJ: Rutgers University Press, 1997], 226).

55. Toril Moi, *Sexual/Textual Politics* (London: Methuen, 1985), 61.

56. There are instances of a fusion of feminist Lacanian theory with literary history and the "big four" nineteenth-century novelists, e.g. Robyn Warhol, "The Look, the Body, and the Heroine of *Persuasion:* A Feminist-Narratological View of Jane Austen," in *Ambiguous Discourse: Feminist Narratology and British Women Writers,* ed. Kathy Mezei (Chapel Hill: University of North Carolina Press, 1996), 21–39; Beth Newman, "'The Situation of the Looker-On': Gender, Narration, and Gaze in *Wuthering Heights,*" in *Feminisms,* ed. Warhol and Herndl, 449–66.

57. The quote is from Woolf, "Women and Fiction," in *Collected Essays,* 4 vols. (New York: Harcourt Brace, 1967), 2:143.

58. Popular biographies of Victoria from collections of the 1860s[e.g., 5; 220] or the 1880s[e.g., 282; 673] emphasize her feminine goodness rather than sovereignty. In 1888, Ewart declares that "goodness has been her real greatness" (27).[270] Few give her credit for the sagacity of her rule or for authorship.

59. Oliphant, "The Literature of the Last Fifty Years," *Blackwood's Magazine* (June 1887), reprinted in *Prose by Victorian Women,* ed. Andrea Broomfield and Sally Mitchell (New York: Garland, 1996), 401–2, 416–18, 392–94.

60. I find it more than coincidental that Sandra Gilbert and Susan Gubar ("Introduction to the Second Edition: The Madwoman in the Academy," *The Madwoman in the Attic* [New Haven, CT: Yale University Press, 2000]) depict their bicoastal bias as newcomers to Indiana University in 1973 in terms of Steinberg's famous cartoon map (xvi–xvii). The task of the introduction is to explain the "geography" of early feminist literary studies (preeminently their own), much as I attempt to do here. Further citations to *Madwoman* appear parenthetically.

61. I wrote critically of Woolf's "Mt. Rushmore of Jane Austen, Charlotte and Emily Brontë, and George Eliot" (*Greatness Engendered* [Ithaca, NY: Cornell University Press, 1992], 10).

62. Gilbert and Gubar themselves urged attention to women poets, while explaining the predilection of women writers for the new domestically adapted genre, the novel. *Shakespeare's Sisters* (Bloomington: Indiana University Press, 1979), xvi–xxii.

63. Considerable recent feminist study of Victorian poetry, including poetic narrative, is displacing the fiction monopoly (e.g., Dorothy Mermin, *Godiva's Ride: Women of Letters in England, 1830–1880* [Bloomington: Indiana University Press, 1993]; Yopie Prins, *Victorian Sappho* [Princeton, NJ: Princeton University Press, 1999]; Angela Leighton, *Victorian Women Poets: Writing against the Heart* [Charlottesville: University Press of Virginia, 1992]), but teaching texts of poetry or nonfiction prose are slow in coming.

64. I had become friendly with both Margaret Homans and Adrienne Munich at conferences. My affection, gratitude, and admiration, as well as a familiarity with their work on this topic, did make it a bit sensitive to agree to review their "Victoria" books, with the addition of Houston's study, in the journal that Adrienne coedits.

65. See my "The Mother of All Cultures: Camille Paglia and Feminist Mythologies," *Kenyon Review* 21 (1999): 27–45.

66. Elaine Showalter, *Inventing Herself: Claiming a Feminist Intellectual Heritage* (New York: Scribner, 2001), 278–83, 303–19; further citations in the text. Paglia attacked the student for impersonating her in a skit. The attack is one of the misdeeds she mentions in *Vamps and Tramps* (New York: Vintage, 1994), 231. See my essay, "Mother of All Cultures," 29.

67. The right locations are Paris, 1968; the 1970 MLA with Florence Howe and the Women's Caucus; Douglass College at Rutgers, the "center of the new women's studies initiative" (257, 270–72).

68. Ann Jernberg and Phyllis B. Booth, *Theraplay: Helping Parents and Children Build Better Relationships through Attachment-Based Play,* 2d ed. (San Francisco: Jossey-Bass, 1999); Wayne C. Booth, *For the Love of It: Amateuring and Its Rivals* (Chicago: University of Chicago Press, 1999).

Bibliography of Collective Biographies of Women, 1830—1940

Prefatory Note

This bibliography, compiled with the assistance of Christopher Jackson, Karen Dietz, Erin O'Connor, Sarah Whitney, Christine Bayles-Korstch, Margaret Cooke, and Regan Boxwell, is an exhaustive inventory of books published in English between 1830 and 1940 that present three or more women's lives in more than skeletal outline (reference works are generally excluded). Other contributions to this subgenre may lurk under misleading titles or cataloging. I do include some closely related books that feature men and women or that take the form of poetry, drama, lectures, historiography, catalogs or encyclopedias, advice or advocacy, and even historical fiction. These exceptions are warranted for various reasons: they feature a series of representative, named women of history (including sacred or legendary history); they affirm new constituencies (e.g. a "Who's Who" of the women of a region or organization); they are written by someone who contributes to this subgenre; or they closely relate to other volumes or varieties of prosopography represented here. Such relevant but formally divergent works are marked by the shorthand "NOT."

In the appendix, I provide a chronological index of collective biographies (table A1) according to the number of the item in this bibliography. The chronological index provides information for the chart of rates of publication (fig. A1), also in the appendix. In order to compare the representation of certain eminent women as well as to measure the standing of certain women across time, I have designed a "Pop Chart" (table A2) that culls the most common subjects from nonspecialized collections during three twenty-year periods of activism on women's rights and roles: 1850–70, 1880–1900, and 1910–30.

To conserve printed space, I shorten many titles and omit most title variations and annotations. This skeletal version is for the reader's convenience as a first reference. Readers inquiring further or citing this bibliography should consult my online "Annotated Bibliography of Collective Biographies of Women" (http://etext.lib.virginia.edu/WomensBios/), searchable for different purposes. There, annotations begin to interrelate the works, identify the presenters, list the contents, and describe the volumes in other ways. In either format, the bibliography is a starting point for the study of publications in this mode. I do not claim to have seen or read all the works.

Works published anonymously are alphabetized by title unless authorship is known. Pseudonymous works are listed under the pseudonym. The publication data includes the date of every edition or reprint through 1940 that I have traced, though I have not attempted complete histories of each work. Unless otherwise stated, I cite the first listed date/edition when discussing books in the text. The online version at times indicates the holding or the source of the information. Entries followed by "PC" are general collections that contribute to my Pop Chart (table A2).

Chronological Selection of Early Examples

1st century A.D. Plutarch. *Mulierum virtutes* (Concerning the virtues of women). 1:340–84 in *Plutarch's Morals Translated from the Greek by Several Hands.* Edited by William W. Goodwin. Introduction by Ralph Waldo Emerson. Rev. ed. 2 vols. New York: Athenaeum, 1870.

1361–75. Boccaccio, Giovanni. *De claris mulieribus/Concerning Famous Women.* Translated by Guido A. Guarino. New Brunswick, NJ: Rutgers University Press, 1963.

1372–86. Chaucer, Geoffrey. "The Legend of Good Women." In *The Works of Geoffrey Chaucer.* Edited by F. N. Robinson, 480–518. 2d ed. Boston: Houghton Mifflin, 1961.

1405. Pizan, Christine de. *The Book of the City of Ladies [Le Livre de la cité des dames].* Translated by Earl Jeffrey Richards. New York: Persea, 1982.

1443–47. Bokenham, Osbern. *A Legend of Holy Women [Legendys of Hooly Wummen].* South Bend, IN: University of Notre Dame Press, 1992.

1521. [Ravisius, Textor]. *De memorabilibus et claris mulieribus aliquot diversorum scriptorum opera.* Paris.

ca. 1610–15. *The Lives of Women Saints of Our Contrie England, Also some other lives of holie women written by some of the auncient fathers.* Early English Text Society. London: Trubner, 1886.

1624. Heywood, Thomas. *Gynaikeion: or, Nine Bookes of Various History Concerninge Women: inscribed by ye names of ye nine muses.* London: Adam Islip. Also published anonymously: *The Nine Muses,* 1700.

1639. Rivers, George. *The Heroinae; or, The Lives of Arria, Paulina, Lucretia, Dido, Theutilla, Cypriana, Aretaphila.* London: Printed by R. Bishop, for John Colby.

1640. Heywood, Thomas. *The Exemplary Lives and Memorable Acts of Nine of the Most Worthy Women of the World: Three Iewes, Three Gentiles, Three Christians.* London: Printed by Thomas Cotes, for Richard Royston.

1642. Scudéry, Madeleine de. *Les Femmes illustres ou les Harangues heroïques.* English ed.: *The Female Orators; or, The Courage and Constancy of Divers Famous Queens, and Illustrious Women, Set Forth in Their Eloquent Orations, and Noble Resolutions: Worthy the Perusal and Imitation of the Female Sex. English'd from the French edition of Monsieur de Scudéry.* London: T. Tebb, 1714.

1647. Le Moyne, Pierre. *Galerie des femmes fortes.* English ed.: *The Gallery of Heroick Women.* Translated by Marquesse of Winchester [John Paulet]. London: by R. Norton for Henry Seile, 1652.

1651. Gerbier, Charles. *Elogium Heroinum, the Ladies Vindication; or, The Praise of Worthy Women.* London: Printed by T. M. & A. C. and sold by William Raybould.

1657. Gent, J. H. [Thomas Heywood]. *The Generall History of Women, Containing the Lives of the Most Holy and Profane. . . .* London: Printed by W. H. for W. H. A reissue of *Gynaikeion.*

1665. Brantôme, Pierre de Bourdeille, Seigneur de. *Le Livre des dames.* English ed.: *The Book of the Ladies; or, Lives of Illustrious Dames.* Reprinted as *The Book of the Ladies (Illustrious Dames): With Elucidations on Some of Those Ladies by C. A. Sainte-Beuve.* Translated by Katherine Prescott Wormeley. Illustrated with Portraits from the Original. London: W. Heinemann, 1899.

1671. *A Catalogue of Virtuous Women.*

1686. [Shirley, John]. *The Illustrious History of Women.* London: J. Harris.

1687. Burton, Robert [i.e., Nathaniel Crouch]. *The History of the Nine Worthies of the World.* London: Crouch, 1703; 1727. Other publishers: 1738; 1759; 1776. NOT

1688. Burton, Robert [i.e., Nathaniel Crouch]. *Female Excellency; or, The Ladies Glory: Illustrated in the Worthy Lives and Memorable Actions of Nine Famous Women, Who Have Been Renowned Either for Virtue or Valour in Several Ages of the World.* London: Nathaniel Crouch. 2d ed., London, 1704. 3d ed., London: Bettesworth & Batley, 1728. 4th ed., Burton, *The Female Worthies; or, the Ladies['] Glory,* Dublin: Cross, 1765.

1727. *The Lives and Amours of Queens and Royal Mistresses, with some Intrigues of Popes, Extracted from the Histories of England, France, Turkey, Spain and Italy.* London.

1752. Ballard, George. *Memoirs of Several Ladies of Great Britain: Who Have Been Celebrated for Their Writings or Skill in the Learned Languages, Arts and Sciences.* Oxford: Printed by W. Jackson, for the author. 2d ed., London: Printed for T. Evans, 1775. Reprint edited by Ruth Perry. Detroit: Wayne State University Press, 1985.

1752. Serviez, Jacques Roergas de. *The Roman Empresses: or, the history of the lives and secret intrigues of the wives of the twelve Caesars* . . . Translated by Bysse Molesworth. Dublin: George Faulkner. Title variant: London: R. Dodsley.

1755. Amory, Thomas. *Memoirs: Containing the Lives of Several Ladies of Great Britain. A History of Antiquities, Productions of Nature, and Monuments of Art. [etc.]* London: John Noon. Possibly identical to the following.

1755. Amory, Thomas. *Memoirs of Several Ladies of Great Britain: Interspersed with Literary Reflexions, and Accounts of Curious Things.*

1766. *Biographium faemineum: The Female Worthies; or, Memoirs of the Most Illustrious Ladies, of All Ages and Nations, Who Have Been Eminently Distinguished for Their Magnanimity, Learning, Genius, Virtue, Piety, and Other Excellent Endowments . . . Containing (Exclusive of Foreigners) the Lives of above Fourscore British Ladies . . . Collected from History, and the Most Approved Biographers, and Brought Down to the Present Time.* . . . 2 vols. London: Printed for S. Crowder, and J. Payne.

1770. Stretch, L. M. *The Beauties of History; or, Pictures of Virtue and Vice, Drawn from Real Life: Designed for the Instruction and Entertainment of Youth.* 2 vols. London: for author. 2d ed., Dublin: Marchbank, 1775. 3d ed., London: E. & C. Dilly, 1777. 5th ed., London, 1782; 1787; 1794; 1802; 1813; 1815; 1833.

1772. La Roche-Guilhen, Anne, Mlle de. *The History of Female Favourites: Of Mary de Cadilla . . . Livia . . . Julia Farnesa . . . Agnes Soreau . . . and Nantilda.* . . . Amsterdam: 1697; London: Printed for C. Parker.

1777. Gibbons, Thomas. *Memoirs of Eminently Pious Women, Who Were Ornaments of Their Sex, Blessings to Their Countries and Edifying Examples to the Church and World.* 2 vols. [London: Backland].

1799. Pilkington, Mary Hopkins. *Biography for Girls; or, Moral and Instructive Examples for Young Ladies.* London: Vernon & Hood, 1800. Subtitle variant: Philadelphia: Johnson & Warner, 1809.

1803. *Eccentric Biography; or, Memoirs of Remarkable Female Characters, Ancient and Modern. Including Actresses, Adventurers, Authoresses, Fortune-Tellers, Gipsies, Dwarfs, Swindlers and Vagrants: Also Many Others Who Have Distinguished Themselves by Their Chastity, Dissipation, Intrepidity, Learning, Abstinence, Credulity, &c., &c.: Alphabetically Arranged: Forming a Pleasing Mirror of Reflection to the Female Mind.* Ornamented with Portraits of the Most Singular Characters in the Work. London: Printed by J. Cundee, sold by T. Hurst. Worcester, [MA]: Printed by Isaiah Thomas, 1804. With title variant: 1805.

1803. Gibbons, Thomas, and Daniel Dana. *Memoirs of Eminently Pious Women: Who Were Ornaments to Their Sex, Blessings to Their Families, and Edifying Examples to the Church and World.* Abridged from the Large Work of Dr. Gibbons, London by Daniel Dana. Newburyport, [MA]: Printed for the Subscribers by Angier March. See 1777.

1803. Hays, Mary. *Female Biography; or, Memoirs of Illustrious and Celebrated Women, of All Ages and Countries, Alphabetically Arranged.* 6 vols. London: R. Phillips. 1st American ed., 3 vols., Philadelphia: Birch & Small; Fry & Kammerer, 1807.

1803. [Stewarton]. *The Female Revolutionary Plutarch: Containing Biographical, Historical, and Revolutionary Sketches, Characters, and Anecdotes/by the Author of "The Revolutionary Plutarch" and "Memoirs of Talleyrand."* 3 vols. London: Printed by J. Harding for J. Murray, 1806. 3d ed., London: Murray, 1808.

1804. Betham, Mary Matilda [1776–1852]. *A Biographical Dictionary of the Celebrated Women of*

Every Age and Country. London: Printed for B. Crosby; Tegg & Castleman; and E. Lloyd, Betham, & Warde, Printers.

1804. Jerment, Rev. George, ed. *Memoirs of Eminently Pious Women, Who Were Ornaments of Their Sex, Blessings to Their Countries and Edifying Examples to the Church and World by Thomas Gibbons.* Rev. ed. 2 vols. London: Ogles. See Gibbons (1777), Gibbons and Dana (1803), and Burder, Gibbons, and Jerment (1815).

1804. Pilkington, Mary Hopkins. *Memoirs of Celebrated Female Characters Who Have Distinguished Themselves by Their Talents and Virtues in Every Age and Nation: Containing the Most Extensive Collection of Illustrious Examples of Excellence Ever Published. In Which the Virtuous and the Vicious Are Painted in Their True Colours.* Embellished with Portraits. [London]: Albion.

1807. Fraser, Donald, comp. *The Mental Flower Garden; or, An Instructive and Entertaining Companion for the Fair Sex. In Two Parts. Containing: 1. A Variety of Entertaining and Moral Dialogues, Partly Original, Calculated for Misses from Eight to Twelve Years, A Collection of Useful Rules Relative to Genteel Behaviour, and a Polite Address. Poetic Pieces. Devotional Poems, Writing Pieces, &c. 2. Miscellaneous Essays, Worthy the Perusal of Women, at any Period of Life. To Which Are Added, Interesting Sketches of Female Biography....* New York: Southwick & Hardcast. NOT

1807. Pilkington, Mary Hopkins. *Memoirs of Celebrated Women of England: Including Also Those Who Have Distinguished Themselves by Their Talents and Virtues in Every Age and Nation: Containing the Most Extensive Collection of Illustrious Examples of Feminine Excellence Ever Published: In Which the Virtuous and the Vicious Are Painted in Their True Colours.* London: Albion.

1810. Aikin, Lucy. *Epistles on Women, Exemplifying Their Character and Condition in Various Ages and Nations: With miscellaneous poems.* Boston: Wells & Wait.

1815. Burder, Samuel, Thomas Gibbons, and George Jerment. *Memoirs of Eminently Pious Women of the British Empire.* New ed., embellished with eighteen portraits, corr. and enl. by the Rev. Samuel Burder. 3 vols. in 1. London: Ogles. Philadelphia: J. J. Woodward, 1834; 1835; 1836.

1817. Cox, Francis Augustus. *Female Scripture Biography: Including an Essay on What Christianity Has Done for Women.* 2 vols. London: Gale & Fenner Hamilton. New York: James Eastburn. Boston: Lincoln & Edmands, 1831. 2d ed., London: John Snow, 1852. See 205.

1818. Aikin, Lucy. *Memoirs of the Court of Queen Elizabeth.* London: Longman, Hurst, Rees, Orme, & Brown. 2 vols., 1819.

1821. Hays, Mary. *Memoirs of Queens: Illustrious and Celebrated.* London: Allman.

1821. [Roberts, Mary.] *Select Female Biography: Comprising Memoirs of Eminent British Ladies, Derived from Original and Other Authentic Sources.* London: Arch. 2d ed., London: Harvey & Darton, 1829.

1822. Aikin, Lucy. *Memoirs of the Court of King James the First.* Boston: Wells & Lilly.

1822. Belson, Mary [afterward Elliott]. *Female Biography; or, Virtue and Talent Exemplified in the Characters of Eminent British Females.* London: Darton.

1822. Sharp, T., and John Stanford. *The Heavenly Sisters; or, Biographical Sketches of the Lives of Thirty Eminently Pious Females, Partly Extracted from the Works of Gibbon, Germont, and Others, and Partly Original: Designed for the Use of Females in General, and Particularly Recommended for the Use of Ladies' Schools. To which is Added, a Memoir of Mrs. Abigail, Wife of the Late President Adams, and a Sketch of the Active Life of Mrs. Sarah Hoffman.* New Haven, CT: N. Whiting.

1825. Dyce, Alexander. *Specimens of British Poetesses; selected and chronologically arranged.*

1825. Taft, Zachariah. *Biographical Sketches of the Lives and Public Ministry of Various Holy Women: Whose Eminent Usefulness and Successful Labours in the Church of Christ Have Entitled Them to Be Enrolled among the Great Benefactors of Mankind: In which Are Included Several Letters from the Rev. J. Wesley Never before Published.* 2 vols. London: Kershaw. Leeds: 1825; 1828. 3 vols. in 1, London: Kershaw, 1835; 1838.

1826–27. Prudhomme, Louis Marie. *Répertoire universel, historique, biographique des femmes célèbres.* . . . Paris. Title variant: Paris: Lebigre, 1830.

1827. Lee, Anna Maria. *Memoirs of Eminent Female Writers, of All Ages and Countries.* Philadelphia: J. Grigg.

1828. Hemans, Felicia. *Records of Woman: With Other Poems.* Boston: Hilliard, Gray, Little & Wilkins; Edinburgh: W. Blackwood; London: T. Cadell.

Alphabetical Bibliography, 1830–1940

1. Abbot, Willis J. *Notable Women of History: The Lives of Women Who in All Ages, All Lands and in All Womanly Occupations Have Won Fame and Put Their Imprint on the World's History.* Philadelphia: John C. Winston, 1913. PC

2. Adams, Charles, and Daniel P. Kidder. *Women of the Bible.* New York: Lane & Scott for Sunday-School Union; Carlton & Phillips; Phillips & Hunt; Cincinnati, OH: Walden & Stowe, 1851; 1854. 4th ed., New York: Carlton & Porter, Sunday-School Union, 1856; 1868.

3. Adams, Charlotte Hannah. *Women of Ancient Israel.* New York: National Board of the YWCA, 1912; 1913. 3d ed., 1916.

4. Adams, Elmer Cleveland, and Warren Dunham Foster. *Heroines of Modern Progress.* New York: Sturgis & Walton; Macmillan, 1913; Sturgis, 1915; 1918; 1921; 1922; 1926; 1939. PC

5. Adams, Henry Gardiner, ed. *Cyclopaedia of Female Biography: Consisting of Sketches of All Women Who Have Been Distinguished by Great Talents, Strength of Character, Piety, Benevolence, or Moral Virtue of Any Kind; Forming a Complete Record of Womanly Excellence or Ability.* London: Groombridge, 1857. Glasgow: Forrester, Stockwell, 1866. London: Routledge, 1869. All page citations in text are to the 1869 ed.

6. Adams, William Henry Davenport. *Celebrated Englishwomen of the Victorian Era.* 2 vols. London: F. V. White, 1881; 1884; 1900. PC

7. ———. *Celebrated Women Travellers of the Nineteenth Century.* London: Sonnenschein, 1883; 1887; 1889; 1903; 1906. New York: Dutton, 1903.

8. ———. *Child-Life and Girlhood of Remarkable Women: A Series of Chapters from Female Biography.* 2d ed. London: Sonnenschein, 1883; 1885; Sonnenschein & Lowery, 1887. New York: Dutton; London: Sonnenschein, 1895. PC

9. ———. *Exemplary Women: A Record of Feminine Virtues and Achievements.* London: 1882. Abridged from *Woman's Work and Worth.*

10. ———. *Famous Beauties and Historic Women: A Gallery of Croquis Biographiques.* 2 vols. London: C. J. Skeet, 1865. PC

11. ———. *Some Historic Women; or, Biographical Studies of Women Who Have Made History.* London: J. Hogg, [1891]. [1890–99]. PC

12. ———. *Stories of the Lives of Noble Women.* London: T. Nelson, 1877; 1880; 1882; [1911]. Same contents as *The Sunshine,* below, but adds Charlotte Brontë.

13. ———. *The Sunshine of Domestic Life; or, Sketches of Womanly Virtues, and Stories of the Lives of Noble Women.* London: Nelson, 1867; 1868; 1869; 1873; 1876. Boston: 1882. London: 1891. Republished as *Stories of the Lives of Noble Women.* PC

14. ———. *Woman's Work and Worth in Girlhood, Maidenhood, and Wifehood: With hints on self culture and chapters on the higher education and employment of women.* London: J. Hogg, 1879; 1880. New York: Cassell, Petter, Galpin, 1880; 1884. Chicago: Rand McNally, 1884. PC

15. ———. *Women of Fashion and Representative Women in Letters and Society: A Series of Biographical and Critical Studies.* 2 vols. London: Tinsley, 1878.

16. Addition, Lucia H. Faxon. *Twenty Eventful Years of the Oregon Woman's Christian Temperance Union, 1880–1900: Statistical, Historical and Biographical Portraits of Pioneer Workers.* Portland, OR: Gotshall, 1904.

17. Adelman, Joseph Ferdinand Gottlieb. *Famous Women: An Outline of Feminine Achievement through the Ages, with Life Stories of Five Hundred Noted Women*. New York: Ellis M. Lonow, 1926. New York: Rogers, Pictorial Review, Woman's World, 1928.

18. Adeney, Walter Frederic. *Women of the New Testament*. London: Service & Paton; J. Nisbet, 1899. London: J. Nisbet; New York: T. Whittaker, 1901; 1906. Title variant: *Women and the Church in America*.

19. Aguilar, Grace. *The Women of Israel; or, Characters and Sketches from the Holy Scriptures and Jewish History, Illustrative of the Past History, Present Duties, and Future Destiny of the Hebrew Females, as Based on the Word of God*. London: Groombridge, 1845; 1853. New ed., Boston: Hickling, Swan & Brewer, 1857. 2 vols., New York and Philadelphia: Appleton, 1850; 1851; 1852; 1853; 1854; 1857; 1860; 1862; 1864; 1866. London: Groombridge, 1857. London: Groombridge; New York: Appleton, 1870. London: Groombridge, 1871; 1872; 1873; 1874; 1875; 1876; 1878; 1879; 1881; 1884; 1886. New York: Appleton, 1871; 1874; 1875; 1878; 1879; 1881; 1883, 1887. London: Routledge; New York: Dutton, 1879. 1 vol., New York: Appleton; London: Routledge, 1889; 1891; 1892; 1897, [1900?]. New ed., New York: Appleton, 1907; 1913; 1917.

20. Aikman, Duncan. *Calamity Jane and the Lady Wildcats*. New York: Holt, 1927.

21. Alec-Tweedie, Mrs. [Ethel]. *Women the World Over: A Sketch Both Light and Gay, Perchance Both Dull and Stupid*. London, 1914. New York: Doran, 1914, [1915].

22. Alexander, Julia McGehee. *Mothers of Great Men: Sketches*. Charlotte, NC: Observer, 1916.

23. Alger, Rev. W. R. *The Friendships of Women*. 3d ed. Boston: Roberts, 1867; 1868; 1870; 1872; 1875; 1882; 1885.

24. Alldridge, Lizzie. *Florence Nightingale. Frances Ridley Havergal. Catherine Marsh. Mrs. Ranyard ("L.N.R.")*. London, Paris, New York and Melbourne: Cassell, 1885; 1887; 1889; 1893. 3d ed., New York, 1887. 4th ed., New York, 1889. 5th ed., New York 1890; 1893. 6th ed. as *The World's Workers: Florence Nightingale, Frances Ridley Havergal, Catherine Marsh, Mrs. Ranyard*.

25. *The American Book of Beauty: with Illustrations on Steel, by Eminent Artists; Edited by a Lady*. New York: Wilson, 1845. Subtitle variant: *Or, Token of Friendship*, Hartford, CT: Andrus, 1845.

26. An American Lady [Ann Hasseltine Judson]. *Sketches of the Lives of Distinguished Females: Written for Girls, with a View to Their Mental and Moral Improvement*. New York: Harper, 1833. Reprint 1837. By Ann Hasseltine Judson, 1847; 1854.

27. American Sunday-School Union. *Notable Women of Olden Times*. Philadelphia: American Sunday-School Union, 1852.

28. *America's Twelve Great Women Leaders during the Past Hundred Years as Chosen by the Women of America; a Compilation from the Ladies' Home Journal and the Christian Science Monitor*. Chicago: Associated Authors, 1933.

29. Anderson, Rev. James [of Edinburgh]. *The Ladies of the Covenant: Memoirs of Distinguished Scottish Female Characters, Embracing the Period of the Covenant and the Persecution*. London: Blackie, 1850; 1851. Glasgow: Blackie, 1852; 1853; 1855; 1857; 1862. New York: Redfield, 1851. 2d ed., Clinton Hall, NY: Redfield, 1853; 1855. New York: Armstrong, 1880.

30. ———. *Ladies of the Reformation: Memoirs of Distinguished Female Characters, Belonging to the Period of the Reformation in the Sixteenth Century . . . England, Scotland, and the Netherlands*. London: Blackie, 1854. London, Edinburgh, Glasgow, New York: Blackie, 1855. New York: Blackie, 1857.

31. ———. *Memorable Women of the Puritan Times*. 2 vols. London, [etc.]: Blackie, 1861; 1862.

32. Anderson, William. *Model Women*. London: Hodder & Stoughton, 1870.

33. *Appleton's Portrait Gallery of Women: Celebrated in History, Poetry, and Romance, for Beauty, Character, and Heroism*. New York: Appleton, 1875. As: *World Noted Women Celebrated in History, Poetry, and Romance for Beauty, Character, and Heroism*, 2 vols., New York: Appleton, 1881.

34. Armytage, A. J. Green [or Green-Armytage]. *Maids of Honour: Twelve Descriptive Sketches of Single Women Who Have Distinguished Themselves in Philanthropy, Nursing, Poetry, Travel, Science, Prose*. With Portraits. London and Edinburgh: Blackwood, 1906.

35. Arnaud, Raoul. *In the Shadows: Three Heroines of the Revolution*. Translated by Noel Fleming. London: Hamilton; New York and Newark, NJ: Barse, 1928.

36. Ashton, Carrie May, comp. *Glimpses of Sunshine in Woman's Century*. [Rockford, IL: Morning Star, 1880s?].

37. Ashton, Sophia Goodrich. *The Girlhood of Celebrated Women: Women of Worth and the Mothers of the Bible*. 2 vols. in 1. New York: World, 1877.

38. ———. *The Mothers of the Bible*. Boston: Jewett, 1854; 1855. New York: Sheldon, Lamport & Blakeman, 1855; Tilton, 1859; 1865; Appleton, 1866. Forms part of 37 above.

39. Asquith, Emma Alice Margaret [Countess of Oxford and Asquith], ed. *Myself When Young: By Famous Women of To-Day*. [2d ed.] London: Muller, 1938.

40. Atkinson, Emma Willsher. *Memoirs of the Queens of Prussia*. London: Kent, 1858.

41. Bacon, David Francis, ed. *Memoirs of Eminently Pious Women of Britain and America*. New Haven: D. McLeod, 1833. Evident reference to Gibbons/Jerment/Burder.

42. Badley, Mary Scott. *Leaves from Lucknow*. [New York]: Rindge Missionary Literature, [1880–1900?].

43. Baker, Franc. *Historical Sketches of the Northwestern Branch of the Woman's Foreign Missionary Society of the Methodist Episcopal Church*. Chicago: Jameson & Morse, 1887.

44. Bald, Marjory Amelia. *Women Writers of the Nineteenth Century*. Cambridge: Cambridge University Press, 1923.

45. Baldwin, George Colfax. *Representative Women: From Eve, the Wife of the First, to Mary, the Mother of the Second Adam*. Philadelphia and New York: American Baptist Publication Society, 1855. New York: Sheldon, Lamport & Blakeman, 1855; 1856; 1857; 1860; 1885. New York and Boston: Sheldon, Gould & Lincoln, [1900–1938?].

46. Balfour, Clara Lucas Liddell. *The Bible Pattern of a Good Woman*. London: Partridge, [1867]. NOT

47. ———. *Moral Heroism; or, The Trials and Triumphs of the Great and Good*. London: Houlston & Stoneman, 1846; 1848. Philadelphia: American Sunday-School Union, 1850. NOT

48. ———. *A Sketch of Charlotte Elizabeth*. London: Cash, 1854. This is part of the following.[49]

49. ———. [Biographical series of pamphlets: Elizabeth Smith, Hannah Kilham, Ann H. Judson, Mrs. Barbauld, Hannah More and Her Sisters, Mrs. M. L. Duncan, Mrs. Sherman, Mrs. Trimmer, Sarah Martin]. London: Cash, 1854.

50. ———. *The Women of Scripture*. London: Houlston & Stoneman, 1847; 1850; 1851.

51. ———. *Women Worth Emulating*. New York: American Tract Society; London: Sunday-School Union, 1877.

52. ———. *Working Women of the Last Half Century: The Lessons of Their Lives*. London: W. & F. G. Cash, 1854; 1856; Bennett, 1860. 3d ed. as *Working Women of This Century: The Lesson of Their Lives*. London and New York: Cassell, Petter, & Galpin, 1868. Possibly the pamphlets above rebound in single volume with the addition of Charlotte Brontë. All page citations in text are to the 1868 ed. PC

53. Barker, Nettie Garmer. *Kansas Women in Literature*. Kansas City: Meseraull & Son, 1915.

54. Barnard, David Nowell. *Biblical Women: Giving a Correct Biographical Description of Every Female Mentioned in Scripture, With Explanatory Remarks*. Cincinnati, OH: Hart, 1863.

55. Barnes, William Goodman. *Women in the Bible*. London: Marshall, [1920–29?].

56. Barrington, E. [i.e., Lily (Moresby) Adams Beck]. *The Ladies! A Shining Constellation of Wit and Beauty*. Boston: Atlantic Monthly, 1922. London: Fisher, 1922; 1923. London: Benn, 1927. NOT

57. Barton, William E. *The Women Lincoln Loved*. Indianapolis: Bobbs-Merrill; London: Melrose, 1927.

58. Batley, Dorothea Sibella, and Annalice Mary Robinson. *Devotees of Christ: Some Women Pioneers of the Indian Church.* 2d ed. London: Church of England Zenana Missionary Society, 1937. 3d ed., [1938–59?].

59. Beach, Seth Curtis. *Daughters of the Puritans: A Group of Brief Biographies.* Boston: American Unitarian Assoc., 1905; 1907. London: Philip Green, 1907.

60. Beaird, Miriam G. *Notable Women of the Southwest: A Pictorial Biographical Encyclopedia of the Leading Women of Texas, New Mexico, Oklahoma, and Arizona.* Dallas: Tardy, 1938.

61. Beale, Lucy Redd Preston, ed. *The Virginian: Woman's Edition.* Benefit of Virginia Board of Woman Managers, Cotton States and International Exposition. [Lynchburg, VA]: n.p., 1895.

62. Bearne, Catherine M. *Four Fascinating Frenchwomen.* Illustrated. London: Unwin; New York: Brentano, 1910.

63. ———. *Heroines of French Society, in the Court, the Revolution, the Empire, and the Restoration.* London: Unwin, 1907 [1906]; New York: Dutton, 1906; 1907.

64. ———. *Lives and Times of the Early Valois Queens.* Illustrated. New York: Dutton, 1898. London: Unwin, 1899.

65. ———. *Pictures of the Old French Court; Jeanne de Bourbon, Isabeau de Bavière, Anne de Bretagne.* Illustrated by Edward H. Bearne. London: Unwin; New York: Dutton, 1900.

66. ———. *A Royal Quartette.* London: Unwin, 1908. New York: Brentano, 1909.

67. Beaton, Cecil. *The Book of Beauty.* London: Duckworth, 1930.

68. Beaton, Rev. Donald. *Scottish Heroines of the Faith: Being Brief Sketches of Noble Women of the Reformation and Covenant Times.* London and Glasgow: Catt; Adshead, 1909.

69. Beaumont, E. de. *Women and Cruelty.* London, 1905. (Edouard de Beaumont, *L'Épée et les femmes* [1881]; Chevalier d'Eon de Beaumont, celebrated "hermaphrodite" featured in various English works, 1860s–1900, and in Andrew Lang, *Historical Mysteries* [London: Smith, Elder, 1904].) NOT?

70. Beedy, Helen Coffin. *Mothers of Maine.* Portland, ME: Thurston Print, 1895.

71. Bell, Margaret. *Women of the Wilderness.* New York: Dutton, 1938.

72. Ben-Asher, Naomi. *Great Jewish Women throughout History.* New York: Education Dept., Hadassah, 1939. As: *The Jewish Woman throughout History: A Course of Lectures in Seven Outlines.* New York: Hadassah, n.d. Jersey City: n.p., n.d.

73. Bennett, Helen Christine. *American Women in Civic Work.* New York: Dodd, Mead, 1915; 1919.

74. Betham-Edwards, Matilda Barbara [1836–1919]. *Mid-Victorian Memories . . . with a Personal Sketch by Mrs. Sarah Grand.* London: Murray; New York: Macmillan, 1919. NOT

75. ———. *Six Life Studies of Famous Women: With Six Portraits Engraved on Steel.* London: Griffith & Farran; New York: Dutton, 1880. PC

76. Bethune, George Washington. *The British Female Poets: With Biographical and Critical Notices.* Philadelphia: Lindsay & Blackiston, 1848; 1849; 1853; 1854; 1858; 1865; New York: Butler, 1849; Allen, 1869; Hurst, 1848, [1860–69?]; Crowell, n.d. As: *Pearls from the British Female Poets,* New York: World, 1875.

77. Bhattacharyya, Panchanan. *Ideals of Indian Womanhood.* With a foreword by A. Chaudhuri. Calcutta: Goldguin, 1921.

78. Biddle, Gertrude Bosler, Sarah Dickinson Lowrie, et al., eds. *Notable Women of Pennsylvania.* Philadelphia: University of Pennsylvania Press, 1942.

79. Binheim, Max, and Charles A. Elvin, eds. *Women of the West: A Series of Biographical Sketches of Living Eminent Women in the Eleven Western States of the United States of America.* Los Angeles: Publishers Press, 1928.

80. *A Biographical Record of Queensland Women: A Representation of Every Sphere.* Brisbane: Webb & Elliott, 1939.

81. Birrell, Francis, ed. *Six Brilliant English Women.* London: Gerald Howe, 1930. PC

82. Black, Helen C. *Notable Women Authors of the Day.* Glasgow: D. Bryce, 1893. London: n.p., 1893; Maclaren, 1906.

83. Blackburne, E. Owens [i.e., Elizabeth Casey]. *Illustrious Irishwomen: Being Memoirs of Some of the Most Noted Irishwomen from the Earliest Ages to the Present Century.* 2 vols. London: Tinsley, 1877.

84. Blackwell, Elizabeth. *Pioneer Work in Opening the Medical Profession to Women: Autobiographical Sketches.* London and New York: Longmans, Green; Hastings: Barry, 1895. As: *Pioneer Work for Women.* Introduction by Millicent Fawcett. London: J. M. Dent; New York: Dutton, 1914. NOT

85. Blain, Alexander C. *Heroines of History: Eleven Little Plays of Great Women.* London: Epworth, 1939. NOT

86. Blair, Gertrude. *Historical Sketches of Southwest Virginia Pioneer Women, 1750–1940.* Virginia Federal Writers' Project. Roanoke, VA: n.p., 1940.

87. Blair, Ruth, comp. *Georgia Women of 1926.* [Atlanta?]: Georgia Department of Archives and History, 1926.

88. Blashfield, Evangeline Wilbour. *Portraits and Backgrounds.* New York: Scribner's, 1917. PC

89. Bleackley, Horace William. *Ladies Fair and Frail: Sketches of the Demi-Monde during the Eighteenth Century.* With Sixteen Illustrations. London and New York: Lane, 1909; 1925; Dodd, Mead, 1926.

90. Blessington, Marguerite, Countess of [1789–1849], ed. *The Book of Beauty or Regal Gallery.* London: Bogue, 1848; 1849. New York: Appleton, 1848; 1849. As: *Heath's Book of Beauty* (an annual), London and New York: Longman [etc.], 1834–36; 1839; 1840; 1842; 1846.

91. Bloss, Celestia Angenette. *Heroines of the Crusades.* Muscatine, IA: R. M. Burnett, 1852; 1853. Detroit: Herr, Doughty & Lapham, 1853. Rochester, NY: Lippincott, 1853; 1881. Auburn, NY: Alden, Beardsley, 1853; 1854; 1855; 1857. New York: J. C. Derby, 1853. New Orleans: Burnett & Bostwick, 1853; 1854. Philadelphia: Lippincott, 1887.

92. Blunt, H[ugh] F[rancis]. *The Great Magdalens.* New York: Macmillan, 1928. PC

93. ———. *Great Wives and Mothers.* New York: Devin-Adair, 1917; 1923; 1927. PC

94. Boehme, Harry. *Women of the Bible.* Richmond, VA: Presbyterian, 1922.

95. Boggie, Jeannie Marr Manson. *Experiences of Rhodesia's Pioneer Women: Being a True Account of the Adventures of the Early White Women Settlers in Southern Rhodesia from 1890.* Bulawayo, Southern Rhodesia: Philpott & Collins, 1938.

96. Bolton, Sarah Knowles. *Famous Leaders among Women.* New York and Boston: Crowell, 1895. PC

97. ———. *Famous Types of Womanhood.* New York: T. Y. Crowell, 1886; 1892. All page citations in text are to the 1892 ed. PC

98. ———. *Lives of Girls Who Became Famous.* New York: T. Y. Crowell, 1886; 1914; 1923; [1925?]; 1930; 1936; 1938; 1939; 1941; 1949. PC

99. ———. *Successful Women.* Boston: Lothrop, 1888. PC

100. Bothmer, the Countess A. von [Marie], ed. *The Sovereign Ladies of Europe.* With 153 Illustrations. London: Hutchinson, 1899. Philadelphia: Lippincott, 1900.

101. Bradford, Gamaliel. *Daughters of Eve.* Boston and New York: Houghton Mifflin; Book League of America; New Home Library; Lincoln Historical Society, 1930; 1942. PC

102. ———. *Portraits of American Women.* Boston and New York: Houghton Mifflin, 1919. PC

103. ———. *Portraits of Women.* Boston and New York: Houghton Mifflin, 1916. PC

104. ———. *Wives.* New York and London: Harper, 1925.

105. Brailsford, Mabel Richmond. *Quaker Women, 1650–1690.* London: Duckworth, 1915.

106. Brandt, Johanna. *The Petticoat Commando; or, Boer Women in Secret Service.* London: Mills & Boon, 1913.

107. *Brave Women: [Bible Stories for Children].* Wellington, NZ: Reed, [1940s?].

108. Brawley, Benjamin Griffith. *Women of Achievement: Written for the Fireside Schools, under the Auspices of the Woman's American Baptist Home Mission Society.* Chicago: Woman's American Baptist Home Mission Society, 1919. PC

109. Braybrooke, Patrick. *Some Goddesses of the Pen.* London: Daniel, 1927. Philadelphia: Lippincott, 1928.

110. Brickdale, Eleanor Fortescue. *Golden Book of Famous Women.* London and New York: Hodder & Stoughton, 1919. NOT; PC

111. Brightwell, Cecilia Lucy. *Above Rubies; or, Memoirs/Memorials of Christian Gentlewomen.* London: Nelson, 1865; 1871. London and New York: Nelson, 1869; 1878; 1879; 1887. Nashville: A. H. Redford, for the M.E. Church, 1874; 1875; 1890; Southern Methodist, 1880; 1883. As: *Memorial Chapters in the Lives of Christian Gentlewomen.* London: Book Society, 1871–73.

112. Bristol, Frank M[ilton]. *Heroines of History: Typical Heroines of Mythology, of Shakespeare, of the Bible.* New York and Cincinnati, OH: Abingdon, 1914.

113. Brockett, Linus Pierpont, and Mary C. Vaughan. *Woman's Work in the Civil War: A Record of Heroism, Patriotism, and Patience.* Philadelphia: Zeigler, McCurdy; Boston: R. H. Curran, 1867. As: *Heroines of the Rebellion; or, Woman's Work in the Civil War: A Record of Heroism, Patriotism and Patience.* Philadelphia: Hubbard, 1888.

114. Brooks, Elbridge Streeter. *Historic Girls: Stories of Girls Who Have Influenced the History of Their Times.* New York: Putnam's, 1887; 1891; 1904; 1915. PC

115. Brooks, Elizabeth. *Prominent Women of Texas.* Akron, OH: Werner, 1896.

116. Brooks, Geraldine. *Dames and Daughters of Colonial Days.* New York: Crowell, 1900.

117. ———. *Dames and Daughters of the French Court.* New York: Crowell, 1904. London: Unwin, 1905.

118. ———. *Dames and Daughters of the Young Republic.* New York: Crowell, 1901.

119. Broughton, Len G. *The Representative Women of the Bible and the Representative Women of To-day.* Philadelphia: Pepper, 1903. New York and London: Armstrong, Hodder & Stoughton, Eaton & Mains, Doran, 1907. Cincinnati, OH: Jennings & Graham, 1907. London: Hodder & Stoughton, 1908.

120. Brown, Hallie Quinn. *Homespun Heroines and Other Women of Distinction.* Xenia, OH: Aldine Publishing, 1926. PC

121. ———. *Our Women Past, Present, and Future.* Xenia, OH: Eckerle, 1925; 1940.

122. Brown, Louise, et al., eds. *A Book of South Australia: Women in the First Hundred Years.* Adelaide: Rigby, 1936. Illustrated and coedited by Beatrix Ch: [sic] de Crespigny, Mary P. Harris, Kathleen Kyffin Thomas, Phebe N. Watson. Published for the Women's Centenary Council of South Australia; Pioneer Women's Memorial Fund. NOT

123. Browne, Phyllis [i.e., Sarah Sharp Heaton Hamer]. *Mrs. Somerville and Mary Carpenter.* London and New York: Cassell, 1887; 1889; 1890; 1893. NOT

124. Browne, William Hardcastle, comp. *Famous Women of History: Containing Nearly Three Thousand Brief Biographies and Over One Thousand Female Pseudonyms.* Philadelphia: Arnold, 1895. NOT

125. Bruce, Charles, ed. *The Book of Noble Englishwomen: Lives Made Illustrious by Heroism, Goodness, and Great Attainments.* London and Edinburgh: Nimmo, 1875; 1878; 1891. New York: Cassell, Petter, & Galpin, 1878. PC

126. ———. *Inspiring Lives: Biographies of the Great among Women.* Edinburgh: Nimmo, Hay, & Mitchell, 1897. Selections of preceding collection.

127. Buchanan, Isabella Reid. *Women of the Bible.* Minneapolis: Colwell, 1924. New York and London: Appleton, 1924; 1925; 1927; 1931; 1934; 1938; 1940.

128. Buckland, Augustus Robert. *Women in the Mission Field, Pioneers and Martyrs.* London: Isbister; New York: Whittaker, 1895.

129. Bunyan, Elizabeth. *Heroines Worthy of the Red Cross: Florence Nightingale, Elizabeth Fry.* London: Dean, 1883. NOT

130. Buoy, Charles Wesley. *Representative Women of Methodism.* New York: Hunt & Eaton; Cincinnati, OH: Cranston & Curts, 1893.

131. Burchard, Samuel Dickinson. *The Daughters of Zion.* New York: Taylor, 1853.

132. Burder, Samuel. *Female Biography: Biography of Remarkable Females*. Philadelphia, 1835. Possible title variation on Gibbons/Jerment/Burder.

133. Burdett-Coutts, Angela Georgina, Baroness, ed. *Woman's Mission: A Series of Congress Papers on the Philanthropic Work of Women by Eminent Writers*. Royal British Commission, Chicago Exhibition, 1893. London: Sampson Low, Marston, 1893. NOT

134. Burke, John. *The Portrait Gallery of Distinguished Females: Including Beauties of the Courts of George IV and William IV*. 2 vols. London: E. Bull/Bull & Churton, 1833.

135. Burns, Jabez. *The Mothers of the Wise and Good*. London: Houlston & Stoneman, 1846. Boston: Gould, Kendall & Lincoln, 1850. 4th ed., Boston: Gould & Lincoln, 1851; 1855. New York: Sheldon, Blakeman, 1855. PC

136. Burroughs, Nannie Helen. *Making Their Mark*. Washington, DC: National Training School for Women and Girls, n.d.

137. Burton, Margaret [Ernestine] Hill. *Notable Women of Modern China*. New York and Chicago: Revell, 1912.

138. Bush, Annie F. *Memoirs of the Queens of France: With Notices of the Royal Favorites*. 2 vols. London: Colburn, 1843. Philadelphia: Cary & Hart, 1847; Hart, 1851. Subtitle variants: Philadelphia: Parry & Macmillan, 1854; 1855; Keystone, 1890.

139. Butts, Sarah Hariet, comp. *The Mothers of Some Distinguished Georgians of the Last Half of the Century*. New York: J. J. Little, 1902.

140. Cairns, C. C. *A Book of Noble Women*. London and Edinburgh: Jack, [1911]; [1912]; 1913. PC

141. Cameron, Isabelle Dorothea, comp. *The American Book of Beauty*. New York: Russell, 1904. Compare Anonymous [By a Lady], New York: Wilson, 1845.

142. Canadian Women's Press Club. *Who's Who at the Third International Congress of Women Held in the Buildings of the University of Toronto, Toronto, Canada, June 24th to 30th, 1909*. [Toronto]: Toronto Branch of the Canadian Women's Press Club, 1909.

143. Carey, Rosa Nouchette. *Twelve Notable Good Women of the XIX Century, with Twelve Portraits*. London: Hutchinson; New York: Dutton, 1899; 1901; 1904. PC

144. Carr, Kent. *Girls Who Were Famous Queens*. Illustrated by P. B. Hickling. London: Partridge, [1915].

145. ———. *Women Who Dared: Heroines of the Great War*. London: Partridge, 1920.

146. Carron, Guy Toussaint Julien. *Young Ladies' Mirror; or, Models of Piety Proposed to the Imitation of Young Ladies Who Aspire to Christian Perfection*. Translated by Rev. Edward Peach. Philadelphia: M. Fithian, 1834. As: *Pious Biography*, 2d ed., Philadelphia: Cummiskey, 1834.

147. Cary, Alice, and Phoebe Cary, eds. *The Josephine Gallery*. Illustrated by Thomas Bailey [Aldrich?]. Philadelphia: Lippincott, 1858; 1859; 1864; 1869. New York: Derby & Jackson, 1859; 1861.

148. Cather, Katherine Dunlap. *Girlhood Stories of Famous Women: Clothilde of Burgundy, Judith of France, Dagmar of Denmark, Eleanor of Poitou, Philippa of Hainault, Jacquelin of Hainault, Yolanda of Aragon, Isabella of Portugal, Elizabeth of England, Mary of Scotland, Vittoria Colonna, Marie Antoinette, Louise Vigée, Martha Washington*. Illustrated. New York and London: Century, 1924. PC

149. Caulkins, Frances Manwaring. *Eve and Her Daughters of Holy Writ; or, Women of the Bible*. New York: American Tract Society, 1861.

150. Chadwick, John White. *Women of the Bible*. New York: Harper, 1900.

151. Challice, Annie Emma Armstrong. *French Authors at Home*. 2 vols. London: Booth, 1864. NOT

152. ———. *Illustrious Women of France, 1790–1873*. Illustrated. London: Bradbury, Agnew; New York: Scribner, Welford, 1873. London: n.p., [1900s?].

153. ———. *The Sister of Charity; or, From Bermendsey to Belgravia*. 2 vols. London: Bentley, 1857. NOT

154. [Chambers, William, ed.] *Lives of Eminent Women and Tales for Girls, from Chambers' Miscellany*. London and Edinburgh: Chambers, 1886. PC

155. Chapin, Clara Christiana Morgan, ed. *Thumb Nail Sketches of White Ribbon Women.* Chicago: Women's Temperance Publishing Association, 1895.

156. Chapman, Mrs. E. F. [Georiana Charlotte Clive Bayley Chapman], and Harriot Georgina Hamilton-Temple-Blackwood of Dufferin and Ava. *Sketches of Some Distinguished Indian Women.* London and Calcutta: Allen, 1891.

157. Chapman, William. *Notable Women of the Covenant: Their Lives and Times.* London: Swan Sonnenschein, 1883.

158. ———. *Notable Women of the Puritan Times.* London: Swan Sonnenschein, 1883; Sonnenschein, Lowrey, 1887.

159. ———. *Notable Women of the Reformation: Their Lives and Times.* London: Swan Sonnenschein, 1884.

160. Chappell, Jennie. *Four Noble Women and Their Work.* London: Partridge, 1898. Subtitle variants: London: Partridge, 1910; London and Glasgow: Pickering & Inglis, 1933. PC

161. ———. *Noble Work by Noble Women: Sketches of the Lives of Baroness Burdett-Coutts, Lady Henry Somerset, Miss Sarah Robinson, Mrs. Fawcett, Mrs. Gladstone.* London: Partridge, 1900; 1910. PC

162. ———. *Noble Workers: Sketches of the Life-Work of Frances Willard, Agnes Weston, Sister Dora, Catherine Booth, the Baroness Burdett-Coutts, Lady Henry Somerset, Sarah Robinson, Mrs. Fawcett, and Mrs. Gladstone.* London: Partridge, 1910. A reissue of two earlier volumes.[160; 161]

163. ———. *Women Who Have Worked and Won: The Life-Story of Mrs. Spurgeon, Mrs. Booth-Tucker, F. R. Havergal, and Pandita Ramabai.* London: Partridge, 1904. London and Glasgow: Pickering & Inglis, n.d., 1928. PC

164. [Charles, Elizabeth Rundle]. *Sketches of the Women of Christendom by the Author of "Chronicles of the Schönberg-Cotta Family."* English ed. New York: Dodd, Mead, 1880. London and New York: Pott, 1880. London: Society for Promoting Christian Knowledge (SPCK); New York: Young, 1889; [1900?]. PC

165. ———. [Mrs. Rundle]. *Three Martyrs of the Nineteenth Century: Studies from the Lives of Livingstone, Gordon, and Patteson.* London and New York: SPCK, Young, 1885; 1886; 1887; 1891; 1895; 1899; 1906. New York: Dodd, Mead, [n.d.]. NOT

166. ———, ed. *The Women of the Gospels: Meditations on Some Traits of Feminine Character Recorded by the Evangelists: Selected from the Works of Chrysostom, Augustine, Calvin, Jeremy Taylor, and Other Writers.* London: Seeley, Jackson & Halliday, 1868.

167. Charlotte Elizabeth [Charlotte Elizabeth Phelan, afterward Tonna]. *The Female Martyrs of the English Reformation.* New York: Taylor, 1844.

168. Child, Lydia Maria Francis. *The Biographies of Madame de Staël and Madame Roland.* Ladies' Family Library, ed. Lydia Child, vol. 1. Boston: Carter & Hendee, 1832.

169. ———. *Biographies of Lady Russell and Mme Guyon.* Ladies' Family Library, ed. Lydia Child, vol. 2. Boston: Carter & Hendee, 1832.

170. ———. *Good Wives.* Ladies' Family Library, vol. 3. Boston: Carter & Hendee, 1833. As: *Biographies of Good Wives.* New York and Boston: Francis, 1846; 1850; 1855; 1859. London: Griffin, 1859. As: *Celebrated Women,* 1858; 1861. As: *Married Women: Biographies of Good Wives,* New York: C. S. Francis, 1871; 1900. PC

171. ———. *The History of the Condition of Women, in Various Ages and Nations.* Boston: Allen; London: Simpkin, Marshall, 1835. Boston: Otis, Broaders, 1838; 1840; 1843. New York and Boston: Francis, 1835; 1845; 1849. NOT

172. Chubbuck, Emily E. [afterward Judson]. *Missionary Biography: The Memoir of Sarah B. Judson, Member of the American Mission to Burmah, by Fanny Forester.* With an introductory notice by Edward Bean Underhill. New York: L. Colby; London: Aylott & Jones, 1848; 1849. New York: Sheldon, Lamport & Blakeman, 1855; Sheldon, 1872. London: Nelson, 1854; 1860. NOT

173. Clark, Rev. David Wasgatt. *Portraits of Celebrated Women: With Brief Biographies.* Cincinnati, OH: Poe & Hitchcock, 1863. PC

174. Clarke, Mary Cowden. *World-Noted Women; or, Types of Womanly Attributes of All Lands and Ages.* New York: Appleton, 1857; 1858; 1868; 1871. PC

175. Clayton, Ellen Creathorne [afterward Needham]. *Celebrated Women: Stories of Their Lives and Examples, Literary, Social, & Historical: A Book for Young Ladies.* London: Dean, 1865; 1870; 1875. PC

176. ———. *English Female Artists.* 2 vols. London: Tinsley, 1876.

177. ———. *Female Warriors: Memorials of Female Valour and Heroism, from the Mythological Ages to the Present Era.* 2 vols. London: Tinsley, 1879.

178. ———. *Notable Women: Stories of Their Lives and Characteristics: A Book for Young Ladies.* London, 1859. London: Dean, 1860. London, 1875. PC

179. ———. *Queens of Song: Being Memoirs of Some of the Most Celebrated Female Vocalists Who Have Performed on the Lyric Stage from the Earliest Days of Opera to the Present Time.* 2 vols. London: Smith, Elder, 1863. New York: Harper, 1864; 1865; 1867; 1869.

180. ———. *Women of the Reformation: Their Lives, Faith and Trials.* London: Dean, 1861.

181. Clayton, Roberta Flake. *Pioneer Women of Arizona.* n.p., 1900.

182. Clement, Jesse, ed. *Noble Deeds of American Women: With Biographical Sketches of Some of the More Prominent.* Buffalo: Derby, 1851; 1852; 1854; 1855; 1856; 1857. Rev. ed., Boston: Lee & Shephard, 1851. Auburn, NY: Miller, Orton & Mulligan, 1854; 1855; 1856; 1857. New York: Saxton, 1858; 1861. Boston and New York: Lee, Shephard, 1869; 1873; 1875. PC

183. Clissold, Henry. *Last Hours of Christian Women; or, An Account of the Deaths of Some Eminent Christian Women of the Church of England: From the Period of the Reformation to the Beginning of the Present Century.* London: SPCK, 1853.

184. Cochelet, Louise ["Mme Parquin"]. *Lives of Celebrated Women.* [London: Bentley, 1833]. NOT

185. Cochrane, Jeanie Douglas. *Peerless Women: A Book for Girls.* London: Collins' Clear-Type Press, [1905]. PC

186. [Cochrane, Robert.] *Lives of Good and Great Women.* London, n.d. New York: Ward & Drummond, n.d. [1889–1900?]. PC

187. Code, Joseph Bernard. *Great American Foundresses.* New York: Macmillan, 1929.

188. Cole, M[argaret] Postgate. *Women of To-day.* London and New York: Nelson, 1938; 1946.

189. Coles, George. *Heroines of Methodism; or, Pen and Ink Sketches of the Mothers and Daughters of the Church.* New York: Carlton & Porter, 1857. New York and Cincinnati, OH: Phillips & Hunt, Walden & Stowe, 1883.

190. Collier, Margaret Wootten [Mrs. Bryan Wells Collier]. *Biographies of Representative Women of the South, 1861-[1938].* 6 vols. [College Park? GA]: Margaret Collier, [1920–38]. NOT

191. *Collins's New Biographical Series,* 8 vols. Vol. 6, *Eminent Women.* Illustrated. London and Glasgow: Collins's Clear-Type Press, [1909].

192. Concannon, Helena [Walsh]. *A Garden of Girls; or, Famous Schoolgirls of Former Days.* London and New York: Longmans, Green, 1914. Subtitle variant: New York: Benziger, 1928. PC

193. ———. *Irish Nuns in Penal Days.* London: Sands, 1931.

194. ———. *Women of "Ninety-Eight."* Dublin: Gill; St. Louis: Herder, 1919; 1920; 1930.

195. Cone, Helen Gray, and Jeanette L. Gilder, eds. *Pen-Portraits of Literary Women by Themselves and Others.* 2 vols. New York: Cassell, 1887. Boston: Educational Publishing, 1900.

196. Cook, Vallance Cole. *Queens of the Bible.* Illustrated. London: Kelly; Epworth, 1907.

197. Cook, Howard Willard. *Makers of Modern American Poetry: Women.* New York: Mentor Assoc., 1920.

198. Cooper, William Ricketts [Secretary of the Society of Biblical Archaeology]. *Heroines of the Past: A Lecture Delivered at the Working Men's Institute, Leighton Buzzard, 23 February, 1875.* London: S. Bagster & Son, 1875. NOT

199. Corkran, Alice Abigail. *The Romance of Woman's Influence: St. Monica, Vittoria Colonna, Madame Guyon, Caroline Herschel, Mary Unwin, Dorothy Wordsworth and Other Mothers, Wives, Sisters, and Friends Who Have Helped Great Men.* London: Blackie, 1906; 1912.

200. Costello. Louisa Stuart. *Memoirs of Eminent Englishwomen.* Illustrated. 4 vols. London: Bentley, 1844.

201. Courtney, Janet Elizabeth Hogarth. *An Oxford Portrait Gallery.* London: Chapman & Hall, 1931. NOT

202. ———. *The Women of My Time.* London: L. Dickson, 1934.

203. Courtney, W. L. *The Feminine Note in Fiction.* London: Chapman, 1904.

204. Covington, Ava Marie. *They Also Served: Stories of Pioneer Women of the Advent Movement.* Washington, DC: Review & Herald, 1940.

205. Cox, Francis Augustus. *Female Scripture Biography: Including an Essay on What Christianity Has Done for Women.* 2 vols. New York: James Eastburn, 1817. London: Gale & Fenner/Hamilton, 1817. Boston: Lincoln & Edmands, 1831. 2d ed., London: John Snow, 1852.

206. Craven, Mary. *Famous Beauties of Two Reigns: Being an Account of Some Fair Women of Stuart and Georgian Times.* London: Nash, 1906; 1907. New York: James Pott, 1907.

207. Creighton, Louise. *Some Famous Women.* Illustrated. London: Longmans, Green, 1909; [1923?]. PC

208. Crocheron, Augusta Joyce. *Representative Women of Deseret: A Book of Biographical Sketches, to Accompany the Picture Bearing the Same Title.* Salt Lake City: Graham, 1884.

209. Crosland, Mrs. Newton [Camilla]. *Memorable Women: The Story of Their Lives.* Boston: Ticknor & Fields; London: David Bogue, 1854; 1856; 1857. London: Kent, 1858. New York: Putnam's, [1860s?]. London: n.p., [1860]. Rev. 4th ed., London: Griffin, Bohn, 1862. London: J. Blackwood, 1870. PC

210. Cruse, Amy. *Boys and Girls Who Became Famous.* London: Harrap, 1929. New York: Harcourt, n.d. NOT

211. Culpepper, John B. *Some Women I Have Known.* Louisville, KY: Pickett; Pentecostal, 1902.

212. Cunliffe, Owen. *Titled Americans: A List of American Ladies Who Have Married Foreigners of Rank.* New York: Street & Smith, 1890.

213. Cumming, Rev. *Ministering Women, Their Lives, Perils and Devotion.* London: Dean, [1864?].

214. Daffan, Katie. *Woman in History.* New York and Washington, DC: Neale, 1908.

215. Da Libra [Daniel L. Brain]. *Women Types of To-Day.* London: Stock, 1907.

216. Daniel, Sadie Iola. *Women Builders.* Washington, DC: Associated Publishers, 1931.

217. Danker, Albert. *Heroines of Olden Time.* New York: [Chapple & Tozer], 1875.

218. Dark, Sidney. *Twelve Great Ladies.* London: Hodder & Stoughton, 1928; 1929. PC

219. ———. *Twelve More Ladies; Good, Bad and Indifferent.* London: Hodder & Stoughton, 1932.

220. Darton, John Maw. *Famous Girls Who Have Become Illustrious Women: Forming Models for Imitation for the Young Women of England.* 4th ed. London: Virtue, [1860–69?]; 1864. Title variant: London: Sonnenschein & Allen, 1880; 1884. PC

221. ———. *The Heroism of Christian Women of Our Own Time.* New York: Carter, 1882; Allison, 1893. Title variant: London: Swan, n.d.

222. Daughters of the American Revolution. *Chapter Sketches: Patriots' Daughters.* Edited by Mary Philotheta Root. New Haven: Connecticut Chapter, DAR, 1904.

223. ———. *Chapter Sketches: Patron Saints.* Edited by Mary Philotheta Root. New Haven: Connecticut Chapter, DAR, 1901.

224. ———. *Outstanding Iowa Women.* [Iowa: DAR, 1920–30].

225. ———. *The Pioneer Women of Wyoming: An Address before the Wyoming Valley Chapter, D.A.R.* By Frederick C. Johnson. Wilkes-Barre, PA: n.p., 1901.

226. ———. *Some North Carolina Heroines of the Revolution.* By Richard Dillard. [Raleigh]: North Carolina DAR, 1909.

227. Davis, Elizabeth [Lindsay]. *Lifting as They Climb.* Washington, DC, and Chicago: National Association of Colored Women, 1933.

228. ———. *The Story of the Illinois Federation of Colored Women's Clubs, 1900–1922.* [Chicago: n.p., 1922?]. Des Moines, IA: [Bystander Press], 1925.

229. Dawson, Edwin Collas. *Heroines of Missionary Adventure: True Stories of the Intrepid Bravery and Patient Endurance of Missionaries in Their Encounters with Uncivilized Man, Wild Beasts, and the Forces of Nature in All Parts of the World*. London: Seeley, 1908; 1909; 1917; 1919; [1930?]. Philadelphia: Lippincott, 1909.

230. ————. *Missionary Heroines in Many Lands*. [Extracted from *Heroines of Missionary Adventure*.] London: Seeley, Service, 1912.

231. Deans, R. Storry. *The Trials of Five Queens: Katherine of Aragon, Anne Boleyn, Mary Queen of Scots, Marie Antoinette, and Caroline of Brunswick*. Illustrated. London: Methuen, 1909; 1910. New York: Brentano's, 1910.

232. De Beck, Alexis Maria. *Women of the Empire in War Time*. London: Dominion of Canada News, 1916.

233. Dell, Floyd. *Women as World Builders: Studies in Modern Feminism*. London, 1913; Chicago: Forbes, 1913.

234. De Vere, Aubrey. *Heroines of Charity: Containing the Sisters of Vincennes, Jeanne Biscot, Mlle Le Gras, Madame de Miramion, Mrs. Seton, the Little Sisters of the Poor, etc., etc., with a Preface*. London: Burns & Lambert, 1854. New York: D. & J. Sadlier, 1855; 1860; 1878; 1885; 1887. New York: P. J. Kenedy [sic], 1896; 1904.

235. Dibdin, Emily. *Outline Lessons on Women of the Bible*. London: Church of England Sunday School Institute, [1900s?]

236. Dickes, William. *Women of Worth: A Book for Girls*. London: Cassell, Petter, & Galpin, 1854; 1859. London: Hogg, 1864; Virtue, [1865–75?]. New York: Townsend, 1860; 1861; Gregory, 1863; Allen, [1870–79?]. New ed., 1886. Subtitle variant: Boston: Lee & Shepard, 1889. London: Hogg, 1904. PC

237. D[isosway], G[abriel] P. *Our Excellent Women of the Methodist Church in England and America*. New York: J. C. Buttre, 1861; James Miller, 1873.

238. Dobson, Austin. *Four French Women*. New York: Dodd Mead, 1890; 1891; 1895. London: Chatto & Windus, 1891; 1893. Toronto: Musson; San Francisco: Robertson, 1900.

239. Dolman, Frederick. *Ladies of Sydney*. Sydney, Australia: n.p., [1890s?]. NOT.

240. Done, Willard. *Women of the Bible: A Series of Story and Character Sketches of the Great Women Who Have Aided in Making Bible History*. Salt Lake City: Willard Done, 1900.

241. Doran, Dr. [John]. *Lives of the Queens of England of the House of Hanover*. 2 vols. New York: Redfield; London: Bentley; Boston: Niccolls, 1855. 4th ed., London: Bentley, 1861; 1875. Boston: Niccolls, 1864; 1911; 1913. New York: Widdleton, 1865; Armstrong, 1880. Philadelphia: McKay, 1890.

242. Douthit, Mary Osborn, ed. *The Souvenir of Western Women*. Portland, OR: [Anderson & Duniway], 1905.

243. Dowie, Ménie Muriel, ed. *Women Adventurers*. London: Unwin; New York: Macmillan, [1890?]; 1893. Reprints of four biographies, 1740–1876.

244. Dunbar, Agnes Baillie Cuninghame. *A Dictionary of Saintly Women*. 2 vols. London: Bell, 1904–5.

245. Eagle, Mary Kavanaugh Oldham, ed. *The Congress of Women, Held in the Woman's Building, World's Columbian Exposition, Chicago, U.S.A., 1893; with Portraits, Biographies and Addresses*. Chicago: American; Conkey; Monarch; Benham, 1894. Denver: Westley, 1894. Chicago: Reeve; International, 1895. NOT

246. Earle, Alice M. *Colonial Dames and Good Wives*. Boston and New York: Houghton, Mifflin/ Riverside, 1895; 1896; 1904; 1924. New York: Macmillan, 1895; 1924.

247. Eddy, Daniel Clarke. *Daughters of the Cross; or, Woman's Mission*. New York: Dayton & Wentworth, 1854; 1855. The two following Eddy collections are closely similar.

248. ————. *Heroines of the Missionary Enterprise, or Sketches of Prominent Female Missionaries*. Boston: Ticknor, Reed & Fields, 1850. London: A. Hall, Virtue, 1854. Title variants: Boston: Estes & Lauriat, 1881; Wentworth, 1866. London: Walter Scott, [1886].

249. ————. *The Three Mrs. Judsons, and Other Daughters of the Cross*. Boston: Wentworth, Hewes, 1859. Boston: Thayer & Eldridge, 1860.

250. Edgar, John George. *Noble Dames of Ancient Story*. Illustrated by James Godwin. [New York: Cassell, 1853–54?]. London and Edinburgh: Gall & Inglis, 1870.

251. Egermeier, Elsie Emilie. *Girl's Stories of Great Women*. Anderson, IN: Warner, 1930; 1952. PC

252. Egle, William Henry. *Some Pennsylvania Women during the War of the Revolution.* Harrisburg, PA: Harrisburg Publishing, 1898.

253. Eldershaw, Flora. *The Peaceful Army: A Memorial to the Pioneer Women of Australia, 1788–1938*. Sydney: A. W. Baker, 1938.

254. Eldorado [pseud.] *Women I Have Loved*. London: n.p., [1912].

255. Ellet, Elizabeth Fries Lummis. *The Court Circles of the Republic; or, The Beauties and Celebrities of the Nation, Illustrating Life and Society under Eighteen Presidents, Describing the Social Features of the Successive Administrations from Washington to Grant*. Hartford, CT, and New York: J. D. Denison, 1869. Philadelphia: Philadelphia Publishing, 1869; 1872.

256. ———, *[The] Pioneer Women of the West*. New York: Scribner; Philadelphia: Coates, 1852; 1854; 1856; 1890; Porter & Coates, 1873; 1875; 1880; 1886; Winston, 1900.

257. ———. *The Queens of American Society*. New York: Scribner, 1867; 1868; 1870. Philadelphia: Porter & Coates, 1867; 1873.

258. ———. *Women Artists in All Ages and Countries*. New York: Harper; London: Bentley, 1859.

259. ———. *The Women of the American Revolution*. 2 vols. New York: Baker & Scribner, 1848. 2d ed., 3 vols., New York: Baker & Scribner, 1849–50. 5th ed., 3 vols., New York: Baker & Scribner, 1852–53; 1854; 1856; 1861. 2 vols., Philadelphia: Jacobs, [1900].

260. ———. *The Eminent and Heroic Women of America*. Illustrated. New York: McMenamy, Hess, 1873. A one-vol. reprint of volume[259] above, plus about twenty additional subjects. Reprint, New York: Arno, 1974. All citations to Ellet's *Women of the American Revolution* are taken from this 1974 reprint.

261. Ellington, George [pseud.]. *The Women of New York*. New York: New York Book, 1869; 1870. Burlington, IA: Root & Smith, 1869. NOT

262. Ellis, Sarah Stickney. *The Mothers of Great Men*. London: Bentley, 1859; Chatto & Windus, [1874]. Edinburgh: Nimmo, 1902.

263. ———. *The Women of England: Their Social Duties, and Domestic Habits*. 11th ed. London: Fisher, 1839. NOT

264. Elwood, Anne Katherine Curteis. *Memoirs of the Literary Ladies of England, from the Commencement of the Last Century*. 2 vols. London: Colburn, 1843. Philadelphia: Zieber, 1845.

265. *Eminent Women in Australia* [Mrs. Sophie Corrie]. Sydney: [Brooks], [1912?]. NOT

266. *Eminent Women Series*. [Edited by John Henry Ingram]. London: Allen, 1883–95. NOT

267. *English Churchwomen of the Seventeenth Century*. London: Burns; Derby: Mozley, 1845. New York: Sparks, 1846; Stanford & Swords, 1847; 1849.

268. Entwistle, Emily E. [afterward Whimster]. *Heroines of Unknown Ways: A Book for Leaders of Senior Girls*. London: United Council for Missionary Education, 1917; 1924.

269. Erskine, Mrs. Steuart [Beatrice]. *Beautiful Women in History and Art*. London: Bell, 1905.

270. Ewart, Henry, ed. *True and Noble Women*. London and New York: Whittaker, 1888; 1889; 1896. PC

271. Faber, Ernst. *Famous Women of China*. Shanghai: Society for the Diffusion of Christian and General Knowledge among the Chinese, 1890.

272. *Facts to Correct Fancies; or, Short Narratives Compiled from the Biography of Remarkable Women*. Written for Children, by a Mother. London: Harris, 1840. New York: Francis, 1845; 1846. London: Grant & Griffith, [1800s?]. Reprinted as "James Miller," *Short Stories from the Lives of Remarkable Women: Being Narratives of Fact to Correct Fiction, As Related to Her Children*. New York: Miller, 1861.

273. *Famous Girls*. London: 1870.

274. *Famous Women of History*. [Lynn, MA: Lydia E. Pinkham, 1920s?].

275. *Famous Women of the World*. [Monticello, IL: Pepsin Syrup Co.], 1920. PC

276. Farmer, Lydia Hoyt. *The Girls' Book of Famous Queens.* New York: Crowell, 1887; 1892; 1915; 1927. London: Harrap, 1927; 1928.

277. ———, ed. *The National Exposition Souvenir: What America Owes to Woman.* Introduction by Julia Ward Howe. Chicago: Charles Wells Moulton; Buffalo, NY: n.p., 1893.

278. Farningham, Marianne [Mary Anne Hearne—.]. *Women and Their Work: Wives and Daughters of the Old Testament.* London: Clarke, 1906.

279. Farrance, E. H. *Twelve Wonderful Women: The Romance of Their Life and Work.* London: Pickering & Inglis, 1936.

280. Faulhaber, Cardinal Michael von. *Women of the Bible.* London: Coldwell; Westminster, MD: Newman, 1938.

281. Fawcett, Millicent Garrett, Dame. *Five Famous French Women.* 1905. London and New York: Cassell, 1908.

282. ———. *Some Eminent Women of Our Times.* London, New York, and Edinburgh: Macmillan, 1889; 1894. PC

283. Fea, Allan. *Some Beauties of the Seventeenth Century.* 2d ed. London: Methuen, 1906; 1907.

284. Felton, Rebecca Latimer. *The Romantic Story of Georgia's Women.* As Told to Carter Brooke Jones in the Atlanta *Georgian.* [Atlanta]: Atlanta Georgian and Sunday American, 1930.

285. Ferrero, Guglielmo. *The Women of the Caesars.* London: Century/Fisher Unwin/Putnam; New York: Loring/Century/Putnam; Chatauqua, NY: Chatauqua; n.p.: Corner House, 1911. New York: Putnam; Chatauqua, NY: Chatauqua, 1925. New York: Loring & Mussey, 1935.

286. Ferris, Helen Josephine, and Virginia Moore. *Girls Who Did: Stories of Real Girls and Their Careers.* New York: Dutton, 1927; 1933. PC

287. Ferris, Helen Josephine. *This Happened to Me: Stories of Real Girls.* New York: Dutton, 1929; 1938; 1942.

288. ——— et al. *When I Was a Girl: The Stories of Five Famous Women . . .* New York: Macmillan, 1930; 1931. PC

289. ———. *Five Girls Who Dared.* New York: Macmillan, 1930; 1931. PC

290. Festing, Gabrielle. *On the Distaff Side: Portraits of Four Great Ladies.* London: Nisbet; New York: Pott, 1903.

291. ———. *Unstoried in History.* London: Nisbet, 1901.

292. Fielding, William John. *Woman—the Warrior.* Girard, KS: Haldeman-Julius, 1928.

293. *Fifty Famous Women and the Lessons of Their Lives.* London: Ward, Lock, [1850?]. Title variant: London: Ward, Lock, & Tyler, 1864; 1876; Ward & Lock, [1879]. PC

294. Finch, Barbara Clay. *Lives of the Princesses of Wales.* 3 vols. London: Remington, 1883.

295. Finden, W[illiam]. *Beauties of Byron; or, Portraits of the Principal Female Characters in Lord Byron's Poems.* London: Tilt; Philadelphia: Wardle, 1836; 1850. London: Tilt, 1865. NOT

296. ———. *Gallery of the Graces: A Series of Portrait Illustrations of British Poets.* London: Tilt, 1837; David Boquet [1830s?]. NOT

297. Finden, W[illiam], [and Edward Francis Finden]. *Portraits of the Female Aristocracy of the Court of Queen Victoria.* London: Hogarth, [1839]; n.p., [1842–49?]. Reprint, 2 vols. [1849?]. Probable alternative title for the volume that follows.

———. *The Book of the Boudoir; or, The Court of Queen Victoria.* London: Tilt; Philadelphia: Carey & Hart, [1840s?].

298. Findlay, Jessie Patrick. *Spindle Side of Scottish Song.* London: Dent; New York: Dutton, 1902.

299. Fittis, Robert Scott. *Heroines of Scotland.* London: Paisley/Gardner, 1889.

300. Forrest, Mary. [Julia Deane Freeman]. *The Women of the South Distinguished in Literature.* New York: Derby & Jackson, 1860; 1861; Richardson, 1865; 1866. London: Richardson, 1866.

301. Forsyth, James S. *The Women of the Bible.* London: Robert Banks, 1896.

302. Foster, Mary Dillon. *Who's Who among Minnesota Women.* [Saint Paul, MN]: Foster, 1924.

303. Fowler, William Worthington. *Woman on the American Frontier: A Valuable and Authentic History of the Heroism, Adventures, Privations, Captivities, Trials, and Noble Lives and*

Deaths of the "Pioneer Mothers of the Republic." Title variants (overlapping publication data): *Frontier Women: An Authentic History . . . ; Pioneer Women of America.* Hartford, CT: Scranton, 1876; 1877; 1878; 1879; 1880; 1881; 1883; 1886; 1891; 1896. Chicago: Beach; Stamford, CT: Longmeadow, 1877. Syracuse, NY: Gill, 1881. San Francisco: Bancroft, 1884.

304. Freeland, Mariet Hardy. *Missionary Martyrs.* Chicago: Arnold, 1892.

305. Frost, John. *Heroic Women of the West: Comprising Thrilling Examples of Courage, Fortitude, Devotedness, and Self-Sacrifice among the Pioneer Mothers of the Western Country.* Title variants: *Daring and Heroic Deeds of American Women* and *Pioneer Mothers of the West.* Philadelphia: Hart, 1854; Evans, 1859; 1860. Boston: Lee & Shepard, 1869.

306. Furniss, Harry. *Some Victorian Women: Good, Bad, and Indifferent.* London: Lane; New York: Dodd, Mead, 1923.

307. Fyvie, John. *Comedy Queens of the Georgian Era.* London: Constable, 1906. New York: Dutton, 1907.

308. ———. *Some Famous Women of Wit and Beauty: A Georgian Galaxy.* New York: Pott; London: Constable, 1905.

309. ———. *Tragedy Queens of the Georgian Era.* London: Methuen, 1908; 1909. New York: Dutton, 1909.

310. Gaddis, Maxwell Pierson. *Saintly Women and Death-Bed Triumphs.* New York and Pittsburgh: Phillips & Hunt. Cincinnati, OH, and Chicago: Walden & Stowe, 1880.

311. Galley, Lucile Vessot. *Famous Women: Character Representation—an Historic Entertainment.* Ottawa: n.p., 1916. NOT; PC

312. Gardner, Rev. James. *Memoirs of Eminent Christian Females.* Philadelphia: Lindsay & Blakiston, 1844. Edinburgh: Johnstone & Hunter, 1852. PC

313. Gardner, J. E. *Marriage and Maternity; or, Scripture Wives and Mothers.* London: Kegan Paul, Trench, 1881.

314. Garner, Leah Beach. *Pioneer Women of Genesee County.* [Flint, MI]: DAR, 1935.

315. Gearey, Caroline. *Daughters of Italy.* London: Simpkin/Marshall, 1886.

316. ———. *Three Empresses.* London: Digby & Long, 1893.

317. ———. *Two French Queens, and Other Sketches.* London: Digby & Long, 1896.

318. Gerard, Frances A. *Some Celebrated Irish Beauties of the Last Century.* London: Ward & Downey, 1895.

319. ———. *Some Fair Hibernians.* London: Ward & Downey, 1897.

320. Gibson, Ellen E. *The Godly Women of the Bible.* New York: Truth Seeker, 1881.

321. Gilchrist, Annie Somers. *Some Representative Women of Tennessee.* Nashville: McQuiddy, 1902.

322. Gilder, Rosamund. *Enter the Actress: The First Women in the Theatre.* London: Harrap; Boston and New York: Houghton Mifflin, 1931.

323. Gillogly, Mrs. L. L. *A Sketch of the Women of Utah.* Macon, GA: Republican, 1891.

324. Gilman, Agness Geneva. *Who's Who in Illinois: Women-Makers of History.* Chicago: Eclectic, 1927.

325. Gilmore, Rose Long. *Davidson County Women in the World War, 1914–1919.* Nashville: Advisory Council; Foster & Parkes, 1923.

326. Gleichen-Russwurm, Alexander Freiherr von. *The World's Lure.* Translated by Hannah Waller. New York and London: Knopf, 1927. PC

327. Glover, Elizabeth Rosetta Scott, Lady. *Great Queens: Famous Women Rulers of the East.* London: Hutchinson, 1928.

328. Goldsmith, M. L. *Seven Women against the World.* London: Methuen, 1935.

329. Gollock, G. A. *Daughters of Africa.* London and New York: Longmans, Green, 1932.

330. Good, James Isaac. *Women of the Reformed Church.* [Philadelphia?]: Sunday School Board of the Reformed Church in the United States, 1901.

331. Goodrich, Frank Boott. *Women of Beauty and Heroism*. New York: Derby & Jackson, 1859; 1861; 1879–80. As: *World-Famous Women* with variant subtitles. Philadelphia: Moore, 1871; Ziegler, 1879; 1880. [n.p.]: Publishers' Union, 1891. PC

332. Goodrich, Samuel Griswold. *Lives of Celebrated Women*. Boston: Thompson, Bigelow & Brown; Taggard & Thompson, 1843. Philadelphia: Thomas, Cowperthwait, 1844; 1846. Boston: Hickman, 1844; Thompson & Brown, 1845. Subtitle variant: *By the Author of "Peter Parley's Tales."* 2 vols. New York: J. Allen, 1844. Boston: Bradbury & Soden, 1844. Also 1 vol. New York: J. Allen, 1844. Boston: Pierce & Rand, 1848; Rand & Mann, 1849; Rand, Cornhill & Reynolds, 1852; 1853; 1854; 1856; Rand & Reynolds, 1855; Rand & Avery, 1856; Bradbury & Soden, 1856; Higgins & Bradley, 1856; 1857; Taggard & Thompson, 1864; Locke, 1876. PC

333. Goodsell, Willystine, ed. *Pioneers of Women's Education in the United States*. New York and London: McGraw, 1931.

334. Gordon, Lydia L. *From Lady Washington to Mrs. Cleveland*. Boston: Lee & Shephard; New York: Dillingham, 1888; 1889.

335. Gordon, John Campbell, Ishbel Maria Gordon, and Harold Copping. *The Women of the Bible*. London: Religious Tract Society, 1927; Lutterworth, 1937.

336. Gracey, Annie Ryder ["Mrs. J. T. Gracey"]. *Eminent Missionary Women*. New York: Eaton & Mains; Cincinnati, OH: Curts & Jennings; Chicago: Missionary Campaign Library; London: n.p., 1898.

337. ———. *Medical Work of the Woman's Foreign Missionary Society: Methodist Episcopal Church*. Dansville, NY: Bunnell, 1881. NOT

338. Graham, Harry J. C. *A Group of Scottish Women*. London: Methuen; New York: Duffield, 1908.

339. Gray, E. Conder. *Wise Words and Loving Deeds*. London: Marshall Japp, 1880. New York: Carter, 1881. PC

340. Green, Harry Clinton, and Mary Wolcott Green. *The Pioneer Mothers of America*. 3 vols. New York: Putnam's, 1912.

341. Green, Mary Anne Everett [Wood], ed. *Letters of Royal and Illustrious Ladies of Great Britain*. 3 vols. London: Colburn, 1846. NOT

342. ———. *Lives of the Princesses of England from the Norman Conquest [to 1670]*. London: Colburn, 1849–55; Longman; Colburn, 1857. 4 vols., London: Longman, 1867.

343. Greenwood, Alice Drayton. *Lives of the Hanoverian Queens of England*. London: Bell; New York: Macmillan, 1909–11.

344. Grégoire, Pierre Marie, and Charles Piccirillo. *Maidens of Hallowed Names*. Woodstock, MD: College of the Sacred Heart, 1881; 1882. New York: Kenedy [sic]/Excelsior Catholic, 1883; 1889; 1893; 1901; 1905.

345. Gribble, Francis Henry. *Women in War*. London: Low, Marston, 1916. London and New York: Dutton, 1917.

346. Gribble, Leonard Reginald. *Queens of Crime*. London: Hurst & Blackett, 1932.

347. Griffith, Rev. Patrick. *Christian Mothers: Saviours of Society*. Dublin: Browne & Nolan, 1923. 2d ed., 1926.

348. Griggs, Edward Howard. *Syllabus of a Course of Six Lectures on Types of Womanhood Studied from Autobiography*. Philadelphia: American Society for the Extension of University Teaching, 1900. NOT

349. Griswold, Rufus Wilmot. *Female Poets of America*. Philadelphia: Baird, 1847; 1852; 1853; Carey & Hart, 1849; Parry & McMillan, 1854; 1856; 1858; 1859; Moss, 1860; 1863. New York: Miller, 1873; 1874; 1877; Collier, 1869; 1877; 1892.

350. ———. *The Republican Court; or, American Society in the Days of Washington*. New York: Appleton, 1854; 1855; 1856; 1859; 1864; 1866; 1867; 1868; 1879. NOT

351. Grosvenor House. *Historical Loan Exhibition: Memorials of Some Notable Women*. London: Odhams, 1905. NOT

352. Guedalla, Philip. *Bonnet and Shawl: An Album.* New York: Putnam's; Crosby Gaige, 1928. London: Hodder & Stoughton, 1928; 1929; 1930. PC

353. Guerber, Helene Marie Adeline. *Empresses of France.* New York: Dodd, 1901; 1906.

354. Hack, Mary Pryor. *Christian Womanhood.* London: Hodder & Stoughton, 1883. Boston: Gannett, 1884. PC

355. ———. *Consecrated Women.* London: Hodder & Stoughton, 1880; 1892. Philadelphia: Longstreth; Toronto: Wesleyan Book Room, 1882. PC

356. ———. *Faithful Service: Sketches of Christian Women.* London: Hodder & Stoughton, 1885. Possible duplicate of *Christian Womanhood.*

357. ———. *Self-Surrender: A Second Series of "Consecrated Women."* Philadelphia: Longstreth, 1883; 1893. London: Hodder & Stoughton, 1892. PC

358. Haggard, Andrew Charles Parker. *Women of the Revolutionary Era; or, Some Who Stirred France.* London: Paul, 1914.

359. ———. *Remarkable Women of France, 1431–1749.* London: Paul, 1914.

360. Hale, Sarah Josepha [Buell]. *Lessons from Women's Lives.* Edinburgh: n.p., [1867]; Nimmo, [1870]. London: Nimmo, M'Farlane & Erskine, 1877. Edinburgh: Nimmo, 1880; Nimmo, Hay & Mitchel, 1889. PC

361. ———. *Sketches of American Character.* Boston: Putnam & Hunt, 1829; 1830; Carter & Hendee, 1830; Hunt, 1831; Russell, Odime, 1833; Bradley, 1838. Philadelphia: Perkins, 1838; 1840; Perkins & Purves, 1843. NOT

362. ———. *Woman's Record; or, Sketches of All Distinguished Women, from "The Beginning" till [Until-London ed.] A.D. 1850: Arranged in Four Eras—with Selections from Female Writers of Every Age.* New York: Harper, 1852; 1853. London: Sampson, Low, 1853. Title variants: New York: Harper, 1855; 1870; 1872; 1873; 1874.

363. *Half a Hundred Radcliffe Women: What They Have Given to the World.* [Cambridge, MA]: Radcliffe College, 1900s.

364. Hall, Geoffrey F. *Moths Round the Flame: Studies of Charmers and Intriguers.* London: Methuen, 1935. New York: Holt, 1936.

365. Hall, Mrs. Matthew. *Lives of the Queens of England before the Norman Conquest.* 2 vols. New York: Miller, 1843. Philadelphia: Blanchard & Lea, 1854. New York: Miller; Worthington, 1859. Boston: Brown, Taggard, & Chase, 1859; Brown, 1862; Taggard & Thompson, 1863; 1864; Thompson, Bigelow & Brown, 1871. As: *The Queens before the Conquest.* London: Colburn; Hurst & Blackett, 1854.

366. ———. *Royal Princesses.* London, 1848. As: *The Royal Princesses of England, from the Reign of the George the First.* London and New York: Routledge, 1871.

367. Hamaguchi, Tan. *Some Striking Female Personalities in Japanese History.* [London: n.p., 1903].

368. Hamel, Frank. *The Dauphines of France.* London: Paul, 1909; 1910. New York: Pott, 1910.

369. ———. *Fair Women at Fontainebleau.* London: Nash; Bell; New York: Brentano, 1909.

370. ———. *Famous French Salons.* London: Methuen; New York: Brentano, 1908; 1909; 1911.

371. Hamilton, Catherine Jane. *Notable Irishwomen.* Dublin: Sealy, Bryers & Walker, [1904].

372. ———. *Women Writers: Their Works and Ways.* 2 vols. London: Ward, Lock, 1872; 1892–93. New York: Ward, Lock, & Bowden, 1893.

373. Hamilton, Cicely Mary. *A Pageant of Great Women.* [London]: Suffrage Shop, 1910. PC

374. Hampton, William Judson. *Our Presidents and Their Mothers.* New York: Aste, 1918. Boston and New York: Cornhill, 1922. NOT

375. Hammond, Lily Hardy. *In the Vanguard of a Race.* New York: Council of Women for Home Missions/Missionary Education Movement of the United States and Canada, 1922. NOT.

376. Hanaford, [Mrs.] Phebe Ann [Coffin]. *Daughters of America; or, Women of the Century.* Augusta, ME: True; Knowles; Des Moines, IA: Co-operative, 1882. Augusta, ME: True; Cincinnati, OH: Forshee & McMakin; Appleton; Alanson; Boston: Russell, 1883. Des Moines, IA: Woodruff, 1884. Augusta, ME: True, 1889. Probable new title for the following. PC

————. *Women of the Century*. Boston: Russell, 1876; 1877.

377. Hanson, [Mrs.] E. R. *Our Woman Workers*. Chicago: Star Covenant Office, 1882; 1884.

378. Hansson, Laura Marholm. *Modern Women.* Translated by Hermione Ramsden. London: Lane, 1895. Title variants: London: Lane; Boston: Roberts, 1896. New York: n.p., 1896. PC

379. ————. *We Women and Our Authors*. London: Lane, 1898; 1899. NOT.

380. Hare, Christopher [pseud. of Marian Andrews]. *The Most Illustrious Ladies of the Italian Renaissance*. London and New York: Harper; Scribner, 1904.

381. Hargrave, Mary. *Some German Women and Their Salons*. London: Laurie; New York: Brentano, 1912; [1915?].

382. Harkins, Edward Francis, and Charles Haven Ladd Johnston. *Little Pilgrimages among the Women Who Have Written Famous Books*. Boston: Page, 1901; 1902. Title variant: Boston: Page, [1906].

383. Harris, Minnie Smith. *The Women of the Bible*. Ojai, CA: n.p., 1934.

384. Harrison, Eveleen. *Little-Known Women of the Bible*. New York: Round Table, 1936.

385. Hart, John Seely. *The Female Prose Writers of America*. Philadelphia: Butler, 1851; 1852; 1855; 1857; 1864; 1866; 1870.

386. Hartley, Cecil B. *Three Mrs. Judsons: The Female Missionaries*. Rev. ed. Philadelphia: Evans, 1860. Title variant: Philadelphia: Potter, 1863; Keystone, [1860s?]. New York: U.S. Book, [1860s?].

387. Harvey, Frances Vernon. *The Six Maries: Devotional Readings*. London: 1912; Skeffington, 1930–51.

388. [————]. *Women Helpers of Their Nation*. London: Skeffington, 1916.

389. Haskell, Thomas Nelson. *Women of the Bible*. Denver: Reed-Wheelon, 1892.

390. Haskin, Sara Estelle. *The Upward Climb: A Course in Negro Achievement*. New York: Council of Women of Home Missions, 1927.

391. Hatchard, Fanny Vincent Steele [Mrs. Goodwin Hatchard]. *Mothers of Scripture for Mother's Meetings*. 2d ser. London: Hatchards, 1875.

392. Hays, Frances. *Women of the Day: A Biographical Dictionary of Notable Contemporaries*. London: Chatto & Windus; Piccadilly. Philadelphia: Lippincott, 1885.

393. Hayward, Charles F. *Women in the Mission Field*. London and Glasgow: Collins' Clear-Type Press, n.d. Same as next record?

394. ————. *Women Missionaries*. London: Collins' Clear-Type Press, n.d.

395. Headley, Phineas Camp. *Historical and Descriptive Sketches of the Women of the Bible*. Auburn, NY, and Buffalo, NY: Derby & Miller, 1850; 1852; 1853. Buffalo, NY: Miller, Orton & Mulligan, 1853; 1854; 1856. Boston: Lee & Shepard, 1850; 1876. New York: Saxton, 1859; Appleton, 1865.

396. Hedemann, Baroness Franzisca von. *Love Stories of Court Beauties*. Illustrated. New York: Doran, 1917.

397. Henrici, Lois Oldham. *Representative Women: Being a Little Gallery of Pen Portraits*. Kansas City: The Crafters, 1913. PC

398. Herbert, Mary Elizabeth, Baroness. *Wives, Mothers, and Sisters in the Olden Time*. 2 vols. London: Bentley, 1876. 1 vol., London: Bentley, 1885. NOT

399. Hernandez, Carlos. *Mujeres celebres de Mexico*. San Antonio: Lozano, 1918; 1919. NOT

400. *Heroines of the Cross*. Kilmarnock, Scotland: J. Ritchie; London: Hubert, 1930.

401. *Heroines of Mormondom*. Salt Lake City: Juvenile Instructor, 1884. NOT

402. Herrington, Walter Stevens. *Heroines of Canadian History*. Toronto: W. Briggs, 1909; 1910.

403. Hewitt, Mary Elizabeth Moore. *Heroines of History*. New York: Cornish, Lamport, 1852; Sheldon, Lamport & Blakeman, 1855; Sheldon, 1859. See Jameson;[454] also pub. as the following.

————, ed. *Lives of Illustrious Women of All Ages*. Philadelphia: Evans, 1860; Davis, Porter & Coates, 1866. PC

404. Higgins, Sophia Elizabeth [Mrs. Napier Higgins]. *Women of Europe in the Fifteenth and Sixteenth Centuries.* 2 vol. London: Hurst & Blackett, 1885.

405. Hill, Josephine O. *A Souvenir of World's Fair Women and Wives of Prominent Officials Connected with the World's Columbian Exposition.* Chicago: Blocher, 1892.

406. Hilton, Agnes Aubrey. *Tales of the Women Saints of the British Isles.* London: Wells Gardner, Darton, 1909.

407. *Historical Tales of Celebrated Women.* London, 1860; Burns, Oates & Washbourne, [1910–19]. NOT

408. Holland, Mary A. Gardner. *Our Army Nurses: . . . 1861–1865.* Boston: Wilkins, 1895; Loundsberry, Nichols & Worth, 1897.

409. Holland, Rupert Sargent. *Historic Girlhoods.* 2 vols. Philadelphia: Jacobs; Macrae, Smith, 1910. PC

410. Holloway, Laura Carter [Langford]. *The Ladies of the White House.* New York: U.S. Publishing, 1870; 1872. Subtitle variants: Philadelphia: Bradley, 1880; 1881, 1883; 1884. 2 vols. New York: Funk & Wagnalls, 1886.

411. ———. *The Mothers of Great Men and Women, and Some Wives of Great Men.* Illustrated. New York: Funk & Wagnalls, 1883. Philadelphia: Calypso, 1883; 1887. Baltimore: Wharton, 1883; Woodward, 1889; 1891; 1892. PC

412. ———. *The Woman's Story, by Twenty American Women.* New York: Alden, 1888; 1889. Troy, NY: Nims & Knight. New York: Hurst, 1889. NOT

413. Holt, Sarah Emily. *Memoirs of Royal Ladies.* 2 vols. London: Hurst & Blackett, 1861.

414. [Hope, Eva]. *Queens of Literature of the Victorian Era.* London: Walter Scott, 1886.

415. Hopkins, Tighe. *The Women Napoleon Loved.* London: Nash; Leipzig: Tauchnitz; Boston: Little, Brown, 1910.

416. Hoppner, John, Charles Wilkin, and Andrew White Tuer. *Bygone Beauties.* London: Leadenhall; New York: Scribner, 1883. London and Melbourne: Eyre & Spottiswoode; Simpkin, Marshall, Hamilton, Kent; New York: Scribner's, n.d.

417. Horner, Joyce Mary. *The English Women Novelists and Their Connection with the Feminist Movement (1688–1797).* Smith College Studies in Modern Languages, 11. Northampton, MA: [Dept. of Modern Languages, Smith College], 1929–30. NOT

418. Horsley, Reginald. *Women of Worth in the Victorian Era.* London: Chambers, 1912.

419. Horton, Edith. *A Group of Famous Women.* Boston and New York: Heath, 1914. PC

420. Horton, Robert Forman. *Women of the Old Testament.* New York: Whittaker; Herrick, 1897. London: Service & Paton, 1898; Nisbet, 1897; 1899; 1911.

421. Houssaye, Arsène. *Philosophers and Actresses.* New York: Redfield, 1852; 1853; Dillingham, 1886. NOT

422. How, Frederick Douglas. *Noble Women of Our Time.* London: Isbister, 1901.

423. Howe, Julia Ward, ed., with Mary Hannah Graves. *Sketches of Representative Women of New England.* Illustrated. Boston: New England Historical, 1904.

424. Howitt, Mary, ed. *Biographical Sketches of the Queens of England, from the Norman Conquest to the Reign of Victoria; or, Royal Book of Beauty.* London: Bohn, 1851; 1856; 1862; Virtue, 1862; 1866; 1868; Rutter, 1865. Chicago: Wasson, 1901.

425. Hubbard, Elbert. *Little Journeys to the Homes of Famous Women.* [Vol. 3.] New York and London: Putnam's, 1897. Little Journeys to the Homes of the Great Series, New York: Putnam's, 1894–97. East Aurora, NY: Roycrofters, 1898; 1901; 1908. New York: Wise; E. Aurora: Roycrofters, 1911; 1916; 1923. *Little Journeys to the Homes of the Great,* Vol. 2: *Famous Women,* New York: Wise, 1923–28. Cleveland: World, 1928. PC

426. ———. *Three Great Women: Being Little Journeys.* East Aurora, NY: Roycrofters, 1908. New York: Wise, 1928. Excerpt of above.[425]

427. Hughes, Hugh. *Female Characters of Holy Writ.* 2d ser. London: Hamilton, Adams, 1846; Warne, 1866.

428. Huie, James A. *Records of Female Piety.* Edinburgh: Oliver & Boyd; London: Simpkin, Marshall, 1841; 1842. Edinburgh: Oliver & Boyd, 1845.

429. Hume, M. *Queens of Old Spain.* London: Richards, 1906; 1911. New York: McClure, Phillips, 1906; Doubleday, 1911.

430. Humphrey, Mrs. E. J. *Gems of India; or, Sketches of Distinguished Hindoo and Mahomedan Women.* New York: Nelson & Phillips; Cincinnati, OH: Hitchcock & Walden, 1875.

431. Humphrey, Grace. *The Story of the Elizabeths.* New York: n.p., n.d. Philadelphia: Penn, 1924; 1926.

432. Hunter, Fannie McDowell, and Aaron Merritt Hills. *Women Preachers.* Dallas: Berachah, 1905.

433. Huntington, Faye. *Stories of Remarkable Women.* Boston: Lothrop, 1887. PC

434. Hurd-Mead, Kate Campbell, and Elizabeth Burr Thelberg. *Medical Women of America.* New York: Froben, 1933.

435. Imbert de Saint-Amand, Arthur Léon, Baron. *Marie Antoinette at the Tuileries, 1789–1791.* New York: Scribner, 1891. In French, Paris: Dentu, 1882; 1885; 1888; 1892. NOT

436. ———. *Marie Louise and the Decadence of the Empire.* Translated by T. S. Perry. New York: Scribner, 1890; 1891; 1899; 1902. London: Hutchinson, 1890. NOT

437. ———. *The Revolution of 1848.* Translated by Elizabeth Gilbert Martin. With portraits. New York: Scribner, [1895]; 1900; 1901. London: Hutchinson, 1893. NOT

438. ———. *Women of the Valois Court.* Translated by Elizabeth Gilbert Martin. New York: Scribner, 1893; 1894; 1895; 1897; 1898; 1899; 1900; 1909. London: Hutchinson, 1893. NOT

439. ———. *Women of Versailles: The Court of Louis XIV.* Translated by Elizabeth Gilbert Martin. New York: Scribner, 1893; 1900; 1901; 1911.

440. ———. *Women of Versailles: The Court of Louis XV.* Translated by Elizabeth Gilbert Martin. New York: Scribner, 1893; 1894; 1898; 1901; 1906; 1911.

441. ———. *Women of Versailles: Last Years of Louis XV.* Translated by Elizabeth Gilbert Martin. New York: Scribner, 1893; 1899; 1900; 1901.

442. Ingham, Mrs. W. A. [Mary Bigelow James Ingham]. *Women of Cleveland and Their Work.* Cleveland: Ingham, 1893.

443. Irwin, Inez Haynes [Gillmore, Inez Haynes Irwin]. *Angels and Amazons: A Hundred Years of American Women.* Garden City, NY: Doubleday; Doran, 1933; 1934.

444. Irvine, E. Marie. *Certain Worthy Women.* Sydney: New Century, 1939.

445. Irvine, Mary D., and Alice L. Eastwood. *Pioneer Women of the Presbyterian Church, United States.* Richmond, VA: Presbyterian Committee of Publication, 1923.

446. Izard, Forrest. *Heroines of the Modern Stage.* New York: Sturgis & Walton; London: Macmillan, 1915.

447. Jackson, Pearl Cashell. *Texas Governors' Wives.* Austin, TX: Steck, 1915.

448. James, G[eorge] P[ayne] R[ainsford], ed. *Memoirs of Celebrated Women.* 2 vols. London: Bentley, 1836; 1837. 1 vol., Philadelphia: Carey & Hart, 1839. London: Routledge, 1876.

449. Jameson, Anna Brownell. *A Commonplace Book of Thoughts, Memories, and Fancies, Original and Selected.* London: Longman, 1854; 1855. New York: Appleton, 1855. London: Virtue, 1877. NOT

450. ———. *Characteristics of Women, Moral, Poetical, and Historical.* London: Saunders & Otley, 1832; 1833; 1835; 1836; 1846; 1858. New York: Saunders & Otley, 1837. Annapolis: J. Hughes, 1833. Philadelphia: Carey, Lea & Blanchard, 1833. New York: Wiley, 1833; 1848; 1850. Boston: Phillips, Sampson, 1853; 1854. New York: Derby, 1854; Appleton, n.d. Boston: Ticknor & Fields, 1846; 1853; 1857; 1859; 1863; 1864; 1865; 1866. Boston and New York: Houghton Mifflin, 1883; 1885; 1887; 1888; 1889; 1891; 1892; 1896; 1898; 1899; 1900; 1911. London: Routledge, 1865; 1870; Bell, 1879. Boston: J. R. Osgood, 1875; Houghton, Osgood, 1879. Philadelphia: H. Altemus, 1899. As: *Shakespeare's Heroines: Characteristics of Women, Moral, Poetical, and Historical.* London: Bell, 1889, 1891, 1903, 1905, 1908, 1911; 1913; 1916;

1924; Newnes, 1897; Dent, 1901; 1904; Nister, n.d., 1905; Aldine, 1904. New York: Dutton, 1901; n.d.; 1905; A. L. Burt, 1905. Philadelphia: H. Altemus, n.d.; 1899.

451. ———. *Legends of the Madonna: As Represented in the Fine Arts.* London: 1852. Boston: Ticknor & Fields, 1853; rev. ed., 1861. London: Longman, Brown, Green, & Longmans, & Roberts, 1857; 1872; 1885; 1890; 1899. Boston: Houghton, Osgood, 1879. Boston and New York: Houghton, Mifflin, 1895; 1896; 1897. London: Unit Library, 1904. All page citations in text are to the 1872 ed.

452. ———. *Memoirs of the Beauties of the Court of Charles II.* London: Bentley, 1833. 2 vols., London: Colburn, 1838; 1851; Bohn, 1861. Title and subtitle variants; as: *The Beauties of the Court of Charles the Second.* Philadelphia: Carey & Hart, Waldie, 1834. As: *Anna Jameson and Sir Peter Lely: Court Beauties of the Reign of Charles II.* London: Hotten, 1872.

453. ———. *Memoirs of Celebrated Female Sovereigns.* London: Colburn & Bentley, 1831; Saunders & Otley, 1834; 1840; Routledge, 1869; 1870; 1880. New York: Harper, 1832; 1834; 1836; 1837; 1840; 1842; 1844; 1845; 1848; 1854; 1858; 1862; 1868; 1871. London and New York: Fowle, 1900. As: *Celebrated Female Sovereigns.* 2 vols. By subscription. [New York]: Werner, 1910; Superior, 1916.

454. ———. *Lives of Celebrated Female Sovereigns and Illustrious Women.* Edited by Mary E. Hewitt. London: Routledge, 1839; 1870; 1890. Philadelphia: Porter & Coates, 1870; Coates, [1900s?]. Title and subtitle variants: Rochester, NY: Graves, [1870?]. New York: MacLellan, 1910.

455. ———. *Memoirs of the Loves of the Poets.* London: Colburn, 1829. Subtitle variants: London: Colburn & Bentley, 1831. New York: Harper, 1833. 2 vols., London: Saunders & Otley, 1837. Boston: Russell, Odiorne, 1833; Ticknor & Fields, 1829; 1857; 1858; 1861; 1863; 1864; 1866; 1878; Osgood, 1875; 1879. Philadelphia: Lea & Blanchard, 1844. Boston and New York: Houghton Mifflin, 1881; 1885; 1888; 1889; 1890; 1891; 1892; 1894; 1898; 1900. Alternate titles: *The Romance of Biography* and *Memoirs of Women Loved and Celebrated by Poets.*

456. ———. *Sacred and Legendary Art.* London, 1848; 1857. 2 vols., Boston: Ticknor & Fields, 1866. 2 vols., London: Longmans, Green, 1870. Fifty-seven listings in WorldCat database. NOT

457. ———. *Sisters of Charity: Catholic and Protestant; and the Communion of Labour.* London: Longman, Brown, Green & Longmans, 1855; 1859. Boston: Ticknor & Fields, 1857. NOT

458. ———. *Visits and Sketches at Home and Abroad: With tales and miscellanies now first collected, and a new edition of the "Diary of an Ennuyée."* New York: Harper & Brothers, 1834. As: *Sketches of Art, Literature, and Character,* Boston: Ticknor & Fields, 1857; 1858; 1859; 1864; 1865; 1866; 1885; Osgood, 1875; 1876; 1880. Boston and New York: Houghton Mifflin, 1881; 1883; 1885; 1888; 1896; 1898; 1911. NOT

459. ———. *Winter Studies and Summer Rambles in Canada.* Toronto: McClelland & Stewart, 1838; 1923. London: Saunders & Otley, 1838. New York: Wiley & Putnam, 1839. Reprinted and abridged: *Sketches in Canada; and Rambles among the Red Men.* London : Longman, Brown, Green, & Longmans, 1852. Toronto: Nelson, 1943.

460. Jay, William. *Lectures on Female Scripture Characters.* New York: Robert Carter, 1854; 1856.

461. Jenkins, John Stilwell. *Heroines of History.* Auburn, NY, and Buffalo, NY: Beardsley, 1851. Peoria, IL: S. H. and G. Burnett, 1852; 1853. Auburn, NY: Alden, Beardsley; Rochester, NY: Wandser, Beardsley, 1851; 1852; 1853; 1857. Chicago: Kerr, Doughty & Lapham, 1853. New York: R. Carter, 1854. Rochester [NY] and New York: Alden & Beardsley; J.C. Derby, 1855. New Orleans: Burnett & Bostwick, 1854. New York: James Sheehy, 1883. Hartford, CT: J. Betts, 1879. PC

462. Jerrold, Clare Armstrong Bridgman. *The Early Court of Queen Victoria.* London: Nash; New York: Putnam's, 1912.

463. Jerrold, Walter, and Clare Jerrold. *Fair Ladies of Hampton Court.* London: Long; Boston: Little, Brown, 1911.

464. ———. *Five Queer Women.* London: Brentano's, 1929. PC

465. Johnson, Joseph. *Brave Women and Their Deeds of Heroism.* London: Gall & Inglis, 1860. Title variant: Edinburgh: Gall & Inglis, 1875. PC

466. ———. *Clever Girls of Our Time and How They Became Famous Women* . . . London: Darton & Hodge, 1862; 1863; 1864; 1865. Title variant: London: Gal & Inglis, 1862; [1880–90?]. PC

467. ———. *Heroines of Our Time.* London: Darton, 1860. PC

468. ———. *Noble Women of Our Time.* Edinburgh and New York: Nelson, 1882; 1886. London, Edinburgh, and New York: Nelson, 1889; 1891. PC

469. ———. *Willing Hearts and Ready Hands.* London, Edinburgh, and New York: Nelson, 1869; 1873.

470. Johnson, Reginald Brimley. *Some Contemporary Novelists (Women).* London: Leonard Parsons, 1920.

471. ———. *The Women Novelists.* London: Collins, 1918; 1922. New York: Scribner, 1919.

472. Johnstone, Grace. *Leading Women of the Restoration.* London: Digby, Long; 1891; 1892.

473. Josephson, Sadie. *Adjustment Histories of Six Jewish Women.* Graduate School of Jewish Social Work. New York: n.p.; 1937. NOT.

474. Junot, Laure, Duchesse d'Abrantès. *Memoirs of Celebrated Women of All Countries.* London: Churton, 1834. Philadelphia: Carey, Lea, & Blanchard, 1835.

475. Katznelson-Shazar, Rachel. *The Plough Woman: . . . of Palestine.* New York: Brown, 1932.

476. Kavanagh, Julia. *English Women of Letters.* 2 vols. Leipzig: Tauchnitz, 1862. London: Hurst & Blackett, 1863.

477. ———. *French Women of Letters.* 2 vols. Leipzig: Tauchnitz; London: Hurst & Blackett, 1862.

478. ———. *Woman in France during the Eighteenth Century.* 2 vols. London: Smith, Elder, 1850; 1864. Philadelphia: Lea & Blanchard, 1850. New York: Putnam, 1893.

479. ———. *Women of Christianity, Exemplary for Acts of Piety and Charity.* New York: Appleton; London: Smith Elder, 1852. New York: Appleton, 1858; 1860; 1864; 1866; 1869. PC

480. Keary, Margaret R. *Great Scotswomen.* [Glasgow] and London: MacLehose, 1933.

481. Keeling, Annie E. *Eminent Methodist Women.* London and Edinburgh: Kelly, 1889; 1893; 1897. Title variant.

482. K[elty], M[ary] A[nn]. *Biography for Young Ladies.* London: Kendrick, 1839.

483. Kelty, Mary Ann. *Memoirs of the Lives and Persecutions of the Primitive Quakers.* 2d ed. London: Harvey & Darton, 1844. NOT.

484. Kendrick, Miss M., and Mrs. L. M. Child. *The Gift Book of Biography for Young Ladies.* London and Edinburgh: T. Nelson, 1848. London: T. Nelson, 1849; 1850. London and Edinburgh: Nelson, 1854. PC

485. Ker, Cecil. *Women Who Have Made Good.* New York: Platt & Peck, 1916. PC

486. *The King's Daughters: The Life Stories of Three Noble Women Distinguished for Their Service in the Cause of Christ.* London and Glasgow: Pickering & Inglis, [1930].

487. King, Hannah T. *The Women of the Scriptures.* Salt Lake City: Deinford, 1878.

488. King, William C., ed. *Woman, Her Position, Influence, and Achievement throughout the Civilized World.* Springfield, MA: King-Richardson, 1901; 1902; 1903.

489. Kirkes, C. *Biographies of Great and Good Women.* Translated by H. Kitayama. Tokyo: n.p., 1889. PC

490. Kirkland, Winifred Margaretta, and Frances Kirkland. *Girls Who Became Artists.* New York and London: Harper, 1934.

491. Klein, Hermann. *Great Women-Singers of My Time.* London: Routledge; New York: Dutton, 1931.

492. Knapp, Samuel Lorenzo. *Female Biography.* Philadelphia: Wardle, 1833; 1836; 1842; 1843; 1846. New York: Carpenter; Baltimore and Phoenix: Wood, 1834. Philadelphia: Sower, Barnes & Potts, 1868.

493. Kohut, George Alexander. *Some Jewish Heroines.* [n.p., 1920s?].

494. Lamb, Kathryne Etheleen. *Bloomingdale Women's Souvenir.* Bloomingdale, IN: Lamb, Rockville Tribune Print, 1908.

495. Lancelott, Francis. *The Queens of England and Their Times.* 2 vols. London: Daly, 1856. New York: Appleton, 1858; 1892; 1894; 1895.

496. Lane, Margaret Stuart. *Stories of Famous Women.* London: Humphrey Milford, Oxford University Press, 1920. Bungay, Suffolk: Clay, 1931. PC

497. Latour, Therese Louis. *Princesses, Ladies and Adventuresses of the Reign of Louis XIV.* Paris: Figuière, 1923. London: Kegan Paul; New York: Knopf, 1924.

498. ———. *Princesses, Ladies, and Republicaines of the Terror.* London: Kegan Paul; Paris: Figuière, 1930.

499. ———. *Princesses, Ladies, and Salonnieres of the Reign of Louis XV.* London: Kegan Paul, 1927. New York: Knopf, 1928.

500. Lawrance, Hannah. *Historical Memoirs of English Female Sovereigns.* 2 vols. London: n.p., 1838–40. Title variant.

501. ———. *The History of Woman in England....* London: Colburn, 1843. NOT

502. Lawrence, Una Roberts. *Pioneer Women.* Nashville: Sunday School Board of the Southern Baptist Convention/Broadman, 1929; 1948.

503. Leach, Rev. Charles. *Mothers of the Bible.* London: Nisbet, 1888; Stockwell, 1908. New York: Revell; Chicago: Bible Institute Colportage Assoc., 1900.

504. *Leaves from Our Lives: Columbian Souvenir.* Grand Rapids, MI: Dean, 1894.

505. Lee, Anna Maria. *Memoirs of Eminent Female Writers.* Philadelphia: Grigg; Desilver; Towar & Hogan, 1827.

506. Lee, Edmund. *Some Noble Sisters.* London: Clarke, 1892.

507. Lee, Elizabeth, and Mrs. C. G. F. [Lucy Blanche] Masterman. *Wives of the Prime Ministers, 1844–1906.* New York: Dutton; London: Nisbet, 1918.

508. Levinger, Mrs. Elma Ehrlich. *Great Jewish Women.* New York: Behrman's Jewish Book House, 1940.

509. Lenski, R[ichard] C[harles] H[enry] [1864–1936]. *Outstanding Women of the Bible.* Columbus, OH: Book Concern, [1900s?].

510. Lewis, Agnes Smith. *Select Narratives of Holy Women.* London: Clay/Cambridge University Press; New York: Macmillan, 1900.

511. Lewis, Howell Elvet. *Women of the Bible: Rebekah to Priscilla.* Manchester: Robinson, 1904.

512. Lewis, Thomas H. *Women of South Africa.* Cape Town: Le Quesne & Hooten-Smith, 1913. NOT

513. Lindsay, Effie Grout. *Missionaries of the Minneapolis Branch of the Women's Foreign Missionary Society of the Methodist Episcopal Church.* [Minneapolis: n.p.], 1904.

514. *Lives of Celebrated Women.* New York: Allison, 1875; 1890; Lovell, 1910. PC

515. Logan, Mrs. John A. [Mary Simmerson Cunningham Logan]. *Thirty Years in Washington; or, Life and Scenes in Our National Capital.* Hartford, CT: Worthington, 1901. With additional chapters: Minneapolis: Baldwin, 1908; 1909. Cleveland: Barnum, 1908. NOT

516. ———. *The Part Taken by Women in American History.* Wilmington, DE: Perry-Nalle, 1912. NOT.

517. Loliée, Frédéric. *The Gilded Beauties of the Second Empire.* Adapted by Bryan O'Donnell. London: Long, 1909. London: Long; New York: Brentano's, 1910.

518. Lord, Fred Townley. *Great Women of the Bible.* New York: Harper; London: Cassell, 1939; 1941.

519. ———. *Great Women in Christian History.* London: Cassell; 1940.

520. Lord, John. *Great Women.* Vol. 7 of *Beacon Lights of History* by John Lord. New York: Clarke, 1886. PC

521. Lotz, Philip Henry, ed. *Women Leaders.* New York: Association Press, 1940.

522. Love, Cornelia Spencer. *Famous Women of Yesterday and Today.* Chapel Hill: University of North Carolina Press, 1932; 1936; 1938.

523. Luckett, Margie Hersh, ed. *Maryland Women.* 3 vols. Baltimore: King, 1931–42.

524. Lugrin, Nellie de Bertrand, and John Hosie. *The Pioneer Women of Vancouver Island, 1843–66.* Vancouver Island: Women's Canadian Club of Victoria, 1928.

525. Luigini, Frederico. *The Book of Fair Women* (1554). Translated by Elsie M. Lang. London: Werner Laurie; New York: J. Pott, 1907.

526. Lundholm, Rev. Algot Theodore. *Women of the Bible.* Rock Island, IL: Augustana, 1923–26; 1927; 1948; 1954; 1957; 1961.

527. Mabie, Hamilton Wright, and Kate Stephens, eds. *Heroines That Every Child Should Know.* New York: Doubleday, Page, 1907; 1908; Grosset & Dunlap, 1908; [1915]. As: *Heroines,* Garden City, NY: Doubleday, Page, 1912; Doubleday, Doran, 1928. PC

528. McCabe, Joseph. *The Empresses of Constantinople.* London: Methuen; Boston: Badger, 1913.

529. ———. *The Empresses of Rome.* London: Methuen; New York: Holt, 1911.

530. McConnell, Thomas Maxwell. *Eve and Her Daughters, or, Heroines of Home.* Philadelphia: Westminster, 1900; 1905.

531. McCook, Henry Christopher. *The Women Friends of Jesus.* New York: Fords, Howard, & Hulbert, 1886. Subtitle variant: London: Hodder & Stoughton, 1888; 1890.

532. McCormick, Henry. *The Women of Illinois.* Bloomington, IL: Pantagraph, 1913.

533. McCracken, Elizabeth. *The Women of America.* New York and London: Macmillan, 1904. NOT

534. McCraith, L. M. *The Romance of Irish Heroines.* Dublin: Talbot, 1913; 1930. New York and London: Longmans, Green, 1913.

535. Mackay, Rev. William Mackintosh. *The Woman of Tact: And Other Bible Types of Modern Women.* Cincinnati, OH: Jennings & Graham; New York: Eaton & Mains, [1910]. As: *Bible Types of Modern Women* with variant subtitles. London and New York: Hodder & Stoughton, 1912; 1919; 1920. New York: Doran, 1920; 1922; 1935. Garden City, NY: Doubleday, Doran, 1929.

536. MacSorley, Catherine Mary. *A Few Good Women, and What They Teach Us.* London: Hogg, [1886].

537. Macurdy, G[race] H[arriet]. *Hellenistic Queens.* Baltimore and London: Johns Hopkins University Press; H. Milford, Oxford University Press, 1932.

538. ———. *Vassal-Queens and Some Contemporary Women in the Roman Empire.* Baltimore: Johns Hopkins University Press, 1937.

539. Madden, Maude Whitmore. *Women of the Meiji Era.* New York and Chicago: Revell, 1919.

540. Maguire, Yvonne. *The Women of the Medici.* London: Routledge; New York: Dail; Macveagh, 1927.

541. Mahan, Jabez Alexander. *Famous Women of Vienna.* Vienna: Halm & Goldmann, 1929; 1930. New York: Stechert, 1930.

542. Majors, Monroe Alphus. *Noted Negro Women.* Jackson, TN: Lynk; Chicago: Donohue & Henneberry, 1893.

543. Mann, Mary Ridpath. *Royal Women.* London and Chicago: McClurg, 1913.

544. Mansfield, Estrith. *Famous Women of Oxfordshire.* Oxford: Slatter & Rose, [1932?].

545. Marble, Annie Russell. *Notable Women of the Bible.* New York and London: Century, 1923. London: Sampson & Low, 1926.

546. Martin, Margaret [1807–69]. *Heroines of Early Methodism.* Nashville: Southern Methodist, 1887; M.E. Church/South, Smith & Lamar, 1915.

547. Martyn, Sarah Towne Smith. *Daughters of the Cross.* New York: American Tract Society, 1868.

548. ———. *Women of the Bible.* New York: American Tract Society, 1868.

549. Mary Theodore, Sister. *Pioneer Nuns of British Columbia.* Victoria: British Columbia, 1931.

550. Masefield, Muriel Agnes [Bussell]. *Women Novelists from Fanny Burney to George Eliot.* London: Nicholson & Watson, 1934.

551. Mason, Amelia Ruth Gere. *Women of the French Salons.* London: Unwin; New York: Century, 1891.

552. Matheson, George. *The Representative Women of the Bible.* New York: Armstrong; Doran; Cincinnati, OH: Jennings & Graham, 1907. London: Hodder & Stoughton, 1907; 1908.

553. May, Caroline. *The American Female Poets.* Philadelphia: Lindsay & Blakiston, 1848, 1849; 1850; 1853; 1854; 1856; 1859; 1865. Title variant: New York: Allen, 1869; World, 1875; 1876.

554. Mayer, Gertrude Townshend. *Women of Letters.* 2 vols. London: Bentley, 1894.

555. Mayhew, Abby Shaw, and Mabel Cratty. *[Biographies].* By Young Women's Christian Associations. New York: YWCA, 1915–29.

556. Mayhew, Experience. *Narratives of the Lives of Pious Indian Women Who Lived on Martha's Vineyard More Than One Hundred Years Since.* Boston: Gerrish, 1727; New England Sabbath School Union, 1800; Loring, 1830.

557. Mayne, Ethel Colburn. *Enchanters of Men.* Philadelphia: Jacobs, 1909. London: Methuen, 1909; 1912. New York and London: Putnam, 1925. PC

558. ———. *Browning's Heroines.* London: Chatto & Windus, 1913; 1914. New York: Pott, 1914. NOT

559. Meade, June [pseud.]. *Three Women of France.* London: Hurst & Blackett, 1933.

560. Melville, Lewis [i.e., Lewis Saul Benjamin; 1874–1932]. *Maids of Honour.* Illustrated. London: Hutchinson; New York: Doran, 1927; n.d.

561. ———. *More Stage Favourites of the Eighteenth Century.* 2 vols. London: Hutchinson, 1929.

562. ———. *Regency Ladies.* London: Hutchinson, 1926. New York: Doran, 1926; 1927.

563. ———. *Stage Favourites of the Eighteenth Century.* London: Hutchinson, 1928. Garden City, NY: Doubleday, Doran, 1929.

564. ———. *The Windsor Beauties.* London: Hutchinson; Boston and New York: Houghton Mifflin, 1928.

565. Menzies, Louisa. *Lives of the Greek Heroines.* London: Bell, 1880.

566. Menzies, Sutherland [i.e., Elizabeth Stone]. *Memoirs of Distinguished Political Women.* 2 vols. London: King, 1873; 1875.

567. ———. *Royal Favourites.* 2 vols. London: Maxwell, 1865; Harrison, 1866; Truscott, 1870.

568. Metcalf, Henry Harrison. *New Hampshire Women.* Concord, NH: New Hampshire Publishing, 1895.

569. Meyers, Robert Cornelius V. *World-Famous Women.* Philadelphia: Ziegler, 1897. As: *Victoria, Sixty Years a Queen,* Philadelphia: Ziegler, 1897. Other title and subtitle variants: Philadelphia: Ziegler, 1897; 1901. PC

570. Michael, Charles D. *Heroines: True Tales of Brave Women.* London: S. W. Partridge, [1900?]. PC

571. Michelet, Jules. *The Women of the French Revolution.* Translated by Meta Roberts Pennington. Philadelphia: Baird, 1855; 1859.

572. Middleton, Meade [Fannie H. Bent]. *Five Women of England.* Philadelphia: Presbyterian Board, 1880. PC

573. Miles, Alfred H., ed. *A Book of Brave Girls at Home and Abroad.* London: Stanley Paul, [1900–1929?].

574. Miller, Basil William. *Meet the Women of the Bible.* Kansas City, MO: Beacon Hill, [1900s?]. Dallas: Chandler's, 1955.

575. Miller, Florence Fenwick. *In Ladies' Company.* London: Ward & Downey, 1892. PC

576. ———. *Portraits of Women of the New Testament.* London: Allenson, 1916.

577. Miller, Thomas E. *Portraits of Women of the Bible.* 3d ed. London: Allenson, 1910.

578. Minnigerode, Meade. *Some American Ladies.* London and New York: Putnam, 1926. PC

579. Montgomery, Lucy Maud, Marion Keith [i.e., Mary Esther Miller MacGregor], and Mabel Burns McKinley. *Courageous Women.* Toronto: McClelland & Stewart, 1934.

580. Moore, Frank. *Women of the War.* Hartford, CT: Scranton; Chicago: Treat; San Francisco: Bancroft; Cincinnati, OH: National, 1866; 1867; 1869.

581. Moore, Henry Charles. *Noble Deeds of the World's Heroines.* London: Religious Tract Society, [1903].

582. Moore, Virginia. *Distinguished Women Writers.* New York: Dutton, 1934.

583. Moreland, Sinclair. *The Texas Women's Hall of Fame.* Austin, TX: Biographical, 1917.

584. Morgan, Henry James, ed. *Types of Canadian Women.* Vol. 1. Toronto: Briggs, 1903.

585. Morgan, Lady. *Woman and Her Master: A History of the Female Sex from the Earliest Period.* London: Colburn; Bryce; Philadelphia: Carey & Hart, 1840. Paris: Galignani; Baudry's European Library, 1840. London: Bryce, 1855. NOT

586. Mortemar, Julie de. *Folly's Queens.* [New York]: Fox, 1882.

587. Morton, Henry Canova Vollam. *Women of the Bible.* London: Methuen, 1940; 1941. New York: Dodd, Mead, 1941; 1946; 1952; 1956; 1963.

588. Mossell, Mrs. N. F. [Gertrude E. H. Bustill]. *The Work of Afro-American Women* (1894). Philadelphia: G. S. Ferguson, 1908.

589. Mossman, Samuel. *Gems of Womanhood.* London and Edinburgh: Gall & Inglis, 1870. Title variant: London and Edinburgh: Gall & Inglis, [1880–94]. PC

590. Mozans, H. J. *Woman in Science.* New York and London: Appleton, 1913. NOT

591. [Mozley, Anne.] *Tales of Female Heroism.* London: James Burns, 1846. 2d ser. London: Lumley, 1856.

592. Mundell, Frank. *Heroines of the Cross.* London: Sunday-School Union, [1897]; [1900s?].

593. Murch, Sir Jerome. *Mrs. Barbauld and Her Contemporaries.* Bath: Printed for private circulation by W. Lewis, 1876. London: Longmans, Green, 1877. [1887?].

594. Murray, E. C. Grenville. *Young Widows.* London: Vizetelly, 1886.

595. National Council of Women in India. *Women in India: Who's Who?* Bombay: n.p., 1935.

596. Neely, Ruth. *Women of Ohio.* Cincinnati, OH: Clarke, 1937. [Chicago]: Clarke, 1939. [Springfield, IL]: Clarke, 1940.

597. Nellist, George Ferguson Mitchell. *Women of Hawaii.* [Honolulu]: Langton Boyle, 1929.

598. Nevin, Adelaide Mellier. *The Social Mirror: A Character Sketch of the Women of Pittsburgh and Vicinity . . .* Pittsburgh: Nevin, 1888.

599. Nevin, James Banks, ed. *Prominent Women of Georgia.* Atlanta: National Biographical, 1928.

600. Northcroft, Dorothea Mary. *Women at Work in the League of Nations.* London: Page, 1923; Page & Pratt, 1925. Keighley, England: Wadsworth/Rydal, 1926; 1927; 1928.

601. Northrop, Henry Davenport. *Famous Women of the Bible.* Harrisburg, PA: Minter; Philadelphia: Moore; Chicago: Wabash; Louisville, KY: Pentecostal, 1898.

602. Norval, Leigh. *Women of the Bible.* Nashville: M.E. Church, South, 1889; 1890.

603. *Notable Women of Affairs.* New York: Women's Syndicate, 1925.

604. *Notable Women of Olden Time[s].* New York and Philadelphia: American Sunday-School Union, 1852.

605. *Notable Women of Our Own Times.* London and New York: Ward, Lock [1883].

606. *Noted Women the World Over.* London and New York: Butterick, 1898.

607. Oliphant, Margaret, et al. *Women Novelists of Queen Victoria's Reign.* London: Hurst & Blackett, 1897.

608. O'Mahoney, Katherine A. O'Keefe. *Famous Irishwomen.* Lawrence, MA: Lawrence Publishing, 1907.

609. O'Malley, I[da] B[eatrice]. *Great Englishwomen.* London: Bell, 1933.

610. ———. *Women in Subjection.* London: Duckworth, 1933. NOT

611. Omori, Annie Shepley, trans. *Diaries of Court Ladies of Old Japan.* Boston and New York: Houghton Mifflin, 1920. London: Constable, 1921. Tokyo: Kenkyusha, 1935. NOT

612. "One Who Knows Them." *Girls and Their Ways.* London: Hogg, 1881.

613. O'Reilly, Bernard. *Heroic Women of the Bible and the Church.* New York: Ford, 1877. Title variant: New York: Kennedy, 1877; Dewing, 1889; 1893. Chicago: Hyland, 1889. New York: Kennedy, 1894; 1896; 1899; 1903; 1905.

614. Overton, Grant M. *Women Who Make Our Novels.* New York: Dodd, Mead, 1918; 1925; 1927; 1928; 1931; Moffat, Yard, 1919; 1920; 1922.

615. Owen, Mrs. Octavius Freire [Emily]. *The Heroines of Domestic Life.* London and New York: Routledge, Warne, & Routledge, 1861; [1877]. PC

616. ———. *The Heroines of History.* New York: Carlton & Phillips; Cincinnati, OH: Hitchcock & Walden, 1854; 1856. London and New York: Routledge, 1854; 1858; [1877]. PC

617. Padwick, Constance E. *Heroines of Healing.* [London]: UCME, 1915. Title variant: London: UCME, 1922; Edinburgh House, 1927.

618. ———. *White Heroines of Africa.* [London]: UCME, 1914.

619. P[ardon], G[eorge] F[rederick]. *Illustrious Women Who Have Distinguished Themselves for Virtue, Piety and Benevolence.* London: Blackwood, 1861; 1868.

620. Parkes, Bessie Rayner. [Bessie R. Belloc]. *Historic Nuns.* London: Duckworth, 1898; 1899. St. Louis: Herder; Edinburgh and London: Sands, 1911.

621. ———. *Vignettes: Twelve Biographical Sketches from the Englishwoman's Journal.* London and New York: A. Strahan, 1866. PC

622. Parkman, Mary R. *Heroines of Service.* London and New York: Century, 1917; 1919; Appleton, 1938. PC

623. Parry, Emma Louise. *Woman in the Reformation.* Philadelphia: Lutheran, 1882.

624. Parton, James. *Daughters of Genius.* Philadelphia: Hubbard, 1885; 1886; 1888. New York: American, 1890. Related works follow.[628–30] PC

625. ———. *Eminent Women.* New York: Alden; Philadelphia: Hubbard, [1880s?]. New York: International; n.p.: Edgewood, 1880. New York: Lovell, 1890. PC

626. ———. *The World's Famous Women.* New York: Alden; American, 1888. Philadelphia: Hubbard, 1889. New York: Lovell; n.p.: Edgewood, 1890. New York: International, [1890s]. PC

627. ———. *Fanny Fern: A Memorial Volume.* New York: Carleton, 1873; 1874. NOT

628. ———. *Noted Women of Europe and America.* Hartford, CT: Phoenix, 1883. Boston: Wilson, 1884. PC

629. ———, ed. *Some Noted Princes, Authors and Statesmen of Our Time.* New York: Crowell; Columbus: Estill; Norwich, CT: Bill, 1885; 1886. NOT

630. Parton, James, et al. *Eminent Women of the Age.* Hartford, CT: Betts, 1868; 1869; 1871; 1872; 1873; 1877; 1879; 1888; Park, 1880. Chicago: Gibbs & Nichols, 1869. PC

631. ———, et al. *People's Book of Biography.* New York: Virtue & Yorston, 1868; 1873. Hartford, CT: Hale, 1868; 1869. NOT

632. Pavry, Bapsy. *The Heroines of Ancient Persia.* Cambridge: Cambridge University Press, 1930.

633. Payne, Gertrude Irene. *Famous Women.* Toledo, OH: YWCA, 1913; 1915.

634. Peay, Emily Clough. *Lives Worth Living: Studies of Women, Biblical and Modern. . . .* Chicago: University of Chicago Press, 1915; 1916; 1921; 1923.

635. Peacock, Virginia Tatnall. *Famous American Belles of the Nineteenth Century.* Philadelphia and London: Lippincott, 1900; 1901.

636. Pennock, Meta Rutter, ed. *Makers of Nursing History.* New York: Lakeside, 1928; 1940.

637. Pepper, Mary Sifton. *Maids and Matrons of New France.* Toronto: Morang, 1901; 1902. Boston: Little, Brown, 1901.

638. Philip, Robert. *The Marthas; or, The Varieties of Female Piety.* New York: Carter, 1836; 1848; Appleton, 1836; 1837; 1844; 1847.

639. ———. *The Marys; or, The Beauty of Female Holiness.* London: Virtue, 1835; 1838. New York: Appleton, 1836; 1837; Carter, 1851.

640. ———. *The Mothers of Scripture.* London: Ward, Lock, & Tyler, 1870.

641. Pickrell, Annie Doom. *Pioneer Women in Texas.* Austin, TX: Steck, 1929.

642. *Pioneer Women Teachers of Texas.* n.p.: Delta Kappa Gamma Society, Alpha State Organization, 1940.

643. Pitman, Mrs. Emma R[aymond]. *Heroines of the Missionary Field.* [London] and New York: Cassell, 1880.

644. ———. *Lady Missionaries in Foreign Lands.* New York: Revell, 1887; 1889. London: Partridge, 1889. Title variant: London: Pickering & Inglis, [1880s?]; 1929.

645. ———. *Missionary Heroines in Eastern Lands.* London: Partridge, 1884; 1895. New York: Revell, [1890s?]. London: Pickering & Inglis, 1932.

646. ———. *Lady Hymn Writers.* London and New York: Nelson, 1892.

647. Polkinghorne, Ruby Kathleen, and Polkinghorne [i.e., Mabel Irene Rutherford]. *Stories of Famous Women.* London: University of London Press, 1933.

648. Pomeroy, Sarah Gertrude. *Little-Known Sisters of Well-Known Men.* Boston: Estes, 1912.

649. Pool, John J. *Woman's Influence in the East.* London: Stock, 1892.

650. Pope-Hennessy, Dame Una Birch. *Three English Women in America.* London: Benn, 1929.

651. Portigliotti, Giuseppe. *Some Fascinating Women of the Renaissance.* Translated by Bernard Miall. London: Allen & Unwin; New York: Brentano's, 1929.

652. Pratt, Edwin A. *Pioneer Women in Victoria's Reign.* London: Newnes, 1867; 1897. PC

653. Presbyterian Church. *This Is My Story: Presbyterian Church (USA) Women in Ministry.* [Louisville, KY: Woman's Task Force of The Convenant Fellowship of Presbyterians, 1900s?].

654. Prichard, Thomas Jeffery Llewlyn. *The Heroines of Welsh History.* London: Cash, 1854.

655. *Queen Victoria and Other Excellent Women.* London: Religious Tract Society, [1903].

656. Ragg, Laura M. *Women Artists of Bologna.* London: Methuen, 1907.

657. Rait, Robert S., ed. *Five Stuart Princesses.* London: Constable; New York: Dutton, 1902; 1908. London: Westminster, 1922.

658. Ranelagh, Frank [i.e., Robert Folkestone Williams]. *Maids of Honour: A Tale of the Court of George I.* 3 vols. London: Colburn, 1845; Kent, 1861. NOT?

659. Rappoport, Angelo Solomon. *The Fair Ladies of the Winter Palace.* London: Holden & Hardingham, 1914.

660. Ravenel, Florence Leftwich. *Women and the French Tradition.* New York: Macmillan, 1918.

661. Raymond, Ida. [i.e., Mrs. Mary T. Tardy]. *Southland Writers.* Philadelphia: Claxton, Remsen & Haffelf nger, 1870. As: *The Living Female Writers of the South.* 1872.

662. Read, Thomas Buchanan, ed. *The Female Poets of America.* Philadelphia: Butler, 1848; 1849; 1850; 1851; 1852; 1855; 1857; 1864; 1866; 1867. New York: Worthington, 1887; 1890; Hagermann, 1894.

663. Reed, Myrtle. *Love Affairs of Literary Men.* New York: Putnam's, 1907. NOT

664. ———. *Happy Women.* New York: Putnam's, 1913. PC

665. Reed, Ruth. *The Negro Women of Gainesville, Georgia.* Athens: University of Georgia Press, 1921.

666. Reeves, Winona Evans. *The Blue Book of Iowa Women.* [Mexico, MO: Press of the Missouri], 1914.

667. *Remarkable Women of Different Nations and Ages.* 1st ser. Boston and Cleveland: Jewett, 1858. PC

668. Reynolds, Myra. *The Learned Lady in England, 1650–1760.* Boston and New York: Houghton Mifflin, 1920.

669. Rhodes, Nora M. *Life Stories of Some Women Missionaries.* Elgin, IL: General Mission Board, Church of the Brethren, [1937?].

670. Richards, Samuel Alfred. *Feminist Writers of the Seventeenth Century.* London: Nutt, 1914. M.A. thesis, University of London.

671. Richardson, Jerusha D[avidson Hunting] [Mrs. Aubrey Richardson]. *Famous Ladies of the English Court.* London: Hutchinson; Chicago: Stone, 1899.

672. ———. Mrs. *Women of the Church of England.* London: Chapman & Hall, 1907; 1908.

673. Richmond, Euphemia Johnson Guernsey. *Woman, First and Last: And What She Has Done.* 2 vols. New York: Phillips & Hunt; Cincinnati, OH: Cranston & Stowe, 1887. PC

674. Ritchie, Anne Isabella [Thackeray]. *A Book of Sibyls*. London: Smith Elder; New York: Harper; Leipzig: Tauchnitz, 1883. PC

675. Robbins, Alice Emily. *A Book of Duchesses: Studies in Personality*. London: Melrose, 1913.

676. Robbins, Mary La Fayette. *Alabama Women in Literature*. [Selma, AL: Selma Printing], 1895.

677. Roberts, Margaret. *Women of the Last Days of Old France*. London: Warne; New York: Scribner, Welford & Armstrong, 1872.

678. Robertson, Mrs. Clyde. *Fifty Famous Women*. Atlanta: Emory University Press, 1936.

679. Robertson, Eric S. *English Poetesses*. London, Paris, and New York: Cassell, 1883.

680. Robins, Edward. *Twelve Great Actresses*. New York and London: Putnam, 1900.

681. Rogers, Cameron. *Gallant Ladies*. New York: Harcourt Brace, 1928. PC

682. *The Roll of Honour for Women*. London: "Gentlewoman" Offices, 1906.

683. Rolt-Wheeler, Ethel. *Famous Blue-Stockings*. London: Methuen; New York: Lane, 1910; 1911.

684. ———. *Women of the Cell and Cloister*. London: Methuen; Milwaukee: Young Churchman, 1913.

685. Romieu, E., and G. Romieu. *Three Virgins of Haworth*. Translated by R. Tapley. London: Skeffington; New York: Dutton, 1930.

686. Ross, Ishbel. *Ladies of the Press*. New York: Harper, 1936. New York: Arno, 1974.

687. Ross, Janet. *Three Generations of English Women*. 2 vols. London: Murray, 1888. 1 vol., London: Unwin, 1893.

688. Rowton, Frederic. *The Female Poets of Great Britain*. London: Longman, Brown, Green, and Longmans, 1848. Philadelphia: Carey & Hart, 1849; Baird, 1853; 1854; 1856. Philadelphia: n.p., 1859. As: *Cyclopedia of Female Poets*, 1874; Dayton, OH: Alvin Peabody, 1883.

689. Russell, Lady Constance Charlotte Elisa Lennox. *Three Generations of Fascinating Women*. London: Longmans, Green, 1904; 1905.

690. Russell, Rev. Matthew. *The Three Sisters of Lord Russell of Killowen and Their Convent Life*. London and New York: Longman, 1912.

691. Russell, William. *Eccentric Personages*. London and New York: Avery; London: Maxwell, 1864; 1865. New York: American News, 1866; 1888. NOT

692. ———. *Extraordinary Women*. London: Routledge, 1857. London and New York: Routledge, Warne & Routledge, 1860; 1864. PC

693. Ryburn, Jessie D., Ellen S. Bowen, and Mrs. J. W. Walker. *Women of Old Abingdon*. [Pulaski, VA: B. D. Smith & Bros.], 1937.

694. Ryley, M. Beresford. *Queens of the Renaissance*. London: Methuen; Boston: Small, 1907; 1908.

695. Sadlier, Anna Theresa. *Women of Catholicity*. New York: Benziger, 1885; 1917.

696. Sainte-Beuve, Charles Augustin, ed. [with commentary]. *The Book of the Ladies, by Pierre de Bourdeïlle, Abbé de Brantôme*. Translated by Katherine Prescott Wormeley. Boston: Hardy, Pratt, 1899; 1902. New York: Collier; London: Heinemann, 1899. Boston: Millet, 1909. As: *Illustrious Dames of the Court of the Valois Kings*, New York: Lamb, 1912.

697. ———. *Portraits of Celebrated Women*. Translated by H. W. Preston. Boston: Roberts, 1868; 1880; 1885; 1895. New York: Little, 1895; Putnam, 1925. PC

698. Sanderson, Edgar, and John Porter Lamberton, John McGovern, Joseph Morgan Rogers, Laurence E. Greene, et al. *Famous Women*. Vol. 5 of *Six Thousand Years of History*. 10 vols. New York and Chicago: DuMont, 1899. Chicago and Philadelphia: Universal History, 1900. Philadelphia: DuMont, 1900. New York: DuMont, 1902. Philadelphia: Nolan, 1906; 1907; 1913.

699. Sangster, Margaret Elizabeth Munson. *The Women of the Bible*. New York: Christian Herald, 1911.

700. Sargeant, Charlotte Eliza. *A Book for Mothers: or, Biographic Sketches of the Mothers of Great and Good Men*. London: n.p., 1850.

701. [Scanlan, Nelle Margaret]. *Boudoir Mirrors of Washington*. Philadelphia and Chicago: Winston, 1923.

702. Schmidt, Minna Moscherosch. *400 Outstanding Women of the World and Costumology of Their Time*. Chicago: Schmidt, 1933. NOT

703. Scott, Eleanor. *Adventurous Women*. London: Nelson, 1933.

704. ———. *War among Ladies*. Boston: Little Brown, 1928.

705. Scouller, Mildred Marshall. *Women Who Man Our Clubs*. Philadelphia: Winston, 1934.

706. Scruggs, Lawson Andrew. *Women of Distinction*. Raleigh, NC: L. A. Scruggs, 1893. PC

707. Sell, Henry T. *Studies of Famous Bible Women*. New York: Revell, 1925.

708. Semple, James Alexander. *Representative Women of Colorado*. Denver: Alexander Art; Semple, 1911; 1914.

709. Senior, Maud Mary. *Some Women of the Gospels*. London: Sheldon, [1940–49?].

710. ———. *Women Pathfinders*. London: Sheldon, 1940. Same as next?

711. ———. *African Women Pathfinders*. London: Sheldon, 1940.

712. Sergeant, Philip Walsingham. *Dominant Women*. London: Hutchinson, 1929; 1930. PC

713. ———. *Rogues and Scoundrels*. London: Hutchinson, 1924. New York: Brentano's, 1927. NOT

714. Serviez, Jacques Roergas de. *The Roman Empresses*. 2 vols. in 1. London: Walpole, 1899; 1909. New York: Nichols, 1913; American Anthropological Society, 1925; Dingwall-Rock, 1932. Title variant: New York: Wise, 1935.

715. Sewell, Daisy Elizabeth McQuigg. *Ideal Womanhood: A Bible Study....* Austin, TX: Firm Foundation, 1927; 1936; 1947.

716. Sheridan, Clare. *Russian Portraits*. London: Jonathan Cape, 1921. As: *Mayfair to Moscow*. New York: Boni & Liveright, 1921.

717. Shorter, Susan I. *The Heroines of African Methodism*. Jacksonville, FL: Chew, 1891.

718. Sigourney, Mrs. L[ydia]. H[untley]. *Examples from the Eighteenth and Nineteenth Centuries*. 1st ser. New York: Scribner, 1857. NOT.

719. ———. *The Girl's Own Book*. 1837; London: Nelson, 1852. NOT

720. ———. *Great and Good Women*. Edinburgh: Nimmo, [1866]; 1871; Nimmo, Hay & Mitchell, 1885. PC

721. Simpson, Harold, and Mrs. Charles Braun. *A Century of Famous Actresses, 1750–1850*. London: Mills & Boon, 1913.

722. Simpson, Helen Macdonald. *The Women of New Zealand*. Wellington, NZ: Dept. of Internal Affairs, 1940.

723. Sinclair, May. *The Three Brontës*. London: Hutchinson, 1900; 1911; 1912; 1914; 1933. Boston and New York: Houghton Mifflin, 1912; 1913; 1914.

724. Singleton, Esther, ed. and trans. *Famous Women as Described by Great Writers*. New York: Dodd, Mead, 1904; 1907.

725. Skaer, Georgia Blaney. *The Women of the Bible*. Kansas City, MO: Burton, 1927.

726. Skidmore, Margaret A. *Women Pioneers in Sheffield Methodism*. [Sheffield]: n.p., n.d.

727. Skinner, Charlotte. *Sisters of the Master*. London: Partridge, [1900s?].

728. ———. *Uncrowned Queens*. London: Partridge, [1900?].

729. Smith, Daniel, comp. *Gems of Female Biography*. New York: Nelson & Phillips; Cincinnati, OH: Hitchcock & Walden, 1850. New York: Carlton & Porter; Lane & Scott, 1852; Carlton & Phillips, 1854; 1856. PC

730. Smith, George Barnett. *Noble Womanhood: A Series of Biographical Sketches*. [London]: SPCK; New York: Young, 1894; 1912. PC

731. ———. *Women of Renown*. London: W. H. Allen, 1893. PC

732. Smith, John Frederick. *Romantic Incidents in the Lives of the Queens of England*. New York: Garrett; Dick & Fitzgerald, 1853.

733. Smith, Mary Ann. *The Holy Women of Old*. Edinburgh: John Anderson, 1897.

734. Snell, Frederick John. *The Girlhood of Famous Women*. Illustrated by Margaret Tarrant. London: Harrap, 1915; 1920; 1922.

735. Snyder, Rev. Harvey Albert, and Ethel Wendell Trout. *Girls of the Bible.* New York: Holt, Rinehart & Winston, 1929.

736. Soissons, Comte de. Guy Jean Raoul E. C. E. *Seven Richest Heiresses of France.* London: Long, 1911.

737. ———. *Six Great Princesses.* London: Holden, 1913.

738. Sokolnikova, Galina Osipovna Serebriakova. *Nine Women: Drawn from the Epoch of the French Revolution.* Translated by H. C. Stevens. Introduction by Mrs. Sidney Webb. [New York: Ballou]; London: Cape, 1932.

739. Somerville, Rose. *Brief Epitomes of the Lives of Eminent Women.* London: Women's Printing Society, 1886; [1896]. PC

740. Sparrow, Walter Shaw, ed. *Women Painters of the World.* London: Hodder & Stoughton; Toronto: Copp Clark; New York: Stokes, 1905.

741. Spaull, Hebe. *Women Peace Makers.* London: Harrap, 1924.

742. Spielmann, Mrs. Meyer A. *Jewish Women Writers.* London: n.p., 1913.

743. Spofford, Harriet Elizabeth Prescott, et al. *Three Heroines of New England Romance.* Boston: n.p., 1895.

744. Spofford, Harriet Elizabeth Prescott. *A Little Book of Friends.* Boston: Little, Brown, 1916. PC

745. Sprague, William Buell, and Jonathan Mayhew Wainwright, eds. *The Women of the Bible.* New York and Philadelphia: Appleton, 1849; 1852; 1855. Title variant: New York and Philadelphia: Appleton, 1850; 1851.

746. Staal, Gustave. *The Bible Gallery.* London: David Bogue, 1847.

747. Staley, John Edgcumbe. *Famous Women of Florence.* London: Constable; New York: Scribner, 1909.

748. ———. *The Dogaresses of Venice.* New York: Scribner, 1910.

749. ———. *Heroines of Genoa and the Rivieras.* New York: Scribner, 1911; 1912. London: Laurie, 1911.

750. ———. *King Rene d'Anjou and His Seven Queens.* London: Long; Hutchinson, 1912. New York: Scribner, 1912. NOT

751. Starling, Elizabeth. *Noble Deeds of Woman.* London: Hookham, 1835. 2 vols., Philadelphia: Carey, Lea & Blanchard, 1836. Title variant: London: Bohn, 1848. Boston: Phillips, Sampson, 1850. London: Bohn, 1858; 1859; 1864. Boston: Crosby, Nichols, Lee, 1860. London: Bell, 1864. Boston: Hale & Whiting, 1881; 1883. London: Bell, 1891. All page citations in text are to the 1848 ed. PC

752. Steele, Eliza R. *Heroines of Sacred History.* New York: Taylor, 1841; 1842; 1844; 1850; 1851; 1853.

753. Steinman, George. *Althorp Memoirs; or, Biographical Notices of . . . Six Ladies . . . in the Picture Gallery of . . . Earl Spencer.* [Oxford]: Printed for private circulation, [J. Parker], 1869.

754. Stevens, Abel. *The Women of Methodism.* New York: Carlton & Porter; Phillips & Hunt, 1866; Carlton & Lanahan, 1869; 1874. London: William Tegg, 1876.

755. Stewart, Agnes M. *Tried in the Furnace.* Vol. 1, *The Three Elizabeths.* London: Burns & Oates, 1869. Title variants: Baltimore: n.p., 1873. Philadelphia: Kilner, 1912.

756. Stitch, Wilhelmina [i.e., Ruth Collie]. *Women of the Bible.* London: Methuen, 1935.

757. Stone, Gilbert. *Women War Workers.* New York: Crowell; London: Harrap, 1917. NOT

758. Stowe, Harriet Beecher, et al. *Our Famous Women.* Hartford, CT: Worthington, 1883. Hartford, CT: Worthington; Chicago: Nettleton, 1884. Title variants: Hartford, CT: n.p., 1886; 1888. PC

759. Stowe, Harriet Beecher. *Woman in Sacred History.* New York: Ford, 1873; 1874; 1876. London: Sampson Low, Marston, Low, Searle, 1874. New York: Alden, 1878; 1888. As: *Bible Heroines,* New York: Fords, Howard, & Hulbert, 1878.

760. Strachan, Annie S. *Famous Women in Scottish Story.* London: Butcher, [1909].

761. Strachey, Ray. *The Cause.* London: Bell, 1928; 1929.

762. Strang, Lewis C. *Famous Actresses of the Day in America.* Boston: Page, 1899; 1906.

———. *Famous Prima Donnas.* London: Page, 1900; 1906.

763. Strickland, Agnes, and Elisabeth Strickland. *Lives of the Queens of England, from the Norman Conquest.* 16 vols. London: Bell, 1840–48. 5 vols., New York: Miller, 1843. 12 vols., London: Colburn, 1844–49. Rev. ed., 8 vols., London: Colburn, 1851. 12 vols., Philadelphia, 1859; 1864; 1869; 1877 (abridged); 1882; 1885. Abridged ed., 1 vol., London: Bell & Daldy, 1864; 1867. New York: Harper, 1867; Knox, 1885; 1886. 6 vols., London, New York, and Bombay: Bell, 1882; 1883; 1884; 1889; 1893. Edited by Caroline G. Parker. New York: Harper, 1883; 1889; 1892. Philadelphia: Lippincott, 1892; 1893; Barrie, 1902–03. 6 vols., London: Nash, 1905; Bell, 1904–8. Rosalie Kaufman's abridgement, 3 vols., Boston: Estes & Lauriat, 1882–84. Chicago and New York: Werner; Akron, OH: Saalfield, 1895. Akron, OH: Saalfield, 1903.

764. ———. *The Queens of England: A Series of Portraits. . . .* New York: Appleton, 1851.

765. ———. *Lives of the Queens of Scotland and English Princesses.* 8 vols. Edinburgh and London: Blackwood, 1850–59. New York: Harper, 1855–59. Edited by Rosalie Kaufman, *The Queens of Scotland,* 2 vols., Boston: n.p., 1886–87. Boston: Estes & Lauriat, 1887; 1894. Abridged, Chicago: Werner, 1895.

766. Strickland, Agnes. *Lives of the Last Four Princesses of the Royal House of Stuart.* London: 1870. London: Bell & Daldy; New York: Scribner, 1872.

767. ———. *Lives of the Stuart Princesses.* London: Bell, 1872.

768. ———. *Lives of the Tudor Princesses.* London: Bell; Longmans, Green, 1868; Bell, 1888.

769. ———. *Lives of the Tudor and Stuart Princesses.* London: Bell, 1868–72; 1888; 1902; 1907. Combines the two previous volumes.

770. ———. *Memoirs of the Queens of Henry VIII and His Mother, Elizabeth of York.* Philadelphia: Blanchard & Lea, 1853.

771. Swain, Anna Canada. *Pioneer Missionary Heroines in America.* New York: Baptist Board of Education, Dept. of Missionary Education, 1932.

772. Sweetser, Kate Dickinson. *Ten American Girls from History.* New York: Harper, 1917.

773. ———. *Ten Girls from History.* New York: Duffield, [1912]. New York and London: Harper, [1912]; 1919. PC

774. ———. *Famous Girls of the White House.* New York: Crowell, 1930. Rev. ed., New York: Crowell, 1937.

775. Tabor, Margaret Emma. *Four Margarets.* London: Sheldon, 1929.

776. ———. *Pioneer Women.* 4 vols. London: SPCK, 1925. 2 vols., London, New York, and Toronto: Sheldon, Macmillan, 1925–33. Printed as four series. PC

777. ———. *Pioneer Women.* 2d ser. London, New York, and Toronto: Sheldon, Macmillan, 1925; 1927; 1929. PC

778. ———. *Pioneer Women.* 3d ser. London, New York, and Toronto: Sheldon; Macmillan, 1930. PC

779. ———. *Pioneer Women.* 4th ser. London: Sheldon, 1933. PC

780. ———. *The Saints in Art.* New York: Stokes, 1908; Dutton, 1913. London: Methuen, 1908; 1913. NOT

781. Taft, Lorado. *Women Sculptors of America.* New York: Mentor Assoc., 1919.

782. Taft, Zachariah. *Biographical Sketches of the Lives and Public Ministry of Various Holy Women.* 2 vols. London: Kershaw, 1825. Leeds: 1825, 1827; 1828. 3 vols. in 1, London: Kershaw, 1835; 1838.

783. Tallentyre, S[tephen] G., [and Evelyn Beatrice Hall]. *Women of the Salons.* London and New York: Longman, 1901. New York: Putnam, 1926.

784. Taney, Mary Florence. *Kentucky Pioneer Women.* Cincinnati, OH: Clarke, 1893. NOT

785. Tappen, Kathleen B., and Bernice T. Morris. *Prominent Women in Latin America.* Washington, [DC]: U.S. Office of Inter-American Affairs, Research Division, 1944.

786. Telford, John. *Women in the Mission Field.* London: Kelly, 1895.

787. Tennessee Federation of Women's Clubs [FWC]. *Woman's Work in Tennessee*. Memphis: Jones-Briggs/Tennessee FWC, 1916.

788. Terhune, Albert Payson. *Superwomen*. New York: Ainslee Magazine; Moffat, Yard; World Library; Cleveland: International Fiction Library, 1916. PC

789. ———. *Wonder Women in History*. London and New York: Cassell, 1918. PC

790. Thayer, Bethia Hayward. *Brockton Women*. New York: Albertype, 1892.

791. Thayer, William M[akepeace]. *The Poor Girl and True Woman*. Boston: Gould & Lincoln; New York: Sheldon, Blakeman; Cincinnati, OH: Blanchard 1858, 1859; 1861. Title variants: Boston: Gould & Lincoln; New York: Sheldon, Blakeman; Cincinnati, OH: Blanchard, 1861; 1863; 1864. New York: Crowell, [1880–1900?].

792. ———. *Women Who Win*. New York, London, and Edinburgh: Nelson, 1896; 1897; 1898; 1901; 1908. Possible rev. ed. of above.[791] PC

793. Thomas, Henry. *Wild Women of History*. Girard, KS: Haldeman-Julius, 1937.

794. Thompson, Henry [1797–1878]. *The Life of Hannah More: With Notices of Her Sisters*. Philadelphia: Carey & Hart; London: Cadell; Edinburgh: Blackwood, 1838. Stuttgart: Steinkopf, 1847.

795. Thompson, Henry Adams [b. 1837]. *Women of the Bible*. Dayton, OH: U[nited] B[rethren], 1914.

796. Thoms, Adah B. *Pathfinders: A History of the Progress of Colored Graduate Nurses*. New York: Kay, 1929.

797. Thomson, Mrs. A. T. [Katherine Byerley] [1797–1862]. *The Queens of Society*. By Grace and Philip Wharton [pseud.] 2 vols. London, 1860. New York: Harper, 1860; 1861. London and New York: Routledge, 1867; 1870; 1872; 1876. 2d ed., 2 vols., New York: Stokes; Worthington; London: Jarvis; Philadelphia: Porter & Coates; Coates, 1890. PC

798. Thomson, Katherine. *Celebrated Friendships*. 2 vols. London: Hogg, 1859; 1861.

799. Thormanby. [Willmott Willmott-Dixon]. *Dainty Dames of Society*. 4 vols. London: Black; New York: Stokes, 1903. London: St. Andrew's; New York: Brentano's, [1900–1910?].

800. ———. *Queens of Beauty and Their Romances*. 2 vols. London: Hutchinson; New York: Appleton, 1907.

801. Thornton, Ella May. *Georgia Women, 1840–1940*. Atlanta: n.p., 1941.

802. Thornton-Cook, Elsie Prentys. *Her Majesty: The Romance of the Queens of England, 1066–1910*. London: Murray, 1926; 1928. New York: Dutton, 1927; 1928.

803. ———. *Royal Elizabeths*. London: Murray, 1928; 1930. New York: Dutton, 1929.

804. ———. *Royal Marys, Princess Mary and Her Predecessors*. London: Murray, 1929. New York: Dutton, 1930.

805. Tillotson, John. *Lives of Illustrious Women of England*. London: Holmes, 1853. Subtitle variant: 1855. PC

806. Timpson, Thomas. *British Female Biography*. London: Aylott & Jones, 1846.

807. ———. *Female Biography of the New Testament*. London: Ward, 1834.

808. ———. *Memoirs of British Female Missionaries*. London: Smith, 1841.

809. Tomkinson, E. M. *Sarah Robinson, Agnes Weston, and Mrs. Meredith*. London and New York: Cassell, 1887; 1889; 1890; 1893.

810. Trollope, Thomas Adolphus. *A Decade of Italian Women*. London: Chapman & Hall, 1859.

811. Trowbridge, W[illiam] R[utherford] H[ayes]. *Court Beauties of Old Whitehall*. London: Unwin; New York: Scribner, 1906.

812. ———. *Daughters of Eve*. London: Chapman & Hall, 1911; 1912.

813. ———. *Seven Splendid Sinners*. London: Unwin, 1908; 1924. New York: Brentano's, 1908–10; 1924. PC

814. Turnock, Sarah Elizabeth. *Women of the Bible*. London: Burroughs, [1899].

815. ———. *A Woman's Tour in Palestine*. Manchester: Heywood, 1907. NOT

816. Tweedie, W[illiam] K[ing]. *The Early Choice: A Book for Daughters.* London, Edinburgh, and New York: Nelson, 1855; 1857; 1859; 1860; 1862; 1863; 1864; 1866; 1868; 1871. Boston: Dover, Lothrop, Day, 1865; Lothrop, 1869. Cincinatti, OH: Poe & Hitchcock, 1866; Hitchcock & Walden, 1869. Cincinnati, OH, and New York: Jennings & Pye; Eaton & Mains, [1870–1910?]. PC

817. Tytler, Sarah [i.e., Henrietta Keddie]. *The Countess of Huntington and Her Circle.* London: Pitman, 1907. Cincinnati, OH, and New York: Jennings & Graham; Eaton & Mains, 1907. NOT

818. ———. *Girlhood and Womanhood.* London: Isbister, 1880. London and New York: Ward, Lock, 1895. NOT

819. ———. *Heroines in Obscurity.* London: Strahan, 1871.

820. ———. *Papers for Thoughtful Girls: With Sketches of Some Girls' Lives.* Edinburgh: Daldy, Isbister, 1862; 1875. London: Strahan, 1863; 1865; 1866; 1870. Boston: Crosby & Nichols, 1864. New York: Crosby & Ainsworth, 1865. Boston and New York: Woolworth, Ainesworth, Barnes, 1868. Boston: Estes & Lauriat, [1870–79?]; 1880. Nashville: A. H. Redford for M.E. Church, 1875. London: Isbister, 1881; [1890].

821. ———. *Six Royal Ladies of the House of Hanover.* London: Hutchinson, 1898; 1899.

822. ———. *Tudor Queens and Princesses.* London: Nisbet, [1895]; 1896. New York: Whittaker, 1896.

823. Tytler, Sarah [i.e., Henrietta Keddie], and J. L. Watson. *The Songstresses of Scotland.* 2 vols. London: Strahan, 1871.

824. Underwood, Sarah A. Francis. *Heroines of Freethought.* New York: Somerby, 1876.

825. Upton, George Putnam. *Woman in Music.* Boston: Osgood, 1880. Chicago: McClurg, 1886; 1889; 1892; 1895; 1899. Chicago and London: Paul & McClurg, 1909.

826. Upton, Harriet Taylor. *Our Early Presidents: Their Wives and Children.* Boston: Lothrop, 1890; 1891. NOT.

827. Villiers, Elizabeth [i.e., Isabel Mary Thorne]. *Love Stories of English Queens.* Philadelphia: Mckay; London: Paul, 1924.

828. ———. *Our Queen Mothers.* London: Melrose, 1936.

829. ———. *Women of the Dawn: A Sketch of Early British History.* London: Heath, Cranton, 1936.

830. Vincent, Arthur, ed. *Lives of Twelve Bad Women.* London: Unwin; Boston: Page; New York: Brentano's, 1897. London: Unwin, 1911. PC

831. Vizetelly, Edward. *The Warrior Woman.* London: Treherne, 1902.

832. Wadmore, S[arah] J[ane]. *Centenary of Portland, 1834–1934: Book of Remembrance of the Pioneer Women . . .* [Portland, Victoria, Australia]: n.p., 1934.

833. Wakeford, Constance. *The Wounded Soldiers' Friends.* London: Headley, 1917.

834. Walford, Lucy Bethia. *Four Biographies from 'Blackwood': Jane Taylor, Elizabeth Fry, Hannah More, Mary Somerville.* Edinburgh: Blackwood, 1888.

835. ———. *Twelve English Authoresses.* London and New York: Longmans, Green, 1892; 1893.

836. Walker, Albert. *Eminent Women: With Lessons from Their Lives.* London and Otley: William Walker, [1877].

837. Walker, Cornelius Irvine. *The Women of the Southern Confederacy during the War 1861–5 [sic] . . . Virginia, North Carolina, South Carolina, and Georgia.* Charleston, SC: n.p., 1906. NOT.

838. ———. *The Women of the Southern Confederacy during the War 1861–5 . . . Alabama, Florida, Tennessee and Mississippi, together with Arkansas memorial.* Charleston, SC: n.p., 1908.

839. Walker, Harriette Hammer. *Busy North Carolina Women.* Asheboro, NC: Harriette Hammer Walker, 1931.

840. Wallace, Archer. *Mothers of Famous Men.* London: n.p.; New York: Smith, 1931. London: Epworth, 1938.

841. Wallas, Ada. *Before the Bluestockings.* London: Allen & Unwin, 1929. New York: Macmillan, 1930.

842. Walsh, James Joseph. *These Splendid Sisters*. New York: Sears, 1926; [1927].

843. Walsh, Walter. *The Women Martyrs of the Reformation*. London: Religious Tract Society, 1905; 1911.

844. Walters, E. W. *Heroines of the World-War*. London: Kelly, 1916; Epworth, 1919.

845. Waters, Clara Erskine. *Heroines of the Bible in Art*. Boston: Page, 1900; Nutt, 1900; 1901; 1909.

846. ———. *Women in the Fine Arts*. Boston and New York: Houghton Mifflin, 1904; 1905.

847. Watson, Henry Clay. *Heroic Women of History*. Philadelphia: Gihon, 1854; 1855; Potter, 1861; 1885. PC

848. ———. *Romance of History: As Exhibited in the Lives of Celebrated Women*. Philadelphia: Gihon, 1857. Possible alternate title to above?[847]

849. Watson, P[aul] B[arron]. *Some Women of France*. New York: Coward-McCann, 1936.

850. Weaver, Anna Crowell. *A Chaplet of Memories*. n.p.: Woman's Missionary Society of the United Evangelical Church, 1915. NOT?

851. Weiss-Rosmarin, Trude. *Jewish Women through the Ages*. New York: Jewish Book Club, 1940.

852. Welch, Alice Kemp [or Kemp-Welch]. *Of Six Mediaeval Women*. London: Macmillan, 1903; 1913.

853. Weld, Horatio Hastings, ed. *The Women of the Scriptures*. Philadelphia: Lindsay & Blakiston, 1848. Title variant.

854. Wells, Emmeline Blanche Woodward. *Charities and Philanthropies: Woman's Work in Utah*. Salt Lake City: Cannon, 1893.

855. Whale, Winifred Stephens. *Women of the French Revolution*. London: Chapman & Hall; New York: Dutton, 1922.

856. Wharton, Anne Hollingsworth. *Colonial Days and Dames*. Philadelphia: Lippincott, 1895; 1908.

857. Wharton, Morton Bryan. *Famous Women of the New Testament*. New York: Treat, 1889; 1890.

858. ———. *Famous Women of the Old Testament*. New York: Treat, 1889.

859. Wheeler, Mary Sparkes. *First Decade of Woman's Foreign Missionary Society of the Methodist Episcopal Church*. New York: Phillips & Hunt, 1881; 1883. New York: Cranston & Stowe; Cincinnati, OH: Phillips & Hunt, 1884.

860. White, Mary Culler. *Stylus Photographus: Pictures of the Bible Women and Scholarship Girls of the China Mission*. Nashville: M.E. Church South, 1922. NOT

861. Whiting, Lilian. *The Golden Road*. Boston: Little, Brown, 1918. NOT

862. ———. *Women Who Have Ennobled Life*. Philadelphia: Sunday-School Union, 1915. PC

863. Whitmore, Clara H. *Woman's Work in English Fiction from the Restoration to the Mid-Victorian Period*. New York: Putnam's, 1910.

864. *Who's Who of Indian Women, International*. 1st ed. Madras: National Biographical Centre, [1900?].

865. Wickham, Gertrude Van Rensselaer. *Memorial to the Pioneer Women of the Western Reserve*. 5 vols. in 3. Cleveland: Savage, 1896–97. 2 vols. in 1, Cleveland: Women's Dept./Cleveland Centennial Commission, 1896; [1924?].

866. Wigmore, Sheila. *Australian Pioneer Women*. [Sydney: Australian Broadcasting Commission], 1933.

867. Wild, Laura Hulda. *Bible Character Studies: Women of the Bible*. Chicago: International Committee of YWCA, 1898.

868. Willard, Frances Elizabeth, and Mary A. Livermore, eds. *A Woman of the Century*. Buffalo, NY, Chicago, and New York: Moulton, 1893. Rev. ed. As: *American Women*, 2 vols., New York, Chicago, and Springfield, OH: Mast, Crowell & Kirkpatrick, 1897. NOT

869. Williams, E. W. *Heroines of India*. [London]: UCME, n.d.

870. Williams, Hugh Noel. *Five Fair Sisters: An Italian Episode at the Court of Louis XIV*. London: Hutchinson, 1906.

871. ———. *Later Queens of the French Stage*. London: Harper; New York: Scribner, 1906.

872. ———. *Queens of the French Stage*. London: Harper; New York: Scribner, 1905.

873. ———. *Rival Sultanas*. London: Hutchinson; New York: Dodd, 1915.

874. ———. *Unruly Daughters: A Romance of the House of Orleans*. London: Hutchinson; New York: Putnam, 1913.

875. ———. *The Women Bonapartes*. London: 1908.

876. Williams, Isaac. *Female Characters of Holy Scripture*. London: Rivingtons, 1859; 1862; 1869; 1870; 1873; 1878; 1884; Longmans, Green, 1890; 1909.

877. Williams, Jane. *The Literary Women of England*. London: Saunders & Otley, 1861.

878. Williams, Mary A. Barnes. *Fifty Pioneer Mothers of McLean County, North Dakota*. Washburn, ND: Washburn Leader, 1932.

879. Williams, S. W. *Queenly Women, Crowned and Uncrowned*. Toledo, OH: Hood, [1880s?]

880. Williamson, Emma Sara. *The Book of Beauty (Era King Edward VII)*. London: Hutchinson, 1902. NOT

881. ———. *The Book of Beauty (Late Victorian Era)*. London: Hutchinson, 1896; 1897. NOT

882. Williamson, William Henry. *Annals of Crime: Some Extraordinary Women*. London: Routledge, 1930.

883. Willing, Jennie Fowler. *God's Great Women*. Louisville, KY: Pentecostal, [1910s?].

884. Willing, Thomson. *Dames of High Degree*. Boston and London: Knight, 1896.

885. ———. *Some Old Time Beauties after Portraits by the English Masters*. Boston: Joseph Knight, 1895.

886. Willson, Arabella M. Stuart. *The Lives of Mrs. Ann H. Judson and Mrs. Sarah B. Judson: With a Biographical Sketch of Mrs. Emily C. Judson, Missionaries to Burma*. Auburn, NY: Derby & Miller, 1851; 1852. Auburn, NY, and Buffalo, NY: Miller Orton & Mulligan, 1854. New York: Saxton, 1858; 1860. Title variant: Boston: Lee & Shephard, 1855; 1869; 1875. New York: Saxton, 1855; 1860. All page citations in text are to the 1858 ed.

887. Wilmot-Buxton, Ethel Mary. *A Book of Noble Women*. Boston: Small, Maynard; London: Methuen, 1907.

888. Wilson, Helen, [Mrs.]. *Brave Days: Pioneer Women of New Zealand*. Dunedin and Wellington, NZ: Reed, 1939. NOT

889. Wilson, R. McNair. *Women of the French Revolution*. London: Hutchinson, 1936.

890. Wilson, Violet Alice. *Queen Elizabeth's Maids of Honour and Ladies of the Privy Chamber*. London: Lane, 1922.

891. ———. *Society Women of Shakespeare's Time*. London: Lane; New York: Dutton, 1924; 1925.

892. Wilson, William. *Heroines of the Household*. London: Cassell, Petter, & Galpin, 1864. New York and London: Virtue, 1869. London: Strahan, 1870. London and New York: Routledge, 1880. PC

893. Winthrop Normal College, Columbia, SC. *Catalogue . . . 1892–93, With the Exercises of Peay Memorial Day, May 12, 1893, Including Sketches of the "Historic Women of South Carolina."* Columbia, SC: Calvo, 1893. NOT

894. Wise, Daniel. *Some Remarkable Women*. Cincinnati, OH: Cranston & Stowe; Jennings & Pye; New York: Phillips & Hunt; Eaton & Mains, 1887. PC

895. Wister, Mrs. O. J. [Sarah Butler Wister], and Agnes Irwin, eds. *Worthy Women of Our First Century*. Philadelphia: Lippincott, 1877.

896. Witt, Henriette de. *Dames of High Estate*. Translated and edited by Charlotte M. Yonge. London and New York: Warne, 1872. NOT

897. Wittenmyer, Annie. *The Women of the Reformation*. New York: Phillips & Hunt; Cincinnati, OH: Cranston & Stowe, 1885.

898. *Wives and Mothers of the Bible.* London: SPCK, 1883.

899. *Woman: In All Ages and in All Countries.* 10 vols. Philadelphia: Rittenhouse, 1907–8. The volumes themselves are unnumbered but are cataloged (and will be cited in text) as follows: Vol. 1, *Greek Women,* by Mitchell Carroll. Vol. 2, *Roman Women,* by Rev. Alfred Brittain. Vol. 3, *Women of Early Christianity,* by Rev. Alfred Brittain and Mitchell Carroll. Vol. 4, *Oriental Women,* by Edward B. Pollard. Vol. 5, *Women of Mediaeval France,* by Pierce Butler. Vol. 6, *Women of the Romance Countries,* by John R. Effinger. Vol. 7, *Women of Modern France,* by Hugo P. Thieme. Vol. 8, *Women of the Teutonic Nations,* by Hermann Schoenfeld. Vol. 9, *Women of England,* by Bartlett Burleigh James. Vol. 10, *Women of America,* by John Rouse Larus.

900. *Women of Attainment: . . . of Rochester.* Bk. 1. Rochester, NY: Rochester Museum, [1940?].

901. *Women of the Bible.* Illustrated. New York and London: Harper, 1900.

902. *Women of Canada.* Montreal: Women of Canada, 1930.

903. *Women of History, by Eminent Writers.* London and Edinburgh: Nimmo, 1866; 1870; 1873; 1885.

904. *Women of Leadville.* [Leadville], CO: Nowland, 1897.

905. *Women of the Old and New Testaments.* Philadelphia: Lindsay & Blakiston, 1848. New York and Philadelphia: Appleton, 1851.

906. *Women Prominent in the Literary and Cultural Life of North Carolina.* Charlotte, NC: n.p., 1914.

907. Women's Centenary Council, Victoria, Historical Committee. *Records of Pioneer Women of Victoria, 1835–60.* [Melbourne]: n.p., 1937.

908. *Women Who Conquer.* Stirling: Drummond's Tract; London: Partridge, [1919].

909. Women's Christian Temperance Union. *Thumb Nail Sketches of White Ribbon Women: Official.* Chicago: Women's Temperance Publishing, 1895.

910. Woodhouse, Airini Elizabeth, ed. *Tales of Pioneer Women.* Christchurch, London, and Auckland: Witcombe & Tombs, 1940.

911. Woods, Mrs. Matthew. *Some Women of the Pre-Raphaelite Movement.* [Philadelphia: Browning Press, 1914].

912. Woodward, Ida. *Five English Consorts of Foreign Princes.* London: Methuen, 1911; 1912.

913. Woolfall, Lila Graham Alliger, and Ruth E. Adomeit. *The Pocket History of the Ladies of the White House.* New York: Woolfall, 1898. Published under pseudonym Olga Stanley. Title variant: Washington, DC: Bureau of National Literature and Art, 1903.

914. Woosnam, Etty. *The Women of the Bible: New Testament.* London: Partridge, 1880; 1889; 2 vols. in 1, 1881–84.

915. ———. *The Women of the Bible: Old Testament.* London: Partridge, [1880–89?].

916. Wooten, Mattie Lloyd, ed. *Women Tell the Story of the Southwest.* San Antonio, TX: Naylor, 1940.

917. Wortham, Hugh Evelyn. *Three Women: St. Teresa, Mme de Choiseul, Mrs. Eddy.* London: Cassell, 1929. Boston: Little, 1930. PC

918. Wright, Richardson Little. *Forgotten Ladies.* Philadelphia, London: Lippincott, 1928. PC

919. Wyman, Lillie Buffum Chace. *Girls in a Factory Valley.* [Pamphlet from article; caption: "Detached from *Atlantic Monthly,* Sept. 1896."] N.p., 1896.

920. Wyndham, Horace. *Feminine Frailty.* London: Benn, 1929. PC

921. Wyzewa, Teodor de, and C. H. Jeaffreson. *Some Women, Loving or Luckless.* London and New York: Lane, 1909.

922. Yardley, Margaret Tufts, comp. *The New Jersey Scrap Book of Women Writers.* Newark, NJ: Advertiser, 1893.

923. Yonge, Charlotte Mary, ed. *Biographies of Good Women: More Precious Than Rubies.* 1st ser. London: Mozley/Masters, 1862. 1st ser., 2d ed., London: Mozley & Smith, 1876. Probable contents of vol. 1, below.[924]

924. ———. *Biographies of Good Women: Chiefly by Contributors to "The Monthly Packet."* Edited by the Author of *The Heir of Redclyffe.* London: Mozley, 1862. 2d ser., London: Mozley, 1865. 2 vol., London: Innes, 1892. "3d and cheaper issue," London: A. D. Innes, 1893. PC

925. ———. *A Book of Golden Deeds of All Times and All Lands.* Gathered and Narrated by the Author of *The Heir of Redclyffe.* 1864; 1865; 1866. Boston: Sever, Francis, 1869; 1870; 1873. London: Macmillan, 1874; 1876; 1877; 1879; 1881; 1882; 1885; 1888; 1892. New York: Hurst, [1890s?]; Allinson, [1890s?]. Chicago: Donohue, Henneberry, [1899?]. All page citations in text are to the 1892 ed. NOT

926. ———. *Womankind.* New York: Macmillan; London, Mozley & Smith, 1877. New York: Macmillan, 1882; 1890. NOT

927. Yonge, Charles Duke. *The Seven Heroines of Christendom.* London: Mullan, 1878; Sonnenschein, 1878; 1879; 1888; 1891.

928. Yu, T'ing-shih. *A Book of Famous and Beautiful Chinese Ladies from All Antiquity.* n.p., 1898.

929. Zaidi, Syed Mohammed Hasnain. *Quoranic Purdah and Distinguished Muslim Women.* Calcutta: n.p.; 1932.

930. Zirndorf, Henry. *Some Jewish Women.* Translated from the German. Philadelphia: Jewish Publication Society of America, 1892.

$\mathcal{A}ppendix\ to\ \mathcal{B}ibliography$

TABLE A1. CHRONOLOGICAL INDEX OF COLLECTIVE BIOGRAPHIES

Date	Numbered Items in Alphabetical Bibliography	Total Number of Items
1830	361, 556	2
1831	205 (first published 1817), 361, 452, 453, 455	5
1832	168, 169, 450, 453	4
1833	26, 41, 134, 170, 184, 361, 450, 452, 455, 492	10
1834	146, 452, 453, 458, 474, 492, 806	7
1835	132, 171, 450, 474, 639, 751, 782	7
1836	295, 448, 450, 453, 492, 638, 639, 751	8
1837	26, 296, 448, 450, 453, 455, 638, 639, 720	9
1838	171, 361, 452, 459, 500, 639, 782, 794	8
1839	263, 297, 448, 454, 459, 482, 500	7
1840	171, 272, 361, 453, 500, 585, 763	7
1841	428, 752, 763, 808	4
1842	297, 428, 453, 492, 752, 763	6
1843	138, 171, 264, 297, 332, 361, 365, 492, 501, 763	10
1844	167, 200, 297, 312, 332, 453, 455, 483, 638, 752, 763	11
1845	19, 25, 141, 264, 267, 272, 297, 332, 428, 453, 658, 697, 763	13
1846	47, 135, 170, 267, 272, 297, 332, 341, 427, 450, 492, 591, 763, 806	14
1847	26, 50, 138, 267, 297, 349, 638, 746, 763, 794	10
1848	47, 76, 90, 172, 259, 297, 332, 366, 450, 453, 456, 484, 553, 638, 662, 688, 751, 763, 853, 905	20
1849	76, 90, 172, 259, 267, 297, 332, 342, 349, 484, 553, 662, 688, 745, 763	15
1850	19, 29, 47, 135, 170, 248, 259, 293, 295, 342, 395, 450, 478, 484, 553, 662, 700, 729, 745, 751, 752, 765	22
1851	2, 19, 29, 135, 138, 182, 342, 385, 424, 452, 461, 639, 662, 745, 752, 763, 764, 765, 886, 905	20
1852	19, 27, 29, 91, 182, 205, 256, 259, 312, 332, 342, 349, 362, 385, 395, 403, 421, 451, 459, 461, 479, 604, 662, 719, 729, 745, 765, 886	28
1853	19, 29, 76, 91, 131, 183, 250, 259, 332, 342, 349, 362, 395, 421, 450, 451, 461, 553, 688, 732, 752, 765, 770, 805	24
1854	2, 19, 26, 30, 38, 48, 52, 76, 91, 138, 172, 182, 209, 211, 234, 236, 247, 248, 250, 256, 259, 305, 332, 342, 349, 350, 365, 395, 449, 450, 453, 460, 461, 484, 553, 616, 654, 688, 729, 765, 847, 886	42
1855	29, 30, 38, 45, 91, 135, 138, 170, 172, 182, 234, 241, 247, 332, 342, 350, 362, 385, 403, 449, 457, 461, 571, 585, 662, 745, 765, 805, 816, 847, 886	31
1856	2, 45, 52, 182, 209, 256, 259, 332, 349, 350, 395, 424, 460, 495, 553, 591, 616, 729, 765	19

Date	Numbered Items in Alphabetical Bibliography	Total Number of Items
1857	5, 19, 29, 30, 45, 91, 153, 174, 182, 189, 209, 332, 342, 385, 450, 451, 455, 456, 457, 458, 461, 662, 692, 718, 765, 816, 848	27
1858	40, 76, 147, 170, 174, 182, 209, 349, 450, 453, 455, 458, 479, 495, 616, 667, 751, 765, 791, 886	20
1859	38, 147, 170, 178, 236, 249, 258, 262, 305, 331, 349, 350, 365, 395, 403, 450, 457, 458, 553, 571, 688, 751, 763, 765, 791, 798, 810, 816, 876	29
1860	19, 45, 52, 172, 178, 209, 234, 236, 249, 300, 305, 349, 386, 403, 407, 465, 467, 479, 692, 751, 797, 816, 886	23
1861	31, 147, 149, 170, 180, 182, 236, 237, 241, 259, 272, 300, 331, 413, 451, 452, 455, 615, 619, 658, 791, 797, 798, 847, 877	25
1862	19, 29, 31, 209, 365, 424, 453, 466, 476, 477, 816, 820, 876, 923, 924	15
1863	54, 173, 179, 236, 349, 365, 386, 450, 455, 466, 476, 791, 816, 820	14
1864	19, 147, 151, 179, 213, 220, 236, 241, 293, 332, 350, 365, 385, 450, 455, 458, 466, 478, 479, 662, 691, 692, 751, 763, 791, 816, 820, 892, 925	29
1865	10, 38, 76, 111, 175, 179, 236, 241, 295, 300, 395, 424, 450, 458, 466, 553, 567, 691, 816, 820, 924, 925	22
1866	5, 19, 38, 248, 300, 350, 385, 403, 424, 427, 450, 455, 456, 458, 479, 567, 580, 621, 662, 691, 720, 754, 816, 820, 903, 925	26
1867	13, 23, 46, 113, 179, 236, 257, 342, 350, 360, 580, 652, 662, 763, 797	15
1868	2, 13, 23, 52, 166, 174, 236, 257, 350, 424, 453, 492, 547, 548, 619, 630, 631, 697, 768, 769, 816, 820	22
1869	5, 13, 76, 111, 147, 179, 182, 236, 255, 261, 305, 349, 453, 469, 479, 553, 580, 630, 631, 753, 754, 755, 763, 769, 816, 876, 886, 892, 925	29
1870	19, 23, 32, 175, 209, 236, 250, 257, 261, 273, 360, 362, 385, 410, 450, 453, 454, 456, 567, 589, 640, 661, 766, 769, 797, 816, 820, 876, 892, 903, 925	31
1871	19, 111, 170, 174, 331, 365, 366, 453, 630, 720, 769, 816, 819, 823	14
1872	19, 23, 111, 172, 255, 362, 372, 410, 451, 452, 630, 661, 677, 766, 767, 769, 797, 816, 896	19
1873	13, 19, 111, 152, 182, 237, 256, 257, 260, 349, 362, 469, 566, 627, 630, 631, 755, 759, 816, 876, 903, 925	22
1874	19, 111, 262, 349, 362, 627, 688, 754, 759, 925	10
1875	19, 23, 33, 76, 111, 125, 175, 178, 182, 198, 217, 236, 241, 256, 391, 430, 450, 455, 458, 465, 466, 514, 553, 566, 820, 886	26
1876	13, 19, 176, 293, 303, 332, 376, 395, 398, 448, 458, 553, 593, 697, 754, 759, 797, 824, 923, 925	20
1877	12, 37, 51, 83, 303, 349, 360, 376, 449, 593, 613, 615, 616, 630, 763, 836, 895, 925, 926	19
1878	15, 19, 111, 125, 234, 303, 455, 487, 759, 876, 927	11
1879	14, 19, 111, 177, 236, 293, 303, 331, 350, 450, 451, 455, 461, 630, 925, 927	16
1880	12, 14, 29, 42, 75, 111, 164, 220, 241, 256, 303, 310, 331, 339, 355, 360, 410, 453, 458, 466, 565, 572, 625, 630, 643, 697, 791, 818, 820, 825, 892, 914, 915	33
1881	6, 19, 33, 42, 91, 248, 303, 313, 320, 337, 339, 344, 410, 455, 458, 466, 612, 751, 791, 820, 859, 914, 915, 925	24
1882	9, 12, 13, 23, 42, 221, 344, 355, 376, 377, 435, 468, 586, 623, 763, 791, 914, 915, 925, 926	20
1883	7, 8, 19, 42, 111, 129, 157, 158, 189, 266, 294, 303, 344, 354, 357, 376, 410, 411, 416, 450, 458, 461, 605, 628, 674, 679, 751, 758, 763, 791, 859, 898, 914, 915	34
1884	6, 14, 19, 42, 159, 208, 220, 266, 303, 354, 376, 377, 401, 410, 466, 628, 645, 758, 763, 859, 876, 914	22
1885	8, 23, 24, 42, 45, 165, 234, 266, 356, 392, 398, 404, 435, 450, 451, 455, 458, 466, 624, 629, 695, 697, 720, 763, 791, 847, 897, 903, 925	29
1886	19, 97, 98, 154, 165, 236, 248, 256, 266, 303, 315, 410, 414, 421, 466, 468, 520, 531, 536, 594, 624, 629, 739, 758, 763, 765, 791, 825, 915	29
1887	7, 8, 19, 24, 42, 43, 91, 111, 114, 123, 158, 165, 195, 234, 266, 276, 411, 433, 450, 466, 546, 593, 644, 662, 673, 765, 791, 809, 894, 915	30

Date	Numbered Items in Alphabetical Bibliography	Total Number of Items
1888	99, 113, 266, 270, 334, 412, 435, 455, 458, 466, 503, 531, 598, 624, 626, 630, 687, 691, 758, 759, 768, 769, 791, 834, 915, 925, 927	27
1889	7, 19, 24, 111, 123, 164, 236, 266, 270, 282, 299, 334, 344, 360, 376, 411, 412, 450, 455, 468, 481, 489, 602, 613, 626, 644, 763, 809, 825, 857, 858, 914, 915	33
1890	11, 24, 45, 111, 123, 138, 212, 238, 241, 243, 256, 266, 271, 436, 451, 454, 455, 466, 514, 531, 602, 624, 625, 626, 662, 791, 797, 809, 820, 826, 857, 876, 926	33
1891	11, 13, 19, 114, 125, 156, 165, 238, 266, 303, 323, 331, 411, 435, 436, 450, 455, 468, 472, 551, 717, 751, 826, 927	24
1892	11, 19, 97, 266, 276, 304, 349, 355, 357, 372, 389, 405, 411, 435, 450, 455, 472, 495, 506, 575, 646, 649, 763, 790, 825, 835, 924, 925, 930	29
1893	24, 82, 123, 130, 133, 221, 238, 243, 266, 277, 316, 344, 357, 372, 437, 438, 439, 440, 441, 442, 478, 481, 542, 613, 687, 706, 731, 763, 784, 791, 809, 835, 854, 868, 893, 922, 924	37
1894	11, 245, 266, 282, 438, 440, 455, 495, 504, 554, 588, 613, 662, 730, 765, 791	16
1895	8, 45, 61, 70, 84, 96, 124, 128, 155, 165, 238, 245, 246, 266, 318, 378, 408, 437, 438, 451, 495, 568, 645, 676, 697, 743, 763, 765, 786, 791, 818, 822, 825, 856, 885, 909	36
1896	11, 115, 234, 246, 270, 301, 303, 317, 378, 451, 458, 613, 739, 792, 822, 865, 881, 884, 919	19
1897	19, 126, 319, 408, 420, 425, 438, 450, 451, 481, 569, 592, 607, 652, 733, 791, 792, 830, 865, 868, 881, 904	22
1898	11, 64, 160, 252, 336, 379, 420, 425, 438, 440, 450, 455, 458, 601, 606, 620, 792, 821, 867, 913, 928	21
1899	11, 18, 64, 100, 143, 165, 379, 420, 436, 438, 441, 450, 451, 613, 620, 671, 696, 698, 714, 791, 814, 821, 825, 925	24
1900	6, 19, 45, 65, 100, 116, 150, 161, 164, 170, 181, 195, 238, 240, 256, 259, 348, 363 (1900s), 437, 438, 439, 441, 450, 453, 455, 503, [509], 510, 530, 570, 573, 635, 680, 698, 723, 728, 762, 791, 799, 845, 864, 901	42
1901	18, 118, 143, 223, 225, 291, 330, 344, 353, 382, 422, 424, 425, 437, 439, 440, 441, 450, 488, 515, 635, 637, 698, 783, 792, 799, 845	27
1902	139, 211, 262, 298, 321, 382, 436, 488, 573, 637, 657, 696, 698, 763, 769, 831, 880	17
1903	7, 119, 290, 367, 466, 488, 573, 581, 584, 613, 655, 763, 799, 852, 913	15
1904	16, 114, 117, 141, 143, 163, 203, 222, 234, 236, 244, 246, 370, 380, 423, 450, 451, 511, 513, 533, 689, 724, 763, 799, 846	25
1905	59, 69, 117, 185, 242, 244, 269, 281, 308, 344, 351, 432, 450, 530, 573, 613, 689, 740, 763, 799, 843, 872	22
1906	7, 18, 34, 63, 82, 165, 185, 199, 206, 278, 283, 307, 353, 382, 429, 440, 682, 698, 762, 763, 799, 811, 837, 870, 871	25
1907	19, 59, 63, 119, 185, 196, 206, 215, 283, 307, 525, 527, 552, 573, 608, 656, 663, 672, 694, 698, 724, 763, 769, 799, 800, 815, 817, 887, 899	29
1908	66, 119, 185, 214, 229, 281, 309, 338, 370, 425, 426, 494, 503, 515, 527, 552, 588, 657, 672, 694, 763, 780, 792, 799, 813, 838, 856, 875, 899	30
1909	66, 68, 89, 142, 191, 207, 226, 229, 231, 309, 343, 368, 369, 370, 402, 406, 438, 515, 517, 557, 573, 696, 714, 747, 760, 813, 825, 845, 876, 921	30
1910	62, 160, 161, 162, 231, 343, 368, 373, 402, 407, 409, 415, 453, 454, 514, 517, 573, 577, 683, 813, 863	21
1911	12, 140, 241, 285, 343, 370, 407, 420, 425, 429, 439, 440, 450, 458, 463, 529, 573, 620, 683, 699, 708, 723, 736, 749, 812, 830, 843, 912	28
1912	3, 137, 140, 199, 230, 254, 265, 340, 381, 387, 418, 462, 516, 527, 535, 557, 573, 648, 690, 696, 723, 730, 749, 750, 755, 773, 812, 912	28
1913	1, 3, 4, 19, 106, 140, 144, 233, 241, 397, 407, 512, 528, 532, 534, 543, 558, 590, 633, 664, 675, 684, 698, 714, 721, 723, 737, 742, 780, 852, 874	31

Date	Numbered Items in Alphabetical Bibliography	Total Number of Items
1914	21, 84, 98, 112, 192, 358, 359, 419, 558, 618, 659, 666, 670, 708, 723, 795, 906, 911	18
1915	4, 21, 53, 73, 105, 114, 144, 276, 381, 407, 446, 447, 527, 546, 555, 617, 633, 634, 734, 850, 862, 873	22
1916	3, 22, 103, 232, 311, 345, 388, 425, 450, 453, 485, 555, 576, 634, 744, 787, 788, 844	18
1917	19, 88, 93, 229, 268, 345, 396, 407, 555, 583, 622, 695, 757, 772, 833	15
1918	4, 374, 399, 471, 507, 555, 573, 614, 660, 789, 861	11
1919	73, 74, 102, 108, 110, 194, 229, 399, 407, 471, 535, 539, 555, 573, 614, 622, 773, 781, 844, 908	20
1920	55, 145, 190, 194, 197, 224, 275, 470, 496, 535, 555, 573, 611, 614, 668, 734	16
1921	4, 77, 555, 573, 611, 634, 665, 716	8
1922	4, 55, 56, 94, 224, 228, 374, 375, 471, 535, 555, 614, 617, 657, 734, 855, 860, 890	18
1923	44, 55, 56, 93, 98, 190, 207, 306, 325, 347, 425, 445, 497, 526, 545, 555, 600, 634, 701	19
1924	55, 127, 148, 224, 246, 268, 302, 425, 431, 450, 497, 526, 555, 713, 741, 813, 827, 865, 891	19
1925	89, 98, 104, 121, 127, 190, 228, 285, 425, 526, 555, 557, 573, 600, 603, 614, 697, 707, 714, 776, 777, [869], 891	23
1926	4, 17, 55, 87, 89, 120, 224, 347, 425, 431, 526, 545, 555, 562, 578, 600, 776, 783, 802, 842	20
1927	20, 56, 57, 93, 109, 127, 190, 276, 286, 324, 326, 335, 390, 425, 499, 526, 540, 555, 560, 562, 600, 614, 617, 713, 715, 725, 776, 777, 802, 842	30
1928	17, 35, 55, 79, 92, 109, 163, 192, 218, 224, 276, 292, 327, 352, 425, 426, 499, 524, 527, 555, 563, 564, 573, 599, 600, 614, 636, 681, 704, 761, 776, 802, 803, 918	34
1929	55, 187, 190, 210, 218, 287, 352, 417, 464, 502, 535, 541, 555, 561, 563, 573, 597, 641, 644, 650, 651, 712, 735, 761, 775, 776, 777, 796, 803, 804, 841, 917, 920	33
1930	67, 81, 98, 101, 194, 224, 229, 251, 284, 288, 289, 352, 387, 400, 417, 486, 498, 534, 541, 632, 685, 712, 774, 776, 778, 803, 804, 841, 882, 902, 917	31
1931	127, 193, 201, 216, 288, 289, 322, 333, 387, 491, 496, 523, 549, 614, 776, 839, 840	17
1932	219, 329, 346, 387, 475, 522, 537, 544, 645, 714, 738, 771, 776, 878, 929	15
1933	28, 160, 227, 286, 434, 443, 480, 559, 609, 610, 647, 702, 703, 723, 776, 779, 866	17
1934	127, 202, 383, 387, 443, 490, 550, 579, 582, 705, 832	11
1935	285, 314, 328, 364, 387, 535, 595, 611, 714, 756	10
1936	98, 122, 279, 364, 384, 387, 522, 678, 686, 715, 828, 829, 849, 889	14
1937	58, 335, 473, 538, 596, 669, 693, 774, 793, 907	10
1938	39, 58, 60, 71, 95, 98, 127, 188, 190, 253, 280, 287, 387, 522, 622, 840	16
1939	4, 58, 72, 80, 85, 98, 444, 518, 596, 888	10
1940	58, 86, 121, 127, 204, 387, 508, 519, 521, 587, 596, 636, 642, 709, 710, 711, 722, 851, 900, 910, 916	21

Note. This table lists the item numbers of books in the alphabetical bibliography, 1830–1940, under each year in which publication has been confirmed, whether as a reprint or a new edition. (Some related works are included in the alphabetical and thus in this chronological tally.) Publication dates can be elusive or ambiguous, however. I have interpreted inclusive dates conservatively to avoid inflating the rates of publication in figure A1. Thus a work said to have been published [1880–1900?] will not be entered every year but at intervals or under the most likely publication date(s) according to other evidence.

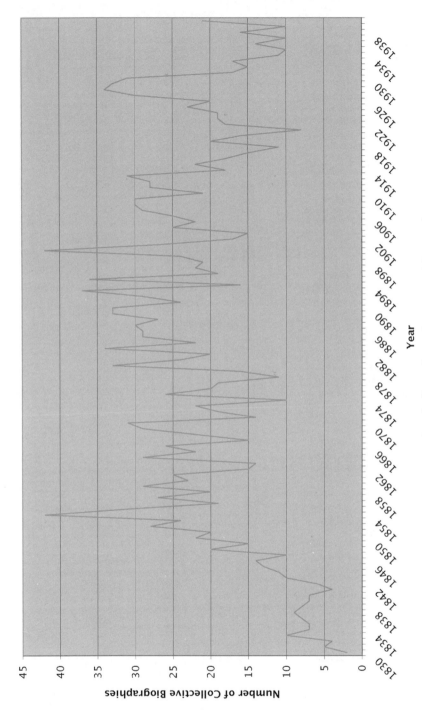

Fig. A1 Number of collective biographies per year (1830–1940)

TABLE A2. POP CHART: MOST COMMON SUBJECTS FROM NONSPECIALIZED COLLECTIONS

Area of Renown/Name	1850–70	1880–1900	1910–30	Total
Paragon:				
Joan of Arc	13	16	9	38
Philanthropy/reform:				
Elizabeth Fry	14	14	8	36
Hannah More	14	11	1	26
Sarah Martin	9	11	0	20
Frances Willard	0	6	9	15
Mary Lyon	0	6	8	14
Julia Ward Howe	0	4	7	11
Lucretia Mott	2	4	5	11
Susan B. Anthony	1	3	5	9
Mary Carpenter	0	7	2	9
Angela Burdett-Coutts	0	5	2	7
Dorothea Dix	1	4	1	6
Jane Addams	0	0	5	5
Amalie Sieveking	1	4	0	5
Nursing reform:				
Florence Nightingale	7	11	15	33
Sister Dora	0	10	5	15
Clara Barton	0	5	9	14
Queens/rank:				
Queen Victoria	4	14	11	29
Lady Jane Grey	14	8	5	27
Queen Elizabeth I	9	8	6	23
Isabella of Spain	13	5	4	22
Marie Antoinette	9	4	7	20
Mary Queen of Scots	9	4	5	18
Maria Theresa	9	6	2	17
Martha Washington	5	8	3	16
Empress Josephine	7	4	5	16
Catherine II of Russia ("the Great")	5	2	6	13
Anne Boleyn	8	3	1	12
Cleopatra	3	3	5	11
Mary Washington	5	6	0	11
Queen Christina of Sweden	3	5	2	10
Zenobia	4	3	3	10
Madame de Maintenon	5	3	1	9
Cornelia	4	3	1	8
Louisa of Prussia	1	3	4	8
Dolly Madison	0	3	5	8
Mary, Countess of Warwick	6	2	0	8
Queen Anne	2	4	1	7
Empress Eugénie	2	5	0	7
Madam de Miramion	2	4	0	6
Princess Alice	1	4	0	5
Margaret of Anjou	4	1	0	5
Literature:				
Charlotte Brontë	8	15	4	27
Louisa May Alcott	0	10	11	21
Harriet Beecher Stowe	3	11	7	21
Elizabeth Barrett Browning	3	8	8	19
Margaret Fuller	4	6	6	16

Area of Renown/Name	1850–70	1880–1900	1910–30	Total
George Eliot	0	9	3	12
Fanny Burney	4	5	2	11
George Sand	0	6	4	10
Jane Austen	0	4	5	9
Anna Letitia Barbauld	5	4	0	9
Felicia Hemans	4	5	0	9
Sidney Lady Morgan	2	7	0	9
Mary Sidney, Countess of Pembroke	5	4	0	9
Frances Ridley Havergal	0	8	0	8
Madame de Sévigné	5	2	1	8
Frederika Bremer	3	4	0	7
Maria Edgeworth	1	5	1	7
Jane Welsh Carlyle	0	5	1	6
Lydia Maria Child	2	4	0	6
Mary Russell Mitford	1	5	0	6
Frances Trollope	0	5	1	6
Emily Brontë	0	5	0	5
Adelaide Procter	0	5	0	5
Role in revolution:				
Lady Rachel Russell	14	7	2	23
Madame de Staël	10	9	4	23
Lucy Hutchinson	13	8	0	21
Madame Roland	11	7	3	21
Charlotte Corday	6	2	3	11
Lady Fanshawe	5	4	0	9
Lady Grisel Baillie	4	3	1	8
Madame de Lafayette	2	5	1	8
Emilie Lavalette	5	1	0	6
Gertrude van der Wart	4	1	0	5
Arts:				
Jenny Lind	2	7	10	19
Rosa Bonheur	2	4	9	15
Harriet Hosmer	3	4	3	10
Sara Siddons	2	3	5	10
Angelica Kaufman	2	6	1	9
Charlotte Cushman	0	5	2	7
Elizabeth Smith	5	2	0	7
Madame Rachel	1	5	0	6
Fanny Mendelssohn	0	4	0	4
Rescue/adventure/exhibit:				
Pocahontas	7	6	3	16
Grace Darling	5	7	3	15
Margaret More Roper	7	4	2	13
Lady Mary Wortley Montagu	4	6	1	11
Flora MacDonald	5	2	3	10
Nell Gwyn	4	2	3	9
Lola Montez	0	0	7	7
Laura Bridgman	2	4	0	6
Ninon de l'Enclos	0	0	5	5
Science/learning:				
Caroline Herschel	2	10	4	16
Harriet Martineau	2	9	2	13
Mary Somerville	0	11	2	13
Elizabeth Carter	4	5	0	9

Area of Renown/Name	1850–70	1880–1900	1910–30	Total
Vittoria Colonna	2	2	**4**	8
Maria Mitchell	0	**6**	2	8
Marie Curie	0	0	**6**	6
Religious mission:				
Anne Hasseltine Judson	**8**	6	0	**14**
Monica	**5**	4	1	10
Anne Askew	**5**	4	0	9
Catherine of Siena	1	**4**	3	8
Mary Bosanquet Fletcher	3	**5**	0	8
Madame Guyon	**4**	3	1	8
Elizabeth Rowe	**6**	2	0	8
Susannah Wesley	3	**5**	0	8
Saint Elizabeth of Hungary	2	1	**4**	7
Countess of Huntingdon	**5**	1	0	6
Elizabeth Burnet	**5**	0	0	5

Note. To prepare this chart, I compiled the tables of contents of all nonspecialized collective biographies of women published in English during three periods: 1850–70, 1880–1900, 1910–30. The intention was to cull manageable samples, from the periods of highest publication rates across the entire time frame of my bibliography, of collections that ostensibly were open to any noteworthy female subject. Specialized collections of queens, nurses, Scotswomen, or Quakers might include some of the above subjects (and thus would show that the total rates of appearances for Victoria, Nightingale, MacDonald, Fry, or others were higher during these decades), but these specialized books contribute less directly to the comparison of the merits of all women. I did draw from some wide-ranging English or American collections and some that designated roles or qualities (e.g., wives, good women) but that spanned countries or centuries. To be entered on the chart, a subject had to appear in four or more general collections in at least one period and, with few exceptions, to appear in more than one period.

The highest total for each subject appears in bold type, and the subjects are ranged in descending order of their total appearances in all three samples. I sorted the subjects according to my assessment of the type they best represent, though several could occupy more than one category. A characterization of the assortments in these books emerges in the rankings of the categories according to the score of their leading exemplar. Thus, although "nursing reform" would have followed "science/learning" if Florence Nightingale were not counted, Nightingale's type—often represented by herself—was exceptionally prominent and closely followed "philanthropy/reform." Joan of Arc is an enduring paragon, combining sanctity with the functions of reform, revolution, and adventure (including combat), as well as the historical prominence of the queens and women of rank. To have placed her in "religious mission" would have catapulted that category to the top, misrepresenting the other more perishable models listed there. Some kinds of heroines are missing; biblical women, extremely popular, and fictional or notorious women, less popular, usually appear in specialized collections.

43, 53, 62–64, 93, 117–19, 135–36, 153, 145, 160, 163–72, 202, 203–9, 248; female subjects of, 7, 9, 58–61, 93, 104, 117–19, 135–36, 153, 145, 160, 163–72, 202, 205, 208, 248; War of Independence, 104, 121–22, 124–25

Amigoni, David, 80, 242, 291n88, 335n19, 335n29, 337n49, 338n66, 339n80

anachronism, 33, 35–36, 39, 50, 94, 246, 279

ancestry, 78, 86–88, 239, 276, 279, 281

Anderson, Amanda, 272, 343n52

Anderson, Benedict, 12, 287n39, 297n148, 332n56

Anderson, Marian, 57, 97

Andrews, William L., 291n86

angels: as feminine ideal, 22, 127, 128, 130, 168, 180; holy, 190; in the house, 141

Anglo American, 2, 16, 43, 93, 121, 136, 164, 172, 176, 183–89, 215, 262, 273, 278

Anne, Queen, 262

Anne of Austria, 26

Anne of Bohemia, 254

anonymity, 55, 57, 92–94, 195, 209, 226, 232, 240, 243; of groups in collective biographies, 92–93, 124. *See also* names

anthologies, 4, 6, 11, 17, 30, 141, 182, 205, 219–21, 240, 272

Anthony, Katharine, 234

Anthony, Susan B., 16, 58, 139, 289n61, 341n12

anthropomorphism, 12. *See also* persona; prosopopoeia

antiquity. *See* period: classical

apology, 8–9, 47, 52, 54, 62, 65–66, 88, 178, 216, 232, 276

Appiah, K. Anthony, 299n17

Arabs, 201, 202, 209

archetypes, 44, 91–92, 110, 115. *See also* types; typology

Arendt, Hannah, 338n66

Arkwright, Mrs., 306n83

Armstrong, Nancy, 5, 284n12, 314n47, 315n56

Arnold, Matthew, 46, 180, 335n27

Arnold, Thomas, 329n10

art, 28, 44, 189–90, 192–95; history of, 178, 180–81, 187–95, 239; Italian, 176

Artemisia, 293n106

Arts and Crafts movement, 46

Arundel, Countess of, 122

Ashby, Ruth, 293n107

Ashton, Sophia Goodrich, 57, 206

Asia: Asian/Asian American, 32, 202, 204, 208; China 26, 32, 207. *See also* orientalism

Askew, Anne, 97, 310n13

Aspasia, 70, 91

assassins, 108, 111–16, 230, 260

Astell, Mary, 231

athletics/athletes, 74, 81

Atwood, Margaret, 326n25

Aubrey, John, 17–18, 231, 293n108

audience, 4, 12–13, 47, 49, 81–83, 151–54, 165, 178–79, 180, 183, 187, 234, 249, 264. *See also* reader

Auerbach, Nina, 271, 325n20, 344n50

Augustine, Saint, 17, 240, 298n10, 339n75

Austen, Jane, 25, 142, 228, 229, 231, 279, 334n17

Australia, 30, 57, 138, 143, 151, 158–60, 208–9; as origin of female subjects, 57

authors/authorship, 23, 30, 142, 189, 206, 221, 233, 267, 270–72, 273–74; death of the author, 239–40

auto/biography, 20, 80, 184, 228, 239, 243, 277

autobiography, 12, 17, 76, 81, 87–88, 143, 156–57, 235, 241, 243; female, 20, 184, 187, 205, 231, 240–41, 243, 280; male, 20, 52, 221, 240–41; proportions of male or female, 20; quantity compared to studies of biography, 20, 233, 243; studies of, 4, 5, 17, 20, 233, 240–41, 243

autonomy, 234, 237, 238–42, 246, 248, 251–52, 278–79. *See also* agency; individualism

Baako, Sekou Molefi, 309n111

Backscheider, Paula, 4, 283n6, 284n10, 303n51, 335n21, 336n35, 338n64

Bahktin, Mikhail, 80, 307n89

Baillie, Joanna, 18, 231, 327n45, 330n23

Bal, Mieke, 312n29

Balfour, Clara Lucas, 72, 136, 140, 142, 146, 148, 316n4, 317n8, 317n18, 323n73

ballads, 14, 100, 139, 230

Ballard, George, 6, 14, 30, 55, 199, 210, 231, 294n112, 295n126

Balmanno, Robert, 301n41

Banks, Louis Albert, 288n53

Barbauld, Anna, 18, 84, 138, 229, 316n4

Barker, Juliet, 74, 303n52

Barlow, T. Oldham, 320n43

Barnett, F. L., 216–17

Barrett, Jerry, 151–54, 320n43

Barrymore, Ethel, 323n78

Barthes, Roland, 313n33

Bartoli, Giuseppe, 311n18

Barton, Clara, 21–22, 58–59, 90, 126, 129–33, 138, 165, 215, 316n4, 320n38, 321n52, 321n63

Bartscherer, Joseph, 287n46

Barzun, Jacques, 20

Baudrillard, Jean, 288n47, 288n50, 304n65

Bauer, Carol, 326n25

Baym, Nina, 23, 28, 204, 284n11, 292n94, 294n113, 295n127, 295n129, 317n16, 328n1, 329n18, 329n20

Beaufort, Margaret, 66, 301n36
Beaumont, Charles de (Chevalier d'Eon), 84, 308n103
beauty (as type), 21, 32, 68, 72, 96, 114–16, 177, 209, 212, 218, 248, 254–55, 257, 259
Beauvoir, Simone de, 279
Becket, Thomas, 339n75
Beecher, Catharine, 59
Beerbohm, Max, 229, 303n61
Behn, Aphra, 228, 229, 334n8
Bell, Quentin, 234
Bell, Susan Groag, 283n6
Bell, Vanessa, 334n11
Benstock, Shari, 240–41, 338n69
Berlant, Lauren, 289n59, 304n64
Bernhardt, Sarah, 310n11, 341n12
Bernikow, Louise, 88, 309n117
Berry, Mary, 310n11
Besant, Annie, 317n12
Betham-Edwards, Matilda, 232–33, 333n6, 334n18
Bethune, George W., 42
Bible: heroines of, 21, 31, 71–72, 89, 92–93, 208, 212; Judith, 71–72, 108–20; Mary Magdalene, 193–94; recommended reading, 52–53, 71–72, 137, 144, 151, 158, 203–4, 270
Bickley, Frances, 297n149
Bildungsroman, 61, 236
biographers: female, 3, 6–9, 19, 105, 158, 166, 169, 186–87, 225–26, 229, 234, 235, 236, 239; homosocial bonds with subjects, 233, 239, 250; male, 3, 7, 229, 233–38. See also presenter
biography: as an art, 236, 237; brief or long, 3, 6, 18, 251–52; as epic hero, 234–39; good for you, 50–53, 62, 180, 234; as history, 10–11, 18, 20, 32, 50, 75, 220, 226, 229, 234; as literature, 10, 50, 73, 75–76, 226, 227, 234; as memorial or funeral rite, 12, 59, 82–83, 186–87, 237–38, 245; as narrative or rhetorical exchange, 4, 9–10, 18, 47, 50, 53, 80, 83, 137, 150–54, 156, 160, 165, 167–69, 183, 186–88, 214, 218–19, 233, 238, 240, 242, 243, 249, 265, 279; pure biography, 234, 238; realism in, 8, 25, 51, 57, 74, 75–76, 191, 227; selected speech, action, traits as form of, 247. See also didacticism; reader
biography, collective. See collective biography
biography, history of, 74, 222, 225; modernist, 23, 46, 225, 233; nineteenth-century, 73, 180; studies or criticism of, 5, 17, 20, 23, 75–77, 225–26, 233–40, 243; twentieth-century, 73
biography, individual, 3, 4, 10, 17, 73, 228; female, 20, 30, 75, 167, 186, 225, 229, 232,

233, 245; male, 17, 20, 227–28, 230, 233; proportions of male and female, 20, 230, 234
Bird, Isabella, 159
Birrell, Francis, 229
birth, 9, 24, 80, 236–237, 251, 268
Black History Month, 14, 288n54
Blackwell, Elizabeth, 59, 126, 129–30, 206
Blanche of Castile, 26
Bleackley, Horace William, 72, 297n149
Bloom, Harold, 278
Bloomsbury, 222, 226, 229
Boadicea (also Boudicca), 94–95, 293n106, 341n12
Boardman, George D., 168
Boccaccio, Giovanni, 2, 26, 311n18
Bodichon, Barbara Leigh Smith, 139, 143, 244, 319n32, 326n25
body, 12–13, 237, 238, 274; as personhood, 76, 242; of prone male, 22, 90, 111–12, 115, 119–20, 125–26, 128–31; of upright female, 111–12, 115, 119–20, 125–26, 128–32. See also woman's body
Bolton, Sara Knowles, 57, 160, 164–65, 322nn62–63, 327n43, 341n12
Bond, Cynthia D., 221, 332n49, 333n67
Bonheur, Rosa, 8, 37–38, 85, 97, 145
book, design: gift books or annuals, 29, 177; organizing principles of, 40–46, 58–61, 91–97, 190, 203–9, 219, 221, 251, 254–55, 268; physical description of, 7, 23, 28–29, 33, 39, 40, 46, 58–61, 70, 94–97, 203, 207, 209, 221, 254–55; printing, 2, 28–29; prize, 95, 310n8
book, as icon, 133, 151–54
Boorstin, Daniel, 304n65
Booth, Alison, 324n3, 327n33
Booth, Marilyn, 6–7, 285n19, 292n99
Booth, Phyllis B., 345n68
Booth, Wayne C., 339n84, 345n68
Bora, Catherine de (wife of Martin Luther), 299n16
Bordo, Susan, 343n44
Bornstein, Diane, 293n107
Bosanquet, Mary [afterward Mrs. Fletcher], 301n34
Boswell, James, 47, 104, 233, 235, 236, 289nn64–65, 337n44
Bothmer, Countess A. von, 252–53, 342n28, 343n34
Botticelli, Sandro, 110–11, 313n39
Boulding, Elise, 11, 286n31, 319n36
Bourdieu, Pierre, 12, 287n37, 299n17
Bouy, Charles Wesley, 31
Bowen, Catherine Drinker, 234
Bowler, Mabel, 289n66
Bracebridge, Mrs., 139

Carpenter, Mary, 92, 128, 138–43, 146,
    160–63, 199, 263, 317n9, 321n48,
    321nn51–52, 321n55, 321n57, 333n8
Carr, Emily, 287n38
Carr, Kent, 296n131
Carroll, Lewis, 271
Carter, Eliza, 91, 230, 232
Carter, Gayle Jo, 307n93
Casper, Scott E., 295n128, 298n8, 329n19
Casteras, Susan P., 342n25
Castle, Cora Sutton, 212–13, 331n41,
    331n42
castration anxiety, 108–9, 111–12
catalogs, 14, 177, 183, 190, 196, 212
Catherine of Aragon, 258
Catherine of Siena, 230
Catherine II of Russia (Catherine the Great),
    62, 69, 70, 91, 253, 296n135, 308n103
Catholicism, 31, 38, 43, 94, 106, 180, 189, 251,
    258. See also Christianity; religion
Catt, Carrie Chapman, 41, 296n140
Cattell, J. McKenn, 212
Cavendish, George, 336n39
Cazotte, Elizabeth, 108
celebration. See commemoration
celebrity: historical, 94, 104, 144, 204;
    nineteenth-century, 59, 99, 115, 123, 150,
    177, 185–86, 188–89, 267;
    twentieth-century, 74, 77, 81–82. See also
    fame
Cezelli, Constance de, 315n65
Chadwick, Whitney, 291n83
Chalon, A. E., 343n34
Channing, William Ellery, 184, 306n79,
    322n61
Chapman, Hester W., 234
Chapman, Maria Weston, 327n36
Chappell, Jennie, 57, 285–86nn24–25, 315n68,
    341n14
character, 15, 64, 76–77, 151
charity. See philanthropy
Charles I, 105, 257
Charles II, 106, 312n23, 342n24
Charles Stuart, Prince, 102–5
Charlotte, Princess of Wales, 53, 68
Charlotte, Queen, 150, 163
Charlotte Elizabeth, 316n4
Charmley, John, 305n76
Chartist movement, 79, 140, 341n11
Chase, Karen, 315n59
Châtelet, Madame Emilie du, 308n108, 318n25
Chaucer, Geoffrey, 14, 17, 26, 86, 302n41,
    311n18
Cher, 303n55
Cherry, Deborah, 143, 318n21
Chevreuse, Duchesse de, 310n13
Chicago, Judy, 288n56

Child, Lydia Maria: abolitionism, 199, 205;
    Good Wives, xv–xvi, 32–33, 53, 62–65,
    100–103, 168, 296n130, 299n16, 306n83,
    311n18, 311n21, 312n25; as presenter, 56,
    68, 294n114, 299n16; as subject, 58–59, 68,
    297n153, 328n1
children: childhood as focus of biography, 33,
    34, 206; children's literature, 24, 29, 30, 33,
    47, 53, 56, 66, 67, 69, 131, 205, 207–8, 210,
    229, 247; subjects having, 100–101, 102,
    149–50, 168, 254, 260, 267, 277
Chiomara, wife of Ortiagon, 117
Chisholm, Captain Archibald, 159
Chisholm, Caroline, 138, 158–60, 162, 317n14,
    321n48, 321n52
Chodorow, Nancy, 241
Christ, Carol T., 335n27
Christianity: as most advanced religion, 16, 31,
    62, 66–67, 188, 201, 203–5; Protestantism,
    11, 79–80, 145; women as models of, 8–9,
    52–53, 93, 96, 166, 188, 203–5, 248; and
    women's status, 143. See also Catholicism;
    Methodists; Quakers; Unitarians
Christie, R. C., 210, 330nn32–33, 331n35
Christina of Sweden, Queen, 68, 69, 253,
    311n21
Churchill, Caryl, 15, 288n55
Chute, Marchette, 234
Cibber, Theophilus, 18
citations of famous women, 83–88, 139–42,
    145, 175, 182–84, 229–30, 232–33, 244,
    275–76, 279
civilization, 4, 11, 84, 136, 165
civil rights, 16, 29, 140, 199, 264
Civil War (U.S.). See war: Civil War (U.S.)
Cixous, Hélène, 194–95, 326n28, 328n51,
    328nn53–54
Clark, Rev. David Wasgatt, 169–70,
    323nn72–73
Clark, Samuel, 18, 38, 293n108
Clarke, Mary Cowden, 35–39, 56, 70–71, 177,
    194, 258, 302n41, 325n24, 326n26, 341n12
class: economics, 84, 127–30, 135–40, 146–48,
    158, 161–62; and gender, 84, 90, 92, 98–99,
    103–4, 121, 127–30, 135–40, 158, 192;
    recognition of middle class, 4, 28, 74,
    230–31, 243–44; recognition of working
    class, 16, 20, 44–45, 74, 78–79;
    transcendence of, 9, 11, 44–45, 98–99,
    249–53, 273
class disguise (cross-dressing), 101, 103–4,
    265–66
Claudine, Roman virgin, 2
Clayton, Ellen, 44, 49, 57, 302n40, 312n28
Clayton, Jay, 327n28
Clément, Catherine, 328n51,53
Clement, Clara Erskine (Waters), 111

Clement, Jesse, 55, 93, 97, 118, 124, 145, 309n5, 315n54, 317n6, 341n14
Cleopatra, 35, 62, 70, 71, 120, 194, 258, 296nn133–34, 323n72, 341n12
Clifford, James L., 234, 288n47, 330n32, 335n22, 335n24, 336n33, 336n36, 338n59
Clinton, Bill, 82
Clinton, Hillary Rodham, 308n101
Clough, Anne, 229, 333n8
club movements. See women's club movements
Cobbe, Frances Power, 8, 85–86, 142, 146, 162–63, 209, 268, 274, 308n107, 317n19, 318n29, 321n55, 326n31, 335n27
Cochrane, Jeanie, 248, 315n68, 317n9, 321n53, 321n55
Cockburn, Henry, 290n73
Cockshut, A. O. J., 233, 335n22, 335n24, 337n43
Cogan, Frances B., 319n34
Cohen, Daniel A., 315n63
Coleridge, Samuel Taylor, 191, 193
Coleridge, Sara, 263
Coles, Robert, 300n19
collaboration: as coauthorship, 6, 53, 55, 57–58, 71, 186–87, 208–9, 211, 214, 219–21, 246–47, 274; and community, 55, 58, 136, 178, 196, 219–21, 269, 277–78; as interpersonality, 4, 8, 191, 244, 280–81; and rivalry, 183, 186–87, 246–47
collecting, 2, 3, 4, 10, 12, 13–14, 94, 244, 270
collective biography: African American, 52, 87; benefits of, 3, 9–10, 53, 62, 97; children in, 100–103, 151–52, 159, 161–62, 168; contributors to, 6, 182
collective biography, female: African American, 22; Australian, 30, 159–60; bias of, 10–11, 226; Chinese, 26; Egyptian and Arabic, 6–7, 26, 199, 218, 202; French, 26, 42, 115, 202; history of, 2, 3, 5, 7, 19–20, 25–47, 49–50, 142; Irish, 42; and male, 3, 4, 5, 6, 11–13, 74, 226; medieval, 26; neglect of, 3, 5, 17, 19–21, 84–85, 143, 177, 225, 228, 236; nineteenth-century, 7, 19, 142, 195, 202–10, 217; proportions of male and, 16–18, 211–13; publication rates by nation, 7; publication rates by year, 28–29; twentieth-century, 7, 19, 172, 182, 211–13, 228, 279; universal, 27, 203–6, 208–10
collective biography, female, tropes in: birth, 9, 24, 251–52, 267; body, 24, 97, 107, 157; death, 24, 98–99, 157, 165–69, 171–72, 213; deeds, 24, 30–31, 42, 97, 167, 207, 222, 267; family, 25, 97, 107, 149, 165, 171, 212, 252–53, 268; influence, 24, 97, 106, 107, 121, 128–29, 133, 149, 254; love, 25, 97, 165; prestige, 24, 46, 97, 99, 108, 123, 133,

149, 163, 165; rank, 27, 44, 46, 212, 248, 269; religion, 24, 27, 55, 97, 149, 267; virtue, 27, 42, 55, 93, 251, 252–53, 258; vocation or work, 24, 42, 44, 66, 97, 127–33, 149, 158, 166–67, 169–72, 182, 212, 215
collective biography, form of: alphabetical, 40, 203–6, 210–11; categories or types, 91–99, 190, 207, 249, 251, 253, 262, 268; illustrations, 7, 15, 33–41, 166, 207, 209, 217, 254–62, 268; long narrative or brief incident, 15, 42, 98–99, 249, 251–52; preface, 8, 21, 47, 52, 279; spatial or geographical, 40, 42, 160, 208–9; table of contents, 6, 40–41, 54, 58, 61, 91–97, 190, 220; temporal, 40–42, 249, 253, 254, 259; titles, 32, 41, 55, 91–97, 249, 250; universal, 42, 242; varied media, 14, 74, 81–83; vocational, 58, 79, 97
collective biography, as history, 3, 10–12, 18, 19–20, 25, 28, 42, 49–50, 66–67, 90, 100, 160, 204, 208, 220, 242, 248, 264, 273, 278–79
collective biography, history of: ancient, 17–18; early modern, 17–18, 28, 49, 79, 210; eighteenth-century, 84; lasting or ephemeral, 16; modernist, 238; nineteenth-century, 18, 28, 74, 79, 211
collective biography, cf. individual, 18, 226, 228, 240; neglect of, 73, 226, 228; as self-help, 77–80, 90, 156, 158, 180, 193, 195, 210, 220, 248. See also prosopography
Colley, Linda, 11–12, 199, 286n35, 328n4
colonization and colonial context, xvi, 90, 118–19, 141, 143, 151, 158–60, 200, 256
Colonna, Vittoria, 8, 341n12
Columbus, 331n52
commemoration: anniversary, 275; centennial, 30, 245; regional, 214
committees, 139, 150–51, 157, 159–60, 162–63, 216–17
community, 3, 4, 11, 14, 50, 54–55, 79, 275; imagined, 12–13, 58, 77, 247, 254. See also nationhood
competition, 14, 50, 57, 64, 78, 177, 180, 183, 198, 226, 232, 278, 279. See also nations, as rivals
compilation. See collecting
compiler. See presenter
Comte, Auguste, 296n139
conduct literature, 5, 21, 25, 53, 77, 80, 93, 108, 172, 248, 265, 272
Confederacy, 105
conferences, 240, 245–46, 275–76
confession, 74, 80, 117, 151, 177, 240
Conrad, Susan Avery Phinney, 295n129, 328n1
Constance of Bretagne, 191

emigration: and emigrants, 138, 151, 158–60, 205; ships, 138, 151, 158–60

empire: British, 66–67, 119, 210, 254, 263–64; colonization, 119, 151, 158, 199; expansion of, 208, 249–50, 253, 262, 263–64; U.S., 15, 208, 213, 248

encyclopedias, 3, 31, 74, 177, 190, 198, 203–7, 208–13, 221

Engels, Friedrich, 326n29

English Civil War. *See* war: English Civil War

entertainment (biography as literature), 21, 53, 179, 227, 234, 235, 237–38

epic, 61, 90, 125, 159, 233, 247

epitaph, 15, 166, 288–89n59

epithets, 13, 90–91, 93–94

Eponina, 21, 100–101, 311n18

Epstein, William H., 20, 233, 292n89, 333n2, 338n64

Erasmus, 107

Erskine, Mrs. Steuart, 180, 325n23

escape, 101–4. *See also* captivity

essays, 46, 85–86, 139, 141, 228–29, 231–32, 235–36, 243–44, 246

essentialism. *See* sameness (universal gender); women: nature of; women: universal sameness of

Estefan, Gloria, 81

Esther, 26, 109, 293n106

ethics, 4, 73, 75–77, 226, 227, 234, 243

ethnicity, studies of, 3. *See also* difference: social; diversity, cultural; race studies

ethnography, 76

eugenics, 11, 198, 205, 209, 210, 212–13, 250

eulogy, 3, 12, 237

Europe, female collective biographies of, 7, 18, 20, 26

Evangelicalism, 9, 29, 57, 79, 143–44, 169, 188

Evans, Mary, 12, 287n41

evolution (social theory), 200, 210. *See also* eugenics

Ewart, Andrew, 291n81

Ewart, Henry, 153–56, 201, 263, 320n43, 321n53, 321n59, 341n14, 343n34, 343n37, 344n58

example: argument by, 2, 84–86, 182; women's biography as, 2, 3, 4, 156, 162, 165, 176, 179, 182. *See also* exemplification; modeling

exceptions, 10, 13, 70, 82, 84–85, 90, 93, 184, 267–68, 272. *See also* class; elites

execution, 96, 101, 105, 107, 115–16

exemplification, 51, 53–54, 63, 69, 71, 72–73, 90, 107–8, 199, 202, 216, 242, 249

exoticism, 92, 112, 116, 123, 170, 194, 198, 199, 209, 254. *See also* orientalism

Ezell, Margaret J. M., 6, 230, 284nn15–16, 290n74, 295n126, 334n14

face, 12–13, 182, 215, 217, 247, 270, 273

Fairbanks, Mrs. Caroline Fuller, 217

Faithfull, Emily, 301n34, 319n32

fame, 3, 4, 7, 10–11, 13, 17, 47, 61–62, 75, 94, 107, 157, 187, 212, 236, 247; incompatibility with feminine virtue, 61, 66, 68–70, 72, 232, 250, 252, 253, 258, 269; peril of, 61, 68, 70, 72, 89, 185–86, 232, 250, 252–53, 277, 280; transience of, 17, 57, 139–44, 157–58, 161, 172, 180–81, 185, 186–87, 205, 213, 219–20, 222, 225–26, 234, 238, 242, 244. *See also* celebrity

family, 79, 96, 107, 160, 212, 253, 266–67

Fanshawe, Lady, xvi, 10, 105–6, 311n19, 312n25

Fanshawe, Sir Richard, 105–6

Farmer, Lydia Hoyt, 297n146

Farrington, Jan, 308n101

fashion, 257; model, 33, 81, 259

Faton, Jeanette, 297n151

Fawcett, Millicent Garrett, 56, 142, 229, 326n31, 327n43, 334n11

Felski, Rita, 325n21

female biographies. *See* biographers: female

feme sole (single or legally independent woman), 44, 85–86, 109, 146, 164, 212, 246, 254, 271–72

femininity: as embodied, 17, 237–38, 241, 242, 243, 252, 276, 280; as gender ideal, 3, 95, 140, 163–64, 244, 250, 264; as personal, 17, 239, 242, 280; as private, 17, 78, 95, 187, 235, 238–39, 242, 243, 262, 264, 270. *See also* body; gender; personal vs. political; private vs. public; spheres, separate

feminism, 16, 32, 46, 70, 75, 78, 84–85, 146–47, 163, 172, 177, 179, 181–82, 185, 188–89, 198, 245–47, 278–80; "difference," 32, 55, 181, 187, 253; Langham Place, 143

feminist studies, 4, 5, 20, 22, 78, 139, 143, 176, 181, 193, 194–96, 227, 239–41, 245–48, 269–75; of autobiography, 240–41; of biography, 19–20, 236, 239–40; of literature, 6, 23, 57, 140–43, 176, 182, 272–75; as recovery, 5, 6, 78, 83, 88, 139, 176, 181–82, 195–96, 197, 225–26, 240, 243–44, 269, 271–72, 274–75, 278–79; of women's history, 10–11, 20, 28, 179. *See also* recovery, feminist

femme fatale, 108, 111, 115

femmes fortes, 26

Fenwick, Gillian, 211, 331nn36–37

Fern, Fanny (Mrs. James Parton), 58

Ferris, Helen, 172

ffolliott, Sheila, 293n103

Fielding, Henry, 51, 298n9

Fielding, Sarah, 233

Finden, William and Edward Francis, 33

61–68, 77–83, 128, 141, 142, 156, 158, 160, 165, 187, 207
modeling, by women: of middle class men, 141, 149, 173; of middle class women, 146, 162–63, 166–73, 244, 248–49, 252–53, 268; of working class or poor men, 141, 146, 151, 156–58, 173, 244; of working class or poor women, 148–57, 158–60, 173, 265–66
models: literary characters as, 22; negative, 44, 53, 62, 66–73, 83, 112, 115, 122, 149, 207, 247, 248, 250–51, 253, 267
modernity, 7, 136, 189, 236–37; and modernism, 226–27
Modleski, Tania, 298n7
Moers, Ellen, 182, 324n8
Mohr, Nicholasa, 81, 308n96
Moi, Toril, 273, 328n55, 344n55
Mojon, Bianca Milesi, 301n34
Molza, Tarquinia, 95
Monaco, James, 77, 304n65
Monica (mother of Augustine), 91
monitors (teaching assistants), 137, 150–51, 153
Monkman, Leslie, 326n32
Montagu, Lady Mary Wortley, 199, 310n11
Montague, Elizabeth, 96, 310nn10–11
Montfort, Jane de (or Jeanne) (Countess of), 122, 311n19, 330n23
monuments, 14, 166, 226, 233, 238, 242
Moodie, Susanna, 183
More, Hannah, 4, 53, 144, 203, 206, 242, 311n17, 317n8, 318n20, 321n47, 321n49; former celebrity of, 18, 72, 316n4, 333n8; as type of instruction, 72, 93, 97, 138, 144, 156, 162, 164, 203, 318n25, 322n61, 327n43
More, Martha, 317n8
More, Sir Thomas, 107, 312n28
Moretti, Franco, 284n12, 298n6
Morley, John, 211, 336n49
Morris, David B., 300n19
Morris, Edmund, 303n58
Morris, Esther, 289n61
Morris, Virginia, 111, 313nn40–41
Morrison, Toni, 307n90
Morse, Ruth, 293n99
Mossell, Mrs. N. F. (Gertrude), 215–16, 218–21, 331–32nn47–49
Mossman, Samuel, 94–97, 103, 151, 310n9, 311n10, 310n15
Mother Theresa, 138
mothers and motherhood: famous women as, 92, 100–101, 149–50, 159–60, 248, 249, 251, 265, 270; of great men, 30–31, 91, 221; obscure, 136, 146; patriotic, 124, 141; as type, 212, 248, 257, 272, 277. See also maternalism; World Mother

Mott, Lucretia, 16, 58–59, 199, 289n61, 320n39, 341n17
Motte, Rebecca, 122
Mou, Sherry J., 293n99
mourning, 12, 15, 100, 245, 261, 264. See also performance; spectacle
multibiography. See collective biography; prosopography
multibiography, mutual, 7, 58–61, 176, 182–89, 206, 214–15, 218, 220, 241, 246, 276–80
Munich, Adrienne, 246, 265, 270–72, 278, 340n9, 342n22, 343n41, 343n45, 344nn48–49, 344n51, 345n63
Murasaki, Lady, 341n12
murder, 21, 69, 108, 111, 118, 120, 253
Murphy, Emily, 287n38
Murray, Charles, 212–13, 331n43
Murray, Fanny, 72
museums, 14, 178, 220, 245
Musset, Alfred de, 31

Nadel, Ira Bruce, 331n36, 335n19, 337n53
Najmi, Samina, 198, 314n47, 323n74, 328n3
names: in lists or catalogs, 83–88, 115, 221–22, 227; as part of persona or biography, 2, 89, 111, 161, 190, 192, 217, 247; plural, 13, 230, 232–33, 242, 268, 270, 272, 273; in prosopography, 13–16, 182, 184; and renown, 4, 89, 98–99, 203–4, 232, 237, 260; women's hidden, 211, 221. See also anonymity
Namias, June, 314n49
Namier, Sir Lewis, 10–11
Napoleon, 69, 95–96, 102, 296n137, 309n8, 312n25; Napoleonic era, 43
Napolitano, Jo, 307n94
Narayan, Uma, 338n65
narratability, 4, 81, 118, 167, 187, 251–52, 254, 259–60, 263, 269
narrative: constructing national history, 12–13, 49–51, 53, 77, 99, 125, 199, 247; constructing subjectivity, 27, 49–50, 53, 77, 195, 218, 240–42; duration, 42; episode or phase of a life, 98, 150, 154, 166; *fabula*, 111, 150, 154, 192; form of, 3; life span in, 69, 99; scene vs. summary, 100–101
narrator, 4, 47, 53, 177
National Association for the Promotion of Social Sciences, 162, 188
National Association of Colored Women, 214, 219
nationalism, 31–33, 42, 43, 202–8, 210, 251–52
nationhood (community), 3, 12, 14, 26, 55, 61, 62–65, 71, 79, 98, 125, 142, 169, 199, 240, 264, 269. See also community
nations: non-European, 20, 199, 202, 204; relations among, 9

nations, as rivals: for biography, 30, 210–11, 235–37; for great women, 30, 31, 62–65, 93, 169, 212–13, 251; for status of women, 201–9, 212–13

Native Americans, 45, 117–19, 124, 179–80, 184, 200–202, 204, 218; imperiled, 118–119, 124–25, 200

Nayder, Lillian, 310n8

Nazianzen, Saint Gregory, 191

Neff, Mary (hired nurse of Hannah Duston), 118, 314n50

Nelson, Claudia, 284n11, 292n97

New Age, 78, 80

New Criticism, 234, 239

New England as cultural center, 8, 213

New Woman, 64, 172

Newcastle, Duchess of, 294n112

Newgate prison, 148–49, 151–53

Newman, Beth, 344n56

Newman, Cardinal, 17

Newman, Louise Michele, 200, 286n25, 286n32, 319n34, 328n5, 332n54

Newton, Judith Lowder, 284n12

Nicholson, Linda, 304n62

Nicolson, Harold, 74, 227, 229, 234, 237, 286n28, 302n46, 333n3, 335n27, 337nn47–49, 337nn50–51

Niemeyer, Andrea de, 307n90

Nightingale, Florence: as Lady with the Lamp, 125–27; and other subjects, 8, 36–38, 64, 69, 127, 133, 139, 147–48, 150, 162, 169–70, 228, 247, 248, 258, 296n135, 312n28, 316n4, 317n9, 320n38, 321nn48–49, 321n52, 341n12, 341n17, 343n32; as preeminent subject, 71, 138, 169, 268–69, 290n66, 342n22; as professional reformer, 71, 139–42, 164, 228, 244; as type of nursing, 21, 64, 129, 253; and war, 121, 127, 129, 133, 286n30

Nithsdale, Countess of, 102, 311n19

Noble, Marianne, 305n70

Nord, Deborah Epstein, 139, 160, 317n13

Northrop, Amanda Carolyn, 331n42

nostalgia, 239, 276

Novarr, David, 234, 235

novels, 274–76; Adam Bede, 155, 320n46; vs. biography, 5, 21, 50, 56, 68, 75–76, 108, 119, 138, 156, 176, 233, 236, 238, 268, 272; Bleak House, 139; The Bondwoman's Narrative, 221; female plots in, 24, 61, 273; Flush, 228, 231, 234; Heart of Midlothian, 98 155; Little Dorrit, 155; Middlemarch, 258; The Mill on the Floss, 61; North and South, 107, 139, 161; Orlando, 227, 234, 270; Romola, 107, 312n27; To the Lighthouse, 210; The Years, 128

Novitz, David, 300n19, 302n46, 335n27, 336n34, 336n36

Novy, Marianne, 327n44

nursing/nurses, 21, 44, 59, 62, 120, 125, 128, 129, 131, 135, 165, 274

Nussbaum, Felicity, 289n64, 337n44

Nussbaum, Martha, 339n84

obscurity, 4, 5, 227, 233, 242–44

obstacles. See adversity

Octavia, 94–95

Ohmann, Richard, 304n65

Ohrn, Deborah Gore, 293n107

O'Keefe, Georgia, 97

Okker, Patricia, 295n122

Oldfield, Sybil 2, 20, 283n2, 292n91, 293n99, 294n110, 295n120, 296n137

Oliphant, Margaret, 57, 84–85, 177, 182, 184, 186–87, 229, 234, 274, 300n23, 308n104, 318n27, 326n31, 327n40, 327n42, 333n8, 334n22, 336n38, 345n59

Olney, James, 241, 338n75

omission, 4, 8, 54, 168, 196, 204, 215, 217–18, 232, 242–44, 257, 276, 279

Opie, Mrs., 229

orientalism, 198, 200, 208, 209, 252. See also exoticism

origin/originality, 80, 82, 85, 167, 227, 237, 270, 276, 277, 278

Origo, Iris, 234

Owen, Emily (Mrs. Octavius Freire Owen), 71, 112

Owens, Darrel E., 309n111, 314n43

pageant, 13–14, 64, 229–30

Paglia, Camille, 278, 280, 345n66

paintings, 109–11, 115–16, 151–53, 193–94, 256

Palmer, Mrs. Bertha M. Honoré, 216, 218, 248, 316n1, 332n52, 332n59

Palmerston, Lord, 343n39

panegyrics, 82, 196, 236, 280

pantheons, 87, 218

Pape-Carpantier, Marie, 232, 301n34

Parini, Jay, 303n57, 336n35

Pariseau, Esther (Mother Joseph), 289n61

Park, Mungo, 95

Park, You-me, 304n64

Parker, Gail Thain, 278

Parker, Pamela Corpron, 284n11, 300n25

Parkes, Bessie Rayner, 56, 62, 65, 139, 143, 188, 229, 301n34, 319n32, 326n25

Parrington, Vernon Louis, 19, 290n77

Parton, James, 19, 34, 37, 38–39, 56, 58, 169–70, 268, 343n40

Partridge, S. W., 290n66